FILEY: FISHING, FAITH AND FAMILY SINCE 1800

FISHING FAMILIES OVER THE LAST TWO CENTURIES

IRENE E ALLEN
ANDREW A TODD

BLACKTHORN PRESS

Blackthorn Press, Blackthorn House
Middleton Rd, Pickering YO18 8AL
United Kingdom

www.blackthornpress.com

First published as *Filey: A Yorkshire Fishing Town*
by Allen and Todd, Ramsbottom, 1985

2nd Edition June 2021
Reprinted May 2022

ISBN 978 1 906259 64 8

The cover photograph, with detailed caption, is reproduced on page 29.

CONTENTS

ACKNOWLEDGMENTS

Crown Copyright Images on pages 73, 74, 176, and 177 are reproduced by courtesy of The National Archives, London.

Personal thanks for help with this new edition to Alan Avery, Joanne Cammish, Peter M Duncan, Stephen Eblet, Ian Elsom, Michael Fearon, Mary Harding, John D Ireland, Jeff Meek, Steve Midwood, and Graham Taylor.

Every reasonable effort, in good faith, has been made to establish copyright for photographs reproduced in this book. If determined, this has been acknowledged in italicised square brackets *[ ]* at the end of each caption. There are, however, many copies of most local photographs spread throughout the town, and this has handicapped this process.

ABBREVIATIONS

FA	Filey Archives
FFF	Filey Fishermen and their Families (Facebook site compiled by Vicky Bradley)
FM	Filey Museum
JC	Joanne Cammish
SE	Stephen Eblet
SMHC	Scarborough Maritime Heritage Centre

N1, R34 etc – these codes refer to people on the JENKINSON[1] family tree (Appendix E)

Where a source is used regularly, an abbreviated reference appears in the footnote in the form Smith (1932). Full details for each are given in *Sources*.

Maps and diagrams are my own work, and I am responsible for any errors.

There will inevitably be mistakes in a book which relies so extensively on personal recollections, and my interpretations of them. If you spot any, please contact the author direct at *aatodd1846@gmail.com*. I will also welcome fresh facts, photographs or stories, however small, that you want to contribute to any new edition.

---

[1] The 15 core Filey fisher surnames, listed and defined in Chapter 4, are always in block capitals.

INTRODUCTION TO THE SECOND EDITION

Much has changed in the 35 years since Irene offset-printed, collated and stapled this book's first edition in the living room of our terraced house in Ramsbottom, and we sold copies in Wray's, on Filey's Belle Vue Street. Most obviously, digital technology has allowed me to revise and send copy for this edition through cyberspace to a publisher in Yorkshire, whilst access to 21st Century photo-printing techniques has created a greatly enhanced product.

In the early 1980s, Irene and I wrongly assumed that Filey was unique: we had never encountered any town or village with such a small core of long-established families, closely linked through bewildering patterns of intermarriage, strong communal values, nonconformist religion, and traditional fishing practices, in essence centuries old. We did not have the overview of fishing history to appreciate how Filey fitted into the national picture. I now realise that other fishing stations, on the Yorkshire coast, and at many locations nationwide, have near identical features.[2] Several villages on the north-east Scottish coast, alongside the Moray Firth, are mirror images of Filey, even down to the superstitions of the fishermen.[3]

Our 1985 local family history soon became known as 'the JENKINSON book', since it focused on Filey's arterial family, to whom just about every native of the town was and is connected, and usually many times over. The recent explosion in the online availability of census returns and parish registers, however, has allowed me to widen findings way beyond this spinal family.

Since the early 2000s, the digital revolution has also brought social media sites into being, and in these lie thousands of photographs and snippets of previously little-known family and local history material. A growth in local awareness has been accompanied by an urge to conserve. Filey's commercial fishing has declined in inverse proportion to interest in it: new local research facilities have sprung up - Scarborough's Maritime Heritage Centre, the Filey Museum and the Town Archive. The amount of information available has been matched in quantity by the enthusiasm and helpfulness of the volunteer staff.

The subject matter of this book may be historical, but there are underlying themes very familiar today. The phrase 'global capitalism' was unknown in the 19th Century; but Filey fishermen knew perfectly well how unrestrained free market forces in the shape of trawlers impacted destructively on natural resources, traditional communities and long-established ways of life. Impersonal companies, with loyalties only to shareholders, have gradually displaced the family-based fishing which sustained Old Filey until comparatively recently. By 2019, 29% of

---

[2] Frank (2002); Thompson et al (1983).

[3] Barron (2009); Blaikie (2002).

the UK's fishing quota was owned by just five families, all on the *Sunday Times* Rich List, whilst one Dutch multinational, operating a single vast ship, held a further 24% of the English quota. The smallest boats, ie those under 10 metres, comprised 79% of the fleet, but could catch only 2% of the fish.[4]

If you have seen a local butcher, newsagent, bakery, or any family shop put out of business by a supermarket or chain - well, you will appreciate the frustrations of those Filey fishermen who complained fruitlessly to 19th Century government inquiries into trawling's destruction of fishing stocks.

Another trend away from localism has been the virtual extinction of dialect, and the spread of a handful of conurbation accents, like those of Tyneside, Leeds, Manchester, the West Midlands and the Thames Estuary. Filey's very special parish priest, Canon AN Cooper, spotted this trend and wrote about it profusely after 1880 in the course of a 55 year ministry. And it continues: the accents and dialect of 1980s Filey are noticeably less apparent on my most recent visits.

One of the joys of preparing the 1985 edition was the inclusion of so many direct quotations from Filey people of the past, preserving the heritage encoded in their speech. I have greatly expanded this element, keeping this account personal, in that I have tried to illustrate as many of the general themes through the individual lived experience. I have generally followed a 70-year rule of anonymity where a topic might be considered 'delicate', and I sincerely hope that this two-generation span should be a sufficient *cordon sanitaire* to spare embarrassment for any existing descendants. I do apologise if I have ever inadvertently got this wrong.

There are omissions – I have for example not attempted to include Filey's part in World War II, because I know that the topic attracts plenty of current research interest. The town's fishermen were more heavily involved in the Great War, though this is not to discount Filey's World War II part. Some 1,456 fishing craft were requisitioned nationally, between 1914 and 1918, primarily as minesweepers. The 1939-45 figure was 215.

Irene and I owed particular thanks to Michael Fearon, that original driving force at Filey Museum, who introduced us to so many informative people in the early 1980s, all acknowledged at the back of this book. That generation, truly part of Old Filey, has now gone, and I doubt if anybody has done as much as Michael to preserve its memory. Stephen Midwood has also been a great and authoritative help in making so many excellent photographs available from Filey Archives.

Irene died in 2016, so when Michael contacted me in February 2018 with a request to republish this book, I saw it as a perfect opportunity for a long-needed updating, dedicated to her memory . . . and thanking her for making such a fascinating town a genetic part of our family's life.

Andrew Todd, Ramsbottom, April 2021

---

[4] *The Guardian*, 9th May 2019.

1 A GRAVEYARD INTRODUCTION

'You would imagine any man mad, from all that you see around you, who would think of trusting himself to the ocean.' Charles Dickens (1851) touring east coast graveyards.

Ovver t'North Ridin'

We just caught it in time. A dozen or so cobles were still launching daily off the beach beyond the Coble Landing; long-lines were baited in a few sheds behind Queen Street cottages; many men wore the distinctively patterned blue Filey gansey as knitted and worn by generations of their ancestors; and the surnames that dominated the parish churchyard were still very much in evidence in the cluster of streets just a few hundred yards away over Church Bridge. We had stumbled upon the small, self-contained Filey fishing community, barely altered in its fundamentals in more than two centuries, and seemingly to be here forever.

It was the early 1980s, we were delving into Irene's family history, and had just discovered the significance of her mother's second Christian name, Jenkinson. Irene's great grandmother, Rachel Cammish JENKINSON (P69)[1] belonged to a fisher family which had lived on Mitford Street. As we looked at the town's records, we had been overwhelmed by the commonness of the surname: in the 1871 census returns, recording the population at the peak of Filey's fishing industry, there were 103 JENKINSONs, all in fisher families. The parish registers were full of them, but identities initially seemed impossible to disentangle because the fishing population shared a confusingly small range of names.

Now, in the summer of 1982, we'd crossed the bridge which led over Church Ravine and into St Oswald's churchyard, passing between Yorkshire's historical East and North Ridings.[2]

1.1: A delightful portrayal of two greying crewmates, potting for crabs in the twilight of their fishing years. One hauls in the *tow* of pots, precisely portrayed, as is the coble's registration number.

Treasured Memories Of
A DEARLY LOVED HUSBAND, FATHER
AND GRANDFATHER
ROBERT PEARSON HUNTER
DIED 30TH JUNE 1995 AGED 78 YEARS

---

[1] Numbers like P69 refer to the pedigree charts in Appendix E.

[2] 'Crossin' ovver t'North Ridin' ' has been a characteristically ironic Old Town euphemism for death and burial beyond memory. It survives, despite the small adjustment to the county boundary in 1889 which brought the churchyard into the East Riding.

JENKINSON, Edmund, 33, Queen Street.

JENKINSON, George, fisherman, 5, Providence Place, Queen Street.

JENKINSON, J. W., 18, Spring Road.

JENKINSON, James S., 3, Providence Pl.

JENKINSON, John, 4, Queen Street.

JENKINSON, John M., 7, Spring Road, Queen Street.

JENKINSON, Charles, 6, Church Street.

JENKINSON, Fanny, 2, Ebenezer Terr.

JENKINSON, John Robert, fisherman, 5, Clifford's Yard, Mitford Street.

JENKINSON, John Robt., 3, Reynold's Yard, Mitford Street.

JENKINSON, John W., fisherman, 16, Spring Road, Queen Street.

JENKINSON, Grace, 93, Queen Street.

JENKINSON, Matthew, carpenter, 2, Hope Cottages, The Beach.

JENKINSON, Matthew, carpenter, 4, Sand-hill Lane, Queen Street.

JENKINSON, Matthew Crompton, labourer, 4, Chapel Yard, Mitford Street.

JENKINSON, Ross, 1, White's Yard, Queen Street.

JENKINSON, R., fisherman, 3, Clifford's Yard, Mitford Street.

JENKINSON, R., fisherman, 11, Queen Street.

JENKINSON, R. C., fisherman, 59, Mitford Street.

JENKINSON, Thomas, fisherman, 1, Marriner's Terrace, Mitford Street.

JENKINSON, Thomas, senr., 7, Marriner's Terrace, Mitford Street.

JENKINSON, Thos., 9, Raincliff Avenue.

JENKINSON, Thomas, fisherman, 31, Queen Street.

JENKINSON, Thos. Robert, fisherman, 57, Mitford Street.

JENKINSON, Susannah, 43, Mitford Street.

JENKINSON, Wm., 11, Mitford Street.

JENKINSON, William, fisherman, 5, Queen Street.

JENKINSON, Mrs. Frances H., 5, Cromwell Avenue.

JENKINSON, Richard C., 59, Queen Street.

JENKINSON, Mary E., 2, Sandhill Lane, Queen Street.

JENKINSON, Miss M. E., 1, St. Kitts, The Beach.

JENKINSON, Mrs. R. C., 6, Stockdale's Yard, Queen Street.

1.2: From WH Smith & Son's 1923 *Filey Directory* - by the 1860s, JENKINSON had become the most common surname in Filey, and remained so 100 years on. The number of non-fisherman JENKINSONs amongst the entries reflects the post-1870s decline in the town's fishing industry.

The yard mesmerised us, as it had another visitor a couple of lifetimes before. John Cole had first encountered 'Romantic Filey' in 1822, and his fine book, *History and Antiquities of Filey*, the town's first proper guide, included transcriptions of many inscriptions from gravestones since lost. At that time, an intriguing memorial fashion was just seeding here: there were by 1982 many stones that carried monumental representations relating to the everyday work of harvesting the sea. Here, sculpted in stone, was a record of nearly two centuries of fishing practice. I have seen nothing like it before or since.

On several stones was the ever-present coble, the bread-and-butter craft used by so many men the year round on the north-east coast, to catch whatever was seasonally available. Here also were several yawls, with petrified images of sails straight from the 1870s, whilst more elaborate rigs featured on later stones.

In 2018, when preparing this second edition, I revisited the yard, the first time in 36 years. Boats had evolved even more, as had the art of the monumental masonry that records them. Now there were carvings of trawlers with modern radar, only a stride away from Castle JENKINSON's 1882 memorial, with its timeless but eroding image of a lug-rigged coble.

1.3: [Left] Finely carved maritime imagery dating from 1823 - the earliest example at St Oswald's. The rudder was a metaphor for the guidance and direction offered by scripture and prayer. Local masons turned the generic Christian anchor of hope into an anchor drawn from everyday local design. The Tindalls were sailors – Peter's son died in the West Indies.

[Right] Richard Cammish Overy's coble *Harriet*, from which he drowned off Robin Hood's Bay on 6th October 1908 - a beautifully accurate representation of an east-coast craft, originating in Anglo-Saxon times. The triangular jib sail was an 18th/19th Century feature.

There were warts-and-all insights into the characters of the people commemorated by these inscriptions, often caught in wry and quirky fishing metaphors that would amuse their departed subjects. One of my favourites is Bob *Tewy* HUNTER's (**1.1**) whom Irene and I had first met and spoken to one July morning, in his Queen Street cottage, in 1983 (see **30.3**). *Tewy* had been characteristically ganseyed, having spent the early morning crabbing in his coble *Morning Star*. His epitaph reads:

> My sails are split, my main mast gone,
> My soul has fled the deck,
> And here beneath this damp cold stone
> My body lies a wreck.

Certain dates appeared on more than one stone: 29th October 1880, 6th March 1883, 14th December 1896, 25th November 1925, 29th June 1948 - each evidence of some catastrophe out at sea, and always the same clutch of surnames. Two or more on each date were usually from the same family. Nor on these inscriptions and carvings was there any shying away from the grim reality of how these men had died whilst earning their living. I am unaware of any carvings of pithead winding gear or miners' picks on the stones of any victim of Lancashire's great colliery disasters. Yet in many of these St Oswald's cases, a widow had commissioned an accurate image of the boat from which her husband had drowned, a reminder in stone for all time - even the boat's registration number is often minutely reproduced on some of the modern stones.

1.4: Economic necessity, ie dependent families and paltry work opportunities, obliged Filey widows to remarry quickly if they could. Their names, therefore, rarely appear on the same gravestones as their drowned husband's. But some remained widows for the rest of their lives.

The longest widowhood I have encountered in St Oswald's yard is the 55 years of Isabella CAMMISH. Her son, Francis, was also lost at sea, from *Trio*, in 1895. None of the six crew, or the boat, has ever been found. The yawl's loss remains unexplained.

Many of the men commemorated here were, of course, condemned to 'a grave in the great ocean cemetery', their families left with an irredeemable sense of loss.

These memorials reveal an intriguing feature of this community - that these fishing families had been giving their children surnames as Christian names since the 1820s. And from the 1830s, they were giving *second* Christian names too. Both practices were rare in the working-class before the 20th Century. Nationally, the perpetuation of the names of parents and grandparents fell out of fashion especially after World War I. But not in Filey, judging from recent St Oswald gravestones.

Also, the art of the maritime pun continues undiminished: witness Thomas Williamson BAXTER (died 1989, 'safely anchored'), John Richard Hanson (1968, 'With the Heavenly Pilot, he crossed the Bar') and Richard Jenkinson Haxby (died 2005, 'Upon the tide you drifted now you're anchored safe and sure'). William Jenkinson Watkinson Mainprize (died 2008) is evidence that 'triple surname' christening was occurring into the 20th Century.

First Impressions: First Questions

Why did this small community use such names? Were they all interrelated, as the limited number of surnames implied? Could the jigsaw of these families be assembled? How long had they been in Filey Old Town? *How* did they endure the staggering occupational mortality rate revealed so starkly on these stones?

During their earliest decades in the town, the JENKINSONs were so spectacularly fertile that they now figure on just about every family tree in Filey. When talking family history to a local chap in the churchyard in 2018, I asked if he were a JENKINSON. 'We all are!' he replied. They were our initial focus, but became the spine of a far wider interest in the ancestry and history of this fishing community. In the process, we have made some intriguing discoveries:

SARAH SAYERS,
DIED NOV. 1, 1921, AGED 78 YEARS.
AT REST.

ALSO, WILLIAM SAYERS,
BELOVED HUSBAND OF THE ABOVE,
WHO WAS LOST AT SEA MARCH 6, 1883,
AGED 47 YEARS.

1.5: [Left] The final evolution of the yawl. William SAYERS was lost off *Denison* at Spurn, one of nine Filey men who drowned in the Great March Gale of 1883, reckoned by contemporaries as the worst of the 19th Century. This carving may well represent the doomed boat. The jib and staysail to the fore increased capture of wind power and assisted tacking. His widow Sarah (née Chadwick) lost her father, two brothers and husband to the sea.[3]

Fine detail like the topsails above each gaff **[Right]** suggest that the mason was closely advised by a crew member, and did not rely on generic templates of boats. This carving is on John COLLING's gravestone - he died at sea, probably of natural causes, on the yawl *Dorothy*, 26th April 1902, and was buried at St Oswald's three days later.

For at least two centuries, Filey's fishing population multiplied from a core of 15 surnames. In addition, several incoming fisher names have been integrated from elsewhere along the east coast, especially from north Norfolk. Generations of intermarriage created a community in which all were interrelated, and usually several times over. *All* JENKINSONs descend from the pedigrees shown at the end of this book, ultimately from the 1778 marriage of Robert and Margaret JENKINSON. Between 1779 and 1795, this couple produced seven marrying children. By the 1840s, early marriages, fertility, rude health, good luck in the daily gamble at sea, and prosperous fishing livelihoods engendered over 32 grandchildren, who themselves produced similarly-sized families. By the 1980s, there were well over 1,000 descendants of this Clapham Junction of a couple, mostly living in or near Filey.

Hence all 33 JENKINSONs in the extract from the 1923 *Filey Directory* (**1.2**) were their direct descendants, or married to one. Identical concentrations of fishing populations in one cluster of streets and yards have been noted in many coastal villages. In north-east Scotland, married children in fishing villages were even accommodated in new extensions to existing houses.[4]

---

[3] *Redux*, 29th Oct 2019.
[4] Blaikie (2002) pp27-8; Thompson et al (1983) pp245-6.

1.6: Perhaps one of John Sumpton Fox's beautifully carved inscriptions. John JENKINSON (N10) was the last of the five 'Clapham Junction' sons: their average lifespan (73 years) is testimony to the sound health of this fishing community – and *their* good luck. John's occupation, proudly proclaimed on the stone, his 'Calling' from God, is equivalent testimony to the community's spiritual health, long lost in modern Britain – how many grave carvings of 'accountant', 'banker', or 'management consultant' do you see?

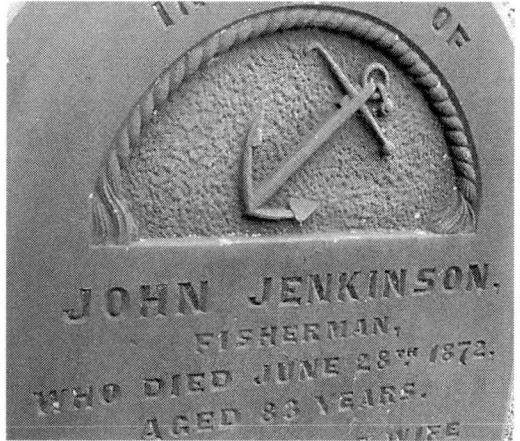

From a simple attempt to trace a direct family tree, our interest escalated into a massive search through every available source to untangle the innumerable JENKINSON fisher families. Since then, the vast increase in the availability of source material has made it possible to widen the scope of the project into a portrait of the now vanished fisher way of life in Filey Old Town.

Postscript: Who carved the Filey Stones?

1.7: A set of bricklayer's tools, perfectly carved in 1877 by John Sumpton Fox, on the 181st stone he completed, perhaps to commemorate a fellow craftsman and friend.

Where did this remarkable art form of depiction of fishing vessels come from? There are a few anchor and boat images at Hinderwell St Hilda's, in which parish lies Staithes, in many ways Filey's twin. But these are mostly on the memorials of master mariners. Some Norfolk coastal graveyards have a few.

But Filey's collection is unique in scale and quality. The first distinctive anchor/rudder motif dates from 1823 (**1.3**). Filey's signature empty coble design, code for a drowning, appears in the 1860s. The real flowering comes in the later 19th Century with accurately rigged yawls.

The whole genre seems to be home-grown, but by whom? There are few stonemasons in the Filey census returns: none lasted long. The most substantial was William Freeman, on Church Street in the 1851 returns, and employing three men. His location implies that the business focused on monumental masonry. John Sumpton Fox probably learned his trade with Freeman, living his whole life on Church Street. Francis, his elder brother, became a bricklayer. Their father, also John, was a joiner, then parish clerk at St Oswald's in the 1830s/40s. He may have encouraged his son to specialise in monumental masonry, aware of the prices that well-carved gravestones commanded. John Sumpton too became parish clerk, a position which surely ensured he was well placed to obtain commissions.

1.8: John Sumpton Fox in his Mitford Street workshop, 1877/8. The narrow stone to the right, with the cross, is to be carved with his son's name. *[JC]*

Note mason's mallet, left. Fox's three year-old son, Francis, died in 1877.

John Sumpton, a very skilled sculptor, was 'a memorable part' of Old Filey according to his 1901 *Parish Magazine* obituary. His 'prominent shop', rebuilt on the old footings, like for like, is now *Shrimpers Cottage.* It stands at the Church Street end of Mitford Street (once called Chapel Street).

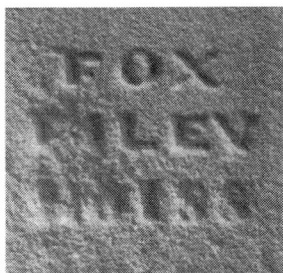

1.9: The memorial to the monumental mason's son. It is incised number 188, first on the left beyond the main gate of St Oswald's churchyard. *[JC]*

John Sumpton carved several hundred stones in a career of over 40 years, and many were for fishermen. Most are edged with his initials. I have a hunch that he had a hand in those polished puns. Whoever did devise them crafted graphic poetry, even when the usual rich veins of fishing and navigation were irrelevant to the deceased's background. One of my favourites is that of William Watkinson, sexton at St Oswald's for 32 years, which reads

A door keeper in the House of my God.

2 A MOMENT IN TIME: FILEY, MONDAY 4TH APRIL 1881

The Filey that Irene and I caught a vanishing sight of in 1982 may be all but gone. But 101 years before, the town must have been an intriguing place to come to. Just consider the many outsiders, especially clergymen, who could not resist writing up their fascinated impressions. This chapter invites you back to one 'Moment in Time', when the old Filey fishing way of life was just past its peak. Please suspend incredulity, see some very familiar *and* unfamiliar things, and walk in the shoes of an imaginary visitor coming to the town for the first time.

Monday 4th April 1881 – when you arrived in Filey, the chances are you came by train. This is far faster than the coach which was the only means of travel until 34 years ago. But let one dissatisfied visitor of 1868 describe his experience at Seamer:

> The dreary call of 'Zee-Mur', with a very long 'Zee' and a very strongly emphasised 'Mur' which seems as though it would never reach your locked door to let you out – the covered sheds in which the prevailing wind blows just the same on one side as on the other; the futile waiting room for ladies, and all the many miseries that beset a shelterless, foodless, and unsightly Junction where everybody has to change . . . .[1]

Imagine this Monday morning in 1881 that you are over that ordeal, and enjoying a spring holiday at one of the many hotels or lodging houses on The Crescent in Filey's New Town. Yesterday, the proprietor requested your personal details to enter onto his census schedule, for over this weekend the census has been held.

Most visitors explore the Old Town, the old fishing quarter, for it is always described in the Filey guidebooks. The main street may be known as Queen Street at the seaward end, and King Street to the west, but there's nothing royal about the mounds of droppings – horse-drawn carts deliver to shops, and shires are brought daily from a nearby stable behind *The Grapes* to haul cobles out of the sea. The street is covered in gravel, brought from the foot of the cliffs.[2]

What a contrast with the neatly laid out New Filey, where you are staying. The strange mix of buildings in the Old Town follows an irregular street line, and if there *is* a pavement it is often very narrow. There are grocers, butchers, fish sellers, bakers/confectioners, tailors, drapers, hatters, a shop for children's clothes and toys, a dressmaker, fruiterer, coal merchant, an eating house, and four inns. Some inhabitants have had no call to venture more than a few hundred yards in their lives.

---

[1] Pettitt (1868).
[2] Filey Enclosure Award (1788) p3.

2.1: The extreme west end of Queen Street c1900, originally the Town Street. Note the irregular street line, varied ages and styles of building, the long-gone crowdedness of the scene, and the sheer quantity of young children, consequent upon early marriage amongst the fishing community, and the low mortality rate. *[SE]*

The shops advertise 'no fancy prices for visitors'. But the reality may be different. 'We expect him to be made of money,' is the real attitude of the traders towards the visitor,

> and ready to part with it too. Our old postmaster rightly hit off the situation when he replied to a visitor who had discovered a penny wrong in his change, 'Oh, if you have come here to make a row over a copper, we don't want you *here*.'[3]

Money-conscious shopkeepers are not the only locals who have reservations about trippers, for day visitors are associated with 'hard-boiled eggs and bottles of beer they brought out with them from home':

> A very large number enjoy themselves after their own fashion, which sometimes does not allow them to get even as far as the amusements on the sands, but tempts them into the first public-house they come to, and there they remain till the time arrives for their train to return.[4]

---

[3] Cooper (1910) p50. The St Oswald's parson was describing the situation in 1910, but it seems unlikely that things were much different 29 years earlier.

[4] Cooper (1908) pp31-5, writing of 20 years before.

2.2: Further east along Queen Street, early 20th Century. A boy in 'short' trousers stands outside JW Freeman's *Crown Hotel*, no 52. Notice the gravel surface of the street, and the heaps of unidentifiable detritus, some possibly emanating from horses. *[SE]*

By far the most noticeable buildings on the main street are the pantile-roofed terraces of tiny fishermen's cottages, with the many yards and 'rents' which have been built behind them. The Local Board simply refers to these side terraces by numbers, although they acquire familiar names amongst the fisher people.

'Primitive and fishy'

You cannot mistake the one and only trade of the men in the Old Town. 'The very smell of the streets is of fish, and every wall and post is pressed into the service of drying and fettling the nets and lines.'[5] Tarring, tanning and barking are central to the fisherman's life - his nets, lines, and over-clothing must be boiled up regularly to resist the corrosive action of seawater, even dog faeces going into the mix to soften the material. Streets are streaked with dull red channels, as waste water runs from the outhouses at the backs of the cottages which have coppers. Smell and smoke emanate from the fish-curing houses; clouds from smouldering oak and ash chippings waft out of the herring houses. Add to this the mixed stenches of decaying cutch (a tarry preservative they boil) pig styes, manure and open ashpits.

The Local Board in 1881 makes even *this* situation worse, its contractors being reported recently as having removed night soil only once every six or seven weeks, instead of the required six or seven days. And these unpleasant operations are not only at night, as their own bye-laws stipulate: their carts are about 'at all hours.'[6]

---

[5] Sokell (1899); Cooper (1886) p38.
[6] *Scarborough Post*, 4th April 1879; *Scarborough Mercury,* 5th April 1879.

2.3: New Filey, as seen in 1858 from south of Bentley Gill, above what is now Glen Gardens. As early as this, a clear 'spin' is being concocted to represent Filey as a select resort for the bourgeoisie. The white-sailed cobles are presented as attractions for visitors, part of the seaside scenery and a genteel leisure opportunity, rather than the means of ordinary families earning a living. Fishing coble sails were dyed brown.

Add to repugnant smells the disagreeable sight of butchers slaughtering animals in full public view, and you sense why some visitors do not chance down the Town's oldest street.[7] It is as well for Filey's growing visitor trade that old and new towns are geographically separate. Hoteliers and lodging-house keepers will tell you how superior Filey is in relation to Scarborough, where visitors have to lodge by the harbour, very close to all these smells of the fishermen's trade.

The interiors of the cottages, however, are cosy and neat, for the women are 'cleanly in their homes'. Tiny windows leave interiors gloomy, but the plainness of the flag-floored interior is alleviated by the fire always burning in the range, an abundance of mugs, plates and dishes on the dresser and the near-universal pot and brass ornaments.

---

[7] Such public executions were actually of great interest to those locals with nothing better to occupy them. There is an engaging account, almost certainly of Filey Old Town, of the unsupervised 12 year-old son of one visiting family who, on an errand, joined a crowd 'gathered round a narrow entry, as it thrilled to watch the pole-axing of a bullock, and sheep after sheep seized and killed . . .' . George thought how tame was building sand castles, or riding donkeys, or even listening to Pierrots, compared to what he had seen that Wednesday afternoon' (Cooper, 1910, pp91-2).

2.4: Three-man cobles, for inshore line-fishing, mounted on old artillery carriages. Beached beyond are three yawls, six-man deep-sea boats, which use the same lining technique to fish the Dogger Bank. Note the coble's brown, part-raised sail, and its mast well for'ard. The photograph must date from after 1870, for the yawls are gaff-rigged (see **9.5**, page 109). *[SE]*

As you walk down Old Filey's main street, and observe the many cottages in its adjoining Yards, Terraces and Places, you will meet no men of fishing age: males between ten and 70 plus have been at sea for hours. But behind cottage or bait house doors, you will hear constant chatter and laughter. Scores of women and youngsters have, since the early hours, been baiting lines with mussels, whelks, cockles, lug worms – indeed with anything likely to tempt a bite. If it's a fine day, some may have escaped the gloom of their cottages to sit outside and knit ganseys with neighbours, either for their menfolk or even for sale.

A self-contained community naturally talks a good deal about itself, *callin*, rumour and snooping being inevitable - but the women will not gossip about other fisher families to strangers.[8] ['You couldn't tell them anything, you could see an accident happen and go in there to tell her about it and she knew all about it' recalled George Burton of the 1920s, reckoning his grandma's and his aunt's house were 'like modern news agencies'.]

---

[8] This reluctance to tittle-tattle to strangers about neighbours was still apparent in the 1980s. As we talked to one elderly Queen Street couple, the old fisherman occasionally lapsed into gleeful gossip about Old Town families. His wife quickly silenced him with a disapprovingly raised voice!

2.5: 'A tale of two cities' – pre-Great War upper middle-class visitors take the sea air by the Coble Landing – note cameras, right. A fisherman nonchalantly puffs at his pipe. He awaits another customer - a sail round the bay costs 2s 6d an hour. *[SE]*

The Fishing

You'll soon realise that there are two separate types of fishing going on here. The offshore men sail 30 miles or more out in their 60-foot decked yawls to the Dogger Bank, a truly wild ground when an easterly whips up its infamously heavy seas.

Two women are walking up from their cottage on King Street - 62 year-old Sarah Mainprize with daughter Sarah Wright, 36. Both are fishermen's widows, forced to eke out a living by charring, probably in the New Town. Few in Old Filey ever visit The Crescent, with its villas and fashionable lodging houses, built only 30 odd years ago. It is a foreign country, as any child will tell you, for they are in trouble if they stray so far. 'What's thoo want down there?' mothers will say. 'There's nowt down there for thoo, keep thiself at this side.'[9] Indeed, with about 20 shops along its main street, and a market every Friday, women have no call to leave the Old Town at all, unless they are off up the coast bait-gathering.

The older Sarah may be reflecting how completely her life changed seven years ago when her husband George, along with his nephew George JENKINSON and son-in-law George JOHNSON, were thrown from their coble by a huge wave, and drowned off The Brigg within sight of their terrified families and friends. Their bodies have never been found, and if they were it would have taken weeks, even months, before they were washed up somewhere. That could be miles away. Prior to their loss, mother and daughter would have been baiting daily too. On the census form last night, Sarah Mainprize recorded her married status as 'widow' for the first time - a sad word for her daughter, too, to be using for herself - at just 36.

There is a tight interweave amongst Filey's fishing families, through marriage and shared ownership of boats. Families gain identity from their boats, men fishing with brothers, sons, nephews and in-laws. Inevitably, given the frequency of loss, there

---

[9] 'And you'd maybe get a clout for going.' (Ned Wright, born c1890, in Frank, 2002, p48.)

are many mothers and daughters widowed by the same storm. Like the two Sarahs, they may live together for financial and emotional support. And these widows would not be human if a part of them did not resent neighbours who anxiously but successfully wait all night at the railway station during a big storm, getting news at last by telegraph that their husbands and sons have safely reached some harbour like Hull or Grimsby along the coast. It is no surprise that anxious eyes regularly glance at the sky over the North Sea, and at the cone and drum which hang from the Coastguards' flagstaff at the end of Queen Street. Their positions signal weather forecasts telegraphed daily from the Meteorological Office in London.

The fearful potency of unpredictable weather has made itself very apparent in the last few months. The storm of October 1880, just six months ago, showed that it is not just the three-man cobles that are swamped and lost in a heavy sea. Whilst fishing for herring, drifting with the swell to keep a mile or two of nets taut on the warp line, the Filey and Scarborough yawls were overwhelmed by one of the worst storms in years. Fifteen men were lost, ten swept off the *Eliza*, including her master, Ross JENKINSON. No body has ever been found, for the *Eliza* went down a long way out. A corpse could turn up in some trawl wherever the sea might take it, but probably too decomposed to be recognisable. Ross's widow, Eliza, now lives alone, just round the corner, on Reynolds Street. How will she be feeling, writing out her 1881 census schedule?

A cold spring has followed some of the severest winter weather in living memory. The great easterly blizzard and snowfalls of mid-January were the worst of the century, closing hundreds of miles of railway, burying trains, uprooting thousands of trees and killing over 100 people on land. It is unimaginable what such weather can do to boats five hours sail away on the cod fishing grounds of the deadly Dogger, let alone to tiny three-man cobles that go out every winter. [10] Almost at the bottom of Queen Street, you'll pass another cottage full of recent grief, the former home of Richard RICHARDSON. He was a shareman on the *Eliza*, and drowned along with his eldest son Richard. Two widows now live here: Ann was 'lucky': she at least has two children of working age, so will not have to go charring in New Filey. Her daughter-in-law Betsy Ann, married just three years, has a two-year old daughter. Like many toddlers on this street, she will have no memory of her father or grandfather.

The more successful and provident fishermen belong to one of the town's friendly societies, but many earn too little to make the regular dues that entitle their widows to a few shillings a week of modest support. Dramatic and poignant tragedies always lead to a public subscription in the town. The sum raised will be boosted if the loss has occurred during the visitors' season, or before Christmas, and might finance an annuity of a pound or more a week per widow.

---

[10] JM Stratton & Jack Houghton Brown, *Agricultural Records* (John Baker, 1969); see the *Wikipedia* entry for the Blizzard of January 1881; in that year, the worst storm of the century was to be just two years away, the Great March Gale of 1883.

2.6: The 'Fisherman's Look-out', a row of benches at Cliff Top, summer 1930: **L to R –** Seamer-born Isaac Walker Ethell (71); Robert Jenkinson COLLING (79) with his grandson, who has the same name; Thomas Chapman (79); William *Ino* Crawford (82); William Stubbs ROBINSON (87); Healand SAYERS (79) and William Watkinson (80). *[FA]*

Unfortunately, the worst losses occur in the Winter and Spring Fishing, when there are few visitors here. Today may just be warm enough for the retired fishermen, men in their seventies and eighties, to be at the 'Fisherman's Look-out'. They are used to harsh weather, and this vantage point at the Cliff Top affords a panoramic view, miles out to the North Sea horizon. Visitors listen to them incredulously as the old men identify homecoming cobles before strangers are even aware of a speck bobbing on the tide.[11] The smallest group of ex-fishermen will contain hundreds of years of aggregated experience, for each man will have been at sea for 60 or more years.[12] Despite the exciting vista from the Cliff Top, there is a sombre reminder nearby of how dangerous the Bay can be: a gas lamp was erected over 20 years ago, with a seaward-facing red pane, as an aid to the town's fishermen.[13]

Fishing has work for both sexes and all ages. There is even light work for the elderly. Watch the group of experienced ex-fishermen on hand as the cobles are launched in the early hours, and beached later in the day, for an onshore wind can

---

[11] These old timers loved 'yarning'. As Sokell puts it in his 1899 *Guide*, 'here you will be informed as to the elements, past, present and future; for depend upon it, if you are at all talkative, you will be the one to tire first . . . '.

[12] The JENKINSON brothers William and John (N8 and 10) born in 1786 and 1791, were still going to sea in 1863, according to their evidence to two government appointed commissioners. William stated that he had been a fisherman 'upwards of 70 years', c1793, suggesting he'd been fishing since seven (*Sea Fisheries Commission, 1863-6*).

[13] The latest version of this lamp, visible so far out to sea as to figure on maritime charts, was apparently unseen by the driver of the wagon that reversed into it around 2015.

2.7: Two generations of touting – **Left:** a post-fishing *spawer* offers a bracing sea-trip. Note rickety stage. 'Going for a sail, sir?' From 'Sketches at Scarborough', *The Graphic*, 14th October 1871. **Right:** unnamed barefoot pre-fishing boys at a loose end. *[FA]*

bring a boat broadside into the beach, and she will be swamped. Old men also help to bait lines, and make and repair herring nets. In the summer, they will be out with grandsons, potting for crabs and lobsters. It is illegal now to have young boys working at sea, though some trawler skippers seem to ignore the law. Ever since Mr Gladstone's government passed the new Education Act last summer, all children under 10 have to be at school. The poorer families resent this loss of income, and many youngsters have to be up baiting lines before school to make up.

The Beach

You'll be struck by how many children there are in the Old Town: fishermen marry young, have big families, and their children don't die off like those in the factory towns. In the season, they can be a real nuisance, pestering to act as guides for visitors, or offering rides in granddad's wagon, in return for a few coppers.[14] Fortunately, the older men who tout for fishing trips are more considerate:

> There is one thing about the Filey fishermen, they can ask a civil question and understand a negative or affirmative answer, and we cannot look upon them as seaside pests, as they take it for granted that if your answer be No! you mean it.

---

[14] 'A dozen boys will beset you as you go down from the sea wall to the sands, "Carriage sir. Take you to The Brigg for a shilling sir . . . ".' (Pettitt, 1868).

> The charge for men and boat is only 2s 6d an hour, and some two or three can join in one boat and each have a line at the same cost; but it is as well to remember that nature, if kind to you, likes you to be kind in return, and the price of an ounce of tobacco, rest assured, is acceptable.[15]

And consideration works both ways, for the visitor

> is allowed to ask endless tiresome questions and receive civil answers, free of charge, from men who have, perhaps been up all night, but still manage to keep their tempers . . . .

You may even risk clambering up onto one of the mobile 'stages' for a trip round the bay in a coble, with one of the ageing ex-fishermen. There are strict limits on how many visitors can be in one boat, if the council inspector is ever around.

There are lots of ways down to the beach – along this coast, many of the pathways down from the cliffs have been created by women bait-gatherers, or smugglers. There is plenty to do on the sands, for bicycles and even horses are available for hire. Be careful that you do not collide with the many donkeys that give rides, for they have hard lives as it is.

But the greatest attraction of Filey beach is its sea-bathing, and female visitors need have no fear of impropriety: the town's bye-laws of 1869 stipulate that no bathing machine hired by a man shall be within 150 yards of one containing females. And as to any peeping toms amongst the coarser fishermen, the regulations specify that:

> No person shall moor, sail, or row, any boat or vessel within the distance of two hundred yards from any Bathing Machine which any person shall be using for the purpose of bathing therefrom.

The Local Board is equally protective of the morals of the young, requiring that 'No female of ten years or upwards, shall bathe on the sea shore . . . without a Bathing Dress.' Equally, boys are dissuaded from lewd behaviour by the insistence that none over 12 'shall bathe without drawers.' The moral tone of the beach is further protected by the ban on bathing machines being out on the Sabbath.[16]

From Filey, there is a fine walk to Bempton, where four or five men,

> make their living by descending the cliffs to gather the birds' eggs, which they sell on arrival at the top again at the price of a penny each if you take them as they come, or fourpence if you pick them. The rest are sent into the West Riding where their white is useful in certain dyeing manufactories. For a consideration the men will let anyone try what it is like to hang over the cliffs suspended by a rope. Even ladies have been known to descend, but in these days ladies seem more venturesome than the men.[17]

---

[15] Sokell (1899); Smith (1932) p199.
[16] Allison (1854).
[17] Cooper (1900) p26.

2.8: The gentle peace of a sunny English holiday morning, perhaps an Edwardian summer, shortly before all was to change in the Great War, when German mines were to float in the bay. Just visible is the 'Children's Corner', where parents get away for an adult break, their youngsters perhaps hearing stories. It is an encumbered society - note the antique prams, the many umbrellas, and the black clothing! The one unchanging feature of beach convenience 110 years ago was the deckchair. A single yawl discreetly lies at anchor. *[FA]*

Yawls and cobles will by now be long gone with the morning tide. But you may spot some of the older men, perhaps accompanied by young boys, bobbing in cobles just offshore, over the rocky seabed by The Brigg, checking their pots for crabs and lobsters and replacing any mouldy bait. Being April, the sea has started to warm up from the winter, rousing the dormant shellfish from the sandy seabed. The crabbers will maybe get 6d for a crab with a five-inch shell.

Along the front are any number of stalls selling dressed crab and crabs' legs on to visitors, but a law of 1877 now bans the sale of any undersized shellfish. As every fisherman here will tell you, stocks of everything in the sea are down, and they blame the trawlers. For the last 50 years, these have been dredging up *everything* from the seabed – a by-catch of shellfish, spawn, and very young hatchlings.

This is why the yawls are away far more. Apart from the summer/autumn herring season, these big boats used to fish for five days and be back every Saturday. But to get the greatfish like cod, the deep-sea men must now go much further afield and live on their yawls far longer. If you were to speak today to the two census enumerators who are trudging Filey's streets and farms collecting the household schedules, you will learn that the man of the house is missing from scores of fisher cottages. There are far more women than men recorded in our recent censuses, and many are widows, because of the high mortality rate of the fisherman.[18]

But 40 or more fisherman were away from home on Sunday night, when the census is supposed to be timed. They should therefore have been entered on forms elsewhere. And they were, but that is another story, which we'll pick up later.

Modern Postscript: the Filey Donkeys

God's dumber creatures were experiencing extremes of treatment in Filey 140 years ago: any 21st Century concept of animal rights was only ever going to receive the shortest of shrifts from a community whose livelihood was rooted in the mass harvesting of living creatures. But there was a wanton heartlessness in attitudes to the local seabird population, and the town's hapless beach donkeys, which can only make us grateful for more enlightened times. Mercifully, a small but vociferous minority increasingly drew attention to the pointless cruelty that they witnessed on the cliffs and the beach.[19]

A Torquay vicar was so incensed by what he had seen at Filey in 1901 that he wrote to a Scarborough newspaper. His account appeared in the St Oswald's *Parish Magazine* that November:

> . . . the pleasure of the visit was marred by the brutality which those who had the donkeys for hire showed . . . every boy [seeming] alike brutal with the poor beasts, and a small boy of six was given a stick with which to belabour a weary and broken looking animal who was drawing a load of Lawn Chairs for local performers.

Nor did these animals have any seasonal rest, for once the summer months were done, they were walked to Flamborough for the Winter Fishing, pannier baskets of cod replacing children as they plodded up to the village from the North and South Landings, and on to the railway station four miles inland. Then as now, worthy causes attracted local celebrity attention, in this case the 'genial and kind hearted actress' Madge Kendal. Perhaps as a result of the publicity that this 'woke' local woman brought to the plight of these beach beasts, she attracted the attention of an anonymous, dying donor.

2.9: 'Mrs Kendal', the Filey actress moved by cruelty to donkeys. *[SE]*

---

[18] The 1895 loss without trace of the yawl *Trio*, with crew of six, highlighted Filey's loss to the sea of 45 fishermen in the previous 15 years. Nationally, of every 83 fishermen, one was killed each year. This occupational death-rate was twice that of a railway shunter, the second most dangerous employment (*Scarborough Gazette*, 30th May 1895).

[19] Changing 19th Century attitudes towards sea birds are considered in ch14.

2.10: Donkey rides on Filey Beach, c1903. Note the sticks with which a Torquay vicar had seen 'the poor beasts' struck by a boy of six, two years before. On the right is Mark Russell, born in 1891 on Murray Street, son of fish merchant Thomas. Mark went on to run a garage. *[FA]*

Though this physician had never been to the town, he paid for an Aberdeen granite trough, and in 1905 Mrs Kendal ceremoniously commended it to the local donkeys before 'a great crowd'. Madge having grandly cut the ribbon, one of the donkeys took the opening drink. Mrs Kendal hoped that the gift would have some effect on the donkey boys in the treatment of their animals, Mr Maley, chairman of the Urban District Council, declared the local authority would keep the trough in constant order, and Mrs Kendal presented each donkey boy with a new sixpence.[20]

'It is not often that Filey appears in the pages of *Punch*', remarked Canon Cooper in the next *Parish Magazine*. But it just had, in the form of this wry observation:

> The watering places are at length waking up to the necessity of providing attractions for visitors. In Filey last Thursday Mrs Kendal opened a drinking trough for donkeys.

Did the efforts of the anonymous donor and the local actress move the hearts of the boys? Alas no, judging from a *Parish Magazine* report three years later of the town's RSPCA June branch meeting. Cooper, to his credit, was chairman. Captain Riddell of Gristhorpe Hall was clearly an animal activist, who had been lobbying on the issue – he had spoken of the ready way in which he had been met by donkey owners and carriage proprietors. Captain Kerr VC had seen several cases of cruelty last summer. Money was made on the beach in the mornings, and the donkeys had to do 'half a dozen journeys in the time of one'. Eighteen years before he had seen 'a gross case of cruelty' and initiated a prosecution before the Bridlington magistrates. On his return to Filey he had been stoned by the fisher boys as 'his recompense'. Ever the optimist, willing to reward rather than punish, Mrs Kendal offered a prize 'to the donkey boy able to make his donkey go without beating it.'[21]

---

[20] Shakespearean actress Madge Kendal (1848-1935) lived at *White Lodge Hotel*, Filey, for around 40 years (*Yorkshire Post*, 11th Sept 2019).

[21] *Parish Magazine*, Sept 1905; Aug 1908.

3 COMMUNITY LIFE IN THE OLD TOWN

'This prosperous watering-place was, little over thirty years ago, an insignificant fishing village,' declared Black's tourist guide in 1862. For most of its history, Filey was an agricultural parish centred on just a couple of streets, where farmhouses and fishermen's cottages were grouped on or near springs - in the 1970s, during demolition, a brick-lined well was discovered under a shop opposite the *Crown Hotel*. In the 19th Century, this historic nucleus evolved into a closely packed fishing quarter, the Old Town, the final outline of which is clearly visible on the map of 1891 (**3.4**). The railway's arrival in 1846-7 helped the growth of New Filey - an entirely separate residential/tourist accommodation quarter to the south of these fishing streets.

Enclosure and the Evolution of the Filey Old Town Community

There is no archaeological or historical evidence to show how the fishing quarter evolved in the distant past, or indeed how old it is. What we see in 19th Century photographs is mostly terraces erected by builders of that period.

3.1: The old *Pack Horse Inn* (later *The Crown*) on Queen Street is a reminder of the importance of pack teams for taking fish, day and night, inland to the towns of Lancashire and Yorkshire. The thatched roof seems distinctly rural, a reminder that Filey was still primarily an agricultural village well into the 19th Century. By the time of this late Victorian view, the Local Board of Health had introduced limited street gas lighting. Electricity only reached the town in July 1930. *[FA]*

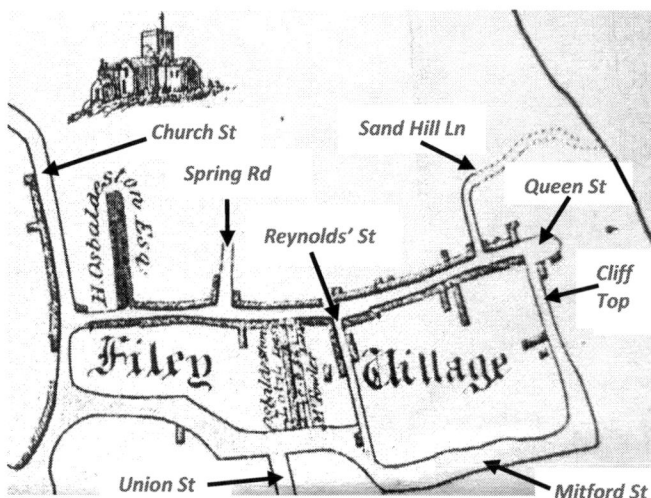

3.2: The earliest street map of Filey: an estate plan of 1835, labelled with modern names.

Mitford Street, the southern extent of the Old Town, was known as Back Lane as late as 1855. 'Fishermen's Road' (later Sand Hill Lane) led down to the landing. *[FA]*

There is evidence elsewhere that fishermen's cottages were built communally prior to any wedding. At Staithes, in 1924, one old man recalled how he had

> heard old people say that their grandparents told them . . . that when they were young it was the usual thing, when two people were going to get married, for the whole community to join together to build them a house . . . without this mutual assistance it would not have been possible for the poorer people to have obtained a house . . . . The only pay they got was an invitation to the covering-in supper.[1]

This account may take us back to the 18th Century, when we have little idea of how Filey was set out. At Robin Hood's Bay, Storm (1991, p25) has found Edward ROBINSON dividing his house amongst sons in 1739. Perhaps Filey parents too extended existing houses, to accommodate marrying children, as happened on Scotland's north-east coast. These arrangements would involve no extra rent if part of a house's yard were built on. Old luggers, broken up on the beach, provided much building material in the 19th Century, their tall masts being incorporated as roof timbers in many existing Old Town houses.

Behind the houses on the town's main street lay their 'yards', the ancient crofts or *garths* stretching north or south, once probably used for livestock, especially poultry. Mrs Mary Sugget, a resident of the town for most of the 19th Century, recalled the Filey of her youth as 'one main street with yards'.

The development of Filey Old Town was a by-product of changes in local farming: we must remember that the village was essentially agricultural until well into the 19th Century, with fishermen's cottages inserted. But the 1841 Census shows that most farmers had ceased to live in the town centre as a result of the complete reconfiguring of the layout of Filey township in 1788-91.

---

[1] Frank (2002) p43. 'Covering-in' was the local term for the final roofing of the cottage.

3.3: A 'six-row' terrace on Spring Road, shortly before demolition c1971, one of many built to house fishing families as the town grew in the 19th Century. Erected on the old farming 'rents' and yards of the original village, these side streets created the familiar herring-bone plan of the Old Town (**3.4**) fossilising the medieval village's layout. Originally Spring Row, 12 cottages were recorded here in the 1881 Census, eight of which were occupied by fishing families. Spring Road is now an uninhabited access route from Queen Street to Ravine Top, but its name suggests it was an ancient path from the medieval village to its main springs and wells in Church Ravine. *[FA]*

Villages in lowland England had usually been farmed since Anglo-Saxon times in large, unfenced communal fields. In these, each farmer had a portfolio of approximately acre-sized strips scattered across the arable land of the parish. By the late 18th Century, rising urban populations were now accessible by turnpike roads, and farmers wanted to produce surpluses to profit from town dwellers. But this was difficult because of this ancient pattern of landholding.

Nobody knows why Dark Age agriculture developed in this disintegrated fashion. It may have resulted from a fossilisation of the annual taking in to cultivation of surrounding land by the earliest Anglo-Saxon settlers. Each year's intake would have been distributed amongst the families in the settlement. An important feature of this system was the various common grazing rights enjoyed by all tenants – in Filey, on the stubble of the three big open fields after harvest, and on the Common Moor and Ox Pasture. Lanes and roads had evolved into broad rights of way, to allow a way to be picked through the mudscape, with greenswards (grass edges) also customarily available for communal grazing.

The privatisation of communal assets was not invented in the 1980s. The *zeitgeist* of the late 18th Century was to push for consolidation of these pre-Conquest hotchpotches of farms into unified holdings. Communal rights of access to stubble, pasture, greensward and woodland were extinguished and the three great open fields partitioned, ie enclosed, into separate, unified farms. In this way, *all* the land became privately owned. This marketisation of agriculture changed Filey's landscape forever, in just three years, 1788-91.[2]

---

[2] Filey Inclosure, Commissioners' Award (1791). Copy at SMHC.

3.4: The 25-inch Ordnance Survey map of 1891 reveals a fleshing out of the basic two street skeleton apparent in the 1835 plan (**3.2**). Note the 'fishbone' plan of terraces, built on the farming rents and yards which lay behind the main village street. Later editions show 'Fixed Light (Red)', the famous lamp at the east end of Queen Street, the first version of which was erected in the 1850s as a navigation aid.

Farm buildings had been in the village centre, clustered along what is now Queen Street. These were mostly sold after 1791, to finance replacements out on the new landholdings. A trace of this process of change is revealed in Filey's 1840/1 electoral register, which lists a butcher, not a farmer, living in a 'farmhouse' just off Church Street. This was George Gofton, whose profits from the weekly sale of meat to yawl crews presumably financed Gofton's Yard, built alongside.

By the 1840s, most farmers had moved out to their consolidated farmholdings in the rural parts of the parish, beyond the village and its livestock enclosures. But farming remained enmeshed with the Old Town fisher streets well into the 20th Century. In September 1905, one man was fined 2s 6d for allowing seven pigs to stray in West Street (now West Avenue). The Appleby family's *Manor Farm*, home of the shire horses which assisted at the launching and beaching of cobles until the 1950s, was wedged behind *The Grapes*. It seems to have been producing milk in the 1930s, and 'there were cows all over' when the herd was brought to the farm from outlying fields at milking time. *Manor Farm* presumably held the various grass fields, and the cow pasture shown on the 1867 plan (**3.5**). And Church Farm, north of The Ravine, still harvested each year, deaf gravedigger Jimmy Douglas famously sitting astride the threshing machine, cutting lengths of binder string, as fisher boys dropped fleeing mice onto the rim of his hat. [3]

---

[3] Fearon (2008) p44; Edmund *Eddie* CAMMISH; Terence COLLINS.

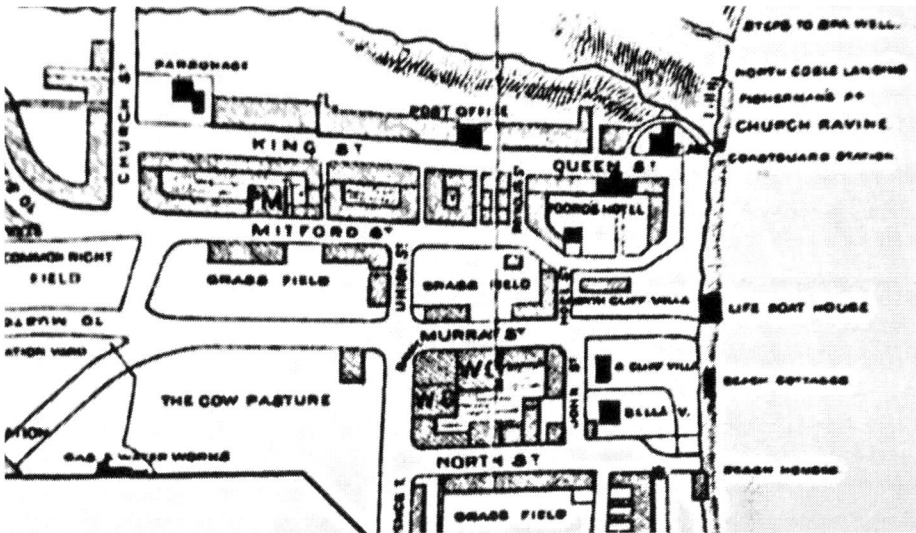

3.5: As late as March 1867, when this rough plan was drawn, there were several remnants of the old farming landscape very close to the town centre. The grass fields were presumably meadows producing winter feed (Rev Arthur Pettitt, *Map of Filey and its Neighbourhood*, 1868).

Quite independently, the village's fisher population grew, and the old livestock yards could be now be used to build baiting and storage sheds.[4] The new cottage that Thomas ROSS lived in around 1800, for example, had a 'bark and tan house'.[5] In the 1830s/40s, men with money used the yards behind their houses or shops to build terraces of small cottages. This gave the Old Town its distinctive 'fish bone' appearance **(3.4)**. Without enclosure, these yards, ideally shaped for housing, and for many fishing-related processes, would not have been available.

Infilling and rebuilding led to changes in some street names from one decennial census to another, and the gradual appearance of the many 'yard' names. It was no longer sufficient to identify a location as simply 'Queen Street'. For example, the 1841 census returns record ship owner James Mosey on what became Queen Street. The 22 cottages of Mosey's Yard (later known as Providence Place) follow on immediately after his house in the enumerator's book.

---

[4] An enthusiastic researcher could follow the evolution of some of these 'yards' from the 1788 enclosure award through to 19th Century maps and printed sources. Fish dealer John Clifford, for example, owned a 'farmstead' according to the 1840/1 electoral register. This can only be the 'Messuage, Tenement and Garth' owned by another John Clifford in 1788, of less than one eighth of an acre. Surely this is Clifford's Yard? The modern, apparently timeless fishertown townscape is actually a recent gloss on a medieval agricultural landscape.

[5] Mark Parker, *Filey to Grimsby: A Family Fishing Story* (Typescript, Filey Archives, 2005).

3.6: A rare view of *Jenk Alley* (Providence Place). Standing on what was actually the site of a medieval livestock yard are **L to R**: Isabella Bielby (*Bella*) Wyvill, son Jimmy *Bass* Wyvill, and daughter Mary E Cammish Wyvill, of no 2. See this family in the 1939 'census', **13.7**. *[Dave Bradley]*

Similarly, Skelton's Yard (opposite Reynolds' Street) is next to Robert Skelton's street-front joinery premises. In a community where there were no street signs, the old name of the livestock yard, or the name of the current owner, would simply be applied in everyday speech to the terrace built on it.

Isolation, Community and Cooperation

The Yorkshire Coast north of Flamborough is a succession of *wykes* (bays) between *heads*, *nabs* and *nesses* (headlands) which isolate settlements. One or more *becks* empty into each bay, usually down steep and incised gorges. Like most fishing settlements on this inhospitable sea edge, Filey nestles by the north end of its bay, shielded from the harshness of the north-easterlies by a headland. Excavation of a site on Queen Street in 1976 exposed traces of buildings from the mid-10th Century. Cottages duck the winds with low-pitched roofs, forced close together by the constraints of the terrain. The physical challenge of launching and beaching boats, in such locations, and geographical remoteness, would, from the

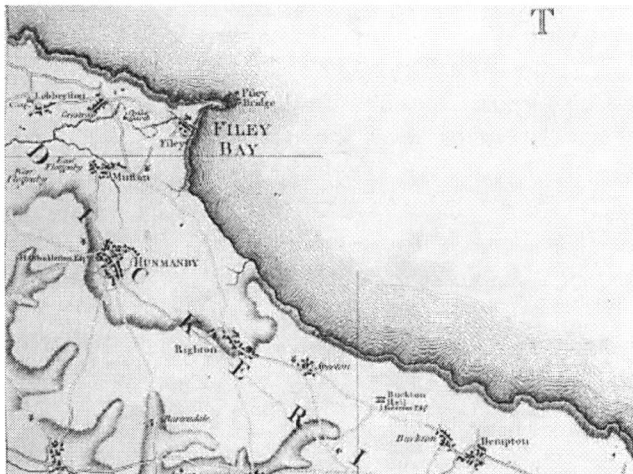

3.7: Before the turnpike era, as Jeffery's county map of 1771 shows, Filey had been merely a village at the end of rough country lane. A century later, Filey's road access to the world was a loop off the main north-south coastal road. 'See what a curve the railway has to make in order to touch it,' observed Canon Cooper in 1886.

3.8: The agricultural geography of the original medieval village, with animal and poultry yards behind each house, fitted the needs of a fishing community like a glove. These former livestock or vegetable plots could accommodate sheds for baiting ('back 'ouses') and barking, whilst their length was ideal for unravelling lines and nets. **L to R:** Jack COLLING, his brother *Bill Bullocky* (William Johnson COLLING) and Jack CAMMISH mend salmon nets in Reynolds Yard, alongside no 11, looking north towards Queen Street, shortly before the clearance of the site in the 1970s. *[Barry Robson]*

earliest times, require communal cooperation. Geographical isolation created strong community identity, but also translated into a robust instinct for collective action – like the instances in the 1790s of Filey men engaging in paramilitary self-protection against hostile foreign privateers (pp148-50).

A century after these French and Dutch incursions, more mundane threats occasioned the same collective response. A major fire broke out on The Crescent in October 1890, to which the Local Board's fire brigade only managed to respond after four and a half hours. Several houses could have been engulfed, but for the intervention of a team of fishermen. Matthew *Walsher* JENKINSON (O40) took the lead, perhaps, because he was a 60 year-old skipper. They scaled the roofs and pitched a steady supply of buckets of water onto the flames. Human chains of lady visitors passed these along, putting several men 'into the shade', as the *Filey Post* put it. No major damage was done, other than to the away-day jaunt of gloating crowds from Scarborough who had 'poured off the 2.54 train expecting to see the best part of little Filey in ruins.'[6]

---

[6] *Victorian Filey* (undated typescript, *FA*).

Writing at the end of the 19th Century, and sensing the imminent extinction of this intense communality, Canon Cooper wryly caught its appealing flavour:

> We can now boast an Urban Council, an Act of Parliament for improving the place, and last season we actually had a burglary! This may seem a queer proof of progress; so it must be said that, not so many years ago, when all the inhabitants were related to another, there was not a lock and key in our parish. Folks went in and out of one another's houses and took what they wanted as a matter of course.[7]

Traces survived well into the 20th Century. Good neighbourliness was especially remembered with nostalgia by those who had lived in the Old Town. Speaking of the 1920s, Lizzie Cammish HUNTER recalled running errands as a child for *Old Brazzy*, once his wife had died, and doing out his ashes. His great niece, Evelyn WILLIS, read him a chapter of the Bible every night. *Lizzie* herself was fondly remembered years after her death for throwing pennies to children.

Compactness contributed to this close community spirit. George Burton, born in Richardson's Yard, reckoned its 16 cottages would fill an area occupied by only three modern houses and gardens. These typical 'yard' cottages had a main room downstairs, perhaps two bedrooms above, and an attic in the roofspace. Personal privacy was unheard of.

The Old Town's 19th Century censuses consist almost entirely of nuclear families, ie just parents and children. A two-roomed cottage in which out-of-season fishing gear might also be stored left no space for grandparents, though they were invariably close by, usually in the same yard or row. But lodging with a married daughter was often the only way on for a fisher widow. *Redux* cites an especially congested cottage, that of the SAYERS household in Ocean Place. William and Susannah (née CAPPLEMAN) had brought 13 children into the world, the ten survivors all still at home at the time of the 1861 Census. The eldest, William junior, was 24. The youngest, Robert Edmond, had been baptised just a couple of months before. Yet somehow there was still room for Susannah's 86 year-old mother, Jane, formerly a Staithes Webster.[8]

Ocean Place became Reynolds Yard in the 1860s, and the family was still there, same cottage, no 12, in 1871.[9] One of the 13 children was Jane, unmarried (the return disobligingly recorded her as a 29 year-old lunatic). A remnant was there in 1911, Jane and two unmarried brothers. But by 1917, Frank and Robert Edmond

---

[7] Cooper (1900) pp48-9.

[8] Jane had been a widow for 40 years, her husband Thomas being lost with two others when their coble was upset in a gale. At 91, and poorly sighted, Jane too had a violent end, falling to her death one December afternoon in 1865, into the cellar of the *Grapes Inn*. The new landlord, Francis ROBINSON, had the hatches open 'the full breadth of the footpath', clear evidence of how narrow the pavement on King Street was (*Redux*, 18th Nov 2018). Today that would have occasioned a prosecution for criminal negligence.

[9] It is possible to determine continuity by noting down neighbours in each census.

3.9: 'Nobody ever knocked'. The Old Town's good neighbourliness was fondly recalled to us in the 1980s. 'People helped one another,' Lizzie Cammish HUNTER said. Part of the 'Haxby Cluster' on Chapel Street, c1890 – Elizabeth Ann (née JENKINSON) and lay preacher Matt Crawford Haxby (seated); **Left**, rear, over the wall, famous ranter preacher Matt Haxby, father of Matt Crawford, who lived on one side, according to the 1891 Census. **Right**, standing to his right William ROSS and Mary Elizabeth (née WILLIAMSON), neighbours on the other. In June 1858, William ROSS had found religion after surviving a truly traumatic night in a capsized coble (pp230-4). By the time of this photograph, he was part-owner/skipper of the yawl *Tranquility* (**9.7**). *[SE]*

were dead, yet she remained. Somehow this old woman got by, despite her serious mental health problems. *Someone* local must have been helping: there seems to have been no question of banging her up in Dean Road workhouse or the county asylum. In the 1920s, Reynolds Yard was known colloquially as *Jane Sayers Yard*, and remained so into the 1980s, long after Jane had died.[10] Places are only called after residents when everybody knows each other well.

George Burton reckoned his grandma's door was always open: 'nobody ever knocked', he told us.[11] Every day, her niece, Bella Wheeler, called in - 'short tongued' ie always talking, whether or not it was wanted, something of a 'worry woman' (hardworking, trying anxiously hard). As *Bella* walked in, she always called out, 'No Aunt Liz, I isn't gan ter stop'.

---

[10] Terence COLLINS. Jane died in 1930, aged 87, in the house where she had been born.
[11] George's grandmother was Elizabeth Ann CAPPLEMAN (née COLLING) 1847-1939.

Grandma was 'a bit of a critic': 'Praise the Lord,' she would remark wryly from her rocking chair.

The town's strong community spirit was sometimes punctuated by discord, as in this incident reported in the *Filey Post* (20th October 1877). A confrontation between fishermen Rickman Skelton and Matthew JENKINSON had got sufficiently serious to reach the local magistrates' court at Bridlington. Skelton kicked away JENKINSON's pail,

> . . . pulled off his coat, and for a quarter of an hour dared him to fight, and essayed to strike at his wife. Complainant stood with his hands in his pockets, and when defendant found that he could not provoke complainant to fight he struck him in the face. The bench advised both parties to settle the matter, as they were neighbours, and they retired to do so.

No doubt the justices sensed this discord had a long history, best resolved *within* so cohesive a community. And there were social sanctions. As late as 1900, Cooper could describe an Old Town punishment extant within living memory:

> If anyone offended, there was a penalty at hand far more dreaded than any rigours of the law. The fisherwomen *ran the culprit into the sea*. Joining hands, like children at play, only making an unbreakable chain, they chased the offender down the cliffs to the very edge of the sea, and there drove him again and again into the waves until the women thought he had been ducked enough.[12]

Cole (1828, p144) describes another traditional method of community intervention in the district, more psychological, and usually nocturnal, which continued well into the 19th Century. Known as *Riding the Stang*, its purpose was

> to ridicule any boisterous quarrel between married parties, when several boys preside as judges, riding the Stang which consists of a pole carried on the shoulders of the lads, and across it is mounted the chief speaker, beating a pan with a thick stick and repeating some doggerel rhymes.

Contrary to common belief, this was not only to protect women from domestic violence, but also to encourage over-gentle husbands to keep their wives in order, physically if necessary. (A *stang* was a prod or 'sting'.) Admiral Mitford, Lord of the Manor of Hunmanby, banned it in 1860, but it was recorded in parts of Holderness as late as 1899.[13]

Social Class within the Fishing Community

I have a sense that one historian's comment about Whitby in 1817 could probably have matched Filey. Dr Young had been impressed by

> the distinctive nature of manners . . . they had an 'ancient simplicity'. One facet of this that caught his attention was that, 'gentlemen of the first respectability'

---

[12] Cooper (1900) pp48-9.

[13] Robin Gilbank, *The Prettiest Liar: The Life of Dr W Pritchard* (East Yorkshire Local History Society, 2012) pp59-60.

would go shopping and carry home 'with their own hands' their purchases.[14]

Classlessness was inherent in the maritime culture – men muck in on boats. And at Filey, without the range of professions at Whitby, this must have been even more pronounced. The many nostalgic accounts of the east Yorkshire fishing suggest that class division only crept in as trawling reduced the shareholding gearman to a waged maritime labourer.[15]

Traditionally, the gearmen shared much the same tasks when fishing, diminishing any class division between owners and crew. The system produced skipper-entrepreneurs who rose from the same class as the crew.

There had always been social distinctions, reflected in the gradations of housing in the Old Town. In 1841-2, rents ranged from three or four pounds for the 'Holy Year' (ie beginning Lady Day, 25th March) to the more typical £2 10s or two pounds. So what kind of accommodation did the modest rent of one pound give 'Widow Bulmer' – but maybe this sum had been charitably reduced?[16]

'Many of the masters of yawls and others *middlin weel* off', noted Rev Shaw, 'stop at home during winter and employ themselves in leisurely repairing their nets and other gear.' Members of this Filey labour aristocracy were moving away from the old fisher streets. There were now,

3.10 Robert and Elizabeth CAMMISH, a couple 'middlin weel off', in Sunday best. Robert wears an unpretentious, heavy cotton moleskin overcoat, hardwearing and windproof, with velvet collar. Elizabeth's black gros grain skirt is durable rather than flashy. Her blouse is cotton, not silk, as befitted a woman who ran the St Oswald's Mothers' Meetings for 30 years, and contributed to each child's 'bags full of good things' at the yearly School Treat. *[JC]*

---

[14] Storm (1991) p12.

[15] Trawler skippers in Hull and Grimsby moved away from those parts of the town dominated by the crews, and frequented their own pubs and clubs (Friend, 2010, p62).

[16] Rector of St Oswald's Cottage Rents, 1841-2 (East Yorkshire Record Office, DDU/17/14).

> excellent houses [on Chapel Street[17]] several of which have been lately erected,
> and are the property of fishermen who by industry, frugality, and religion, have
> risen from poverty to circumstances of comfort and comparative wealth.[18]

It is not clear from the standard genealogical sources whether this betterment was
creating a class structure amongst the Filey fishermen. As late as the editions of
1915 and 1923 (**1.2**) WH Smith's *Directory* simply listed 'fishermen', making no
distinction between a coble crewman and a yawl or drifter owner; and before
1891, British census returns similarly fail to distinguish between skippers and
crewmen. Richard Haxby was unique in describing himself as 'Master Fisherman'
in the 1871 Census. But our 1980s informants, alive between the Wars, definitely
recognised social gradations. One described the *Laffy* line as:

> . . . an upper crust sort of JENKINSON family . . . always had a bit of money, always
> lived in decent houses, didn't live down the yards . . . .

And the descendants of Richard Cammish *Dick Sled* JENKINSON

> . . . weren't ordinary common or garden like we were . . . a bit of money . . . Sally
> went to college.

Interestingly, none of this was said with resentment or bitterness. These men were
known to have worked for their money, for the diligence and application of
individuals was visible, and respected. Those who had crewed for them
understood their skill as fishermen. The class edge may also have been dulled by
common membership of Chapel, the community divide being more between
saved and unsaved, than between rich and poor.

One rich source which can shed light on the financial outcome of many men's
lives is the freely accessible online *Calendar of Probate Grants, England &
Wales, 1858-Present*. Owners and skippers invariably left wills. Copies of these
public documents can be downloaded by anybody, at £1.50 each.[19]

The evolution of a kind of 'labour aristocracy' amongst Filey's working
fishermen can also be traced from the many photographs that survive from the
late 19th and early 20th Centuries. They wear the gansey as a mark of their
working heritage, but the cut of their clothing often sets them apart (**3.10**).
Robert CAMMISH (1851-1925) came from at least two generations of
skipper/owners - he commissioned (1890) and owned the yawl *Diligence*.

Yet one senses that Robert and his wife had few airs or graces. Family lore
catches the no-nonsense character of this unpretentious couple, relating how

---

[17] This part of Back Lane was the location of the *Bethesda* Primitive Methodist Chapel
from 1825.

[18] Shaw, *Rambles* (1867) p5; *Our Filey Fishermen* (1867) p113. 'Middling' was a term
first used in the late 16th Century to denote those above the labouring classes, often
with inherited capital, and able to save on a regular basis to improve their position.

[19] The *Calendar of Grants* gives name, date of death, address, and occupation of the
deceased, together with the names of executors and value of the deceased's estate.

Robert regularly walked from Filey to his boat at Scarborough, despite his age. His family, keen to preserve him from all those miles, reputedly nailed his sea boots to the floor. Joanne CAMMISH, married to one of Robert and Elizabeth's great grandsons, neatly sketches the character of them and their peers as

> very ordinary people who didn't show money . . . no one showed money, they all wanted to appear equal even if they weren't - that to this day is a very Filey thing.

Elizabeth was sufficiently accomplished to supervise the purchase of 'suitable books' for the women's library. And yet despite so active a parish life, she somehow managed to look after their 13 children!

The herring boom may have been a catalyst to the emergence of this *middlin weel off* sub-class. The fishery had existed for centuries, but began to expand in the 1830s, bringing prosperity to those who adapted quickly. 'Hauls of £100 a week were frequently made,' reported Canon Cooper.[20] The profits of good seasons, like those around 1833-4, allowed groups of fishermen to pool savings and commission new boats, a level of commitment that drew extra investment from local tradesmen.

Take George JENKINSON (N12) who took a risk and bought the first yawl, built speculatively by Robert Skelton at Scarborough in 1833. By 1836, after just two years, George could make his nephew, Matthew (O7) skipper, but as owner he retained one share of the profits, a kind of pension fund, until 1846. Owners could pass wealth and status down their family line. Often, they filled the Primitive Methodist Chapel offices, or became lay preachers.

By the later 1800s, the sons and grandsons of men who had profited from the herring boom had moved into Filey's newer streets. Most fishermen lived in the tiny cottages of the Old Town, still tipping human waste into communal ashpits. But if we link census returns and directories with the 1891 map (**3.4**) we can see which fishermen were *weel hefted wi' brass*. They were in the larger houses with the luxury of backyards and toilets (even if they were in the yards) on Chapel Street, Mitford Street, Reynolds' Street, Hope Street, and Union Street.[21]

Billy Butter Watkinson, who left nearly £3,000 in 1915, according to the *Calendar of Probate Grants*, had made good money from buying into steam early, and ended up at *Seadale House*, on the prestigious Grove Terrace. Richard Ferguson *Clicker* CAMMISH entered the fish wholesale trade, formed the Filey United Steam Trawler Company in 1918, and progressed from Cambridge Yard in 1911 to Raincliffe Avenue by the time of his death in 1940. His estate was valued for probate at over £15,000, the equivalent of around £600,000 today.

---

[20] Cooper (1886) p35.

[21] See **3.9** for families with the mod-con of a backyard. Another member of this class was the 'A DOUGLAS' listed in Bulmer's 1892 *Directory* on Mitford Street. He is identified in newspaper reports as the entrepreneur Arthur Douglas, first man in Filey to fit an auxiliary petrol engine to a herring coble.

It may be that the key gradation in fishing communities was pedigree. Filey fish salesman Ben Simpson spoke to the 1863 Sea Fisheries Commission of 'proper bred fishermen'. These *belonged:* they were part of the knot of interrelationship, multi-generation descendants of 'Core families'. Outside this caste of course were the Johnny-come-lately, casual, immigrant, top-up crewmen, the deck-labourers.[22]

Social elevation sometimes came as a result of transitioning from fishing to fish dealing/curing. There were many 19th Century instances of fishermen with modest origins living eventually in some of the most prestigious addresses of the town. One was Jenkinson Haxby, a 14 year-old fisherman in the 1841 Census, and living with seven other family members in what was probably a two-bedroomed cottage in Mosey's Yard; by 1871, still a fisherman, he and his wife were on Chapel Street; but in Bulmer's 1892 *Directory*, he was a retired fish dealer, at the genteel *Clarence View*, on Belle Vue Street. The bald fact is that the dealers needed to keep fish prices down in the Coble Landing auctions if they were to prosper. Here indeed was the clash of economic interests which invariably created class division. Dealers like Jenkinson Haxby, however, had come from the same streets as the fishermen whose catches they bought. An especially charismatic, senior member of the Chapel network, Haxby's shared social and religious bonds probably blunted the class divide, at least in his immediate generation.

It is no coincidence that the oldest, core families, with freehold property in the electoral registers of 1836 and 1841, are the offshore skippers and owners, or the men who later moved beyond fishing into curing and fish dealing. They may well have had farm property which financed their fishing success, those that survived or benefited from the great enclosure changes after 1788-91. More detailed research in census returns, directories and pre-1858 probate records could track individuals from these electoral records, connecting them with property owners who had appeared in the enclosure award referenced in footnote 2, on page 23.

The losers from the national enclosure process were those whose parcels of land could no longer sustain them without the customary common rights. They ended up as wage labourers, either on farms or in the growing towns. In Filey, however, it may have been different, for inshore fishing was available to anyone who could raise the capital to commission or buy a coble.

Queen Street or King Street?

Finally, a longstanding puzzle needs resolving. In the early 19th Century, street naming in many towns was simply an oral consensus amongst locals. But from the 1840s, governments legislated to counter the public health dangers associated with urbanisation, permitting towns to elect local boards of health. These were the forerunners of our local authorities. Clearly, 'nuisances' such as unsanitary dwellings and malodorous accumulations of refuse and sewage could not be pinpointed until streets displayed name boards, and houses carried numbers.

---

[22] They were outside Filey's class system. See below, pp68-72, **10.9.**

3.11: [**Above**] The fishermen's cottages at the western end of Town Street, Main Street, King Street or Queen Street, depending on the year! There is just one street light in view. The date seems to be around 1900, in the middle of a sunny summer's day. **3.12:** [**Below**] This view from the other end of this fishermen's terrace was probably taken in the 1920s. A gas lamp standard has appeared at last. Note traditional pantiles – Filey poet Edward Anderson wrote in 1800 how in the Wolds area 'old thatched cottages have ta'en their flight And new tiled houses now appear in sight'. [*FA*]

> *Town Street* at the time of enclosure in 1788-91
>
> *Main Street* (western end) - 1841 Census
>
> *King Street* (seaward end) - 1841 Census
>
> *Queen Street* (all) - 1851 Census; and 1857-8 trade directories
>
> *King Street* (*westward* end) *Queen Street* (seaward end) - Pettitt's Map, 1868;
>   Ordnance Survey map, 1891; and 1891 Census
>
> *Queen Street* (the whole street) - *Bulmer's Directory*, 1892, and thereafter
>
> **3.13:** A century of confusion - how Queen Street's name changed in the 19th Century. Despite the creation of a local board in 1868, Filey's 'Fishermen's Street' drifted inconclusively through several identities until the 1890s.

Another necessity in growing towns was public street lighting. Clark (1982, p15) quotes Arthur S Umpleby, stationmaster at Staithes and talented dialect poet, who penned these lines in 1934 looking back to traditionalist dislike of official moves at *Steeas* to illuminate 'theeas neets as black as Spanish':

> 'Leets? Leets?' they sez, 'ye want ni leets,
>
> Them's nobbut for awd women
>
> Beeath t'meean and stars cums oot at neets
>
> An nowther wants ni trimmin.'

3.14: Looking west, early 1950s, from what was Queen Street into the older, narrower stretch of the main street known as King Street, the junction with Reynolds' Street marking the split. Note the advertisement, *For Your Throat's Sake Smoke Craven 'A'*! [SE]

4 FISHING AND FAMILY

'I've traced my family tree right back eight generations on both sides and all of them went to sea.' Jim Haxby (1935-2018)

Even the most superficial examination of Filey's parish registers from the late 18th to early 20th Centuries confirms two exceptional features of the town's fishing community:

1. A **small stock of 15 surnames** dominated the town for well over a century. The commonest, JENKINSON, comprised 4.5% (one in 22) of Filey township's 1871 population.
2. The fisherman's **marriage horizons** – ie how far away he looked for a wife - rarely extended beyond the Old Town, or the fishing trade. He did not 'marry out', and often chose first and second cousins as a bride.

In short, the genetic stock remained largely unchanged over generations.

Compare this with an average English rural parish of the same period:

1. Only one third of surnames survived for more than 50 years.
2. A village's commonest surname rarely totalled over 1% of the population.
3. Marriage horizons often extended to neighbouring parishes, so that new blood was regularly introduced.

1 Filey's Core Fishing Families – the Famous Fifteen

Surnames almost universally stayed put in fishing communities, a handful always dominating each settlement. They became sufficiently localised to be an instant badge of origin, even today. The commonest name in each north-east Yorkshire fishing village is shown in bold in **4.1**. We might expect that the commoner a name in a village, the longer it must have been there – ie Filey's JOHNSONs should have been as common as herring, since anyone born with that name alive in the town today will be able to claim continuous descent from at least the reign of Elizabeth I.

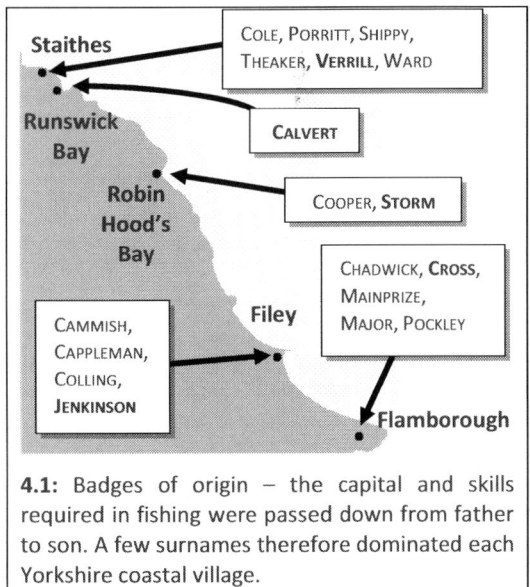

4.1: Badges of origin – the capital and skills required in fishing were passed down from father to son. A few surnames therefore dominated each Yorkshire coastal village.

BAXTER	6	HUNTER	5	RICHARDSON	4	SCALES	4
CAMMISH	20	JENKINSON	34	ROBINSON	9	WILLIAMSON	2
CAPPLEMAN	16	JOHNSON	9	ROSS	3	WILLIS	6
COLLING etc	16	LANE	2	SAYERS	7		

4.2: Continuity from the 18th to the 20th Centuries – Filey's core Old Town fishing surnames, with the number of fishermen bearing each of the 15 in the 1881 census returns. These core names accounted for about two thirds of Filey's fishing population. Similar patterns are found in most traditional fishing communities. In Robin Hood's Bay for example, Storm (1991, pp46-8) found five core names predominating throughout the two centuries prior to 1851.

But in comparison with the four most common names shown in **4.2**, they were lightweights, despite this ancient lineage. Of the 244 fishermen in the town's 1881 census returns, only nine were JOHNSONs, ie 3.7%, one fisherman in 27. The true heavyweights were the JENKINSONs, with 34 males of fishing age - 14%, or one in seven. Yet this surname had only been present since the mid-18th Century: profusion depended on the roulette wheel of fertility, child gender and chance early drownings. All can skew a fisher surname's survival, especially in the decades after its arrival in the parish. Robert and Margaret JENKINSON, whose 1778 marriage is the ancestral Clapham Junction of the Old Town, appear on most of its 20th/21st Century family trees. All five of their surviving sons married, went forth, and multiplied. By the 1820s, 19 grandsons were maintaining a truly exponential rate of increase.[1] At Filey, the fishing families seem to have been distinct from those which provided the town's handful of sailors: a summary at the Scarborough Maritime Heritage Centre, of crew lists of 1747-50, containing Filey men, revealed virtually none with the 15 core fisher names.

Fishing families at Filey were generally profuse breeders, more so than other working people. The fisherman married early, and remarried promptly if widowed, for he could not be self-sufficient without a wife. There were also plenty of employment prospects within fishing for his children, rendering sexual restraint unnecessary. In addition, by the later 19th Century, whole broods often made it to adulthood, defying a national infant mortality rate of 16.5%, or one in six (1900). There was nurture from a large extended family, and in contrast with industrial towns, access to fresh air, and a protein rich diet. The Medical Officer's Report for 1896 declared Filey 'nearly free from infectious diseases'. The water supply quality was 'excellent, quite equal to any town on the coast'.[2] Sanitation was bad, but crucially, geology protected the wells down Church Ravine, the main water supply. Human waste went to the sea, rather than into the water table.

---

[1] I'm using the term *exponential* specifically of a surname that increases in number appreciably faster than the rate of population increase in the parish.

[2] *Driffield Times*, 9th Jan 1897.

4.3: The 'Clapham Junction' of an exponential family, c1881 – the 'Obbies, as they were usually known. John ROBINSON stands patriarchally in waistcoat and cravat, by his yawl's corfe, with four sons and three grandsons. The surname was mostly borne by brickmakers in Filey, the fishing line hanging on by a thread – just one ROBINSON fisherman in 1841, and three in 1871. But John *'Obbie* (mutton chop whiskers) born in 1814, had four sons, shown here, which in turn generated nine fishing ROBINSONs by 1881, and 13 by 1911. John's six-man yawl *Maud Florence* was crewed entirely by his own ROBINSON family, 13 year-old 'Boy' John probably standing between grandfather John and father William. By the 1920s, William CAPPLEMAN reckoned 'the *'Obbies* were one of the best-known families in Filey, there were a lot of them.' *[FA]*

Until the 1870s, an ever-increasing fishing population was sustained by what appeared to be the infinite resources of the sea. This fishing population expanded on a very limited base of surnames because entry into the trade was difficult.[3]

This was for several reasons. The skills of seamanship took years to acquire. Fish seller Ben Simpson told the 1863 Sea Fisheries Commission that there were only 130 'proper bred fishermen' in Filey.[4] It is unclear what he thought about the rest. A marine natural selection culled those who fell short – the incompetent and foolhardy were unlikely to survive.

Interestingly, the extreme concentrations of surnames that characterised the Yorkshire fishing villages can also be found in north-east Scotland, where similar fishing was practised, but not on the East Anglian coast, where shellfish were the main catch. The simple gear and undecked craft used to catch crabs, lobsters and

---

[3] Appendix B summarises the known individual histories of each of these surnames.
[4] The number suggests he was referring to the owners and gearmen of the town's yawls.

shrimps cost a fraction of the gear needed to catch fish offshore.[5] Non-fisher families could easily move into the trade, bringing in new surnames. In contrast, a Filey offshore boat and its gear had to be a long-term family investment, owned and crewed by brothers, sons and sons-in-law. Boat shares passed down generations, Yorkshire fishing villages practising partible inheritance, not the conventional primogeniture – ie ensuring that all sons benefited from the wealth at death of their father, not just the eldest. This led to high concentrations of surnames since younger sons had no need to migrate to find work. Another factor keeping families and their surnames in situ may have been secure property tenancies, as seems to have been a factor in Robin Hood's Bay.[6]

2 Restricted Marriage Horizons - Fisher Family Intermarriage

Similar factors, capital and skills, explain the remarkable pattern of intermarriage in Yorkshire coast fishing villages. The more remote the settlement, the more pronounced it was: thus *all* the 44 fisher women who bore Robin Hood's Bay commonest name, Storm, married maritime husbands in the period 1789-1897.[7] The bride had to bring skills to the enterprise, and ideally a boat share as a dowry.

JENKINSON **Grooms** - 34, *all* fishermen	**Their Brides** - 27 were daughters of fishermen
JENKINSONs **Brides** – 31, *all* daughters of fishermen	**Their Grooms** - 20 were fishermen, one a fishmonger, one a labourer, but son of a fisherman

4.4: How Filey fishing families 'married in' - JENKINSON marriage partners, 1813-1908 - 79% of JENKINSON grooms married fishermen's daughters; 71% of JENKINSON brides married men from the fishing trade.

Intermarriage amongst Filey fishermen was sufficiently pronounced to be a source of mirth along the coast. Captain Sydney Smith told us how his father, who worked for years with Filey men in Scarborough Harbour, concluded 'Kick one, they all limp'. Inbreeding allegedly produced a lack of intelligence. One Scarborough story told how the crew of a Filey coble landed a ling. 'What'll we do with it?' one man asked, looking down at it. 'Cut it in three', came the reply, 'and have half each'.

---

[5] Thompson et al (1983) pp184-5.

[6] Storm (1991) pp26-7, 83. Filey lay in the Manor of Hunmanby, so research into its court records might shed light on the issue of security of tenure.

[7] Malcolm Smith, 'The Demography of Coastal Communities' (*Local Population Studies*, 70, Spring 2003, p63).

Similar stories are of course often told to the detriment of neighbouring communities. The rural parts of Hinderwell parish saw their Staithes fishing fellow-parishioners as 'a funny lot' – 'You've heard of the village idiot? Well Staithes has got six.'[8] And with Darwin's *Origin of Species* and natural selection in the air, contemporary scientific opinion was also concerned about the genetic non-diversity of self-contained communities, not least about the risks of fisher inbreeding. Identical appearance was considered a giveaway. Commenting in 1885 on the fisher families of the Ards Peninsula, County Down, a local newspaper noted:

> The young men seldom venture outside the limits of the village in their search for a wife, hence a strong family likeness prevails . . . .[9]

Pritchard, however, noted in 1854 the health, 'good stature and robust frame' of the Filey fisherfolk, observing that such interbreeding would normally produce a 'diminutive and unhealthy' population. And Canon Cooper (1886, p31) defended his parishioners with characteristic tongue-in-cheek flair:

> . . . the percentage of idiots is under the average of the rest of the kingdom, for with our population we ought to have five lunatics in the parish, whereas we have but four people who could be described as of weak mind.

Was this his notion of a compliment!

The eight key reasons for this ingrained pattern of intermarriage shed much light on the Old Town community's way of life:

a) The wife's skills kept the man afloat - the primary explanation was economic. Family involvement was indispensable to the fishing enterprise, and the wife in particular was the key support worker, managing the whole shore-based process.

> i) Whilst the men and older boys were at sea, the wives and daughters collected bait, perhaps roaming many miles if supplies were short.

> ii) They *skeined*[10] whatever came shelled, and baited thousands of hooks daily, assisted by retired fishermen – a mix of dexterity and experience.

> iii) The same workforce, and those of pre-fishing age, made and repaired nets.

> iv) Crucially, the wife's financial management determined whether the family floated or sank.

---

[8] Clark (1982) p33.

[9] Blaikie (2002) p24; Smith (2003) p64.

[10] Using a sharp knife to remove molluscs like mussels, whelks and limpets from their shells, so that they can be put on hooks.

v) Even fish curing, though a specialist male trade, required unskilled assistance since the process involved the gutted catch being dried in the sun on rocks and hillsides: in the peak herring months of July to September every spare pair of hands was turning the fish and shooing away sea birds.

In these circumstances, it was inevitable that a fisherman would marry a woman whose upbringing had schooled, and resigned her to so demanding a life.

b) Marriage as a capital investment: a share in a boat – Blaikie's study of five fisher parishes in north-east Scotland, found that the traditional system of shares in boats led to families encouraging sons to marry daughters of fellow crew members. This may have happened in Filey. The practice kept boats in the family, prevented profits going to non-family members, and kept guarded a lifetime's priceless capital asset - the fisherman's skill and knowledge of grounds.[11]

As with a farmholding, boat ownership offered economic security, and could not be allowed out of the family. The 49th Psalm notes of farmers: 'They call their lands after their own names.' Similarly, calling the boat after your parents, grandparents or female relatives confirmed its centrality to the family business. This emphasis on family lineage partly explains that custom of giving children the maiden surnames of mothers and grandmothers as first and middle names.

Filey fishermen invested large sums of money in their boats, numbers peaking in the 1860s. Unsurprisingly, government commissioners found it difficult to reconcile this with claims that trawlers had been ruining their livelihoods. Whilst some of the funds came from Scarborough and Filey traders, it seems likely that intermarriage buoyed up what the fishermen themselves could invest, by preventing resources being lost to outsiders. It is possible that any marrying-out had the aim of gaining an infusion of capital into the family business.

The desirability of keeping boat shares in the family may even have led to men marrying their brother's widow. Though this remained illegal until 1921, it did happen. Edmond JENKINSON (P52) is one Filey example, and there are probably more. This pillar of the Primitive Methodist movement evidently thought nothing of marrying his sister-in-law Mary (née Maulson) after the death of John, his elder brother. Clearly, nobody cared about this obsolete prohibition.[12]

---

[11] Most men built up a huge memory of such trade secrets, but Richard Cammish JENKINSON (*Dicky Hoy*) was far more meticulous: 'I have a lot of books like this and they're going to be left to our Tom,' he told Terence COLLINS, referring to the daily notebooks he had kept for over half a century of coble fishing (ch15).

[12] It was of course Henry VIII's insistence on such a marriage being against scripture that led to the 16th Century's equivalent of *Brexit*, the Break with Rome. This is probably why such unions remained illegal for nearly four centuries. In practice, however, it became the norm for individual clergymen to decide whether they were willing to marry such couples. Once the marriage had been performed, there was no way of challenging its legality.

c) Lack of working contact with non-fisher people – fishermen could not court at sea. Cooper characteristically summed it up concisely:

> ... fishermen have no market to attend, and no Martinmas week[13] where they are thrown into other company as the countrymen are, the consequence being they intermarry among themselves to a far greater extent than other folks (1886, p31).

Also, by the 18th Century, Filey had become that rare phenomenon, a truly specialised fishing village. Most full-time fishermen lived in the fishing quarters of coastal towns, supplying fresh food to their land-based neighbours throughout the year. But the difficulties of transport for so perishable a commodity meant that isolated coastal villages, with no such adjacent demand, could usually make only a part-time living from fishing. Fishermen were famous for having extra jobs.[14] But Filey men, fishing year-round, met no women other than Filey fishergirls.

Historically, there was high demand for fish: it was cheap; meat was in short supply in winter. The medieval Catholic church insisted on 'lean days' for the 40 days of lent (no sex, no meat), on Fridays (the day of crucifixion) and on any number of saints' days. Nearly half the calendar in pre-Reformation Britain joylessly consisted of such fast days. Only 'cold food' (fish, waterfowl) could be eaten. And after 1562, Wednesday too was a 'fish day', to nurture seamanship.

By the 18th Century, though Catholicism survived only in pockets, there remained high demand for fish. And the coasts of Yorkshire, Northumbria, and Scotland's north-east uniquely managed to tap into it all year round, sustaining full-time fishing employment. In the case of the Yorkshire coast, there were nearby inland towns, where harvest failure could produce disorder.[15] There was also a growing middle-class demand for fresh fish in the nearby industrial towns. As early as the 1780s, rapidly moving trains of packhorses were taking the Yorkshire catch as far afield as the mushrooming towns and cities of Lancashire, working in relays day and night. As late as 1924, a Sledmere historian could identify a field where Filey and Flamborough trains stopped to take on fresh packhorses. From about the same time, salt came from Cheshire in packhorse panniers to dry-cure Yorkshire fish for in London, Newcastle, Spain, and even for West Indian slaves.

Coble was king on the north-east coast, adaptable for all-year fishing. Fishermen switched from whitefish to shellfish and salmon, according to the season. Even

---

[13] Martinmas, 11th November, was traditionally the end of the agrarian year. Agricultural workers of both sexes attended 'hiring fairs' to secure a position for the following year.

[14] As the local economy slumped, fishing was the backstop, quickly abandoned when the brisk times returned. The men of the Kent's Isle of Thanet, for example, were described as 'amphibious animals . . . equally skilled in holding helm or plough' (Thompson et al, 1983, p13).

[15] In the late 18th and early 19th Centuries, Hull was sufficiently worried about food supplies and possible 'bread riots' to pay bounties to fishermen for landing catches.

the high wages offered on the land during harvest months could be trumped by the earnings offered in the same weeks by the summer herring fishery. Indeed, it returned enough in good years to provide capital to purchase boats.

This exclusive fisher economy meant that in coble country, men had little contact with non-fisher women. When fishermen did marry from further afield, it was invariably to fisher girls from nearby fishing stations. The annual movement of the herring shoals brought fishermen into contact with single women, the seasonal gutters at each landing port. 'Herring girls' from as far afield as the Scottish Isles were recruited by fish merchants, though many went only to the nearest landing point. The marriage in 1778 of Robert JENKINSON to Margaret 'Truckles' at Great Yarmouth, both from Yorkshire, must have been a consequence of this fleeting, annual chance to meet a non-Filey woman.[16]

Jim Haxby summed up how this Old Town mating pattern survived into his time, referring to Ted *Funk* CAPPLEMAN, and how it preserved Filey fisher culture:

> . . . before the [second] War, they all were fishermen's wives or daughters that did the skeining, nobody ever kem in from out of town. And then after the War people married into fishing families, they 'ad to learn to skein . . . .

> She was Irish, was Rose, never seen a mussel and she was another one that kem into Filey and learnt to skein, so that Ted could go to sea . . . . That was part of the deal. It was wi' me . . . I saids to 'er before we were married, I'm gooin' to go to sea . . . you'll need to skein . . . another thing, if I 'ave any kids, they'll be christened at Filey Methodist Chapel. I was talking about this to me son, he smiles at me . . . 'e says, I said exactly the same thing . . . it 'ad to be. If yer wife din't skein you din't go to sea that was it.

Nor were fisher girls likely to click with out of parish suitors, despite much essaying out into the outside world in search of bait. You need only read some of Arthur Munby's diary observations of his 1869 encounter with Filey flithergirls on Scarborough station to appreciate how utterly alien they appeared to the rest of the world. Their distinctive attire alone provoked amazement and mockery.[17]

d) The mismatch between the tidal and the solar day - who else was up with the tide? Fisher families were a mysterious night-people, constantly in one another's company, in the same few streets and alleys, sleeping at the dictates of the tides, weather and fish. Launching occurred between 3.00 and 5.30am. Women got up with the men, to dovetail bait-gathering, *skeining* and baiting with the fishing trips.

Crewmates had sisters and daughters, and many couples must have met in the half-light of the dawn, during the team effort of carrying lines and kegs to the boats. Such common tasks, and shared understanding of the skills, hardships and

---

[16] *Truckles* was probably a southern version of the Staithes *Trattles* – see p102, fn5.

[17] See below, p359.

dangers of the trade must have lubricated many budding romances, guaranteeing an ease between couples. As in mining communities, fisher streets developed a social cohesion which naturally propelled its men and women into neighbourhood romance and marriage.

e) The social isolation of the Old Town was partly a result of the movement of the farming population out of the town. Before the enclosure of 1788-91, there was probably far more social contact and intermarriage between fisher and farmer people. Storm has identified a pattern of segregation resulting from enclosure at Robin Hood's Bay. Dowries from pre-enclosure marriages may account for the number of fisher surnames owning property outside the fishing streets, and these could ultimately have been the germ of a family owning a lugger rather than a coble. Property of course has always secured credit.[18]

Even more isolating was the near universal assumption that fisher streets were socially and sanitarily unattractive. A national class prejudice dismissed all fishing communities as full of ageing, basic, functional cottages, which generated unsavoury, foul-smelling waste. The science of microbiology only evolved late in the 19th Century: previously, the Miasmatic Theory of disease dominated medical thinking. 'Bad air' (miasma) was believed to cause all the killers of the time - cholera, typhoid and typhus. Infection was spread simply by the smells emanating from rotting organic matter, and the fishing trade generated this in quantity.[19] Filey's less attractive organic matter included pigs' bladders and sheep's stomachs, tarred to act as buoys for longlining; whilst dog excrement was boiled up with the tanning solution used to preserve sails.[20] Walcott reported how nets and sails were regularly tanned,

> a small outhouse being attached to the rear of the fishermen's cottages for the purpose. In Old Filey, the roads are streaked with channels of a dull red colour, being the effect of the waste water of this boiling apparatus.

Rev Pettitt noted in 1868 how the 'Fisherman's Road' down to the beach was 'odoriferous with the refuse from the cobles landed there'. Herring were smoked throughout the night in the curing houses, ready for the morning trains. Cod, ling and skate were dry-cured in summer, spread out by the shore on every rock and stretch of grass, *sweated* in one large pile for ten to twelve days, and finally dried out in the sun, possibly on lines across the street.[21] It is as well for the New Town's tourist-trade livelihoods that the summer visitors were lodged well away from these delights.

---

[18] Storm (1991) pp20-1, 28.

[19] In 1859, Nairn's newspaper noted the fishertown's 'dunghills', and that its cottages had a mortality rate nearly double that of the rest of the town: there, 'epidemic disease enters first, tarries the longest, and commits its mightiest ravages'. Filey Old Town had a low mortality rate but this may not have countered such hostility.

[20] Frank (2002) pp95-6; Smylie (2015) p163.

[21] Cole (1828) pp94-6. Skate, dried to 'horn hardness', was a unique Filey product.

4.5: The distinctive Filey fishing culture also survived for so long because of the compactness of the Old Town. The large share in raising children usually taken by grandmothers, and the multi-generational, open-air nature of the community's work and leisure, encouraged social contact across the full age range, as in this early 1920s view of the Cliff Top. Any way of life dies when there is no contact across the generations. The three men are (**L to R**) Robert CAMMISH, William *Ino* Crawford, and William ROBINSON. *[JC]*

Unsurprisingly, such fishing quarter sights and smells were associated with social undesirability. Eyemouth was described in 1862 as

> a fishing village pure and simple, with all that wonderful filth scattered about which is a sanitary peculiarity of such towns. The population . . . are rough, uncultivated, and more drunken in their habits than the fishermen of the neighbouring villages.[22]

Fishermen in the Banffshire fishing town of Buckie on the Moray Firth were considered 'low . . . little thought of', prone to fighting with farm labourers and amongst themselves; in Peterhead, fishermen were expected to walk on a different side of the street, away from townsfolk.[23] It is unclear if such antipathy existed in Filey: though we encountered no personal memories in the 1980s of hostility towards the town's fisher people, it may historically have been different.

For antipathy was a common feature of such relations elsewhere. Early 20th Century 'stinking Steas' was dismissed by neighbouring Hinderwell as a rough community of *quair* fishing folk below the steep cliffs. In Buckie, townsfolk, known disparagingly as *granders* by the fishermen, lived quite separately, and fights were recorded. Fisticuffs between high-spirited fisherboys and farm boys were a particular problem. On the Yorkshire coast, children's fights were accompanied by reciprocated terms of abuse such as 'cod' and 'turnip head'.

---

[22] 'The Fisher Folk of the Scottish East Coast', *Macmillan's Magazine*, No36, Oct 1862. At least one of Filey's core fisher surnames, COLLING, came from Eyemouth.

[23] Barron (2009) pp32-3; Thompson et al (1983) pp248, 251.

None of this offered fertile ground for romance and courtship. According to Clark, it was 'until recently' a popular notion at Staithes that 'foreigners' attempting to court one of their women were 'summarily run out of the village.'[24]

A lifetime's association with fish also impacted on one's personal freshness. 'I used to skein in our bait shed in Queen Street,' said one Filey woman this century. 'I would pop into Frankie Dee's afterwards . . . the looks I would get because of the smell on my clothes certainly woke the shoppers up.' Into the 20th Century, fisher girls taken on as herring gutters along the east coast found the carpets in their lodgings removed to counter the smell of fish.[25] 'We stank of fish despite baths!' a fishgutter from the old Aberdeen fishing quarter of Torry told a friend of mine in the 1980s. 'Only fishermen would go out with us!'

f) The cultural separateness of the fisher community - geographically and socially isolated populations inevitably build up their own popular cultures. In Filey Old Town, these were reinforced because so much time was spent communally in a public, open air environment, sharing what Alan Storm has called at Robin Hood's Bay 'the intimacy created by the physical compactness'. The attire of the Old Town, and its dialect terms, were only its *obvious*, separating features. The fishermen even had their own football club.[26]

Far deeper were the age-old beliefs, considered in Chapter 22, almost certainly of pre-Christian pedigree. At core was a visceral conviction that there was a proper time and place for everything. Any upset of this natural order would end badly. Given the uncertainty and risks of the trade, how could the fishing culture not seek to influence weather by trying to please the unseen forces that had control over them?

An unbridgeable gulf opened up over this body of folklore between the fisher folk and their more land-bound contemporaries. It was easily mocked as simple and primitive by those who did not face the risks of a maritime occupation. The annual rhythm of communal rituals and revels by which the Old Town celebrated special occasions also separated it from the local cultural mainstream.

And what of the collective memory store, passed down the long, slow centuries? This shared body of tale and truism was simply inaccessible to those who did not depend on the sea for their livings. What might be dismissed as 'Filey Death Tales' by those working safely on the land were deeply ingrained reminders of the daily risks that the fisherman took to win a living. These community histories came down the generations, from an ancient past - as late as the 1820s, Cole

---

[24] Clark (1982) pp50, 33.

[25] Smylie (2015) p171.

[26] Filey Red Stars played only local friendlies, the problems of the sea's attrition on the squad, and the coordination of kick-offs with the tides possibly causing difficulties in compiling the Saturday team sheet. The club merged in 1893 with Filey Town (Tradesmen) FC to form Filey United, forerunner of the present Filey Town.

wrote of the great storm of 1696, 'emphatically called "The November Gale" . . . an oft repeated story, related by those of the last generation to their children when assembled around the blazing hearth on a November's night.' How could such a cultural heritage not set apart those brought up in it?[27]

g) The race apart - early in the 17th Century, James VI reputedly claimed that the inhabitants at one end of the town of Nairn could not understand those at the other: the fisher families spoke Scots, a variation of Anglo-Saxon, whilst the rest spoke the Gaelic of the Celts.[28] Fisher communities were often seen as alien, but even other fishermen classed Filey's as different. One woman, presumably an outsider, could state as late as 2005 that 'she knew Filey had an evil past and a strong connection with the devil'. But the prejudices worked both ways: a Filey resident also repeated in 2005 the local belief that should a Filey person lead a dissolute life, 'the devil would arrive in his carriage to collect the soul of the deceased person – and deliver it to Scarborough.'[29]

To Captain Sydney Smith, Filey men were different – they were strict Primitive Methodists, and in contrast to other crews, 'no drink and no swearing on board. Nor would they sail on Sunday or Good Friday.' United so solidly by occupation and belief, how could such men not expect sons and daughters to bind their families further into this community? Tommy Flynn called them a 'race apart'. For one thing, each man was referred to only by his Filey nickname: 'you never knew his proper name', his wife told us. Disdaining the universal blue, they reputedly even had a distinctive violet tinge in their ganseys. These knitted pullovers carried an esoteric code, symbols of belonging, passed on at the hearth or doorstep, where the women collected to knit, often following a family pattern, a mesh of anchors, cables, rope ladders, and shells, with sleeve rings repeated to record the number of a man's children.

The 'race apart' tag may have been true. Some fisher communities were of different linguistic stock to their neighbours. Sussex fishermen had strong affinities with their French and Dutch equivalents; those of Beer in Devon had a 'language of their own'; in the Cromarty peninsula, the fishermen had a distinct dialect which seemed more akin to Norse and Dutch. As late as the 1980s, a friend of mine who worked on North Sea oil rigs regularly heard Peterhead fishermen talking over the radio, and assumed for years that they were Scandinavians, a characterisation common to much of the fisher stock of the British east coast, especially north of the Humber.

The survival of another, probably equally apocryphal story says much about popular perceptions in neighbouring fishing communities of the apartness of Filey fisher folk. An old Filey woman decided to use the railway for the first time.

---

[27] The storm of November 1696 wrecked 200 colliers (Godfrey & Lassey, 1982, p7).
[28] Barron (2009) p7.
[29] Friend (2010) pp203, 210.

'Where are you going?' asked the booking clerk. 'Mind your own business', she retorted, 'just like all your family . . . I'll walk'.

Insularity bred dismissive shibboleths about nearby communities, older men reserving an especial contempt for the larger fishing towns, where less skilled, less traditional fishing practices were to be found. 'There was fishermen in Scarborough, but they don't fish,' was a universal view amongst older men as late as the 1980s, reckoned Terence COLLINS. And Sydney Smith told us how Old Isaac ROSS, chapel-keeper, expressed similar Filey prejudices about Whitby:

> 'I hear'd ye's goin' on thee holidays', someone might say to him.
>
> 'Aye', he says.
>
> 'Where's tha goin'?'
>
> 'I'm goin' 'e laiks. Goin' t'Whitby.'
>
> 'There's nay laiks at Whitby!'
>
> 'Don't thoo believe it,' Old Isaac would say, 'there's a bloody sight mair laiks than works at Whitby!'   [*laiks* is dialect for 'larks']

h) 'Ranter Chapel' - Primitive Methodism, 'the Harbour of comfort', gelled the fisher families socially as well as spiritually: *Ebenezer Chapel* on Union Street was remembered by our 1980s informants as the hub of their childhood and teenage social activity. Services, classes, bazaars, processions, fish-pie suppers – chapel life threw so many young men and women together. Historically, religious sects have maintained purity of belief by seeking marriage partners within their faith. In addition, certain chapters in the Old Testament implicitly approve of family intermarriage: in Genesis, both Esau and Jacob married first cousins, whilst Abraham married his half-sister. In the 1980s, we heard no memories of family pressure to 'marry in'. After the 1820s religious revival, however, in so patriarchal a society, the strength of example alone, and the unconsciously received messages of preachers and teachers, may have created customarily unchallengeable marriage horizons amongst fishing families.

Virtually all birthplaces in the town's 19th Century census returns are 'Filey', revealing very little movement along the immediate coastline into the town.[30] Wives were local. Other isolated fishing villages as far apart as the Marshside near Southport in Lancashire (shrimping) and the Shetlands display this lack of marrying out. Almost invariably, the pattern of intermarriage is associated with the centrality of wives and daughters as land support, a small number of surnames, and nonconformity in religion.[31] The next chapters examine how this hermetically self-contained culture played out in the family history of the Old Town.

---

[30] The number of fishermen in Filey born in the town only dropped below 88% during the peak years around 1870/80 when outsiders were attracted; by 1891 it was back to over 90% (Friend, 2010, Table 8).

[31] Thompson et al (1983) pp75-83; pp334-8.

5 THE FAMILY HISTORIAN'S GUIDE
TO THE OLD TOWN

Identity Confusion

*'Are you number one or number twelve?' Dr Simpson asked, on hearing that his
next appointment was Mary JENKINSON.*

Mary Elizabeth ROBINSON (R15) told us about this visit to the surgery as a
teenager, before the First World War. The same problem applied to other core Filey
surnames. Identifying individuals in any historical record is confounded if several
people carry the same first and second names. It is little consolation that this
identity confusion was experienced in most communities as a daily reality.[1] We
explored in Chapter 4 how immobile Filey fisher surnames have been, and how
they have mushroomed in number.[2] Filey's population grew, but only a limited
number of Christian names were in common use at the time. The doppelganger
phenomenon was inevitable. The JENKINSON family was the most pronounced
instance, with CAMMISH a close second.

Since the 1980s, when we first wrote up this research, it has become clear that Filey
was far from unique in its incidence of such identity confusion. During the 18th
Century, the stock of Christian names popular in Britain had fallen to probably its
lowest level in the last thousand years. Where the surname stock was as limited as
Filey's, the results were a complete breakdown in the conventional use of Christian
name and surname as means of individual identification.[3] In the year 1900, there
were ten JENKINSONs with a first name *John*, eight with *Matthew*, six apiece with
William, *Thomas* and *George*, five called *Richard* and four *Robert*. At virtually any

---

[1] Filey seems to have had the edge. Alan Storm found 'bewildering' the existence at
Robin Hood's Bay of 23 fishermen or sailors, from the 17th to the 20th Centuries, called
Isaac Storm. Several Filey combinations must have at least matched that (Storm, 1991).

[2] The limited research into surname turnover suggests that in this respect, Filey and
other fishing communities are exceptional: in one Warwickshire parish, for example,
typical of arable England, between 1561 and 1860, only a third of names persisted for
more than 50 years, whilst just 5% survived beyond 250. Nor is Filey the most extreme
example of a community being dominated by a few surnames. In the shrimping village
of Marsh Side, on Lancashire's Ribble estuary, 90% of the population shared just five
surnames in 1841 (Thompson et al, 1983, p83). On some Scottish islands, over half the
population bear one surname.

[3] Fishing communities in north-east Scotland were also badly affected. Typical was
Portessie, on the south coast of the Moray Firth, where according to the 1881 Census
59% of the population shared just four surnames. The commonest, Smith, was carried
by 41%. Unsurprisingly this coast featured inheritable by-names, known as *tee-names* in
Scotland, in exactly the same way as Yorkshire's fishing villages (Blaikie, 2002, p23).

time after about 1850, there would be at least six John JENKINSONs of fishing age. As late as 1970, there were five Tom JENKINSONs in the town. In the early 20th Century, 48 Mrs JENKINSONs were reputedly on the books of the friendly society, the Shepherds' Club. Many Filey women took in holiday visitors during the summer, and it became a standing joke how unsuspecting newcomers arrived at Filey station with their bags asking for directions to Mrs JENKINSON's.

Surnames as Christian Names

One solution was to increase the stock of Christian names, and this may account for the use of the maiden surname of a bride as a first name. The practice wasn't new. It can be found in various places at least as far back as the 16th Century. There may have been some church resistance to this straying from conventional first names, but never any legal rules.[4] But since the practice began amongst the landowning elites, and was often copied by their tenants, local power realities silenced clerical disapproval. By the late 18th Century, it had percolated downwards, being adopted by some of Filey's tradesmen and farmers. Fisher families took it up just as the 19th Century turned (**5.1**). In the 1841 Census, 19 Filey families had at least one man bearing a surname as a Christian name, around half belonging to the fishing community. The oldest example, Crumpton Skelton, was a 70 year-old publican, though some of his extended family were fishermen.

For some reason, female babies were never given a surname as a sole Christian name. Perhaps the risk of boys and girls bearing identical names would have added a new twist to identity confusion. In a patriarchal society, the priority was to register family descent in the male line. Perhaps the need for identification was greater in what would now be termed safety-critical environments like the open sea. Perhaps the reckoning and accounting of fish sales, provisioning, boat construction and repairs demanded clear identification. More likely, surnames simply did not make for very feminine-sounding first names.

Invaluably for Filey family historians, maiden names adopted as Christian names have cascaded down several generations in many families. The surname *Edmond*, for example often rendered as Edmund (incorrectly, according to some purists) has been a favoured JENKINSON Christian name well into the 20th Century, notably amongst the *Eamen* branch (**5.2**). The Thwing surname *Castle* became a Christian name in the ROSS family at Filey and Bridlington, and in the Mainprize families at Filey and Scarborough.[5]

---

[4] In 1991, Iceland introduced an official register of approved given names to limit the introduction of new names into national culture; I know of no other example.

[5] The origin of the name in these Filey families was Thomas Castle of Flamborough, originally of Thwing. One daughter, Mary, married a Filey JENKINSON, Thomas. Her sister Ann married Isaac ROSS at Flamborough in 1827: this is the wellspring from which flow the ROSS fisher families at Filey, and their frozen food offshoot (see p248).

Bulmer CAPPLEMAN 1791	David **Dunn** CRAWFORD 1817	Francis **Wilson** BAXTER 1834
Cappleman CAMMISH 1801		**Skelton** FENBY 1837
Crumpton SKELTON 1801	**Morton** CHAPMAN 1816 (burial, aged 9 mths)	Robert **Jenkinson** CRAWFORD 1837
Wilson CAMMISH (name of the father) 1803 baptism	**Sumption** JOHNSON 1817 (burial, aged 3 wks)	**Brown Marshall** COOLING 1837
Bayze (ie **Bayes**) SCALES 1808	**Bayze** (ie **Bayes**) COWLING 1820	Robert **Cammish** COOLING 1839
Rickman SKELTON (groom) 1810	**Castle** JENKINSON 1824	Richard **Cappleby** SIMPSON 1839
Edmond JENKINSON 1811 (from age in 1841 Census)	**Rickman** FENBY (groom) 1827	**Edmond** CRAWFORD 1839
Nesfield Glaves CRUMPTON 1813	**Jenkinson** HAXBY 1827	**Castle** ROSS 1840
Cappleman FELL 1814	William **Cappleman** CAMMISH 1831	John **Pockley** CAPPLEMAN 1841
Edmond CAMMISH 1815 (from age in 1841 Census)	Thomas **Cappleman** SIMPSON 1833	**Ross** JENKINSON 1841

5.1: First appearance in St Oswald's registers, for each Filey fisher family, of children or bridegrooms with surnames as Christian names, up to 1841. The practice began in 1791. For no clear reason, girls were never given surnames as *first* Christian names.

By the 20th Century, surnames as first Christian names had fallen out of fashion in Filey, with the exception of *Edmond*. Nesfield Crompton (1900) and Irene's uncle, Castle Mainprize, familiarly *Cas*, born in 1912, are very late examples.

Middle Names

The custom of giving a child a surname as a *second* Christian name effectively replaced it. The practice can be found in County Durham in late 18th Century parish registers. It may initially have been a way of including the surname of a father in the name of an illegitimate child. But the fashion grew of giving legitimate children, especially sons, the mother's maiden surname as a middle name. The first instance amongst Filey's fisher families was in 1813, but it grew in popularity in the 1830s. Filey's 1823 religious revival may have generated a greater sense of family. Connection to a relative, locally respected within the Primitive Methodist community, could have been significant in this way.

Such a naming pattern securely ties each generation to its predecessors. We found that about half the JENKINSON couples perpetuated a wife's maiden name in the names of their children, as did other Old Town families. This has persisted well into the 20th Century. Grandmothers' maiden names were often used too. The example shown on page 54 (**5.2**) is exceptional in that Thomas Cappleman *Titch* JENKINSON (R85) received a *great* grandmother's maiden name 70 years after the marriage from which it derived.

The tree also shows the origin of the name *Ross* as a Christian name amongst the JENKINSONs and their related families.

Surnames were only given to girls as *second* Christian names, perhaps because the lead name retained the sense of femininity. The first fisher example I found was Sarah Cappleman JENKINSON (1844, P43). Pairings of a traditional female first name with a fisher surname as a middle name have produced some truly sonorous compounds, oozing with family history - Rachel Cammish CAPPLEMAN, Frances Haxby COWLING, and Dorothy Scales JENKINSON. In all, the Old Town used 30 surnames as Christian names. About a fifth of all the 400 or so JENKINSONs on our pedigrees (Appendix E) had a surname as a first Christian name, and these were mostly the core 15 fisher surnames. A family might be satisfied with one of their babies perpetuating a maiden name, but some went further. Mr and Mrs Matthew Crompton JENKINSON (Q43) took the preservation of ancestral linkage seriously enough to give seven of their eight children the middle name *Crompton*, but this was a special case. He had been deprived of his 'real' surname, being born just before his parents' marriage.

Entity-naming

In 1863, William and Elizabeth George, a Welsh couple in Manchester, followed a new middle-class fashion and gave their baby son both the Christian name *and surname* of his maternal grandfather, David Lloyd. I call this *entity-naming* because the identity of an actual person was commemorated in the baby's full name, *David Lloyd* George.[6] The practice can also be found in north-east England, and in parts of Lowland Scotland, particularly from the 1820s, but I suspect many other pockets. They have a predictive quality in that when we realise *entity-naming* is being practised, we know the likely name of a parent *somewhere* back along a female line. In Filey, the practice may have been an especially emphatic way of indicating respect for religiously devout grandparents. In 1856, for example, to preserve the identity of two celebrity relatives, both called George JENKINSON, one little Mainprize was given the fine entity-name of George Jenkinson Mainprize. The George JENKINSONs in question had each been eminent members of the town's Primitive Methodist Society.

By-names

Working class men were often known by nicknames, communally determined from early life, often in jovial honour of some distinguishing characteristic: once given, they could stick to at least one of the man's children.

---

[6] Following another middle-class fashion of the time, this future prime minister decided that his credibility as a lawyer would be enhanced if he migrated his second Christian name to become part of his surname. Any number of double-barrelled surnames evolved in this way. The practice was especially common in Wales, where surname stock was limited to a small number of patronymics like *Davies*, *Evans* and *Jones*.

Thomas m Mary
JOHNSON ROSS

m 1804

John m Mary
JENKINSON EDMOND
1791-1872 1788-1856

m 1810

m 1816

*Thomas m Rachel
JENKINSON JOHNSON
1817-90

*Edmond m Mary William m Mary
JENKINSON CAMMISH CAMMISH CAPPLEMAN
1811-41

Cousins?

Ross JENKINSON 1841-80

Nancy JENKINSON 1840-63

m

Edmund JENKINSON 1839-1910

John m *Elizabeth
CAMMISH JENKINSON
Ranter bn1828
Jack

Edmond Ross
JENKINSON
1862-92

m

Isabella§ CAMMISH
Bell Taffy
1860-1938

Susannah§ CAMMISH
1869-1954
m Robert
JENKINSON

Ross JENKINSON
Reas
1881-1959
m Susannah
SAYERS

Thomas Cappleman JENKINSON
Titch
1885-1963
m Mary Jane
CAPPLEMAN

Edmond JENKINSON
Eamen
1890-1965
m Mary Cammish
CHAPMAN

Richard Cammish JENKINSON
Snosh
1892-1961
m Lily
JOHNSON

Edmund Ross bn1904

Mary Elizabeth Cappleman bn1917

John William Chapman bn1912

Edmund Ross
Eamen
bn1915

Thomas Chapman
Eamen
bn1919

Frank Chapman 1929-99

Edmund Ross 1920-2

Edmund Ross bn1924

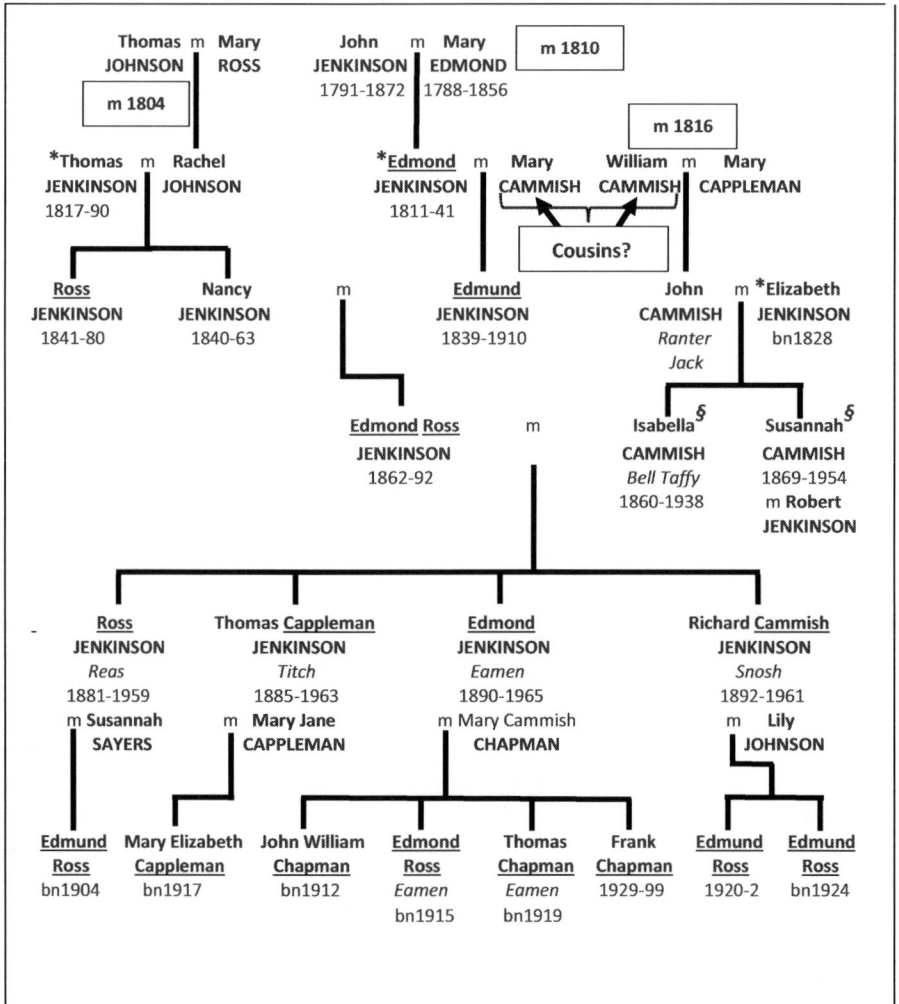

5.2: The *Eamen/Eamon* JENKINSONs: cousins four times over. Note in particular:

a) Intermarriage between cousins (the three JENKINSONs marked* were first cousins, and their JENKINSON grandparents therefore appear three times on the direct ancestry of everyone in the two most recent generations on this tree). Note that the bottom two generations were also cousins on the CAMMISH side — Mary and William would have been first or second cousins;

b) Origins of surnames used as Christian names (instances underlined);

c) Double family marriage (first cousins Robert and Edmond Ross JENKINSON married sisters Isabella§ and Susannah§ CAMMISH);

d) How the by-name *Eamon/Eamen* originated from a marriage of 1810.

A good example is *Old Naz* (Thomas Robert JENKINSON, Q44) who reputedly had a surly disposition. Whilst *Naz* himself went just by the nickname, his children took it after their Christian name. Thus daughters *Mary Naz* and *Sally Naz* acquired it irrespective of their personalities. Mary ROBINSON's cousin, *Gertie Penny* (Q33), inherited her father's by-name, *Bill Penny*, even though it was unnecessary for identity purposes - there was never any other adult Gertrude JENKINSON in Filey to be confused with. The nickname's origin is a mystery. Occasionally a man didn't take his father's by-name: *Dick Black* JENKINSON (R138) took his maternal grandfather *Jack Black's* by-name, not his father's, for he was born two years before his parents' marriage. These names could trickle down generations: Jim's Haxby's brother, Richard Jenkinson Haxby, first got called *Tabsy* by the ageing George SCALES, who knew it as the boy's grandfather's by-name.

5.3: Fisher by-names were once not broadcast beyond the community, for as long as a man's identity was secret, he could not be 'claimed' by the sea. Now they appear on gravestones. Note the symbolically empty coble. The Church of England in the 21st Century has become less tolerant of nicknames in churchyards.

IN LOVING MEMORY OF
DEAR PARENTS AND GRANDPARENTS
THOMAS JAMES (CHICK)
CAMMISH
15-11-1908. - 2-1-1989

Jack Black JENKINSON's by-name (P93) may have derived from *black*, dialect for squall, perhaps a reference to the man's terse turn of phrase. Robert Pearson HUNTER inherited *Tewy* from his risk-taker of a father George William. Cooper reckoned it came from the dialect word meaning restless. Thomas JENKINSON (Q108) was always known as *Laffy* because of his light-hearted disposition. Bob Wheeler related how he fell for Thomas's jocularity – *Laffy* and his pals sat on the wall of butcher Old Tom Haxby's field, throwing stones at the apple tree to bring down fruit. Bob and others were 'sent ovver t'wall' to fetch it. Old Tommy used ter come up wi' his steek sayin' he was gonna murder us, if he catched us.' The name, and perhaps the humour, passed on to his son, Thomas Gordon (R140) so dad morphed into *Old Laffy*, the usual pattern in these cases of father-son inheritance. William Johnson (*Bill Bullocky*) COLLING (**3.8**, **21.6**) reckoned his name derived from working with cattle as a youth, though others may have felt it fitted his strong, solid frame. Who will ever know?

Some names were corruptions of a surname used as a Christian name – *Denk* for Jenkinson; *Lano* for Lane, as in the case of Bob Lane Wheeler, *Laffy's* apple fetcher; *Reas* was applied to Ross JENKINSON (R83), and *Eamen*, given to his brother Edmond (R87). These nicknames also percolated down the generations, as did *Buggins* – George JENKINSON (P91) was *Old Jossie Buggins,* whilst his son, Frank Cappleman (Q90) became *Bonzo Buggins* after his acquisition of the famous seal. Delightfully, the seal's name has become an inheritable name itself, the latest bearer *Jackie Bonzo* living now (2019) on Queen Street.

Inevitably, names often had maritime and fishing connotations: *Billy Trummy's* (William JENKINSON, Q46) reputedly resulted from his early use in Filey of a trammel net.[7] The *Bass*, applied to at least two Jimmy Wyvills, presumably derives from the dialect term for a handwoven net, often used to carry bait. *Dicky Hoy* (Richard Cammish JENKINSON, Q45) was probably so called because he coordinated efforts to get his coble onto the launching carriage with the shanty-like chant *hip a hoy*. William *Barla* JENKINSON (R65) had the *barls* (ie sea boils and ulcers) caused by stiff oilskin cuffs and collars rubbing against wet skin. This was why fishermen wore mufflers round the exposed neck, and bandaged their wrists with a knitted band of wool. William Cappleman CAMMISH, lost with *Research* in 1925, was *Coddy*, which can only derive from cod.

Indiana Jack seems to have been John Crawford, master of the yawl *Indiana*.[8] William CAMMISH was reputedly impressed into the crew of a Royal Navy ship whilst fishing for herrings near Whitby. He supposedly carried the name *Traf* on his return to Filey: tradition has it that he had served at Trafalgar. A descendant, *Traf* CAMMISH, is still fishing today. Alas, the National Archives' on-line database of men who served at Trafalgar (21st October 1805) draws a blank for a William CAMMISH. Nor is there a large gap in baptisms around 1805 for children of William and Ann/Nancy CAMMISH, the most likely candidate for *Traf*. Despite so eventful a life history, *Traf* seems to have survived long enough to have been enumerated in the 1861 Census aged 77, though he did declare himself a 'Worn out Fisherman'! This man gave evidence to the Sea Fisheries Commission in October 1863. He had given up fishing '14 or 15 years ago'. What a shame neither of the commissioners asked him, 'What did you do in the War?'

Filey's core fishing surnames are unrepresented in the Trafalgar database, probably because just about every fisherman in the town was enrolled after 1803 in the local naval reserve, the Filey Fencibles, and therefore spared foreign service and impressment.[9] Perhaps *Traf* was a generic nickname for former Naval seamen. Many families may proudly but misguidedly hand down such retrospective claims to service at Britain's most famous naval victory.

---

[7] A compound net of different meshes was used to catch fish at every depth. The trammel was attached to the foot of an ordinary drift net to catch bottom feeding fish. Strung between two boats, a stretch of sea could therefore be trawled of virtually everything in the water. *Trumming*, a Flamborough practice, was frowned upon in Filey.

[8] Kath WILKIE points out that Jack died in 1908, just three weeks after *Indiana* was broken up. It is a moot point if his attachment to the yawl influenced this coincidence.

[9] Nor does one other Trafalgar legend hold up to scrutiny. The report of John Wheeler's award of long service in the Naval Reserve (March 1910) contains the assertion that 'Wheeler's great grandfather was boatswain on the *Victory* and fell in action with the great commander at Trafalgar' (Nellist, 1913). See *Trafalgar Ancestors*, on the National Archives' website. Ten Wheelers served at the battle, but none are recorded in the data base as being on the *Victory*. The number of jack tars at Trafalgar would have been many times greater than the 18,000 mustered if all naval family legends were true!

George Whiteley Boynton (1842-1922) probably got *Baltic* from regular voyages taking cured herring to Baltic ports, with trees tall enough to provide masts as a backload.[10] Frank, George's son, inherited his dad's penchant for physical forcefulness and became *Rammy*. Fortunately, this was 'confined to the football field'.[11] *Baltic's* grandson (**5.4**) inherited his name, but his nickname from a footballing father.

5.4: Name from Granddad, by-name from Dad.

The by-names were used universally, for they were better recognised than a man's true name. Even the *Filey Post* occasionally referred to the fishermen only by their nicknames, evidence that they were the most accurate identifiers. Similarly, they were often used by the compiler of the Cappleman Accounts Book (1872-93) - it would be poor business practice to be hounding the wrong CAMMISH or JENKINSON for an unpaid bill. By the 1970s, they were figuring in some St Oswald's inscriptions, reflecting a diminution of the gravitas and solemnity which had traditionally characterised graveyards (**5.3, 5.4, 5.5**). In parts of north-east Scotland, fishermen's by-names were even included in the census enumeration books, effectively evolving into their official names. The Nairn surname *Main* had proliferated so much that rate demands had to be addressed according to men's by-names. To prevent similar confusion, when Mains emigrated, the men's by-name sometimes actually became their surname, retained even on the other side of the Atlantic.[12] This is rather like being present at the medieval surname Big Bang, when second names sprang up spontaneously to identify individuals.

Names that don't perform this discriminatory job have no further use, and people and organisations find ways to augment them. As population grows, the state in particular needs greater precision: wartime identity numbers became our NHS numbers in 1948; we have unique National Insurance numbers; and countless organisations guarantee uniqueness with user names and 'strong' passwords.

These by-names were often tinged with dry Filey irony: *Titch* (Thomas Cappleman JENKINSON, R85) was so called because he was the tallest man in Filey. Many arose at school. Three Tom Crimlis cousins were in the same class. One teacher asked 'Tom Crimlis' a question, and all three stood up. 'So he called them *Tommy A*, *Tommy B*, and *Tommy C*', explained Richard Haxby, 'and they stuck till they died.'

---

[10] George was a mariner when he married in 1864. Several Filey men were involved in the Baltic trade with Scandinavia and Russia – see below, pp98 (footnote 14) and 298.

[11] *Redux*, 4th Nov 2019. For the elder George Whiteley's fisticuffing, see pp99-100 and 411-2. As with the *Naz* sisters, a family nickname might not be applicable to the personality of its new owners!

[12] Blaikie (2002) p23; Barron (2009) pp52-3.

5.5: Fisher communities attached by-names to wives, sons and daughters, and these nicknames could be retained throughout life, despite marital surname change. *Tina Tint,* incidentally, confirmed that the family shared Filey's sardonic sense of humour when she explained that the incongruous mound of vegetables piled in her dad's coble celebrates his love of growing cabbages.

Thomas *Tint* JENKINSON (R60) got his nickname because his stock response to accusations of school misbehaviour was 'tint me'! His son inherited, and it percolates down the line. 'I'm *Tina Tint,*' his delightfully-named granddaughter told me in 2019, as she tended her father's grave at St Oswald's, 'even though I'm married!' (**5.5**). Women often acquired their husband's by-name: 'Good morning, *Mrs Fatty'* was Mary E CAMMISH's normal greeting from shopkeepers on Queen Street! Offence was neither intended nor taken.[13]

Not everyone inherited their nickname, for the father's might be trumped by some distinctive characteristic in the son. Brothers Matt, Frank and Tom CAMMISH, sons of *Tosh*, were *Tooter, Tosh* and *Chicken* (**5.3**). *Chicken* was another of those Filey irony names – 'an 'ard case,' according to Jim Haxby. But more importantly, Tom had a 'nose like a chicken,' though he was the sort of man nobody would risk telling that to. Fisherman's Choir conductor, Stuart CAMMISH also got *Chicken* - same family. *Frankie Tosh* was unkindly also known as *Lord Lascelles*, a certain haughtiness of manner evidently being reminiscent of George V's son-in-law, a regular Filey visitor.

Ignorance of Common Ancestry

Anyone with fisher ancestors in Filey is related to everyone else probably several times over. We saw in Chapter 1 that all the Filey JENKINSONs descend from one 18th Century couple who married in 1778, four of whose sons were still alive in 1860.[14] Yet we found in our researches that any notion of this common origin had long since disappeared, despite all the family bonds of occupation and intermarriage. If we asked one JENKINSON about some other family living a few houses away, on Queen Street or Mitford Street, we would be told, 'Oh, they

---

[13] James *Fatty* CAMMISH (1887-1970) was well-built, but not especially overweight!

[14] Mass descent from a common ancestor is very common in fishing communities. One remarkable example is provided by the *Main* fisher family in the town of Nairn. A 2004 sampling revealed identical genetic profiling across 10 haplotypes (DNA variants) strongly suggesting that all 15 fishermen in the project descended from one man living between 500 and 1,000 years before (Barron, 2009, pp56-8).

weren't related to us'.[15] Unaided memory about ancestors rarely stretches back more than two or three generations; beyond that, knowledge is usually confused and sketchy, if it exists at all. The relational status even of living members of the wider family is lost if the point of connection lies beyond three generations. *Gertie Penny*, daughter of William Hall JENKINSON (*Bill Penny, P27*, the eccentric shooter of sea birds) was a regular visitor to the JENKINSON childhood home of Mary Elizabeth ROBINSON - she was a cousin of Mary's father. Yet despite Mary Elizabeth's expertise on Filey families, she told us how:

> She used to come to our house. I wondered why she used to come because I didn't know they called her JENKINSON. She always got *Penny*. If you hear their proper names it stops you.

Two Filey COLLINGs, William Cammish and William Johnson (*Bill Bullocky*), both in their twenties, were involved in a shipwreck off Newfoundland, in 1947. Of 22 other crew on board, it fell to *Bill Bullocky*, the only surviving man on watch, to attempt to rescue his Filey mate. Nearly 70 years later, he related how

> 'e was a cousin more or less . . . 'is father and my father were cousins, like, so 'e was sort of 'alf cousin.

In fact, they were second cousins, their fathers, Matthew Jenkinson and William Johnson COLLING, being grandsons of fisherman George COLLING, who had married Ellis (ie Alice) Simpson in 1844, 103 years before.[16]

Things are changing. In the space of just three decades, appreciation of common ancestry and collateral relationship has become widespread. The sources for family history we used in libraries and record offices in the 1980s are now readily available online, whilst genetic genealogy is becoming increasingly accurate, and affordable, in its ability to pinpoint common ancestors in the male, surname line.

Patterns of Marriage, Birth and Illegitimacy

'The appearance of the woman at church in the character of a bride is not *followed by her appearance a few weeks later in the character of a mother. The records of illegitimacy are lowest among the Jews, but I doubt if theirs are lower than ours.' Canon Arthur N Cooper (1886)*

It is clear that Old Town fisher families were conscientious in having their children baptised - only one or two JENKINSON child burials, for example, had no

---

[15] For example, Foster Holmes JENKINSON (R37) and Elizabeth Jenkinson Allen (née Hoggarth) were fourth cousins, born at Filey within a year of each other, brought up within a stone's throw in the Old Town, at school together and later living in the same part of Scarborough. Yet they were completely unaware that they were related.

[16] See below, pp305, 407-8, for further details of the 1947 wreck of the *SS Langleecrag* off Newfoundland, and of *Bullocky's* unsuccessful attempt to rescue his Filey friend/cousin.

corresponding baptism, perhaps because the baby had died within hours or days. Every JENKINSON child in the 1841, 1851 and 1861 Censuses had been baptised. The Primitive Methodist Chapel accounted for many baptisms after that.

The concentrated nature of the Old Town, and the fact that the St Oswald's minister and his officials lived close by, must have encouraged a high rate of baptism. At Gosforth, in Cumberland, the 'real old families' were keen to have their children's arrival in the village officially recorded,[17] and Filey was no different. Another persistent feature was the annual birth peak in September and the trough in June/July, to be expected as long as Yorkshire offshore fishermen were involved in the two months of the autumn herring fishery.[18]

Early marriage - the truism 'no man can be a fisher and want a wife' was common in north-east Scotland, but applicable to all traditional fishing communities. It accounts for the pattern of early marriage amongst fishermen, their low illegitimacy rates, and prompt remarriage. In communities where men and women had known each other since childhood, opportunities for a new marriage were rife. Put baldly, sexually mature fishermen did not spend long unwed. Fishing villages were geographically constricted settlements, in which secret trysts were nigh on impossible and the close presence of watchfully upright grandparents may have been a factor in discouraging sexual incontinence.[19]

Illegitimacy is popularly associated with paternal abandonment, but modern research has found that it was far more likely to be the result of an interruption to the normal sequence of events marking a couple's progression to marriage. Pre-nuptial sexual intercourse was a norm in working-class communities, pregnancy simply bringing urgency to what had already been intended.

But marriage might be impossible in the absence of accommodation, a fall in earnings, illness, or death. In communities where housing stock was in short supply, the death of grandparents was often quietly anticipated to free up a cottage for younger family members. In fisher villages, however, readily expandable housing stock and economic demand for wives removed many of these interruptions. If anything, there were likely to be far more incentives to marry than obstacles – like the availability of steady work, a financial share in a boat, close community and strong family life.[20] There was also potent social disapproval of a man abandoning a pregnant woman whose parents were probably related to his own, with likely physical consequences off her male relatives!

[17] Storm (1991) p35.

[18] Storm (1991) p154. This was the pattern at Robin Hood's Bay, 1780-1840, when dates of birth were given in the baptismal register. Filey must have been the same, given that over a hundred men were missing from late September to November each year.

[19] Thompson et al (1983) pp212-3, 234; Storm (1991) pp189-92.

[20] Kenneth M Boyd, *Scottish Church Attitudes to Sex, Marriage and the Family 1850-1914* (Donald, 1980).

Unsurprisingly, fishing communities were renowned for low rates of illegitimacy, as Cooper implied. Where there were distinct fishing and non-fishing populations in a parish, the contrast could not have been clearer. At Robin Hood's Bay, between 1653 and 1840, the 'Bay' rate of illegitimacy (ie the fishing community) was a third of the 'Country' part of the parish. Similarly, at Filey, we found just eight illegitimacies in 150 years on the whole of our *JENKINSON* pedigree.

Many of the actual instances of illegitimacy could simply have been the result of delays in marriage occasioned by lengthy fishing absences. Nor does there appear to have been great social disapproval of such occurrences where delay was in good faith. The widespread use of surnames as second Christian names often clarifies the paternity of illegitimate children and confirms this pattern. For example, this entry figures in the St Oswald's baptismal register:

> 6th March 1856 John Williamson illegitimate son of Elizabeth ~~WILLIAMSON~~ JENKINSON.

A later entry in the St Oswald's marriage register clearly relates to this child's parents, probably after his father's moneyed return from the Norfolk fishing:

> 22nd November 1856 John WILLIAMSON, fisherman, son of John WILLIAMSON, fisherman, married Betsy JENKINSON, daughter of Thomas JENKINSON, fisherman.

Similarly, Edward Scales (*Neddy Rasp*, Q35) was born prior to the marriage of his parents, Edward SCALES and Sarah Jane JENKINSON. After their marriage, his parents accurately recorded him in the 1881 Census as Edward Scales JENKINSON. In many similar cases, such a pre-marital indiscretion would have been concealed by a diplomatic sleight of hand, ie entering him on the schedule with his father's surname. The fact that his parents did not suggests that such illegitimacy, if followed by a marriage, involved no stigma. It may also indicate that in a very close community, of which the census enumerator would be part, no one could conceal such a situation. Significantly, Edward Scales JENKINSON saw no reason to pretend he was a SCALES throughout his 65 years. He became a respected and leading member of the Primitive Methodist Chapel.

Rates of Bridal Pregnancy were no different from other working-class communities, so in this regard, Cooper's boast about Filey brides only becoming mothers after a respectable interval was unfounded. Nationally, around a third of 19th Century brides were expecting the couple's first child. There were 77 Filey marriages between 1813 and 1908 involving brides or grooms carrying one of a sample of seven fisher surnames. Twenty-three of these couples had a child baptised within 8½ months of the marriage. This small sample suggests about a third to a quarter of brides in 19th Century Filey Old Town were pregnant when they married, a figure which corresponds to the general findings of population historians. This is the normal yardstick by which pre-marital conception is measured. *Monkey Island*, the hill behind the Lifeboat House, was according to Terence COLLINS, the favoured place to engineer it.

6 FILEY AND FAMILY MIGRATION

We have already seen that Old Filey's glacial rate of surname turnover made it exceptional. Many of its 20th Century names had been in the town for over 250 years. But equally exceptional were the long distances that its few incoming surnames had travelled. Nationally, inland migration rarely involved journeys from places more than a day's walk away. People rarely died more than a few miles from where they had been born.[1] Movement in and out of Filey, however, predictably extended almost exclusively *along* the coast, between fishing stations, as if the hinterland did not exist. And the distances covered by migrating fishermen and their families could extend to scores, and even hundreds of miles.

The 1851 Census reveals both short distance Yorkshire fisher immigration into the town, and far longer moves, like the four Norfolk-born men in the Old Town - this East Anglian drift to the Yorkshire coast had intensified by the time of the 1861 and 1871 Censuses. Some of the core Old Town names had originated from even further afield, and long before the census period. This makes determining their origins far harder.

Migration of Fisher Families

Few working-class men ever saw towns and villages as distant from their homes as offshore fishermen. Filey men had been following herring down to East Anglia since at least the 17th Century, and probably far longer. British deep-sea fishermen regularly experienced such widened horizons, and the recognition of more attractive fishing could lead to permanent migration. How else can we explain the prevalence of the surname *Abbs* in a group of coastal parishes around Cromer in Norfolk? The original bearers must have originated from the Berwickshire village near Eyemouth which has given its name to the nearby St Abbs Head, familiar to listeners of the BBC's Shipping Forecast.

From the late 19th Century, overfishing and chronic shortages of bait prompted movement from the Yorkshire coast to the steam trawling ports of Aberdeen, Grimsby, Milford Haven and Fleetwood.[2] But no group of fishermen could outdo the Cornish for mileage: in a remarkable annual circumnavigation of the British coast, many St Ives lugger crews followed the herring shoals northwards in the Irish Sea, landing catches in Irish ports, then made for the Clyde, if necessary dragging their boats by rope along the Forth and Clyde Canal, emerging in the

---

[1] Based on data provided by family history researchers about 73,864 residential movements in the lifetimes of 16,091 people born between 1750 and 1930 (Colin Pooley & Jean Turnbull, *Migration and Mobility in Britain since the Eighteenth Century*, UCL Press, 1998).

[2] Thompson et al (1983) pp10-11.

Firth of Forth to join the Scots herring fleet on its southwards course along the North Sea coast. And finally home via the Channel.[3]

Three factors could persuade a fisherman to transfer his family along the coast:

1 'Fish swims' was how one Filey coble fisherman explained the unpredictability of the quarry. Fishermen follow fish, and if stocks deplete or habits change, then longer voyages to the fisheries are avoided by relocation. In the mid-19th Century, for example, herring were inexplicably shoaling longer off the north Yorkshire coast. Fish-buyers took up residence in Scarborough, and competition between them pushed up the quayside prices offered to boats. Consequently, many Norfolk men now spent longer fishing off Yorkshire, and settlement often followed. By 1861, a fifth of Scarborough fishermen were East Anglia born.[4] The small influx of Norfolk men into Filey occurred at a similar time.

News of the fortunes of relatives and friends who had already migrated reached home by letter or word of mouth, and acted as a powerful draw. Migration was rarely solitary, and several families might make the same move, though not necessarily at the same time. This is why clusters of incomers from the same district or even village are often found in a town's census returns. Irish escapees from the Potato Famine of the 1840s huddled in the same London, Liverpool or Manchester streets, reflecting the same community instincts that grouped fishing families together in Scarborough's Old Town.

2 The Attraction of Beaches and Harbours – overcrowding at landings undermined earnings and could be dangerous. Regular passage along the coast alerted fishermen to better locations. In the 19th Century, the move from beach fishing stations to nearby harbours, whether by offshore or inshore men, was a trend along most of the British coast. In Yorkshire, Whitby drew Coles, Theakers and Verrills from Staithes, Storms from Robin Hood's Bay, and Dukes from as far afield as Flamborough.[5] Northumberland coble fishermen left traditional beach-launching villages like Beadnell for nearby Seahouses and Amble. Harbours saved the hard work, expense and risks of beach launching and landing; there was no need to immerse oneself waist-deep in water. Ballast, normally removed to minimise weight at launching, could be left permanently in the coble.

Filey's population grew, crowding at the landing got worse, facilities deteriorated, and cobles moved to Bridlington and Scarborough.[6] Similar problems drew the town's offshoremen to these harbours (**7.3**) their yawls being berthed there permanently.

---

[3] John McWilliams, *The Cornish Fishing Industry: An Illustrated History* (Amberley, 2014).

[4] Margaret Gerrish, 'Who followed the fish to Scarborough Fare?' Part 3, *Yorkshire History Quarterly*, Vol 3, No 3 (Feb 1998).

[5] Frank (2002) p38.

[6] In 1897, the Coble Landing, used by 150 fishermen, was 'in bad repair' (*Driffield Times,* 9th Jan 1897).

6.1 The Filey removal van – imagine moving family and furniture in a 17½ foot coble like *St George*, or sailing c700 miles to South Wales in so small a boat. *[FM]*

The crews could now easily sail out in the great-lining months, from Monday to Saturday, walking or catching the train home for the weekend. Richard JENKINSON's (O8) was one of the first Filey families to settle at Scarborough's 'Bottom End' permanently, as early as the 1820s (Appendix E, Chart **E2**). The considerable JENKINSON fisher clan now in the town descend from them. By 1881, there were dozens of CAMMISH, CAPPLEMAN, COLLING/COWLING, JENKINSON and SCALES families in the old town fishing streets - Castlegate, Sandside and Quay Street - all shown in the census as fishermen born in Filey.

Bridlington Harbour (*Quay*) in Hilderthorpe, a mile from the old town, also attracted Filey men, but later. About a dozen families moved there with several of the town's offshore fleet between 1877 and 1881, as plans for harbour facilities at Filey came to nothing.[7] But most commuted. The Filey men in *Quay* were inshoremen, and had appeared in the Hilderthorpe fishing streets by 1881 and 1891. Seven 'core' Filey fisher names are there, CAMMISH, CAPPLEMAN, COLLING/COWLING, JENKINSON, JOHNSON, ROSS and WILLIAMSON, as well as non-core Filey families, Martin, Scotter and Simpson. These were the years of decline, and most migrants were probably chancing the coble-trawling for which Bridlington had become a centre.

3 Long Distance Migration – demand in growing English towns brought Scottish fishermen down the east coast, hence Filey's COLLING/COWLING, Crawford, Donkin (a corruption of Duncan) and ROSS families. Later, fishing

---

[7] Robinson (1987) pp90-1; Parkin (1989) p20; see also below, ch7.

boats were also drawn to the Yorkshire coast from as far away as Devonshire. Brixham men probably pioneered use of the beam-trawl. With no regional market for large quantities of fish, the Brixham men moved to south coast ports like Ramsgate, landing catches for the London market. Devon, Kent and Essex men took their trawling further along the coast to Lowestoft in Suffolk, and from the 1830s, trawler owners like John Gidley from Ramsgate (1835) and the eminently successful Robert Hellyer, later Britain's largest, from Brixham (1855) were working the Dogger Bank out of Hull.[8] Scarborough was later seen as preferable to Hull, as landing there avoided the 24 mile sail up the Humber. An interesting sequel to this account of coastal migration is the move of Scarborough men to Hartlepool and Aberdeen after 1900, where there was more room. Some may have had Norfolk, and perhaps even Kentish or Devonshire ancestry.[9] In the Great War, the Government sent all Scarborough trawlers to Aberdeen to protect food supply from U-boat attack. By then, the Granite City's steam engineering expertise was a big advantage.

The 19th Century herring boom prompted return voyages of a thousand miles or more. Cornish and Manx boats landed catches as far afield as north-east Scotland. Shetlanders came to East Anglia. Fleetwood crews might originate in the Hebrides. Some courted and married women who were taken on to gut and pack the catch. Several Filey wives in the 1851 returns were born in Staithes and Robin Hood's Bay. Sometimes, the marriage took place at Yarmouth, as in the case of Robert JENKINSON and Margaret 'Truckles', at the end of 1778's season.[10]

Unmarried fisherwomen could travel far greater distances than inland single women, finding that herring gutting offered an ideal dating opportunity, as well as seasonal income, at east coast fishing stations. Gangs of women were recruited by fish-merchants from as far afield as northern Scotland, and Northumberland villages like North Sunderland and Beadnell - the descendants of these fisher girls can be found as far south as Yarmouth.

The Filey Fishing Diaspora

Short distance movement of wife, children and household possessions was not difficult. Captain Smith remembered George Jenkinson Mainprize using his coble *Annie Elizabeth* in the early 1920s to move his household, lock stock and barrel, from Filey to Scarborough. 'We've come to live here', he announced, as the newcomers docked in the harbour. But Filey inshoremen could cover far larger distances than the Mainprizes in search of better fishing. Coastal journeys of truly prodigious distances were undertaken if men heard that trawling companies were taking on hands. Moves might be seasonal, and reversible; or a short move might break the Filey bond, and be the stepping stone to a longer one.

---

[8] Frank (2002) p20; Parkin (1989) p80.

[9] Robinson (1984) pp331-3; Captain Sydney Smith; Godfrey (1974) pp13-14.

[10] Margaret was almost certainly a *Trattles*, from Staithes. See below, p104, fn5.

As local catches declined, one adventurer tried his luck in South Wales: 32 year-old Joseph Watkinson was the only Filey man in Milford Haven in the 1911 Census. He had acquired a Pembroke Dock wife, on an earlier visit. They had briefly moved back to Scarborough, before returning to Milford Haven by 1911.

Several Filey men gave up fishing to move to Hull for work on tugs or lighters. Bridlington was often a staging point.[11] Appendix E also reveals JENKINSON moves to the North-east (John Adamson, Q65), tip of a larger Filey iceberg. Fishermen from Whitby and Staithes could find work in the heavy industries of Teesside, 20 miles away, lodging in the week. Yet there was no such temporary work near Filey. Alternatives involved seasonal migration, like those men who tried Milford Haven. William CAPPLEMAN recalled how a lot of Filey fishermen moved to Brimington, in Derbyshire, when fishing was bad in the early 1920s, to work at the Stanton and Staveley Coal and Ironworks. Some, came back, but several remained.

The Norfolk Migration: the Puzzle of the Missing Fishermen

A string of coastal villages in the vicinity of Cromer accounts for the origins of much of Filey's later 19th Century fisher immigration. But many of these villages, given as birthplaces by settlers in Filey in the censuses, have *no* fishermen living there in earlier returns. How is this mystery to be explained?

The fishing histories of Filey and north Norfolk are very similar. The parallels are reflected in the appearance of the fishing settlements - be prepared for a startling *déja vu* when visiting the two areas (**6.2**). Norfolk inshoremen worked from three-man family cobles, particularly from Sheringham and Cromer. 'Gaps' in the cliffs and dunes allowed other villages further east to work off the flat, sandy beaches, primarily to pot for shellfish in the summer. Ancient boundaries ensured that each parish had at least a few hundred yards of coastline for this purpose, even though the village might be a mile or more inland.

The explanation for the missing fishermen, however, lies in the pattern of Norfolk's *offshore* fishing. As in Yorkshire, large dual-purpose vessels great-lined for white fish, and pursued herring shoals in summer/autumn. Their shareowning crews accepted a lifestyle which took them away from home for weeks at a time. But bad harvests and war with France from 1793 to 1815 pushed up bread prices; demand increased for fish, especially herring; and east coast fishermen began to follow the annual shoals further and longer. Yorkshire boats then specialised in long-lining, so there was a gap for outsiders, and this may have drawn East Anglian men northwards before the great herring boom of the 1830s.[12]

---

[11] See Robert JENKINSON (P65), Appendix E, **E5**. Lighters (from 'to lighten, unload') were small craft, loading and unloading boats in the Humber, or for local coastal trade.

[12] The lack of a fishing tradition on the Yorkshire coast south of Flamborough drew East Anglian families to Withernsea in the later 18th Century (Robinson, 1987, p10).

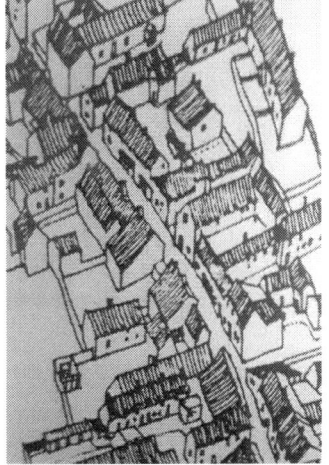

6.2: Norfolk County Cousins: there is so much in common between Yorkshire fishing communities and their Norfolk equivalents, suggesting long-term social and economic connections between the two coasts.

Above: Gravestone of a Cromer fisherman, Old Cemetery, 1880, with carving of a local lugger. I have yet to find any such Norfolk grave carving on a stone as old as those in Filey's churchyard.

Top right: Modern-day Blakeney, with its fishermen's cottages, side alleys and sheds, is identical to Filey's Old Town before the hollowing out of the 1930s.

Right: Queen Street's identical Norfolk twin – Jetty Street, Cromer.

Then the fish changed their habits. In the 1850s and early '60s, herring shoaled off Yorkshire far longer than was normal either before or since.[13] The season's start had moved forward from July/August to early June. It continued into the autumn 'home fishing' off East Anglia, which lasted until the end of November.

Add to this the presence of shellfish, the vulnerability to silting of Norfolk's slow-moving rivers and landing creeks, and the Yorkshire grounds increasingly became attractive to East Anglian fishermen. By the 1860s, the 'Norfolk Fleet' of 40 or more large luggers, 12 men to a boat, were sailing 'down north' for the season, early enough in the year for 54 East Anglian fishermen to be in Scarborough on census night, 7th April 1861.

---

[13] As late as 1869, 34 Filey yawls, still fitted out for herring drifting, were out on 25th-26th Oct just 30 miles ENE of Scarborough when they were struck by a great gale. See ch10 for reference to Kendall's account, in his *God's Hand in the Storm* (1870).

These 'Great Boats' carried small crab boats on deck, usually returning with live stock to bolster breeding populations in Norfolk waters.[14] The East Anglian luggers were known as *Lowstermen* (ie 'Lowestoft men') by Yorkshiremen.

In the 1980s, we had heard local traditions in Filey of how inshoremen left Norfolk and came north to more reliable, gently sloping Yorkshire beaches. The physical geography of the north Norfolk coast allegedly made inshore fishing difficult. Marram grass had been planted to stabilise the dunes, but this increased the gradients and therefore increased the risk of the boats 'pooping' as they were beached – ie being swamped and pounded to pieces if the tide swung them broadside to the waves.[15]

Alas, no corroborating evidence has ever come to light to substantiate these attractively simple explanations for the Norfolk migration to Yorkshire fishing stations. The true explanation lies with the *joskins*.

Yorkshire's *Joskins*

Filey fish-salesman Benjamin Simpson made it clear when giving evidence to the 1863 Sea Fisheries Commission that it was the casual wage labourers from offshore fishing, *not* coble fishermen, who settled in Filey from East Anglia:

> We have had some who have come here from the south but they have not got boats or anything of that kind.

The newcomers from East Anglia were unskilled agricultural labourers, laid off once the harvest was in, and recruited from a coastal hinterland up to ten miles deep. Until the 1860s, they were taken on by Norfolk luggers to help with the 'home season' of herring fishing. Their main qualification was the immense strength that enabled them to haul in a couple of miles of calf-thick warp, and sodden, fish-filled drift nets. Capstans were introduced in the 1850s, but though this eased much of the labour, the nets still had to be lifted out of the water by hand. Only men used to constant, back-breaking manual labour could slog round on a wet, heaving deck for up to 12 circular miles, forcing round the seven-foot capstan bar or spike.

These deckhands, outside even the classless system of the Norfolk shareman crew, were derided as *joskins* (ie 'yokels', 'bumpkins'). They were deemed too smelly to share the cabin, and so ate on deck and slept on nets in the hold. Gradually, *joskins* were hired by Yorkshire boats, presumably for the Norfolk fishing initially. Here they were treated even less kindly, being insulted with the worst aspersion of all, 'farmers'! I know of no crew photographs which include them. Nobody on shore seems even to have bothered to find out what their names were, although these must have been known to their crewmates.

---

[14] Gerrish (1998) p96. Into the late 20th Century, the nickname *Yorkshiremen* continued to be applied to the light brown crabs sourced for East Anglian waters in this way.
[15] Fran Weatherhead, *North Norfolk Fishermen* (The History Press, 2011) pp7, 29-30.

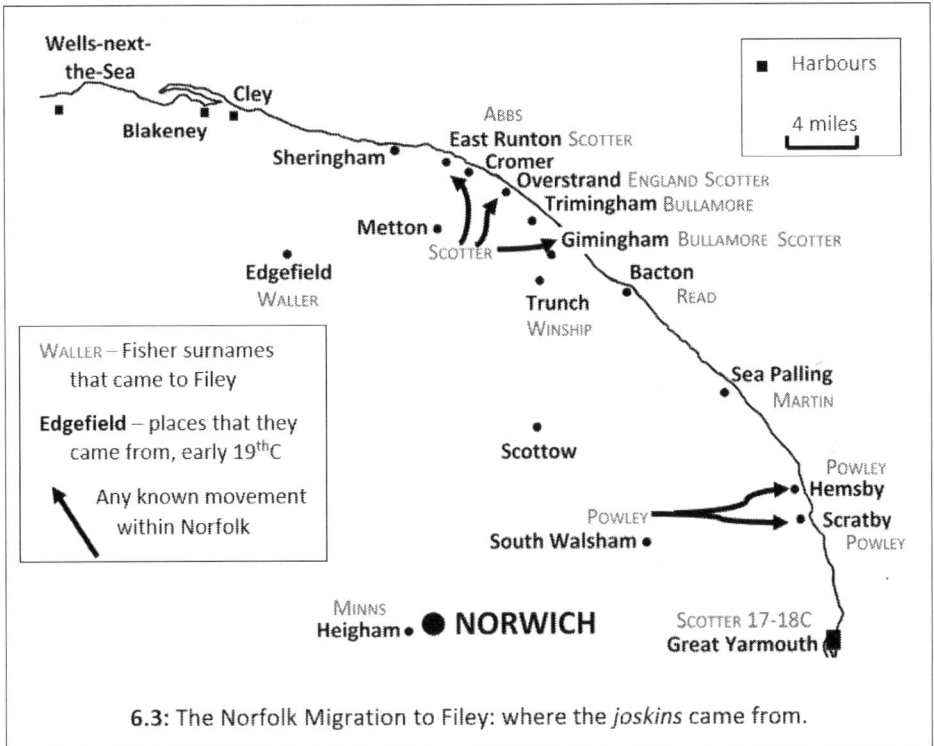

Wells-next-the-Sea
Cley
Blakeney
Sheringham
ABBS
East Runton SCOTTER
Cromer
Overstrand ENGLAND SCOTTER
Trimingham BULLAMORE
Metton
Gimingham BULLAMORE SCOTTER
SCOTTER
Edgefield
WALLER
Bacton
Trunch READ
WINSHIP
Sea Palling
MARTIN

Harbours
4 miles

WALLER – Fisher surnames
that came to Filey

Edgefield – places that they
came from, early 19th C

Any known movement
within Norfolk

Scottow

POWLEY
Hemsby
POWLEY Scratby
South Walsham • POWLEY

MINNS
Heigham • ● NORWICH
SCOTTER 17-18C
Great Yarmouth

6.3: The Norfolk Migration to Filey: where the *joskins* came from.

The day-to-day reality of their status only came to light with their deaths. When in October 1880 local Yorkshire newspapers reported the loss with both crews of the Filey yawls *Eliza* and *Sarah*, 12 Filey men were named, but with them died the names of the remaining eight victims, four from each boat, clearly casuals, listed as 'unknown'. Even 20 years later, the St Oswald's window dedicated to those 40 fishermen 'lost at sea and whose bodies have never been recovered' described seven of the 1880 missing as 'strangers'.[16]

Many would be *joskins*, probably leading a very mobile lifestyle, frequently moving between Norfolk and Yorkshire. During the spring, when the censuses were held, they would be labouring on farms in their home parishes, the local enumerators not considering their few months of autumn fishing worthy of record. In the absence of clear guidelines, there was no national consistency as to whether second occupations were recorded on 19th Century census schedules.

---

[16] *Scarborough Mercury*, 30th Oct 1880. The window is discussed below, pp132-3. *Redux* has identified two of the waged men as George and Henry Field, their Australian great great niece Rosemary Barrett having traced them to Barton-upon-Humber, where they are recorded on a gravestone. They were sons of sailor and coastguard, James Field, whose long life had already taken him from Great Yarmouth to Ramsgate and Immingham, mirroring aspects of many fishermen's lifetime migrations.

In the mid-1860s, the Yorkshire herring season suddenly contracted, as unpredictably as it had extended a decade before, but by then many *joskins* had spotted more opportunities in Scarborough than in their home county. They also began to appear in Filey as lodgers, local share crews grudgingly accepting that they usefully topped up the number of hands available at brisk times.

Without the earnings to amass capital, and without ancestral ties to the Old Town, many, like the Bullamores, moved to the fishing streets of Scarborough, where there was waged offshore work on the trawlers. There were 78 East Anglian fishermen in the town's 1871 returns, 22% of the Scarborough fishing total[17], whilst temporary wage labourers such as herring-gutters and packers, and *rully* (lorry) men also came up from Norfolk for the season.

The Scotters, Powleys and Wallers: Offcomers who Prospered

6.4: Reuben Scotter (1820-1910) another Filey 'Clapham Junction', but who lived and died in Norfolk. He belonged to the class of East Anglian agricultural labourer /fisherman that provided casual crew for yawls in the herring season. *[David Scotter]*

Some Norfolk men who came to Filey, notably the Wallers, Powleys and Scotters, did achieve greater economic and social integration in the town. They had come from the same modest *joskin* origins, usually in family groups, and found Filey wives from the community. If they happened to be on a yawl, voyaging away from home on census night, they can actually be found enumerated with Filey crews. Four were on board such yawls in the 1881 returns for Grimsby Fish Dock.

By the late 19th Century, the Scotters had eased into the Old Town fisher life more than any other Norfolk migrants. Three brothers, George, Robert and Mark, had come from East Runton to Filey in the 1860s and '70s, working as fishermen: 19 of their 21 children are known to have married in Filey, and into many of the core families. The increasing use of their surname as a second Christian name confirms their presence. The 1915 *Filey Directory* has 11 Scotter entries.

---

[17] Janet Sellars, *Yorkshire History Quarterly*, Vol 3, No 3 (Feb 1998).

Their father, Reuben (**6.4**) was a Filey 'Clapham Junction', even though he never settled in Yorkshire. Typically *joskin*, Reuben worked as an agricultural labourer and fisherman. And equally *joskin*-like, he had contact with the north-east coast. A family memory holds that he tramped to Yorkshire, probably to find work. On arriving home in Norfolk, he found his wife in the workhouse. Being on the cusp of pauperism was another time-honoured *joskin* characteristic.

Reuben's wife, Sarah née Bullimore *[sic]*, belonged to another migrant family that came to Filey: word about the town's opportunities evidently spread through Norfolk kinship networks, hence the move of the three Scotter sons to Yorkshire. The brothers, like the Wallers and Powleys, readily settled into the Filey community because they were a fit amongst the Old Town families. Seamanship rather than muscle qualified them for 'berths' on Filey yawls.

Another little-known fit, attracting Norfolkmen to east Yorkshire, was the preponderance of Primitive Methodism in the northern part of their county. The rural poor, the social soil from which the *joskins* came, were natural adherents to Ranterism. In its chapels, there was an equality utterly lacking in their everyday existence, for the landlords and farmers who controlled their lives did not worship there. All three of Filey's successful Norfolk families, the Scotters, Powleys and Wallers, had this religious culture in their East Anglian backgrounds.

We will be examining the powerful New Testament doctrine of God's 'Calling' in Chapter 23. Briefly, it gave men a spiritual as well as material incentive to take the risks of enterprise, and to work hard. For was their occupation not God's will, and would he not provide for them if they followed it? Two of Reuben's sons fit this upwardly aspirant profile. George Scotter rose to mate on the yawl *Amelia*, whilst his youngest brother, Mark became skipper of the *Susie*. Both men died violently at sea, matching another, depressingly familiar Filey tradition - George with all the crew on *Integrity*, in the Great March Gale of 1883, and Mark at the hands of a German machine gun in 1917. George left a wife and six young children; Mark's at least were grown up.[18]

In one generation, Mark had achieved the unachievable, complete acceptance! Few offcomers got the 'very well attended' send-off accorded to him. He was of course seen as a war hero, 'one of the best of our brave fishermen who risk their lives to obtain food for their fellow countrymen.' He had been a chapel Sunday School teacher too.[19]

---

[18] David Scotter, *Spawned in Norfolk Caught in Filey*, posted in three parts on the *Looking at Filey* site in 2011; *Scotter* is a place name surname, deriving from Scottow, 15 miles south of Cromer, ten miles from the sea. The surname's spelling followed that of the village until the 19th Century; but the southern accent gives little stress to final syllables, hence the shift to *Scotter*. The village of Scotter, in north Lincolnshire, is an unlikely alternative origin. The surname was primarily in Great Yarmouth in the 17th and 18th Centuries.

[19] *Scarborough Mercury*, 24th Aug 1917; see also ch28.

In Loving Remembrance of
George Scotter
The beloved Husband of
Elizabeth Scotter of
Filey who was lost at sea
March 6 1883
Aged 37 Years

Farewell my friends - and wife so dear
Farewell my children too.
I leave you to my Fathers care
Who will provide for you.

6.5: Carefully embroidered samplers, like mourning cards, were common features of Victorian bereavement. These personalised family memorials were especially important where there was no grave on which to focus grief. Note the core Ranter belief that God's providence could be relied on. Middle brother Robert may *also* have been lost to the sea - his death seems never to have been registered. *[FM]*

With children married into Old Town families, and many grandchildren, Mark had truly 'arrived'. Similarly, three Waller brothers, born in Edgefield, Norfolk, 1855-61, also sons of an agricultural labourer/fisherman, came to Filey together, and married Old Town girls, a Haxby and two Wheelers.[20] William became master of the yawl *William Clowes*, one of ten Filey boats based at Bridlington but recorded at Grimsby in the 1881 returns. James, his younger brother, was with him. They were successful enough to rise well above the *joskin* class, later becoming fish-dealers in Sculcoates, Hull.

The Powleys had the same background. William (1828-1908) was from the rural labouring proletariat, from which personal drive raised him. In his early thirties, he was master of a 29-ton offshore fishing boat in Yarmouth; in the mid-1860s he took the risk of bringing his family to Filey, left fishing to become a fish merchant – and by 1891 was also the town's Primitive Methodist chapel-keeper.

William CAPPLEMAN recalled another group of East Anglians in Scarborough, boat engineers from Lowestoft. As Halewood and Dagenham were to the British car industry in the 1960s, Lowestoft had been most associated with steam drifter technology, and provided the niche skills in demand as steam supplanted sail.

Finally, not quite East Anglia, but from the next county – the 1st Battalion Huntingdonshire Cyclists was used to patrol the Yorkshire coast between Scarborough and Spurn Point after 1914. The stretch south of Flamborough was vulnerably flat, and accessible to invading German forces. Most of the battalion went to France in 1916. George W Fairey, Sid R Hollis, and Ralph Watson later settled and married in Filey, as did Herbert G Lovitt, the only one who, as a fish-merchant, took up work related to fishing. His business continues (2021) at 7, Mitford Street, a century on. The 1921 Census, available in January 2022, will almost certainly reveal more examples.

---

[20] The 1861 census returns for Edgefield show them three doors from 'Ranter's Chapel'.

7 A Moment in Time: Grimsby Fish Dock, Monday 4th April 1881

In Chapter 2, we imagined the experiences of a visitor to Filey in the week following the taking of the census in 1881. We saw that many fishermen were away from home that weekend. In fact, they were about 60 miles south, having spent the Saturday and Sunday nights sleeping on board their yawls, moored together in the world's premier herring station, Grimsby's state-of-the-art fish dock. Let's now return in our imaginations to that Monday morning 120 years ago. As in Chapter 2, I've used footnotes to anchor our visualisation in reality, citing source material which supports this time travel .

Apart from the nine Filey great-liners at Grimsby at first light, this first Monday in April 1881, the dock is empty, for the trawlers normally using the harbour are out at sea on the fishing grounds, only docking here every few weeks. Masters of any vessels likely to be at sea during Sunday night, 3rd April, were given a census form, as they set sail. They were told to complete it that night as close to midnight as possible. These forms were to record the key biographical detail of each crew member, and were to be handed in once the boat docked. (7.1).

One of the skippers is Primitive Methodist lay preacher, Edmond JENKINSON (P52). Neither he nor any of the other Filey boats will be at sea on the Sunday. But few of the other boats observe the Sabbath, which is why the dock is so empty this morning.

7.1: An 1881 Census schedule for vessels away from their home port - Edmond JENKINSON's handwritten list of the crew of his yawl *Welcome Home* captures the uniqueness of Filey's fishing practice: all men are Filey-born, and are bewilderingly interrelated. The skipper's son and nephew are on board, whilst John *Ranter Jack* CAMMISH and son are related twice over to the skipper by marriage. Three of the crew are sharemen. This is a 'Sunday Boat', with two lay preachers on board.

The skipper is unfamiliar with the spelling of the Little Boy's *Wyvill* surname. John, 16, is responsible for the most menial jobs on board, like peeling potatoes and brewing tea. *[National Archives]*

Hundreds of trawlers are out fishing - once back in dock, in a few days' time, their skippers will hand in the completed forms, recording their positions on census night – these will include 'Dogger Bank', 'Silver Pits', 'fishing grounds 70 miles NE of Spurn' and some locations even further out in the North Sea.

As the small Filey fleet prepares to sail this Monday morning, many of the trawlers will be racing to dock, hoping to catch the first fish-trains. These stand four-abreast, waiting to be loaded, 15 tons per van, 13 trains a day, rushing their perishable stock to London and other big cities. They can be smelt as they pass!

7.2: Edmond JENKINSON's handwritten description of his 31 ton yawl *Welcome Home*. The skipper was given the form at Bridlington. He records his boat's precise geographic position at midnight, Saturday 2nd/Sunday 3rd April - 'mored [sic] in Grimsby Dock'. [National Archives]

The nine Filey 'liners and codmen' will be a source of amusement to the trawlermen, virtually unchanged in design, rigging or fishing methods since the 1830s. They are old-timers, with traditional lug rigging.

From March to June, the Filey boats continue their traditional pattern of sailing to the grounds on a Monday morning, and returning at the end of the week. They may sail further and fish longer because of falling catches. But somehow, these nine floating heritage centres manage to make a living.

One of the Filey skippers, William JENKINSON (O14) has been fishing the North Sea since the 1820s. He will tell you that in those days his father and uncles were landing many more 'great fish', their name for big cod, than they ever can now. Sixty years on, each yawl may shoot twice as many lines - maybe seven miles in all - but fewer fish are landed. Fortunately, the Sheffield railway company's rates are far cheaper than those of the old packhorse masters. Grimsby has fast railway links to every British city, demand for cod is high, so earnings justify the Filey men's voyage south.

Apart from their outdated rigging and quaint line-fishing, the biggest contrast between the Filey boats and the trawlers here is the make-up of the crew.
Trawling requires fewer skills than lining, and men are waged rather than on shares.

Each trawler has taken on its nomadic crew at Grimsby, where men from any east or south coast port congregate for work. They are mostly strangers to their shipmates.[1] The Filey yawls, however, are crewed almost wholly by Filey men. Thus Edmond JENKINSON's *Welcome Home* is moored next to *Lucy*, its 69 year-old master William JENKINSON also having two sons on board.[2]

All the Filey boats have been laid up over winter in harbour at Scarborough or Bridlington. It may be tempting to fit out for great-lining early in the year, especially if earnings were poor the previous year. But even in March, when the boats re-emerge, these skippers know from family experience just how dangerous the North Sea can be in winter. Like many Filey men, Edmond JENKINSON has no memory of his father, for he was lost in a sudden squall off a coble in December 1841, when his son was just two.[3]

Those shooting or taking in lines from a yawl's coble are especially at risk: this is how William JENKINSON, on *Lucy*, lost his son William, off *Jane and Elizabeth* in 1867 (see below, p121). Cobles can be overwhelmed in any month, and within sight of shore - in 1858, Edmond JENKINSON's elder brother, also William, was lost in a June squall just one mile off land (see below, pp 230-4).

Most of the yawls will give up great-lining in early summer, fitting out with drift nets to fish the herring shoals along the east coast. Until about 30 years ago, Yorkshire's offshore fleet followed the herring southwards from home waters every September. They landed catches at Yarmouth, remaining away from home for about two months. Many wives and children accompanied their menfolk to maintain running repairs on the nets. In recent years, however, many Filey men have returned to great-lining for the final months of the year, once the local Banks group herring are past their peak.

---

[1] In Grimsby's New Clee fishing quarter, the fishermen come from Barking, Brixham Gravesend, Great Yarmouth, Lowestoft, Hull, Scarborough, and Sheringham. A few were even born in Grimsby (Friend, 2010, Appendix 7).

[2] This list of sources used for this historical fantasy should reduce the need for too many footnotes. The chapter's family history content is based on parish registers and census returns; for North Sea fishery working conditions, and its massive mortality rate, Dyson (1977); technical detail - Robinson's extensive thesis (1984, online) which uses customs house vessel registers, harbour commissioners' minutes, government and parliamentary reports, and local newspapers; for Grimsby Fish Dock - Edward Gillett, *A History of Grimsby* (Oxford University Press, 1970); eyewitness accounts of the storm of October 1869 are in Kendall (1870); Bridlington Harbour (known to Filey men as *Quay*) is covered in David & Susan Neave's *Bridlington: an Introduction to its History and Buildings* (Dalesman, 2000).

[3] *Hull Advertiser and Exchange Gazette*, 31st Dec 1841. It is as well Edmond does not know that he is just 11 years away from losing a fourth member of his family, and another namesake – Edmond Ross - with the herring coble *Unity* (1892).

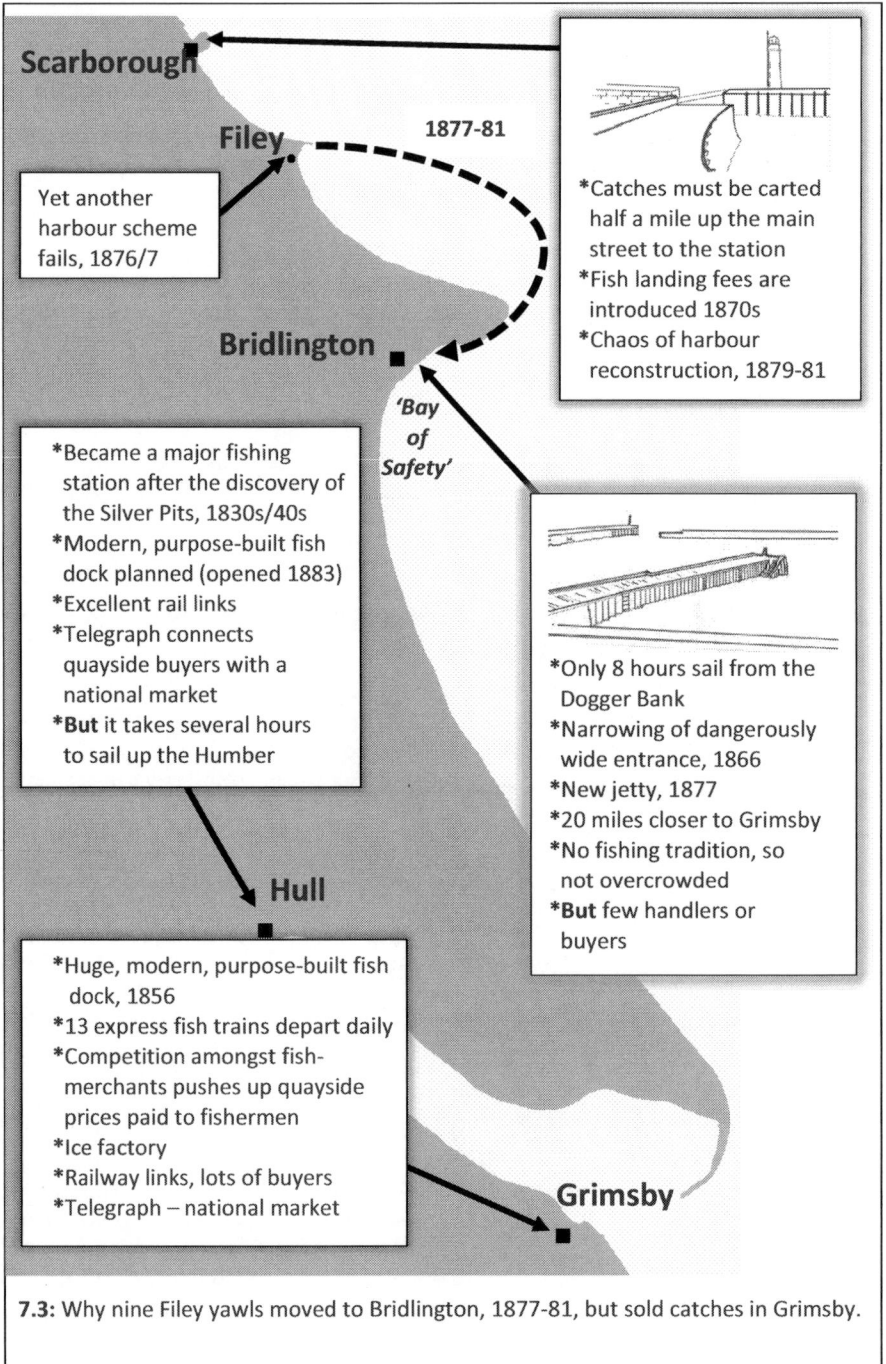

Scarborough

Filey

1877-81

Yet another harbour scheme fails, 1876/7

*Catches must be carted half a mile up the main street to the station
*Fish landing fees are introduced 1870s
*Chaos of harbour reconstruction, 1879-81

Bridlington

'Bay of Safety'

*Became a major fishing station after the discovery of the Silver Pits, 1830s/40s
*Modern, purpose-built fish dock planned (opened 1883)
*Excellent rail links
*Telegraph connects quayside buyers with a national market
***But** it takes several hours to sail up the Humber

*Only 8 hours sail from the Dogger Bank
*Narrowing of dangerously wide entrance, 1866
*New jetty, 1877
*20 miles closer to Grimsby
*No fishing tradition, so not overcrowded
***But** few handlers or buyers

Hull

*Huge, modern, purpose-built fish dock, 1856
*13 express fish trains depart daily
*Competition amongst fish-merchants pushes up quayside prices paid to fishermen
*Ice factory
*Railway links, lots of buyers
*Telegraph – national market

Grimsby

7.3: Why nine Filey yawls moved to Bridlington, 1877-81, but sold catches in Grimsby.

The Move to *Quay*

When not driving for herring off East Anglia, Filey fishermen have traditionally returned home each weekend to land their catches, discharging onto Filey sands. Their yawls can be brought up to lie on the beach, or safely ride at anchor in the bay at high tide, even in heavy seas. But the risks of this practice were revealed in 1860, and well within the memories of most of the Filey men here today, when 13 anchored yawls were torn from their moorings by a freak Whit Monday storm. Ten crashed onto the rocks at Speeton. Scarborough's harbour offers safer anchorage in bad weather, so it is no wonder that during subsequent years, many Filey yawls moved there, their crews either walking or travelling in by train each Monday morning. The harbour attracts many more fish-buyers than Filey, so there is competition. This brings better prices for the fishermen. Unfortunately, docking at Scarborough has its own problems: all catches have to be carted nearly a mile up the steep main street to the station. Any large landings of herrings often result in a wild race of carts to catch the next train departure.

For a long time, Bridlington's harbour has afforded no protection from rough sea, the waves rushing in through the wide entrance, but in 1866, the North Pier was extended to narrow the gap. In 1877, a timber jetty replaced the long-decrepit stone one, finally making the dock fit for an offshore fishing fleet. Many fishermen have now settled at *Quay*, including outsiders like the Newbys from East Anglia. The Filey yawls we met at Grimsby on census weekend have been based at *Quay* since about 1877, but these men do not want to leave Filey - they travel in by train every week or two.[4]

The World's Largest Fish Dock: seeking the Almighty's Assistance

Grimsby Fish Dock, the largest in the world, is a railway phenomenon. The Manchester, Sheffield and Lincolnshire Company's line reached the town in 1859, but the dock had opened three years before. The resulting growth has been extraordinary: Grimsby, dismissed in 1819 as a 'miserable little port', had just one boat in 1833. By 1877, 505 fishing boats were registered here. Most were large trawlers, with huge 38-foot beam-trawls. The beams are so long they must be lashed to the sides of the hull to allow them to pass through the harbour entrance.

In the last few years, even this scale of trawling has got more intensive - beams of 48 feet length are in use, now with wider nets, capable of trawling three tons of fish in a single haul.[5] Initially, the railway offered cheap rates for fish to attract

---

[4] Once the move had been made, landing catches on Filey beach virtually ceased. By the late 1870s, boats paying the 3d 'discharging' fee to the Lord of Hunmanby Manor were usually bringing coal or timber (*Fishing Project*, Box 6, *FA*). The size of the fishing population at Bridlington also reflected the move - in 1891, four times as many fishermen were living at *Quay* as in 1851.

[5] See below, **12.1**, p151, for an explanation of how a beam-trawl was used.

Yorkshire boats. There is an ice factory, and the fish dock has recently been extended to cover 11 acres. The telegraph system, another railway creation, connects the many fish-buyers with dealers anywhere in the country. Competition pushes up the prices paid to fishermen. No wonder this weekend's Grimsby Dock census schedules will record boats registered as far afield as Lowestoft, Yarmouth, Cornwall, Leith, Glasgow and the Irish port of Dundalk.

But there are risks for the unwary. Prices here move quickly: they collapse instantly if catches are large, and only the first men in benefit. It can be barely worth the voyage some years: the Filey men were paid £2 16s for a score of large cod just three years ago, but less than a pound the following year. Of the price you receive at the quayside, 40% and often a lot more, can go in railway rates, whilst competing foreign fish importers are charged a fraction of this, to attract their custom. All catches go at the sender's risk. At worst, the whole of a boat's profits can go in charges. But 50 years of railways have created national markets, and rapid sale and distribution are crucial if these traditional fishermen are to compete with the huge trawling fleets.

The more successful skippers enter into agreements with quayside fish-dealers – these wily operators get good prices by using contacts, reputation and sales expertise. So the Filey liners are especially grateful that with them is one of their own, Jenkinson Haxby, a fisherman for 30 years and a yawl owner. His elder brother, Richard, is here on his yawl *Frances and Elizabeth* with two members of the family. Indeed, the Haxbys are related in some way to virtually *all* the 46 Filey men on these nine boats.

At 52, a respected preacher of the Filey Primitive Methodist Society, *Denk* Haxby is trusted both by the Filey sharemen, and the buyers to whom he will sell their catches. The fishermen are strong believers in God's ability and disposition to advance the affairs of His Chosen, and may have seen Jenkinson Haxby's decision to take up fish-selling as divinely engineered!

At this distance in time, we cannot know why a man gives up the sea to become a fish-dealer. Perhaps the free travel for fish-merchants offered by the Sheffield company alerted Jenkinson to a glowing business opportunity. Perhaps he could build up a marketing network inland, using his chapel contacts. All the fish- dealers in Filey have started as working fishermen, with all its risks - the next voyage could be the last. Perhaps this has finally convinced him, for his family, like that of Edmond JENKINSON's, has been serially affected by losses at sea.

Three of the town's fishermen on average drown each year. Just 12 years ago, three generations of Haxbys, at least six in number, had a particularly terrifying, close collective brush with that grim statistic, when their three yawls were caught in the gale of 25-26th October 1869. All 34 of the town's boats were 30 miles out, on the Great Dogger Bank.

7.4: Jenkinson Haxby (1827-1908) the 'Bishop of Filey', so highly respected on land as rarely to be referred to by his fisher by-name, *Denk*. Even a 19th Century photograph captures the commandingly calm presence and aura of this special man. He must have been difficult to say 'no' to, whether in the Union Street Chapel, or in a dockside haggle! Even at 13, he was able to recruit his father and mother to a class meeting. 'Leading his father, he proposed a detour in order to call upon an uncle. "Uncle," he said, "father is coming to the class to get pardoned. Will you come, too? Put on your coat. The Lord has sent me to ask you".[6] *[FA]*

The waves would have dashed the yawls onto the shore, had they risked coming anywhere near port. Instead, they endured two days of gigantic seas. Jenkinson's elder brother, Richard, on his yawl *Unity*, had the unnerving experience of witnessing the final moments of the Scarborough's *John Wesley*. His account was used by Rev Kendall in *God's Hand in the Storm* (1870):

> She had on board 10 lives, men and boys; soon she disappeared from human view, sinking through the violence and the winds and waves, and her crew all perished.

We can only guess how deeply his story became entrenched into family lore. Jenkinson, also in that storm, as skipper of *Felicity*, similarly believed he was going to die. He had told his crew:

> I think we have done all we can to secure our safety . . . the best thing each one can do now is to seek a full preparation for another world.

Jenkinson's brother Matthew was also on *Felicity* and broke into tears as his son and nephew, just 11 and 12, sang a hymn when all seemed lost. Nearby, on *Ebenezer*, their nephew, Richard, had faced an even more certain end as a large steam-packet sliced into his yawl in the chaos of the storm. Somehow, 200 or more Filey men and boys survived those traumatic two days. But plenty of *Denk's* family members have not been so lucky: in 1859, he had watched helplessly as another brother, Frank, together with the two SAYERS brothers, were swept off one of *Ebenezer's* corfes as the lines were being hauled in. Their bodies were never recovered.

This grim family event may well have been in Jenkinson's mind this April weekend of 1881, for it had occurred 22 years to the day last Friday. Frank's widow, Susannah, Jenkinson's sister-in-law, and their only son, also Frank, were next door neighbours on Chapel Street. Jenkinson and his wife, Sophia, will have been regular comforters to this sad little family.

---

[6] *Primitive Methodist Magazine*, 1905/153 (*My Primitive Methodists* website).

As longstanding members of the Filey Primitive Methodist Society, and lay preachers, the male Haxbys have seen it as a Christian duty to urge their neighbours to accept these losses at sea as God's will. But such spiritual reassurance must have felt hollow to a lot of local people after last October's Great Gale when young Frank too, just 23, was lost off the yawl *Felicity* near Withernsea. Like most men lost like this, his body was never found. Perhaps it was as well that his mother, Susannah, had herself died three years before. The inscription on the family gravestone, a characteristically Victorian mix of the melodramatic with the poignant, will have moved any Filey fisher widow. Many are denied the solace of a grave to visit on anniversaries and birthdays, so the erection of a stone at least is a priority if loved ones are never given up by the sea:

> I cannot bend beside his grave
>
> For he sleeps in the secret sea
>
> And not one gentle whispering wave
>
> Will tell the place to me

The Filey men's trusted fish-dealer Jenkinson Haxby is childless. His wife, Sophia, may have told him she feared a lonely widowhood. Perhaps she has been arguing passionately for some time for Jenkinson to concentrate on investing in boats, like the fish-merchant Bulmers, Crawfords and Simpsons who now live in some of the more prestigious houses in Filey. They have ploughed back decades of sales commission into boat shares.

Fishing from Grimsby in the later 19th Century: 'a Rum, Hard Life'

Jenkinson probably required little persuading: the Filey offshoremen are well aware that in their grandfathers' day, the luggers only needed to go out 30 or 40 miles to the deep water *outsand* at the edge of the Dogger Bank. Now, as the trawlers have destroyed stocks, boats must take more risks, sailing further and staying out longer to earn their living. Some of the Grimsby boats fish 300 miles or more from land. Jenkinson must realise that traditional great-lining cannot survive much longer. Filey crews may soon have to give up their opposition to trawling.

Four years ago, steam paddle tugs began out of North Shields, and now up to 20 north-eastern steam trawlers work at Scarborough. They exceed even the sailing trawlers in damaging the yawls' lines and drift gear. Trawling depletes stocks and forces the Filey boats to stay out later in the year. The new steam trawlers drag even longer beams, their huge nets leaving wider trails of seabed destruction, indiscriminately scooping up spawn and young. What if the trawlers start to go after herring too, the traditional fisherman's great earner?

These Filey men have always disliked trawling, and nothing they have seen in Grimsby since they started here in the 1860s has reduced their loathing. This is a new and unfamiliar world. Trawling is largely unskilled, the crews are mostly on wages, and the urge is to cut costs - companies own the new boats and fish only to pay shareholders a dividend. The trawler crews call these smacks 'floating workhouses'. And the Filey men have seen first-hand the appalling conditions in which these men labour up to 18 hours a day. Being on a fixed wage, trawlermen lose any anticipation of the 'big catch', for all that means to them is heavier work.

Most men on trawlers never remove their bulky oilskins, somehow sleeping in wet bedding. One Scarborough sailing trawlerman recalled being 'all sodden to the skin, in spite of our oilskins and thick clothing'. These trawlers are out 'for eight and ten weeks at a time, and never dry for a minute, day or night.'[7] The men cannot even remove their thigh length boots, since dampness shrinks the leather and they will never get them back on. They sleep in the stoopingly cramped, unventilated, pitch dark cabin, hatches permanently shut to minimise the ingress of the sea. And they don't see their families every weekend – if they have one. Few do. In contrast, Filey men value such contact; several are preachers and do not want to miss the services on a Sunday.

Every man on these Filey yawls has learned the skills of seamanship and fishing on his father's or uncle's boat. That's why now, in 1881, each Filey boat has at least one Boy, the son of the skipper or of a gearman. It's not an easy apprenticeship, but there is none of the cruelty that is so common on the trawlers.

In complete contrast, the trawling apprenticeship system exploits some of the most vulnerable children in British society. Apart from the Filey yawls, there are *no* family boats here: trawling requires only a handful of skilled men on board, and the costs of the mass harvesting of North Sea fish can therefore be screwed down to a minimum by the employment of boys as young as 11.[8] Many are orphans or runaways, or brought from workhouses, the masters glad to be rid of their cost to the local poor rate. There are cases of these boys being lodged in Grimsby brothels between voyages. They are often paid throughout their seven year 'apprenticeships' with a few *dabs*, small flatfish. This is an invisible world - virtually no one on land knows how bad conditions for these children are, but just occasionally there surfaces a straw of evidence of the brutality meted out to them.[9]

---

[7] 'Old Ben', in Wood (1911).

[8] By 1872, there were actually *more* apprentices on the Grimsby trawlers than there were fishermen.

[9] We can never know if the handful of cases, like that of Osmond Brand, hanged at Armley Jail in 1882 for the murder of his smack's 14 year-old cook, was actually the tip of a sinister iceberg. The case was described by the judge as the most atrocious he had ever heard. It was widely reported in the Yorkshire newspapers, and makes distressing reading, even 140 years later. It can only have been received with a keen but outraged interest by those Filey men who had encountered the trawling industry first hand at Grimsby (Dyson, 1977, pp117-8; *The Murder of William Papper*, Hull Bullnose Heritage Group website).

7.5: Nothing quite captures the on-board Filey family fishing culture as well as this delightful portrait of the crew of William JENKINSON's old yawl *Lucy*, c1900, at Scarborough. The boat has now passed on to his sons, but little else has changed. Clearly a happy boat – smiles are rare on pre-20th Century photographs, yet Jack, the Boy, is virtually laughing, whilst *Marky Jenk* has a wry semi-smile! Back row, **L to R**: Jack Crimlis[10]; Frankie BAXTER; front row, **L to R**: Mark Baxter JENKINSON (P32); his son, *John Willie* JENKINSON (Lay preacher, Sunday school teacher and superintendent, Q41); *Marky's* brother, Richard Cammish *Old Baggy* JENKINSON (P35), skipper; and William C CAMMISH ('the Yorkshire Baritone') spending a day of his school holidays on board.

Body language suggests young William C was close to the skipper - perhaps a great uncle? Few trawler crews would have had such an ease with one another. Maybe Frankie was related through Ann BAXTER, mother of Mark and Dick JENKINSON. Dick holds a shave hook scraper, for recaulking? *[FA]*

One boy's recent death (1878) was reported to the Hull police as

> Suicide - the skipper threatened to thrash him for misconduct and he jumped overboard.

One wonders how many similar instances are not reported so honestly. Faced with years of such a life, it is hardly surprising that many of these boys abscond - 258 were *imprisoned* in just 1877 at Grimsby, often with hard labour. Plenty of boys

---

[10] Jack Crimlis joined the Royal Navy, and drowned in the Red Sea, 1907, trying to save a shipmate. He is commemorated on St Oswald's gravestone G/705.

preferred even this to the sea. It was only last year (1880) that Parliament outlawed the imprisonment of apprentices.[11]

Another hazard is the 'boxing' system, so called from the wooden boxes which small boats use to transport the catch from the trawler to a 'cutter'. These tiny craft are at grave risk if the sea turns rough, which cannot be avoided since the cutter meets each trawling fleet daily. This fast-sailing boat then runs the fish to market here in Grimsby, or in Hull.

An elaborate and precisely choreographed procedure allows a hundred or more little boats, in turn, to row into position windward to the cutter. They must then 'board the fish' quickly to the larger boat. With surging waves tossing a 14-foot boat up to 45° from the vertical, the risks can well be imagined:

> The cutter rolled like a thing demented and with a press of small boats around it, all heavily loaded with fish, the dangers and chaos can be imagined. Once he got alongside, the fisherman in the boat balanced himself lightly and lifted a box of fish to waist height. Then, in the split second that the cutter's rail dipped low towards him, and paused before beginning its upward travel, he laid the box of fish half across it. The man on deck steadied the box as the fisherman let go. As the rail soared upwards the box slid off it and the man on deck guided it to a soft landing.[12]

One big risk was the crushing of the smaller craft if the cutter rolls onto it. Boxing in winter is especially dangerous, boats colliding and being swamped in the heavy sea, so that men and boats are lost together. Eleven Hull apprentices died in this way between 1878 and 1882.

There was a huge strike by 700 fishermen at Grimsby only last year, when the trawler-owners (some of whom are millionaires) tried to introduce year-round boxing, even in the wild winter months. The Filey men will have soon picked up the hostility the crews feel towards the skippers and owners in trawling ports. Such a split does not exist amongst shareman crews.

---

[11] Maltreatment of children in mines and mills was exposed 40 years earlier, but continued at sea to the very edge of 21st Century memory. The horrors of the trawling industry remained inaccessible to official gaze. But the inhumane treatment these children suffered must have been common knowledge at Grimsby Fish Dock, and we can only guess at the impressions the Filey men took away with them. Men like Edmond JENKINSON, whose yawl *Welcome Home* was regularly there, knew well enough how important it was to keep children in line, yet the accounts of his strictly disciplinarian control of the Filey's Union Street chapel scholars were related to us with fondness and respect as recently as the 1980s, by those who had been in his classes. How close we are to a past more akin to the 18th Century than anything we know. Perhaps this barbarity is yet another reason why Filey men disliked trawling. Maritime apprenticeships were only abolished in the 1930s.

[12] Dyson (1977) p120.

Reefing the mainsail and fell overboard.	Drowned - drawing a bucket of water and fell overboard.
Sick and while leaning over the side of the vessel, fell overboard.	Taking in the jib and washed overboard by heavy sea.
Knocked overboard by a block.	Emptying a bucket of ashes and fell overboard.
Struck by handle of winch when heaving the gear and killed.	Boat capsized returning from the cutter.

7.6: The risks of being an apprentice at sea: a tiny sample of the causes of death at sea of fisherboys reported to the Hull police, in just *five* years 1878-82.[13]

And what will our Filey codmen make of the *copers,* often Dutch, that cruise the North Sea selling spirits, cigars and tobacco to any boat they pass? Rum and gin can be had for as little as 1s 6d a pint, so toxic, one seaman noted, that it 'burnt yer inside like vitriol'. Skippers might frown on the trade, but contact with these 'floating grog ships' is often unavoidable.

Only last year, the Scarborough newspaper reported how John Sheader, master of a Scarborough yawl, wanted to exchange a basket of herring for water but somehow his men received four bottles of spirits. Most of this was drunk immediately, and the boat was nearly lost in the drunken knife fight that followed. Much of the attraction of the grog ship is that merchandise can be easily smuggled ashore without payment of duty.

'I've been all through it: it's a rum, hard life; I'd as soon be a convick *[sic]* as go through it all again', one Norfolk trawlerman was to recall in 1909, summing up a lifetime in the North Sea fishery. Recruited from some of the country's most deprived and emotionally stunted children, and accustomed to a life at sea for up to eight weeks at a time, for four-fifths of the year, many of these trawlermen slip easily into a life of unattached anomie, without family ties. The high earnings and Grimsby's low moral tone lead many to fritter away their wages on drink and prostitutes.

Even the skippers can fall into this lifestyle, and it is well known that they must remain teetotal if they are to become successful owners. Many trawler crews are simply beyond the close community life that the Filey men sail back to. Later this year, a missionary will sum up his impressions of the crews he met on a North Sea cutter:

> . . . rough, unkempt and boisterous . . . utterly careless and Godless . . . language coarse, profane and disgusting.

---

[13] *Report of Hull Fishermen Drowned or Dying at Sea, 1878-82 (mariners-l.co.uk* website).

We have no record of what the Filey men made of the Grimsby wage fishermen in 1881, but their impressions may not have been very different. Perhaps the most significant thing about the Filey crews this census weekend is that 45 of the 46 men spent Sunday night on their boat, having half-assembled on one to hold a service. How many seamen do *that* when they are in dock?

A Look into the Future

1891 - ten years on, and the spring census finds no Filey boats at Grimsby. But William JENKINSON's *Lucy* is still at sea, as it was in 1881, now moored on census night at Hull's St Andrew's Dock, exclusively surrounded by steam-powered trawlers. The yawl had left Filey eight days before, carrying long-lines and nets. And though William, now nearly 80, is no longer at sea, sons Mark and Richard, on board ten years ago, are now skipper and mate. All six crew are Filey-born of course. The photograph of c1900 (**7.5**) probably includes most of that 1891 crew.

1901 - the only Filey yawls to be caught away from home by the census will be William Jenkinson *Billy Butter* Watkinson's *Good Intent* and Richard Crawford's *Brothers*. Anchored in Grimsby Fish Dock, and still observing the Sabbath, this pair of floating museums of mid-19th Century fishing practice occasion wonder in the eyes of the steam trawlermen moored nearby. Grimsby is the epitome now of the raw, late-Victorian capitalist fishing industry. The trawler crews who toil for weeks at a time are of course a waged mix from every port on the east coast. In contrast, these two ghost ships are family concerns, seven sharemen in all, and all 11 crew are Filey men, most bearing one of the town's core fisher surnames.[14]

'T'ord yalls' now eke out a pittance of a living for their crews, at the bottom end of the market, precariously great-lining for cod throughout the winter months. They have just switched to haddock from the Dogger, landing their catches weekly at Grimsby, where the prices beat Scarborough's. They pay a toll of 7s 6d to leave the Fish Dock. You have to wonder if they have caught enough to pay even that sum.

Yet one of these men, *Billy Butter*, is a man of vision, and in 12 years time he will be taking a great step forward into the future, the first in the district, abandoning the sailing technology of generations of Filey men and risking steam.

---

[14] Each recorded in the census as 'working on own account'.

8 FILEY'S OFFSHORE FISHING: 1: GREAT-LINING

Great-lining for 'Greatfish'

Until the great fall-off in stocks began in the mid-19th Century, offshore fishermen worked 30 or more miles out, whereas inshore, coblemen stayed within a few miles of the coast. The split between the two types of fisherman wasn't hermetic: once the luggers were laid up for the winter, the crews could use their two corfes (*calfs* in local dialect) for winter fishing, whilst coble fishermen might be taken on as extra waged crew at the height of the herring season. Some offshoremen took to cobles when their catches plummeted.

These three-man boats cost a fraction, maybe a tenth, of the offshore luggers or yawls.[1] And they could be worked from the beaches. Men could live at home, and not be at sea, or in a harbour town, for days at a time.

Modern fishing is based on the trawling principle, which in the North Sea dates from the 1830s. Previously, **demersal** (sea bed) fish like cod were caught by hooks (lining); whilst **pelagic** (surface) fish, especially herring, were snared in drift nets.

1 Typically 2 or 3 feet long after 6 years, but can be as big as a man	**2** Can live 30 years, but are mostly caught after four, *just* as they can spawn	**3** Larger cod spawn in cold, shallow, northern offshore waters . . .
8 Smaller cod, below 20-30lbs, live inshore all year round		**4** . . . coming inshore from autumn until early spring
7 Cod will eat virtually anything, but the best bait was mussels and lamprey eels	**6** They are demersal, feeding and breeding at the sea bottom	**5** Cod feed greedily in the 'spring run' prior to swimming northwards to breed

8.1: The Atlantic Cod: main quarry of the lining fisherman, one of the few fish that stayed fresh long enough to reach shore in a fit condition for curing. 'Voracious eaters', they have been known to reach 200lbs in Arctic waters.

---

[1] Yawls were a shorter, faster version of the lugger, and appeared at Scarborough in the 1830s. Sources for 'great-lining' include Cole (1828); Cortis (1860); Dyson (1977); Frank (2002); Pettitt (1868); Pritchard (1854); Robinson (1984, 1987); Shaw, *Our Filey Fishermen* (1867); Sea Fisheries Commission (1863-6); Thompson et al (1983); and Walcott (1862).

8.2: A late 19th Century view of Filey beach and landing, illustrating the two traditions of line fishing. Four yawls are moored to points on firm land, not sand (four lines just visible). They may be landing catches or taking on supplies. Note their corfes, and horse drawn carts. Several cobles, masts raised, are anchored in the bay. *[FA]*

Filey's traditional specialism, offshore and inshore, was line-fishing for 'white fish', especially cod, but also ling and skate. But cod was king, fat free and long lasting once salted and dried. It was cheap and nutritious, yet known as 'the beef of the sea'. There was status in fishing for cod, even though it was easy to catch, for it would eat anything and so took greedy, terminal bites at whatever the fisherman baited on his snoods. Before the import of ice, halibut and turbot rotted too quickly, as did haddock – but those at least could be used as bait. With few natural predators, apart from seals, cod stocks never diminished – at least not until the appearance of trawlers in the North Sea in the 1830s – New England folklore had cod as the fish that Christ multiplied to feed the 5,000. Maybe its fertility associated it with sexuality in many languages – in English, we have *codpiece*.[2]

Offshore boats used 'great-lines', or 'big lines' ('cables' at Staithes) thicker in diameter than a coble's, as the fish they sought were larger. Ironically, transport innovation boosted the traditional system of great-lining – the railways socially deepened and expanded the market.

Filey's concentration on cod dated from the mid-17th Century - the Dutch, the maritime super power of the day, paid the first two Stuart kings for a monopoly of

---

[2] Kurlansky (1998) pp35-6, 40-2.

8.3: The *calf* off a Staithes yawl, landing a cod, 1909. Sketched from life by marine artist JJR Bagshawe, the drawing shows why large cod were called 'greatfish'. A six-footer of 211lbs was caught by line off Massachusetts in 1895. As the cables extended miles from the yawl, its corfe would rarely be hauling in as near to safety as this.[3]

the North Sea herring fishery. The obvious alternative was the large cod which helpfully congregated in the shallows over the Great Dogger Bank each summer. The closest landing point was Filey, just 30 or 40 miles away.

The best grounds were kept as secret as possible – Bayman's Hole, 27 miles off Scarborough, at 44 fathoms (264 feet) the deepest part of the North Sea, could be identified by leadline. This 'big area of deep' was good for big cod and ling. The sandy Whitby Fine Ground Bottom was ideal for turbot.[4] Each three-masted lugger acted as a floating base, 'riding the waves out'. A skilled piece of seamanship, known as 'heaving to the wind', kept the boat stationary: sails were set to, so that the action of the wind on one was balanced by the action on the other, whilst the tiller was roped at 90° to the leeward (ie to the downwind). The two sail/oar-powered cobles, usually known as corfes, could then shoot the lines, in opposite directions from the lugger, and later haul them in.

Historically, each great-line or cable was 700 yards in length, and originally carried 140 snoods, around 1,500 in all (see Figure **15.8**, page 207). Bait varied depending on the fish being targeted. Writing in 1932, Smith reckoned yawls each took up to 100lbs of frozen bullock liver when going to the Dogger for haddock. Pettitt records how each morning the crew baited a few lines with mussels, limpets and the like to catch haddock and herring. Whatever these few lines caught was cut up to bait the remaining lines, ready to hook cod, ling and skate.

The lugger made for the Dogger, and here its two support corfes ventured out to shoot the lines. This had to be in calm conditions, but the time spent miles out in an open boat exposed crews to sudden weather deterioration. Usually, two men worked each, the skipper handled the lugger, and it was left to 'the lad' to bait a second set of lines. Yawls had only one *calf*, as they were built with herring fishing as the main activity. These later boats will be considered in more detail in the next chapter. The same timetable survived into the age of steam. A few lines would be baited at Scarborough until 9.00pm, ready for the next day.

---

[3] Joseph John Ridgard Bagshawe, *The Wooden Ships of Whitby* (Horne, 1933). Sketch reproduced in Frank (2002). Bagshawe died shortly after this fishing voyage, aged 39.
[4] Graham Taylor.

Staithes	Runswick	Whitby *	Robin Hoods Bay	Scarborough *	Filey	Flamborough	Bridlington *
19	3	0	4	5[5]	7	3	0

8.4: The number of luggers at Yorkshire's fishing stations, 1825, according to the *Registers of Shipping* of the three ports of entry, marked * (Robinson, 1984, p78).

Eating only began when the work was done. Local boys often helped: George CAPPLEMAN, born in 1889, remembered Captain Sydney Smith as 'a kid who used to come aboard and help us.' Such helpers would be rewarded with 'a bit of fish and 'tater for their suppers.' Captain Smith himself fondly remembered at seven years old (1914) cracking whelks for Jack *Sled* JENKINSON. The shells, one to six inches long, were put on a stone and struck with a mallet. The tail was the best part for bait, so Jack would constantly remind him: 'Crack tails, laddy'. There was a row if you didn't. Captain Smith was paid 3d a sack, a rate which reflected how thin traditional great-lining had got in its last years.

An inshore coble could fill all available space with its catch in just a few hours, and was out and back in a day. In contrast, the luggers and yawls fished for days. Cortis noted in 1860 that the offshore boats usually worked in pairs:

> In the middle of the week all the fish caught is put on board one yawl, which takes it to market – Hull, Scarborough, or Filey – leaving a Coble and three men with her partner to fish for the remainder of the week when she follows (p60).

Stocks diminished after the 1830s and '40s as the railway-generated mass market spawned indiscriminate, industrial fishing. Trawlers swept up fish whatever their age, and even eggs. Originally each of the five shareholding crew on a lugger brought three lines, but by the 1860s, one man was shooting six, ie two miles of line, double what their fathers had done, just to catch as much.

Few traditional fishermen wanted anything to do with trawling, despite its spread throughout the North Sea after the 1830s. Filey supplied the quality end of the market, and the better the fish, the better they travelled; reputedly, it was even tastier after two days, and always better in winter.[6] Though the British preferred fresh, cod was famed for not turning if salted and well dried. Some palates found

---

[5] This figure seems to include Filey boats operating from Scarborough, for Cole (1828) gives Filey's complement of luggers as 12.

[6] As we saw in ch4, there was a well-developed network of packhorse routes to northern cities as early as the 1780s.

Lug-rigged - ie four-cornered sails, hanging like *lugs* (ears) from the yards

Yard arms lashed obliquely to each mast and able to be swung according to the wind direction

Mizzen lets boat sail into a head wind

Cabin aft, where the crew ate and slept

Clinker built, ie planks overlap to allow swelling when wet

Manual, 'hand-spike' capstan for hauling in herring drift nets

Rope room; and well, to keep fish alive

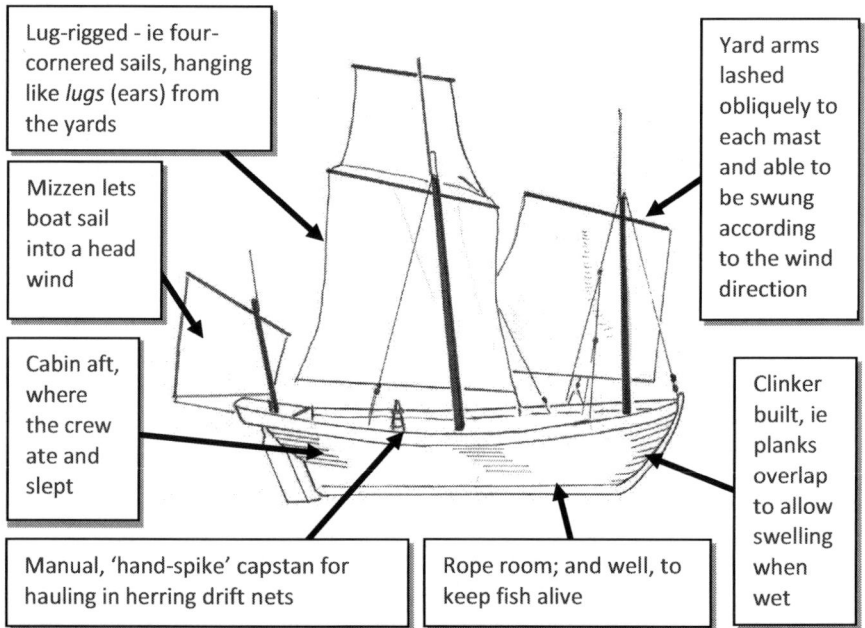

8.5: The three-masted lugger, or *farm* ('five-man boat'), the offshore workhorse of Yorkshire, in its final form as built from c1770 to c1850. These solid boats were 50-60 feet long, and weighed c50 tons. Having evolved from the smaller coble, they had become floating fishing bases, with features that allowed them to stay at sea for days. The leaner, shallower, faster two-masted yawl evolved from this design in the 1830s.

the increased flakiness of lightly-salted cod more appetising. Turbot, haddock and halibut were sold on Filey sands, but cod and ling went for curing. Filey fish merchant David Crawford told the 1863 Sea Fisheries Commission that hooked fish went to market 'with all the gloss and scales', earning the fisherman 1s 6d or two shillings each; but trawled cod were always bruised, and brought just '6d and 9d apiece'.[7] Liners used essentially the same method, whether from a 60-foot lugger, on the Dogger Bank, five hours out, or on a 20-foot coble off The Brigg.

'The Nursery of our Maritime Defence'

Nervous after Britain's defeat by the rebellious American colonists, the government extended its bounty system, a common wartime expedient, to encourage the national fishing industry and boost the number of fishermen. From 1786, 46 shillings were paid for each barrel of fish caught, and to prevent fraud, registers of offshore British vessels were introduced at the same time. 'Fishing boats and

---

[7] Cole (1828) pp93-4. The 1863 evidence of Crawford suggests that buyers like himself would pay a shilling a head extra for lined cod 'without even looking at it'.

merchant ships, with their crews, are the antecedents of men-of-war and naval armaments,' declared Walcott in 1862, 'the nursery of those elements of our maritime defence.'

Government customs houses administered the bounty scheme. Principal ports, 'ports of entry', supposedly the only legal landing place for all imports, registered existing boats working from them, including lesser nearby harbours, and new ones as they were built. The registration numbers of Filey fishing boats therefore carried Scarborough's *SH* prefix.[8] It is remarkable that tiny communities like Filey and Staithes outranked the fishing fleets of their respective ports of entry **(8.4)**.[9] The explanation is that Whitby focused on whaling, and Scarborough on shipbuilding, whilst Bridlington provided pilots and provisions for passing ships, leaving the specialism of fishing to these small neighbours.

Giants of the Deep: the Three-Masted Luggers

Scarborough's *Register of Sailing Fishing Vessels*, which starts in 1786 with this enhanced bounty scheme, lists the boats that great-lined along this stretch of coast. Until the 1830s, these were exclusively three-masted luggers, 50 to 60 feet long, 50 tons in weight, and built from several acres of locally grown oak **(8.5)**. They had evolved from the smaller inshore cobles, reaching their final, fully decked form by the late 18th Century. Almost flat-bottomed, to allow beaching in shallow bays, they lay deep enough in the water to remain stable in heavy seas. Design details are scant, for builders worked 'by eye' and with the use of scaled down models, not plans. We have to rely on statements given by the oldest fishermen to the 1863 commissioners. William JENKINSON (N8) born in 1786, and aged 77 when he gave evidence, reckoned 'they had just begun to get decked boats' when he had first gone to sea 'upwards of 70 years ago'.

Below deck was a 'wet well' compartment amidships, with holes drilled in the hull. These kept the catch just about alive, in freely circulating water - until they were 'knocked on the head' as they were to be sold. 'High end' fish like cod sold better fresh. Other spaces below deck were fairly watertight, on account of the decking. This countered swamping: luggers, consequently, did not usually have to run for shore in bad weather.

The Scarborough *Registers* indicate that 15 or so luggers had been registered at the port during the 1780s, mostly built in the town's harbourside yards. Seven were owned by Filey men, for the town was the second most important offshore fishing station on the Yorkshire coast **(8.4)**. Most luggers survived 30 years at sea, the

---

[8] The *Registers*, now at The National Archives, Kew, record design, dimensions, ownership and name the captains. They therefore chronicle the changes in fishing boat design, and pinpoint which Filey men were involved with which specific craft.

[9] Filey was literally a village: between 1821 and 1831, its population rose from just 888 to 1,128. Staithes was about the same.

record being set by William Edmond's 1773-built *Providence* - she eventually became a coaster, and was lost after *90 years* of work in 1863, with all hands. Family names amongst the Scarborough fleet included Robert Edmond's *Robert and Mary* (1787) marking his marriage to Mary Healand in 1781.

Despite the ungainliness implied in their name, the great lug-rigged sails brought a major edge over competitors. They gave the speed to get catches quickly to shore to secure market advantage, and to escape to harbour in the worst storms. In 1902, a Cornish lugger sailed the 600 miles to Scarborough in 70 hours or less, a speed that might challenge a modern racing yacht. The rig also allowed a boat to sail very close to the wind, permitting headway in even the toughest conditions. Three-masted luggers were also known as 'Five Man Boats' or *farms* (ie *far-man boats* as locally pronounced). A sixth man might be taken on as cook. Extra waged crew were needed in the herring season.

The Boy

Captain Sydney Smith, a Boy (ie 'apprentice') on steam fishing boats, reckoned the crew's attitude to 'the lad' was simply 'his fault, whatever went wrong'. According to Jim Haxby, the Filey way was for teenagers to learn the trade offshore - on a lugger, yawl, or steam drifter - even if they later fished from cobles. Boats took on a Big Boy and a Little Boy, and one line each was shot for them. As their fish were hauled in, the tail was nicked, and the sale proceeds were their wage. Initially they worked with the cook, but in later years crews usually cooked for themselves. They then 'worked their way in all jobs', as Jim put it.

'Taking a Share': Patterns of Boat Ownership

Scarborough's *Register of Sailing Fishing Vessels* reveals varied sources of finance for Filey's offshore fleet. A lugger cost perhaps £600 in 1800, whilst an 1830s yawl, two thirds the size, was reckoned to cost £500; with sails, ropes, auxiliary coble, two sets of lines, and nets, this rose to £1,000. Over half the capital came from working fishermen, the profits of one or two good seasons - such as those around 1833/4, but especially 1837 - sufficient to stimulate the commissioning of new boats. Two or more fishermen often co-owned a boat, because of the high initial costs.

The *Registers* classify fishermen as 'subscribing owners', ie actively involved in the work of the boat. But capital also had to come from 'non-subscribing owners' like local gentry ('gentleman speculators'), farmers and tradesmen.

These men got a share of the fishing profits, and probably a guaranteed market for their products. Filey baker William Newton clearly profited from high wartime bread prices, for he bought into three luggers between 1815 and 1818 **(8:6)**. He could expect to sell half a hundredweight of bread weekly to each. In turn, skipper and sharemen gained from the arrangement for they could be sure that any goods or services provided would be promptly and carefully delivered.

Name	Built	Owners		Skipper
Endeavour	1792	Ann WILLIAMSON Richard RICHARDSON	both of Filey	Richard RICHARDSON
Zephyr	1801	Richard CAMMISH of Filey		Richard CAMMISH
Isabella	1815	William DUNN yeoman Cornelius RAILEY William NEWTON baker Chris GRUNDON gamekeeper of Hunmanby	all of Filey	Charles DUNNING
Dunn's	1815	William DUNN fishmonger William NEWTON baker	both of Filey	John CRAWFORD
Diligence	1817	John CAMMISH fisherman William SMITH boatbuilder Herbert STALKER ropemaker of Scarborough	both of Filey	John CAMMISH
Scarborough	1818	William NEWTON baker of Filey		Robert SCALES
Herring perhaps a re- registration of the 1787 boat, after new owners had bought in	1820	Marmaduke CAMMISH fisherman William CAMMISH fisherman John Hill COULSON shipowner of Scarborough William DARLEY gent of Whitby William PECK farmer of Beverley	both of Filey	Marmaduke CAMMISH
Providence perhaps a re- registration of the 1773 boat	1822	John CRUMPTON fisherman Jane DIXON widow George SMITH master mariner of Scarborough	both of Filey	John CRUMPTON

8.6: Summarised entries in the Scarborough *Register of Fishing Vessels* relating to Filey's fleet of three-masted luggers in the 1820s. Women are likely to have been heiresses of deceased owners.

Banks were wary of investing in any 'business start-up' as risk-ridden as fishing. The financing of luggers and yawls therefore relied on personal connection: Filey fish merchant Benjamin Simpson told the 1863 commissioners how fishermen 'look out for a friend to take a share'. Such 'friendship' bonds might extend to East Anglia, Great Yarmouth fish merchants investing in Filey boats involved in the annual autumn voyage to the Norfolk herring fishery.

This could have been a natural extension of the commercial relationship of merchants contracting with Yorkshire fishermen, agreeing to pay *steerage money* for the season – effectively travel expenses to sail down from home. In return, the Yorkshiremen had to sell them their catch at a fixed rate.

The Share System: a Cooperative at Sea

There were seven shares in a lugger according to Cole, each entitling the holder a seventh of the profits. The owners, which often included the skipper, jointly had one – the owners' share could be subdivided as far as 64[ths] ('doles' at Staithes) which might be traded, or passed on to heirs, including widows. A second share paid expenses - repairs, maintenance and sundries, like the set annual 21 shillings to the rector of St Oswald's as a tithe on the fish caught and landed at Filey. Another expense was the 2s 6d *Scar rent* which each lugger was paying yearly in 1841-2 to moor and land catches on Filey beach. The smaller yawls paid 1s 9d. The remaining shares normally went to the skipper and 'sharemen', the adult crew: also known as 'gearmen', they 'took a share' by providing the lines.

This joint, financial involvement of skipper and crew, a forerunner of the cooperative, did not lend itself to the divisive capitalist model that came with trawling, then rampant throughout the offshore fishing trade. The Filey 'codmen' would see its abuses at Grimsby in the 1870s, and would not have liked the change, for the traditional system suited them:

1 The share system was essentially **egalitarian**: since men relied exclusively on the success of 'the venture', there was no wage bargaining to create class consciousness. There was little economic hierarchy, shareholders being equally exposed to the gluts and mischances of a season. Non-seagoing owners could trust the shareholding crews of their boat not to slack or be careless.

2 Skippers were usually **fellow shareowners**; former skippers sank their accumulated savings from good years into a boat whose crew they knew and trusted. Rising from the ranks, and therefore starting as ships' boys, skippers might have decades of experience at sea. Those with temperate habits succeeded. One 20th Century East Anglian fisherman, used to the system, quoted by Dyson, summed up simply his own personal experience of skippers:

> . . . they weren't uppish or ought like, they were just people . . . . They would pick you up and give you a lift home . . . . They mixed with you.

3 Filey's fishermen **belonged to a boat and to a family**. Retired skippers who were part-owners often made a younger relative or in-law the next skipper. The share system was thus indissolubly linked to the family support system that kept the boats at sea. The common practice of naming boats after parents, or close female relatives, emphasised this sense of family identity.

On the Moray Firth, the share system meant 'a boat attached to every house'. The need to retain boat shares within families may explain the pattern of multiple marriage, often seen at Filey, two siblings marrying two siblings, or first cousins. In this way, the children would become first or second cousins twice over, doubly binding the families genetically and economically.

The Lugger's Year

Great-lining, the 'Spring Fishing', began between February and mid-March as the weather eased, and continued until mid-summer when the Banks Group of herring appeared from the north. These shoaled off the Yorkshire Coast from July till late September.[10] Until c1850, and for about six weeks, Yorkshiremen then went south to join the Yarmouth fishery. This annual voyage to East Anglian waters lapsed in later years, though some Filey men continued into the 20th Century. Once back in Scarborough, the luggers were laid up, or over-wintered, at a pound a week, for about three and a half months. This was a dangerous season to be out on the North Sea, made more so by the fact that all the local harbours – Whitby, Scarborough and Bridlington – were tidal. Any boat caught in a violent winter storm at low tide, or in a heavy high tide, had several terrifying storm-tossed hours to wait before it could get safely into harbour.

This annual calendar varied: reports of good herring catches drew boats away from great-lining early, and the opposite could apply. In lean times, the Filey luggers might be fitted out as early as January. They would stay safe by fishing well south of their usual grounds until May, landing catches at Hull, Boston and Lynn, only returning to Filey every few weeks to bark their lines.

The Shift to Scarborough and Bridlington

Writing in 1868, at Filey's fishing peak, by which time luggers had largely been replaced by the smaller yawls, Rev Arthur Pettitt was moved deeply by the sight of the town's 34 strong offshore fleet setting out for the grounds:

> The many boats that lie about the low cliffs - and the busy sails that hurry to, and from, the larger craft at anchor in the Bay - will arrest your attention . . . . You will scarcely fail to observe that, early in the week, the larger boats take their departure in silent dignity - one after the other - in marvellously direct course, till the last in their turn drops below the horizon line, where the rest have gone before; that, day after day, one or two have returned . . . and that on Friday or Saturday, all are back again - with their foremasts laid to rest and looking precisely alike.

These Monday morning departures were grand affairs, and a great visitor attraction in the Filey offshore glory days. Wives and daughters carried provisions, including bait and kegs of water, down the steep paths to the resting boats, ready for the week's fishing. This could not be done on the Sunday, for Lord's Day observance had been paramount in Filey since the 1820s.

---

[10] See below, p99, and Figure **10.1**, p116.

8.7: Nineteenth Century lithography at its best - a print of the remains of the Filey first-class fleet, below Speeton Cliffs. A hurricane, 'truly the worst ever . . . came so suddenly upon the coast that, in ten minutes, the calmness of the Bay and neighbouring waters was changed to a boiling flood' (*Scarborough Mercury*, 2nd June 1860). Note the similarity of the hulk in the foreground to an Anglo-Saxon or Scandinavian longboat.

On return, the boats could be anchored in the bay, masts dropped to reduce exposure to the wind, and catches taken to the beach by corfe. Luggers and yawls could also be beached for maintenance, discharging and loading. Nets were be repaired and tanned. Men then stayed with their families, and most attended chapel.

'Owing to the protection afforded by the Brig *[sic]*,' warned the Admiralty's survey of British coastal waters, 'there is a fair riding in the bay with the wind as far out as NNE, but no vessel should remain in it with the wind to the eastward of that point.'[11] Such winds were seasonally predictable - *usually*. But once-in-a-generation weather in 1822 wrecked two anchored luggers. The risk-taking was more severely punished on Whit Monday 28th May 1860 when 22 of Filey's 23 yawls were anchored in the Bay (**8.7**). Walcott clearly spoke to witnesses before writing his 1862 account:

---

[11] *North Sea Pilot*, Part III, East Coast of England (1889) p119.

> ... there had been a fierce gale of wind from the north, which lasted from 2am until 6am, when a sudden hurricane swept over the bay from the SW, lashing up the sea into sheets of foam. The fishermen, who had clustered along the cliffs waiting for the lull, ran to their cobles and gallantly launched out to save their yawls; owing to the driving spray, the sea was so dark that they could barely see the distance of a boat's length with the greatest difficulty, but at the most imminent risk, they scrambled into the yawls which lay nearest; and, with one or two crews crowding into single vessels, succeeded in saving the greater number; while one intrepid fellow actually got a little sail set [ie the *mizzen*], triumphantly rounded Flamborough Head, and carried his salvage into Bridlington.

Two yawls drifted onto the rocks; one was driven onto the beach; and one was actually carried round Flamborough Head and 20 miles beyond. Nine [one account said 13] were totally wrecked. Losses were put at £10,000.

Some crews now embraced the advantages of Scarborough Harbour. By 1867, several yawls were kept there, the men commuting from Filey each Monday. Provisions, lines and ballast were easier to load in a harbour, whilst the presence of more buyers boosted quayside prices. Also, the outer pier was let out to fishermen for dry curing. Since 1844, all railway companies had to run a daily 'Parliamentary', for workmen, 1d a mile, but this was not cheap, and some men continued to walk. Whether the vessels were at sea for days at a time, or in Scarborough overnight, the crew slept on board all week. The boats often sailed to Filey and beached, to load the provisions. Onlookers regularly commented on, but never seemed to photograph, the fishermen's descent on Filey Station, and their arrival at Scarborough. William CAPPLEMAN relates how:

> ... they used to walk up to the station with a *bass* in one hand and a japanned box in the other, and in this box the wives 'ad done all the baking and it was full of light and short ... all sorts of things.[12]

Into the 20th Century, the army arrived around 8.15am. Tommy Flynn recalled up to 70 of them, in fishing gear, walking down Eastborough, *meat* tins on shoulders - *me-at* [food in general] had two syllables. Men poor enough to have to eat fish all week maintained the appearance of a well-stocked tin by putting a brick in it. Filey currant cake was included as a luxury, often dished out to poor Scarborough lads who helped out at the harbour – to them, it was known as *corran*.

Food remained a crucial consideration for the demanding physical labour of offshore fishing. Each man cooked his own meal in turn. Bacon, eggs, skate, meat and potato pie (depending what had come with them in the *meat* tins on the Monday) would follow one after another into the same panful of fat. Even in the later years, as white fishing declined and the weekly pattern disappeared, Filey men were still known at Scarborough for their disciplined routine, setting off to the grounds early, and returning late the same afternoon.

---

[12] A *bass* was a net normally used for carrying bait.

Holiday diarist JS Wane recorded the weekly trek to Scarborough:

> We went to Whitby on the 9.28am train, by which all the Filey fishermen travel to join their ships. A very short train it was that steamed into the station and a very large crowd wanting places. Every true fisherman in the Old Town seemed to be there, each with bronzed face, roughly shaven, and each wearing his blue jersey and carrying his oblong tin box. They swamped the train, all but the solitary first class compartment (Monday 7th September 1908).

Rather less well known is the equivalent commute to Bridlington. We know it must have taken place, for the families of the 40 Filey men on board those nine yawls in Grimsby Fish Dock in the census of 1881 were enumerated in Filey that night. The move took place in the late 1870s. One piece of corroborating evidence is the reported prosecution of George *Baltic* Boynton for brawling on Bridlington station in October 1877, 'wilfully interfering with the comfort of the passengers':

> George Knaggs, porter, stated that defendant and a number of other fishermen were on the platform arguing about a boat, when defendant struck one of the others and a fight ensued. Defendant was turned out of the station but returned and renewed the disturbance. Fined £1 including costs.[13]

The move to harbours might be expected to have led to a dilution of Filey individuality, as the men were exposed to this outside world. There were some adjustments needed which didn't always work out. Graham Taylor, herring drifting from Scarborough in the 1960s, told me how the crew hit upon the idea of throwing nets over railings by the Harbour: 'we ended up tanning a car', he said.

The Senior JENKINSON Line: the Master Mariners

The senior branch of the JENKINSON family on the extreme left-hand side of the pedigree (Appendix E, Chart **E1**) uniquely left fishing, and Filey, in the early 19th Century - the town spawned a small number of mariners as well as fishermen. Captain William JENKINSON (N2) was already a master mariner at Hull in the 1790s, and on a visit home during the war with France quickly organised some fishermen to repel an attack on a collier in the bay.[14] His son, Captain Edmond JENKINSON (O4) continued the upward social trajectory, marrying Mary, sister of substantial Muston farmer Christopher Hutchinson,[15] whilst Edmond's only son, John William JENKINSON (P1) warranted an entry as 'Esq of London' in the columns of the *Filey Post* of 21st September 1867.

---

[13] Parkin (1989) p15.

[14] William JENKINSON was one of several Filey skippers who left fishing for the Baltic trade from Hull. For his successful resistance to hostile attack on the collier, at the age of 20, see p151. A St Oswald's gravestone records his death at Kronstadt, Russia, in 1844. Several such Filey cases can be found in the *Register of Shipowners, Part Owners and Masters of Scarborough Ships 1747-1920* (transcript at Scarborough Library).

[15] In the 1861 Census, Hutchinson, of Muston Hall, listed himself as 'Farmer of 256 acres'.

9 FILEY'S OFFSHORE FISHING:
2: DRIFTING FOR HERRING

In the 1980s we were fortunate to speak to two men, Tommy Flynn of Scarborough and George CAPPLEMAN of Filey, then in their eighties and nineties respectively, who had fished for herring from some of the last yawls. Their recollections, and information given by Captain Sydney Smith, helped us to build up a picture of 19th Century herring fishing techniques.[1]

From the 1830s to 1913, the herring shoals were the great earner: in those eight decades, Yorkshire fishermen reckoned line-fishing just sustained them, whilst herring was 'the harvest', supplying capital for new boats and equipment.

Little was known of the herring's annual migration cycles: up to the 1920s many believed that the fish swam to feed and winter around the North Pole. Later it was thought they circumnavigated the British Isles each year. In fact, they spent much of the year in deep water, different 'stocks' coming to breed in shallow waters, closer to shore, particularly in three distinct North Sea locations, each at a specific time. Helpfully, they spawned in sequence down the coast (**10.1**, page 116):

1.   **the 'Buchan stock'**, off north-east Scotland, from June to September

2.   **the 'Banks group'**, off the Durham/Yorkshire Coast, July to September

3.   **the 'Downs stock'**, the Norfolk fishery, from October to December

Each group engaged in a gigantic feeding rotation taking hundreds of millions of fish over scores of miles. The females increased in size and edibility, mature eggs making up a fifth of their body weight, in readiness for spawning. Nobody was interested in 'spent' herring.

What were called 'walls of fish', ten or more square miles in area, swam with the current within a 40-mile corridor, southwards along these three western edges of the North Sea: 'the water before them curls up, as if forced out of its bed.'[2] For the half year between spring and autumn, fishermen willing to travel could make a good living from the 'silver darlings'. The shoals came close enough to shore to be netted from cobles, but those swimming further out could only be harvested from more robust craft like luggers, and their successors, the yawls.

---

[1] This account also relies on Dyson (1977); Frank (2002); Robinson (1984, 1987); Shaw, *Our Filey Fishermen* (1867); and Christopher Unsworth, *The British Herring Industry: The Steam Drifter years 1900-60* (Amberley, 2013).

[2] Oliver Goldsmith, *An History of Earth and Animated Nature* (J Nourse, 1774).

1 The Scots discovered the secret Dutch cure of immediate gutting and barrelling in brine

2 Abolition of the tax on salt, 1825, after lobbying by chemical manufacturers, cut its price

3 Better preservation opened up more distant markets, in Russia, Eastern Europe and the Baltic

8 The speed of rail made salt-based cures unnecessary. 'Lighter cures' of smoking preserved taste and spread the popularity of herring

4 Stocks of white fish fell as trawling spread to the North Sea in the 1830s. Catches fell, and herring became an alternative, at least in the summer

7 Railways reached Whitby (1836), Scarborough (1846) and Filey (1846-7), opening up a mass market. London could now be reached within a few hours

6 Lighter cotton nets woven in Musselburgh on power looms replaced bulky hemp nets in the 1840s. Yawls could now carry twice the number - up to 130

5 Large French herring boats started to appear off the east coast in the 1820s, buying catches off local boats. This rekindled the local herring fishery

9.1: Why Yorkshire's offshore fleets became more involved in the Yarmouth herring fishery from the 1830s. 'Bloateropolis', as Yarmouth was later nicknamed, was a money-spinner which got these Yorkshiremen through the lean months of the Winter Fishing.

Yorkshire's Involvement in the North Sea Herring Fishery

As the regional maritime superpower, the Dutch dominated the North Sea fisheries until the late 18th Century. English boats had been fishing for herring since the 13th Century, but their North Sea involvement fell away as the English Civil War and wars with the Dutch started a 17th Century disengagement. Dutch and French control of the fishery forced Yorkshiremen to specialise in great-lining for white fish.[3] In any case, salted herring, 'the pork of the sea', went off quickly, and was not a dish of choice in Britain – 'chewing a salty dishcloth, full of fish bones' was one later verdict. It was seen as the 'food of the poor', often distributed by parish overseers to the starving.

---

[3] It is likely that Dutch involvement in the annual North Sea herring fishery explains the early 17th Century arrival in Filey of the surname CAPPLEMAN. See Appendix B.

High wartime bread prices in the 18th Century reawakened local involvement, as herring prices rose. Yorkshire luggers now drove for herring, at least during those summer weeks when the shoals were accessibly off their own coast. Also, nets could be fetched out of winter storage early if cod prices were low.

The Yorkshire season traditionally began on midsummer's day, 21st June, as local boats joined the hunt for the Banks group of shoals at the mouths of the Tyne or Tees. As the group moved south, catches were landed at Whitby, Scarborough, Filey and Bridlington. The Scarborough season began on 15th July when the buyers arrived from harbours further north. The core weeks were in August and September, when boats from Scotland, Yorkshire, East Anglia and even Cornwall used Scarborough harbour. 'You couldn't get any more boats in,' Tommy Flynn recalled. The shoals were close enough for a fishing voyage to be completed overnight. Bridlington Circuit Methodist minister George Shaw, in a much-quoted account of an overnight herring trip on a Filey yawl in the summer of 1866, relates how the boat had left Filey Bay at 2pm, started shooting nets around 7pm, and was selling the catch at Scarborough by 10am the next morning.

The Scarborough season finished in late September as the focus of the fishery moved south. Since the 12th Century, the great Free Fair of Herring had been held at Great Yarmouth, from Michaelmas (29th September) to Martinmas (11th November). The Yorkshire fishermen had choices once the shoals left their coast:

1. Sail south to the spawning season of the Downs stock, for a further seven weeks, landing catches at Grimsby, Yarmouth and Lowestoft. Fishing from the last two was rated the most profitable: the herring were closest to shore and full of spawn. An East Anglian fish merchant usually paid 'steerage money' to secure all the Yorkshiremen's catch. After particularly lean years, 1848-50, Cortis (1860) reckoned that Filey men increasingly fished in deeper waters to the east, and gave up the trip south.

2. Return to Filey's offshore specialism of great-lining for cod until the winter lay-up, continuing to fish from Filey or Scarborough by the week.

3. Lay up in Scarborough Harbour for the winter, and go coble fishing.[4]

In 1828, Cole recorded that all 12 of the Filey luggers were following option one, and this is borne out by the muster roll of the Filey Sea Fencibles dated 20th September 1803.[5] Wives and children accompanied the fleet to assist with dockside running repairs to nets as the menfolk fished, and perhaps as gutters.

---

[4] 'We start in the back part of July and we laid up last week', Edward SCALES of Filey told the Sea Fisheries Commissioners on 1st Oct 1863 (ie option three). The introduction in 1750 of government bounties for boats committing to 90 continuous summer/autumn days of herring fishing may have boosted Filey participation. The bounty ended in 1830.

[5] See Appendix A. Fisher reckons 12 went to Yarmouth in 1806 (*History*, 1970) *Fishing and Shipping* ch, p2.

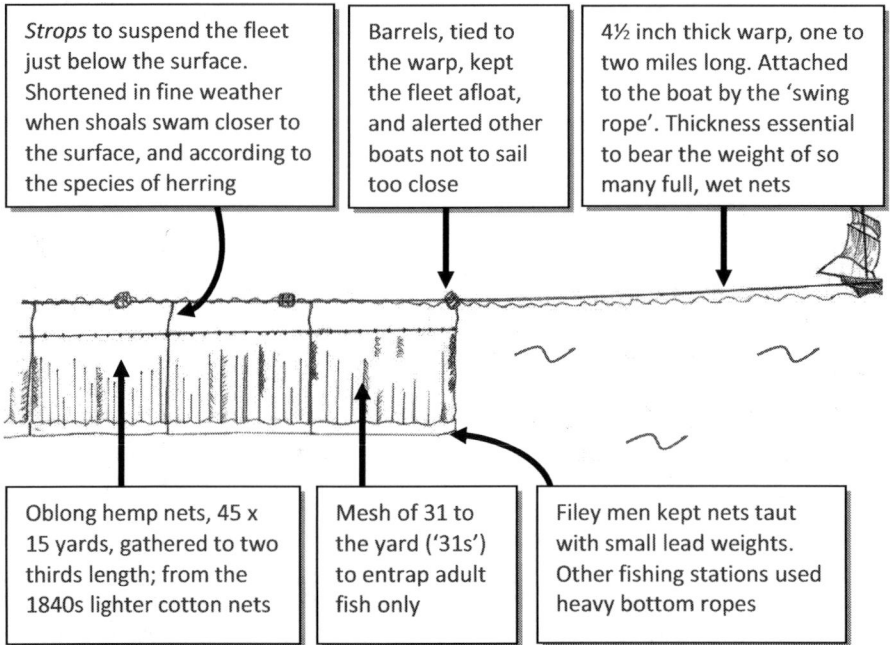

Strops to suspend the fleet just below the surface. Shortened in fine weather when shoals swam closer to the surface, and according to the species of herring	Barrels, tied to the warp, kept the fleet afloat, and alerted other boats not to sail too close	4½ inch thick warp, one to two miles long. Attached to the boat by the 'swing rope'. Thickness essential to bear the weight of so many full, wet nets

Oblong hemp nets, 45 x 15 yards, gathered to two thirds length; from the 1840s lighter cotton nets	Mesh of 31 to the yard ('31s') to entrap adult fish only	Filey men kept nets taut with small lead weights. Other fishing stations used heavy bottom ropes

9.2: A typical fleet or drift of 60 herring nets rose to 120 or 130 by the 1860s, as lighter cotton came into use, and the need to increase catch potential rose as fish stocks fell. The whole fleet could weigh two tons, far more when wet, or full of fish.

Yorkshire's herring fleet (maybe 60 boats) mustered in Filey Bay for two days, making final preparations. As Richard Harland puts it, 'a night or two of revelry and feasting, and then they were gone.'

There are tantalising hints of Filey involvement in the Norfolk autumn fishery at least 70 years before the great herring revival of the 1830s. Robert JENKINSON, from whom the majority of 20th Century Filey fishing families descend, married Margaret Truckles at Great Yarmouth, on 1st November 1778.[6] In these last days of the Free Fair, merchants were settling up before the northern luggers sailed home, and a man might have enough to start a separate household.

---

[6] Margaret had presumably come down with a lugger. I've found no other instance of her surname – it was probably a southern version of the Staithes name *Trattles*. East Anglians would pronounce this *Trackulls*; and even in Yorkshire it was misspelt outside Staithes. A witness from the village became *Turttles* in the 1863 Sea Fisheries minutes of evidence!

Another clue is the 1803 claim of John CAPPLEMAN of Filey that he had not missed the 'Yarmouth fishing' for 45 years. It is likely that this Filey involvement dated back far longer.[7]

Drift Nets

Herring cooperated with their hunters by gathering in monster shoals, conveniently rising each evening to feed on the clouds of plankton which flourished in the shallow waters of the British coast. They were caught in the Dutch-designed drift net, oblongs of mesh invisible to the fish in the darkness. Fleets of 60 or more drifted as a continuous giant curtain just below the surface, each gathered to two thirds length. Known also as gill nets, they were traditionally made in Bridport, Dorset, of local, American or Baltic hemp.

But they were expensive - Walcott (1862) reckoned £30 each, well beyond the budget of an ordinary fisherman, for warps had to be bought too. As each gearman needed two fleets, it usually fell to women and retired fishermen to weave them at home. The three or four gearmen were responsible for 'netting' the boat, so they each provided a third or quarter of the fleet. The time involved in knitting 30 drift nets, each around 700 or so square yards, defies calculation.

Every two or three weeks, one fleet was boiled in hot water coppers, with a tannin-rich preservative like oak bark chippings, or blocks of dye from the Acacia Catechu tree, from which the name *cutch* derived. Quinine was also used in the barking process, to kill off infection.[8] Some families had tan or bark houses to the rear. The nets were washed, dried and stored in attics after the herring season. Walcott describes the weekly routine:

> The nets are generally soaked in tan from Saturday night, on the return of the fishing-yawls, until Wednesday morning, when the women spread them out to dry upon the slope of the common-land under the north cliff of Old Filey.

Few families had the facilities to treat large items like sails, so an occasional communal barking took place, on common land, with a large tank over a bonfire. A big pit behind the *Station Hotel* was in use for this purpose as recently as the early 1950s, families collecting wood from Church Ravine to fill it with fuel.[9] Linseed oil and even dog faeces were mixed in to ensure the sails were supple enough to work.

---

[7] CAPPLEMAN was attempting to secure the release two of his crewmen from impressment into service on a Royal Navy warship – see below, pp146-8. Staithes boats were sailing to East Anglia at least as early as 1651 (Clark, 1982, p49). There is also strong evidence of such 17th Century involvement at Filey – see p448.

[8] Terence COLLINS reckoned that the rising cost of this bark, from the South American cinchona (quina-quina) tree, used as an anti-malaria drug since the 1630s, was one of the reasons for the adoption of nylon nets.

[9] Eddie CAMMISH.

9.3: The unmistakable architecture of a bark house, possibly also used for baiting, behind Church Street. The best known example is on *Teddy Rent*, which runs from Queen Street, immediately right of the Museum, to Mitford Street.

This unglamorous additive also acted as a fixative for the dye. Along with the oak chipping or *cutch*, this rich cocktail gave the sails their distinctively deep red-brown, tarry appearance. Ropes, rigging, lines and even smocks, trousers and sou' westers were also later tipped in, but perhaps separate to the excrement!

The Early Yawls, 1833-c1850

As the herring fishery escalated, local lugger design altered rapidly, for drift net fishing had become the priority over great-lining. The *Registers* indicate that a new, shorter type of lugger, soon to be known as a *yawl*,[10] appeared in 1833 **(9.4)**. Scarborough boatbuilder Robert Skelton had speculatively built a version of a craft associated with Cley and Cromer. He must have observed these Norfolk boats landing herring near his yard on Sandside. The middle mast was removed to create space for fishing operations, and to deploy extra nets. These 'two-masted luggers' were lighter, sacrificing speed and stability for manoeuvrability. Skelton was taking a big risk, for it would have been 'on the 'stocks' (under construction) for months - he had only six men and five apprentices according to the 1851 Census. But after 1834 the yard was somehow building ten more, again for Filey and Scarborough men. No one seems to have anticipated that these craft were less resistant to heavy seas than the luggers they were to replace.

---

[10] Possibly originating from the Dutch *jol*, a Jutland boat, but nowadays meaning a dinghy. In Filey, it seems to have been pronounced *yall*, rhyming with *shall*.

Space below deck for crew's cabin, warp-room and well-room, fish room, net-room, and salt-cribs

No mainmast - more room amidships for extra nets and for the corfe

Traditional lug rigging continued until the 1870s

Lug sails

Mizzen mast well aft to maximise working space

Fluted stern - short hull meant less drag

Length c35 feet, lighter (c20-30 tons) to increase manoeuvrability

Gangway in bulwark used for launching the boat's corfe

Flattened hull allowed boat to rest nearly upright on a beach

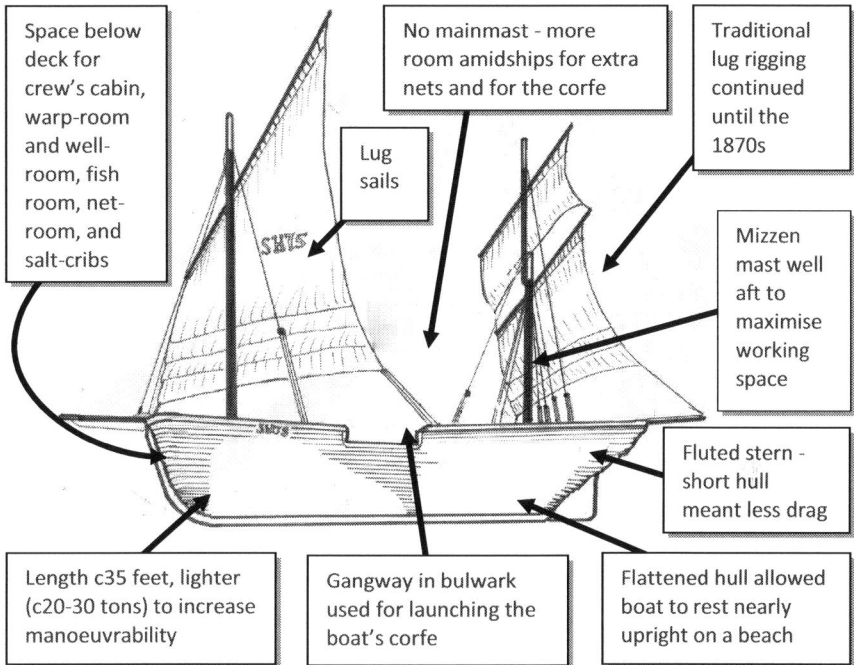

9.4: The early yawl – effectively a 'two-masted lugger', as built at Scarborough after 1833 and up to c1850. Used by offshore fishermen including those from Filey. The cabin provided refuge when the alarm 'water's coming' warned of danger. There were bunks, and a coal stove where 't'lad' cooked the *meat* brought by the crew.

The original, *Integrity*, had been snapped up by George JENKINSON (N12), the youngest of five brothers, a man who, unusually for Filey, was not a hidebound fishing traditionalist. Elder brother Thomas, however, stuck to the old ways, taking delivery in 1848 of *York*, one of the last three-masted luggers to be built in Scarborough. (Ben Simpson's *Robert Newton*, 1850, was lost in the May Hurricane just ten years later, despite being named after a nonconformist divine. This misfortune propelled him out of fishing, and into fish buying and selling.)

The first yawls were small enough for one man to be able to finance, without partners. These boats therefore made possible a high point of east-coast individualism, with a crew of sharemen to spread the costs of lines and nets. Yawls needed fewer crew, and usually had only one corfe. A section of bulwark could be removed to allow its launching and retrieval. 'The cabin of the yawl is of comfortable dimensions,' observed Walcott (1862) 'and fitted with four beds, each capable of holding two persons, one fisherman always being on deck at a time to keep watch, who wakes his mates in case of danger by giving three loud stamps upon the deck.'

The Later Yawls, c1850-1917

After 1850, fishing proprietors started to commission larger yawls, eventually almost double the length of the 1830s prototype. The cost rose, and the old lugger model of two or more partners owning each boat was revived. The fully evolved Yorkshire yawl was adaptable – faster than a *farm*, easier to handle, yet still robust in heavy seas, though not in fierce gales. It was an early factory ship, needing fewer trips back to port, having facilities to salt and store herring for up to five days, and keep white fish alive in wells.

When lining, there was, as George CAPPLEMAN put it, 'no stopping', and when the calf was out working the lines it had been difficult for the skipper and boy to handle the original lug rigging. For this reason, from the 1870s onwards, the yawls were 'dandy-rigged', easier to handle, but at the expense of the boat's speed. Also, dandy-rigging reduced the ability of the boat to lie close to the wind, increasing the risk of it being driven onto the land by a sudden easterly.

Herring Heyday: Midsummer Nights on a Filey Yawl

Walcott (1862) describes the routine in the Yorkshire season, the Filey yawls returning to replenish each weekend:

> On the arrival of the yawls, the men may be seen carrying down large black tubs slung upon a pole, full of tan scalding hot, while their wives and daughters hurry along with kegs full of fresh water for the use of the boatmen in their next cruise. Two stone of beef and meal for dumplings, sea-pies, sweet cakes, 0.5 cwt of bread, and a quarter pound of tea, form the weekly provision for the commissariat. Each yawl carries from six to eight water-kegs, besides a huge cask holding as much water again, which is refilled as occasion demands at Scarborough or Whitby.

I have yet to encounter a more polished account of high season, offshore drifting than George Shaw's chapter 'Out with the Herring-Fishers' in his *Our Filey Fishermen* (1867). He contrasted two very different voyages in the Scarborough season of 1866. The fishing ground was 25 to 30 miles out, four or five hours sail. Shaw was especially impressed by the sense of human community of purpose amongst those so far out on one of the world's most dangerous seas:

> . . . and about two o'clock, pm, the vessel was sailing gently out of the Bay, with her bow towards the open sea. Several yawls and herring cobles were steering in the same direction, and here and there we passed a fishing-boat bound for Filey or Scarborough, two of which were apparently loaded with fish.

Shaw had first confirmed with the skipper that the boat would be back before Sunday, and would not be proceeding to sell at Grimsby!

Spotting the Shoals

As the sun dropped in the west, herring fishermen knew to look for 'signs' of the 'sparkling millions', as a *skoal* surfaced - a greasy surface, oil droplets, the light milky brown of floating plankton, the sea's reddish colour, or maybe that peculiarly phosphorescent glow, known at sea as 'fire', visible at 30 yards even on a dark, moonless night. Old hands reckoned they could smell the shoals.

But the presence of the fish's many predators was the most obvious alert: a fast-forming cloud of seabirds on the horizon, diving gannets, solan geese, conger eels, seals, porpoises, certain types of shark and dolphin, and any toothed species of whales. The 'blow fish' might be the size of the boat, and dangerous when close, but Shaw could only share the crew's excitement as calls of 'a *Santariman*' greeted the sight of a surfacing whale:

> . . . not more than a hundred yards from our vessel - blowing a large mass of water up into the air. While we were watching him, a shout apprised us of the appearance of another 'big fellow' on the other side of us. The delight of the fishermen knew no bounds, who informed me that 'wherever them chaps was, there was generally plenty of herrings.'[11]

The best swims were reckoned to appear in the brightness of a full moon, and after south-westerly gales. It was believed that they were more likely to strike the nets in a light breeze, rather than in a calm spell. In reality, we now know that herring 'came upstairs' primarily when its principal prey, the copepod, was shoaling at the surface. These are tiny crustaceans, less than a tenth of an inch in length.

Shooting the Nets

During the day, herrings stayed in deep water to avoid their predators, only surfacing as daylight receded. The fleets of net were shot in the dim light of dusk or dawn, fishermen believing that herring vision was impaired in the half-light. Swimming near the surface open-mouthed, the fish ran into the nets as they fed. In the 1840s, a fleet was usually 60 nets. By the 1860s, railway-induced rising demand, lighter cotton nets, and thinner swims meant that the largest of the luggers and yawls were shooting up to 130 nets. On Shaw's 1866 trip, a two-mile drift of 120 nets was now ready in the warp-room, nets tied together end to end. Each shareman was about to risk up to a thousand pounds worth of gear in the North Sea, if he'd bought them. Usually homemade, they still represented a huge family expenditure in time, so each man's nets were distributed regularly along the fleet (*abc abc abc* etc) to spread the risk of loss.

---

[11] It is a mystery how the name of the Pacific's Sanitarian whale become the generic term in Filey for the creature. Also called *Santallamant*. Shaw suggests *blow fish* was a Cromer term.

It took the crew up to an hour to pay out the warp, another man attaching 100 barrels, whilst a second tied the precious nets, as the huge rope passed over the yawl's starboard side. The weight of a couple of tons of fleet made this process exhausting. It was shot at right angles to the tide, and outwards 'to the horizon', so that the warp remained under tension. The boat drifted, 'hanging on to the nets', 'the long winding line of corks looking like a serpent in the sea', warp and fleet taut so that the adult fish swam inescapably into the mesh.[12]

Supper

The fleet was left to drift through the shoals until dawn, the herring snared by their own gills: there was time to eat and relax. One fisherman described the joy of it:

> You'd just sit there – it used to be lovely. You'd wait maybe two to three hours. You'd just sit there rocking. And you could fall asleep. You could stretch out on the boards and have a doze . . . .[13]

Shaw's description of this interlude is especially delightful, catching a rarefied, comradely male atmosphere, that mix of practicality and banter. The size of the mealtime portions clearly exceeded what he was used to at the manse:

> You sit down upon the deck, a piece of boiled beef, smoking hot, is brought up, and one of the men - the master most likely - commences to 'cut it up'. And he does cut it up, and no mistake, and hands you a piece, that looks sufficient for half-a-dozen meals. He tells you . . . that it's 'a *lang tahme* between then and supper.' To this is served bread - home made, and worth the name of bread - cabbage, potatoes, or carrots. Should there be a little sea on, you will have some difficulty to keep your plate on your knee - for a table is out of the question - or if you keep your plate, it is likely you will lose your meat or potatoes.

The meal even extended to dessert:

> After the meat comes round dumplings, which, for the sake of security, are served in basins, and the treacle can is handed round and you help yourselves. After this you have a 'dish o' teaa' if you feel disposed, intoxicating drink is out of the question, most of the men being teetotallers . . . .

Once again, Shaw was struck by the sense of comradeship:

> After supper, we gathered round the fire for a chat, previous to turning in for a nap. I should like you to have seen the picturesque group we made. It was a scene for a painter. Talk of comfort and contentment. I never saw it equalled.

---

[12] *Warp* - from early German/Dutch, 'bent, twisted' ie made of several threads; barrels were only one type of float. Also used were corks, inflated dog, goat and sheep skins, all orifices stitched watertight, and even bullock bladders. In Buckie, Morayshire, dogs were bred specially, little realising their life's ultimate purpose (Dyson, 1977, p180).

[13] Weatherhead (2011) p125.

'Dandy' (ie triangular) sails stretching from main mast to bowsprit – these aided stability, but at the expense of 'heaving to'

A 'gaff' (ie spar) rises from each mast to hold the main sail. The canvas can then be larger, as it is supported on all four sides

Gaff-rigged sails, and dandies, are fixed and therefore easier to control than the earlier lug sails

Deeper hull increases head space below deck, increasing capacity, but also the cost of construction

Length now up to 70 feet (c40-50 tons) greatly increasing catch capacity

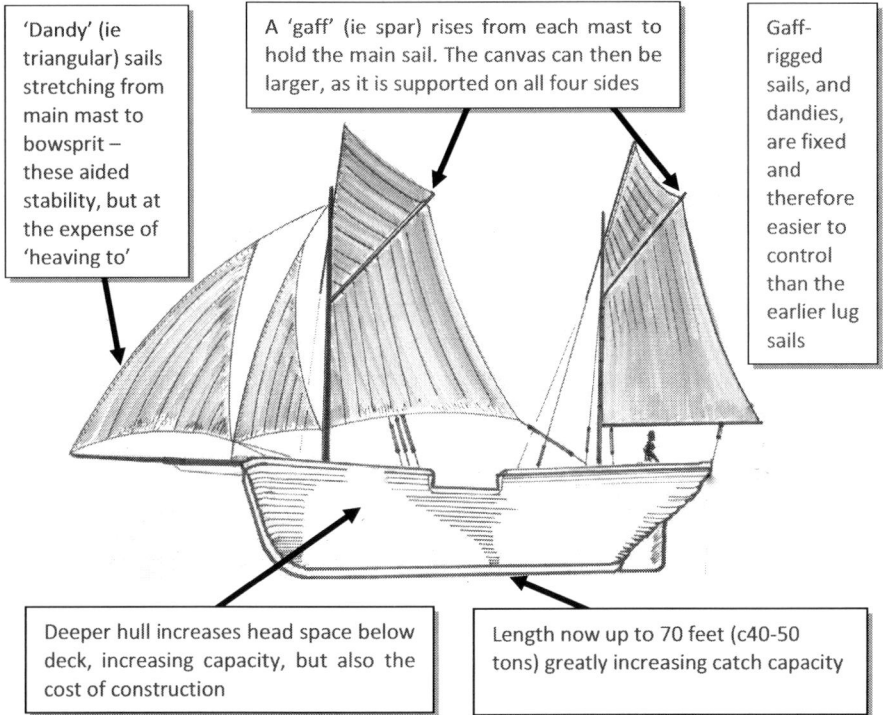

9.5: The later yawl, c1850-1917, with the dandies and gaff-rig used after c1870. This arrangement was now a closer type of 'fore-and-aft' rig, ie set along the line of the keel, and better suited to sailing in a head wind than sails rigged square to it. But the increase in sail area, and height of the mast, probably decreased safety in gales.

He was also mesmerised by a deep calm, and the dots of light, each a boat carrying a lantern set in a timber and seven feet above deck. Did the Filey men on board share this sense of the mystical, or had they long since ceased to notice?

> About ten o'clock, I went on deck, and sat down to muse. It was getting dusky, and the signal-lights from the vessels around us, presented a sight indescribably novel and beautiful. Not a sound was to be heard, or a breath of wind felt. While sitting I saw, faintly glimmering through the distance, the far-famed Flamborough Light.

'Looking on'

In fine weather, the yawl's corfe 'looked on', hauling up a sample net every quarter mile to monitor how many herring were meshed. But in the usual poor conditions, a 20-foot coble bobbing on the North Sea, inspecting two miles of nets, was simply too exposed. The sampling was therefore restricted to hauling in the nets nearest the vessel.

Shaw succeeded in persuading the skipper to let him risk a few hours of 'looking on' in the coble, another very special experience, once the tide had turned:

> Shortly after midnight I was awakened by a loud stamping of feet upon the deck, and found that it was the signal for the hands to look on . . . .

> And now the boat was pushed off from the vessel, and there we were, in a frail coble, out upon the wide sea. Never shall I forget the scene. The moon had risen and was shining with undimmed splendour. Not a cloud was to be seen. Our path lay directly along the line of silvery brightness caused by the reflection of the moonbeams upon the water.

The surrounding boats, all from the Filey fleet, would of course have all been known to each other, but even men from other communities along the coast fell in with the comradely spirit when so far out at sea:

> The men pulled along for some time, and not a word was spoken. Here and there we could perceive a boat leaving a vessel on a similar errand to our own. As we neared them, or others passed who had examined their nets, we hail'd them with a word of good cheer, or inquired, Do you find anything? The reply from one or two was, 'Lots, on 'em.' This caused the men to pull with renewed vigour . . . we pulled to the 'fleet', and took in a barrel, by which we hauled up the warp, which one of the men thrust over the bow of the coble . . . .

Graham Taylor has probably come closest to this intangible sense of closeness between these fishermen of a lost age when he spoke to me in 2018 of the sense at sea of 'the intimacy of darkness'.

Shaw clearly brought them good fortune:

> In the small portion I saw there were scores of herrings entangled in the meshes, which lashed the water with their tails and presented a beautiful appearance. Putting the warp overboard we went about another quarter of mile [sic], and examined another net with the same result, and after repeating the process two or three times, finding herrings in every instance, rowed for the vessel . . . .

The Catch

The hard labour now began. Each net weighed about 28lbs, so the full fleet came to well over a ton, even when dry. Now sodden, and full of fish, hauling them and two miles of arm-thick warp took the crew four to eight hours of back-breaking work on the traditional 'hand-spike' capstan:

> The men went to the capstan and commenced turning it round. By this means the warp was drawn in; as it came on board one man loosed the barrels, another 'paid' it into the hold, and two others shook the herrings out of the nets on to the deck, part of which fell through an opening into the well beneath. When they accumulated so as to be in the way, I shovelled them down. This process lasted about three hours. At length the whole fleet was in and we captured about 30,000 herrings.

Everyone to hand worked the capstan, though probably not Shaw! But he couldn't resist italicising the 'I' when describing his shovelling of the fish, revelling no doubt in this opportunity to rough it! The sails were immediately hoisted, and as the yawl sped for the market, the hard, physical work of the *scudding* of the nets began - corners held over the hatch by four men and shaken, to empty all fish into the fish-room below. The decks were cleared and washed, and the barrels lined up ready for the next night's work.

Meanwhile, down in the dank, dark forrard warp-room, one of the least pleasant jobs was underway. Coiling the warp, as it came in, took hours, as jelly-fish and octopuses were detached. Jim Haxby heard from his father how on the 1920s/30s steam drifters the Boy was put down in this darkness, to deal with the two miles or so of this immense, heavy rope as it came in. 'Terrible job especially in bad weather, it was dark, sometimes they had a candle sometimes they hadn't.'

Mercifully, the drudgery of the hand-spike capstan was soon to end. In 1876-7, the steam capstan appeared on fishing boats. A small steam-engine turned a large drum, with an unmistakable 'puffing and clicking'. Initially, few were installed, for why spend a capital sum when *joskins* could be hired at 18s a week? But as the traditional rope warps gave way to steel cables, and more nets were shot, the 'iron man' became essential. It also hoisted the huge sails, allowing even greater expanses of cloth to be used. Thus bigger boats could fish, bigger catches landed, and the cycle of overfishing was accelerated. Few people realised that the herring fishermen would, in the next century, effectively outfish their own livelihoods.

Back to Shore

Breakfast could be a huge meal, perhaps a dozen herring and mackerel each. George Burton recalled one 20th Century Filey crewman who often breakfasted on 18 herrings when out drifting. With seven men on board, and appetites like this, the cook had a huge task of frying. One 19th Century trawlerman wrote how:

> . . . willingly obedient to the summons, we tumble below again and fall hungrily upon tea, bread and butter, and herrings - herrings freshly caught, gutted, beheaded, deprived of tails, slashed with jack-knives latitudinally so that when a huge dishful of them is placed on the floor, piping hot from the boiling fat in which they have been fried, we can bend down and help ourselves, and with our fingers strip the delicious morsels from the bones and eat them.[14]

Shaw's timings indicate that the whole enterprise had been completed in just 20 hours, of which 16 or so had been intense physical labour:

> About ten o'clock the same morning we reached Scarborough, and a sample of herrings, taken promiscuously from the heap, was sent on shore by a man in the coble, whom I accompanied. We landed at the pier and proceeded to the place of business. The herrings were thrown on the ground, a bell was rung, a crowd of

---

[14] Wood (1911) quoted in Dyson (1977) pp156-7.

buyers and others collected, and the lot knocked down at 6s and 9d per hundred, a capital price, and we moved off gratified to think that our night's fishing had netted something like £90.

When the shoals were too far off to allow a return the same day, herrings had to be salted at sea. They commanded a lower dockside price than fresh fish.[15] During the summer months, it made sense to land the catches at Filey each morning. But unloading by corfe took so long that the yawl could not be back amongst the shoals that night. This was one of the reasons why Filey men left the town.[16]

The Lottery

'The herring-fishing is quite a lottery business,' William CAMMISH told the 1863 commissioners, summing up 60 years of experience. So it was in summer 1866. Shaw opted to come out on a second night's fishing. Everything was done as the night before, although the wind was too strong for the coble to look on:

> One or two nets were hauled up, but we found nothing in them. After three hours of hard work the whole fleet was got on board, but we did not get as many fish as would serve for our breakfasts. In this emergency, we had to fall back again upon beef and fruit pies!

Several of the crewmen would be sharemen, and would have lost money that night. The *joskins*, simply wage labourers, were taken on in the high season in anticipation of big catches, at a fixed 18s to 20s a week with food. They had to be paid whatever the catch. An odd *thin* night could be subsidised by previous successes, but skipper and gearman faced real hardship if more nights left the drift so empty. A consolation was the ever-present dream of landing with a huge catch, when everyone else had encountered thin swims, and prices were soaring.

'Bread and butter and herrings in his grimy fist'

We do not know how comfortably Rev Shaw rubbed along with those Filey men in 1866 - a social and educational gulf must have gritted the ease of their companionship. Could he *really* connect with an ordinary fisherman? Perhaps JJR Bagshawe, though writing nearly 40 years later, bridged the gulf more effectively. How graphically he caught the sweaty exhaustion of the herring fishery, in this earthy observation of a Scottish drift fisherman:

> After a hard night at sea and a busy morning getting rid of his fish he may sit for a few minutes on deck with a mug of tea and some bread and butter and herrings in his grimy fist - there is no time to wash and water is scarce. The signs of fatigue are plain on his face, which is begrimed with galley smoke and channelled by perspiration, and plain in his heavy, stumbling feet and bent back.

---

[15] Herring were sold by the *cran*, ie four baskets each of about two dozen, total c100 fish.
[16] Cortis (1860) pp56-7.

9.6: One response to the herring revival of the 1830s was the herring coble, at 40 feet twice the size of a normal coble. Filey had 21 by 1878, each shooting 60-65 nets. Decked at the front, above a small cabin (the *cuddy*) with four bunks, Scarborough and Filey men knew them as *mules* – ie a cross between coble and lugger. Here, a mule (also known in Filey as a *splasher*) is being manoeuvred on the Coble Landing, c1900, probably in readiness for launching. The children may belong to the crew, perhaps having carried the buckets down. The small boys to the right seem to have been *sandpoking* - one has an empty bottle, and a hooked line. Another herring coble is in the background. *[FA]*

> Twenty minutes at most he will allow himself. Then, with his blackened clay stuffed into his mouth, he wearily starts afresh.[17]

Such men were the backbone of this immense industry, so productive that in the 1860s around a *thousand tons* of herring, concentrated into just a few weeks, were dispatched annually from Filey alone. Yet this was a fraction of the total carried inland by rail from the Yorkshire coast at that time. Nevertheless, North Sea herring stocks seemed safe from the destruction imposed on their white fish cousins. They seemed living proof of nature's infinite bounty. A large 'egg mat' laid by many individual fish, perhaps seven million eggs per square metre, ensured proliferation, despite being a tempting mass of readily obtainable protein for many predators.

The shoals did not diminish yet, even though as few as 1% of larvae survived to become juvenile fish. Even fewer reached spawning age, a handful per million eggs. Herring escaped the attentions of industrial-scale steam trawling until the eve of the Great War. Did the survival of the medieval technology of the drift net spare them the overfishing that was decimating other species?

---

[17] From Joseph John Ridgard Bagshawe, *The Wooden Ships of Whitby: being some account of the fishermen and fishing craft, and the traffic, past and present, of the North Sea* (Horne & Son, 1933) quoted in Dyson (1977) pp193-4.

Shaw's excursion of 1866 probably reflects the height of Yorkshire involvement in the herring fishery. The North Eastern Railway's freight tonnages in the 1850s and '60s, indicate that Filey was landing between a quarter and a third of all the herring caught between Bridlington and Berwick. At the same time, Filey was one of the dwindling number of small local stations still to be joining the 'Yarmouth Fishery'. But by about 1890, most owners had sold their yawls or reverted to the great-lining that they knew best. The town's withdrawal from the herring fishery was very rapid, a viciously effective competitor, the *Zulus*, appearing from Scotland in 1879. Scarborough was a busy herring port until 1914, but now Scots boats dominated. A couple of Filey's herring-house buildings survive in 2021, all that remain today of the town's extensive involvement in this fishery.[18]

No list of raw statistics quite catches the scale of the east coast herring harvest in its brief heyday as one tiny 1868 newspaper item from the height of the Yorkshire season. The signalman at Malton had passed herring specials from Scarborough totalling 135 vans in a single day, and a further 77 vans from Whitby. Each vehicle had drain holes on account of the oiliness of the load, and in consequence the rails were left so greasy that the first train the following morning lost three quarters of an hour, skidding up the three mile-long Goathland incline on the Whitby to Pickering line.[19]

Shaw's two nights out on that unnamed yawl clearly made a lifelong impression on him. He is one of many authors who have attempted to capture in words that intangibly special sense of the fisherman's community at sea, inevitably beyond those who had never been on a working, wooden sailing fishing vessel many hours sail out on the North Sea.[20]

Michael Fearon has come as close as most to capture the uniqueness of the daily experience of these long dead Filey fishermen:

> To be on the deck of a yawl and see round about some other vessels and to know many of the members of their crews, must have been, however familiar, an experience which would compensate in some degree, for the hard work which lay ahead.

Here is the appeal that the traditional livelihood of sailing boat fishing held for the Filey fisherman. It was hard and dangerous, but the comradeship, the sense of a small, intermeshed community magically extended onto the waves, hard to express in simple words, rendered this a way of life so appealing that he never wanted it to change. For the traditional fisherman's conservatism was rooted in hard-gained experience.

---

[18] *Herring Hill*, the cobbled slope down to the beach from Ravine Road, is also a remnant.
[19] *Scarborough Gazette*, 26th Aug 1868.
[20] Edmund Crawford's evidence to the 1863 Sea Fisheries Commission indicates that the whole of the Filey fleet, herring cobles included, got as close as possible to any shoal that was detected. Each boat would therefore have been within sight of the rest.

9.7: Few shots capture the scale and majesty of a large yawl as well as this late 19th Century gem. *Tranquility* was built at Scarborough in 1866, at the peak of Filey's offshore fishing. She marked the last phase of the yawl's evolution - 59 feet long, and converted to dandy-rig, possibly by the previous owner (note lowered dandy sail coiled behind the bowsprit). Skipper/part owner William ROSS and two crewmen are cleaning the hull of barnacles and weed, since 'drag' impeded speed. Filey beach was a poor man's dry dock, such shots probably catching a boat moored for this fee-free basic maintenance rather than for the discharge of a catch. Compare with **9.5**. There had been one night in 1858 which taught ROSS to be an especially careful fisherman (ch17). It also probably taught him to be an avid avoider of risk. Certainly he avoided change – it is likely that he continued great-lining from *Tranquility* until she was broken up in 1915. *[FA]*

When a man's occupation pitches him so completely and indiscriminately at the mercy of massive natural forces, he has only two things to fall back on: what has been passed on from previous generations; and whatever experience has seared itself into his and his crewmates' practical memory. With probably the highest death toll of any British fishing station, it is no surprise that Filey stood out as one of the least willing to innovate. And fishermen in general were hardly the most innovative of men!

This conservatism was about to be challenged. Our accounts of great-lining and the herring fishery in this and the previous chapter represent practice up to the 1870s, the golden peak of Filey's offshore fishing. We shall see in Chapter 13 how this way of life rooted at least in the 17th and 18th Centuries, was about to change dramatically.

10 OFFSHORE TRAGEDY

'The man who gets upset because of wind and weather isn't a man to make a living on the Dogger. He carries his life in his hands, and always expects them to be emptied suddenly.' Scarborough trawlerman, 'Old Ben'[1]

The Dangers of the North Sea: '. . . a Fisher whose Name is Death'[2]

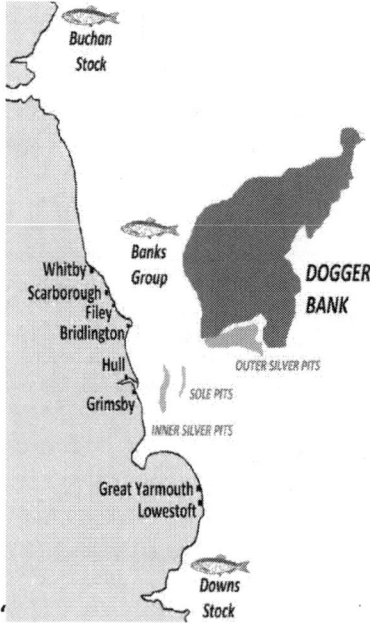

10.1: A 'mega-tsunami' flooded Doggerland, probably in one day, c6200BC. Herring shoal to the west, but many fish, especially cod, live around it.

Doggerland was the huge land mass which occupied the area now covered by much of the North Sea. It was coated in ice several times, glaciers depositing a vast, trenched mound of debris, the Great Dogger Bank.[3] This became a 7,000 square mile island as water levels rose after the last Ice Age, finally to cover it. North Sea coastal populations must now carry the genes of its refugees. Trawlers have been bringing up human artefacts and bones since at least 1931.

The submerged top of the Bank became covered with shifting sand, an ideal home for flatfish. Its sloping edges and nearby hollows sheltered many species of white fish, notably cod. Great underwater cliffs line the Bank's east face. These, and the sudden variations in depth from 50-foot shallows to 120-foot trenches, cause some of the most extreme sea conditions in the world. Add to this a harsh marine climate - snowstorms have even been known out on the Dogger in summer.

---

[1] Quoted in Wood (1911).

[2] This unnerving quotation comes from an especially cheerful poem written by Rev George Shaw (*Our Filey Fishermen*, 1867, pp84-5). I have relied on Dyson (1977) for accounts of the exceptionally dangerous conditions suffered by 19th Century North Sea offshore fishermen – see his chapter, *The Real Price of Fish*; and Wood (1911) for a powerful account of being on the Dogger Bank in The Great March Gale of 1883.

[3] *Dogger*, Dutch for a fishing boat towing a trawl, their trawlers being common on and around the Bank. The name has also been given to the area flooded c6200BC.

According to late 19th Century trawlerman 'Old Ben', fishermen gave these rich grounds such unsettling names as *The Hospital*, whilst one deep basin between two huge sandbanks was *The Cemetery*. Strong westerlies are especially serious on the Dogger, for the waves they stir up can travel great distances and gain a truly terrifying cumulative power.

The Bank is just the worst part of a large, dangerous marine environment. Modern statistics from oil and gas platforms reinforce the most extreme anecdotal evidence of the North Sea's deadliness. The Yorkshire coast in particular has a dire reputation for shipwrecks, with an estimate of over 50,000 vessels lost since 1500. Filey Bay has been chillingly called a shipwreck graveyard, 'drenched in death'.[4] In adverse weather conditions, even aids to navigation could be dangerous. Passing Flamborough Head in the 'thick and hazy' coastal visibility of a February night in 1859, one experienced ocean-going captain made a fatal error. His 621-ton barque struck The Brigg as it entered what he disastrously took to be Scarborough Harbour:

> He mistook the light in the town, which is exhibited for the use of the fishermen, and, unfortunately, supposed it to be the light at Scarboro' Lighthouse, and did not discover his error until too late.

The misleading light was the Gaslamp, then only recently placed at Cliff Top with a red seaward-facing pane. It was known locally in jest as 'Filey Lighthouse', having been erected as a modest navigation aid. Elsewhere on the Yorkshire coast, ironstone deposits could play havoc with compass bearings.[5]

Several factors compounded the risks imposed by the weather:

1 'The Winter Fishing', by its nature, took the boats out into the North Sea's worst weather. The best fish were reputedly caught in November, when conditions could be especially harsh. A run of bad weather kept boats ashore, increasing the temptation to take risks as losses mounted, bait deteriorated, and the shortage of catches temptingly elevated fish prices. This was what happened when a gale hit the Berwickshire coast on Black Friday, 14th October 1881; of 189 fishermen who drowned, 129 were from Eyemouth alone, which lost 23 boats. The expense of money and energy spent baiting miles of lines tilted cautionary judgement, for mussels went 'stale' quickly.

2 Nabs, Nesses and Scars - strong easterlies can drive vessels onto the many rocks and headlands with which the Yorkshire coast bristles. Even beaches could kill - one of the North Sea's worst storms, the Great Gale of 10th February 1871, beached around 30 boats onto the coast at Bridlington, the waves demolishing many as they were caught on the sand. This was the most dangerous part of any escape from the Dogger, for a heavy 'run of sea' could catch and capsize any boat

---

[4] Godfrey & Lassey (1982); Alec Gill, *Lost Trawlers of Hull* (Hutton Press, 1989).
[5] *Scarborough Mercury*, 5th March 1859; *Redux*, 26th Feb 2018; Frank (2002) p197.

rounding Flamborough Head. But if the weather broke as it got landward of Smithwick Sands, these shoals prevented any escape back into the North Sea, and the wind and tide could drive it onto the shore. Around 75 men drowned in that 1871 gale, mostly from colliers, 43 being buried in a mass grave at Bridlington Priory Church. An annual commemorative service is held at the memorial.[6]

3 Tidal Harbours - none of the three local harbours could be entered at low tide, Scarborough being especially dangerous. Just listen to this Admiralty advice:

> Vessels intending to enter the Harbour for refuge should, if practicable, hang off shore until the tide is well up, then, if the wind be northerly, keep just outside the broken water at the castle, and run in before the sea.

A north-easterly could combine with a bay current to drive boats onto the harbour wall, or the adjacent Castle Rocks. 'In case of missing the entrance,' official advice continued, 'the vessel may be beached on the sandy shore abreast, where life is always safe, and vessels generally sustain but little damage.' Filey men knew better. Ben Simpson told the 1863 commissioners how three of the town's boats had been lost with all hands off Scarborough in 1844, probably in such circumstances. The usual response to wild weather was to sail to the Humber, hours away, or 'keep their heads to the sea, and keeping well out.'[7]

4 Man Overboard - men made mistakes, for they got little sleep. 'Freak waves' could sweep the corfe, masts, sails and men into the sea. Sammy Hall of Filey (born 1824) witnessed two crewmates swept overboard in Boston Deeps. The men who survived threw the corfe overboard:

> A coble on board in a violent gale, being driven about is liable to injure the men, or if carried off with a powerful sea, may carry some of the crew along with it; or it might injure the yawl.[8]

Strong winds might swing the mast's boom[9] out of control and knock a man into the sea. When a big sea was 'sweeping on', the shout 'water's coming' meant drop below instantly. Bulwarks were low to allow lines and nets to be shot and recovered, and a man could easily be swept over them, lost to view instantly, and dragged down by the 25lbs weight of several layers of clothing and thigh length, thick-soled, iron-heeled, nail-studded seaboots. Sail-powered boats could not stop or turn: no wonder fishermen were resigned to drowning in such circumstances, and did not bother learning to swim. An impromptu survey of 1898 established that *none* of 40 Filey fishermen questioned were swimmers.

---

[6] John Mayhall, *The Annals of Yorkshire, From the Earliest Period to the Present Time.* (Simpkin, Marshall & Co, 1878, Vol III); Godfrey & Lassey (1982) pp103-5; Richard M Jones, *The Great Gale of 1871* (Mereo, 2013).

[7] Robinson (1984) pp426-7; *Scarborough Evening News*, 20th May 1895.

[8] Kendall (1877) p20.

[9] The *boom*, the spar attached to the foot of the sail, pivoted from the mast and swinging with the wind to harness it as much as possible – from Dutch 'pole' or 'beam'.

1 A 'shelf' sea - huge volumes of ocean forced into a sea of just 300 feet average depth exaggerate tides and waves

2 Strong south-easterlies often drove sailing boats onto the rocky north-east coast

3 The Dogger - trenches and cliffs - sudden changes in depth cause 'broken water' as opposed to the regular waves of a 'running sea'

Why are weather conditions off the Yorkshire Coast so dangerous?

6 'Rogue waves' of up to 60 feet are known to occur in the North Sea every two to three weeks

5 One of the coldest non-polar seas in the world - survival if adrift is far less likely

4 Coastal banks and shoals, exposed in certain tides, can ground boats causing them to be swamped

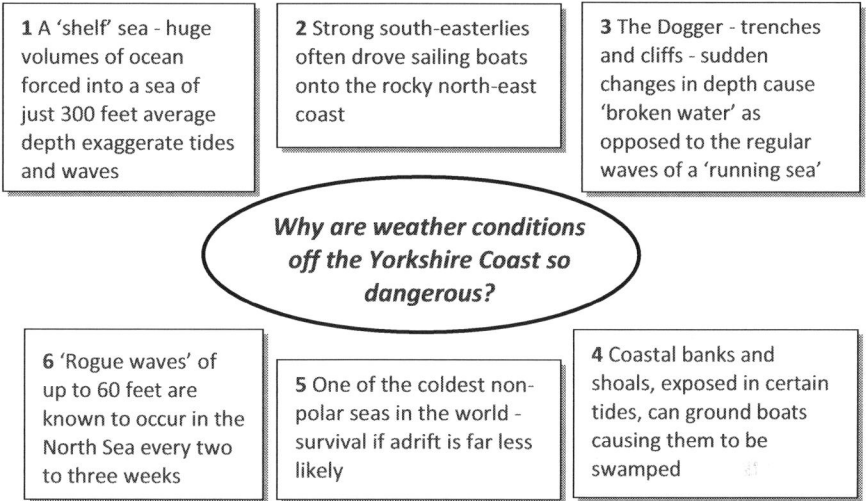

10.2: Since the 1970s, North Sea oil platforms have provided far clearer evidence of meteorological conditions, and seem to confirm the common claim that this shallow stretch of sea is one of the most dangerous in the world.[10]

On average, a British fisherman was washed, knocked or fell overboard *every week* between 1883 and 1893. This was the commonest cause of death amongst the 109 fisher fatalities reported to Hull police over a five-year period, the majority teenage apprentices.[11] Some Filey men were retrieved, risks being taken by crewmen who were friends or relatives, a big advantage to the Filey fixture of 'family boats'. In September 1851, of four men swept off the yawl *Concord*, three were rescued, only Cappleman CAMMISH (50) drowning. The same storm washed two men off the yawl *Ino* - one was retrieved, but Robert CAMMISH (30) was lost. Rescue was impossible in rough circumstances, and men could only watch as a crewmate died. William SAYERS was swept off the yawl *Denison* in the March Gale of 1883, and in a brave display of resignation 'being held up by his oil skin, waved his hand to his son and comrades in the boat, as they were driven away from him by the force of the wind.'[12]

---

[10] A freak 100 metre-wide 'wall of water', the *Andrea Wave*, 21m from crest to trough, the steepest and highest ever recorded, was logged at one platform on 9th Nov 2007, sweeping across the North Sea at 40mph. Just imagine encountering that on a yawl.

[11] *Filey Parish Magazine*, Nov 1898; *Report of Hull Fishermen Drowned or Dying at Sea, 1878-82* (*mariners-l.co.uk* website). This was *before* the duty to report deaths at sea was tightened up in 1883. The true figures revealed the 'Real Price of Fish': in the decade after 1883, a national average of 60 fishermen a year were washed or fell overboard, whilst 27 committed suicide, the simplest means being to take 'the fisherman's walk'.

[12] *Scarborough Gazette*, 2nd Oct 1851; Cooper (1886) p121.

10.3: The gas lamppost with red cover pointing out to sea, so that ships did not see a white light. Below it, left, on a house wall, was the thermometer box. The original 'Fishermen's Look Out' was immediately in front of the early 19ᵗʰ Century Coastguard House. The third storey was removed around 1960. *[FA]*

Running rigging, for controlling sails, or a rope paying out, could snake round a man's foot and whip him overboard. This seems to be what happened in February 1903, when a sudden squall capsized the Filey herring coble *Wild Rose* about five miles off Scarborough:

> Two of the crew, Thomas H[unter] COWLING, the skipper, who is 70 years of age, and T. HOLMES, had just time to scramble into their small boat before the *Wild Rose* went down. Jenkinson COWLING, another of the crew, swam alongside the coble, and the fourth man, John WILLIS, went down with the vessel . . . [probably] thrown against the halyards [ropes] by the lurching of the boat, and, being unable to clear himself in time, was dragged down with it. [13]

5 Thirty Miles out on the North Sea in a Corfe - luggers and yawls were the 'mother' boat, travelling quickly and safely to and from the ground; but once there, huge risks had to be taken by the crew who went out on a *corfe* to shoot and haul miles of great-line. When driving for herring, the cobles were used to inspect up to two miles of drift nets. It takes some guts to be 30 or more miles from the shore, in a 12-foot corfe, and up to two miles from the boat. Manoeuvring slowly by oar power, these men were exposed if the fickle North Sea threw up a storm.

This happened to Jenkinson Haxby's yawl *Ebenezer* in April 1859, his brother, Francis, being out in the corfe with the SAYERS brothers, William and Edmond:

---

[13] *Aberdeen Press and Journal*, 4ᵗʰ Feb 1903; Thomas Hunter COWLING was actually 60.

They had left the yawl about noon, in a coble, to haul their lines. After about 4 hours the yawl lost sight of them. The vessel instantly put about, and on nearing the spot . . . discovered the coble bottom upwards . . . a sudden wave had struck the coble, various articles belonging to the missing men were floating nearby.

One newspaper blamed the victims themselves, because they didn't wear lifebelts:

. . . had these men had them their lives would probably have been saved. Edmond SAYERS was an excellent swimmer, but this could be of little avail, encumbered as they are with clothing and heavy sea boots (*Yorkshire Gazette,* 9th April 1859).[14]

No reporter, of course, had ever tried to perform the fisherman's heavy manual tasks on board a lurching coble in 25lbs of gear, let alone in a lifebelt. Men, for example, involved in the 'boxing' system, could attest how dangerous it was, and how difficult if wearing a belt whilst loading crates of fish from a trawler onto a small boat, pitching and tossing on a rough sea.

In March 1867, the COWLING family was again exposed to the unpredictability of the 'Spring Fishing' weather, when a storm struck several Filey yawls, about 30 miles out. Many fishing boats ran for shelter but Bayes COWLING's *Jane and Elizabeth* had 21 lines out, and he gambled, unsuccessfully. Fourteen were already hauled in, and the coble had set off to get the remaining seven. On it were Thomas Hunter COWLING (the Captain's son), William JENKINSON (P34) and William SAYERS. At this point, 'a tremendous sea rose, filling her with water' and the coble was swamped. She overturned, JENKINSON and SAYERS managed to get onto it, but Tom COWLING was still in the water. Captain COWLING ran the yawl to the scene of the capsizing. 'One of the boys on board got hold of the hair of his head and held him up' and he was eventually pulled in. A second wave swept the others off the coble, and only SAYERS managed to get back on; 'but poor JENKINSON, in attempting to do so, fell backwards exhausted, exclaiming "Lord help me", and was never more seen.'[15] The sea seems to have had a vendetta against the SAYERS, so this escape was unusual.

Statistically, every 19th Century Filey fisherman must have experienced the horror of powerlessly watching and hearing a man drowning. We know, for example, that Thomas Hunter COWLING, saved by his hair, was with William JENKINSON as he drowned, just as he was to be with John WILLIS nearly 36 years later, when the *Wild Rose* capsized. Who knows how many other men he had watched go down, perhaps in the great storms of 1869, 1880 and 1883?

6 Collisions with Larger Ships - larger vessels striking small craft in darkness, fog or snowstorms are a fact of maritime life. Stationary fishing boats were especially vulnerable. Filey men told the 1863 Royal Commission how French boats, 'as big again' as theirs, could 'knock us to pieces'. Collisions caused a third of the 1,066 English and Welsh fishing boat losses between 1880 and 1914.

---

[14] Shaw (*Filey Fishermen,* 1867) pp63-5; *Adventures* (undated, chV).
[15] *Filey Post*, 16th March 1867.

Hull Advertiser and Exchange Gazette 13 May 1865

BOY DROWNED AT SEA.—Captain William Capple-man, of, the fishing yawl Zillah and; Rachel, on his arrival on Wednesday from this fishing ground, reported the loss of a boy, named William Cammish, fourteen years old, on the Dogger-bank. According to the usual practice, six of the crew had gone out of the vessel into two cobbles to fish, leaving the captain and two boys in charge of the yawl, which is constantly kept sailing about in sight of the cobles waiting their return. Whilst in the act of turning the yawl round under sail, the wind blowing strong at the time, the weather sheet broke, struck the boy, and swept him into the sea. Unfortunately the sail wrapped itself round the mast, and before it could be disentangled the lad was borne away to a considerable distance. He struggled hard for some time in the water, crying for help, but before the captain, who used every exertion, could get the yawl round and sail to the spot, he sank.

10.4: Accidents could easily take place when skipper and boy alone were sailing a yawl. This death occurred when the others were out tending lines or nets in the corfes. The child often had to battle with strong wind to work sails. The loss of 13 year-old William CAMMISH, was an especially poignant case. It may well have been politic for the skipper to inflate the boy's age.

This risk of a boat being tossed by a storm wind into the path of a larger vessel was probably one of the reasons why Filey fishermen often contrarily 'ran for shelter' to the nearest enterable port. There was a persistent rumour that one of the most famous losses, that of the yawl *Trio*, which mysteriously vanished without trace in May 1895, had been 'run down' during a huge gale. It was probably running southwards from the Dogger, to the 'Bay of Safety' off Bridlington, or the Humber. The onset of steam increased the unpredictability, speed and power of such collisions: at least sailing craft were subject to the same elemental wind and current directions and strengths.

7 Declining Catches - 'When I went fishing 24 years ago we got as much fish in one day as we could get now in six, and on the same ground', maintained Filey fish buyer David Crawford, in evidence to the 1863 Royal Commission. Fishing became even more dangerous as declining stocks forced men out to more distant grounds, and for more of the dangerous winter months.

8 The Yawl's Design Faults were exposed in a sequence of monster gales, especially in the 1880s and '90s. As fish stocks diminished, a premium was placed on landing the catch quickly. The stability of the lugger was sacrificed for speed – more canvas and taller masts increased 'windage' (ie exposure to wind) but raised the centre of gravity. Reduced draught lessened friction, and also allowed beaching – for unloading or refitting. A parallel development in North America had created the schooner – from the New England dialect word *scoon*, 'to skim lightly over the water'. Elegance and speed are poor consolations for unseaworthiness; and schooners disappeared as crews refused to sail in them.[16]

---

[16] Kurlansky (1999) pp83-6, 128-9.

The Telegraph and 'Fishery Barometers'

Some of the 19th Century's technological advances greatly benefited fishermen. From their earliest days, the railway companies had managed train movements through the newly devised 'electro-telegraph' system. Its wires and poles, once a lineside feature of every railway until the 1970s/80s, had almost immediately been used for a commercial messaging service in addition to train management.

By the late 1840s, weather conditions over a wide area could be communicated almost instantly. This was formalised in 1861, when Robert Fitzroy, head of the government's Meteorological Department, began what he termed 'forecasting the weather'. Headquarters in London received observations from his coastal observers, collated them, and telegraphed them back.[17]

The forecasts were based on readings from government-provided 'fishery barometers'. Communities had to guarantee theirs would be publicly accessible, perhaps at the Coast Guard Station house, 'a better place,' opined the guidelines, 'than in either private or "Public Houses"'. Filey applied for one in 1858, but the letter was annotated in London with a suggestion that the many beneficiaries (95 married and 79 unmarried fishermen) should club together to pay for it:

> It would not be more than 1s 6d a boat and if the Fishermen would not subscribe such a small sum for such a purpose I cannot think they have a claim of the Gov't.

Despite this aspersion, some fishermen bought their own, reckoning that the cost - around a month's fishing income - was worth the lives they could save. Eyemouth in Scotland clubbed together for this purpose. The Meteorological Department reported in 1858 how it was 'esteemed as a faithful monitor by the Fishermen, its warnings having saved them many tempestuous gales'. But even the gravest warning could be ignored if men were desperate for income: as we have seen, Eyemouth was to lose 129 men on Black Friday, 14th October 1881, *despite* the readings of its barometer.

Scarborough smacksman 'Old Ben' admitted that the Great March Gale of 5th-6th March 1883 had been forecast:

> . . . but it came sooner than any of us expected. I was hoping to get out to the Dogger and back home before the weather grew too bad for fishing.

Writing in *Filey Fishermen*, in 1867 (pp76-7), Shaw captured powerfully the communal sense of foreboding that had flooded the Old Town during that year's March gale. Before the telegraph age, it could be days, or even weeks, before the news of the fate of the town's offshore fleet got back. Once the railway opened, news could arrive by wire seconds after boats docked, bad weather electrifying the station telegraph office with an indescribable importance:

---

[17] This account relies on Sarah Dry, *Fishermen and Forecasts: How Barometers Helped Make the Meteorological Department Safer in Victorian Britain* (London School of Economics website, CARR/documents/DP/Diss Paper46).

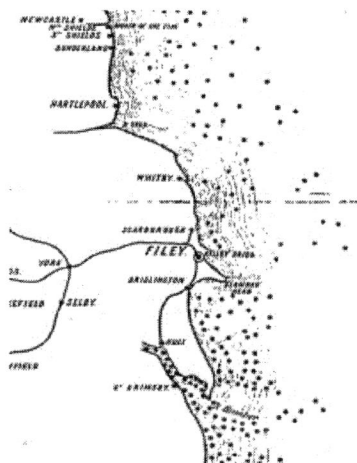

FILEY FISHERY HARBOUR
Map or Chart,

10.5: Project Fear - the case for a harbour of refuge graphically presented in 1876: boats lost or damaged at sea in the year 1875-6 are represented by dots. Titled in sombre, funereal fonts, the appeal was to local sentiment as well as financial gain. A non-tidal fishing harbour was planned. But there were just too many interests in the visitor trade pitched against it. How many seamen's lives would have been saved had a scheme gone ahead?[18] *[FA]*

> On reaching home a few nights ago, from a country appointment, I was distressed to hear that one of our men had been drowned, and that no less than seven of our yawls were missing. You can form no idea of the feeling which prevailed in the place. Women, whose husbands were in the missing vessels, were in a state of intense excitement, and the scene at the telegraph office was really distressing.

The boats would have run south ahead of the wind, but the offices at Hull and Grimsby would not reopen before six the next morning.

> Slowly and silently they returned to their homes, but not to sleep. If ever I prayed earnestly for sailors and fishermen it was that night.

Of course, weather conditions wild enough to threaten a yawl could easily bring down telegraph wires, especially alongside an exposed coastal railway line. The level of tension must have been unimaginable. The community assembly point in such circumstances was the equivalent of the pit head during a colliery disaster:

> Next morning I was at the cliff-top before day-light, but no tidings had been received. The sea was rolling in upon the beach in dark and sullen waves, and the faces of the weather-beaten fishermen looked as gloomy as that of the ocean. Six, seven, eight o'clock arrived, and no news! At last about nine o'clock, the gladsome message was flashed along the wires, and written by the trembling hand of the telegraph-clerk, that six Filey yawls, were safe at Grimsby, and in the Humber. This still left one unaccounted for, but about noon she also was heard of, and a great load of anxiety was removed from many a heart.

The Gale of 25th-26th October 1869: 'God's Hand in the Storm'

A day of fine morning weather, and no warning from the flagstaff - the Rev Charles Kendall's book *God's Hand in the Storm*, first published in 1870, was another of those graphic craftings of fishermen's first-hand accounts of weather

---

[18] Robinson (1984) ch16.

that had tested them to the edge. On Monday 25th October 1869, late in the season, Filey's yawls had set out for herring from Scarborough the men having travelled up by train from Filey. The wind began to rise 30 miles out, and for several days the boats were at the mercy of heavy seas, snowfalls and high winds. George JENKINSON (O16) skipper of *The Good Intent*, a Primitive Methodist lay preacher, must have been one of many who shared Kendall's assumption that something miraculous had happened out on the North Sea that week. JENKINSON and his crew had prayed earnestly, as the waves became 'of mountainous size'. Several of the boats lost their warps and nets:

> I found the Lord very powerfully present, and, addressing the men, I said: 'The best thing that all of you can do is to prepare for another state of existence - that is, for heaven. On Tuesday . . . brother John RICHARDSON asked me what I thought to our being saved? I replied, I believe we shall be saved. I said, considering the praying host we have at sea, and the one on land, it is strange that the gale should continue so long.

By Tuesday evening the worst had passed. 'We easily got in what ropes were left, and then made our way to Scarbro'.' By Saturday they were back in Filey. 'May we all continue to believe in the Son of God, till we have navigated the sea of sorrow, and all land at length in the Harbour of comfort,' concluded JENKINSON, no doubt preaching the very next day on the parallels between maritime travails and the spiritual challenges of life. Whatever forces *were* at work, given the culture of faith that pervaded the Old Town, it can only have been seen as an act of providence that all 34 Filey yawls returned safely.

10.6: An undated print, perhaps 1840s/50s, showing the Coastguard Station with its weather-forecast flagpole. This was the natural coastline at Filey until the construction of the landing for cobles in 1870/1, and the sea frontage later in the century. *[SE]*

The Great Gale, 27th-29th October 1880: the Losses of *Eliza* and *Sarah*

In heavy seas, everything on the deck of a lugger or yawl could be swept into the waves. The small cabin, waterlogged in such a storm, was no refuge - men could only stay on deck, gripping whatever they could, whilst two hung on to the tiller, keeping the bows into the weather. Such a storm struck the entire coast in 1880 from the Thames to the Forth, coincidentally with 1869 in the week beginning Monday 25th October. Altogether, 15 men were swept off vessels in the Filey and Scarborough herring fleets, including Filey's William Wiseman and Francis Haxby.

In addition, two Filey yawls, *Sarah* and *Eliza*, were lost completely, each with all ten crew. Twelve were 'names unknown' – mostly Norfolk *joskins*. All those who may have known the names had drowned too. Ross JENKINSON's *Eliza* was wrecked off Robin Hood's Bay in the ESE gale. *Sarah* had famously drifted off without crew round Flamborough Head in the hurricane of May 1860, yet somehow had been recovered unscathed after a 20-mile unmanned voyage down the coast. But her luck finally ran out in the Great Gale. Other casualties were the piers at Hornsea and Withernsea, demolished by foundering boats.[19]

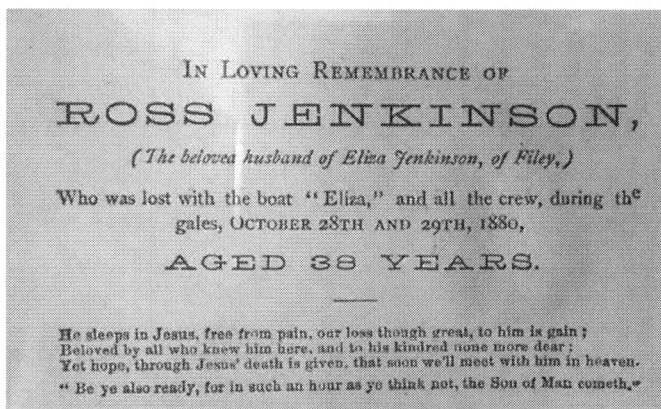

In Loving Remembrance of

ROSS JENKINSON,

(The beloved husband of Eliza Jenkinson, of Filey,)

Who was lost with the boat "Eliza," and all the crew, during the gales, OCTOBER 28TH AND 29TH, 1880,

AGED 38 YEARS.

He sleeps in Jesus, free from pain, our loss though great, to him is gain ;
Beloved by all who knew him here, and to his kindred none more dear ;
Yet hope, through Jesus' death is given, that soon we'll meet with him in heaven.
" Be ye also ready, for in such an hour as ye think not, the Son of Man cometh."

10.7: Privately printed by the family, memorial cards were part of the Victorian middle-class's way of death. Originally sent, with black gloves, to invitees unable to attend, they evolved as a keepsake for all relatives and friends. In keeping with the less florid inclinations of Chapel, the card is plain – no maudlin symbolism in the shape of evergreen ivy, immortal yew trees or angels. It is no coincidence that the two examples at Filey Museum relate to men lost at sea: retained for a century, they had assumed an extra significance, a small substitute for a gravestone, the bodies never having been retrieved. *[FM]*

---

[19] *Scarborough Mercury*, 30th Oct 1880; Godfrey & Lassey (1982) pp105-6; *Redux*, 29th Oct 2017. The ten Filey crewmen lost off *Eliza* and *Sarah* are listed after skippers, Ross JENKINSON and Thomas COWLING, on the 'Fishermen's Window' (**10.9**).

The Great March Gale, 5th - 6th March 1883

And so the depressing catalogue continues. The Black Friday storm of 14th October 1881 which cost Eyemouth a man in every three fisher houses, was localised to the coast north of the Tyne. But even that storm paled in relation to the 'Black Monday' storm which began late in the night of 5th March 1883, reckoned to have been the worst North Sea catastrophe of the century. It was caused by extremes of pressure across northern Europe, causing winds of 80 to 90 knots in the North Sea. Such was their potency that 43 craft were 'knocked down' on the Dogger Bank, mostly above its steep eastern edge. Every boat went down with all hands, some 255 men and boys, and no bodies ever recovered.

The Filey boats were fishing out of Grimsby (see Chapter 7). Two men were lost off the yawl *Amity* 12 miles out, as it ran for shore. One was Frank Haxby, the third of that ill-fated name to be lost in 24 years. William SAYERS was lost off *Denison*. (We had particularly noticed his gravestone (**1.5**) on that first visit to St Oswald's graveyard.) In an unlucky community, the SAYERS and Haxbys were *especially* unfortunate families. One William SAYERS had narrowly escaped drowning on the Dogger in 1867 when washed off the *Jane and Elizabeth's* corfe. His sons or cousins, William and Edmond, had died in identical circumstances in 1859. Perhaps William was expecting such an end.[20] Of the two SAYERS families in Filey's 1851 Census, he was the third of the eight males to drown.

One Filey yawl, *William Clowes*, was saved by the barometer perhaps acquired by Jenkinson Haxby, a previous skipper/owner who had of course lost many relatives to the sea. Seeing a big drop in pressure, the captain decided to flee the Bank, saving his crew from the ensuing mayhem.[21]

Robert Hall's memories of his grandfather suggest that these barometers were prized, perhaps because of such life-saving warnings. *Old Naz* JENKINSON (Q44) spent his last years with Robert's family. The old man had:

> . . . a passion for an old ship's barometer which had to be fixed to the wall when he was living with us . . . . The glass of the barometer was cracked but he would never have it mended because as he used to tell me almost daily it had been broken 'aboard the yawl in *the* March gale'.

Almost certainly, this heirloom had survived the Great March Gale of 1883.

'Old Ben' was skipper of the Scarborough sailing trawler *Uncle Tom*. George JENKINSON's account of the 1869 October gale is highly atmospheric, the terrifying impact of the elements seen through the lens of an unshifting conviction that somewhere in that storm was a presence capable of intervention and rescue. But Old Ben's account of the once-in-a-century onslaught of March 1883, replete

---

[20] He faced his death with almost saintly resignation, as we have seen (p119).

[21] Fearon (2016) p48. Ironically, the yawl reached Filey Bay, but the crew of six had to be taken off by the lifeboat.

with contemporary fishermen's expressions, has no such sense of comfort. It is raw, a graphic evocation of forces capable of dashing large vessels to matchwood, the most powerful portrayal I have read of the elemental dangers that generations of offshoremen experienced out on the North Sea:

> I never saw anything so savage as the great March gale. I have known other breezes as bad in some ways, but never one which brought up such a deadly sea as that, and in such a short time did so much mischief and caused such heavy loss of life.

Ben goes on to explain the smacksman's penchant for understatement:

> . . . bad weather means to him a breeze; if it's a real smashing snorter then he'll let himself go a bit and call it a smart breeze or a hard blow, with a big lump of sea; but the weather has to be something of a hurricane before he'll call it a gale.

He describes how certain parts of the Dogger are deadly in specific winds:

> The northerly or north-westerly edge is very dangerous, for, when a gale is blowing from that quarter, the full force of the waves is driven up against the edge of the Dogger and makes a deadly smother. The Dogger is itself a fatal place just because of this uncommon shallowness. The waves have no depth to swing and roll in, and, having struck the bank, they break into an immense cauldron which is more like a whirlpool than anything else.

This phenomenon was well-known. Another eye witness that Tuesday morning believed a great tidal wave was accelerated by the northerly wind, hitting the rising shallow ground of the northern edge of the Dogger Bank with great force:

> 'I have never seen it curl so high and break . . . waves high enough to fall upon the vessels, smashing in hatches and tearing away masts and the decks with them'.[22]

It was such 'broken water' which truly unnerved seamen, as Ben explains:

> Give any real sailor or smacksman plenty of room and depth, with a true sea running, and he'll be comfortable in his mind; but he gets uneasy when he's caught in broken water. In a true, swinging sea he knows what to expect, but he can never tell when he's going to be knocked down when the water comes from all points at once.

Uncle Tom had been ill-advisedly trawling on *The Cemetery* since 11pm on the Sunday night. But after two or three hours, Ben sensed something:

> I got uneasy, for there was something queer and uncanny in the weather, something that I could not account for and didn't understand at all. North Sea smacksmen work mostly by instinct and the lead. There are barometers and chronometers and such fantastic gear for the big liners, but the old school of fishermen were brought up to use their wits, and to understand the weather became part of their nature . . . .

---

[22] *Burton upon Stather Heritage Group* website, Shipping 120, The North Sea.

When I saw how bad the weather was likely to be I gave the order to haul the trawl, but I had scarcely spoken the words when the *Uncle Tom* gave a heavy lurch and the thick trawl warp was snapped just like a piece of thread. This meant that the whole of the gear, worth about thirty pounds was gone; and that's a heavy loss for poor smacksmen.

Ben took the tiller and headed home off the Bank as quickly as possible. This was a night of severe frost, hail and snow showers. Conditions must have been beyond extreme - imagine hanging on to a tiller exposed to that.

Time after time, we ran before the wind and sea in the darkness, we were swept by a big wave, and I expected every moment that we should be carried overboard, or that some immense mass of water would fall on us and crush us like matchwood. She plunged and rolled and pitched in the most awful manner, but I stuck to the tiller and never let it go except once or twice when the mate relieved me for a few minutes.

Conditions in the morning were no better, and the crew were presented with a frightening prospect:

. . . the shallow waters of the Dogger were just one roaring, foaming plain. I never saw a snarlier sea . . . . At such a time as that, with the freezing wind driving cruelly against your face, it's hard to do more than try and see just ahead of you, but from time to time I looked about me, and occasionally saw just a little dark speck of a smack trying to fight her way off the Dogger and get into deeper and safer water.

Not very far away from me was a Hullman, which had been working on the Bank - it was awful to see the way that the seas were hammering her.

I looked again and the Hullman seemed to be falling into the trough of an enormous wave. You know what it is, I dare say, to be out on the Dogger and to look at another smack not far away which has rushed down the crest of a wave and gone right into the hollow. Often enough she sinks so deep and the seas rise up so enormously between you, that you lose sight of her altogether. I lost sight of the Hullman. I looked again towards the spot where I had last seen her, but not a sign of her was left. She'd been smashed bodily by a huge wave. It was no use being scared by such a sight as that. I stuck to the tiller, and all that day we tore towards Hull.

Boats that weren't 'knocked down' still suffered horrendously:

On board many a smack that day the seas crushed and killed or maimed the poor fellows who had no chance of escape. Decks were swept as clean as if they had been cut by an enormous knife.

They waited two days off Flamborough Head, until smoother water came with a turn of the tide and let them safely into Bridlington Bay. Here, he saw at anchor,

all around a great fleet of ships, many of them crippled. At night they looked like a town lit up.

10.8: 'An iron-bound coast on their lee . . .' Boats could only survive extreme weather by 'keeping their heads to the sea, and keeping well out.' This early 20th Century postcard, *Wreck near Filey*, shows the cost of getting too close to shore in easterlies strong enough to sweep boats to destruction, against rocks like these at Bempton/Speeton. Postcard tastes have changed – imagine sending such a doleful holiday card to your grandma!

There had been heavy losses on the east coast, but Hull and Grimsby suffered most. The national total was said to be 982 men lost, 146 widows and 400 orphans. Many boats disappeared without trace.[23] A board or two of one Scarborough trawler, all that was ever seen of her, washed up on the Norfolk coast three weeks later. When Ben finally reached Hull, he saw the crippled smacks which, like him, had somehow made it back:

> they entirely filled four docks, and some of them were so badly beaten and damaged that it was wonderful that they escaped at all. It was pitiful to see the battered craft - but even that was easier to look on than to go into streets where nearly every house had orphans and a widow.

Few men can have been as ruggedly phlegmatic having brushed so closely with the Rev Shaw's *Fisher whose Name is Death*, but this fortitude did not prevent him ending his account with this poignant recognition of the human cost of what he and his crew had been through:

---

[23] Godfrey (1974, p19) suggests that the Yorkshire toll was over 250 men dead, 43 fishing boats sunk, and 38 seriously damaged.

You can patch up ships well enough, and make them as strong as ever they were - sometimes stronger; but you can't do much with broken hearts - and there were plenty of 'em after that big breeze in March.[24]

By the time of the 1883 Great March Gale, half a century had passed since the first appearance of the early yawls. Almost certainly, these shallower craft did not stand up to weather so well. The earlier luggers may have fared better.

The Tragic Nineties

The drip-feed of Filey drownings was often punctuated by multiple losses when one boat went down. But most swingeing were the clusters, and these came often: in the late 1860s, the early 1880s, the 1890s, and in April 1919.[25] Although regional losses were bigger in the case of the first two, the three Filey disasters of the early/mid-nineties were probably cumulatively the most impactful on the town.

Unity - the need for earnings tempted three herring cobles out to great-line on the fine evening of 27th April 1892, bad weather having kept them ashore all day. Such super-cobles often ventured offshore, but they were small in comparison to offshore boats, far more at risk than a larger yawl. *Unity*, only 20 tons, was by 4am 'a great many miles from land' when a northerly gale suddenly whipped up heavy seas. Coble and crew were never seen again, apart from portions of its corfe, later washed ashore at Speeton Cliffs.[26] None of the four-man crew had subscribed to one of the town's friendly societies, evidence of their hand-to-mouth need to take risks with the weather to earn a living.

Trio - the 125 year-old mystery of *Trio* is a human interest story *par excellence*, the local press speculating for weeks on the circumstances of the boat's loss, with

---

[24] It seemed right that so gifted a writer of prose should be given due acknowledgement, and I was relieved finally to identify 'Old Ben' as I was indexing. Ben Grimmer was of classic *joskin* origin, born in the tiny South Norfolk village of Twait in 1843, son of a farm labourer. The 1861 Census found him tending cows several miles from home; by 1871, he was a fisherman on Quay Street, Scarborough, with a local wife, part of the mid-19th Century Norfolk migration to the Yorkshire coast. Ten years on, and he was master of a sailing trawler, out on the Dogger on census night, 1881. Despite being master for years, he owned no shares, but must have been able to buy his own trawler *Uncle Tom* at a knockdown price in 1886 after at least one owner went bankrupt. His memories were collected and quoted by Walter Wood in his *North Sea Fishers and Fighters* (Kegan Paul, Trench, Trubner, 1911) and are on the SMHC website under *Great Gales of the 1800s*.

[25] On the 15th April 1919, all seven Filey crew were blown up on the drifter *Emulator* when she struck a German mine; six days later, two men drowned when the coble *Annie* was tipped over in the notorious Tide-way which regularly races around the end of The Brigg.

[26] *Driffield Times*, 30th April 1892.

six crew. Had *Trio* been run down by another boat, had she been blown too close to shore and foundered off Flamborough Head, had she been swamped by huge waves? Nobody knew then (May 1895) and the mystery has never been solved.[27]

Trio was last sighted by at least one Hull boat 30 miles off Spurn, probably running southwards from the Dogger Bank for the Humber. Such fleeting reports intensified the mystery. A Grimsby steamer claimed to have seen three men washed off the yawl by huge waves. Thomas Avery JOHNSON drowned with two sons, leaving a wife and five children. Tommy JOHNSON was just 12, yet inherited the role of sole breadwinner in his mother's home. Robert Edmond left a widow, Margaret Baxter née JENKINSON (Q38), with two small daughters. Only Matthew Crawford *Wiggy* CAPPLEMAN drowned unmarried.

The St Oswald's Commemorative Window

There is a touching postscript to the disappearance in 1880 of Ross JENKINSON, his yawl *Eliza*, and its whole crew. These losses did not readily drift out of family memory. Nineteen years later, his widow, Eliza, suggested a contribution from each bereaved family of five shillings towards a new church window recording unrecovered fishermen. Mark Baxter JENKINSON (P32) was also behind the scheme. He and Eliza paid the first contributions towards the cost, and names were collected. Forty fishermen were to be commemorated. The New Testament furnishes much material relevant to the lives of fishermen, the window's subject selected being 'Our Lord calling St Andrew and St Peter'.[28]

Mark Baxter, *Old Marky Jenk*, was a tall, quiet old man, a familiar and sad figure sitting in his doorway at No 2, Sandhill Lane, above The Ravine. To George Burton, as a child born in 1911, he was 'the oldest man I could remember', wearing 'a little hairy hat', round and of sealskin, and light-coloured trousers.

Mary Elizabeth ROBINSON remembered him as a doleful man, without teeth, 'hair down here', and looking like Santa Claus. 'Oh, I'm all run in,' he would say. 'You'd think he would have been about 200 years old,' she told us in 1983. His wife, Mary, was of the tragic SAYERS family, sister of William and Edmond, lost together off the corfe in 1859. Perhaps they shared a sense of the darker side of things: 'shan't have time to die,' was Mary's catchphrase, as she hurried past acquaintances in the street. No doubt many Old Town couples were pessimists.

Mark was 85 at his death in 1920, a man born two years before Victoria became queen, when Filey still had stage coaches. A widower for 28 years, several of his close relatives, and who knows how many crewmates and friends, had been lost at sea.

---

[27] *Scarborough Evening News*, 20th May 1895; *Filey Post*, 25th May 1895; *Scarborough Gazette*, 30th May, 6th June 1895.
[28] *Filey Post*, 25th Nov 1899, 26th May 1900.

10.9: At least 18 Filey fishermen were lost in the Great Storm of October 1880, as listed on the older of the two St Oswald's 'Fishermen's Windows', dedicated on 24th May 1900 to the 40 fishermen 'lost at sea and whose bodies have never been recovered'. Note the anonymity of the 'seven strangers', ie *joskins,* the untouchables of the industry. *[Redux]*

He was old enough to recall Uncle Matthew drown in Boston Deeps (1849); his brother William, off the yawl *Jane and Elizabeth* (1867); his son-in-law Robert Edmond with *Trio*; and son George, drowned with the coble *Mary* in 1896, a few years after his wife died. How could these losses *not* have made him a sad, reflective man? He would be related to most of the names in that glasswork.

New Dangers in the Steam Era

It was not chance that backloaded so many disasters into the last two decades of the 19th Century, for one factor that made fishing increasingly dangerous was the dramatic decline in fish stocks. To earn a return, boats had to go further, and for longer in the year, so that the fishing season was drawn out into more unpredictable weather, thus doubly exposing their crews to danger. Steam vessels were safer in that they were powered independently of the winds that might drive boats to danger on rocks, and could run for shore quickly. But steel parts, moved by steam, brought entirely new risks which were not anticipated.

The steam capstan, introduced in 1876-7, saved much drudgery on herring boats. But the 'iron man' brought new dangers. On 25th July 1914, one week before the Great War, 50 year-old crewman Thomas William *Crow* JENKINSON (P75) was killed in a particularly savage mishap. The steam drifter *Pride of Filey* was 30 miles off Scarborough 'hauling-in' the herring nets, when the steel warp came flying off the drum. Skipper/part-owner Isaac ROSS, and mate Thomas William Lewis, both Filey men, told the coroner how a heavy sea had rolled the drifter over to the port side. With the sudden relief of pressure on the drum, the wire warp flew forward, striking JENKINSON in the stomach. He was thrown to the deck with such force that the back of his skull was fractured.

The owners had only acquired her the previous November, so perhaps this was their first experience of an 'iron man' and its lethal power. Despite surgery, surprisingly available for such an injury as early as 1914, *Crow* died of a brain haemorrhage at Scarborough Hospital some hours later. He left a widow and eight children.[29]

Inexperience was also at the root of an especially gruesome accident on Matthew Jenkinson ROBINSON's drifter *Girl Annie*, as told by William CAPPLEMAN:

> Their engineer was taken ill so they got another bloke to go with 'im and they never insured 'im, and there came real bad weather and 'e was thrown into the engines and 'e died in me grandfather's arms. And they had to pay, they had to go to court and they paid compensation. It would've cost them thousands these days but it cost them about eight hundred pounds apiece. And me mother had just bought 45 Mitford Street . . . . And she had to re-mortgage it to pay the money.

To recoup their cost price (maybe £3,500 around 1900) steam fishing boats had to work year-round, irrespective of weather conditions. So it was on 25th November 1925 when the clapped-out drifter *Research* was swamped, having stuck on a large shoal in Bridlington Bay. Though separated by three full decades, during which the age of sail had been eclipsed by the supposedly far safer technology of steam, the loss of *Research* was nearly identical to that of the yawl *Trio* - both disappeared virtually without trace, and in uncertain locations - no bodies were ever retrieved from either; and each crew was characteristically much interrelated. We will consider Filey's most famous 20th Century disaster in Chapter 13, for its circumstances encapsulate many aspects of the degraded conditions in which the fag-end decline of the town's offshore fishing was being conducted.

As a reminder of these waters' power, it is worth remembering that there have been modern losses in the North Sea and its near-neighbours, of boats with the most advanced design features. Even an 18 month-old 'supertrawler' *FV Gaul*, supposedly designed specifically to withstand these northern waters, seems to have been overwhelmed and sunk in February 1974 by a succession of very large waves in heavy seas. All 36 crew drowned, their bodies never recovered. It took 23 years, even with late 20th Century technology, to find the wreck. As with some of the more mysterious Filey disasters, these losses without trace leave a vacuum that sucks in wild speculation.[30]

Filey's decline as a fishing station had become more evident in the latter years of the 19th Century, though the town's fish-dealers dated the downward spiral far earlier. Their testimony to a series of government inquiries, and that of Filey men whose memories of fishing reached back to the 18th Century, is an exceptionally detailed account of this spiral. We consider this material and the whole issue of decline in Chapters 13 and 16.

---

[29] *Filey Post*, 1st Aug 1914.

[30] An introduction, with *YouTube* links, is at *britishseafishing.co.uk/the-loss-of-fv-gaul*.

11 THE EARLY DAYS OF STATE INTERVENTION

'A Most Unnecessary Attention.' Adam Smith (1776)

Government policy began to impact on British coastal communities to unprecedented degrees around the turn of the 19th Century, and particularly in the 22 years of near non-stop war with France from 1793 to 1815. These maritime populations would have fully agreed with Adam Smith's general dislike of such state intervention, but particularly in three aspects of their lives.

1 Revenue Protection: Cracking down on Smuggling

Fifteen year-old Robin Jewison was taking a horse one night from Sewerby to the *Rose and Crown* at Flamborough:

> By the windmill on the top of Crofts Hill he was stopped by Customs men, who asked if he had seen anything untoward, which of course he had not and then, at the *Rose and Crown*, Robin, who could hear hidden men shifting casks in the cellar below the stable, wondered why the landlady tried so hard to persuade him that her husband was ill in bed. Returning to Sewerby that night he met a cart with muffled wheels, pulled by two horses with padded hooves, and in the darkness heard the voice of the 'ill' landlord, Tant Pockley. 'Now then, Robin, we've seen a lot o' thoo leatly, an' we're alus pleased to see thi, but thoo tak oor advice, see nowt, say nowt, an' hear nowt, an' some fine day thi ord gran'fayther may find summat tiv his likin' iv his corn bin.' And the next morning there it was, a half anker of brandy in Robert Jewison's granary, at Sewerby Fields (Dykes, p58).[1]

In the 18th Century, such episodes had been even more common on the notorious Flamborough coast, but Robin Hood's Bay smugglers paid suppliers better prices, and the 'trade' moved north.[2] When a workman's wage was less than 10 shillings a week, and a fisherman's income barely at subsistence, it was a given from about 1750 until the 1840s that much of the coastal population was actively or collusively involved in nocturnal contraband operations.

Locals viewed the 'trade' as an entirely justifiable, victimless 'social' crime. One Bay man termed it merely 'a disagreement with the government over imports' – hence official actions against it were robustly resented and resisted as intrusions on local livelihoods.

---

[1] The tale dates from 1844. Directory and census evidence associate Tanton Pockley with the *Rose and Crown* in the 1840s, but young Robin Jewison remains unidentified. An *anker*, an archaic Dutch measure, was a cask equal to about 45 bottles. Much of the local detail in this chapter relies on Jack Dykes, *Smuggling on the Yorkshire Coast* (Dalesman Books, 1978) and Graham Smith, *Smuggling in Yorkshire 1700-1850* (Countryside Books, 1994).

[2] Storm (1991) p221.

a) i THE TERRAIN – over 100 miles of indented coastline offered countless obscure landing places for contraband 'imports'

a) ii The remote coastal communities had many little-known bait-gathering descents down to sandy landing beaches, in inconspicuously small bays

b) INCENTIVES – import duties made tobacco, gin and brandy 300% dearer in Britain than in Europe

d) iii Officers were badly paid and easily bribed

d) ii Customs officers stationed singly in fishing villages, were often old and easily intimidated by locals

c) i THE SMUGGLERS - fishermen had uncertain income from the sea. Cash from smuggling contributed to buying boats

d) i THE ENFORCERS - magistrates were wary of jailing offenders, fearing reprisals from local people - and like everyone else they were buyers of contraband

c) iii In home waters, fishermen's cobles could easily out-manoeuvre and outrun customs officers' craft, especially at night

c) ii Cobles met boats from the Continent at sea, taking cargoes ashore for distribution by packhorse, cart, donkey or on foot

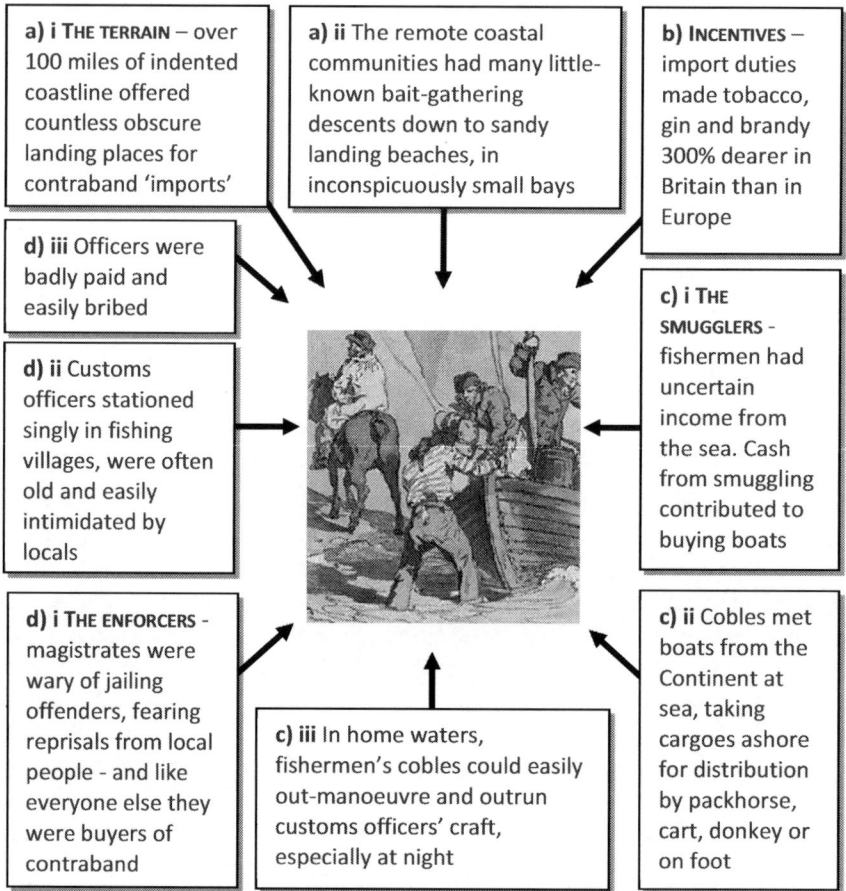

11.1: Why some Yorkshire fishing villages may have been more economically dependent on smuggling than on their catches.

Despite modern preconceptions, there was nothing romantic about smuggling. Bribery and threats or acts of extreme, even terminal violence ensured the only rule of law was that enforced by the contraband *mafiosi*.

a) The Terrain

The government's customs service was administered at the country's 'ports of entry', from customs houses responsible for collection of duties along a stretch of adjacent coast. The records of two of these major ports, Stockton and Whitby, indicate a regional involvement in smuggling on a par with anywhere in the more notorious Channel coast district.

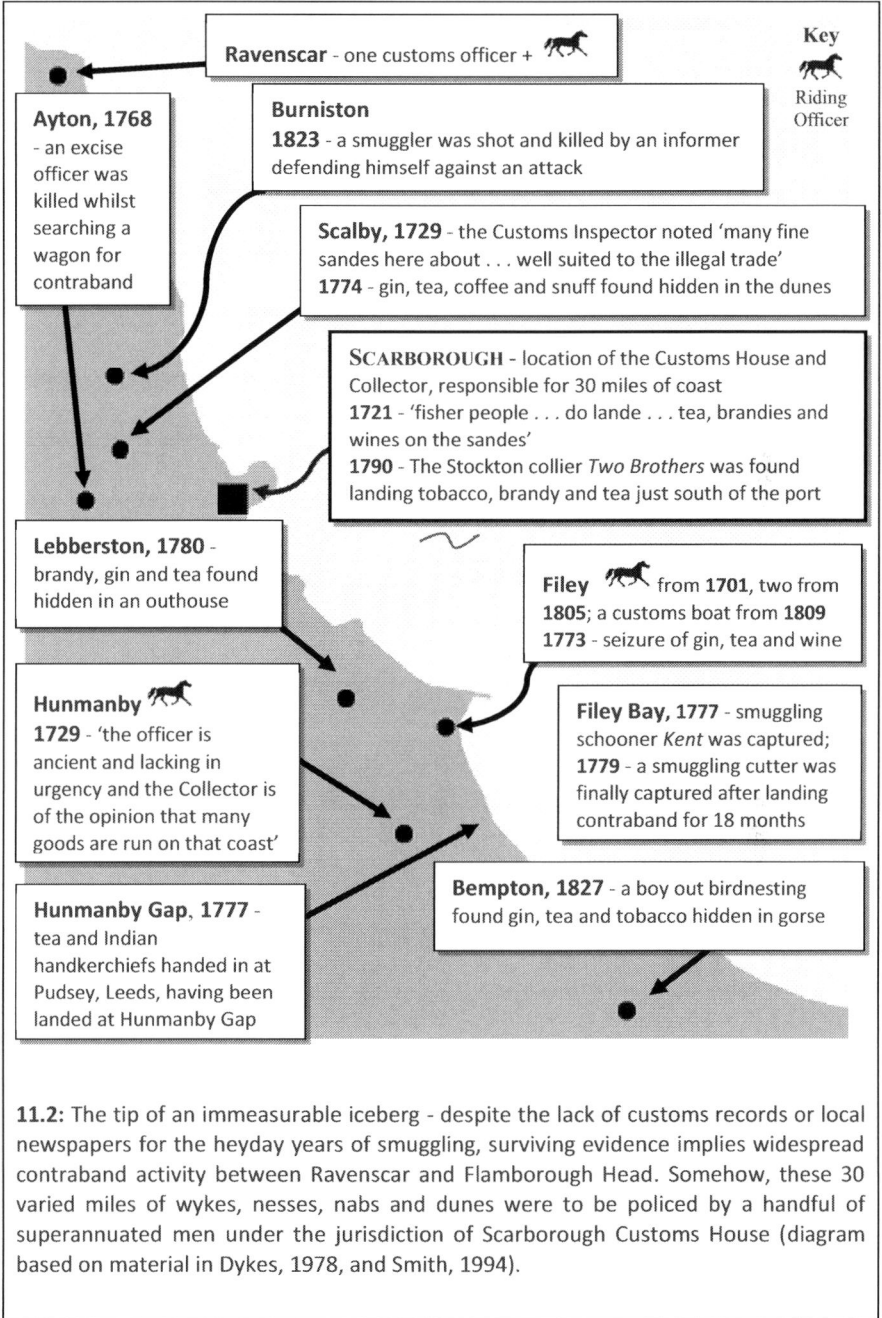

Ravenscar - one customs officer + 🐎

Key
🐎
Riding Officer

Ayton, 1768
- an excise officer was killed whilst searching a wagon for contraband

Burniston
1823 - a smuggler was shot and killed by an informer defending himself against an attack

Scalby, 1729 - the Customs Inspector noted 'many fine sandes here about . . . well suited to the illegal trade'
1774 - gin, tea, coffee and snuff found hidden in the dunes

SCARBOROUGH - location of the Customs House and Collector, responsible for 30 miles of coast
1721 - 'fisher people . . . do lande . . . tea, brandies and wines on the sandes'
1790 - The Stockton collier *Two Brothers* was found landing tobacco, brandy and tea just south of the port

Lebberston, 1780 - brandy, gin and tea found hidden in an outhouse

Filey 🐎 from **1701**, two from **1805**; a customs boat from **1809**
1773 - seizure of gin, tea and wine

Hunmanby 🐎
1729 - 'the officer is ancient and lacking in urgency and the Collector is of the opinion that many goods are run on that coast'

Filey Bay, 1777 - smuggling schooner *Kent* was captured;
1779 - a smuggling cutter was finally captured after landing contraband for 18 months

Hunmanby Gap, 1777 - tea and Indian handkerchiefs handed in at Pudsey, Leeds, having been landed at Hunmanby Gap

Bempton, 1827 - a boy out birdnesting found gin, tea and tobacco hidden in gorse

11.2: The tip of an immeasurable iceberg - despite the lack of customs records or local newspapers for the heyday years of smuggling, surviving evidence implies widespread contraband activity between Ravenscar and Flamborough Head. Somehow, these 30 varied miles of wykes, nesses, nabs and dunes were to be policed by a handful of superannuated men under the jurisdiction of Scarborough Customs House (diagram based on material in Dykes, 1978, and Smith, 1994).

Government enforcement of duty payment operated on a very slender shoestring. Just three customs vessels, two at Newcastle one at Hull, were responsible for policing the whole of the English east coast. The service also had cobles, but these were easily outpaced by the fishermen. And anyone fishing could claim legitimately to be out in the darkness – how then could the odd anker or two secreted under the catch possibly be detected? Many men at the hotspots of Staithes, Runswick and the appropriately named Robin Hood's Bay may have had no other occupation. Fancifully, the law expected *all* exports and imports to be reported to the 'Collector' at the customs house, where duties were to be paid.

In contrast with Stockton and Whitby, there are few Scarborough or Bridlington customs house records for smuggling's peak years. We therefore know next to nothing about illicit trading southwards from Ravenscar, and through Scarborough, Cayton, Filey and Flamborough Head to Bridlington and beyond. There are no newspapers in Scarborough before 1825 or for Bridlington anywhere near that time. But small shafts of evidential light about Scarborough and Bridlington's customs enforcement do shine out from the scantily-recorded darkness (**11.2**).[3] Why after all was there a mounted 'Riding Officer' stationed at Filey from 1701? And why does a staff list of 1757 to 1831 show an officer occasionally stationed at Cayton or Reighton, other than to deal with opportunistic cat and mouse spikes of activity at these remote landing bays?[4]

b) The Incentives

Active involvement in just one night's 'run' could bring a farm labourer or fisherman more in a few hours than several weeks of legal work. 'Show me a fisherman and I will show you a smuggler' was one 18th Century opinion. As we have seen, even a passive role ('see nowt, say nowt, an' hear nowt') earned the Jewison family several pounds worth of spirits in 1844.

Tariffs on some 1,200 imported items, and excise duties on certain home-produced items, were a big source of government income. Duties affected all social classes. Whilst levies on brandy, wine, tobacco, silk and lace might be affordable by the wealthy, those on commonly used goods like candles, salt, soap and tea regressively hit those least able to pay. The price of tea was pushed up tenfold, and cost more in the 1750s (up to 16s per lb) than in the 1950s. The war with France after 1793 brought even higher duties - by 1815, 97% of the price of tea went to the Government. Here were profit margins large enough to tempt *every* member of a coastal community into duty evasion, even those supposedly enforcing the law.

---

[3] A December 2019 search in the online *British Newspaper Archive* for Filey's 19th Century involvement in smuggling yielded no references, although there are a few Filey references in Smith (1994) ch5, and Dykes (1978) ch2. Unfortunately, neither offers clear indications of the primary sources used.

[4] National Archives, CUST91/118.

c) The Smugglers

Canon Cooper had a sensitive if quixotic nose for odd, undated tales of yesteryear, filling his many books with them, however unlikely, and always teasingly sidestepping the absence of any source for these 'facts and fancies'. But one of his most bizarre yarns concerned an unidentified 'great house' on the cliffs at Buckton, the enforced abode of a dwarf, improbably an imbecile Duke of Queensbury. His grace was so immensely strong that, according to local belief, he had to be kept in chains. In later years, when this abode of gothic fantasy had found a more conventional use as a farmhouse, Filey beach-watcher Bob CAMMISH stumbled across a secret passage, unusually exposed by a very low tide. It proved to lead up to the house, and naturally contained a barrel of brandy, which the beach-watcher proceeded to sell off locally 'in ginger beer bottles and jugs at a quarter of the usual price'. The coastguard got wind, Bob was busted, and he co-operated fully. It transpired that the house had cellars and a chain-lift up to an attic. The tale of the chained-dwarf duke was good cover to keep locals away from smuggling activity.[5]

Almost as incredibly, one intriguing piece of family history research reveals that three smuggler members of the East Riding Staveley family were actually Riding Officers under the Bridlington Collector! Conveniently, a Staveley cousin was a Hunmanby grocer at the time, 'a useful trade to move smuggled goods' the researcher notes. At Robin Hood's Bay in the 1720s, the Riding Officer was related by marriage to a smuggling family, whilst one especially big-time contrabander had been a founder of the Methodist chapel. Officers might be 'absent' when a run was taking place in their district. Such local penetrations of the customs service were difficult to expose and eradicate given the *cosa nostra* nature of these networks.[6]

Active and passive involvement were essential features of all four legs of the smuggling 'trade'. Initially, a '**shipmaster**' transhipped legally purchased cargo from the Continent – the risk of boat confiscation meant he expected to earn £250 for just one run. At a prearranged offshore handover point, a couple of 'landers' took the goods, cobles which ran the contraband ashore. Alternatively, a 'spotsman' made the crossing, taking a chance on selling on to a passing boat. A keg of brandy could easily be carried off the beach on a wife's head, as though it were an empty water receptacle. The shipmasters' racy schooners and cutters had any number of ingenious means of concealing their wares, from double hulls, false bulkheads and cavities between decks, to hollow spars and masts.

Secondly, the **landers** secreted their load under known dunes, or in caves. Or they might choose to get the incriminating items off the shore as quickly as possible, rendezvousing with a train of **tubmen**, the third set of players, who stumbled up one of the many bait-gatherer paths with their loaded donkeys. Descendants of these animals would eventually be giving rides to children on local beaches.

---

[5] Cooper (1908) pp191-202.
[6] *staveley-genealogy* website; Storm (1991) pp216-9.

11.3: Filey's extra-legal epicentre, *The Ship Inn*, 78, Queen Street, before its closure in 1910, where crews once legally settled up on Saturday nights, neatly camouflaging less reputable dealings. Smuggling 'county-lines' warehoused Dutch tobacco and brandy for local and regional distribution. Note the famous Filey red lamp. *[FA]*

The tubmen were protected by 'batmen', hefty and armed with staves. A barn, cellar or baiting shed acted as a temporary warehouse, its owner obligingly leaving it unlocked. Some unlikely hideaways were pressed into service in the area - like the crypt of the parish church at Hornsea. Whilst the risk of being badly beaten by a batman or two was enough to protect such places, fabricated ghost stories (or dwarves-in-chains) could explain nightly activity, echoing the spectres associated with houses used by Catholic priests to administer illegal masses in the 16th and 17th Centuries.

This may be the source of the whispered rumours of various hauntings associated with The Brigg, Church Ravine and the churchyard at Filey: a cottage in Church Street with many hiding places and concealed panels was a likely safe house.[7] Flamborough's *Jenny Gallows* is the best-known local ghost, her value to smugglers enhanced by her reputed ability to bring death to those who snooped around the chalk pit in which she had supposedly killed herself. The *Jenny Gallows* story may have acquired a life of its own, for a sighting of this especially nasty spirit was reported near the coast by Danes Dyke as late as 1912.[8]

---

[7] Fearon (2016) p23.

[8] *para normal database.com* website – see under Yorkshire, Filey; *haunted-yorkshire* site, flamborough sightings.

Tubmen paths, like those south of Primrose Valley, and their safe houses, seem fixed in local lore, even though recollections of regular 'runs' are beyond living recall. In 1900, when the peak years of the illicit trade were still part of folk memory, Cooper, could refer to

> one or two cottages behind the *Ship Inn* which still retain the smugglers' holes. These run the height of the house, and must have held a considerable booty. They can only be entered from above. [9]

Pubs were ideal epicentres for local smuggling, cover for the comings and goings of strangers where illicit spirits could merge with legitimately sourced stock. Like Tanton Pockley's *Rose and Crown* at Flamborough, Filey's *Ship Inn* has often been cited historically as a smuggling den. At its closure in 1910, the *Filey Post* produced what would now be deemed a 'Heritage Statement' of its significant features:

> The walls of the inn, which are three and four feet thick, are hollow in many places, and contain all sorts of queer cupboards and receptacles . . . . Amongst the great beams over the kitchen is one which is nothing more than a box with a sliding panel. There is a secret chamber under the hearth-stone, and in a cottage at the rear, which at one time formed part of the inn property, is an upper room with a double floor and peepholes commanding a complete range of Filey Bay.

Further, the report claimed, there had been 'no conviction against its licence' in over 200 years of *T'Oard Ship's* existence.[10] This unblemished record surely reflected the difficulties of policing a closely interwoven community, as well as the effectiveness of the bespoke smuggler-design features listed above.

The fourth, final leg of the trade was the **distribution network** which moved contraband once any heat had died down. This might be big business on a *mafia* scale, with tentacles stretching well inland - in 1779, Thomas Kent of Leeds was described as 'sometimes a smuggler on the coast of Hornsea and Filey'. Legitimately wealthy merchants and tradesmen invested 'working capital', fronted by respectable trading reputations. Men like John Hutton with a 'tobacco factory' at Skelton, York, and a private army of toughs, were openly untouchable.

Such a sophisticated criminal chain was in theory vulnerable to penetration, given that informers stood to gain a third of the proceeds of sale of confiscated contraband. But in reality, the communities involved were too isolated, interrelated, tightly secretive - and frightened - to leak intelligence. The consequences of informing were daunting - in 1823, for testifying against a Stainton Dale smuggler, one witness was viciously dragged around the streets of Scarborough on a ladder, whilst at High Peasholme a mob of 200-300 nearly killed a second informer.

---

[9] Cooper, *Guide* (1900) p29; *Borough Guide* (1912); Nellist (1913); Fearon (2016) p23.
[10] *Filey Post*, 7th Oct 1910.

d) The Enforcers

Unpaid magistrates were the judicial arm which dealt initially with smugglers, but they were members of the community. Imprisonment cost the parish money, and magistrates were some of its biggest ratepayers. They also belonged to a class most likely to benefit from huge savings on the most heavily-tariffed luxury goods. The penal code they administered was ineffective. To avoid expense, government policy in the 18th Century was to escalate the level of punishment in the familiar hope that this alone would deter transgression. After 1736, those who injured officers could expect to be hanged, a penalty extended to any smuggling offence in 1746.

The Landguard, mounted riding officers, did the police work, patrolling their allotted stretch of coast. The new risk of hanging raised the stakes, making the violent elimination of officer witnesses more likely. If cases reached the assizes, jurors became even less likely to convict. Ironically, customs enforcers were as likely to face assault charges as to secure convictions if confrontations had turned violent. The military were occasionally drafted in to assist enforcement, but they inspired no fear. Dragoons were sometimes stationed in twos at various fishing villages, one at Staithes being murdered in 1776. Such men were 'Foreigners' in any district, isolated and vulnerable if they pressed down too heavily.

The difficulties were quaintly spelt out in an account of 1736, quoted by Smith. A customs vessel, *Prince of Wales*, caught a French boat transhipping liquor to fishing cobles off Flamborough. In an attempt to recover other contraband, a party was landed somewhere north of Filey, but had to be aborted. The officials had the legal right of 'rummage', but this was rather harder in practice.[11] The revenue men:

> received some abuse and insult from the fishermen of that place, as well as the mobb of unruly country people that had gathered there . . . . They durst not rummage properly as they were afeared for their lifes, such was the heat of the people against his Majestyies revenue.

Until wartime reforms of the early 1800s, there were very few riding officers patrolling the coastline. No wonder a smuggling cutter captured in 1779 had been landing contraband with impunity in Filey Bay for 18 months. In fact, judging from a surviving customs service staff list, Filey's Landguard was distinctly under strength at the time. The service was clearly a parking lot for retired, ageing military men, superior officers turning a blind eye to their ineffectiveness.

From at least 1757 to 1790, two elderly men acted successively as Filey's riding officer, their tenure ending only with death in service, and of natural causes. Thomas Herbert somehow lasted from 1779 to 1790, though by 1786 'through infirmity not able to do much.' His predecessor, William Hazelwood, had been appointed at the improbable age of 70 in 1757. The Collector at Scarborough judged him 'a very good officer considering his age'. According to the somewhat fanciful

---

[11] 'Rummage' was the legal term for the right to search private property. The job title 'rummage officer' survived in the customs service until 1972.

records of his superior, Hazelwood had aged just 12 years by the time of his death in 1778, 21 years later. The Collector had clearly massaged his returns to conceal the retention of a nonagenarian in a supposedly active patrolling role. Both Hazelwood and Herbert were recruited in wartime, when there would have been a shortage of able-bodied entrants to the service.[12]

Nor were levels of pay likely to attract officers of quality, or to keep them above the temptation to take bribes. In the 18th Century, riding officers were paid between 15s and £1 per week, but this apparent generosity tarnishes drastically given that the officer had to buy his own horse without further allowance, and to saddle, shoe, feed and stable it. At Whitby, in 1723, 'tidesmen/watchers' were paid just 6d a shift for the window of hours when landing could take place. Even the Collector himself received just £50 a year. In 1811, Robert Chew became the 'Coal Meter' at Filey, responsible for assessing the quantity of coal taken out of each collier. Since this was at best a vague and highly subjective estimate, the Meter would have been a saint not to err short, in return for coal or cash.[13]

Tedium and isolation seem to have been central to the work of a customs officer. According to the returns, William Wheeler spent the census night of 1851 alone in the Watch House, Cliff, whilst his wife and children slept at home on Sand Lane. The following visitor account from the 1830s catches precisely this sense of the solitary, unstimulating routine of a coastguard's patrolling duties:

> . . . we almost invariably noticed a person with a gun in his hand loitering about, or lurking among the crannies and huge stones as if to screen himself from observation. He belonged to the Preventive Services stationed at Filey. His employment seemed to be - shooting the rare species of sea birds which haunt the crags; but perhaps his proper business was - to watch for smugglers along the whole line of coast from Flamborough Head to Scarborough Castle which lay open to his view. We have occasionally seen him hemmed in by the tide and almost up to the waist in water. He then became an isolated being, and might appropriately be designated as the hermit of the rock.[14]

Each day's bag would of course augment his paltry pay, being sold on to the town's bird stuffers and hatmakers.

Smuggling's Decline

Wartime led to reforms in the customs service, as state income became a priority. The surviving staff list shows that from the 1790s officers were in their prime, not in their seventies or eighties. Pay was increased, and the Preventive Waterguard was established in 1809. Its galleys now patrolled Filey's inshore waters at night, overcoming the inaccessibility of so many landing places from the landward.

---

[12] National Archives, CUST91/118.

[13] CUST91/118.

[14] John Edwards, *Recollections of Filey* (William Bemrose, 1835) p14.

The Waterguard became known as the Coastguard in 1822. In the 1841 Census, five coastguards were living in the Old Town. For obvious reasons, they lived close to each other, with two families on Spring Row. There were six in the 1851 returns. Their birthplaces ranged the length of the English east coast, and in the case of the Stockdales, from Nottinghamshire, according to family information.[15] None was local. Thomas Crimlisk, from County Donegal had arrived in 1842. The new service was based on coastal watch houses, Filey's being at the end of Queen Street.

Smuggling's disappearance is normally attributed to the removal of the excessive duties that made it profitable. William Pitt's ministry had begun the process in the 1780s. By the 1820s, a pound of candles cost 7d, about a fifth of its 1750s price. In the early 1840s, Prime Minister Robert Peel continued the process, reducing duties on 1,200 items, including sugar. Contemporary laissez-faire economics insisted that free trade was the main route to prosperity and international accord.

But it is more likely that a lessened 'trade' withdrew into its roots, the coastal communities that had spawned it, illicit goods finding a market in the immediate maritime hinterland. The days of mass transportation inland, organised by the Mr Bigs like Kent and Hutton, were over – for pack horses or carts trundling through villages in the dead of night would surely have excited the interest of the county constabulary - the East Riding's force had been set up in 1856.

Sharped-eyed customs officers at Scarborough knew what to look for, especially in the herring season, when the harbour got busy. As late as autumn 1884, a Dutch 'cooper' or 'floating grog ship' had been spotted close to the boats, and the subsequent raid on a sample of herring boats arriving on the Saturday produced 'small quantities of tobacco'. No doubt this was small beer, intended to hoodwink and satisfy the officers who found it. But they smelt some rats:

> A watch was kept upon fishermen leaving the harbour, and Mr Stockdale, having noticed the suspicious appearance of four fishermen belonging to Flamborough, caused them to be examined and about 28lbs of tobacco, a quantity of cigars and Eau de Cologne were found in their possession.

It seems that Robert Skelton of Filey, master of *Rising Sun*, was the biggest of the smelt rats, for the charge sheet escalated to a total of 80lbs of tobacco within his illicit luggage. But most were fined only the value of the goods, and along with the duty, suggesting that the magistrates considered such offences insignificant.[16]

---

[15] John Smith, born in Lydd, Kent, must have been an expert officer, coming from a stretch of coast which was 'virtually in the complete control of smuggling gangs . . . often over 100 strong . . . small private armies quite prepared to do battle with the Revenue and the military alike' (Smith, 1994, p15).

[16] *Driffield Times*, 27th Sept 1884. Perhaps a higher power was less forgiving, for Skelton was lost off the coble *Mary* 12 years later.

New Roles for the Coast Guard

Historically, British governments have handed new functions to existing state institutions rather than create new ones. Thus the Preventive Waterguard became responsible for what little responsibility governments took for the safety of shipping. Its boats gave assistance to shipwrecks, each of its stations having a mortar for shooting a line from shore to ship. Increasingly, these rescues services were taken on by Volunteer Life Brigades, although the Coast Guard was often likely to be first to spot a distressed vessel and give the alert. Coast Guards were also known to rescue sheep that had slipped over cliff edges!

The Coast Guard Station house frequently doubled up as the location for the government barometer, readings from which were dispatched daily by telegraph to the Meteorological Department in London. In the absence of any satisfactory alternative, the resulting aggregated reports of weather conditions were also often displayed at the Coast Guard Station.

2 Impressment, 1664-1815

One of the worst causes of hardship for the family of a fisherman was his impressment for service on a ship of the Royal Navy.[17] Whilst a service pension would be payable at discharge, the Navy gave no assistance to dependants during what were usually many years of absence. In the last resort, wives, children and widowed mothers had to seek parish poor relief.

Britain's fleet was the largest in the world, and the country's main military arm. During each of the country's ten wars between 1664 and 1815, 76 years in all, it had to expand dramatically. Naval service was unattractively lengthy: leave was rarely allowed, since it often led to desertion, so men saw nothing of their families for years. Wages remained frozen from 1653 to 1797, until mutinies forced increases. They were paid six months in arrears, also to discourage desertion, and up to two years late as a wartime economy. In 1755-7, as the fleet went onto yet another war footing, 53% of the Navy's 70,566 men were probably pressed men.

Contrary to popular belief, impressment mostly occurred from boats intercepted at sea. Why sift through the flotsam and jetsam of dockside taverns when someone else had sorted the wheat from the chaff by recruiting a crew for their merchant or fishing boat? In wartime, His Majesty's warships, or his recruiting vessels, could legally stop any merchantman or fishing craft, provided it was homebound. Encountering a man o' war returning from foreign service exposed a civilian craft to the loss of its best crewmen. Since around 50% of jack tars on a given voyage could die through scurvy, warships always returned seriously undermanned.

---

[17] For conditions in the Royal Navy generally in this period, and on impressment in particular, see John Richard Hill, *The Oxford Illustrated History of the Royal* Navy (Oxford University Press, 2002); and Nicholas Andrew Martin Rodger, *The Wooden World: An Anatomy of the Georgian Navy* (WW Norton & Co, 1986).

The Royal Navy's peace time strength of about 50,000 in 1793 rose unprecedentedly to 129,000 during the war with France. This made even greater demands on the civilian seafaring population. At the 1805 peak of the naval war, when British warships alone could repel Napoleon's huge armies, over half their sailors were pressed men.

The Cases of CAPPLEMAN, Crumpton and CAMMISH

Fishermen were supposedly exempt from impressment, since the government was concerned to maintain wartime food supplies. But given chronic manpower shortages, a 'hot press' was often resorted to, so that even legal exemptions from impressment were ignored. How else do we explain the collapse in coble numbers during the war with France from 1793-1815? At Staithes, for example, the wartime number of 42 active cobles had risen to 67 within one year of the end of hostilities.

The reality of impressment for Filey fishermen comes starkly to life through the only two known cases that I have found. The first concerns two Filey offshoremen, and is well documented, thanks to the attempt of fishing boat master John CAPPLEMAN to gain the release of two of his impressed crewmen.[18] In April 1803, the men had been taken off CAPPLEMAN's lugger, *Happy Return* – for them, it had proved to be anything but. Spare crew being in short supply in wartime, the desperate skipper sought the help of Filey Sea Fencibles' commanding officer, Captain James Coutts Crawford.

As a senior and experienced fisherman in his fifties, CAPPLEMAN would be a valuable member of the Fencibles, the wartime territorial navy, and Crawford agreed to intervene, writing to the Admiralty on his behalf. The letter, now in Admiralty records, illustrates how skippers of naval vessels and fishing luggers alike were ultimately competing for the same diminishing pool of experienced seamen:

Scarborough, 5th October 1803

John Cappleman the master of a Fishing Vessel belonging to Filey, and who is enrolled as a Sea Fencible under my command, had his son Thomas Cappleman and another man John Crumpton, both fishermen, impressed out of his vessel in April last by His Majesty's Ship *Carysfort* in consequence of which he has been obliged to lay up his Vessel ever since and has now lost the opportunity of going to the Yarmouth Fishing which is the first he has missed for these 45 years, not being able to procure other men to go in their room. He has a wife and four small children at Filey, and really from what I have stated he is now reduced to great distress.[19]

---

[18] This account relies on Dan Eaton, *Filey: a Town at War?* (*Looking at Filey* website, 2012). His article includes a transcription of the Filey Sea Fencibles muster rolls of 1803, 1809 and 1810, though there is a small mistranscription in 1803's. Scarborough Maritime Heritage Centre holds photocopies of the original rolls, and of Captain Crawford's letter of Oct 1803.

[19] National Archives, ADM/2326 59625.

It is likely that the two were eventually released on the understanding that both joined Filey's Sea Fencibles, for they appear on the muster rolls for 1805 onwards.[20]

Unfortunately, the CAPPLEMANs did not live happy ever after. Scarborough's register of boats indicates that son Thomas had become *Happy Return's* co-owner with his father by 1804, but that she sank in 1806. Thomas was buried at St Oswald's on 7th February 1825, having drowned at the age of 48. His father outlived him by 16 years, buried at Filey on 4th March 1841, at a recorded age of 90.

11.4: Father and son reunited. **Above:** John CAPPLEMAN, one of the few Filey fishermen present at the muster of 18th September 1803 - he and William Edmond were co-owners of the lugger *Happy Return.* They had been unable to go to the autumn Yarmouth Fishing after two of their crew were impressed earlier that year. **Below:** father and son Thomas together in the 1810 Muster List of the Filey Fencibles (signatures to the right). Note that they spelt their surnames differently (ADM 28/7).

The other impressed man fared a little better. Eaton rounds off the story:

> John Crumpton was baptised on 20th June 1779, just three months after Thomas, and the boys must have grown up together; both would have been very useful aboard a naval vessel having spent their lives at sea and being in the peak of physical health. John [died] in September 1844 . . . at a good age of 68 [*sic*].

The second case is anecdotal, handed down for at least 100 years by the time Captain Sydney Smith heard it as a boy. The story claimed that one William CAMMISH had acquired the by-name *Traf* after his return from involuntary service with the Royal Navy during the Napoleonic Wars. Impressed at sea, off a boat fishing for herrings near Whitby, he carried the name because he had served at Trafalgar. We have already looked at the unconvincing evidence on page 56.

---

[20] National Archives, ADM 28, Sea Fencibles Pay Lists, Flamborough Head to the River Tees 1803, 1805, 1808 and 1810 cited by Eaton. They are chance snapshots, each year's covering just four training musters over a period of weeks, and are therefore limited in scope.

The Press Gang

Non-seafarers were rarely seized. But when need was greatest, especially at the outbreak of a war, such norms were ignored. One gang caused notoriety between Newcastle and Hull in the early 1790s, 'especially vigorous in its attentions to the Yorkshire coast'. The popular reaction to its raids eerily anticipated that meted out to the British army in Belfast around the Catholic Falls Road during the 1970s:

> The hostility its activities attracted provoked a riot at Whitby in 1793 and the customary practice of women in fishing communities such as Robin Hoods Bay when they spied its approach was to beat and rattle a drum in such a loud fashion that their men were warned to keep clear. Nevertheless, by one means or another, many of these men were recruited into the Royal Navy.[21]

In a period where riot was the usual avenue for popular outrage, the 602 anti-press gang affrays between 1738 and 1805 made impressment the second most common spark for such collective violence.[22] After the peace of 1815, impressment fell into abeyance, though it was not abolished. Indeed, it was revived in more systematic forms in 1916 and 1939, only disappearing fully with the end of National Service in 1963.

3 The Filey Sea Fencibles, 1803-10

The Threat from French Privateers . . .

In 1793, France had around 75 ships of the line, half Britain's naval strength. French maritime strategy therefore focused on attacking British trade: this had the twin aims of enmeshing the Royal Navy in protection duties, and sapping Britain's financial ability to bankroll allies. During the Anglo-French wars of the 17th and 18th Centuries, France had mobilised private enterprise by authorising ordinary citizens to prey on enemy shipping. In return, the government received a share of the value of captured ships and cargoes.

These irregular naval forces, known as privateers, had a semi-official status which exempted them from charges of piracy. Fishing boats were inevitably vulnerable, given that they had market value, and might be found well offshore. Once captured, they could easily be armed with cannon by their captors and themselves turned into privateers. North Sea luggers, however, were usually far too fast to be outpaced and taken.

To make trouble for her old enemy, France sided with the rebel colonists during the American War of Independence of 1775-83. The threat to Yorkshire boats from American and French privateers led to Filey and Flamborough fishermen coming

---

[21] Robinson (1984) pp62-4.

[22] Nicholas Rogers, *The Press Gang; Naval Impressment and its Opponents in Georgian Britain* (Continuum, 2007) p39.

together for mutual protection as the *Royal Fishing Volunteers*. An improbable contemporary claim put their strength at 500.[23]

The threat reappeared when war broke out again in 1793. Cole's account (1828, page 39) of the predatory appearance of a French privateer in the autumn of 1795 confirms that Filey had become nothing less than a war zone, but that the community could mount staunch collective response:

> . . . the inhabitants . . . hauled their boats aground; and the volunteer infantry of this and neighbouring villages were called out and mustered on the sands, with every other resident who could bear arms. There happened to be a Yarmouth brig ashore at the time toward which the French bore in their well manned boat: at this juncture the infantry fired with great spirit, which so intimidated the enemy that they immediately retreated, and all again subsided into calm.

Such a cooperative spirit of resistance was a natural characteristic of any interrelated fishing community. Many fishermen had probably seen formal as well as volunteer naval service in the American war, so this 'Dad's Navy' was a formidable opponent. In December 1794, fishermen in Filey Bay had seized a grain ship which three French privateer vessels had previously captured.

Also in the 1790s, Captain William JENKINSON (N2), normally based in Hull, was visiting friends in Filey, heard that a Dutch privateer was about to capture a collier, organised resistance, and drove off the attackers by firing 'two or three rounds' with its small guns.[24]

The following account of an action off Scarborough on 9th August 1797 confirms that the fishermen irregulars were especially effective at counterattacks. Their luggers could be reinforced with guns and crew very quickly, and could clearly take privateers by surprise:

> . . . a five-men fishing boat was chased into Scarborough harbour by a small French privateer, appearing to mount four guns, and to be manned with 20-25 men. The

11.5: A Filey resident looks out at us across 200 or so years. Captain William JENKINSON (N2), nephew of Robert and Margaret, from whom all the fisher JENKINSONs descend, was the founder of the line that rose socially. I can't think of many Old Town residents who had their portraits painted! He seems to have been involved in the Baltic trade from Hull, dying in the Russian port of Kronstadt in 1844. *[Kath Wilkie]*

---

[23] Eaton (2012).
[24] Cortis (1860) p24.

privateer was seen very distinctly from Scarborough, and sailed towards Filey Bay. At eleven o'clock, the fishing boat, with about 100 men, armed with all arms and swivels, sailed in quest of the privateer, which they fortunately came up with and captured, and are now bringing her in.[25]

... and the Government's Response

This record of effectiveness must have recommended fishing fleets as an obvious paramilitary resource, and the Admiralty put these volunteer efforts under formal control with the formation from 1798 onwards of 36 companies of Sea Fencibles, each responsible for a stretch of coastline. Nothing was done to implement the scheme in Yorkshire until 1803. The French had attempted minor invasions of Ireland and Wales, but their concentration of a new *Armée d'Angleterre* of 200,000 men around Boulogne and Bruges focused minds. All fencible recruits were to be 'fishermen and other persons occupied in the ports, and on the coast, who, from their occupations are to be unpressed.'[26] Here was the irresistible sweetener - each man was to be given a certificate to exempt him from naval impressment. So a fisherman convicted for smuggling escaped the usual fate, compulsory naval service, if he ran foul of the vigorous wartime attempts to increase customs revenue.

At Filey, the 1803 seizures of CAPPLEMAN and Crumpton, coming right at the beginning of the local company's existence, must have sent many men rushing to enlist. The muster list for 20th September 1803 contains 115 men, 104 of whom regularly attended at least three of the roll's Sunday training days. Seven men in eight seem to have been fishermen (Appendix A). They were split initially into three companies. The commissioned officers were retired or serving naval lieutenants and captains. Each company, around 25-30 men, chose its own petty officer. He kept registers of attendance, known formally as muster rolls, and handed out pay – one shilling a day – following training.

Attached to the first Filey muster roll sent in to the Admiralty is a request for long boats, and nine, or twelve-pound cannon on field carriages. These had to be light, for they would be mounted as bow and stern 'chasers', used in pursuit of privateers simply to disable rigging, so that the boat could be taken. Heavier guns mounted as high would affect a boat's stability. Training in the use of such cannon would be compromised by the Admiralty's notorious reluctance to supply powder for practice use. The guns were muzzle loaders, and the men would therefore drill in 'running' them back and to, and repetitively loading and tamping. One wonders how the fishermen took to this largely unskilled and heavy, monotonous labour. A further source of boredom would be the manning of the beacon lookout midway between Filey and Flamborough.

---

[25] *Oxford Journal,* 19th Aug 1797. Quoted in Eaton (2012). Swivel guns were small cannon, able to rotate on a mounting to allow a very wide arc of range.

[26] Sea Fencibles *Wikipedia* entry. Their oddly ungrammatical title, short for *defencible*, referred to men recruited for home service, for the duration of a war.

It is unclear whether the Fencibles were as unwelcome an initiative as the other two government actions described in this chapter. Despite the obvious benefit of having armed craft at hand in an area prone to privateer plundering, Eaton suggests the Fencibles were not widely popular. At least they acted as a lifeboat service. Filey men would not have relished several years of being forced out to sea each Sunday, on their one day of rest, for a derisory shilling a day.

But the Admiralty seems to have been flexible with the rules. They must have been well aware of the autumnal hiatus in attendance at musters occasioned by the Norfolk fishery, since no attempt was made to conceal it in Captain Crawford's letter of October 1803.

Perhaps the biggest attraction for the men was the prospect of prize and salvage money. As the risk of invasion vanished, with the French naval defeat at Trafalgar, the Fencibles became less significant, and by 1809 the training musters had dropped to one Sunday a month. In 1810, when Filey's unit had shrunk to a single company, there were just 28 names on the list, the final muster being on 4th February. And so shuts a tantalising snapshot of the Filey fishermen of 1803-10 contained in the Fencible muster rolls. Careful use of these listings can reveal lots of hidden genealogical information: linkage to the St Oswald parish registers, grave inscriptions and pre-1858 York wills offers rich leads to anyone wanting to reconstitute the early 19th Century fishing families.[27]

It was to be half a century before Britain set up a pool of volunteer seamen as systematically organised as the Fencibles. Coincidentally, it was the emergence of a second militaristic French emperor, Napoleon III, who frightened the government into setting up the Royal Naval Reserve in 1859. Many Filey fishermen were members.[28]

Let's leave the last word on this little-known piece of the town's history to Dan Eaton who describes these lists as 'a fascinating cross-section of Filey's men taking part in some of the earliest national civic defence duties'.

---

[27] See Appendix A, p439.

[28] Occasional references to reserve volunteers are in the local press – like the granting of long service and good conduct medals to John Wheeler and George Crimlisk in March 1910 (Nellist, 1913).

12 THE OLD WAYS UNDER THREAT:
1: FROM LAISSEZ-FAIRE TO REGULATION

Falling Stocks

'One fisherman told me that they could have taken up cod almost in their hands, and that now they get none.' Rev Arthur Pettitt, evidence to the Sea Fisheries Commission, 1863.

As a Lancastrian, I must be careful not to smile knowingly at the apparent gullibility of this southern-born curate. He had been in post at Filey's Iron Church for a mere nine months. This catered only for the visitor/retirees of New Filey, so perhaps Pettitt was yet to realise that Yorkshiremen, and Yorkshire *fishermen* in particular, have never been given to understating their catch or case!

But the evidence to the 1863 Commission given on 1st October 1863 by the nine Filey fishermen and fish traders, with a collective experience of 400 or more years of the town's fishing catches, consistently described the same dramatic fall-off in the catches of white fish. Fish salesman Benjamin Simpson, and fishmonger Edmund Crawford, named three favourite Filey lining locations and their decline within living memory. This is the only such historical identification I know of:

1 A ground 'six miles off the Spurn', which had yielded '600 or 700 head of cod a day' 20 years before, yet now rarely as many as 80.

2 Dimlington, 'our outsand', 35 miles out, 'in deep water . . . off the edge of the Dogger . . . about clean now'.

3 A sandy ground 'three or four miles' out, consistently declining for 20 years.

Sometimes, it takes just a single incident to bring into relief a massive trend. On Saturday 29th January 1842 the Flamborough and Filey Bay Fishing Company opened a 'shop-cum-stall' alongside what was later Manchester's Victoria Station. By a very tight schedule, fish landed in the afternoon at Flamborough, Bridlington and Filey were carted to the nearest railhead at Hull, to be loaded onto the early morning Manchester train. The fish were on sale within 24 hours of docking, and at around one fifth of the old price. On this first day, the poorer Mancunians flocked to the shop 'in such numbers as to completely obstruct for a time the footpath over the neighbouring bridge'. The entire 3,192 lbs of stock was sold within an hour and three-quarters. By the 1850s, an equally mass rail-served market had been developed in London and the rest of the country.[1]

The inspired pairing of fried fish and potato chips was made some time in the 1860s, any number of Lancashire shops, usually converted from front rooms, claiming to have been the first 'chippy'. The explosion took place after 1870, as such 'takeaway' meals allowed housewives to feed families *and* work long hours

---

[1] Robinson (1984) pp108, 121, 123.

in mills. The genie was truly out of the bottle. An ecological maritime disaster was inevitable.

Whilst the peak landing of catches at Scarborough was reached in the 1890s, Filey's decline as a fishing station is usually dated from the 1870s. Yet well before that, Yorkshire fishermen were adding their voices to a steadily growing appeal for government action against the beam-trawlers which they blamed for the depletion of their fish. Unfortunately, no one then knew if stocks were *truly* in decline: the science was simply not there. But governments had to be concerned because the issue was central to the nation's food supply. Three commissions trawled over the matter between 1863 and 1885.

The most voluminous in terms of evidence taken was the Royal Commission on the Sea Fisheries of the United Kingdom, which sat in 86 UK ports and fishing stations in 1863-4. Just three commissioners asked some 62,000 questions of fishermen, auctioneers, traders, carriers, boat-owners and harbour authorities about stocks and the impact on them of different methods of catching fish. Reporting in 1866, the verbatim minutes of evidence ran to 1,379 pages. The closely summarised evidence of the next inquiry, of 1878-9, ran to 175 pages, whilst the third, from 1883-5, posed 13,000 questions to 224 witnesses. Reading between the lines, all the commissioners were sceptical about fishermen's claims. They were, after all, viewed as a class of men prone to exaggeration.[2] Even today, their claims seem dramatic, localised, and unrepresentative of the wider picture.

But a remarkable piece of academic research has recently analysed this huge body of testimony, concluding that the responses of north-east coast fishermen to the 1863-6 enquiry agreed on an average 64% decline in white fish catches over 55 years. The downward trajectory continued at a faster rate, trawler catches along the same coast falling by a further 66% between just 1867 and 1892.[3] The implication was that a fisherman in the 1890s might in one day be catching one eighth of what his great grandfather could have expected 80 years before.

Bottom Trawling

'All I know is this, before they came there used to be plenty of fish, and now there is very little of any kind.' Benjamin Simpson, evidence to the Sea Fisheries Commission, 1863.

We may not instantly associate trawling with the days of sail, but it was only in the last two decades of the 19th Century that steam trawlers overtook their sailing predecessors numerically. They offered greater range, year-round operation, and

---

[2] The 1879 Report noted that a skipper had landed at Scarborough in the 1830s, laid three soles on the pier, and declared that they were 'the last three in the sea'.

[3] Ruth H Thurstan, Julie P Hawkins & Callum M Roberts, *Origins of the bottom trawling controversy in the British Isles: 19th century witness testimonies reveal evidence of early fishery declines* (Environment Department, York University; Blackwell Publishing Ltd, 2013) - available at *marinepalaeoecology.org* website, *Thurstan-et-al-2013*.

massively enlarged catching power, and would have destroyed seabed fish nurseries even faster, had the devastating beam-trawl not been superseded by the otter-trawl very shortly after steam's appearance.

Bottom alias beam-trawling had spread from the Channel and the Thames Estuary into the North Sea as early as the 1790s. The weight of this necessarily heavy trawl assembly increased with the length of the beam. Before the late 18th Century, sailing vessels were strong enough only to tow a 20-foot beam. But far larger trawls appeared around the 1790s, as Brixham boatyards began to build large, dedicated trawling smacks up to 80 feet long, with 40-foot mainmasts. Devon trawlers could now sail quickly to and from more distant fishing grounds, and tow far larger trawls.

Each year, Yorkshire's local boats were catching herring for the inland or foreign market, just when its resorts were filling up with wealthy visitors, keen to eat local fish. Here was a neglected summer market for white fish. The appearance of this proto-seaside holiday industry may have attracted the southern trawlers. They first landed their catches at Scarborough in the summer of 1831.

The following year, eight trawlers came with the men's families, from Ramsgate, Dover and Plymouth. These brief stays were the beginning of the extensive immigration of Scarborough's 'foreign-born' fisher families. There was much hostility, local fishermen fearing a collapse in prices.

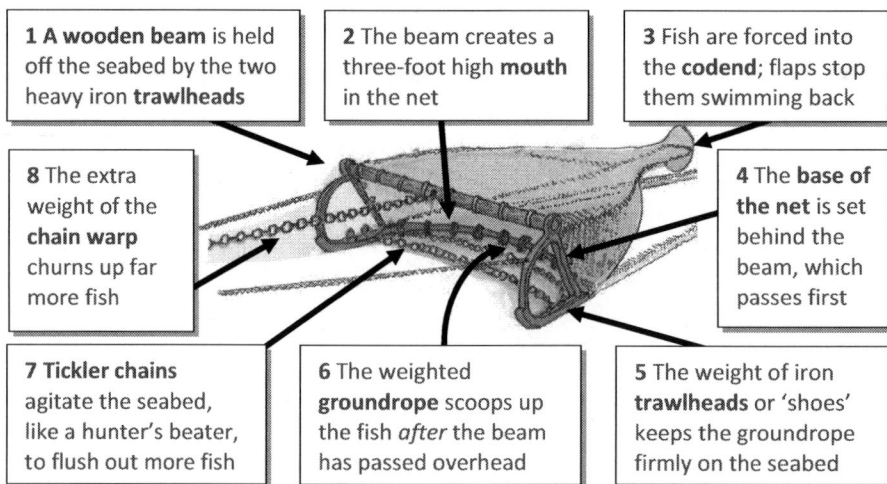

1 A wooden beam is held off the seabed by the two heavy iron **trawlheads**

2 The beam creates a three-foot high **mouth** in the net

3 Fish are forced into the **codend**; flaps stop them swimming back

8 The extra weight of the **chain warp** churns up far more fish

4 The **base of the net** is set behind the beam, which passes first

7 Tickler chains agitate the seabed, like a hunter's beater, to flush out more fish

6 The weighted **groundrope** scoops up the fish *after* the beam has passed overhead

5 The weight of iron **trawlheads** or 'shoes' keeps the groundrope firmly on the seabed

12.1: The seabed devastation caused by bottom-trawling - 'They trawl along the bottom and tear everything that is before them' – a single beam-trawl raked out a 40/50-foot wide, foot-deep furrow, on 20 miles of seabed, in just six hours of fishing.

In 1832 one of the visiting crewmen was stabbed. Despite this hostile environment, the southern trawlers kept coming. There were three reasons, Robinson (1984)[4] suggests:

1 Scarborough's classier visitors relished the sweet, buttery flavour of filleted sole. **The discovery around 1837 of the Silver Pits (10.1)** just 28 miles east of Spurn Head, acted as a magnet for trawlers. In severe winters, cold river currents ran over the sand and gravel beds of the usual estuary habitats of flatfish, and the deep submarine valley of the Pits became their refuge. Beam-trawls easily shovelled up these half-buried bottom-dwellers from the trenches where they lurked for passing prey. Local luggers and yawls were laid up during these cold spells, and rarely went for sole, for lining was not designed to hook them out of such hiding places.

2 **The dredging of Scarborough's harbour in 1844** probably made it worth the risk of fishing all year, not just in 'pit weather', as cold spells were termed.

3 **The first railway into Scarborough, from York (1845)** connected the town with the mass urban markets where the lower quality trawler catches could be sold.

During the 1850s, locally crewed sailing trawlers began replacing the Devon and Kent men as they deserted the town's crowded harbour for Hull. Yorkshire became *the* trawling coast from the 1860s. The Great Northern Railway successfully brought fish to London as fast as other companies could from southern coasts. Up to 1850, only 10% of the North Sea bed was being trawled. By 1900, the figure was about 50%, and by 2000 over 90%.

Filey's hostility to its near-neighbours dates from the mid-19th Century. From the 1830s, a few Bridlington inshoremen were bottom-trawling close to port, over the soft, sandy seabed of their bay. But these were the very beds that traditional line fishermen further north relied on, as cod favoured them for their eggs.[5] Add to this Scarborough's embrace of offshore trawling. These treasons simply reinforced the Filey belief that neither Scarborough nor Bridlington had produced any true fishermen.

The growing involvement in trawling of these local Yorkshire boats, and the invasion from the south, all seemed alarmingly coincident with the collapse in fishing stocks that Filey men were experiencing daily.

---

[4] This account of early North Sea trawling relies on Dyson (1977) chIII; Frank (2002) ch2; Robinson (1984) chs5 & 10; Robinson (1987) chV; *Sea Fisheries Commission* (1863-66); *Sea Fisheries Commission* (1879); and the *Trawl Net and Beam-trawl Fishing Commission* (1885); The International Council for the Exploration of the Sea's *Advice on fishing opportunities, catch, and effort: Greater North Sea Ecoregion* (2019) offers a modern perspective on cod stocks.

[5] By the 1870s, 42 of Bridlington's cobles had switched from lining to trawling. Even arch-conservative Flamborough was turning to coble-trawling in the same decade.

Traditional fishermen were not slow to draw the obvious conclusion, that trawling was the culprit, and needed controlling.

The Traditional Fisherman's Case against Trawling

1 Indiscriminate Fishing - trawling, or *dragging*, of the seabed brought up what was euphemistically termed 'by-catch', fish too inedible or young to be sold. In contrast, traditional fishing gear was 'passive' – it waited for the fish. As Peter Frank (2002, p19) has astutely observed, old-style fishing required fish to be active participants in their own capture, ensuring by a perverse kind of voluntary engagement that they were only taken if they were mature, or decently edible:

> . . . fish caught themselves, whether by taking a baited hook, or unwittingly swimming into a net . . . . Using these methods, a degree of selection was involved: certain baits used in certain places caught certain kinds of fish; drift nets shot at a particular time of year off a particular stretch of coast caught herring.

A number of traditional liners dabbled with trawling. There were 'two or three' Filey boats, cobles presumably, using small beam-trawls each summer, just within the bay, one witness told the 1863 inquiry. But they often returned to the old ways. If line fishing was now so hopeless, why didn't many more line fishermen try, and persist, with trawling, the commissioners wondered? The answer was in their DNA. One witness from Flamborough famously replied:

> We were brought up to hook and line fishing and we cannot think of commencing anything else. We never did anything at this place but fish with a hook and line and follow the herring fishing and the mackerel fishing a little.

In fact, it was the testimony of men who *had* briefly switched that was the most revealing about beam-trawling and fish stocks. Filey's John JENKINSON (N10) had risked the contempt of his fellows about 1835 to start offshore trawling out of Scarborough. He had lasted a year, he told the 1863 Sea Fisheries Commission, having come round to opposing the method:

> We used to trawl for about six hours north or south, and when we took our net we had always a great deal of young fish, spawn, and such like. After we had taken out of it what fish we required we used to take a shovel and shovel the rest overboard.

One contemporary estimate put the level of 'offal' or by-catch at 80%. Filey fishmonger/fisherman Samuel Stockdale dramatically laid out small plaice, dabs and sole discarded from a trawl when the 1878 Sea Fisheries commissioners took evidence in the town. 'These fish are too small to be caught,' he announced; they came up 'suffocated or drowned', and could not be returned live.

2 Destruction of Spawn - the 'soft ground' described by Simpson and Crawford to the commissioners in October 1863 was 'the nursery for the fish'. Now it was 'being constantly trawled over', and had been for 20 years. The 'large quantities of cod' once there in the latter part of March were now gone.

One Brixham trawlerman let the cat out of the bag, describing exactly how the beam-trawl destroyed spawning grounds. He told the Sea Fisheries Commission:

> This ground-rope weighing with the pair of irons to keep it down 250 lbs is dragged over the ground; it goes over the ground at the rate of a tide, and for 20 miles it will scour the ground wherever it goes, and that, in my opinion, is where the destruction is caused. It destroys all the eggs.

Ironically, the smooth, sandy seabeds on coastal shelves that attracted the spawning fish were also a magnet for the beam-trawlers, for their equipment could be badly damaged by a rocky sea bottom. Such disregard for local knowledge, and the local marine ecology, could only pitch the trawlermen diametrically against the liners.

In fact, much of the lost spawn wasn't even laid! Jim Haxby described 20th Century trawlers that 'med a killin', by targeting cod in the March spawning season, for cod roe in particular was misguidedly considered a delicacy:

> Fish can't swim as fast when it's full o'spawn. I've seen Scarborough Market from one end to the other full of boxes of roes[6], millions and thousands of millions of cod. And they say, where's the fish gone?

3 Destruction of Habitats - Scarborough coble fisherman W Appleby, who had also fished by both trawl and line, recalled to the 1885 Trawling Commission a favourite ground covered with clam shells, 'to the back of west rock, that is abreast of Filey'. Fifty years before, the coble could trawl there for two hours and catch '40 and 50 pair of soles in a tide' with a small beam net:

> Well now, you could take the same coble, the same net, the same everything, and trawl over the same ground . . . and I would think we would not get five pair of soles in a tide.

4 Dumping Catches - equally wasteful was the trawlermen's practice of pre-empting market gluts by shovelling overboard all but the best fish. It especially angered line fishermen who could usually sell off most of their catch. Filey men understood the modern concept of sustainability. The traditional saying 'sons to come after, and sons after that' was still remembered in the 1980s.

5 Damage to Equipment - each coble set thousands of yards of lines at a time, and offshore lining craft even more. These lines might lie on the seabed for several hours, the boat several miles away. Miles of crab or lobster pots were equally exposed.

The destructive impact of even one beam-trawl dragged across such a ground can be imagined. William JENKINSON (N8) who dated the trawlers' first appearance locally to 1836/7, told the 1863 commissioners how long-lines would always be 'hauled up' by the trawl, and even dragged as far away as Scarborough.

---

[6] Roes - the fully ripe internal egg masses in the fish's ovaries.

12.2: Unmistakable evidence of beam-trawling by Filey men – small, no-frills beam-trawl, compact enough to be towed by a coble, of the kind described to the Sea Fisheries Commission in 1863. Contrast the simpler, lightweight trawlheads and lack of tickler chain with the standard trawl shown in **12.1**. Note yawl discharging catch. *[SE]*

We can imagine a trawler, probably ignorant of what had happened, being chased by a lining crew who were desperate to retrieve their lines, though JENKINSON had to admit that he personally had never lost lines. It was clear, however, that this was because liners scrupulously avoided trawlers:

> When we fall among the smacks we are afraid to set our lines, and we usually come away.

We were told in the 1980s, that the traditional fishermen may have got their own back. Some of the old gas cookers and other assorted scrap iron *boobies* that befoul the trawls may not have always got to the seabed by accident.

Filey men involved in herring fishing were just as likely to suffer loss. The biggest complaints were levelled at the French, whose huge trawlers, with crews of up to 30, were difficult to argue with. Belgian trawlers were known to carry a sharpened anchor device which could be trailed through any drift in its way.

Several countries had agreed on a three-mile coastal limit in 1822. But did this three nautical mile limit stretch from the cliffs, or from the high or low water mark? Did it include bays and estuaries? International law was scarcely more precise than the 18ᵗʰ Century custom of claiming a cannon-shot distance from the shore as defining the limit. Filey fisherman Edward SCALES told the 1863 inquiry how French boats disregarded the inshore limit:

> Four years since they came right down over our nets, and took all the buoys from them, and destroyed them altogether.

Trawling took place increasingly at night, inevitably encountering the equally nocturnal herring drifters. Each nation's trawlers were supposed to keep three miles from the other's drifters, which in turn should have been lit. All boats had to carry their numbers clearly displayed on both hull and sail, but these were rarely visible in the dark, and Filey men insisted trawlers deliberately painted them on as inconspicuously as possible. In theory, the Admiralty was enforcing the new agreements, but the naval brig *Nautilus* had to police *200 miles* of east coast as far as the Scottish border. By the time of the 1863 inquiry, enforcement still seemed only nominal. There was a gunboat but it had been in Scarborough harbour for two or three weeks, 'keeping a good look out,' SCALES noted in his evidence, with characteristic understated Filey sarcasm.

Inshore trawling remained an issue even after 1889, when British trawlers were also excluded from the three-mile inshore limit. Skippers, were regularly in the *Filey Post*, being fined between £2 and £20 for breaking this law. The most serious penalty was probably the confiscation of nets, which was routinely ordered.

The Case for Trawling

It has been calculated that if no accidents prevented the hatching of the eggs and each egg reached maturity, it would take only three years to fill the sea so that you could walk across the Atlantic dryshod on the backs of cod. Alexander Dumas (1873)

The 19ᵗʰ Century unquestioningly believed in the unconquerable force of nature, whatever increasingly desperate traditional fishermen might say to the three government inquiries about ever-falling catches. Nobody was listening: the various commissions found that

> . . . the populations of the inshore communities had risen, that the number of boats had increased, and that the gross value of catches had also gone up.

British fishing was truly drinking in a last chance saloon of over-exploited, collapsing stocks. The evidence was actually there for all to see, in the shape of the ever-increasing effort that was needed to make a living (**12.3**) and in rising prices as fish got scarcer. So why was there no official acknowledgement until the late 19ᵗʰ Century? There were five main reasons:

1 Laissez-faire - 19ᵗʰ Century British governments were convinced that human productivity only flourished in unfettered competitive markets. An invisible hand, wrote Adam Smith in his seminal *Wealth of Nations* (1776), led the individual 'to promote an end which was no part of his intention', for in pursuing self-interest, 'he frequently promotes that of the society more effectually than when he really intends to promote it.' Put simply, Smith insisted:

> . . . it is not from the benevolence of . . . the brewer, or the baker, that we expect our dinner, but from their regard to their own interest.

When trawlers were, by 1878, often landing three times as much fish as long-liners, wasn't competition making the case for all to see?

2 Food for the Masses - food supply haunted 19th Century Britain, for the country had relied on imports since at least the 18th Century. The 1851 Census revealed that just 22% of its population was engaged in agriculture, the smallest proportion at the time of any country in the world. The 1840s were known as the Hungry Forties, millions suffering from high food prices all over Europe. This was the sobering backdrop to the three inquiries into Britain's sea fisheries, the first beginning just 14 years after Ireland's Potato Famine of 1845-9.

The mass supply of fish by rail in the 1850s changed British diet. It was seen as a cheap, nutritious godsend – dried cod, for example, is 80% protein. London consumed over one thousand million fish a year, around 450 per head of the capital's population. Fish was fried in East End and Soho warehouses, or down back alleys, and peddled around the city by street traders.

The chairman of the 1863-6 Sea Fisheries Commission was the pre-eminent biologist and anthropologist Professor Thomas Henry Huxley (1825-95). He had served a medical apprenticeship in Rotherhithe, a foully squalid part of London dockland, and had seen some of the country's worst poverty, disease and want. Like all Britain's later 19th Century policy makers, he grew up in the shadow of the Potato Blight. This 'Great Hunger' had killed a million people, one in 12 of Ireland's population.

Huxley's commission established that in just ten years, 1854-64, as trawling burgeoned, the annual non-herring catch alone carried by the North Eastern Railway trebled, from 6,130 to 19,600 tons. Filey fish merchant Gordon Douglas might decry the trawled fish landed at Scarborough as invariably 'rubbed, or bruised, or scratched'. But in the context of the mass availability of cheap, trawled, high-protein food for the masses – who cared?

Unsurprisingly, the pleas of the line fishermen for restrictions on trawling got nowhere. If anything, things got worse, for the commission recommended that fishing should be deregulated even more. The Government acted on this advice, so that trawler and liner were left to compete in an open market.

3 The Nursery for British Seamen - another troubling backdrop to the 1863 Commission was the appearance of another Napoleon across the Channel. Styling himself Emperor Napoleon III, this aggressive nephew of the original *Boney* understandably alarmed British governments. Defences were bolstered in the South and rifle volunteer regiments were raised. Britain historically favoured state promotion of fisheries to generate a pool of experienced seamen: they would not restrict a type of fishing that was clearly increasing the number of men at sea.

4 The 'Natural Bounty' Argument - for every line fisherman complaining of depleted catches, someone from the trawling interest claimed the opposite. The 1878-9 Trawling Commissioners were told at Scarborough by Samuel Randal that 'this fishing is as productive as it was twenty years ago'. Their final report noted that 50 times as many herring were devoured by natural predators as caught in nets. As late as 1883, Professor Huxley was insisting that intensity of fishing had no impact on fish stocks. Known as 'evolution's most effective advocate', he had been greatly influenced by Darwin's *On the Origin of Species* (1859). This seminal work insisted that natural selection alone influenced the survival of species, a biological parallel of Adam Smith's 'Invisible Hand'.

All animals outbreed their survival levels, insisted Huxley, especially fish. One cod could spawn *nine million* eggs in its lifetime – only two needed to survive to breed. Mats of herring eggs could be six feet deep on the seabed. The seas were vast: human action had no bearing on the invisible hand of natural predation and selection. Species had an indestructible resilience. Nature could be trusted to find solutions. As Canon Cooper pithily put it, 'Professor Huxley gave the opinion that the contents of the trawl nets had no more to do with young fish than cocks and hens had with Jumbo.'[7] But Huxley's enjoyed guru status in the world of biological science: no wonder the trawlermen came out with some truly bizarre 'natural bounty' claims. J Bartlett's was a peach. This chairman of Brixham's local fishery board waxed lyrically before the 1885 Royal Commission:

> As the crow follows the plough for the worm, so the stirring of the ground brought the fish, and made our fishing ground really prolific, a beautiful provision of nature.

5 The 'Ploughing' Argument - in the absence of any science, this 'tilling' myth of the trawling lobby was hard to counter. The belief had already surfaced at Scarborough in 1878 when Samuel Randal claimed that 'the trawl net stirs up the ground and does good.' The originator of this notion may have been another Bartlett, a Hartlepool trawl-fisher, who had told the 1863 commissioners:

> . . . . the oftener the smacks and the trawls go there the more fish they get . . . wherever we go with our trawls we plough the ground at the bottom of the sea.

The 'ploughing' argument convinced Huxley: how else could it be that a trawler dragging a ground soon after another often caught even *more* than the first?

Traditional Fisherman versus Trawlerman: Who was right?

Unfortunately, no one seems to have told the fish that regularly dragging several hundredweight of beam-trawl over their spawning and living grounds was good

---

[7] The world-famous 6¾ ton circus elephant had died in 1885, as Cooper was writing.

for them. Uncooperatively, their numbers continued to fall, and even trawlermen were coming round to this realisation. One Hull owner had kept notebooks since the earliest days of bottom-trawling – he told the 1885 Commission that prices secured for sole had risen 15 or 20-fold since the '40s. 'The southern part of the North Sea is fished out,' declared another. It got worse: steam power, and the use of the otter-trawl (1895) caught six times more than any sailing trawler.

The problem was not so much the pseudo-science of the 'ploughing' argument as the absence of *any* seabed science. Nobody knew where or when different fish spawned, for no one had ever seen a seabed spawning ground, let alone the effects on it of a beam-trawl. The earliest diving, pioneered in the 19th Century, was for salvaging and ship repair, not for marine ecological investigation. A bounty of cod and haddock resulting from a temporary rise in sea surface temperatures may also have concealed the true impact of trawling on fish stocks.

Modern understanding of marine ecology is still incomplete, but we can now answer some of the imponderables that beset those late 19th Century commissioners. And we are far more aware that species *do* become extinct.

1 Did 'ploughing' increase catches? Only temporarily – masses of dead and dying invertebrates remained in a trawler's fish track after the passage of a beam-trawl's groundrope and tickler chains. These collateral casualties briefly attracted

1 Longer fishing seasons – some lining crews stopped laying up their yawls and began Winter Fishing early, or went trawling	**2 More distant fishing grounds** – 30/40 miles voyages had become 170. The fish had fewer places to hide	**3 Increased size of boats** – new Scarborough yawls averaged 48½ feet in the late 1840s, but up to 70 feet in the '70s

Falling catches, 1840-70: how traditional fishermen survived . . . and made the problem worse

6 Increased number of nets in each offshore herring boat's *drift* - from 60 to 120/130	**5 Double the hooks** were now set on each inshore line, 800–1,000, up from 400-500	**4 . . . and more costly** - £600/700 rising to £850/1,200. Bigger catches were needed to make them pay

12.3: The mid-19th Century's last chance saloon: a vicious cycle of depletion - how fishermen's responses to shrinking North Sea stocks accelerated the decline.

swarms of seabed hyenas. Cod were particularly enthusiastic revellers in such a perimortal beanfeast. A second trawling simply captured these scavengers.

2 Was trawling depleting stocks? Only now are we recognising how important coastal meadows of seagrass are for sheltering and feeding young cod and plaice, and how beam-trawls have chronically damaged these seafloor ecologies. Britain has lost 92% of her seabed meadows since the 19th Century, probably half of that in the last 30 years, though also through pollution.[8]

3 But in time do stocks *eventually* recover after trawling? The link between fish populations and trawling became clear after December 1914 when German submarines laid tens of thousands of mines in the traditional North Sea grounds. Few dared to ignore Admiralty advice to enter these lethal areas. Five near-totally unfished years doubled catches, but only for four or five years. They then fell below 1913 levels, suggesting that intensive trawling had had a chronic impact on stocks.[9] A similarly short-term improvement was demonstrated as a result of the Cod Recovery Plan of 2006-17. Its restrictions led to a fourfold increase in the species. But the return to old levels of trawling after 2015 cut numbers by 31% within four years, according to the *Greater North Sea Ecoregion Report* of 2019.

Trawlers returned too quickly to historically productive grounds, perhaps believing their own 'ploughing' myth. And the *Ecoregion Report* suggests that even after *ten* years of 'fallow', a single trawl damages the ecosystem. Also, there are genetically some 200 different sub-populations of cod, the prince of the catch, inhabiting specific regions, so that fished-out areas are not readily repopulated.

We now know that unlike humans, many species of sea creature produce *more* eggs as they age. This is one reason why four experimental 'no-take zones' established recently after complaints of depletion of shellfish by trawlers have led to dramatic repopulation, once a stock is allowed to age. Lobsters are now over four times more abundant in the small Arran zone, where fishing is prohibited.[10]

In short, the laissez-faire arguments rested on a simple fallacy - that natural resources are infinite. Catches were improving not because the stocks were plentiful but because fishing was getting more efficient.[11] Indeed the North Sea fishery was one of the first major natural resources in Britain to reach through human agency the outer limit of non-sustainability. In this new territory, 19th Century science had no tools to challenge either the free market economic ideas of Adam Smith, or Huxley's 'natural bounty' presumptions which dominated the world of biological science well into the 20th Century. Ironically, Huxley's personal circumstances should have taught him that over-indulgence in a natural resource had consequences. He famously told Darwin in 1873 that he was in need

---

[8] *theguardian.com website*, ENVIRONMENT, 4th March 2021.

[9] Dyson (1977) p274.

[10] *theguardian.com* website, ENVIRONMENT, 25th Feb 2020.

[11] Kurlansky (1998) pp121-2.

of remunerated duties because 'A man with half a dozen children always wants all the money he can lay hands on.'[12]

The tragedy is that Huxley's belief that 'permanent depletion' of a species could never occur had a toxic influence on governments all round the world, and for decades. Britain was the late 19th Century fishing world's Silicon Valley: she had to compete with many nations for North Sea fish; innovation bred there; so British experts had to be listened to. In 1885, Canadian politician and fisheries expert LZ Joncas was repeating Huxley's view that despite the increasing catches of fish in British waters, 'the English fisheries show no sign of exhaustion.'[13] Joncas should have tried to convince a few Filey fishermen.

Hoist by their own Petard: the Fishing Boats Act of 1883

Do you think it will be to the advantage of the fishermen that they should have some government interference with them? – I think not.

You would rather not be interfered with at all? – No.

Edmund Crawford was expressing the universal Filey view in his evidence to the 1863 Sea Fisheries inquiry. This account cannot let the traditional Yorkshire fisherman escape blame entirely for the eventual collapse of North Sea stocks, for he was as hostile to imposed regulation as any trawlerman. He believed passionately in laissez-faire, especially for himself, but saw no inconsistency in demanding government restriction of others. And as the modern world of national and international regulation caught up with him, he did not like it.

In 1883, Gladstone's government tightened up what was seen as the fishing industry's weak regulatory regime. The torturing to death of 14 year-old William Papper on board the Hull fishing smack *Rising Sun*, and the hanging for his murder in May 1882 of its skipper, Osmond Brand, had been the catalyst that uncomfortably catapulted the issue of on-board conditions into public awareness. Brand had claimed that the boy was swept overboard in heavy January seas by the foresail sheet. Only the testimony of the two other apprentices, and corroboration by the mate, sent Brand to the gallows - see above, page 81, footnote 9.

The Fishing Boats Act of 1883 required proper reporting of accidents and deaths at sea, and skippers of boats of over 25 tons to have certificates of competence. Many yawl skippers were at best only lightly schooled, unable to fill in forms, let alone comply with a modern system of regulation. Fines were to be imposed for those not following the rules, and somehow skippers had to pass examinations. Subsequent public meetings at Scarborough and Filey were closely reported, local Liberal politicians bravely trying to explain the benefits of the measure.[14]

---

[12] University of Cambridge, *darwinproject.ac.uk/letter/DCP*, Letter 9126.

[13] Kurlansky (1998) pp123, 130.

[14] *Scarborough Mercury*, 28th Sept, 14th Dec 1883.

They might as well have talked to the fish in the North Sea. With bad weather confining local boats in port for days, 1883 was proving to be one of the worst herring seasons for years. The Filey meeting, bitterly hostile, was held at the Victoria Rooms of the Liberty and Peace Defence League, in Murray Street. The traditional fishermen boiled with anger, convinced they were being regulated because of other people's shortcomings. The chairman pulled not one punch:

> The Act appeared to be one of those meddlesome pieces of legislation that was of no benefit to anyone, except those who would receive large salaries for the work of worrying a lot of hard-working fishermen.

Here was that timeless lament, echoing sentiments that reverberate whenever unwanted regulation is in the air. Impotently, the meeting resolved:

> That the interference of the Board of Trade with the liberty and freedom of the people ought to be put a stop to.

Respected 'community leaders' were present at the Filey meeting: John CAMMISH (probably *Ranter Jack*) Mr Jenkinson Haxby [the journalist added the 'Mr'] and George COLLING. At least two of them were big hitters in the town's Primitive Methodist Society, and their attendance probably tempered excess. But there was no such restraint at Scarborough, perhaps one of the most turbulent meetings ever reported by the *Mercury*: 'The meeting at the Old Town Hall was not characterised by logical and reasoned debate,' it reported euphemistically.

Joshua Rowntree, local Quaker and Liberal (the town's MP after 1886) gamely tried to report the efforts made to consult fishermen. He was wasting his breath:

> 'Some provisions were introduced by the fishermen of Hull' and before he had chance to make his point a fisherman had shouted him down 'We don't want Hull, we want Scarborough and we won't have it'. During the whole of his speech Mr Rowntree, a prominent Scarborough politician, was cat called and hooted at. At times nothing could be heard above the din of the crowd.[15]

Trawler skipper George Marshal perhaps caught the mood of his class precisely:

> I have been a skipper for a long period but never flogged a boy (hear hear from the audience) . . . I do not love the board of trade officials, they generally come round untimely hours, and call meetings in the middle of the week when many skippers were hundreds of miles away . . . there were many skippers here this evening who had never passed an examination, and could not (Hear! Hear! from the audience. Can you take a smack to the Dogger!)

---

[15] The Scarborough Rowntrees, from whom the York chocolate makers sprang, seem to have had a knack for antagonising the town's more vocal elements. An anti-Boer War meeting that they held at Rowntree's Café on Westborough in March 1900 led to such violence that the police at one point withdrew, claiming the situation was too dangerous. The family's grocery shop, store and home were attacked, and the army had to be called out *(guise.me.uk* website, *rowntree/ riots).*

Marshal was old school, appalled at obligations to record activities on his boat:

> Partly this was due to boys being abused on boats. There had been a case in the papers recently concerning a boy who had died on a boat. He had been bullied and the culprits pleaded innocence as they had only been following the orders of the skippers. Boys were often bullied - toughened up and forced into doing the worst jobs. In many ways it was like the army with newcomers forced to pass initiation tests. They would later be accepted.[16]

This remarkable meeting was as much an encounter between alien mindsets as that between Huxley and the Filey long-liners 20 years before. Two irreconcilable gulfs had opened up, one simply being 'how we've always done it' versus the modern world of bureaucracy and regulation. Let Scarborough smacksman, 'Old Ben', sum up this chasm between old and new:

> As a rule, the smacksman didn't own a chart. Give him the lead and a lump of tallow and let him heave it overboard, and he could tell you exactly, from the stuff he brought up, which part of the Dogger he was on, just as you know which street you're in by looking at the name of it on a lamp post.[17]

A second gulf was between rulers and ruled. The *Mercury* journalist caught the nub of the issue in his conclusion:

> The officials and civic dignitaries expected a certain amount of respect for their office and their class. There was an expectation of deference from the lower classes - and that's what the lowly fishermen were to them. It was a curious clash of cultures. A debate between professional politicians and fishermen.

In all this, readers may hear many echoes of the outraged, often nationalistic sentiments of 'Brexit' Leavers, now reverberating throughout Britain as I write this chapter. For underpinning the fishermen's frustration was long-term rage at how their economic interests and way of life had been eroded. It is an enduring sense of alienation – and no coincidence therefore that some of the highest *Yes* votes in the June 2016 EU referendum were clocked up in coastal constituencies.

The bald fact was that in 1883, the role of Filey and other small communities on the north-east coast as fishing stations was visibly vanishing. No wonder people were angry. It was chronic decline, and it brought great cycles of winter poverty and want in Filey for decades.

---

[16] The case Marshal cited so dismissively was probably that of the murder of Charles Newton of Scarborough, reported in April of that year. The 'toughening up and initiation' of this 14 year-old included being hoisted by a line to the masthead of a Grimsby trawler, and then thrown overboard with a rope round his neck (Godfrey, 1974, p21).

[17] Wood (1911).

13 THE OLD WAYS UNDER THREAT:
2: OFFSHORE FISHING'S VOYAGE TO EXTINCTION

'Filey is not now the place for fishermen as it was formerly.' John Sokell (1899)

Filey's Decline as an Offshore Fishing Station

In 1825, with 12 luggers, Filey was second only to Staithes in Yorkshire for great-lining. The domination of the town by the fishing industry was complete – in the 1841 and '51 Censuses, one in ten of the whole adult/child population was a fisherman. The town's offshore boats, the 'first-class fleet', totalled 35 by 1867. There were also 17 herring cobles and 64 inshore long-lining cobles.[1] Fisherman numbers peaked at 202 in 1871, the glory days when great-lining from first-class vessels was concentrated on Filey, Scarborough, and Staithes. But by 1881, the Filey offshore fleet had relocated to Scarborough or Bridlington, those at *Quay* often landing their catches at Grimsby. The yawls were still crewed from Filey, but the town was becoming a holiday resort, with an inshore fishing station tagged on. The 1870s saw a fall in fish prices, as railways opened up American prairies, and flooded Europe with cheap grain. Canning and refrigeration brought meat to the masses for the first time.[2] Some men jumped ship quickly: the 1881 Census found William Edmond JENKINSON (Q59) on his stepfather's yawl *Welcome Home*. Ten years on, and he was a gardener in Derbyshire. But many hung on, through the misery, as Filey's two staple offshore fisheries disappeared simultaneously.

1 The Decline of Great-lining: Shortage of Bait

The fall in fish prices made critical the chronic shortage of bait. In the 1860s, a great-lining crew set off with at least three baited lines (ie 420 snoods, six mussels to the hook) to prime the fishing. Constant dredging of the main mussel beds at Boston Deep and the Tees was exhausting them.[3] The arrival of trawlers brought temporary respite - two Filey fish merchants told the 1863 Sea Fisheries Commission how up to a quarter of a trawler's catch was usually shovelled overboard as by-catch. This offal, juvenile fish 'the length of my finger . . . hardly fit to eat', was passed on to long-liners at sea, at a small cost. But even offal could be sold for human consumption as the Great Northern Railway opened up a mass market in London in the 1850s, and this source of bait disappeared.

It is worth remembering that 35 yawls might shoot over 300 miles of great-line in one day. Nearby stations too had large first-class fleets. No wonder bait was short; no wonder fish stocks were declining.

---

[1] Shaw, *Our Filey Fishermen* (1867) pp110-1.

[2] Frank (2002) p176.

[3] Robinson (1984) ch8.

1 The advantages of the modern fishing stations of Hull and Grimsby meant better prices for catches

2 Falling stocks brought cost advantages for steam over sail, as fishing grounds became more distant

3 Early paddle steamers (1878) were robust enough only to trawl inshore, but they did undermine coble catches

4 But screw-driven steam trawlers (1880s) could reach distant grounds so far accessible only to sailing craft . . .

5 . . . they alone were powerful enough to haul the huge otter trawls capable of catching 30% more per pass

Tonnages of fish transported from Filey by the North Eastern Railway, 1879-1889

1134

1200

1191

TONS

0

1879 1880 1881 1882 1883 1884 1885 1886 1887 1888 1889

8 Shortages of bait raised the costs of great-lining but did not affect trawlers

7 Filey's traditional share system could not raise the capital to afford steam boats

6 Specialist Scottish herring drifters, *Zulus*, outclassed Filey's yawls

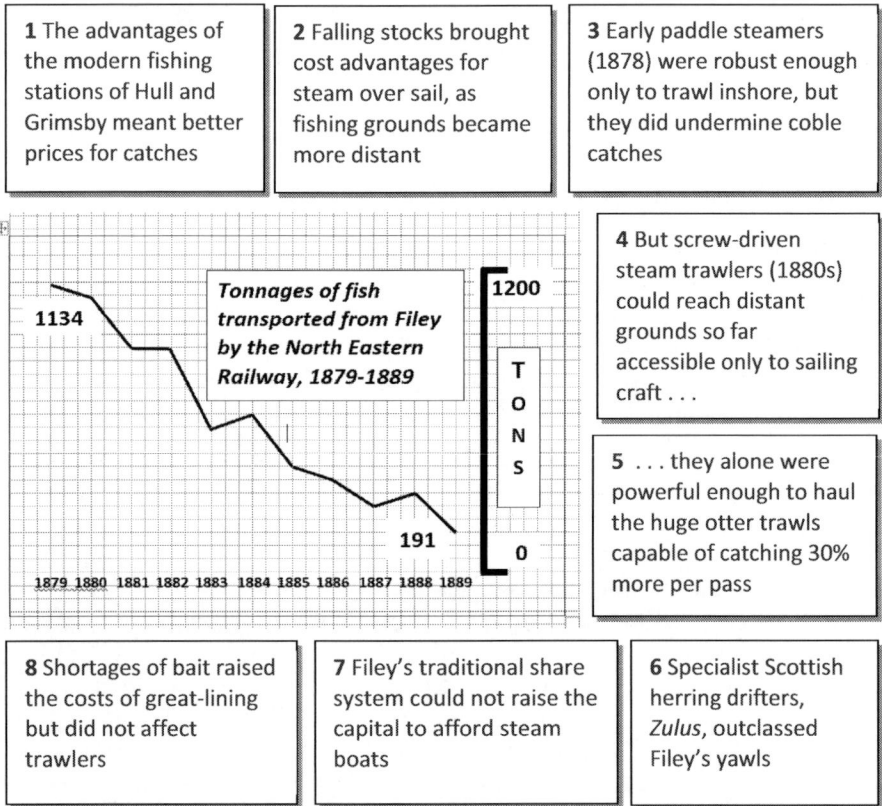

13.1: The decline of Filey's traditional offshore fishing industry in the 1870s and '80s.[4]

2 Filey's Withdrawal from the Herring Fishery

The collapse in railway tonnages from Filey Station (**13.1**), mostly herring, suggests that local yawls withdrew from drifting very suddenly. A Scottish raptor, the *Zulu*, had appeared in 1879, a competitor no less aggressive than the eponymous warriors who were giving British troops a seriously hard time in southern Africa that year. The Scots were reputedly sympathetic to the invaded Africans. Like their fierce warrior namesakes, the Scottish *Zulus* were the speedy giants of fishing craft. Up to 80 feet long, with narrow beam, steeply raked stern, and short keel, they could make 11 knots, and be out and back the same day. The great fleets of drift nets they alone could tow had suddenly become feasible with the invention in 1876/7 of the 'iron man' steam capstan. In contrast, the Yorkshire boats were out overnight, had

---

[4] Table based on Robinson (1984) p358. According to Bill Farline, one Filey stationmaster reckoned that on one day in the 1870s as many as 160 fish vans had left the town.

to salt at sea, and so commanded lower prices, in years when fish generally were selling for less. Whether the swims were thin, or there was a glut, the first boats in made the better price. When bonanza catches alternated with famine, as in the 1880s, *Zulus* were back before glut prices dropped through the floor; if catches had been poor, prices were still highest when the first boats got in.[5]

Late arrival could be a disaster. In 1906, one Eyemouth boat landed a huge catch of around 100,000 herring, yet could not sell at £5 for the lot. 'Herrings were so plentiful,' noted a local newspaper, 'that even the chemical and manure factories had to close their gates against their reception.' Skippers sometimes dumped entire catches. By the early 1900s, Yorkshire yawls were becoming fit only for crabbing, or scrap. In contrast, the last *Zulu* under sail was still drifting in 1939. One that had been motorised only ceased fishing in 1968.[6]

This is the standard version of Yorkshire's abandonment of the herring fishing, but these were Filey men, and there were some diehards. Tommy Flynn worked on Scarborough's last yawls during the Great War. He told us in 1985 how Filey men were characteristically the last to carry on with the tradition of going down to the Yarmouth and Lowestoft autumn herring fisheries from Scarborough. Tommy recalled sailing occasionally to Norfolk with *Jack Sled* JENKINSON (P49) one of the last Filey skippers in at least two centuries to make the annual trip.

Such was the quality of the *Zulus* that they were still being built in 1910, at a time when up to a dozen yawls from Bridlington, Filey and Scarborough were ignominiously crabbing off Holderness. It was as if the fastest-ever steam engine, A4 Pacific *Mallard*, were reduced to shunting coal trucks. But as late as 1908, JS Wane observed some Filey men travelling by train to join their boats at Whitby, where herring were being landed. It was Monday 7th September, so it seems that they were drifting right at the end of the Yorkshire season. The end came after 1914, as German minefields rendered these grounds too dangerous. A yawl's only value was as scrap, as wartime shortages pushed up prices of wood and copper fittings. By 1918, the survivors of the old first-class fleet had been broken up in Scarborough harbour, *William Clowes* enjoying a brief stay of execution until 1922 as the local yacht club's headquarters. According to the 1911 Census, its 67 year-old caretaker, delightfully, was none other than that veritable A4 Pacific of the Dogger, Benjamin *Old Ben* Grimmer.

3 Steam

Steam added the nails to the coffin.[7] The age of steam passed Filey by, for without a dock, steam drifters simply could not function. Yet ironically, Filey men were in its vanguard locally – though at neighbouring stations with harbours.

---

[5] Robinson (1984) pp344-6.

[6] Kate Newland, *The Zulu Herring Drifter* (*bf494.co.uk* website, *assets/1998.pdf*).

[7] This account relies on Robinson (1984), especially ch8, and Captain Sydney Smith.

13.2: *William Clowes*, a 58′ yawl, built by Robert Skelton in 1860, and owned by Jenkinson Haxby, survived until 1922 as the very last of 't'ord yalls'. Photographed in reduced circumstances at Scarborough c1900, its corfe is moored left foreground. On its left, another yawl is apparently being broken up. *[George Scales Collection]*

Steam trawling experiments had been made with tugs in the late 1870s, though they were safe enough only to work within 12 miles or so of shore. But the arrival of screw-driven boats in the 1880s allowed steam-fishing out on the grounds that had so far been accessible only to sail-powered craft. These powerful new boats easily hauled the newly devised otter trawl (c1883) which could sweep up around 30% more per pass than the beam-trawl. Despite the folklore that its name derived from the Normandales' steam trawler *Otter*, the dates don't fit, for this Scarborough boat was only built in 1888.

Trawlers were over 100 feet long, dimensions which strained at the limits of wooden technology: their powerful engines also required steel hulls. Steam power was costly, and so came late to the undercapitalised Yorkshire fishing trade. Scarborough struggled – the harbour was designed for yawls of half the size, it was tidal, unlike Hull and Grimsby, and it was a long way from any coalfield. There had been a rash of local bankruptcies in the late '80s, which undermined any will to invest.

The increased costs were usually met by raising capital through a share issue, investors protected by limited liability. This was the model adopted by Richard Ferguson *Clicker* CAMMISH, whose Filey United Steam Trawling Co Ltd owned four trawlers, and managed others. Operating from 1918 to 1963, from West Pier, Scarborough, and also apparently from *Clicker's* front-room on Raincliffe Avenue, this was a new form of collective ownership, 'with shareholders from across all the fishing-related trades in the town, including not just boat builders but also those supplying provisions for the vessels.'[8] Perhaps it worked as Filey's version of the new market capitalism. It certainly worked for the *Clickers*.

Steam drifters filled a niche at Scarborough. They were 20-30 feet shorter than steam trawlers, fitted the harbour better, yet could haul the great fleets of steel warps and a hundred or more herring nets. Sailing craft had been at the mercy of the wind, lacking manoeuvrability: it was, impossible to shoot lines windward, or fish very close to rocky shore. A change in wind direction or strength could prevent entry into any tidal harbour, leaving the crew stuck with a deteriorating catch, waiting for the next tide. Yorkshiremen got to know steam drifters at the Norfolk herring fishery, which is why the earliest ones were bought from there. Scarborough shipbuilders, however, readily adapted their carpentry skills: up to the Great War, steam drifters were almost entirely made out of oak.

Filey men in particular took to them, and were the first to own them at Scarborough. Whereas trawlers went out for weeks, steam drifters returned to port the same day, with a fresh catch for the best prices. And the crews could retain a family life. Moreover, the annual rhythms of lugger and yawl fitted drifters well, for they could be used for great-lining too. You would *never* see a steam trawler lining. Steam drifters probably gave traditional offshore Filey fishing a few more decades - family crews, direct ownership by one or two men, and gear provided by sharemen.

Of course, a prospective convert to steam needed some technical skill, and access to around £3,500, or at least a partner or two. But the actual fishing processes were barely affected. William JENKINSON (*Billy Trummy*, Q46) his nephew Richard Cammish JENKINSON (R53) and Matthew *Matty Airy* Crimlisk got round the cost hurdle by forming a partnership and dipping into the second-hand market. They bought the doomed *Emulator* on 10th January 1913.

The Watkinsons were the second Filey partnership to get into steam: *Billy Butter*, William Jenkinson (1867-1915) finally sold the yawl *Good Intent* to the breaker's yard in 1913. Then he rented and weeks afterwards bought the 12-year old drifter, *Lord Kitchener* with his two sons.[9]

---

[8] *exploringfileyspast.co.uk* website, *lastoftheline.*

[9] Scales, *A-Z Boat Index.*

13.3: *Billy Butter* Senior, William Jenkinson Watkinson (1867-1915) took steam drifter *Lord Kitchener* 'into the minefields and fished – made a fortune', in Terence COLLINS' words. He was worth £2,915 at his death in 1915, c£170,000 at today's values. *[Photo: SE]*

These Scarborough steam pioneers had reasoned that this new motive power would get them out and back quickly to and from the ever more distant grounds, so that the expense of buying ice could be reduced.

Also, a steam boat's supreme manoeuvrability would help when negotiating the tightly-packed dock at Scarborough.

From Cooperatives to Uber: Leases replace Shares

Only skipper, mate and engineer were skilled – the other drifter crewmen were usually deck hands. But shades of Filey's old cooperative model persisted initially, for even these 'maritime labourers' received a share of the profits if they contributed gear. High initial costs, however, made owners like the *Butter* and the *Trummy* threesomes unusual - most drifters were company-owned, and leased to the skipper.[10] There was far more to go wrong, and insurance was costly. The owners took about half the profits, so the pool from which skipper and crew took their shares was far smaller than on the old yawls. A century in advance, this leasing arrangement anticipated the *Uber* model of operation, owners offloading risk onto workers: if the crew would not accept the terms then somebody else would.

An undated newscutting reports how *Codge* and his crew, on the drifter *Girl Annie* (**13.5, 13.6**), would alone be suffering the cost of the full drift of nets lost in a recent storm. The practice in the brisk period of taking on *joskins* continued on the steam drifters.

---

[10] One informant reckoned the *Butters'* operation later acquired capital through Robert Watkinson's 1922 marriage to Mary Priscilla JENKINSON (Q78). This in turn had come from lay preacher Jenkinson HAXBY's estate. He and wife Sophia had been childless.

Mast retained as a crane to unload the catch	Thin, high funnel ('woodbines') cleared smoke and steam safely away from deck operations	Mizzen sail, hoisted to steady boat when nets were drifting

Steam capstan ('iron man') - a winch to haul in nets

Screw propeller, perfected in the 1880s, stopped the slippage associated with paddle steamers . . .

Steel hulls after WWI and division into watertight sections – far less risk of being swamped in heavy sea	40-50 tons, 80-90 feet - extra length. So more nets, and bigger catches	. . . 9-11 knots whatever the weather, faster journeys from the fishing grounds with a fresh catch, earning best prices

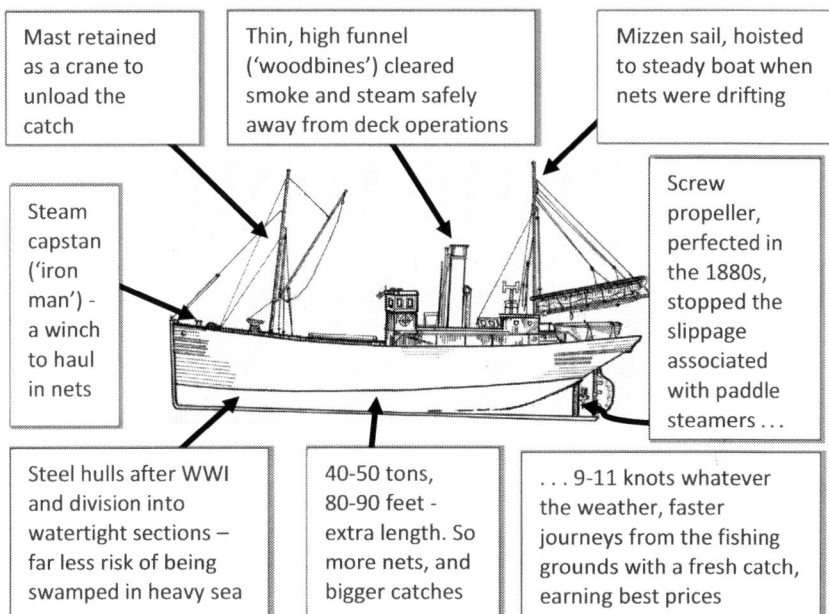

13.4: The steam drifter, c1905, direct successor to the yawl, in widespread use along the British coast from the 1890s to the 1960s, and especially favoured by Filey men. Cost c£3,500, gear c£750, inefficient engine, coal costs therefore high – usually beyond the share system, and therefore often owned and operated by companies.

A new post-war age of diminishing revenue did not support the old share system. Declining catches also created tensions, for wage labour expected payment whatever the catch, even if a yawl 'laid up bad', not having the variable expectation of the shareman in the outcome of any venture. In one tiny makeweight from the *Filey Post* (10th August 1878) we glimpse an early instance of this divergence of economic interest. Filey's George JENKINSON (O39) was experiencing the notorious unpredictability of the herring shoals. Having taken on William French at 21s a week, he told him as the boat was about to set off from Scarborough for a second week's fishing that 'if they did not get any fish he could not pay any wages'. French objected to this change of terms and was put ashore. Bridlington Petty Sessions awarded him a week's wages and two shillings compensation.

After the Great War, the iron laws of unsustainability, barely understood at the time, finally razed herring stocks: the fish's prodigious reproductive capacities might result in shoals measured in miles, but even this fecundity couldn't protect it from a rapidly increasing industrial scale of human predation. In the 1913 season, the number of boats in Yarmouth alone reached an historic peak of 1,006, whilst some *2,000 miles* of drift nets were shot nightly from out of Lowestoft.

13.5: A fine painting of steam drifter, *Girl Annie*, owned by Matthew Jenkinson ROBINSON, but named after the daughter of the skipper Robert *Codge* CAMMISH. Note the signature of George Race, 1928, a talented 'pierhead painter', who speculatively painted such portraits for the seamen who crewed them – like a later seafront photographer! 'The paintings were of a broadside view with the sails set, exact and generally technically accurate.' Pierhead painters had to work quickly, for their prospective clients did not stay long (see *artuk.org/discover/artists/race-george*). [Photo: FM]

Warships were accused of having driven away the herring shoals at Staithes.[11] But the real problem was post-1918 economics: the British herring fishery never recovered from the total loss of the Eastern European and Russian markets in the Great War. Adaptation of the otter trawl for herring fishing added to the arsenal of human assault, and by 1913 the practice had spread to Scarborough and Grimsby. In that peak year, more than a *third of a million tons* of herring were landed at English and Welsh ports. By 1938, this had fallen by two thirds. At Scarborough in the same 25-year period, the tonnage fell from 6,406 to just 307. By 1967, overfishing had all but eliminated the fishery. In that year, Yarmouth - 'Bloateropolis' - landed just one three hundredth of its peak tonnage of 1913. As William Butler Yeats put it, 'The herring are not in the tides as they were of old'.

The Filey extract from the wartime emergency census of 1939, the *National Register* (**13.7**), shows how local men reacted to the collapse of offshore fishing. Many simply moved to an inshore living, coble fishing with two relatives or neighbours, in the Old Town way.

---

[11] Clark (1982) p22.

13.6: The unglamorous reality of offshore fishing - a fine, grittily cheerful shot of the crew of nine of *Girl Annie* (**13.5**). Robert Jenkinson Watkinson CAMMISH is probably seated. *[Ian CAMMISH]*

But some offshore men, like Charles HUNTER, hung on, commuting to nearby ports, fishing as gearmen of sorts on drifters and even trawlers, or being hired by the week. The distress of those who stayed was masked, as men accepted the lower earnings of coble fishing, or summer 'spawing', ie sailing visitors around the bay. A seasonal cycle of Winter Fishing poverty, often mentioned in the local press, was contained only by a widespread, large scale communal generosity (Chapter 20).

The Loss of *Research*, 25th November 1925[12]

Few Filey gravestones anchor the bald reality of offshore fishing's chronic decline in the experience of individual families quite as powerfully as F87, situated appropriately at the seaward end of St Oswald's churchyard. Not one of the six family members named on the stone is buried there, for none has ever been retrieved. Five of them were lost with *Research*, during the Winter Fishing of 1925, and the approaching centenary is likely to prompt many visits to this poignant stone. Its crew of nine, all lost without trace, were scratching out a living on a worn out, unseaworthy steam drifter, at the bottom end of the pyramid of sub-hiring, where maintenance seems to have always been someone else's job.

---

[12] This account uses *Redux's Looking at Filey* website; Kath Wilkie, *Filey Genealogy & Connections;* and *wrecksite.eu.* website. Other sources are cited in the text.

13.7: Old Filey, as glimpsed in the September 1939 *National Register*, a wartime census. Most Filey fishermen worked their own inshore cobles. But Charles W HUNTER was one of many now articled by the week to work on deep-sea boats out of nearby harbours, returning by train at weekends. Note the focus of this quasi-census, which was to enable rationing, and list military potential, eg senior lifeboat experience.[13]

ADDRESS.	SCHEDULE.		SURNAMES AND OTHER NAMES.
	No.	Sub. No.	
1	2	3	4
3 Providence Place	63	4	Jakinson George W
2 Ditto	64	1	Wixsill Crompton
		2	Wixsill Isabella
		3	Wixsill James
			This r
			This r
18 Ditto	65	1	Hunter Charles W
		2	Hunter Helcia

E.D. Letter Code ABEA .... Borough, U.D. or R.D. Filey

Filey's most famous fishing tragedy was a strangely fresh memory for many local people we spoke to in the 1980s. Steam-powered fishing boats were rarely swamped in very heavy sea as so many yawls had been, for they could power to safety. Without extensive rigging, they presented less of a profile to the elements, and so could survive extreme winter conditions.

But even the lower centre of gravity, or the division of the hull into watertight compartments, couldn't save a steam boat from the worst seas. Sometimes that centre of gravity could be *too* low. On this particular day, *Research* succumbed to a fateful combination of unseaworthiness and an exceptionally strong blizzard.

Skipper *Jack Sled* JENKINSON was what sociologists now call a 'remainder', a craft worker whose traditional living has been eclipsed by technological change. Long after the days of sail, *Sled* stuck resolutely to old-school Filey fishing. Not for him the modern, impersonal hiring of whoever might present as crew: he sailed with family and friends in the Filey way. Perpetuation of tradition was to cause a tragedy in its true sense. For this essential aspect of his character led inescapably to the deaths of eight Filey men, five from his family.

The *Sled* family had been dogged by recent tragedy. Just six years before, Jack had lost a nephew and two great nephews when *Emulator* was blown up by a German mine. A third great nephew, Thomas JENKINSON (R54), had been killed in action on the Western Front on 25th April 1915. *Jack Sled's* own son, James Henry Newby, was lost off Ravenscar on 13th December 1911, aged 19.

---

[13] When the Register was released in 2015, the 100-year rule meant that entries for those born after 1915 were redacted , to conceal data on living persons. If someone born after 1915 wasn't blacked out, the assumption is that they were known to have died. *[National Archives]*

O.V.S.P. or I.	M. or F.	BIRTH- Day	Year	S.M.W. or D.	PERSONAL OCCUPATION.	See INSTRUCTIONS.
5	6	7	8	9	10	11
	M	16 Aug 19		S	Fisherman Inshore	
	M	23 April 93		M	Fisherman Inshore	Second Coxswain Royal National Lifeboat
	F	13 Inch 94		M	Unpaid Domestic Duties	
	M	28 ... 16		S	Fisherman Inshore	

record is officially closed.

record is officially closed.

| | M | 31 Jan 04 | | M | Deep Sea Fisherman | Weekly article |
| | F | 18 Dec 07 | | M | Unpaid Domestic Duties | |

He and two other men were out working the nets from the herring coble *Swanland Hall* when its corfe capsized. His father dived off the coble, trying to get all three onto the up-turned hull: *Sled*, unusually for a fisherman, was a strong swimmer, but as he got one onto the hull, another would lose his grip and fall back into the sea.

James left a fiancée, Mary Ellen JENKINSON (Q101), with child. A family account has it that news of his drowning sent her into labour, a daughter Jane Baxter being born days later. One other man who drowned, George SCALES, had been married six weeks.

Sled had frequently sailed in steam drifters: low incomes were forcing fishermen into a risky sector, where raw and impersonal commercialism was king. After the Great War, as catches fell, and pre-1914 overseas markets were not regained, fishing incomes plummeted. Boats generally fell into disrepair, but *Sled* had really reached the fag end of the operational food chain with *Research*. Owned by Melrose, T & Sons of Hull, but managed by the Filey United Steam Trawling Company, the vessel was 'a poor affair, worn out,' Captain Smith told us. It was one of the oldest drifters sailing out of Scarborough.

Terence COLLINS reckoned that for years after, on many an evening, the disaster was a recurring topic of conversation. Everyone agreed that *Research* 'should never have been at sea . . . in Filey Bay in a flat calm you could bend over and wash your hands in't water o'er t'stern.'

The details of that wreck had stayed with people. Of all the hours we spent with Captain Smith, I think this was the one occasion, as he related the story, when I saw him deeply moved. He had known these men personally for over ten years, having baited for them since the age of seven. The last Filey men to see the crew of *Research* alive, Sydney reckoned, were *Denk* Major, and Mark and Reuben Scotter. They were on a steam drifter heading for a harbour as the wind got up.

13.8: In very distinctive seaboots, incongruously near Carr Gate Hill, c1918. Front row, **L to R**: --- RICHARDSON, James *Bass* Wyville, Edmond *Almond* CAMMISH, John Wm S SAYERS, --- Baxter; back row, **L to R**: Robert *Robin Sled* JENKINSON, standing (Q52, drowned from *Research*, 1925), Mortimer SCALES (lost off the coble *Annie*, 21st April 1919 aged 42). *[FA]*

> They passed within 60 yards of the *Research* and Reuben called, 'It's time you were gettin' in, Jack. Run for Brid'. The crew waved to *Denk*, and he waved back. Within an hour, the boat and crew were lost.

Ironically, if they had stayed offshore away from the shoals, or got through the storm to the deeper water near Bridlington, she might have survived. But being so low in the water, *Research* grounded in bad visibility on Smithwick Sands, known to fishermen as *Skitter Sands*, a notoriously dangerous shoal, or sandbank, in the so-called 'Bay of Safety'. They were caught in just a few feet of water, barely a mile south of Flamborough Head. The heavy sea easily swamped her, no trace of the crew ever being found. Two days later, a few pathetic remnants of the drifter washed up off Hornsea – an oilskin, the gaff from the mast, and a shard of wood bearing enough of the boat's Yarmouth registration number to confirm its identity.[14]

A Flamborough man chanced to see a drifter through a telescope, as it headed for Bridlington Bay, over Smithwick Sands. He saw three huge waves strike, intensified by the cross currents around the Head. Close enough to watch the crew scramble up to the boat's highest point, he could only watch in horror as the drifter capsized. Moments later, it had sunk. For days there was no news, but eventually the absence from Scarborough of *Research* was married with this sighting, and her identity was confirmed.

All is chance in such conditions, the loss of a crew of eight contrasting starkly with the good fortune of eight men on the *Arndilly*. This Lossiemouth drifter, returning northwards from the Yarmouth fishing, was literally split in two in the same storm, a passing Hull trawler, *Beryl*, somehow managing to rescue them.[15]

---

[14] WM Rhodes, *Filey a History of the Town and its People* (WM Rhodes, 2017) pp110-1.
[15] *wrecksite.eu* website.

13.9: Left - George Johnson Crimlisk.

13.10: Above - two of these fisher lads are sons of *Jossie Buggins*, Edwin and George JENKINSON, lost with *Research*, but for whom their mother never lost hope. *[FA]*

The sinking was truly a family tragedy, an inevitable consequence of the town's crewing practice, the final big offshore disaster and the worst. *Jack Sled* drowned with sons Robert and George Featherstone Baxter; both were married, *Robin* having six children. Luck ran the other way for *Sled's* remaining son, John Robert, who would have died with them, had it not been for him being ill.

He died in 1958, his widow, Rhoda Margaret, whom we met in 1983, being one of the last surviving people directly connected with that swathe of family drownings. Also lost off *Research* were *Sled's* two sons-in-law, George Johnson Crimlisk and William Cappleman CAMMISH, husbands of daughters Jane Baxter and Lilian.

Two other JENKINSON brothers, Edwin Chapman and George (R116 and R118) sons of John Matthew, *Sled's* distant cousin, also drowned from *Research*. John Matthew was better known in Filey as *Jossie Buggins*. George Burton knew the *Buggins* well. Edwin (*Teddy Fat*) was about 21 at the time of his death: 'he allus had taithwack and a shawl wrapped around his jaw, and always had a bloody great gob full o' taffy . . . and a woodbine at the same time'. George, only 16, was very quiet.

Their deaths, George Burton told us, were deeply felt in the family. Twenty years on, the family loss was still remembered. We found this notice in the *Filey News* of 1st December 1945:

> In Memoriam - JENKINSON - In loving Memory of our two dear sons, Ted and George, lost at sea, Nov 25th 1925. Always in our thoughts. From Mother, Father, Brother and Sister.

In
Loving
Memory
+ of +

JANE B. CRIMLISK
BORN 1885, DIED SEP. 20, 1931,
ALSO, OF HER HUSBAND
GEORGE J. CRIMLISK, BORN 1885
AND HER FATHER & BROTHERS
JOHN R. JENKINSON, BORN 1862
ROBERT JENKINSON, BORN 1890
GEORGE F. B. JENKINSON, BORN 1897
WILLIAM C. CAMMISH, BORN 1895
ALL DROWNED IN THE 'RESEARCH' DISASTER
NOV. 25, 1925.
JAMES H. N. JENKINSON, BORN 1892
LOST AT SEA 1911.
LOVED IN LIFE, TREASURED IN MEMORY.

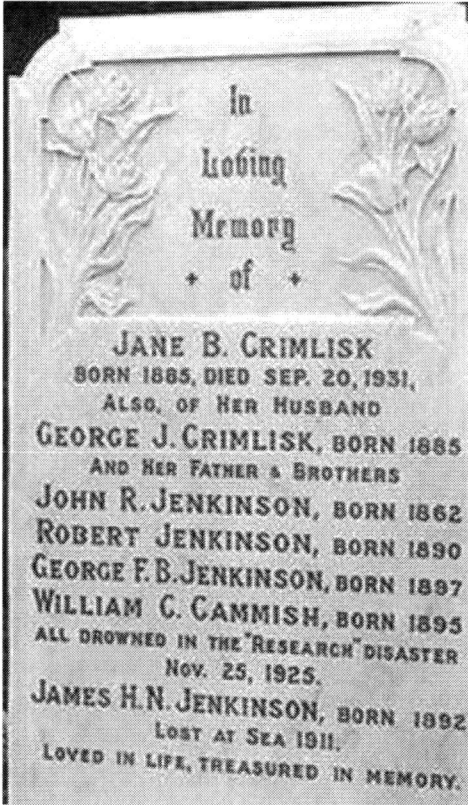

13.11: The *Research* grave F87, when new, in pristine marble – perhaps one of the most famous stones in Filey churchyard. Many disaster memorials were not erected until the death of the widow - this stone dates from after 1931, when George Crimlisk's widow had died. *[FA]*

It is worth noting that before 2013, in the absence of a body, English law would not normally permit registration of death or a grant of probate, insisting that seven years had to elapse without evidence that the person was still alive before death could be legally assumed.

In fact, where death was indisputable, and witnessed, this insistence for probate seems to have been waived, though registration of death was not allowed. So there was official acknowledgement, if not encouragement, that hopes for lost sailors and fishermen should not be abandoned. The eighth man was James Southern, the boat's engineer, only 'taking the berth' because he had six children and it was coming up to Christmas.

It is hardly a surprise that the drownings from *Research* are well commemorated in stone. There are four St Oswald's gravestones, whilst a plaque inside the Church names all Filey fishermen who 'perished at sea and whose bodies were never found' between 1901 and 1948. A quarter of these men were lost with *Research*.

Ten years later, *Research* may have had a radio. But who would have installed one on such a craft in 1925? Certainly, a crew working in such a marginal market would never have had the money even to consider it.

14 'SCARBOROUGH FOR POPULARITY, BRIDLINGTON FOR VULGARITY, FILEY FOR SOCIETY'

This chapter heading, a popular late 19th Century truism, quoted especially in Filey, highlights one key factor in the town's demise as a fishing station. Put simply, there was an irreconcilable incompatibility between the fishing industry, as it was evolving in the 19th Century, and 'leisure and tourism'. Though few may have seen it at the time, once New Filey began to attract what is now called merchant capital, any continuation of offshore fishing was doomed. Quoting an 1873 list of visitors, published in the *Filey Post*, Richard Harland, in his *Society at the Seaside* (c1970) notes the 'small and very select class of visitor' which came,

> . . . from most parts of Britain and included some who claimed Paris, America and Germany as their homes . . . . Clergymen, with wives and families were numerous but the list also included Peers of the Realm and officers from the higher ranks of Her Majesty's Services and other illustrious personages.

'Piquant Rustic Loveliness'

On a single day in 1868, an earl, a cardinal and an archbishop were seen on The Brigg. The town had features which therefore needed careful concealment if such tourists were not to be repelled. For centuries, Church Ravine had been a communal tip for the Old Town, raw sewage finding its way down there until 1857, on its unedifying journey to the sea. FM Fetherston's *Mr Smuggins*, the fictitious late 19th Century middle-class visitor to Filey, probably spoke for many in his dislike of 'the sham donkey drivers, boat lads and riff-raff playing all day on the sands.'

14.1: 'Noblemen, Gentlemen, and others, are especially invited to the above well-known established hotel . . . recently renovated regardless of cost,' boasts an 1854 plug for *The Royal Hotel*. Built in 1848, on Belle Vue Street, its site, until 2020 the *Three Tuns* car park, is now apartments. This 1856 illustration cunningly erases *all* other buildings on the street to create a rural idyll!

'No pets, no riff-raff' seems written very forcefully between any number of lines! *[FA]*

Like modern estate agents selling property near 'rough areas', hoteliers carefully diverted clients away from any horrors. No wonder so many establishments conveyed guests from the station, as Harland shrewdly puts it, 'as speedily as possible to the more attractive parts before their illusions were shattered.'[1]

---

[1] Harland, *Society at the Seaside* (c1970) *Fishing and Shipping*, p2.

14.2: 'This cliff embosom'd bay' - from the earliest years of New Filey's mock Regency existence, the town was determined to image itself as a resort of genteel quality. A key feature of *Project Airbrush* was to massage out of existence any hint of the fishing trade to which the town owed its existence. This 1872 print takes spin to new heights of concealment, not one coble marring this view from above Crescent Hill! Geographical isolation was turned to advantage, a unique selling point for the socially select. *[FA]*

Early on, hotels advertised the facility of 'warm baths', then evidently considered a Ryanair-style add-on. In 1820, 'a portable bath manufactured of tin' could be hired from Mr William Munro, surgeon; the *Foord's* proclaimed 'well-aired' beds . . . wines of the most approved vintages . . . excellent stabling and lock-up coach houses'; whilst *The Commercial* offered billiards, markedly up-market from any contemporary equivalent of bar-snooker.

Deference to the quality reached deeply into Filey's population, despite its Liberal politics. When Viscount Lascelles, the later Earl of Harewood, son-in-law of George V, began to stay there with his family in the 1920s, nothing was too much trouble. Media obsession with the royal family and its various appendages was even more sycophantic a century ago than in the 21st Century. The Royals became yet another element of the Filey 'Visitor Offer'.

An undated late 1920s newscutting, reports how day trippers flocked to the town to fawn over every royal move of the Lascelles guests. A *paparazzo*, not local judging from his elementary spelling error, was lurking, and found Councillor Tom *Titch* JENKINSON (R85) willing to brag and name drop effusively about his preferment to being, by appointment, *spawer* and crab-seller to royalty:

I found Councillor JENKENSON [*sic*] swinging his great rubber thigh boots on the sea front . . . indignant that their guests should be pestered like this . . . . 'They did get a bit of peace when they were sailing with me . . . . Colonel and Mrs Lane Fox were with them. The Colonel has been to Filey before and has had a ride with me.'

Just then Councillor JENKENSON's daughter left her crab stall nearby and came over to tell her father in no uncertain terms to 'pick out four good crabs and dress them and see you leave no bits of shell in. They're for 33 Crescent.'

'That'll be for Royalty, then. They're at 33, Crescent,' replied Councillor JENKENSON.[2]

Those who stood to make a good living from such a clientele had no wish to see Filey become a dock town . . . or coaling station for the Navy, as was considered.

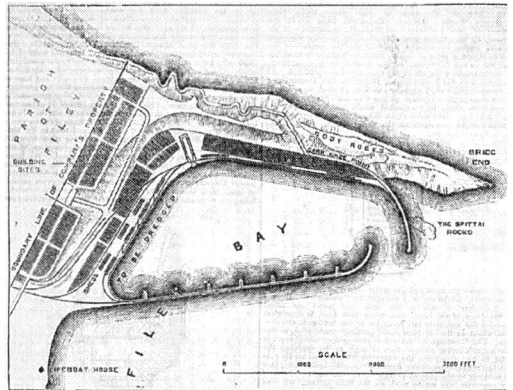

14.3, 14.4: One of several late 19th Century harbour of refuge schemes, most probably that of 1889, which included a tramway to carry fish up to the railway. Carrgate Hill appears to have been earmarked for a tramway or dock branch; and the cliffs of Carr Naze were to lose a big slice to accommodate a line of dock buildings. We can almost hear the peacefulness of St Oswald's churchyard being detonated by the labouring exhaust of a stationary winding engine, hauling wagons up the Ravine tramway incline! *[FA]*

The cliffs north of The Brigg were to be quarried for 'nearly all the materials required'. What would have been left of Filey to visit? Fortunately, the bay was reckoned too shallow. The Old Town and Coble Landing were to be erased, its fishermen presumably condemned to trawling!

---

[2] *Filey the History of The Town and Its People*, Facebook Group, 19th Feb 2020.

There had been a time when the quaintness of the Old Town, and isolation from the modern world, could be discreetly marketed as Filey's Unique Selling Point. As Halliday lyrically waxed in his 1860 Guide:

> . . . their boats are hauled on the beach, and the paraphernalia of nets, spread out to dry, and [the tanning of] the sails with oak bark, the scene is pleasing, and imparts a piquant rustic loveliness to all around.

Even the most creative estate agents, however, would have been hard-pressed to pass off a fish dock as a desirable retreat for cardinals and archbishops, let alone 'Peers of the Realm and officers from the higher ranks of Her Majesty's Services.'

'The Whole Character of the Place has changed' – evading 'Dog-holes'

Canon Cooper, Vicar of St Oswald's from 1880 to 1935, was a keen observer of his parish's secular affairs. Perhaps more than most, he could take an insightful overview of the changing character of the town:

> Dried skate was our special line, and there is extant an advertisement for a parson for our parish, setting forth with wonderful frankness the fact that he would have little else to live upon. To-day you might as well try to find a mammoth as a dried skate. What once were fish-curing houses are now granaries or stores. The women who used to make a living by splitting and drying the fish now earn their money by washing and drying the clothes of visitors.[3]

In November 1897, his widely reported address to the annual parish tea summarised the dramatic changes the town had recently undergone. Thirty years before, Filey had boasted 116 fishing craft:

> Now there are 32 cobles, only two herring cobles, and 24 yawls, and fishing is so bad that men are counted lucky who average a pound a week.

The yawls did not even fish out of the town, for they had been at Scarborough or Bridlington since the 1870s. It was the same elsewhere. Staithes' 1885 fishing fleet of 124 had dwindled to just four just after the Great War.[4] That year, Cooper had written despairingly of the future prospects for Filey's fishermen:

> Nothing saves but the ability to hold your own. May the day be distant when our people have to leave their beautiful bay, their pleasant cottages, their healthy homes, to crowd into some dog-hole in Hull or Shields.[5]

It was the iron fate of so many victims of economic decline. So why did Filey not experience at least *some* of the unemployment, or migration, that hit Staithes, where many of the fishermen had to find work in nearby ironstone mines? The answer was in part because Filey's collapse was not as severe, but also on account of the 'Leisure and Tourism' industry. There *was* life beyond the fishing.

---

[3] Cooper (1900) p48.

[4] Clark (1982) p22.

[5] Cooper (1886) p38.

14.5: Respectable visitors on a Filey-bound charabanc outside Scarborough Station, 1920. Ten years before, Rev Nadin had lamented the 'char-a-bancs, motor busses [*sic*], landaus and wagonettes' dominating the town's streets in their hundreds. *[Photo: FA]*

Within a generation, this rebranding had turned up trumps:

> . . . the outward signs of prosperity are everywhere apparent . . . the whole character of the place has changed: from being a fishing village which let a few lodgings to visitors, it has become a watering-place in which there are a few fishermen.[6]

Cooper wittily summed up the annual cycle of the season's progress:

> . . . more lodgings are taken, the shops engage extra assistants, the postman gets later on his rounds as his bag becomes heavier. . . trains become later on account of the traffic, omnibuses, for which one horse sufficed, now must have two . . . .[7]

The town alas had always attracted the unrefined as well as the primates, princes and peers. As early as October 1802, *The Gentleman's Magazine* noted how Filey was visited by 'the cockney traveller who drives about to stare at things in the North'. But it avoided the worst excesses of gross populism. In 1907, JS Wane saw 'the tunes of that noisy little merry-go-round' as the town's only blemish. He'd had to shelter from a shower in the Post Office doorway – all so English seaside.

The source of the town's prosperity had shifted completely. Gone were the days when offshore fishing generated enough to replenish a wrecked fleet in under three years.

---

[6] Nellist (1913).
[7] Cooper (1900) pp48-50.

14.6, 14.7: The worst fears unfulfilled – the idyllic ideal of this 1872 sketch (**top**) may have been fancifully over-ambitious in its offer of 'unmolested retirement'!

But the view taken at the eve of the Great War (**below**) has respectable families and sand castles everywhere, and no improper bathing attire, 'sham donkey drivers, boat lads or riff-raff' in sight! The eminent toiletry of choice, Pears Soap, clearly had some kind of monopoly franchise on 'bathing machine' advertising space. These contraptions had grown into dangerous monsters – one, trundling out of control down Crescent Hill, had fatally knocked down 65 year-old Mary CAMMISH in 1882. *[FA]*

Now, reckoned Cooper, as many of the landladies had bought houses worth more than a thousand pounds, 'it is obvious there is money in the trade.'[8] There was a gradual shift in Filey Old Town's culture, despite the collapse of the holiday industry in the 1914-18 War: William CAPPLEMAN reckoned that

> in the 1920s, the fishing was finished. That's why me mother told me that whatever I wanted to be I was never going to be a fisherman.

Another significant change that Cooper did not mention was how visitors' expectations of a *full*, uncurtailed week of holidaymaking were altering the character of Filey's Sunday observance. The Bridlington Primitive Methodist circuit minister, however, was less restrained:

> Unfortunately, the peacefulness of the Sabbath day is completely destroyed 'in the season,' because of the scores, not to state hundreds of vehicles, char-a-bancs, motor busses, landaus and wagonettes, which run into the place with their freights of sightseers. This is deplored by the Christian public, but appears to be inevitable.[9]

David Smith (1932) noted a deterioration in the visitors coming to Filey – they had lost 'the power to do nothing. They have not the stamina to spend a quiet Sunday.'

---

[8] Cooper (1900) pp48-50.

[9] Rev Nadin Jefferson, *Christian Messenger (1910, myprimitivemethodists* website.)

14.8: One growth industry in early 20th Century Filey was *spawing*. Messrs CAMMISH (with pipe) and Douglas assist visitors off the stage and onto their coble. By the 1950s, it was two shillings each for adults, one shilling for children and 'a penny out and a penny in' for use of the landing stage. When working men earned only around five pounds a week, these were clearly middle-class prices. *[FA]*

Further to his case, he described a conversation with an earthy Yorkshireman, a gardener, who used decidedly crisper language than anything likely to be in the vocabulary of the Bridlington minister:

'Since t'war,' he said, 'everybody's getten t'fidgets, specially t'women. They can't settle the'rsens, an' they wain't let nobody else settle.

Until the Great War, Smith reckoned, no Filey man would launch a boat on a Sunday, but now, under pressure from visitors, some had begun to.[10] But there were some areas of visitor improvement. Cooper seems to have collected little vignettes of tourist transgression, and could conclude that these were rarer. Writing in 1908 and contrasting visitor behaviour then with that of 20 years before, he reckoned

you rarely see drunkenness, and the imbeciles who used to cut their names on the turf, or wherever a knife or lead-pencil would work, seem to have died out.

And if nowadays they get to the parish church, they are

'not writing their names in the hymn books, not eating their lunch in the pews, nor playing hide and seek round the pillars . . . '.[11]

---

[10] Smith (1932) p198.
[11] Cooper (1908) pp31-5.

Then there was the 'key-overboard' case of around 1880. A party had borrowed the only church key one Saturday to wander round, and gone off for a sail round the bay, meaning to drop it off as they returned to the station. But the man deputed to take custody had suffered seasickness, whisked out a handkerchief as he 'paid tribute to Neptune', the key had come out with it, and dropped it off prematurely - into the sea. Rather than do the decent thing, the cads had made for the station without a word. On Sunday, the whole congregation was sitting on the grass or wandering round the graveyard as a bellringer was sent to the blacksmith to break in. But he was out ferreting, and the service was abandoned.[12] Cooper's implication was that nothing so dastardly could happen now, in the more civilised 1910.

Spawing

Foresighted fishermen, especially those with access to capital, had always had the option of remaining at sea in the far more relaxed branches of the coble business. As Smith put it in 1932,

> The short summer season enables the men who are too old for the hard work of regular fishing to earn a little money to help them over the winter. More valuable still, perhaps, it enables them to get out to sea once more.

As fishing declined, hire charges paid for a coble jaunt round the bay became an increasingly significant component of many more fishermen's income. For years a weekly advertisement in the *Post* (**14.9**) offered to take 'sportsmen and others' out into Filey Bay. Thomas JENKINSON (O50) once a liner, probably owned four cobles, reflecting the varied portfolio generating his income.[13] He appeared in the 1872 *Directory* as a 'Pleasure Boat Owner', and the report of his sudden death (*Filey Post*, 18th May 1895) stated that he had just returned from a crabbing trip. He and son *Tommy Laffy* (P97) were described as 'regular spawers'. There was money to be made in the season, men like James *Fatty* CAMMISH combining spawing with their year-round work. In *Fatty's* case, this was house painting.

TO SPORTSMEN AND OTHERS.

TO BE LET, a first-class PLEASURE BOAT, by the day, week, or month, with an experienced man in attendance, for fishing, shooting, or sailing.

Application to be made to Thomas Jenkinson, Fisherman, No. 8, Hope Street, Filey.

14.9: At 2s 6d an hour, good money could be made from a party of 'sportsmen' who wanted to fish, or shoot sea birds. Or you could book your private party to enjoy 'a glowing summer's evening . . . while you glide along the bosom of the ocean.'[14]

Spawing was another variation on the coble's very varied theme, and several men can be traced in late 19th Century trade directories switching to it from lining. The name presumably originated in Scarborough, where The Spa had been attracting

---

[12] Cooper (1910) pp26-7.
[13] Cappleman Account Book, Oct 1892-April 1893.
[14] Cole (1828) p128.

ailing visitors since the early 17th Century. Filey's equivalent, found on Nab Hill, half a mile north of the town, was reputedly a cure for 'scrofula, dyspepsia and nervousness.'[15] As early as the 1820s, Cole noted Filey's classy attraction of a sail in a coble 'cleaned for jaunts of pleasure' around Bay and Brigg. Smith pointed out that fishing trips brought extra costs for the spawer, for he had to provide bait and fishing equipment, and stood to lose hooks and sinkers if fishing over rock. *Spawers* needed a support staff of several old men who helped with the 'stages', wheeled platforms from which the visitors boarded the cobles. Between the Wars there was one of these contraptions at Bridge Hole, and two at the Coble Landing. A shilling took you out to the buoy, south of the tip of The Brigg. Each 'stage crew' (perhaps two or three men) pushed the stage into the water and to the boat (**14.8**).

14.10: Filey's target market, c1870 – the upper middle-class family, who could afford to commission its own photographer for snaps at sea. The governess perhaps looks attentively on at her little charges, Mother trails a line and hook, Father sports a fashionable cricket cap, and an archetypally 'pork pie' boater-hatted, mutton-chopped, cut-above-the-rest fisherman, apes a Venetian gondolier! *[FA]*

At around 2d a trip, men in their sixties and more, like *Old Jossie Buggins* (George JENKINSON, P95), or a house painter like *Fatty* CAMMISH, spent many 1920s summers working as stagers for 'pleasuring' but also watching for the Local Board's Inspector of Boats and Carriages. As a teenager in the 1950s, Graham Taylor got a pound a day helping out at *spawing*:

> We took anglers to Butlins, on an ebb tide – a 20-minute jolly. The foreshore inspector at Filey didn't know if you were exceeding 12.

Filey Council could fine and refuse a licence to those who transgressed.

At the higher end of the *spawing* market, man and coble were available 'by the hour, day or week' to those eminent visitors who wanted regular sails, often for fishing, or shooting seabirds. *Dabbing* for sole was especially popular.

---

[15] John Marius Wilson, *Imperial Gazetteer of England & Wales* (A Fullerton & Co, 1870-2).

14.11: Promenade Bridge (*Bridge Hole*) built by the Local Board in 1894 to enhance the seafront. This c1910 view may show the day of that annual summer fixture, the two-man coble race. Note how the boats moored just off the beach are facing the same way, and sporting flags, probably for identification. One of the *spawing* stages is just visible under the bridge. *[FA]*

You could enjoy a 'your triumphant march home with your catch hanging by your side.'

> The charge for men and boat is only 2s 6d per hour, and some two or three can join in one boat and each have a line at the same cost; but it is as well to remember that nature, if kind to you, likes you to be kind in return, and the price of an ounce of tobacco, rest assured, is acceptable and well-earned when more than two fish in one boat . . . .[16]

The 'sea fowl' that nested on the many cliffs at Filey impressed visitors as early as the 1820s. Cole delighted in the 'wild harmony' of their collective calls as he was rowed past one promontory. But he was outraged at the indiscriminate shooting of them. He observed

> two or three boats anchoring at different distances, in which were certain *savages* . . . diverting themselves with shooting at these poor birds, as they flew from their nest, or returned to them with food from the sea; destroying not only the parent birds, but leaving their hapless progeny to clamour in vain.[17]

---

[16] Sokell (1899) pp21-2.
[17] Cole (1828) pp83-6.

14.12: Victorian Society enjoyed killing things. 'Savages' (in Cole's words) at *Ackworth House* in deer-stalkers, a key part of 1870-90 hunting fashion. The two fishermen will take them sailing to Speeton Cliffs to shoot sea birds, though controlled since 1869. The house was built as the *Spa Saloon*, and became a lodging-house shortly afterwards. *[FA]*

The birds seem to have been disadvantaged by their naïve assumption that no one would simply kill them for the sake of it. According to one early assassin:

> The birds that sat upon the different ledges in the cliffs, were innumerable; and in less than ten minutes, we had killed twenty-one . . . .[18]

Cole seems to have been a lone voice in decrying such pointless slaughter, if one 1867 *Filey Post* report of local bird-stuffer Richard Lorriman's activities is any guide. He was near The Brigg when he saw a large target flying towards him:

> He at once crept into a crevice of the cliff, and having his gun with him waited until it came within shot, when he fired and brought it down. The bird proved to be a splendid specimen of the Osprey, or Fish Eagle, which from tip to tip of wing measured 5ft 6in, and from beak to tail 2ft 2in.[19]

The implied editorial approval in the account speaks volumes. But opinion was shifting. The writers of local guides were sensing that the slaughter was actually causing damage to the town's prosperity. In 1860, Dr Cortis had accused 'wanton use of the gun' of clearing the cliffs north of The Brigg of breeding birds.

---

[18] John Henry Manners, Duke of Rutland, *Journal of a Tour to the Northern Parts of Great Britain* (J Triphhok, 1796).

[19] *Filey Post*, 14th May 1867.

And in 1899, Filey printer and stationer John Sokell raged against the 'loathsome propensity' to shoot sea birds. Species as rare as the Sea Eagle, he observed, were left 'wounded to die on the ledges . . . or to be washed ashore to die of hunger.'

He had visited the cliffs the previous year

> a fortnight after the close term had ended, when three or four boats were out with murderers in them, sending out their death shots to the parents of the hundreds of young birds visible on the cliffs.[20]

Despite this Hoorah Henry image that these 'huntin and shootin' elites may present to us today, many Filey men almost certainly developed strong relationships with their more solid gentleman visitors. Richard Harland suggests that Filey's fishing community accorded their visitors respect according to their 'quality' rather than their wealth or social status:

> . . . they were proud to initiate their guests into the skills of their craft and several amateur sailors of distinction learned the rudiments of the art in a Filey coble.

Bonds across the Classes

One ex-fisherman who, despite a certain uncouthness, went *spawing* for the aristocracy was *Old Brazzy*, Matthew JENKINSON (P43). George Burton got to know this extremely down to earth man very well. *Brazzy*, he told us, had little grasp of the art of customer relations. Whilst *spawing*, he would think nothing of relieving himself there and then, 'using the world at large' as the fishermen euphemistically termed it![21] 'Now all you lot, look yon road while I attend to myself,' he would announce, if caught short at sea. 'He never bothered about nobody,' George reckoned. Remarkably, *Brazzy* struck up a close friendship with the Irish peer and Tory politician Uchter John Mark Knox, 5th Earl of Ranfurly. This frustrated sailor regularly stayed in Filey around the turn of the 20th Century, at the prestigious *Royal Crescent Hotel* (where else?) to rekindle his love of the sea.

His lordship had been forced to give up a naval cadetship to enter Cambridge. But at Filey, the Earl learned practical seamanship to a level which satisfied even the Cowes' Royal Yacht Club's membership standards. *Brazzy*, who was in the Royal Naval Reserve, was his tutor.

As Filey's guest celebrity, Ranfurly judged the two-man coble race in the Bay in 1890, watched from the beach or promenade by hundreds. Despite his social elevation, the 5th Earl was renowned for 'bonhomie, love of sport, and charm of manner'. He retained *Brazzy* as his boatman each season, shooting, fishing and picnicking with his family on The Brigg. At 2s 6d an hour, it was what every *spawer* dreamt of. Jim Haxby tells the tale:

---

[20] Local MP, Sir Christopher Sykes of Sledmere was mockingly known as 'The Gulls' Friend' because he had introduced the 1869 Bill to limit the wholesale slaughter.

[21] The more tales you hear of *Brazzy*, the more the rudely assertive 'brassiness' implied in the nickname seems to fit; Frank (2002) p54.

When 'e finished, the last night, 'e said to *Brazzy*, now Jenkinson, 'e says, I'd like you and your man to come to our *Crescent 'otel* for dinner.

Righto, maister, what time are we t'come? Seven for seven thirty. Well, they looked at one another 'cos Brazzy 'ad his dinner dead on twelve o'clock.

So away they went, knocked at the *Crescent 'otel* and the two flunkies on the door said, you – tradesmen's entrance. Nobody talked to *Brazzy* like that. 'E said, gerrin there and fetch Lord Ranfurly out 'ere for *Brazzy*. So he came out and there he was in all his regalia, 'is brogues, everything out in the Irish way. Ah, Jenkinson, come on in.

Thus these two unlikely dinner guests appeared incongruously in one of the plushest hotels on the coast, never having been in anything smarter than a fisherman' cottage or baiting shed:

All 'is family was there sat at the table. *Brazzy* ses to 'im, well Jack, 'e says, somebody else must a come in, Jack. Intrigued with all these knives and forks. Never seen, 'e 'ad his broth and dumplin's with a spoon, 'e never bothered with 'owt else.

14.13: An unlikely friendship arose between *Brazzy* JENKINSON and Lord Ranfurly, a Tory peer connected in the highest places, and Governor of New Zealand from 1897 to 1904. *[Wikipedia entry]*

So, owld Jack says, watch Lord Ranfurly, do same as 'im. And there was another thing 'e didn't understand, this bit 'o cloth curled round in a glass. And *Brazzy* weren't gonna touch that becos' 'e didn't know what it was. Anyway, the soup came, and Lord Ranfurly says, serviette Jenkinson? *Brazzy* says, maister, if you can eat one I can eat two.

Improbably, *Brazzy* was invited to stay at the Earl and Countess's London home, and also to accompany them to their Ulster estates for six months, to entertain house guests. It was there that *Brazzy* had his famous encounter with the gas jets: the house had all the modern conveniences - gas lighting included. *Brazzy*, used only to candles, proceeded to blow out a gaslight, and nearly managed to gas the whole household.

Entertaining as these tales are, some scepticism alas may be in order, for lilies may well have been gilded:

. . . a great humourist, *Brazzy* entertained his friends with stories of life in Society and his tales (often embroidered) are still current all in some circles.[22]

Perhaps, in the light of *Brazzy's* genuine if unlikely friendship with Lord Ranfurly, I have been unfair earlier in this chapter, dismissing *Titch* JENKINSON's relationship with Lord Lascelles as that of a fawning toady. Listen to Terence COLLINS' description of the real delight that the royal couple derived from their visits to Councillor JENKINSON's modest home, at 1, Spring Road:

They used to think it was wonderful to sit in a fisherman's cottage and talk for an hour and a half and have their suppers on a table with no tablecloth and have mugs to drink their tea.

14.14: Bathing machines at the foot of what is now the Crescent Hill slipway. Probably an 1890s view, by which time they had become beach changing rooms, rather than vehicles drawn by horse into the sea. (Bathers had wanted not be observed walking into the sea.) Even here, with doors front and back, high levels of modesty were guaranteed by this laagering! Nude bathing had been common, and possible, with decorum, on uncrowded beaches, though as mass seaside tourism developed in the railway age even men were eventually, by 1860, required by law to wear something! The bathing machine had evolved in the later 18th Century 'whereby the most refined female is enabled to enjoy the advantages of the sea with the strictest delicacy.' Beaches were segregated for bathing in Britain until 1901, local authorities taking the law very seriously – see above p17. *[Wikipedia entry; Photo: SE]*

---

[22] Harland, *Society at the Seaside* (c1970).

15 FILEY'S INSHORE FISHING:
1: LONG-LINING FROM THE COBLE

'A boat and harbour in one.'[1]

Along England's north-east coast, the three-man coble has, well into the 20th Century, dominated inshore fishing. Operating on a daily basis, and straying no more than a few miles from the shore, this maid of all work can operate from the roughest beach, and needs no harbour facilities. It can be used the year round, adaptably pursuing whatever edible sea creature is most readily available at any particular time.

We were fortunate in April 1983 to talk to Richard Cammish JOHNSON, of Queen Street, a man in his seventies who had started inshore fishing in the late 1920s. As was the way with most Filey coble fishermen, he had started offshore, on drifters, learning the skills from men far older. One of the delights of engaging with a tightly-woven community is that in the living you are only one removed from many accumulated generations of local knowledge. In that Filey front room, 37 years ago, we were in secondhand contact with local people alive in the 1850s.

In 2018-19, Graham Taylor, well-known as an experienced crewman of the Filey Lifeboat[2], described his coble experiences a generation later, between 1959 and 1974, close to the twilight years of the town's commercial fishing. He sailed mostly in Matt Jenkinson *Lampler* Haxby's cobles *Janet and Carol* and *Britannia*. Jim Haxby (1935-2018) whose memories are contained in the *Oral Interviews* transcripts, in Filey Archives, continues the account almost to the end.

The inshore fisherman could own several cobles: line-fishing required the three-man winter coble, usually about 18-20 feet long; salmon netting warranted a smaller, two-man coble; and a larger, four-man coble was needed to fish for herrings with drift nets. These boats were much cheaper than the luggers and yawls: William JENKINSON (O14) paid £14 10s 0d for a new coble 17½ feet in length on 4th December 1873 according to the Cappleman Account Book.[3] After the Great War, Filey's cobles were normally up to 30 feet, perhaps because petrol engines began to eclipse rowing, making far heavier boats and loads practicable.

---

[1] EW White, *British Fishing-Boats and Coastal Craft* (Read Books, 2011; first published 1952) p13.

[2] Graham joined the Filey Lifeboat crew in 1963. He was mechanic and coxswain at retirement in 1998, shore helper/tractor driver until 2005, and Deputy Launching Authority until 2013. He was awarded an MBE in 1997.

[3] JENKINSON also owned the yawl, *Brothers*, so his new coble, being short, was probably to be used as her corfe.

15.1: Early 19th Century print of a coble on Filey Beach, being pushed 'out of the reach of the tide.' (Walker, 1814).

Some fishermen could not raise even these sums, and relied upon outside capital, being 'employed' as skippers by investors, who took the 'boat share' of the net earnings. David Smith had this arrangement with *Jossie Buggins* and describes it in his 1932 article.

The Design of the Coble

'Two boats are never alike,' Graham told me. 'A boat's alive, and she lets you know when you're steering her.'[4] Cobles were the work of local builders, designed for local conditions, often personalised to the commissioner's specific fishing specialisms.

Filey's cobles had a pronounced *forefoot*, to act as a rudder when the boat backed onto the town's particularly open beach. It was a long-perfected design, dating to the Dark Ages, and often attributed to the Vikings. In fact, its features were found on most North Sea coasts, including Iceland, with shallow, sandy beaches, where wide bays provided little shelter from onshore gales. One Whitby coble builder has recognised its design in the 7th Century Anglo-Saxon Sutton Hoo royal boat burial, discovered in Suffolk in 1939.[5]

Crucially, they were cheap to build, for the clinker technique of overlapping planks doesn't need the careful joinery and caulking of carvel (edge-to-edge) construction. At around 'a pound a foot' in 19th Century Filey, it was within reach of working fishermen with access to just a little capital.

---

[4] Graham provided much of the information in this chapter on coble design.
[5] Frank (2002) pp59-60. Anglo-Saxon, Dutch, or Scandinavian in origin? It is unlikely that we can ever know, although who knows what may be lying preserved in a millennium of estuary mud somewhere?

Square stern steadies the boat as it reverses onto the beach

Clinker-build of overlapped planks (*strakes*) allows 'give' to resist damage when beaching, and in rough sea

Two side keels ('**double drafts**') like the runners on a sledge, allow the boat to be pulled out of the sea without tipping

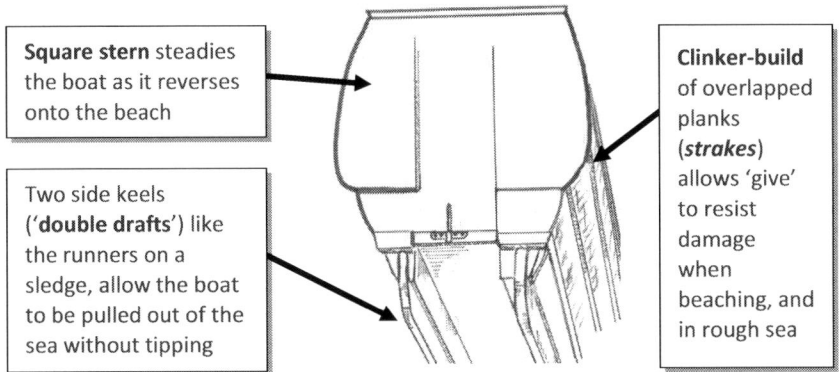

15.2: Clinker construction made the coble cheap, its double-keeled flat bottom made it stable and its lug rig allowed it to sail very close to the wind. Also, it was versatile. This is why scores of villages from the Humber to Burnmouth, five miles north of the Scottish border, could make a year-round, low-tech living from the sea.

Launching

According to an 1853 map, the name *Cobble Landing* was applied only to a stretch of shoreline, the present-day site being referred to as Penny Hill. The actual landing was first built in 1870-1, with timber walls and stone fillings. These materials were in turn replaced with stone in 1930.[6] Launching techniques in 1853 would have been entirely recognisable to fishermen 160 years later and indeed to those 160 years before.

Some fishermen started later, coming 'doon t'beck' in their own time. They would stand around, watching the sea and the weather and then it was 'right, we're off'! *Lanching* was a group effort, a team of elderly fishermen always present. You had to wait your turn, but there were ways of working an advantage for those in a hurry. 'You were shoved into the water in order of arrival,' explained Graham Taylor:

> So you didn't tell anyone what time you were hoping to be away next day. I could hear him getting up next door, so you'd be off quick.

The following timeless account conjures with shivering accuracy the reality of the process on the eve of the tractor age:

> It is 3.30am on a cold mid-winter morning. There has been a fall of snow early in the night. It is pitch dark and very cold. Men in oilskins and sea-boots move about the cobble landing, shovelling snow out of their boats, stowing long baited lines, flapping arms and stamping to get their circulation going . . . . Rumble, rumble,

---

[6] Fisher (*History*, 1970) *Fishing and Shipping*, p3.

rumble – a cobble on wheels is rushing down the paved landing to the sea – now the launchers, standing in the breakers, have got her – they are the older men, no longer strong enough to face the winter fishing in open boats. She is off her wheels and afloat – her crew wade out and board her – she is away through the surf, vanishing in the darkness of the night. It is beginning to snow again.[7]

Up to World War II, Frank, and then George Appleby brought their team of three or four shires down to the Landing every morning bar Sunday.[8] When at rest on the Landing, cobles stood traditionally on old artillery carriages, and so could easily be pushed into the tide. These would be washed away if not hauled back onto the sand quickly. The crew waited for a 'smooth' (a non-breaking wave) then launched into the swell, using oars and a pole (called a *prod* in Filey) to shift the boat off the sand.

15.3: Richard Cammish JENKINSON's *Lily* sits on its carriage, at the head of the queue, waiting for the *Lanchers*, early 20th Century. The timber walls were erected in 1870-1. The all-stone version appeared in 1930. Most of the cobles shown will have been constructed in one of the three boat-building sheds just visible on this side of the new Lifeboat House. The three-storey Coastguard Station, two-storeyed since the 1960s, gable end seawards, is at the end of Queen Street (centre of photograph). *[FA]*

---

[7] Smith (1932) pp193-4.

[8] Fearon (2016) pp15-6. They came from *Manor Farm*, shown as 38, Queen Street in the 1915 *Directory*, but actually behind *The Grapes*.

'Dipping lug' sail can be brought round to either side - the canvas isn't pressed into the mast, but fully catches the wind

Foremast stepped well forward, c6 feet from prow or less, to make room for fishing operations

'Loose-footed' – ie the sail is simply held in place by a rope. Wing-like shape in lower sail and ease of angling ('trimming') catches more wind

The **jib** increases stability, and overall sail area - more wind is caught to power the boat

Rudder acts as a keel, keeps the boat upright, and is **'unshipped'** (removed) for launching and landing, since it projects well below the bottom of the boat

Larch ***strakes*** (planks) formerly locally-grown oak, resist rot when out of the sea

Deep, sharp ***forefoot*** cuts through the waves, converts force of side wind into forward motion, and increases stability

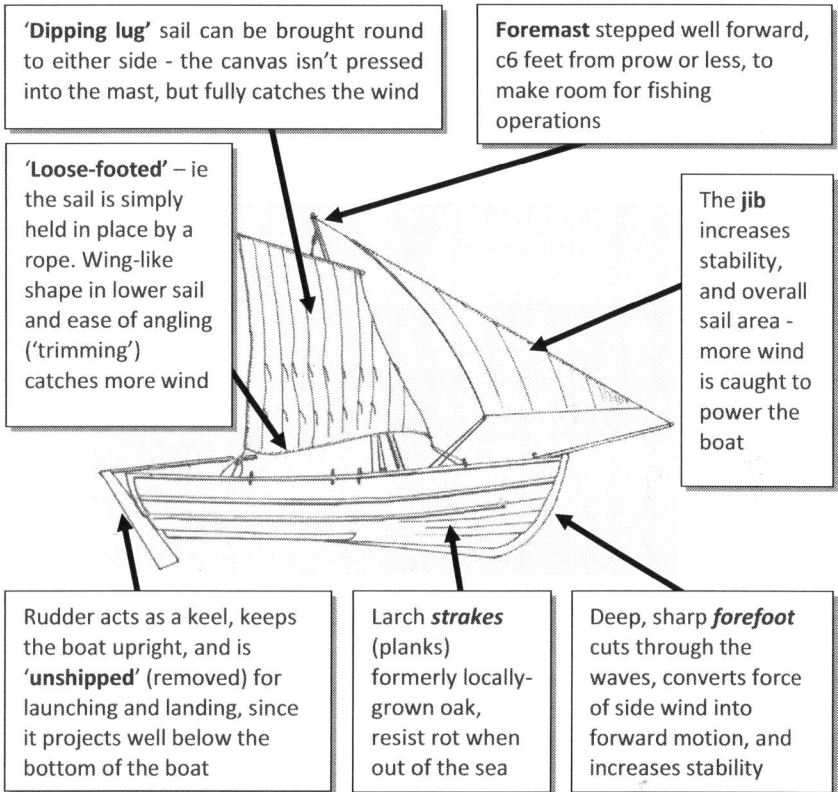

15.4: If luggers were the workhorses, cobles were the donkeys. About 20 feet in length, before motorisation, the same classic, flat-bottomed design had been in use for over 1,400 years, on all coasts around the North Sea.

The dipping lug was designed to be hoisted rapidly, lying ready, in the correct tack position for the wind direction. Hard rowing powered the coble through the tidal flow, the big *forefoot* cutting through the waves to ensure a swift getaway. The rudder was fitted once there was enough depth. Speed was crucial, for if the boat grounded and was caught by a strong tide, it might be brought round by the surf through 90°, tipped over and wrecked by the pounding of the waves. A strong easterly increased the danger. Sometimes the risks were too great. The attempt to launch the lifeboat to help the trawler *Skegness* in 1935 took about three-quarters of an hour - each time the tractor got the boat into the water it was blown back by the wind. A fishing trip would not be attempted in such conditions.

But not everyone necessarily agreed how bad it was. If there were 'dodgy weather', explained Graham,

... we'd all go to the end of Queen Street to see conditions. One woman came and played hell at her husband. 'Go to sea!' she shouted. 'Here's your sea-boots.' 'Go yerself,' was the response.

Maybe the family was truly living from hand to mouth. And the poor woman may have spent hours skeining and baiting. Perhaps this was the last day before the mussels went stale. She faced many disagreeable hours unhooking rotting molluscs simply to start the process again. In the old days, when thousands of limpets had been laboriously prised off distant rocks, the prospect must have been soul-killing. And then there was the heavy labour of getting everything down to the boat again (**15.6**). Even in the best functioning marriages such a dilemma will have caused tensions.

It really was a 'tough trade', for men *and* women. The bald reality was a trade-off between risk and the need to make a living. In the fierce winter of 1962-3, it took Graham three months to earn one pound, his usual daily wage.

Even if it were safe to get off, what if the weather deteriorated and you hit a storm several miles out? Or conditions were just too threatening to land on the return? Even then the risks of damage were not over. The prudent fisherman laboriously pulled his coble up Church Ravine for protection if a northerly gale threatened.

Long-lining

Traditionally, the inshore Winter Fishing began after Hull Fair Saturday, in October, when cod came inshore to feed off moulting crabs as they lost the protection of their shells.[9] It continued until February, but could go on into March or April, when the fish returned to the deeps, beyond the safe reach of cobles.

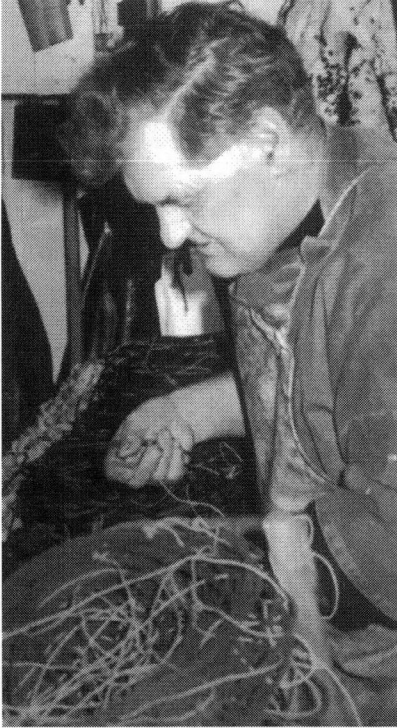

15.5: William Robinson JENKINSON (R3), *Wemp*, was 'shore hand who did all the lines and nets' for the crew of four he fished with. They drowned in a salmon coble, in June 1948, at Primrose Bay. Here, *Wemp* knots white cotton snood cord onto a hempen long line. *[SMHC]*

---

[9] Lines were baited on the Friday – then the midday train to go to Hull Fair on Saturday, home by eight. 'That was their holidays . . . come back, didn't sail on Sunday . . . then Monday morning away you'd go' (Jim Haxby).

These Winter Fishing months of course meant bad weather, 'by far the most perilous' as Cole put it. So why did they go out in the winter? 'Fish decides that', Richard Cammish told us. Cod tasted better in winter, meat was expensive then, and line-caught cod commanded a good price.

Preparation – each of the three-man crew was responsible for his own gear. At Staithes, it was common in the 19th Century for a man to bring three hempen lines, nine in all. Each was 400 to 480 yards long, with a snood (*sneard* in Filey) every five feet, up to 300 per line.[10] This three-foot length of twisted horsehair, hard wearing and flexible, connected a barbed hook to the main-line.

At Filey in the 1920s, Richard Cammish was using four lines, three after Christmas, because of deteriorating weather and the consequent risks of an over-long day. Each was 480 yards long, with 'ten score' (200) hooks, making up to a mile of line for each man. By the 1920s, a new, lighter cotton line would cost about £2 10s. Cotton lines were lighter to carry, and needed less space, whether in the working coble or summer storage in cottage or out house. Smith (1932) reckoned a hemp line cost £3, yet wore out in half the time.

If fishing were poor, the crew might take 18 or 21 lines – say six miles, and thousands of hooks. Dick CAPPLEMAN (*Granddad Cap* as the local children called him) had a bait shed at the back of his Rutland Street house and unravelled his lines by laying them out up the alley to the telegraph pole.

Each man set ten lines, with sneards and hooks, in readiness for the winter season. This guaranteed that two fleets were always available, to provide spares (regular maintenance was necessary) and to allow one to be baited whilst one was in use. The capital outlay even for a coble fisherman was therefore considerable.

15.6: Susannah CAPPLEMAN with *skep*, in an 1896 studio portrait, aged 10. *Skeps, meat* tins and water cans could also be carried from a yoke. Despite such hard labour, she died as Susannah JOHNSON in 1990, aged 104. *[FA]*

---

[10] Frank (2002) pp88-9; *snood* comes from early German, 'rope', 'string'.

Skeining and Baiting – whereas offshore fishermen had plenty of time to catch bait as they sailed out to the fishing grounds, coble crew did not, and needed their lines fully baited, ready to be shot. This added hugely to the labour involved in preparing each day's fishing.

Graham Taylor, like Richard Cammish JOHNSON 40 years earlier, had 200 hooks to the line, baited with up to 1,000 mussels. A 16-stone sack did four lines, and took three hours. As it was baited, each line was coiled onto a *skep* (a wooden or wicker basket lid-shape, a Norse word, related to 'skip'). These were lined with *bents* (marram grass) to keep the bait moist. The *sneards* were precisely stacked so as not tangle as the line was shot. The razor-sharp hooks easily got embedded into a man's hand at sea, and a knife was always on the *thoft*[11] to get one out.

In the 19th Century, bait-gathering, skeining and baiting had been entirely family tasks, wives and daughters preparing each man's lines in the living room or baiting shed (the 'back 'ouse'). But as coble numbers in Filey increased, bait had to be bought in.

'Mussels beats everything', Richard Cammish reckoned, but they were expensive. Six to a hook was the formula, though just one would satisfy a haddock. An economy measure was to bait some hooks with limpets, whelks (from Sheringham) or a piece of squid. But the more bait the more fish: 'the man that pinches his lines for bait, the fish pinch him,' was a fisher saying in Staithes. By the 1960s, the fish had to settle for four or five mussels.

Before Christmas, 'odds and ends' would do, as cod shoaled close to shore, and might be hungry. For strong tides, a 'hard bait' like lug worms or whelks was better, since they stayed firmly on the hook, so that the expense of buying bait could be minimised.[12]

Large Victorian families provided lots of children to *digger* in, ie help out, but smaller families and improved employment opportunities for women forced men to employ their own *skeiners* and baiters. Rates went up - Graham Taylor was paying his skeiners 10 shillings a sack in the '60s, for the two bags his lines needed daily. Typically, the job was done by a couple of women, retired fishermen, or even someone on the dole and 'on the fiddle'.

Some baiters simply got it wrong! Jim Haxby recalled fishing five lines each, one Saturday morning in the 1950s, with his father, and Mark Henry Scotter:

> . . . we started at the 'aul, me dad's line was first, 'e got twenty odd fishes which was all right. Doesn't seem many off two 'undred 'ooks, but they were big fish, workin' sand. Mark's line was next one, 'e got two or three. My line was third one and I think I got mebbe twenty odd, thirty fishes. And that's 'ow it went right through all the lines. Mark's lines din't get anything. And the problem was, the

---

[11] The *thwart* that crossed the body of the coble, on which the two rowers sat.
[12] Frank (2002) pp98, 157-8; Jim Haxby.

> bloke who baited for 'em 'e used to put the mussels in water . . . . You might as
> well put a stone on 'cos all the goodness 'ad gone out o' the mussel. They were
> white . . . the fish din't want 'em . . . no taste.

But some swore by soaking! It was also assumed that bait went 'stale' after a few
days, and one day, at the end of the Winter Fishing, the men were all set to throw
away one putrid lot – it had been baited for three weeks. Jim continues:

> . . . we were finishin', wrappin' up, and I'm telling yer, just to look at 'em coulda
> med yer sick. They were all colours, they were pink, they were green, oh god, they
> were terrible. I says, well we're gonna have to go and gerrem worked. We hated
> cavin', tekkin the bait off again, becos' yer lines were allus mucky . . . it would be
> our final shot of the year, it was March . . . they stunk 'eavens 'igh. And we kem
> back and started the 'aul and we got 120 stone off 'em. It was what was comin'
> away on the tide, fish come to the lines, what they could smell. Didn't matter
> what they could see.

All these baited lines had to be carried down to the Landing on *skeps*. In the old
days, this was also usually women's work. A can of drinking water came on
board too, along with about 20 bags of sand for ballast. This had to be discharged
on landing, or as the catch came in, to ease the work involved in beaching. A few
stones came too, to sink the lines to the seabed.

Overing – as mussels rotted quickly in warm weather, frozen herring or mackerel
were taken in spring and summer, the lines being baited by the crew as they shot.
Two men baited as each long-line was fed over the coble's side, hence the name
'overing'. The risk of getting a hook in your hand was especially high.

Midsummering involved drifting for bait when the herring were shoaling off
Scarborough. Graham described two or three days of very intense work on a keel
boat in the 1960s, smaller than a drifter, with a crew of seven. It began with 20
nets being shot around 10.30pm, 'when they come upstairs'. Around midnight,
most of the men got into the bunks until 5. By then they were at the cod grounds,
perhaps 27 miles out. Then they baited some 25 miles of line, with large,
especially lethal 'Big Baggin' hooks, as each line went over the side. 'We got
only herrings for breakfast,' Graham added. 'Who wants herring for breakfast
when you've been catching 'em all night?' He ended up bringing his own food.

By this time there were just two Filey crews midsummering out of Scarborough:

> We got the bus in, then the Town bus down to the harbour. When we got back,
> and got on the Filey bus, we were so tired that many a time the conductor had to
> wake us. The lucky ones got run in and back in a van.

Choosing the Fishing Ground – 'They had their own spots, where they would
prefer to fish,' Richard Cammish said. He reckoned Jack JOHNSON, with his
brothers *Dicko* and Sam, 'never went beyond the buoy off The Brigg'. They spent
longer at sea, but made a living; they didn't get wet, they avoided several miles of
rowing, and they were safe.

The risks of being caught in bad weather several miles offshore were serious, for it took hours to row back to safety. Only with the fitting of auxiliary motors, in the early 20th Century, did this danger recede.[13] Cole reckoned (1828, pages 97-8) that some men went out as far as 15 miles. But I suspect that each writer had a different figure depending on which fisherman he had talked to, and such talk was strictly governed by what is now termed 'commercial confidentiality'. Skippers were even careful not to identify their location at sea if casuals had been taken on for that trip. Even today, coded talk takes place over the radio to this end. Graham Taylor summed it up:

> On land you'd be the best of friends, but you didn't want them knowing where you'd been. If you came home with a hundred stone of fish, after a good shot, everyone wanted to be shooting over the same ground. 'What sort of trip have you had, lad?' You kept it to yourself if you could. We went because someone before us had found a ground.

Good grounds were kept secret, family knowledge that had been handed down for generations. In pre-literate times, men kept it in their heads for life. One late 19th Century Northumbrian fisherman cited his father's memory for lobster grounds:

> For years he couldn't walk about, just sat . . . . But go and ask him the marks to shoot a length of pots on a certain place, and he could tell ye exactly the marks to use, what water there was there, when to be there and when not to be there.[14]

One man who approached this problem scientifically was Richard Cammish JENKINSON (Q45), universally known as *Dicky Hoy*. Terence COLLINS recounted, with dramatic gravity, how he had received crucial advice as a child from this canny man:

> Now lad if you go to sea when you grow up you keep a BOOK. It doesn't matter what sort of a book it is but you keep a book. You can get one at Annie Wiseman's for a penny. They're red coloured but that doesn't matter, the colour doesn't matter at all. It can be a green one, but get a book. This one's a black one. Look at this book. I have a lot of books like this and they're going to be left to our Tom.

> This book will tell yer what sort of weather it was on a particular day. How strong t'wind was, what quarter it was out of, where t'MOOOON was and that's very important where t'moon was. And whether the wind was backin' or not, what time we went off (if we went off) and where we went, where we shot our lines - on an EBB, never on a flood. All t'other Filey men shut on a flood but we shut on an ebb. Where we shot, what each line gev us. And we put that down when we got ashore, after we've had our tea.

---

[13] Captain Sydney Smith told us how Arthur Douglas Senior of Filey became, in 1902, the first man around Scarborough to fit an auxiliary petrol engine. This was to his herring coble *Jane and Priscilla*, since this fishery's large catches justified the expense.

[14] Quoted on *Islandshire Archives* website.

'And for years and years and years,' added Terence, as though describing revelatory insights from an Old Testament prophet,

> . . . he kept the book. And if the fishing had been bad in that particular part, that day, last year - didn't go again. He went somewhere where it had been good. And he was always t'top coble in Filey was *Dicky Hoy* and he always swore it was 'that booook'.

There were signs to watch for. A 'Saturday moon', for example, was a sure sign of bad weather, retained in memory, according to Shaw through a simple couplet:

> A Saturday's moon
> in seven years is too soon

It was equally vital to know the whereabouts of seabed hazards like submerged rocks, though in the Great War, these had provided refuge from prowling German U-boats and their torpedoes. And gear might be irretrievably snagged on *boobies*, the name given to the numerous wrecks and lost anchors that littered the seabed. Some spots were very well known – Jim Haxby described Fileyman's High Rock three by six miles, in the bay, where 'King Mussel' alone caught fish. Then there was the soft ground south of Flamborough, worked by local inshoremen for generations. Fishermen's tales spoke of a 100 stone of large fish in a day.

Trawlermen found it at the time of the 1849 Sacramento gold rush, and nicknamed it *California* on account of its yields. Long-liners now risked damage to their gear from trawlers, and retreated to rocky inshore 'hard ground' where they were left alone. These Flamborough grounds were subject to 'top tides', a full 18 feet between high and low water. You could get away with a harder bait - whelks, and flithers. But 'big tides' disturbed the lines, snagging them on rocks, making hauling-in 'serious hard work.' 'Dead tides' were far easier to work.

Getting to the Ground - in the days of oar and sail, this might take several hours, depending on wind speed and direction, and the amount of exhausting rowing required. Graham described the extensive set of local 'meets', alignments of landmarks, like the Castle, High Brigg, and the Hunmanby Trees. Recent features were readily used, like the Butlin's clock tower. They sported lovely names, rooted in a coastal landscape known intimately to centuries of fishermen. *Millie Black*, for example, refers to Muston Mill, a windmill having stood since the 14th Century hard by Muston Road, an ancient highway once known as Mill Lane. Kath Wilkie tells how Jim Haxby explained *Millie Black's* puzzling name:

> . . . out in Filey Bay and looking landwards – you've got Muston Mill at the top; and you've got the dark patch of Osborne House and Martin's Ravine underneath it – at the bottom – so there you have the 'mill in the black' or *Mill i' Black*.

Rhymes and aphorisms were used as memory aids to local meets, an oral tradition, time out of mind. But they were also semi-officially committed to print in esoteric maritimese, the Admiralty capitalising on local knowledge, for example:

Myer's house, upon the outline of the land near Speeton, kept well open to the southward of Hunmanby road, bearing SW, ½ S, clears the outer point of the Brig [*sic*].[15]

No charts, said Graham, just 'in the skipper's head, and using compass, watch and leadline'. The *plummet* (Middle English, 'ball of lead') had a tallow-filled hole to pick up seabed sand or mud. Some skippers didn't need one, knowing the bed's landscape by heart. Graham gave an example:

At 10 fathoms, sand becomes High Rock, then Out Rock, then sand, then rock again – reached after 27 minutes at six knots. In fog, you could retrace the route, following that bearing.

If you were after the rock, where sole lurked, 'you followed a perfect line up Carrgate Hill, but once you could see Scarborough Castle behind The Brigg you were on rock.'

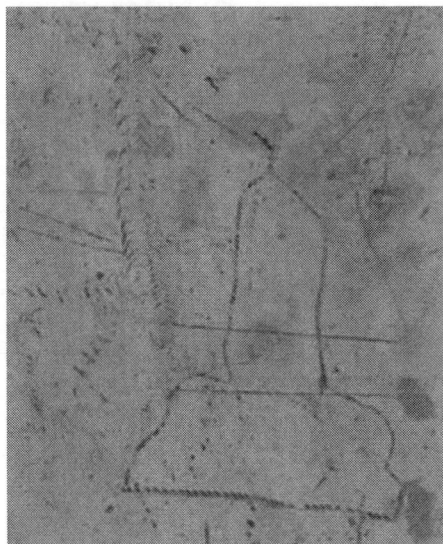

15.7: Work on St Oswald's roof in 2015 revealed 1,482 individual markings in the lead, ranging from sets of initials to images of fully-rigged sailing boats, some dating back to the 17th Century. One is this distinctive profile of the church tower, an undated but timeless representation of what can be seen at sea about half a mile from the end of The Spittals, on the south side of Filey Brigg. It is a well-known meet for fishermen, directing boats in towards the Coble Landing. Note the crudely scratched impression of Church Ravine to the left (*archaeology data service* website). In fog, the church bell was rung, a kind of auditory meet.[16]

This timeless orienteering worked in Filey Bay, but during the Great War, many Filey men had to contend with unfamiliar waters, simply unused to conventional navigation techniques! Smith relates the tale of a drifter, returning to Britain after minesweeping in the eastern Mediterranean, and getting completely lost on the first leg to Malta. They finally got there 'by stopping ships and asking the way, sweeping the bunkers for coal dust'.

---

[15] *North Sea Pilot Part III, East Coast of England* (JD Potter, 1889) p119.

[16] Another 'meet' of sorts was the bell buoy which marked the rocks round The Brigg. Lit in darkness or fog, its bellows produced a draft of air as it rose and fell with the tide. This in turn generated the 'moaning minnie' whistle hoot which reverberated round the Bay.

| Six mussels per hook, or bits of fish, limpets or lugworms | Hook at end of a snood (**sneard**), 3 to 3½ feet of twisted horsehair | Hemp longline, c400-480 yards, with up to 300 *sneards* per line |

Zoom out

Sneard every 5-7 feet

| End of each man's 3 lines marked by buoy (**bowl**) a dog skin stitched and tarred for air tightness | Ebbing tide 360 foot line | Lines shot across the tide as it ebbs. Lines are kept in place with anchors or stones |

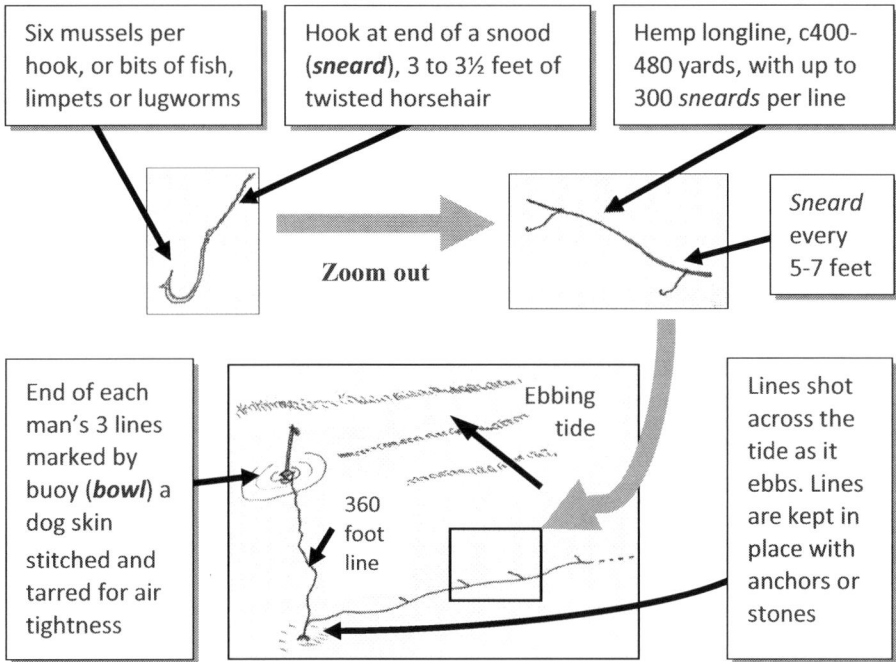

15.8: Shooting lines in the mid-19th Century, three lines per man, 'sweeping' across an ebb tide, downwind. This ensured each *sneard* settled clear of the main line. End to end, the dozen lines stretched three or four miles. Local blacksmiths must have made the hundreds of thousands of hooks that the boats used.

Shooting the Lines was usually done in daylight, probably to reduce accidents with hooks - 'good eyesight, nimble fingers'. Hempen lines sank to the sea bed, but if just sand, intermediate stones were needed where one line met another, to anchor them down – 'the more anchors the more fish'. But lines were not anchored if shooting on rock, to avoid snagging – 'hauling lines off rock is bloody hard work,' one former coble fisherman told me.

Two men 'shot', being careful not to snag round the deep rudder, the third ready to attach the next line, as it was needed. In this way, miles of line were dropped to the seabed, a process that took up to an hour. Fish might be attracted by the movement of the bait, for the lines billowed with the run of the tide. The tidal flow also prevented the lines from settling motionless on the seabed where bait became prey to *varmints* like small crabs or starfish.

Sometimes lines were left overnight, especially in deep winter, if conditions for hauling-in were dangerous, though there was a risk of lines breaking adrift in a swell and being lost. 'It had to be really bad to leave lines,' Graham said.

Hauling-in the Lines - the coble could return to the first buoy at once, and 'haul 'em back' right away. 'Tiding' involved waiting for up to an hour for fish to bite.

According to Jim Haxby, the important part of hauling-in was the art of steering,

> . . . keeping her alongside the line. It was a very difficult job. You just think of wind and tide. That line is there on the bottom of the sea. You've got to 'aul that way, she'll go that way, she'll come over top o' line. That bloke has to be on his toes to keep that boat just there, you can do it with a car, can't do it with a boat. And they were that good that they could do alongside.

> . . . me father would haul the first line, and he was built for 'auling a line, he had arms thicker than what mine are now, and they made it look as though he were pulling a bit of string aboard . . . .

Jim and his dad took it turns. Some men had the knack, some didn't:

> Anyway, I said, when' he gonna 'aul one, Mark? Me father said, if you want him to haul any lines, go to George Cambridge's tonight - that was a plumber's shop and electrician's. I said, what for? He said, get some electric lights, 'cos if he has to 'aul-in lines we'll be here all night.

Mark was perhaps the fall guy on that boat! Coiling a line onto a *skep* as it was hauled-in was called 'Making up'. Jim reckoned it was the hardest job he ever had to learn at sea. The line was supposed to end up piled at a manageably low level – 'mine were up here (indicates head height) like a crow's nest.'

There was no 'average catch'. Men have been known to take 300-400 stone of fish on their lines, and to take next to nothing. If porpoises were 'chasing the sail' they'd eat the cod.

> You'd get down to about thirty or forty stone but the other times made it up when you'd get over 'undred stone . . . . Maybe, northerly winds or nor' west winds and the bottom was stirred up, discolourin' the water so the fish couldn't see the bait . . . .

William Johnson COLLING reckoned 'if the wind was south-east the water used ter clear . . .'. Richard Cammish put it simply: 'fish swims . . . they're like us, going from house te house and street te street'. 'I saw one chap come ashore one day,' Bill Farline told Jim Haxby, he'd 'been off about four in the mornin' an' 'e cam back about four in the afternoon and 'e 'ad one fish.'

Beaching was a visitor attraction, but few watching ever appreciated how dangerous it was, especially if the wind were coming in from the sea. If a coble came in prow-first, the *forefoot* would be the first to ground, and act as a deadly pivot for the incoming surf to wheel the stern through 90°. If the boat tipped, it would quickly fill with water. Catch, craft and crew could all be lost.

To prevent this, an incoming coble was turned through 180°, at a point before the sea broke into surf. Traditionally, this was done with sail, rudder, and oar, then the sail was dropped. Even then, a strong sea might swing it broadside to the shore. Experienced *lanchers*, elderly fishermen, were always in attendance in such conditions.

15.9: These cobles are being beached in what may look like calm conditions, but Matthew *Scrat* HUNTER's *Peggy II* (**Right**) was actually in danger of being swung broadside to the shore. Once the rudder is unshipped, the boat has no means of steering, and keeping headed into the swell. The man in the bow is struggling with a prod to get the stern onto the carriage axle, where chains can secure it. **Left** is *Old Tint* JENKINSON's *Isabella*. [SE]

'And you always got full wellies,' one modern fisherman reckoned. Smith (1932) describes the process:

> Round she goes; we are on the edge of the breakers; the rudder is unshipped; we pole her in; now we hang overside, waiting until our feet touch bottom. The water is cold today – I got one over my boot-tops in launching. We haul her up as each breaker gives us leverage; the launchers are in the water with us, bringing the boat's wheels; backs under her stern we heave her up; chains are made fast; and four powerful horses drag her from the sea to rest with her sisters on the cobble landing.

The boat was wheeled up the beach out of the reach of the tide. In calm weather, all this effort and risk could be avoided if cobles were anchored at the southerly side of The Brigg, where they were protected from dangerous north-easterlies.

Auctioning the Catch on the Coble Landing was often not seen by any visitors, for though the fishing was often completed by noon, on a fine morning, cobles could be away by 3.00am, and back on the landing before 8.00. 'A fish auction on the sand is a marvel of its kind,' Kendall observed in 1871, 'a perfect mystery to the uninitiated; the language and signs baffle the comprehension of mere spectators.' Graham Taylor reckoned the fishermen weren't much wiser:

> We fishermen wouldn't know what was going on. They [the buyers] knew what they were doing when they bid.

Men at smaller fishing stations were at a disadvantage for a single buyer might be able to drive a hard 'take it or leave it' bargain. There were also commonly accusations at Filey that *one* buyer in particular gave his dad better prices! But though three or four fish merchants regularly bought at Filey's Coble Landing, including men from Flamborough and Scarborough, they never bid against each other. It was all pre-sorted – the cartel 'ringed it', as the fishermen put it.

These buyers were masters of their trade. Terence COLLINS summed up Richard CAMMISH, eldest son of the Filey United Trawler Company founder, *Clicker*:

> . . . a very shrewd man said to be the best fish-buyer on the east coast of England. Estimate a pile of fish and he'd be right. Other fish merchants would wait until he'd bid . . . .

Yet the fishermen had some dodges to try in response, judging by these lines from the poem *Buyers and Sellers*, written by Jack *Skeeter* Pearson in the 1930s[17]:

> Baltic sold next; he'd had anchors int' crib;
>
> Cos his crib is a big 'un – it holds fish ad lib
>
> Old *Eamen* then sold, with big uns on t'top
>
> He'd a lot of fish out, but his crib had gone flop.

Jim Haxby describes a typical exchange:

> . . . you'd say to 'em, 'righto, how much?' And they start bidding and sometimes we used to put a bid in, see? Sometimes you were caught out with it, see? Wasn't that yours, Ben? No, I didn't bid. Oh right, you'd better tek it, Bill. You were the bid before. Y'know, you had to be as cute as them.

For once, however, modern developments worked in the inshoremen's favour. Graham described how Matt *Lampler* Haxby 'broke the ring'. Bill Anderson brought cheap, bruised trawl-catch up from Grimsby on his open-backed wagon, the Filey men buying it to bait crab pots. Bill and Matt came to a deal: Bill would buy Matt's fish and take it to Grimsby as a backload. 'It was the first time we got a pound a stone,' Graham said, 'we were not popular!'

Caving was one of the least agreeable jobs, Jim related, for it involved removing 'sour', mouldy bait. First, each quarter-mile line was unravelled:

> . . . when you get the lines 'ome, it's got weed in it, the 'ooks are bent, no 'ooks on. Yer turn it over and lay it straight for the men to come and bait the next morning.

'Reckoning' was done on Saturday night in *The Ship* in the 19th Century. Clark (1982, page 24) was told of the old custom at Staithes of the 'reckoning jug' of ale, which seems to have been an occasion to boast of catch sizes to rival crews.

---

[17] A *skeeter* placed his *skeets* (wooden rollers) in front of the returning lifeboat, repeating the process as the craft moved forward after landing.

15.10: A daily sight on the Coble Landing until the 1960s – preparing for an auction, c1960. The weight of the fish in each row typically added up to ten stone. The largest cod are in the first row and would be sold locally. The rest would be sold at Grimsby, bypassing the local 'ring', the dealers who attempted to keep prices low by not bidding against each other.

Note how each crib – plastic by the 1960s – carries the name of the coble's skipper, for accounting purposes. In this case it is John Robert LANE, who sailed in *Sunbeam*. [FA]

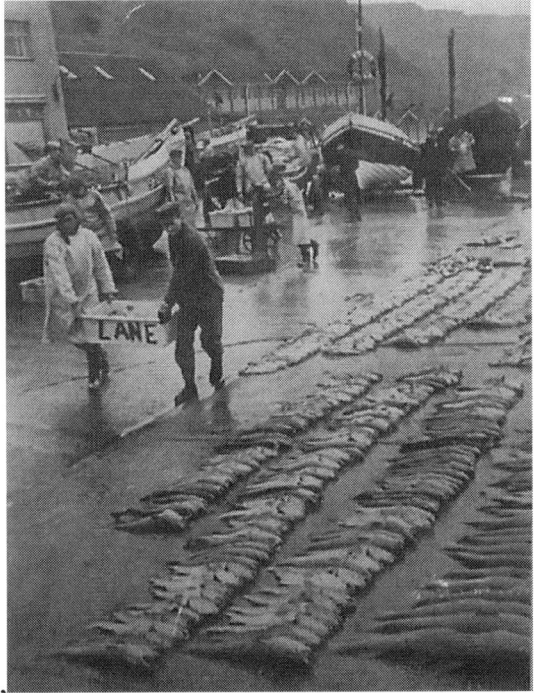

At Filey, by Graham's time, it was done less ritualistically at Friday teatime:

Matt wrote on the back of a cig packet what we got for fish. First, running costs for tractor, fuel were deducted. Then 't'coble took its share . . . .

This went to the skipper as owner, for upkeep and for providing the boat - usually a fifth of the profits, 'a quarter if the skipper was greedy'. This custom, known as 'one for the boat' also rewarded the skipper, who was supposed to know where to find the fish! The rest was shared out amongst skipper and crew. Graham began straight from school, in 1959, on a half share with Frankie *Trab* CAMMISH, since he was not a gearman, but eventually

a three quarterman as I got more experience. Then a full share when I got my lines and pots and I joined *Lampler*.

Long-lining was to survive as an ever-fading shadow of its old self into the early 21st Century. The future lay elsewhere, for by the late 19th Century, the chronic decline in inshore fishing had started to force coble fishermen to concentrate on those branches of their trade which could exploit the summer invasion of visitors. Despite the changes that this new industry brought to the town, it was probably as well that these tens of thousands of visitors *did* come.

16 FILEY'S INSHORE FISHING:
2: ADAPTING TO CHANGE

The Decline[1]

The men whose accounts of coble fishing provide the flesh of the previous chapter represent the vanishing traces of Filey's now extinct inshore long-lining tradition. Several factors undermined it after the 1860s/70s peak.

Coble fishermen, like their offshore cousins, were suffering from the intensive exploitation of dwindling North Sea stocks. By the 1880s, they were taking out twice the length of lines, doubling the number of hooks and bait – yet not catching as many fish. In April 1905, the *Parish Magazine* reported high levels of distress amongst the fisher people,

> some of whom had earned nothing in the past six weeks. This is only partly due to the bad weather, the appalling absence of fish accounting for the rest.

Pots were also catching less, and the Government responded in 1877 by requiring any crab measuring less than 4¼ inches across its shell to be returned to the water. In Yorkshire, this applied between Filey and Bridlington because of the importance of the shell fishery there. Remaining fish stocks were also adversely changing their habits. Herring shoals which had recently stayed off the Yorkshire coast longer and later went south or moved out from inshore grounds to locations only offshore craft could reach safely.

Many inshore Filey men had left the town for Scarborough and Bridlington, on account of overcrowding on the Coble Landing, and to escape the physicality and danger of beach launching and landing. Operating a coble from a harbour saved the hard work, rendered unnecessary self-immersion maybe waist-deep in cold water, and allowed ballast to be left permanently in the boat.

Sailing-trawlers had forced inshoremen off their traditionally productive soft, sandy-bottomed grounds, and onto rock, usually very close to shore. These were waters that trawlers avoided, since rock damaged trawls, and a large boat risked grounding or colliding with headlands. But the appearance of steam tugs with trawls in the late 1870s led to intense fishing of these last long-lining refuges. (The original rationale for tugs had been harbour-manoeuvrability, ideal for close inshore work.) Within a few years, stocks on these grounds had gone the way of the rest of the North Sea.

---

[1] This account relies on Robinson (1984) ch10.

16.1: The Coble Landing, 21st August 1930 – a mingle of inshore fishermen and visitors adds to the general sense of crowdedness. *[FA]*

What the inshoremen *did* catch was costing more. Bait shortages were pushing up prices, at a time when one man needed about 12 bags of mussels a week. Trawling was the solution, for that needed no bait. It was not difficult for a coble to drag a light trawl, and increasingly, traditional fishermen who had railed against trawling now had no choice but to engage in a low-tech sail power version themselves.

Trawling from Cobles

There was a rich irony here, for when a three-mile ban on trawlers was introduced between 1889-91, most inshoremen had welcomed the official acceptance of their longstanding complaints about diminished stocks. Only Bridlington objected - they had been trawling from cobles since 1830, to the disgust of neighbouring communities.

But within a few years, these other places had completely changed their tune. By 1909, local cobles, including seven from Scarborough, were illegally trawling inshore along the Yorkshire coast, no longer able to make a living by lining.

A sole fishery officer was supposed to police the trawling ban, rather difficult when cobles rather than large offshore boats were the main offenders. Since he had no boat, the unfortunate official had to travel by train from his base at Bridlington Quay. But to catch boats in the act of trawling, he needed a boat and crew himself. Traditionalist Flamborough men happily took him out on hire to make trouble for the old enemy.

The Bridlington coblemen took the characteristic fisherman view that no new law was going to stop them fishing in the way they had done for 60 years. Eventually, some were caught, prosecutions resulted, and the prolific bad blood led to threats that there would be nocturnal reprisals against unguarded cobles at Flamborough's two landings. No further Flamborough cobles were hired to the fishery officer.

A 60-foot enforcement steamer was introduced in 1899, but the wily fishermen worked out that the boat had to remain in harbour every twelve hours to rest the crew. Illicit telegrams were sent along the coast giving the all-clear for trawling to commence. To outwit the fishermen, the officer reverted to unobtrusive train journeys to catch them at sea.[2]

Official thinking had at last woken up to the issue of the unsustainability of unlimited fishing. So it was ironic that economic distress was simultaneously turning many traditional fishermen against the very controls they'd been pleading for since the 1860s. One official summed up his frustration in 1914:

> I think there are a lot of fishermen who never look ahead of themselves, if they land a small crab, if they can get a penny for it today they never think that if they left it another year they could get 6d for it. As soon as they get a copper for it they land it.

Flamborough stood out longest against trawling, always traditionalists, but succumbed during the Great War. In 1915, 53 Filey inshore men were allowed to trawl and this continued after the War, especially for Dover sole in June and July. The rare photograph of the beam trawl at Filey (**12.2**) must date from this time. Jim Haxby was one of a number who went trawling nocturnally for sole in the summer:

> They only came out of the sand in the dark. The darker the night the more yer got. So we used to go away at six o'clock, to six o'clock next morning, and it was a cold job. We 'ad all our winter gear on. It was terrible sat there for two hours. So, me and me brother says, well, nights are med fer lovin', days are med fer fishin', so we packed that up and gorrer salmon boat.

Another disincentive was that light trawls were uncompetitive, and the larger motorised boats that were needed to haul bigger gear could not be launched from a beach. This, rather than any principled opposition to trawling, was probably the main reason for the persistence of line-fishing at Filey. But increasingly this played second fiddle to those branches of the trade which could exploit the annual invasion of summer visitors. It was the same all along the Yorkshire coast: those that wished to carry on fishing migrated to the nearest port with a harbour often to fish in larger vessels.

Something that had been unthinkable 30 years before began to affect family life. The 1911 Census shows fishermen whose sons, still at home, had found jobs on land. The traditional craft model based on family labour was breaking down. What is more, fathers were encouraging it. In the late 1920s, William CAPPLEMAN was

---

[2] To date, I have found no evidence of Filey complicity in this Keystone Cops cat-and-mouse activity, but newspaper research may throw it up in future.

urged to get a trade. Twenty years later, Colin JENKINSON's father was dead against his son following him to sea.[3]

It was not until the 1960s that government help made inshore fishing briefly profitable again. Just 14 cobles were working out of Filey in the '50s but this had risen to 18 by the '70s.

Shellfish

In the early 1800s, every north-east coast community had a few elderly fishermen, often helped by youngsters, who specialised in catching crabs and lobsters. Lobsters were the aristocracy of edible shellfish, and commanded 14 times the price of crabs (ie the same per pound as crabs cost per stone). They were a high-end market, and worth transporting at one time by stagecoach as far as York. But they were awkward to deal in – unlike crabs, they had to be boiled alive just before eating, so they travelled alive, and under guard. Only the largest were kept for sale.[4]

This fishery changed as soon as the railway reached Filey, and widened the market. Crabs became popular with holiday visitors, and even small lobsters could now be sold. The season began a week or two after the Winter Fishing ended, mostly crabs till late May, when lobsters appeared. This dovetailed with the salmon season, late June/July. Female and retired family members dressed the catch (removing legs, scooping meat out of shell) and sold direct from seafront stalls, or on regular district fish-rounds. By the later 1880s and '90s, as cod stocks fell and steam trawlers invaded inshore waters, shellfish and salmon became the only prosperous coble fisheries.[5]

Crustaceans favour rocky seabeds, and therefore abounded in the rocks around The Brigg, but rarely in the sandy Filey Bay. Good weather was essential, since the knack was to get 'as close to The Brigg as possible', though the rocks made this risky. Men learned to look out for 'broken water' as a warning sign for their submerged presence. Brigg End Gulley was 'full of lobsters', whilst the south side of Bridlington was good for crabs. A 'crab swell' which stirred up the mud created a cloudy sea, ideal for daytime potting.

The movements of shellfish made them an elusive prey. They spend winters dormant in deep sea mud, only 'starting to creep' inshore for mating as the sea warms to 6°C. Cold winters make for better shellfish seasons. By July they have moved in casts (the collective noun), for safety in numbers, to favoured moulting grounds. Here they grow 20-30% in size, becoming most edible by September to November. The largest are in the deeper water, where they return in the autumn.

---

[3] *Yorkshire Post*, 31st Dec 2019.

[4] Robinson (1984) p41; Frank (2002) p110; Weatherhead (2011) ch4, is useful on Norfolk techniques of crabbing, which were virtually the same.

[5] Robinson (1984) pp415-6.

They are reckoned to build up water content under high water pressure, so the purest meat is found in those that remain in shallows.[6] Unfortunately, the seas were rough when the creatures reached prime edibility, and the risks to gear made the fishery impossible after summer. It was 'a job keeping up with them', Cromer fishermen reckoned. Indeed shellfish got quicker as the summer progressed. Female crabs (hens) improbably journeyed 140 miles along the seabed from East Anglian coastal waters to spawn off the Yorkshire coast. A crab marked 'Yarmouth' was caught off Filey on 7th July 1911, having taken 'several months' to walk the distance![7]

This migration was only fully understood in the 1960s. In the mid-19th Century, East Anglian 'Great Boats' came crabbing each summer off the Yorkshire Coast, returning home with live crabs to replenish the Norfolk populations. We can only guess at the frustrations of these forcibly repatriated crustaceans, given that many of them had only just completed the walk in the opposite direction.

Trunking for Lobsters

16.2: Early 19th Century print of a Filey fisherman baiting a trunk. *[Walker, 1814]*

This was the traditional method of catching shellfish, probably as old as fishing itself. A two-man coble normally went out at night, rarely far from the coast, to shoot a line of trunks, known as a *fleet*. A larger buoy, probably a pig's bladder or dog skin, marked each end of the line. Within half an hour, the coble could be back at the first trunk to start *haling* (hauling) in – silently and gently, so as not to alert any catch. The whole line would be shot up to 15 times a night, strenuous work.

So time-consuming a method couldn't fit the age of the mass market of the railway age, initiated by the opening of the line to Filey (1846). Within a few years, as demand grew, the new technique of 'potting' had eclipsed trunking. Filey made the switch in the 1850s.

Only Flamborough refused to enter the age of mass capture. In 1863, one of its fishermen dismissively told the Sea Fisheries Commission, that 'any tailor or landsman' could lay the new-fangled creel pots. Shellfish fell in price, as a less selective mass market took sales deeper into the social structure - even Flamborough abandoned trunking in the 1870s and '80s.

---

[6] Mike Smylie, *The Perilous Catch: a History of Commercial Fishing* (The History Press, 2015) p104.

[7] CG Brown, *Norfolk Crab Investigations 1969-73* (Ministry of Agriculture, Fisheries and Food, 1975); Nellist (1913). The newly-hatched young drift back to Norfolk on currents.

1 Each crewman lowered 12-15 trunks onto rocks as a tide ebbed. Shallows (a few tens of feet) meant a meatier catch

2 A cork float marked the position of each trunk as it collapsed onto the seabed

3 The trunk was an open collapsible 3-foot bag net, hanging from an iron hoop, 12-20 inches in diameter

4 Lobsters were so agile and fast that a trunk had to be *'haled-in'* rapidly but smoothly before they could escape

6 Bait of stinking fish hung from a bar across the open top. Known to attract lobsters at 50-60 yards

5 Trunks were hauled-in as the tide went out, to lessen the length of the upwards pull

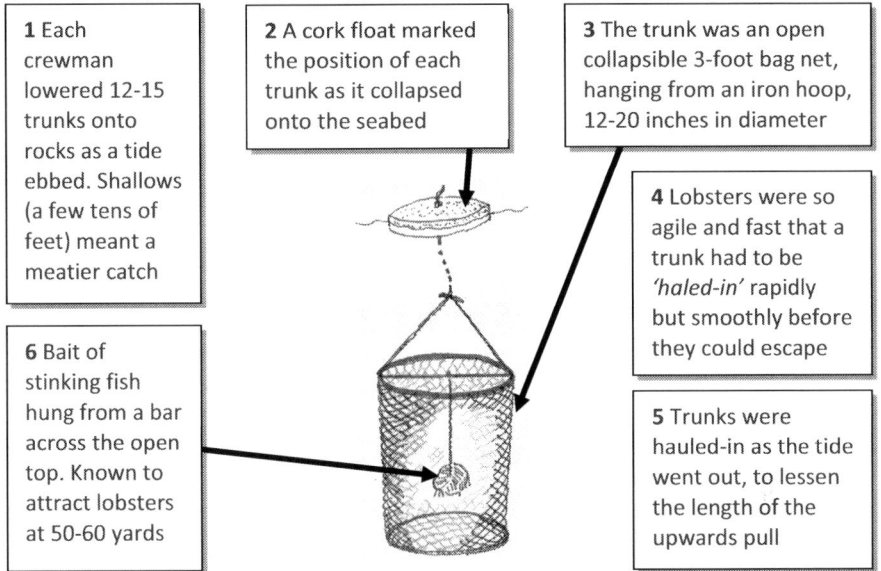

16.3: Trunking - 'lobster snatching with stealth and silence'. The trunk collapsed onto the seabed, so that the lobster could crawl onto the bait. This technique took great steadiness and skill - any sudden movement on the tow (the line) and the lobster could swim out, or flick itself out of the trunk by the tail.

Potting

It is unclear whether the familiar D-shaped creel pot was invented in Norfolk or Yorkshire, but after 1850 their many advantages over the trunk speeded their adoption on both coasts. The pot was an entirely enclosed prison, and could therefore be left for a full day, long enough to trap several crabs or lobsters. Any longer, and crabs would not be attracted, since they objected to rotten bait, whilst lobsters liked it, especially if salty. Herring were poor as bait – they got 'dirty' in the water.

A twice-daily emptying was recommended for lobsters - they were cunning enough to find a way out. Their capture was night work, or just before dawn, for once it was light they could escape from even the best-made pots. The risk of escape from the open trunk during its long ascent was also eliminated. Deeper waters could now be fished, and therefore more grounds exploited.

George Burton told us how younger men were keen to improve their gear. Thomas (*Tint*) JENKINSON (R60) devised a tray on the *eye* of a pot to prevent escapes. 'By God, this'll keep em in, maister,' he said to his uncle, *Old Naz*, 'they won't get out o' 'ere!' The old man wasn't impressed by the elaborate system: 'Aye, you want to get the buggers in first', he commented.

Each of the three-man crew usually contributed 100 pots, 300 in all, and these took three or four days to shoot, in *fleets* of 25. Two fleets could just fit in a coble, so if two trips were possible, 100 pots could be shot in a day, over a scatter of locations. 'Start at the Brigg End, in maybe eight or ten foot of water,' reckoned David Pockley, 'then four and a half, maybe five miles out, in 125 to 130 foot.'[8] Each fleet had some pots from all three crew, so men got branding irons from the blacksmith to burn their initials onto the buoys and wooden pot bases.

There were many advantages to 'working' pots. They were simply fed off the boat attached to the *tow*, and dropped onto the seabed, not lowered. Yet there were skills involved – just different ones from trunking. Success depended on the *tow* being shot on the best ground for tidal and weather conditions. As with long-lining, watch, compass, meets and memory were the keys to locating known grounds. There was no need to spend all night constantly shooting and hauling - men could return to shore once the pots were on the seabed, or lay more elsewhere. A lot of bait was needed, but by-catch and cod-heads could be bought from Scarborough.

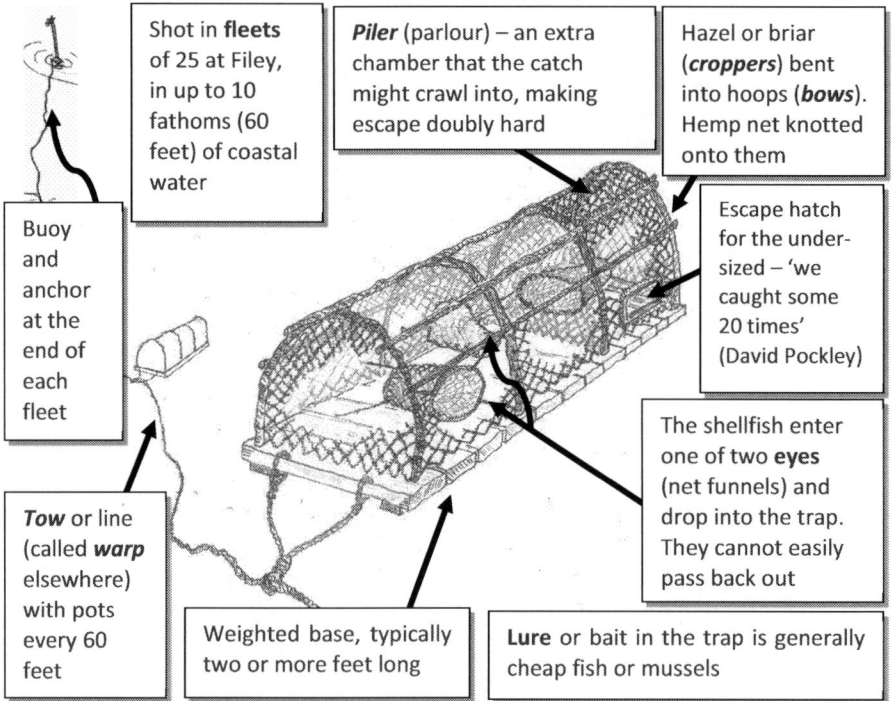

Shot in **fleets** of 25 at Filey, in up to 10 fathoms (60 feet) of coastal water

Piler (parlour) – an extra chamber that the catch might crawl into, making escape doubly hard

Hazel or briar (*croppers*) bent into hoops (*bows*). Hemp net knotted onto them

Buoy and anchor at the end of each fleet

Escape hatch for the under-sized – 'we caught some 20 times' (David Pockley)

Tow or line (called *warp* elsewhere) with pots every 60 feet

Weighted base, typically two or more feet long

Lure or bait in the trap is generally cheap fish or mussels

The shellfish enter one of two **eyes** (net funnels) and drop into the trap. They cannot easily pass back out

16.4: Traditional fleet of pots – each of the crew would have four. A three-mile line of up to 12 fleets, 300 pots in all, sometimes continuous, was therefore shot on the seabed.

---

[8] *Filey: Last of the Coble Fishermen* (*Around and About Yorkshire*, Youtube, Oct 2020).

New skills were developed to work pots. The tidal swell could be used to start hauling-in at a wave's crest, whipping in the slackening *tow* as the boat dropped into the trough, and repeating. Hauling-in was half an hour of hard work, for each pot was weighted. But deftness of touch was no longer needed. In calm conditions, the *tow* could be hauled-in and shot 'under run' [continuously] each pot being quickly emptied of catch as it was pulled in on one side, rebaited, and dropped over the other. The effort was also reduced if pots were attached to the line at least as far apart as the water was deep – say 60 feet apart in 60 feet of water. In this way, there was only ever the weight of one pot to haul.

Men who spent a lot of time shooting and hauling could be identified by the muffler and wristlets of bandages they wore to protect exposed flesh against abrasive oilskins. The lacerated skin broke out in *barls* (salt water boils) on neck, arms and wrists - constant rubbing by the *oilies* exposed it to brine, hence the by-name of William *Barla* JENKINSON (R65).

Like so much of the 19th Century fisherman's gear, pots were made by the men themselves. On 'bad weather days', when fishing was too risky, Filey men collected wild rose briars from local hedge-rows. As recently as the 1960s, the wooden bases, 18 inches wide, were recycled from driftwood. 'Dunnage', ie wood used to pack cargo, was ideal.

'It had to be completely dried out,' explained Graham Taylor, 'then taken to the local joiner who had a circular saw':

> 'How much do we owe you, Mr Townend?'
>
> 'Oh, just fetch us a few crabs some time.'
>
> We had to swear there were no nails in it.

16.5: Filey's cottage industry in pot making, but using modern materials. 'You'd be in a divorce court if you brought a ball of tarred twine in t'ouse' – Jimmy *Bass* Wyvill makes a divorce-proof pot. 'Steel frames, plastic coated, nylon netting. Up at 3.30am, makes pots all day, for everyone' (Graham Taylor). *[Photo: Conrad Newton]*

Or, in Bill COLLING's words, they could drive to the Duchy of Lancaster estate at Cloughton, 'and get *ludded up* wi' wood, which was really cheap . . . saw it up, nail it all together. When it was bad weather, easterly winds . . . it used ter last about ten days . . . we used ter mek fifteen to twenty pots, each man.'

'We'd take out a pair of *croppers* [new branches] and bend them round our 'former' [pattern] whilst still wet,' explained Graham. The netting, too, was hand-braided with hempen twine round the *bows* [the hoops of hazel or briar, known as *bree-ers*]. Man-made fibres were just becoming available in the '60s, so the braiding could actually be done indoors:

> I used to sit here, braiding pots, watching TV. Before that, you'd be in a divorce court if you brought a ball of tarred twine in t'ouse.

The Risks of Shellfishery

16.6: James Wheeler's huge 36lb salmon, caught in Filey Bay, 17th July 1907. *[FM]*

When in use, fishing gear is vulnerable because of its sheer extent. A dozen fleets of pots spaced at 60 feet could be three-miles long. There were always the marker buoys anchored every quarter-mile, at the start of each fleet, but on a ground known to be productive, there was a chance of shooting a line of pots across someone else's.

Even more likely was the risk of a trawler straying inshore, not seeing the buoys, and dragging its beams through a line. Though there were in theory international conventions to keep foreign trawlers out of the three-mile inshore limit, this exclusion did not apply to British trawlers until after 1889, and then only imperfectly.

The best lobsters were close in, but northerlies could create swells in 'short' [shallow] waters strong enough to shift pots off the sea bottom. These could then be smashed up, or swept away on the tide, a rolled-up tangled mass.

If the 6.00pm news forecast strong winds, fishermen went out to get fleets into deeper water. Some were known to be out at 2am if winds got up.[9]

Wrecks were a favourite haunt for lobsters, but there was a risk of lines snagging. Billy ROBINSON, who owned *Windsor Lad II*, discovered what became known as *The Dock* in the 1960s, an especially productive wreck below the cliffs south of Filey. The site was of course kept top secret. Graham Taylor sailed with Matt Haxby who used an early echo-sounder to locate it:

> We heard a whisper on the sounder. The skipper insisted on shooting two fleets, there and back – we needed divers to retrieve them!

Salmon and Sea Trout Fishing

Sand-fishing, also called sand-netting, was another established fishery that increased in significance as lining declined. Salmon and trout are similar in life-cycle and size (up to four feet). They can survive in salt or fresh water, and spend much of the year in bays along the Yorkshire coast, north of Flamborough Head. Deep water around Filey and Bridlington were especially good grounds.

From May onwards, they head northwards, then westwards at Whitby, to spawn upriver in the Esk, one of the most prolific of English salmon breeding streams. Rivers further north are also spawning locations. The law allowed salmon and sea trout to be taken only from May to 31st August. Again, special gear was required for what Yorkshiremen called *fishin' in t'sand*.

If herring was the food of the poor, salmon was a delicacy for the rich. In the 1920s, the fish retailed at anything from 1s 6d to 4s a pound on the Yorkshire coast. At a time when a skilled man earned around two pounds a week and a labourer less than one pound, a top season in a salmon coble could set up a crew for the full year, whatever the winter catch.

Most salmon swim north parallel to the shore, just beyond the breakers, so the net has to be shot several hundred yards, square to the beach. Trout, too, could be caught in the salmon nets. They were less intelligent than the elusive salmon, Richard Cammish JOHNSON told us, and would 'slam in' to the lead net [pronounced *leed*]. Nevertheless, you had to give them 'no room at all' and set the net as close as possible to the shore or they would swim round the lead's edge.

Salmon stocks are unusually vulnerable to over-fishing because of their narrow, predictable migration path. They have therefore long enjoyed legal protection:

> It is obviously possible for man to place some obstruction across a narrow channel in order to stop all or nearly all the salmon in their migration . . . . Salmon can be intercepted like the traffic which passes along a street.[10]

---

[9] Graham Taylor; Malcolm Johnson, *Filey Fishing*, typescript, SMHC (1992) p4.

[10] *Report*, Sea Fisheries Commission (1879).

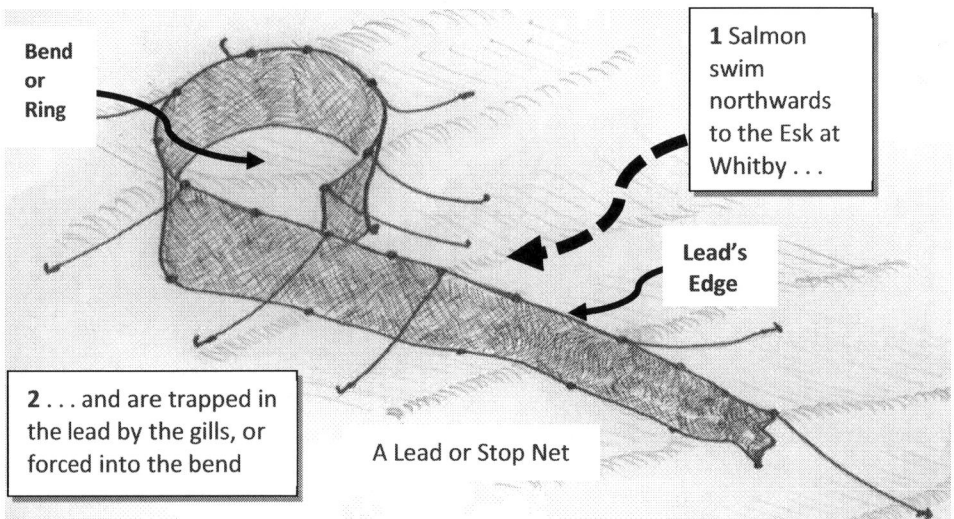

Bend or Ring

1 Salmon swim northwards to the Esk at Whitby . . .

Lead's Edge

2 . . . and are trapped in the lead by the gills, or forced into the bend

A Lead or Stop Net

16.7: Sand-fishing for salmon - a 400-yard gill net, known as a lead or stop net - is anchored to the shore. The coble shoots its net at 90° to the beach, then circles to create the ring or bend, the pocket trap. An invisible curtain of mesh, weighted at the bottom, now dangles vertically from the **cork rope** – kept at the surface by cork floats.

Licences had to be bought, and could be refused by a magistrate. There were also strict limitations on net length and mesh size - no more than 400 yards, and not less than 6½ inches diagonally from knot to knot. (This was later reduced to four inches.) One net was allowed per boat. Unsurprisingly, the temptation in bad years to break the law in quest of these valuable fish could not always be resisted.

Not uncommon were the 1900 prosecutions of three Filey fishermen: William JENKINSON and John BAXTER were fined 2s 6d apiece, with 1s 9d costs, whilst Tom JENKINSON (presumably caught with four times as many fish) copped for 10s and 3s costs.[11] Given that a really big fish might be the weight of a small child, and worth several pounds, these penalties were hardly swingeing. Local magistrates knew how desperate men could be in a bad season.

Unfortunately, one predator cannot be fined. 'Seals take bread from children's mouths,' reckoned Jim Haxby. Conservation which protects one species undermines whatever fishery those creatures prey on.

The 'Tom' clobbered by the beak in 1900 may have been a young Thomas Robert (Q44), brother of Richard Cammish JENKINSON (Q45), a pair better known as *Old Naz* and *Dicky Hoy*. If their catches in the 1941 season were typical, they were in old age a truly formidable partnership, and probably the champions of Filey's salmon fishing fraternity.

---

[11] *Filey Post*, 1st Dec 1900.

The brothers began that May with a 20 pounder, the Filey season's first salmon, and four weeks later had netted a monster of 39½lbs.[12] A very good day might see a coble land 100 salmon. In the 1960s, according to one account, a crew returned with 300 after a day's sand-fishing. But inevitably there were days at a time when a fish wasn't even sighted. A salmon could typically weigh up to 10lbs, but giants of 40lbs or more were known.

Given the prices that salmon commanded, conflict arose if someone tried to fish what was deemed to be somebody else's patch. On the rocks around The Brigg, and below the sea wall, the nets were set out to sea, at intervals of 200-300 yards. Men would pace these distances out if encroachment were suspected, and fights could occur if it were proved. Since salmon and visitors were in season simultaneously, excellent money could be made in just a few weeks by a man with a coble.

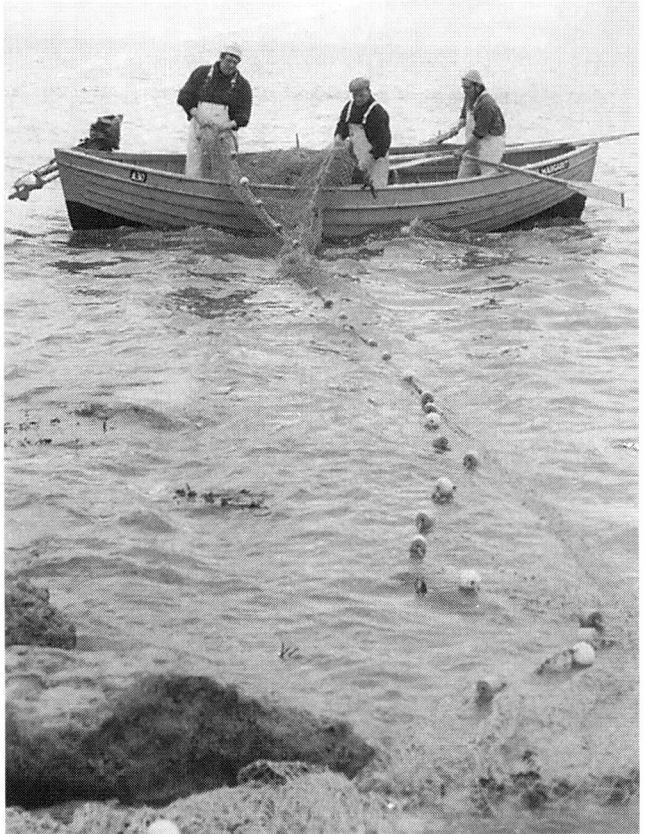

16.8: L to R Richard CAMMISH, *Dickie Tat* CAPPLEMAN, and Jimmy *Bass* Wyvill on the 20-foot salmon coble *Margaret* (*Betsey* until 1960) c1970 – note that it is a 'double ender' (ie no stern) not intended to beach in winter weather. *[FA]*

Once the net is shot, the coble lies at anchor offshore – if the cork floats bob, two men haul-in (as in the photograph) preventing any fish escaping. Most recently, nets were left out, and checked morning and evening. Whatever is already caught in the bend is collected when the net is hauled-in. Salmon in particular were 'very clever'. They would 'touch and poke'. They have been seen to 'sit and watch', weigh up the situation, and then 'work over the top'.

[12] *Filey Post*, 23rd May, 20th June 1941.

16.9: Matthew Crawford Haxby (1859-1936) lay preacher son of the fiery preacher Matt Haxby, repairing a salmon net with a braiding needle. Cork floats lie on the floor, whilst a marker *bowl* (ie a buoy) and anchors are leaning against the yard wall. *[FA]*

To make the most of these boom days, some men were out early in the day for salmon or shellfish, cleaning their boats ready for spawing and shooting parties - before the visitors were even out of bed.

Some were even out with a light beam-trawl when their human catch was back in bed. 'Men who are doing this scarcely get to bed at all, but obtain what sleep they can in their boats,' Smith reckoned in 1932. Where two men were at anchor watching the corks on a salmon net, only one needed to be awake. The triple shift is not an invention of our zero-hours contract, austerity times.

Motorisation and its Hazards

The demands of the Great War brought about a rapid evolution of the internal combustion engine. Its application to inshore fishing was possibly the biggest and most sudden change to which Filey men had to adapt. Filey and Flamborough boatbuilders traditionally made cobles, for inshore lining, salmoning, potting, and spawing, and for offshore herring drifting. The last herring coble in the area powered by sail, *Olive Branch*, was built at Filey in 1913. But unlike the yawls, cobles could be fitted with a petrol engine.

The first around Scarborough was the *Jane and Priscilla*, but a Filey coble through and through. It had been built there in 1879 for Matthew Haxby, the senior preacher, and bought in 1896 by Arthur Douglas, also of Filey. Arthur fitted an auxiliary petrol engine in 1907, but it was little used, for water affected the electrical system and spark plugs.

Motorised fishing increased the number of lines you could shoot, got you back for the best prices, and out of storms, irrespective of wind direction. It also removed much of the seamanship, perhaps leading to a deskilling of the trade. Jim Haxby grew up used to the freedom motors brought:

> We used to work mebbe an hour into sea, mebbe nine or ten mile, January time of year. And we got some really bad weather.

By the 1920s, a petrol or paraffin engine was deemed essential on safety grounds, especially for the Winter Fishing. But in a declining industry, men had to make do – of the remaining 25 cobles at Filey in 1925, Richard Harland (*Fishermen*, 1970) reckoned half were still oar and sail-powered. Many of these boats were worked to the limits of seaworthiness. Smith had little time for motors:

> . . . everybody said I must have one in case of emergency. The weight of the engine in launching and pulling up strained a boat not built to carry it, and by 1930 she was worn out.

And there were other problems. Lines could very easily be sliced through by propeller blades. One story from around 1960 concerns a coble incapacitated when a crab pot jammed the propeller whilst a fleet was being hauled-in. The incandescent skipper refused a tow from another coble. 'F.....g neglect,' he announced back at Filey, 'so I made 'em sail it home.'

An overheating engine in a wooden boat was another accident waiting to happen. Red hot exhaust was known to set a coble on fire. Boat and crew could only be saved by dowsing sea water onto the flames. But the greatest risks emanated from the mindset of men used to a working life so steeped in danger that the explosive properties of petrol or paraffin were disregarded. The Health and Safety Executive, established in 1975, would have been appalled at some of the cavalier ways fuel was treated in these early days. The Kelvin engines fitted to Filey cobles were started by crank, but the generally damp environs made ignition hard work:

> We took the plugs out, put them in a bucket of petrol, set fire to it, then fished them out with your hat, and screwed 'em back in, and squirted petrol into the top of the cylinders. You had to get it going on the Coble Landing. Couldn't risk trying to start at sea.[13]

Men soon did master the new technology. Graham Taylor reckoned Filey marine engineer Edmond Watkinson 'could take a petrol engine apart in his sleep.' For many, however, 20th Century technology was alien and challenging. As late as 1964, Graham recalled men taking sails and oars in reserve, perhaps because of the petrol engine's unreliability – or their own Fileyesque luddism!

---

[13] Graham Taylor, describing some of the pre-HSE practices of the 1960s.

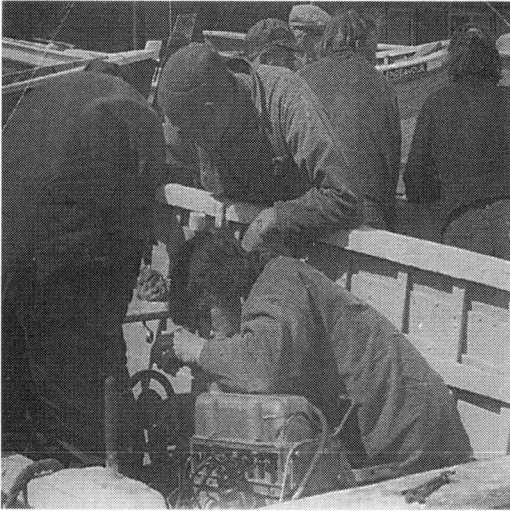

16.10: Edwin G JENKINSON and Michael *Pip* Farline, work on a coble's Kelvin petrol engine, 1970s. *'Pip'* supposedly derived from his 'being round'! *[FA]*

A big improvement was the appearance of diesel engines. Reliant on compression for combustion, they eliminated the electrical sparking so vulnerable to damp. Diesels appeared on the Yorkshire coast as early as the 1930s, but only became common in the '60s. They were 50 and later 80 horsepower.

Jimmy *Bass* Wyvill was the first Filey man to get one. Jim Haxby had a wonderful story about Jimmy *Bass's* father, *Crump* Wyvill[14], who had retired, and it sounds just as well, for he evidently struggled with 20th Century technology:

> . . . 'e was general dogs body runnin' about for 'is son, Jimmy *Bass* . . . one day they kem ashore and they had a bit of trouble with the fuel pipe. So they took the part out . . . . Jimmy went up to 'is father, *Crump*, and says, look I want this part getting' fer tomorrer'. Ring David Brown up tomorrer mornin'. There weren't many 'ad telephones then but *Crump* 'ad. And it was quite unique 'cos 'e allus put a tea cosy on top of it. Whether it was to keep it warm or 'e din't want anyone to see it I don't know. So next mornin' 'e rung David Brown up. 'Ello, is that David Brown? Well, I'm the manager. He says I want a part for our engine we gorroff yer. Yes, can you explain? 'E ses, it's 'ere look, it's in me 'and.

Also, the use of WD40 penetrating oil[15] made the more hazardous methods of starting damp petrol engines unnecessary. A godsend to fishermen, it had reached Britain by the late 1960s. Unfortunately, its applications were not fully understood by the more traditionally minded Filey men. Graham described how the skipper Matt Haxby, took a leap into the modern era around 1970, buying one of the earliest echo sounders. It was a fishing aid, determining sea depth, and locating seabed *boobies*. Alas, there were teething troubles, so Matt sprayed it with WD40:

> That packed it in completely! He took it to the electrical shop in Scarborough. The chap opened it up and saw the mix of WD40 and oil – like tar. He lifted the bin lid and threw it in. *Lampler* went mad!

---

[14] Crompton *Crump* Wyvill (1893-1957).
[15] Originally *Water Displacement, 40th lab attempt*! Developed in California in the 1950s.

One of the most serious mishaps with petrol occurred at Scarborough Harbour in 1935, in those early lackadaisical years. Much of the Filey fishing fleet was very nearly set alight as it lay at anchor, and a young woman had her clothes ripped off.

A pump, operated by 30 year-old Hannah Margaret Groundrill, was used by the fishermen at a garage on North Promenade Landing. Tom *Laffy* JENKINSON Junior (likely to be Q108, or his son Thomas Gordon) described to a local journalist how he wandered up to the pump to have some cans refilled:

> One can had some in, and I forgot to tell her. The can overflowed and to my astonishment flames leapt about a foot from my face, no doubt from the cigarette in my mouth. I covered my face with my cap. Flames were all around. They leapt right to the top of the garage roof. Petrol ran along the road under our boats. Flames quickly followed, scorching several of our boats.

Fortunately, Thomas Wright, almost certainly one of the Filey men, saw what had happened from the amusement arcade opposite, dashed out and

> following the river of flames played a fire extinguisher on the boats as flames licked against the boats' bottom.

Meanwhile, poor Miss Groundrill had caught fire, fainted, and only escaped martyrdom as a result of the quick thinking of some fishermen who presumably could think of no means to save her other than ripping her clothes off:

> It all happened so quickly. I was pumping petrol into the cans when suddenly I was enveloped in flames, the clothes burning on my back. I tried to reach them with my hands, but could not put the flames out. Then someone grabbed hold of me and ripped my burning clothes off.[16]

Such an insight into a far simpler way of life, typical Filey fisherman – a far-off time when the risk-assessment culture had yet to be thought of!

As coble fishing declined in Filey, the Coble Landing boatbuilding industry went too. The Chapmans had been joiners for much of the 19th Century. Son Frank died in 1927, aged only 38, and when his father John William retired, dying in 1930, there was no one to follow. The business had diversified into coffin-making, as did many joiners before the emergence of the modern undertaking business. Billy Guinn had a motor engineering shed there too.[17] Cambridge, the last, seems to have gone before World War II. There had also been a maintenance shed – 'you pushed your coble in there', Graham said simply, of this reliable constant in the fisherman's life.

---

[16] *Leeds Mercury*, 1st Nov 1935, 'Filey Fishing Fleet in Peril from Fire on Promenade Landing', quoted by *Redux*, 7th Oct 2018.

[17] Smith (1932); William CAPPLEMAN.

17 INSHORE TRAGEDY: THE RISKS OF COBLE FISHING

'We have our living to get, and many's the time that we have gone off when it was unsafe.' Elderly Filey fisherman, 1896

Risk is inherent in fishermen's everyday existence – they had to be, in the words of one 16th Century commentator, 'lavish of theyre lives'.[1] Ironically, at any one time, conditions at sea can actually be far worse just a mile or two out than 30 or more from shore. The sea shallows towards the coast, a 'tsunami energy' forces all the violence of any swell into an increasingly diminishing depth, and wave height (amplitude) increases dramatically. The coble, for its size, may be one of the safest boats afloat, but if hit unexpectedly by a very heavy sea, it is as vulnerable as any small craft. The North Sea can work itself up to unimaginable violence inshore: Bulmer's 1892 *Directory* describes large boulders north of Filey Brigg,

> . . . though some of them weigh from 40 to 50 tons, they have been tossed by the force of the stormy waves to a height of 20 feet.

No wonder Filey cobles were disproportionately involved in disaster. When colliers, luggers, yawls and even capital ships of the Royal Navy overwintered in dock, the cobles were out long-lining. And as offshore crews usually took to their corfes too, to eke out a survival income, a maximum number of small craft was out at sea when storms were most common. Men were even desperate enough to be out on Christmas Day: 13 men from Filey drowned in a sudden storm on 25th December 1834.[2] They rarely strayed more than a few miles from the coast, but they were sometimes alone, since knowledge of good grounds was 'commercially sensitive'. Far from help, they were until the early 1900s totally reliant on sail and oar power. Cobles lie low in the water, a rough sea can easily sweep men overboard, or swamp the boat, and in spring this coast is 'much exposed to easterly winds, and greatly annoyed by them'.[3] A man might even have been dragged overboard as a line was shot if a hook caught in his hand. This 1970s Norfolk account of how exposed cobles were in an emergency would probably strike a chord with Filey fishermen of the time:

> . . . we tied an oilskin on an oar and held that up. That's all you had, no flares, no radio, no nothing. Someone would come and see if you were all right, and give you a tow in. We didn't even know what a life jacket was.[4]

Offshoremen didn't wear lifebelts, because they were hamperingly cumbersome. Coble fishermen certainly didn't bother, for they were active for an even greater proportion of any fishing voyage.

---

[1] Frank (2002) pp56-7.

[2] Halliday (1860).

[3] Isaac Leatham, *General View of the Agriculture of the East* Riding (Board of Agriculture, 1794) p7.

[4] Weatherhead (2011) pp15, 104.

Storms force the sea into the decreasing depths close to shore, creating huge waves	The Winter Fishing took place in the most severe of the year's weather	Currents meeting at the end of The Brigg generate the huge waves of the Tide-way

All nearby harbours were tidal, and so could not be entered at low tide to escape heavy seas

In darkness, when cobles were often out, or in fog, they were invisible to large boats and easily run down

As catches declined, men took risks with distance and weather to make a living	Cobles had no decking, and were easily swamped in very heavy seas	Fishermen swept into the sea wore too much clothing to swim or remain afloat

17.1: Three Men in a Boat: why coble fishermen were just as vulnerable as the crews of luggers and yawls, and often more so, despite fishing far closer to shore.

Jim Haxby's great great uncle, Matt JENKINSON (P46) was coxswain of the lifeboat between 1907 and 1915, when it was entirely oar-powered. *Brazzy*, explained Jim, was one of this old school:

> I've 'eard me father say when they used to come down to gerra belt to gerrin the lifeboat, if there's any small men and it was a bad night, 'e'd say, get that belt off, I want someone that can pull. That's the sort of bloke 'e was.

We were frequently told that in the past very few fishermen could swim. Non-swimmers, it was said, would be especially careful at sea, whilst swimmers would be lackadaisical. Is this one of the many highly adhesive stories about the old ways unfounded in fact? In 1898, of an impromptu survey of 40 Filey fishermen, not one could swim. Unless a man were an exceptional swimmer, the weight of his clothing condemned him to drown. His thigh length leather boots alone were an encumbrance and the later *Bulls Eye* rubber versions little better.[5]

---

[5] St Oswald's *Parish Magazine*, Nov 1898. Vulcanisation of rubber was developed in the 1850s, and rubber boots were manufactured in Britain from 1856.

According to Graham Taylor:

> We had that much on to keep warm – trousers, clothes, gansey, smock, old jacket with sleeves cut out, oilskins, balaclava, mittens – except when working. If you went over the side, you had no chance.

One May night in 1902, Richard Douglas (23), with his two brothers, and Isaac Ethell, were drifting in the herring coble *Margaret* a mile off Ravenscar. A sudden wind swung the mast's boom, and it knocked Arthur (20) into the sea:

> A third brother, James (17), shouted 'Art is overboard' and Richard, at the tiller, leapt into the sea without hesitation. Both young men were good swimmers but, hampered by oilskins and seaboots, neither stood a chance of rescue.

The wind took the coble away, and the two other crewmen could not reach them, and may not have been able to see them in the darkness, 'though they could hear their cries in the water for some time'.[6] If a man were lucky, he might grab or be thrown a *bowl* [7], or a plank if the boat were breaking up, but lifebelts were simply not part of the coble's gear. 'It is easy to think you can swim,' Canon Cooper once observed.

> It is one thing to swim across a swimming bath, with an attendant watching on . . .
> It is another thing to swim a mile or two at sea, and at the end reach a shore at the foot of steep cliffs, up which only the sea birds and egg gatherers could climb.

Very often, a crew might be faced with the agonising prospect of leaving several valuable miles of baited line, and running for shore, as bad weather threatened. Taking in lines could so easily be the wrong choice.

How William ROSS survived and became converted

Countless cobles have been lost over the centuries from north-east coast fishing villages, and since their crews often disappeared without trace, the circumstances of the loss are themselves lost. But unusually, one dramatic case of June 1858 is well-documented, for one of the crew, 19 year-old William ROSS, somehow survived. That great recorder of Filey tragedies, the Rev Shaw, published the teenager's account in *Our Filey Fishermen* (1867, Chapter 6). The lost men were John WILLIAMSON (50) and William JENKINSON (P51) aged 21.

It was a fine evening for potting. Having sailed for five miles, an unseasonal squall capsized their boat, somewhere off Reighton. It floated two or three feet under water, virtually on its side. The three managed to get onto her, somehow just clinging onto the submerged hull, sitting/crouching precariously, water presumably up to chest. Let ROSS's own words, as recounted to Rev George Shaw, take up the deepening nightmare:

---

[6] *Redux*, 27th May 2018.

[7] *Bowl* – a buoy or float, to mark off the end of a man's lines. Pronounced as in 'howl'.

The wind now rose, and the water dashed against her very heavy. WILLIAMSON was washed off the boat; but I took an oar from JENKINSON, and pushed it towards him, he took hold of it, and I pulled him to us, and got him on the boat again. Then WILLIAMSON said, 'Let's all shout as hard as we can, likely there may be someone riding under the cliffs' - which were about a mile off - for the Flamborough boats were 'trunking' . . . about there. We shouted until we were hoarse, but no one heard us, and we gave over, thinking it was no use. The wind increased and blew still more furiously. We commenced to sing.

What must William ROSS have felt as John was swept off yet again, and despite frantic attempts to save his skipper, was washed further away? The older man was too exhausted to resist drowning, but somehow he managed to sing too.[8] The unfolding of this tragedy had a profound effect on young ROSS. The son of devout Wesleyan parents, with eight converted siblings, he had somehow remained a non-believer. He had been just 12 when his father, Isaac, had drowned. We can sense his embarrassment, as he had to admit to his godly interviewer, Shaw, that at this time, on the edge of eternity, he had had no faith. Yet JENKINSON never ceased praying, and the sinking WILLIAMSON continued to sing to his god:

> Cover my defenceless head
> With the shadow of thy wing.

I could see just then the top of his sou'-wester out of the water, and a minute or two after he sank, and we saw him no more. When we were left by ourselves, JENKINSON said, 'ROSS, can we pray?' - He was converted you see, sir, and I was not. I said, 'No, I don't know how.' He said, 'then you say the words after me as I say them,' and he began to pray, and I said what he said; then he sang and I sang.

Accepting that there was no chance of help, William ROSS, made two attempts to swim ashore. The prospect of being left alone in the darkness, clinging to a capsized coble, was too much for his remaining crewmate:

When JENKINSON saw me leaving him, he said, 'O Lord, help me, I am left by myself.' I could not bear to hear him say that, and returned, determined not to leave him any more. We both continued to sing and pray, as well as we had strength. It was getting very dark now, and the boat was sinking deeper in the water. At length there was so much wind, and she was so deep, that we floated off her. I could see nothing, but felt for JENKINSON and found him, and discovered that his head was under the water. (The bowl to which he had been tied had shifted and kept him under). I could feel his hair in my hands . . . .

---

[8] The names of these men betray none of the close connections that bound them. The 1851 Census shows the ROSS and WILLIAMSON families as near neighbours, at The Cliff and Mosey's Yard respectively; JENKINSON was weeks away from marrying WILLIAMSON's daughter Elizabeth: whilst ROSS was to marry his second daughter, Mary Elizabeth, in 1865. Typically of the Old Town, a single boat was the focus of a complex social web.

It was very dark, I could feel but could not see him. While struggling in the water I felt a line in my hand, which was fast to the boat, and hauled myself to her. I tried to find JENKINSON, but I could not see anything. The moon was rising and just headed the top of the white cliffs. I had my eyes on that moon and looked towards Filey, wondering if I should ever see them again in this world, and whether any rescue would come, but none came.

A 'billy-boy[9] for the north' passed close by, 'so near that I could have thrown a stone into her', and then a schooner, but ROSS's desperate shouts were lost in the wind and swell. The coble was invisible, just beneath the surface, and alarmingly threatening to sink at any moment. Attached to a buoy, his friend was drifting just feet away, in who knew what state. ROSS tried to lower the sail, believing perhaps that this might pitch the boat over.

I should think nearly two o'clock - I thought I saw a sail in the distance, and concluded it was a boat from Filey coming to seek us. My heart leaped for joy. Alas! Alas! I was doomed to be disappointed again. I soon found it was only the flag flying at the top of the bowl to which I had fastened William JENKINSON . . . But oh, how I longed for the morning.

17.2: A fisherman seems to have conducted a party of mid-Victorian ladies to the edge of The Brigg. They practise some non-still life painting, perched above, and occasionally in, the breaking waves. It is almost certainly the summer season, and was probably like this in June 1858 . . . *[FA]*

At last day began to break, and the first thing I saw was a ship, which seemed to be steering straight in for me. Now I thought I am going to be saved! . . . . The ship came right in, and got nearer and nearer. At last I saw them lower the boat, and I lifted my heart up . . . . The first and only words I could say, were, 'Pull for yon bowl.' They did so, and found JENKINSON's body still tied to it, took it in and pulled for the ship. As soon as we got along-side, they handed me two or three pots of hot coffee over her side, to refresh me. After drinking these, I was taken on board and *shifted* (ie his clothes were changed). This was about half-past four, in the morning.

---

[9] A flat-bottomed coastal trading vessel, from Hull – the nickname *billy-boy* referred to the town's support for William of Orange against James II in 1688-9.

In such poignant circumstances, William JENKINSON's funeral was very well attended. It took ten more days for WILLIAMSON's body to be found and buried.[10]

But long after the formal mourning was over, the events of that night were to have a permanent effect on William ROSS. Perhaps his decision to marry his skipper's daughter seven years later derived from some sense of connection. Both had lost fathers from a coble; indeed, William had actually been alongside Mary's father in his last hours. What a bond between human beings. Something shifted in the man, for, in Shaw's words, he continued thereafter 'steadfast in the faith':

> Each of his brothers are officers in our Filey Society, and one of them, the Rev Castle ROSS is a very promising travelling preacher. Mr John ROSS, a devoted local preacher and class-leader gave me the following account. 'We were, as you may all suppose, very anxious about William, and when noon the next day arrived, had very little hope of his safety . . . . I remember being in my mother's (the house is on the top of the cliff, and commands an excellent view of the bay), when a vessel came into the bay with a flag flying at half mast high. I knew in a moment what that meant[11], and, while mother was in another room, removed my brother's stockings, Guernsey, &c, &c, which were hanging upon the line, and put them out of sight lest my mother should see them, for though I was only a boy when my father drowned, I very well remembered how the sight of his clothes used to affect my dear mother.'[12]

There is so much in this story that takes us into the heart of Filey's psyche – how close to death by drowning every family was; how the death of a husband was usually compounded by the loss of several of a woman's closest relatives; and how its threat was just under the surface of every fisherwoman's consciousness - there were so many simple reminders in the most banal of daily chores.

William, son of Isaac and Ann ROSS, married Mary Elizabeth WILLIAMSON in 1865. He survived to a grand age of 82, his gravestone at St Oswald's recording that he 'entered the higher service' on 21st September 1921. Mary died in 1931, aged 92. They are in the cover photograph, a couple at ease with one another, in middle age (captioned at **3.9**). But the grit that got him through that horror is unmistakably still in his face, thirty-odd years later.

Some men who were out on a coble overnight, in extreme circumstances, did *not* survive. Frank (2002, page 202) cites a 1909 example, a 17 year-old dying through 'heart failure, consequent upon exhaustion, due to exposure and want of food'.

---

[10] There was always large attendance in such circumstances, for every family would have memories of their own grief triggered by a loss: a communal grieving kept feelings healthily in check. WILLIAMSON was the third of three brothers to have drowned at sea.

[11] Clearly, this was how a drowning out at sea was announced.

[12] Isaac ROSS had been lost on 12th March 1851, seven years before - see **21.1**; there is more detail in Shaw, *Scenes and Adventures* (undated) ch1.

17.3: St Oswald's grave carvings commemorating men lost on cobles usually portray an empty boat, mast down, and tossing on a violent sea. Note the accuracy of the detail, with what may be a *bowl* [buoy] in the stern.

This stone records the loss of *Mary-Jane* off Atwick, near Hornsea, 27th November 1879. Unusually, the body was recovered, and buried ten days later.

ROSS, also a young man, 'could not stand' when he was landed: 'they placed me in a carriage and drove me to my mother's. I was very lightheaded after that. It was some days before I was myself again.'

'It came as Black as Night'

People on land could offer some assistance to cobles in distress. If it were suspected that men were in difficulties on account of bad weather, candles were placed in the windows which faced the sea, to guide the boat in.

In the 1860s, William HUNTER (born c1806) and his son were overtaken by a violent storm when out in a coble with Matthew JENKINSON. An attempt was made to 'burn off' the boat - lighting a fire or tar barrel on the sands, to warn the crew to await the launch of the lifeboat. In fact, HUNTER contrarily took this as a guiding light, and got the boat to shore in hazardous circumstances.

In such serious weather, the man at the tiller had to stick there and take his chance, for if he let go, the boat would capsize. Graham Taylor explained how this man literally held the lives of the crew in his hands. If the boat swung 90° to the sea, it would be swamped. He described his closest brush with death in Matt *Lampler's Janet and Carol*, with Peter Warcup, one winter in the 1960s, when the full fury of a terrifying storm suddenly broke over the Filey boats:

> We got really copped once. We were working off The Brigg, ten or 12 cobles, three or four miles out - we started shooting in 18 fathoms . . . and it came as black as night.

> The crucial thing was to keep the boat stable and upright – we had a mizzen sail up to keep it steady and the coble would also be held against the wind if we kept tension in the line we were hauling-in.

> One hauled, one made up, one steered at the helm. Then we'd change round. The skipper was on his hands and knees, with the tiller over his head . . . the wind broke off the mast, and there was nothing to hold us. We spun round out of control -

terrifying. One man on another coble nearby got onto the bottom of the boat and started to pray. We had bilge pumps and we had to use buckets too. We used the engine to get home. We had to leave the lines. It had to be really bad to leave lines. The lifeboat was called out, but within minutes the sea was as smooth as glass. We all think we're tough, but three men in a boat on the North Sea . . . .

After each Christmas, Graham long-lined three or four miles off Flamborough, and only in good weather, four lines per man, even though this reduced the catch - the weather was just too unpredictable: 'At times, you stuck your neck out . . .'.

Filey Bay's Death Traps: the Tide-way and Racing Tides

The Brigg in winter could create daunting conditions: in 1860, Cortis poetically described waves being 'dashed a hundred feet into the air in foam of the most snowy whiteness'.

There was no avoiding The Brigg as a coble came home, and though it offered protection from vicious northerlies, its projection out into the open sea could create desperate conditions for a returning open boat. Its waters should only have been entered at slack tides. But how often must men have launched at dawn in perfect conditions, only to face a foaming cauldron of sea on return? And accidents here could be truly traumatic for anxious relatives waiting on the shore, if they became helpless witnesses to the deaths of their menfolk. The terror experienced by those on the cliff tops in 1865 must have unimaginable when it was reported that 'the boats were out of sight in the deep troughs, then they appeared on the crest of a mountainous wave' (Shaw, undated, Chapter V).

The big risk was the **Tide-way** at The Brigg's end, the strong tidal current to its south that a boat encountered suddenly as it neared home. Many of the coble losses before the age of any newspaper probably succumbed to its violent unpredictability. This happened on 16th January 1874, when a coble was caught in a gale, and had to run for shore. A huge wave thrown up by the Tide-way overturned the boat and threw the crew into the sea. Despite a search, and the proximity to the shore, the three bodies were never found.[13]

Such family disasters were an inevitable result of the Filey family boat practice. It was a given that a son should learn the complicated fishing skills from his father or uncle, and the custom prevailed in the smaller, more traditional fishing stations. An extreme example was the three Douglas brothers, on the four-man herring coble *Margaret*, referred to already in this chapter.

---

[13] *Filey Post*, 24th Jan 1874. The captain of the coble, George Mainprize, had married Sarah JENKINSON (O45) in 1845. He was a great great grandfather of Irene Allen, whose family history drew us into this research project. The coble was likely to have been *John and William*, registered in Mainprize's name at Scarborough in 1869. As we would expect in a Filey family boat, a nephew, George JENKINSON (P80) and son-in-law, George JOHNSON, drowned with him.

17.4: Men might launch in perfect conditions but have to land in sea as rough as this. Chris *Wokkie* Watkinson's *Mary*, is returning to the beach in extreme bad weather during the Winter Fishing, December 1954. The crew are using auxiliary oars and prods to keep her head into the seas – the danger was the boat being swung round broadside to a strong tide, tipped over and dashed apart by the force of the waves. *[FA]*

But even conservative Staithes abandoned the practice eventually, and in most stations some variant was adopted to lessen the risk of family wipe out.[14] One common practice relied on a family's capital accumulation. The eldest son helped his father, but then bought his own boat, father and son having half shares in each, with separate crews. The second son worked with the father, aiming for a third boat. The three would then have third shares in three boats. Thus one loss could not snatch away the livelihood and personnel of the whole family. Yet Filey predictably stuck with the old way well into the modern period - Captain Sydney Smith remembered his father's despairing comment when seeing such an arrangement: 'Look at them . . . three in a coble, and all in the same family.'

Racing tides were as big a threat as the Tide-way. Heavy seas drive into the shallowing bay, the surface currents race over the bulk of slow-moving water below, and crash violently down. The water breaks, creating deadly conditions.

These twin threats were greatest in the wildest months, the hard weeks when poverty forced men out to sea whatever the weather. Five cobles went out on the morning of Monday 14th December 1896, when a storm was anticipated – Winter Fishing catches were usually poor, so prices were high.

Five skippers were gambling on being back before the weather broke - James Wheeler, Edward SAYERS, Peter CAPPLEMAN, Matthew JENKINSON and

---

[14] Frank (2002) p64.

Robert Skelton. The flotilla left the grounds near Speeton Cliff around midday, as the rising moderate ENE breeze portended 'every indication of a storm'. From the cliff top, much of the Filey community saw the lifeboat put off, for the *Mary* was clearly in danger inside The Brigg, where a full tide was running:

> The lifeboat proceeded to the spot, but none of the occupants of the vessel were seen. Those watching the *Mary* saw her struck by a big sea, and she sank immediately after.

Everything went out of sight. It could not be seen whether the men in her were entangled with the cordage or whether they had floated for some little time. But they were lost without trace. Skelton (41) left a wife and two children, as did crewman George Thomas JOHNSON (26) whose little daughter Lily was just three months-old. The third man, George JENKINSON (18) was unmarried. Since all the families lived in the Old Town, the Skeltons at Ravine Top, scores of relatives must have been amongst the crowd of spectators who witnessed the whole episode from the cliffs.

> The sea washed up a piece of the coble *Mary*. A sou'-wester, some oars, and other appliances have also been cast ashore. Asked as to the risk incurred by the *Mary* and the other cobles in putting off in the teeth of the easterly wind, an old Filey fisherman exclaimed, 'We have our living to get, and many's the time we have gone off when it was unsafe.'

Particularly chilling is the account of one eyewitness, who told the journalist how

> . . . a great wave bore down on the *Mary* and literally engulfed her. She did not overturn but together with her occupants was knocked clean down out of sight.

Though a close watch was maintained along the coast between Filey and Flamborough, the three bodies were never recovered.[15]

Gravestones were especially important in preserving memory in such circumstances, even if erected far later than the event itself. The impact of loss in so extreme a case as *Mary* stayed with families for a lifetime: the stone recalling George Thomas JOHNSON's drowning was finally erected decades later, probably at the death of his widow, in 1951. No doubt Lily, who had never known her father, was responsible for ensuring he was not forgotten.

17.5: Crewman George Thomas JOHNSON's modern memorial, one of three Coble *Mary* gravestones at St Oswald's.

---

[15] *Filey Post,* 19th Dec 1896.

It is a powerful experience to have talked to an actual eye witness of something so overwhelming, yet now beyond living memory: in 1983, George CAPPLEMAN, born in 1889, told us he could vividly recall watching the event, as a child, from the cliffs.

The Tide-way was unforgiving. Once a boat capsized, that current, racing strongly round the end of The Brigg, took the men down. It was that terrifying phenomenon of broken water. One coble man who had been in it summed it up:

> Strange things happened in the Tide-way. The sea came at you from all sides – no direction to it. You could feel it pummelling the boat, making it shake. A dollop of sea water suddenly thrown into the boat . . . .

One man survived this modern-day Scylla and Charybdis by grim determination. When the coble *Annie* succumbed on Monday 21st April 1919, returning after a night's crabbing, Mortimer SCALES (aged 42, **13.8**) and Matthew Jenkinson CAMMISH (65) were swept to their deaths, their bodies never retrieved. But in contrast to the Tide-way, Fate ran the right way for John Robert LANE, the third member of the crew: he lived until 1968.

17.6: The Brigg's hard sandstone claw slices three-quarters of a mile out into the wildness of the North Sea from the natural line of coast, splitting incoming tides and swell. This can create entirely contrasting conditions just yards apart, as visible in this timeless Victorian photograph – note the cobles riding in the calm to the right. Currents such as the infamous Tide-way were one especially deadly effect encountered by shore-bound boats. *[FA]*

Somehow, as his crewmates were swept to their deaths, LANE managed to cling to the upturned coble. You have to marvel at the desperation that found handholds on what must have been a deliberately smoothed hull. But with a wife and three young children, he had everything to live for; whilst at 23 and only recently demobilised, he was at the peak of his physical fitness. Good luck also rendered Richard Cammish JENKINSON able to reach him in his coble *Sunstar*.

Newspaper accounts do not specify, but the rescuer must have been *Dicky Hoy*, (Q45) the only Richard Cammish JENKINSON in Filey in 1919 with the experience and skill to navigate a sailing coble in such waters. Fate often seemed to throw eerie ironies into the Filey mix: *Dicky Hoy's* brother and nephew had been blown to nothing on *Emulator*, just six days before. [16]

The Risk of Collision

The *Mary* report reveals how inshoremen, like their offshore cousins, might go out in a flotilla despite the risk of revealing trade secrets about good grounds, for if one got into difficulty in a strong sea, help was at hand. Cobles were historically painted in a distinct livery to facilitate this flocking – Filey's colours were red and blue.[17] Such colouring also increased visibility. This reduced the risk of collision with the large ocean-going boats that used the busy east coast sea lane:

> Fog was the enemy. Up to the late 1960s there were still 'flat-iron tankers', colliers taking coal up the Thames for London power stations – you could hear one coming – that's why you usually kept a knife on the first *thoft* – to cut the lines if you were still shooting.[18]

In early March 1900, the *Hermione*, perhaps 18 feet in length, was struck by the 1,950 tons screw-steamer *Water Lily*. The three JENKINSON crewmen were long-lining, and had not noticed the appearance of the ship, perhaps because of sea mist. They would have been drowned had two other cobles not been nearby.[19]

As the first edition of this book was virtually ready, there came a pointed reminder that even the backstops of radio, electronic navigation aids, sophisticated radio-watch coastguard systems and helicopter rescue could not guarantee safety. On 7th May 1984, the Bridlington coble *Carol Sandra* sank off Flamborough Head, whilst checking crab pots. All four crew were lost. Whilst searching for the missing coble, the £80,000 Bridlington charter-fishing boat *North Wind*, equipped with the latest navigational equipment, was swamped by freak waves in the old way. Three men were lost off her.

---

[16] *Redux*, 21st April 2018.

[17] Fearon (2016) p16.

[18] Graham Taylor. The *thoft* was a *thwart* or cross plank, the seat for the rowers.

[19] *Filey Post,* 10th March 1900. The skipper was Richard Cammish JENKINSON (*Dicky Hoy*).

The Loss of *Lady Shirley*, Primrose Valley, 29th June 1948

Motorisation did reduce the dangers of coble fishing, but the risk remained of being swamped when a strong sea hit the inshore shallows, a danger in any month. One notorious accident, still recalled in Filey sixty-odd years later, is recorded on four gravestones grouped together in St Oswald's churchyard.

William Robinson JENKINSON (*Billy Wemp*, R3) was drowned with *Frankie Tosh* CAMMISH, and with two other CAMMISH brothers, William *Codge* Watkinson and Richard *Sorta* Ferguson. A 'moderate swell' caused by a NNW wind overwhelmed their salmon coble, just yards off the coast at Primrose Valley.

There is much about this sinking, the last big fatality involving Filey men, that seems compellingly intriguing. Characteristically, it involved family tragedy. And just as Fate had kept John Robert JENKINSON off *Research*, 23 years before, so illness spared *Lady Shirley's* owner, Tom *Tint* JENKINSON (R60). He was in bed with pneumonia that summer Tuesday morning, so two, not three, went out. Jim Haxby, 12 at the time, was an eye witness, from the Coble Landing, about half a mile away:

> . . . they shot their net two hours before low water . . . . They kem 'ome for their dinners, put anchors on 'er, and when they went back a lot o' northerly sea 'ad come on and the first of the flood tide. So, they called at the *Daybreak* and took two men outta the *Daybreak* and left *Daybreak* where she was. It's a pity they 'adn't tekken 'er becos' she was by far the better boat. Why they took four men I don't know. I don't think any other fisherman down 'ere will tell you why they took four.

17.7: Luck . . . or Fate? Primrose Valley, 29th June 1948 - **L to R:** the two CAMMISH cousins, *Bill Codge* Watkinson and *Frankie Tosh*, who drowned; and *Tommy Tint* JENKINSON, their skipper, spared the same death through a bout of pneumonia. *Dick Sorta*, Bill's younger brother, stood in for *Tint* that day, and his was the only body never found. *[Photo: Ian CAMMISH]*

17.8: It is as well we do not know the future. Robert *Codge* CAMMISH poses sombrely with his wife, Mary Emily Simpson (née Watkinson, *Em Wokky*) their three sons and two daughters, around the outbreak of the Great War. *[Ian Cammish]*

Back row, **L to R:** Robert Jenkinson Watkinson (1900), Margaret Mary (1899), William *Codge* Watkinson (1902) and Richard Ferguson *Sorta* (1906). Front, Annie Liza *Annie Codge* (1910), stands between her parents. The summer of 1948 was to be hard for *Codge*: his wife died in the May, whilst the two younger boys drowned when *Lady Shirley* was lost, just seven weeks later. The youngest boy, *Sorta*, died in an attempt to rescue his brother and two other crewmates.

In the 1980s, when the events were fresh in many minds, we heard one opinion that the four had 'thrown their lives away' by 'rushing out' at low tide, when there was a risk of grounding. But that is hindsight – all fishing is risk.

Conditions were near-perfect, and changed suddenly, unexpectedly, and unseasonally. The problem with being caught in bad weather when sand-fishing, Jim Haxby reckoned, was that once you started hauling-in, you were locked in:

> Now, if you're caught in dire straits if yer linin' or pottin' you can pick a knife and and chop and get out of it. Not so with a salmon net . . . 'undred meshes deep, four-inch meshes, on top there's a cork rope, on the bottom there's a lead rope. There's no way that you can get that up in seconds and chop. Yer committed, once yer tek 'owld. And they started to 'aul-in, and I saw this 'appen . . . . And one sea kem, knocked 'er broadside on, and the next one filled 'er. Down she went, two hundred yards off the shore.

Several people saw it, including Dick Harland, a teacher, who got there first:

> A good job 'e did, becos' there's 'olidaymaker 'ad stripped off and 'e was goin' in forrem and Dick Harland ran and gorrowld of 'is 'and and said, you goo in there you'll join 'em, there's no way you can swim in that. They were all drowned and Dick *[Tosh]* who was instead of Tom *Tint* JENKINSON was never found.[20]

---

[20] Richard Harland taught at Filey Junior School on Scarborough Road. He was an

Auxiliary coastguard Eddie Belt, was on bad-weather watch on Carr Naze. Through binoculars, he saw one man make it to the beach, shake himself and walk back into the waves. Given his age, it seems Jim's account wasn't considered, but he confirms that this was Richard *Sorta* Ferguson CAMMISH, returning to the upturned boat to rescue his brother and crewmates. In July, at the inquest, the Coroner paid tribute to Sidney Leonard Moon, of Leeds, clearly the man who went into the sea 'in a vain attempt to rescue the fishermen'. It was ironic that Richard's was the only body not found. The other three were found entangled in the net, and were retrieved right away.[21]

Ferrying Gravel

The dangers close to the shore from tidal currents had again been revealed at Scarborough in July 1890. When fishing was bad - and the '90s were bad - an income of sorts could be earned from Scarborough Corporation, raking and shovelling gravel off the shore at Carnelian Bay, two miles south of the harbour, and ferrying it to the West Pier slipway. It was used for road building, and large construction projects like Valley Bridge (1864-5) and the Aquarium (1875-7).[22]

This was hard work, and risky – there were treacherous rocks around Knipe Point. The men were paid by weight, so got in as much load as possible. A coble could manage three tons, at 2s 6d a ton, but this would leave less than a foot of 'freeboard' between gunwales and water. Any waves washing onto the gravel added to the weight, pushing the coble even lower in the sea. As with fishing, the men gambled on the weather, and were always tempted to push their luck – one extra trip, a touch more gravel. Unsurprisingly, many Scarborough cobles sank, with drownings.

The Scarborough coble *Ellen* was owned by Jack Bell, an uncle of Captain Smith's. Jack's mate, Thomas *Filey Tom* CAPPLEMAN (24) also now lived in Scarborough. The boat left in calm conditions for Carnelian Bay at 4.30am on 24th July, with one other coble.

But 300 yards from the East Pier, *Ellen* encountered an extremely choppy sea, likely to be the current known locally as *The Stupe*. Waves splashed into the coble, the gravel got soaked, and within minutes boat and crew had sunk out of sight. Weighed down by heavy seaboots, which may have been impeded by gravel, the men did not surface. Grappling irons retrieved the two bodies within hours.

---

auxiliary coastguard, member of the Rocket Brigade, and Sea Scout organiser. This national scouting movement, like the Boy Scouts, dates from the years of tension with Germany before the Great War, to prepare boys for military experience.

[21] *Redux*, 29th June 2019 (71st anniversary); Jim Haxby.

[22] Marie Belfitt, *The Scarborough Leader*, 11th Aug 1988, quoted by *Redux*, 24th July 2017 (127th anniversary); *Carnelian* is now normally spelt with an *o*.

Calculating the Filey Death Toll

Filey people claim that no maritime community has proportionately lost so many men at sea. This was primarily because the town persisted with line-fishing from cobles. Ironically, in all other respects, the town was very healthy. There is no evidence of cholera or typhoid, the great waterborne cullers of working-class urban populations. Nor was the fisher population vulnerable to poor harvests, with hunger then weakening immune systems, although some died of a particular variety of consumption (tubercolosis) associated with the sea. Put simply, the sea's toll looked high because nothing much *else* killed the adult male population.

Whilst there was clearly a convention that a gravestone was especially necessary where no body was found, the death of menfolk put a memorial beyond most families' means. Sometimes it took years to erect one.[23] There is never an entry in the burial register for an unrecovered body, and most Filey drownings fell into this category. Similarly, civil registration of death, established on 1st July 1837, recorded these only where there was a surviving body. The same precondition existed for a coroner's inquest to be held. There was only limited registering of deaths on board boats before 1880 anyway. Thus the 20 or more JENKINSONs that we know to have been lost at sea are unlikely to be the full number, and this will be representative of all the fisher surnames.

Reports of sea deaths in local newspapers can fill gaps. Many are now accessible via the digitised *britishnewspaperarchive.co.uk*. This source often provides the answer to the mystery of the male members of fishing families who figure only in the register of baptisms, or in the census returns as children. Sometimes, however, these online returns have revealed them in new, migrated lives, away from Filey. They may perhaps have moved to Scarborough or Bridlington, where many Filey fisher families settled in the later 19th Century.

Some single men may have been lost into the more rootless, waged existence of the trawling fleets. Or perhaps they were washed ashore many miles away and buried in some distant churchyard as 'a drowned man'. The sea could be utterly unpredictable with dead bodies. They could be carried large distances: in September 1903, the body of Leonard Mainprize of Flamborough was recovered a month later, nearly 20 miles away at Scarborough.

Nor was there any predictability as to *where* the body might be taken. A now lost gravestone at St Oswald recorded how John CAMMISH (68) was carried in exactly the opposite direction. Drowned in Filey Bay on 22nd December 1824, he was found at Flamborough six weeks later, on 5th February.[24]

---

[23] John and Maisie Crimlisk completed the herculean task of transcribing, indexing and typing the inscriptions on all 1,756 gravestones extant in 1978.

[24] Nellist (1913); *Scarborough Mercury*, 6th Nov 1880.

17.9: The 'Tagged-on' phenomenon - St Oswald's inscriptions are often the only clue to a man's death at sea. Francis Haxby, lost on the Dogger Bank in 1859, when a yawl's corfe was overturned, was only recorded many years after his drowning. Like many young men, he was squeezed into the last scrap of space at the bottom of his parents' stone, and can very easily be missed. Just as the sea has deprived him of any death or burial record, rising vegetation threatens to blot out even this modest trace of his existence.

Some young men simply vanished without trace, abandoning fishing to take up a life on the wider waves. Ironically, their new life only comes to light as it ended in some distant disaster.[25]

Even men who had retired from active employment at sea were not immune to danger. In the 6.30am wetness and darkness of 18th January 1939, a 62 year-old *lancher*, John William Sumpton SAYERS, was hurrying up from the Coble Landing, head down against wild weather. The combined noise of wind, rain and waves deafened him to the rumble of the approaching coble, *Joan and Mary*. He was knocked down, a wheel ran over his head and he died instantly. Why, the Coroner wondered, was no light used when launching the cobles in hours of darkness?[26]

If pressed, the fishermen would probably have said, 'we've always done it like this'.

---

[25] Robert Jenkinson Watkinson (1891) and William Cammish COLLING (1947) are just two of the known examples. See below, pp406-8.

[26] *Redux*, 18th Jan 2018 (81st anniversary). It may be that older launchers were used to the noise made by iron-rimmed wooden wheels. I have heard a suggestion that old bus wheels with soundless rubber tyres were replacing them.

18 BEYOND THE FISHING:
MAKING A LIVING ON THE SHORE

Dependency in Old Age

At what age did men stop fishing? In 1863, the Sea Fisheries Commission heard evidence at Filey from men who had been fishing into their seventies. In the 1841 Census, Isaac ROSS (77) described himself as a fisherman. William CAMMISH, living in Cammish Yard, also 77 in the 1861 returns, described himself with some typical Filey irony as a 'Worn out fisherman'. This remarkable survivor made it to the 1871 Census, by then at Mariner's Place, aged 89, still described as 'fisherman', although this must at most have represented a land-based support role, or even a courtesy title. He died in April 1872.

Retirement could be phased, for it had no set age before 1909, when old age pensions were introduced – initially paid at 70, at 65 from 1948. William JENKINSON (N8, born 1786) was around 77 when he told the 1863 commissioners that he had been out 'a week or two' in the previous herring season. His younger brother, John (N10, born 1791) told the same inquiry that he had given up herring fishing 'about three years ago' but seems to have taken up coble fishing. There were of course many land-based contributions that an old man could make to the family fishing effort, thus staving off the pinch point when the elderly became net consumers of family resources rather than contributors. Even the least physically active could earn something: curing, making and repairing nets, attending coble launchings and beachings, baiting, salmoning, *spawing* - all had economic value. Jimmy *Bass* Wyvill was especially skilled at making crab pots (**16.5**).

Up to 12 men, including the elderly, were needed to help launch and beach the cobles. Each boat contributed a couple of '*lanchers* fish'; these were sold with the rest of the catch, providing a small reward for the old men's work. Those unable to fish could still go potting, young boys accompanying them, apprentice-like: their crab stalls were a distinctive summer feature on the Coble Landing.

Many old fisher people in Filey lived with their children and grandchildren. About a third of all JENKINSON households in the 1881 Census were of this extended type, ie parent(s) living with married children's families. This was exceptional, even amongst fishing communities.[1] Nationally, the late 19th Century union workhouse increasingly became an old people's care home, as age diminished what an old person could earn. In Filey, however, it seems that few people spent their last days there as long as they had somebody to look after them.

---

[1] Blaikie (2002) p27, notes that its rarity within the fishing communities of north-east Scotland was partly because houses were too cramped, and the proximity of the extended family rendered cohabitation unnecessary anyway. Extended families were far less common in the past than many rosy-spectacled views would have us believe.

The whole culture of the fishing community emphasised family, and this may explain this worthy tradition.[2] More prosaically, the versatility of coble fishing, and its many support jobs, offered even the oldest ex-fisherman a modest income.

Fish-Sellers

The seller/dealer was the link between fisherman and fishmonger, from whose shops or stalls the public bought the fish. The more foresighted fishermen, especially those who had capital, worked out that sellers and fishmongers lived in some of the better houses in the town, were spared the intense physicality of fishing, and were unlikely to drown in the course of their work. Men like Jenkinson Haxby (see Chapter 7) seem to have switched from active fishing to selling in early middle age, perhaps on account of family tragedy, the anxieties of wives perhaps adding the final gloss to the attractions of giving up the sea.

One man got into the business by pure chance. According to William CAPPLEMAN, Richard Ferguson *Clicker* CAMMISH won £700 on the Irish Sweepstake, gave up fishing to set up in the fish business, bought trawlers and formed the Filey United Steam Trawler Company in 1918.

Two men had stopped fishing in 1860, Edmund Crawford becoming a fishmonger, whilst Ben Simpson became a salesman. Simpson alone specified it was because his lugger, *Robert Newton*, was lost in the Whit Monday hurricane of that year, but it seems safe to assume that Crawford had given up on 20 years of long-lining in similar circumstances. Simpson seems to have taken a broader interest in the market for even in the 1850s, before his 28 years of active fishing came to an end, he had been travelling to Manchester in some selling capacity.

18.1: One branch of a diversified empire – three generations of Simpsons fish-dealers had built up a chain of three shops in Filey by the 1910s.

This is one - William Simpson's Fish and Game Dealers shop at 8, Belle Vue Street (1908). *[FA]*

---

[2] Of 243 inmates at Scarborough Workhouse on census night, April 1881, in whose union Filey belonged, just two women had been born in the town. Neither had a fisher surname, nor did the 13 year-old Filonian in the Bridlington Workhouse that night.

He alone of the witnesses mentioned that demand for fish had dropped so much during the American Civil War (1861-5) that sellers could barely make a profit. Salesmen had an aptitude for understanding the wider market, and had authoritative knowledge on boat costs, demand and trends. Significantly, of the ten Filey men who gave evidence in 1863 to the Sea Fisheries Commission, two-thirds of it came from just three fish-dealers. Ben Simpson's fish had been going as far as Leeds and Manchester since the 1830s, yet despite the railway, 'as many carts used to go then as now.' The main markets for Filey fish in 1863 were London, Manchester and Nottingham.

Selling was a sophisticated operation. Simpson received daily briefing letters on the state of the different markets. The railway age had led to the introduction in 1840 of the Penny Post, the world's first cheap postal service. Several stretches of independent railway connected the Yorkshire coast with these markets, and the railway companies finally woke up to the value of the mass fish market later in the 1840s and '50s. They agreed cheaper rates and joint charging arrangements, so that men like the Filey sellers paid once, and not to each company. The market boomed. No wonder Crawford and Simpson each founded dynasties of curers/dealers/merchants/mongers which lasted well into the 20th Century.

Jenkinson Haxby pioneered a new occupational niche, travelling with the Filey fleet to broker fish sales on the crews' behalf. It made good money (see his probate valuation, 1908, in Appendix D). Men did not die as wealthy as this without a nose for business, and a certain drive. 'He didn't like anyone saying no to him,' Graham Taylor said of one Filey fisherman turned fish-dealer. They were shrewd: 'they wouldn't bid against each other.'

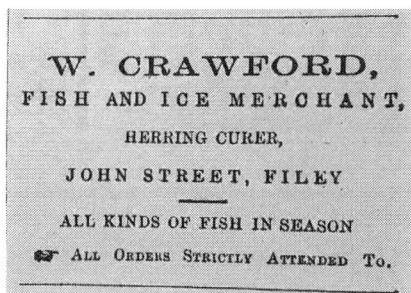

W. CRAWFORD,
FISH AND ICE MERCHANT,
HERRING CURER,
JOHN STREET, FILEY
ALL KINDS OF FISH IN SEASON
☞ ALL ORDERS STRICTLY ATTENDED TO.

18.2: The vanishing world of the local fish merchant/monger - the 1904 advertisement [**left**] features a type of business which fishermen with capital entered as a safer alternative to the sea. Personal service was at a premium – a similar 1901 advertisement for Simpson's 'Fish Game and Poultry' boasted 'Families waited on for orders daily'.

Benny Hoy's 1958 advertisement [**right**] – Ben Cross JENKINSON (R59) a successful fish-merchant, was a son of *Dicky Hoy,* the man whose systematic recording of every fishing trip brought him the popular acclaim of 'top coble' in Filey.

FOR QUALITY FISH
Ben C. Jenkinson
15, HOPE STREET
Tel. FILEY 2140
ORDERS DELIVERED TO ALL PARTS
MAY WE SUPPLY YOU ?

'A very careful man with money,' reckoned one informant, of a fish-merchant he worked for as a schoolboy in the 1950s. I'd better not give either name!

> I picked up fish from the front for his shop. Sixpence an errand. Then me and the other lad laid fillets out in boxes, nailed them down and tied up each box with old fishing line. 'Here, have a shilling,' he might say, 'we've had a really good day.'

This merchant was systematic: he bought on the Coble Landing, brought the fish up to his shop, where the lads packed the orders, six or eight stone, in *Norraway* boxes [Norway, perhaps from the type of wood] between layers of ice. The lads then went with the lorry to the station for the 5 o'clock steam train, which had a fish van, packed with ice, coupled at the rear. The practice continued even when diesel railcars took over, and until 1964 when all goods working ceased at Filey.

> We used the hammer shaft to raise each box while old fish line was passed underneath. One day when we got back to the shop, there was no sign of the hammer. 'Get in the *rully* [lorry] and go back to the station,' [the lads were told]. We held up the train whilst we searched the boxes and we found the hammer under a box, tied in with fishing line! You'd think it were made of solid gold.

A glance at Appendix D reveals that fish-merchants almost invariably died richer, and often far older, than fishermen. Filey's prime seaboots-to-riches story begins with Thomas ROSS (1870-1937) modestly born in Mariners Yard. He famously graduated from Filey fisherman to Grimsby fish-merchant, founding the Ross Frozen Food Group, and becoming the largest trawler-owner of his day in Europe.

18.3: Filey Station in British Railways days, around 1960, with goods shed at north end, into which fish vans were shunted for loading. In the town's heyday, an average of 20 tons of fish were dispatched from here weekly. *[SE]*

Shopkeeping

It may be that yawl owners dabbled in grocery to supply their own boats at trade prices. John JENKINSON (O12) and his enterprising wife *Nan Cooling* (Ann COWLING) managed to multi-task to a formidable extent, an 1860 directory entering him on Queen Street as 'fisherman, grocer, draper, and lodging house'. Somehow, wife Ann must have managed all this land-based trade, between skeining and baiting, whilst her husband was at sea.

One small example reveals that many fishermen were side-lining as grocers out of necessity. In April 1881, Castle JENKINSON (O34) was described as a Filey grocer, when he was fined 5s with 7s costs by Bridlington magistrates for having a pair of small scales 'quarter of an ounce short'. (We can't know of course whether this was an oversight, or deliberate.) Yet in the census of 1881, taken at the beginning of that same month, he styled himself as a fisherman, with no mention of his grocering. The size of the scales suggests tea, coffee and sugar, bought in modest bulk, and sold on to neighbours in small quantities. He died the following year, and his gravestone features a beautifully carved coble – and not a pair of scales in sight! He was skipper of the yawl *Admiral Hope*, which had been wrecked off Bridlington in the October Gale, just six months before this fine.[3]

18.4: Robert (*Bobbin*) CAMMISH and his wife Eva (née COLLING) outside their bootmaking shop, 2, Mitford Street, c1942/3 to which they had just moved, from Reynolds Street. Robert, son of Robert, master of the yawl *Diligence,* was sea sick when out with his father, and suffered from asthma. He gave up any thoughts of the sea, becoming a cobbler and seaboot maker.

Family tradition says the last pair he made was for Tom *Titch* Cappleman JENKINSON (R85). Bobbin's grandson Ian CAMMISH, with his wife Joanne, still have the business, though now *Cammish Outdoors*, at 2c, Mitford Street, over a century on. *[JC]*

---

[3] *Scarborough Mercury*, 30th April 1881; Scales, *Scarborough A-Z Boat Index*. For Castle, grocery was, in short, a survival strategy, at a time when the chronic decline of Filey's offshore fishing was aggravated by storm loss.

Robert CAPPLEMAN (*Bob 'ush*) was another forced to shore by his health. He gave up fishing in the 1890s following an accident when the boat was coming into Bridlington. No longer fit to go to sea, he became a grocer and provision dealer, in one of the fishermen's cottages, no 13, Queen Street, where he and his family lived 'over the shop'. His estate in 1931 was valued for probate at a respectable £485, probably far more than if he'd remained an uninjured coble fisherman.[4]

Fish Curing

Dry Curing had been practised for around 5,000 years - the water in dead flesh encourages the growth of the decay-inducing micro-organisms, but salt soaks it up. Filey's salt was originally brought from Cheshire by packhorse train. Throughout the summer months, cod and ling were laid or hung out to dry on every spare bit of ground in most Yorkshire fishing stations north of Flamborough. The fish were split on landing, salted, and collected when dried into one huge pile to 'sweat' for ten to twelve days. The finished product was known as 'stockfish'.

Filey's speciality was skate, dried to the consistency of horn. House fronts, paddocks, rocks, tenter frames – no doubt the locals got used to the stench, though perhaps it wasn't the best inducement to attract visitors.[5] Winter catches were pickled in brine (*pekel* is Dutch for brine). Herring, the 'pork of the sea', deteriorated quickly on account of its oiliness. Salting might make it edible for six months, but the disagreeable taste of the salt made herring the food of the poor.

The fish's outer skin could be sealed against bacterial penetration by quick smoking. The original **Smoked Cure** required at least 15 days exposure in a smokehouse to slow-burning oak sawdust, herrings in particular receiving such 'hard smoking'. But railways got fish fairly fresh to market within hours, so that preservation became less of a priority for the home market. From the 1840s, an eight hour 'lighter cure' had the dual benefit of retaining the fish's original flavour whilst masking poor quality.[6] Also, the flavour of herring lent itself to the smoked cure, which assisted the 19th Century boom in its fishery. Thus the original hard-cured 'red herring' was ousted by the light-cured kipper, or bloater.

Edward SCALES told the 1863 Sea Fisheries commissioners that there had been no curing houses in Filey 20 years before. But a few fishermen moved into the trade. One clergyman who toured a 'herring house' in 1862 explained its origins:

> One of the principal herring houses is held by a fisherman who lost his yawl during the terrible storm of May, 1860, and who forthwith determined to give up his old occupation. Fortunately, his wife inherited a small patch of land, and upon it he erected his herring-house.

---

[4] Kath Wilkie; census returns; *Calendar of Probate Grants, England & Wales, 1858-Present.*
[5] Robinson (1984) ch2.
[6] Robinson (1984) ch4.

18.5: Judging from the 1914 *Directory*, this was the Crawfords' herring-house on 14, West Parade (later renamed West Road) behind nos 5 to 17, Scarborough Road, near the old Church of England school. Aso known as a smokehouse, it stood by Belt's Yard, and was later Killingbeck's slaughterhouse. Its change of use is evidence of 20th Century changes in diet. *[FA]*

Further research may clarify this man's identity, and the precise location of his enterprise, but it seems safe to assume that here were the seeds of either the Crawford or Simpson curing empires in Filey. The processes in the new enterprise were broken down into an assembly line that we might associate with a 20th Century Midlands car plant:

> The building includes a large shed open to the rafters, which contains casks, boxes, washing-tubs, spits (long sharp pointed pieces of hazel wood), and piles of herrings, and is used for washing and spitting the fish.

> . . . the packer, who strips the herrings off the spit, by twenties at a time, upon the table . . . rapidly places them by fifties in boxes, which a boy quickly covers. On the side next [to] the only window is a wall-ladder, leading into an upper room, where boys, who receive from 5 shillings to 7 shillings a week, are employed in making little packing cases, the boards for which are supplied ready-made from Sheffield.

> Upon the opposite side are two doors, each of which leads into a room open to the roof, higher than the shed, and capable of containing 12,000 herrings.

This was where the actual smoking took place:

> Upon the floor several fires of oak and ash wood are burning and throwing up clouds of smoke; rude racks of wood line the walls on either side, and across these are laid the spits with the herrings strung upon them . . . .

> Four girls, who commonly begin their work at three o'clock in the afternoon, can spit at least 10,000 herrings in two hours upon their spits of hazel wood, at a payment of five shillings among them; and as each spit is covered with twenty fish, it is piled upon a rack. The scene is one of great animation at this hour: one man shovels the fish off the floor of the shed into baskets with open wicker sides, with

a broad flat spade; while another transfers them into a larger swill or basket, which he immerses in a huge tub of cold water, and stirs with both hands to free the scales from salt.

When perfectly clean, the fish are thrown into a long flat tub which is dry, and then quickly spitted by the nimble fingers of the girls . . . .[7]

Walcott's description is the only account I've encountered of a fishing-related, industrialised land trade which was a big employer – just count up the number of workers referred to in the above passage. Much capital was involved, which is why three such houses was about the limit for a fishing station the size of Filey.

The account also illustrates yet another instance of the steady shift of fish-focused activity away from family to employer, in this instance from cottage and croft to commercial herring-house.

Walcott's description also catches a process now virtually out of Filey living memory, having lasted barely 80 years. Blossoming on the back of the herring boom of the 1830s, and from being 'extensively carried out here' in 1872, according to Kelly's *Directory*, herring curing died out in the town after the Great War. The fishery went elsewhere, and fell into decline as eastern European markets were lost. And tastes change: 'who eats herring now?' a Suffolk fisherman asked me in 2018.

On the Beach

Trotting[8]

This more modest land-based occupation, also known as beach-fishing, might attract men who had had enough of coble fishing in the harshest months of the year. A *trot* might be a length of a draw net, or a line with snoods, used to introduce boys to the rudiments of long-lining. George Burton, who knew the three *Buggins* JENKINSON brothers well, recalled how this eccentric family did just a little *spawing* in summer in the mid-1920s, and somehow made winter ends meet by a variety of ruses which kept them away from long-lining. 'Bit do nothing' said one relative in 1984, perhaps a little harshly!

Frank and Jim[9], sons of *Old Jossie*, were in their forties, of fishing age, but in winter they set a *trot* at low water mark - up to 200 hooks. It was anchored to the shore with a stone, cleared of fish and rebaited at each tide. The *Buggins* Brothers stretched their line from the rocks by The Brigg and back towards the Coble Landing, or at Primrose Valley. It could be tended from a rowing boat. Bait could readily and cheaply be found in the sand in the form of lug-worms, and the expert at sourcing these was Jim, 'the last of the original sandpokers'.

---

[7] Walcott (1862).
[8] The word *trot* is of Norwegian origin.
[9] Frank Cappleman and James Scotter JENKINSON (Q90 and 91).

Sandpoking

Throughout the winter months, irrespective of weather conditions, *Jim Buggins* was a familiar sight on Filey beach in the '20s. Woodbine in mouth, wearing a worn out, patched-up oilskin, and invariably accompanied by two dogs, he was always *scratting* with a child's beach spade in the corners where the tide could have washed up coins. He was Filey's prime beachcomber: it was said that 'if *Jim Buggins* had got nowt it was a certainty there was nowt washin' ashore'.

There was a science to it, built up over centuries of survival at the margins. Seaborne material moves south, driven by the direction of the most powerful waves and currents on this coast. A sustained easterly gale stops this movement and washes it up on the beaches. Jim would know exactly when conditions were right for large quantities, especially when the force dropped, or swung to the west.

18.6 One of the best-known residents of Providence Place *(Jenk Alley)* – this shot is likely to be *Jim Buggins,* James Scotter JENKINSON, 'the last of the original sandpokers'. 'No matter what weather,' reckoned George Burton, 'Jim'd be there with two dogs. And his dogs barked all bloody day long - when he was digging worms they'd be stood just in front on him barkin' into his face. I used to say, "how the hell thoo can stand that Jim?" But Jim was a great lover of animals, an even-tempered man who never got 'crazed'.' *[SE]*

Eldest brother *Jossie Buggins*, Jack Matthew JENKINSON (Q89) was another well-known sandpoker, a magus of the shoreline, maybe looking for patches of weed and coal at the tide's edge, which might conceal jet or Baltic amber. He sailed a coble owned by David Smith. During the Great War, the Government paid a pound for any report of German mines washing ashore, anxious to study the mechanisms. Who else but one of the *Buggins* clan would have spotted the first to come ashore on the British coast?

Jossie found it behind The Brigg, driven in by an ENE gale, 'when down the cliff on a rope looking for fishing buoys or anything else of interest which might have drifted in,' wrote Smith (1932), 'a very good corner for such things, but difficult of access.'

Of course, high explosives capable of blowing up a sea-going craft are not the safest of quarry. *Jossie* told Smith about some fishermen, probably Filey men, who

found another mine a little way up the coast. They found difficulty in rolling it
ashore, owing to the horns up on top of it. One of them tried to knock them off
with an oar. Special angels guard such men. The mine did not explode.

The Bonzo-Buggins Partnership

The *Buggins* family found other ways of gaining an income from the sea. Jim and
Frank's *trot* led them to discover and adopt a common seal that became one of the
most famous characters ever to have lived at Filey. Early one morning in late 1927,
on their way to check the *trot,* they found the pup on the beach, very small, probably
about 12lbs in weight. It was christened *Bonzo*, inspired by a contemporary comic
strip cartoon seal. Frank soon became known as *Bonzo Buggins*. Foster Holmes
JENKINSON (R37) wrote down the story for us:

> On my way to school this particular morning, as usual, I went down Providence
> Place (*Jenk Alley*) and saw old *Jossie Buggins* and his sons, Jim and Frank, emptying
> the seal pup out of a sack in which they had carried it from the beach. Opposite the
> houses where they lived in *Jenks' Alley* was a row of baiting sheds, one of which
> they used. They then put the seal in a zinc bath full of sea water.

Planning permission was clearly not an issue in those distant days, and the project
soon needed a relocation. Tom Smith, who owned the land down to the Coble
Landing, let them build a pen. 'They fed the seal all winter and it grew very
quickly,' continued Foster.

18.7: 'Wooden erections at Filey used to house a seal' – a contemporary sketch of
Bonzo's hut by the Coble Landing, 1930s, artist not identified. *[FA]*

I remember going to see it whenever the shed was open. During the winter, they built a wooden hut with a concrete pool inside on the top end of the Coble Landing and in the summer *Bonzo* was moved into his new quarters.

Children fed him fish they'd caught with hook and line.

I think they had tried to get it to go back into the sea again, but *Bonzo* preferred hand-feeding and always refused to leave the beach. He was looked after by Frank, Jim and *Old Jossie*. I understand it wasn't too easy getting fish in summer for him and they used to get fish heads and offal from Scarborough when Filey cobles were crabbing. Eventually, Frank's son Jack (my age)[10] left school and he took a big part in entertaining the visitors who were charged admission to see him. *Bonzo* became very attached to Jack and he could do just anything with the seal. *Bonzo*, by now, was growing huge and they had to build a bigger hut and a larger pool, of course.

Keen to maximise exposure to a larger market, the *Buggins* consortium looked further afield. At some point, the show moved to Bridlington and Scarborough.

One summer I know they had a hut or tent on the West Pier, at Scarborough, thinking that they would earn more money. However, they only tried it once. *Bonzo* would not settle and refused to do his party tricks and the next summer he was back at Filey.

Bonzo's accommodation clearly posed problems: by January 1934, the *Filey Post* reported how Frank was taken to court by Walter West for at least one year's non-payment of rent 'in respect of wooden erections at Filey . . . used to house a seal'. By this time, *Bonzo* was said to be approaching 'the size of the Loch Ness monster', eight feet long and 20 stone. The seal was ordered to vacate the 'premises' within 28 days. He became such a local celebrity that his passing was reported in the *Filey News* on 10th August 1940 under the headline '*Bonzo* is dead'. A delightful sculpture, making *Bonzo* the only Filey resident I know of to attain statuesque status, was on the Coble Landing for many years. *Bonzo* gained a renewed lease of wooden immortality when a fresh likeness was carved in 2020.

The parents of this unlikely family were *Old Jossie* and *Pris*, in Providence Place. Jim lived next door. George Burton, who was a neighbour, remembered *Old Jossie Buggins* (George), born in 1860, as past fishing age, 'a nice old chap, wore a cowboy-style felt hat with a band, and always had a great mug full of baccy.' He baited lines in an agitated manner, dancing from foot to foot, and as the mussels went on the hooks a shot of brown spit would strike the ground. 'It was just as if someone had emptied a tea pot on the floor,' George recalled. Their eldest son, *Jossie Buggins*, who found the German mine, lost sons Teddy and George on *Research* in 1925; their other son, Matthew (*Sailor*) played for York City.[11]

---

[10] In fact, Jack Matthew (R124) was Frank's nephew, one of the two children of brother George William (Q92), who migrated to Sacramento, in California.

[11] *Sailor* JENKINSON, reckoned the second fastest winger in the Football League, played for York 54 times (1930-4) and was also with Scarborough, and Filey Town *[Wikipedia]*.

'Sea-Gift'

By law, beach finds had to be declared to the Receiver of Wrecks, though some laxity was permitted, small takings such as sacks or bucketfuls of coal being allowed. But the authorities drew a line at the sort of widespread plunder that took place on the beaches around Filey in January 1913 when the 1,155 ton *Hawkwood* was wrecked near the King and Queen Rocks, north of Flamborough Head:

> Hundreds of tons of coal have been washed out of the steamer, and scores of men are busy bagging and carting it away to their homes. Cabin doors, lockers, racks and all manner of fittings, besides hatch covers and combings and planking, have also been torn free by the sea and thrown on the beach. In the absence of the coastguard, cartload after cartload of these things have been carried off.

The more enterprising hawked this coal around Filey and its environs. Coastguards and policemen might be posted on the descents to the beaches in cases of large wrecks, but it was hard to stop what was popularly seen as a traditional right to take 'sea-gift'. The risks that men took to get at wrecks on barely accessible rocks were remarkable. Precarious descents included 'The Band'. One 1864 'rocker' on Horse Shoe Rock, at the foot of Lebberston Cliff, could only be reached by 'The Chimney' (the 'Baitgatherer's Descent') a crack, down which a rope hung precariously from a stake, and:

> it was astonishing to see what heavy loads of broken timbers, etc, the men would bring up this place, upon their backs.

> Practically every owner of a horse and cart has found employment there, and farm waggons from remote distances have also been sent by farmers to get what they could.[12]

Some didn't even use a rope. Once the crowds had gone, of course, it would be *sandpokers* like *Jossie* and *Jim Buggins* who mopped up any items subsequently driven ashore. Especially valuable were the physical remains of dead whales which, from time to time, washed up. Not one shred would be wasted. One late 19th Century account describes the recycling of a 30-foot bottle-nose found dead at sea near Whitby:

> Its captors tried to bring it to shore at Whitby, Scarborough, and Bridlington, and had been forbidden to beach it by the authorities. At Filey there were no authorities, and no courtiers to resent the intrusion of the stinking carcass between wind and their nobility.

> I smelt it a mile off. I found a crowd of men, women, and children round it, cutting and slashing away, and filling cauldrons and kettles with the blubber. Under a hot sun, rivulets of oil, white, blue, yellow, and red, meandered through the sands.

---

[12] Pettitt (1868) p41.

This went on for several days, when the fleshy interior and the bones were finally carried away and laid on the land.[13]

Shrimping

Another beach fishery for the mature in years was shrimping, the catch being sold alongside shellfish to tourists. The skilled shrimper preferred the lowest possible tides, pushing his net parallel to the shore, in at least six inches of water.

The 'blade' is angled to cut a couple of inches of sand, where shrimps, crabs or small fish are feeding. They feel the vibration, make a break for it, and the waves sweep them into the net behind the digging blade.

Controversially, some Filey men went shrimping with horse-drawn nets three times the breadth that Matt JENKINSON is using (**18.8**). Coble fishermen did not approve – it looked suspiciously like trawling. After 1870, *Walsher* had been used to more glamorous harvesting of the sea – he and his younger brother William had fished from *Elizabeth and Susannah*, but their yawl had been wrecked behind Scarborough's Outer Pier on 1st February 1884. That date suggests they had come out of the winter lay-up very early (the '80s were hard years) and paid a heavy price.

18.8: A photograph that uniquely catches the decline of Filey's offshore fishing. Matthew *Walsher* JENKINSON, born 1836 (O40) in thigh-waders, c1890s, timelessly with push-net at Filey – a method of scooping up shrimps at the low tide's edge. A few years before he had been master and half-owner of the yawl *Elizabeth and Susannah*. *[FA]*

Fish-Rounds

Women normally hawked that part of the catch not auctioned on the beach, but a few old fishermen sold around the countryside with a horse and cart. Petrol engines later took Filey fish vans as far as the West Riding.

---

[13] Thomas Mozley, *Reminiscences Chiefly of Towns and Villages and Schools* (Longmans, Green, 1885) pp450-1.

When John William JENKINSON (Q41) stopped fishing, he began a fish-round with a pony and flat-cart. He developed a particular rapport with horses. Terence told us about his pony, *Molly*, a fat animal which he 'thought the world of.' *John Willie* lived on West Road but kept the horse on L&NE Railway land later, by Dee's supermarket. Mark BAXTER, *John Willie's* nephew, often took *Molly* from West Road (*Comma Right* – common land - before it was built on) at the end of its working day, and along Scarborough Road to the field.

One evening, Mark wanted to get away quickly, to play football. He therefore took the risk of using the short cut between the doctor's and Jim Taylor's garage. *Molly* was a 'big black fat pony', and it got stuck in this passage. Jim Taylor's office wall had to be taken down to get the horse out.

Molly seemed to endear herself to her owners. Before coming to *John Willie*, she'd belonged to William *Ino* Crawford, a fish-dealer who employed George Burton to deliver around Filey. It was George's job to tend the pony, and to take it back to its close each evening. *Ino* got *Molly* an apple from the greengrocer every day and handed this to George to pass on to the pony at his discretion. 'I used to go round the corner an' eat bloody apple myself,' he confessed.

Some men found it difficult to shake off the habits of the sea once they gave it up. George Burton had a fund of stories about another hawker of fish, *Old Brazzy* JENKINSON (P46), who had a horse called *Paddy*. He would take his horse to William Edward Morley's, the shoeing-smith at 1, Church Street.

> 'Now then Morley,' he would boom, 'where have I to moor him?'
>
> 'Tie him up o'er there,' Morley would reply. 'What d 'ye want doin' at him, Matt?'
>
> 'He wants shoeing,' *Brazzy* would say, 'fore and aft'.

Tom Jenkinson Watkinson, *Brazzy's* great great nephew, related how, with limited equine nous, Matt would hold the bit up to *Paddy's* mouth and say: 'open thee gob, Pad!' 'On one occasion,' Tom writes, '*Paddy* had a bad attack of colic through getting into the corn bin. Matt could not understand why *Paddy* had got access to the corn as he had "moored him off with plenty of cable", good nautical practice with a boat but it had allowed the pony the run of the entire stable.'

One of many stories that we heard in the 1980s about *Brazzy* catches the characteristic 'Yorkshireness' perfectly. On his fish-round out of Filey with *Paddy* and his flat-cart, *Brazzy* regularly encountered a certain parson's wife at Hunmanby, a woman of similar nature to him, it appears. Here is a composite of George Burton and Jim Haxby's versions of the story:

> . . . she always wanted what he hadn't! She used to come out with a great big plate as though she was going to buy all there was, and never bought nowt. She always used to look for what wasn't on the cart and she'd want something that wasn't there. *Old Brazzy* was determined: he went up yah day with every fish in the sea - 'that'll beat her'.

> She came out and kept going round - 'have you this? have you that?' - trying to find
> out something - and then she said 'kippers! thee have nay kippers on t'cart - now if
> I'd known you had any kippers, Mr JENKINSON - we love kippers - I would have had
> five shillings worth.' A hell of an order! 'By God missis,' said *Brazzy*, 'I have you this
> bloody time! Give us yer five shillin's then' – 'e had them strung round 'is neck!

George's version has the kippers stuffed down his trousers.

Harvesting the Air

Just as most Filey men found livings garnering creatures swimming in the sea, a
few did so from those that flew over their heads.

Shooting and Stuffing

The richness of the seabird population which had the misfortune to visit Filey
offered another source of income to retired fishermen. Disapproval of shooting was
expressed as early as the 1820s by more enlightened observers, but these critics
were a minority. A view persisted at all levels of local society that unusual birds
were to be shot at. 'Fifteen cormorants were shot in one year' boasted a late 19th
Century directory. Typical of contemporary opinion was the reaction to the
appearance of a flock of 15 swans in January 1864:

> Immediately riflemen and gunners of all grades, eager for a shot, hastened to the
> spot; but the wily birds took wing, mounted aloft, formed themselves into a line,
> and flew away. They returned in the evening, but none were secured.[14]

One explanation for this urge to kill was the money to be made from 'fowling'. The
market in stuffed birds was reflected by the presence in 1850s trade directories of
a bird preserver. 'Collectors' displayed the rarest casualties in glass cases. Local
bigwig Admiral Mitford of Hunmanby, lord of the manor of Filey, paid his
gamekeeper for bagging an ibis on The Brigg.[15]

An especially ambitious hope was to associate Filey with the grotesque mid/late
19th Century practice for fashionable ladies to wear complete stuffed bird in their
hats. In the space of a few years, Richard Lorriman on Hope Street aped Parisian
fin de siècle elegance by elevating himself from 'bird preserver' to the rather
grander *plumassier* – a dealer in ornamental feathers.[16]

An unlikely participant in this niche trend to ease Filey into the high fashion circuit
was the casually-tailored *Bill Penny*. William Hall JENKINSON (P27) would 'do
a bit of helpin'' with the cobles', as George CAPPLEMAN put it, and then go off
shooting at kittiwakes, geese or grouse.

---

[14] *Scarborough Mercury*, 16th Jan 1864.

[15] Harland, *Society at the Seaside* (c1970).

[16] Kelly's *Directory*, 1872; Bulmer's *Directory*, 1892. In the USA, Extinction Rebellion-type
'feather boycotts' led in 1918 to a legal ban on 'Murderous Millinery', perhaps one of
the very first animal rights' successes.

Any rare avian kill would command a price from a naturalist, or from the *plumassier.*

A fox might bring 'half a sovereign', whilst the coroner paid five shillings for finding a dead human body. *Penny* often accompanied a boat, for it was always followed by flocks of birds when fish-gutting was in progress. Or he'd venture onto the cliffs around Filey. Perhaps it was *Penny*, or the gun happy Lorriman, described as a 'bird stuffer', who was fined by Bridlington magistrates for discharging a gun near the highway at Muston on a Sunday.[17]

Bob HUNTER remembered *Penny* on these shooting expeditions as 'in an old coat, like a tramp', and his bizarre appearance earned him a certain amount of mocking attention. The local wags would shout after him 'Squat, *Penny*, there's a duck', and this alternative by-name of *Squat Penny* stuck. *Penny's* old muzzle loader could be a dangerous weapon to all kinds of living creatures. He claimed to have rammed it full of paper and fired up the chimney to clean out the soot. This also blasted away the chimney pot and brought down a wild goose as a bonus.

Few men can have encountered the deadly *Squat Penny* in more harrowing circumstances than the unfortunate crewman of the Italian ship *Unico* in 1871. At least 14 of his fellows had been washed overboard to their deaths in hurricane winds, and rumour had it at the time that the drunken captain had shot the mate to remove a witness to his own part in the wreck. Whatever the truth of the story, local tradition states that the sole surviving crewman scrambled ashore only to find himself staring into the barrel of *Squat Penny's* kittiwake-blasting musket. Understandably, he thrust his hands into the air in a panic-stricken gesture of surrender.[18]

Penny was probably responsible for the shooting of 'a fine specimen of the sooty shearwater' in November 1888, and his death in July 1908 earned him recognition as 'a noted fowler' – his property was valued for probate at over £350. But his deadly work on rare birds did not die with him, a falcon being reported as shot on The Brigg in January 1911.[19] *Penny* was also a beachwatcher, which was a good deal like *Jim Buggins' sandpoking*. Both kept a keen eye on the tide, looking out for wood and cordage, in which the Coastguard would be uninterested.

Egg Climming

Seabirds were lucky even to reach the stage where they could be shot at, for their eggs offered another harvest crop to coastal settlements. It seems likely that locals had always appreciated this annual and protein-rich variation to their staple fish diet; and although 'egging' is not known to have been practised before the 18th Century, eggs must have been a source of calories since humans first settled here.

---

[17] Cooper (1908) pp197-9; Harland, *Society at the Seaside* (c1970).
[18] Godfrey & Lassey, 1982, p64; Bob HUNTER.
[19] Nellist (1913).

It became illegal to take wild bird eggs in 1954, and to possess them in 1982. But by the early 20th Century there had developed a demand from a number of sources. Filey shops sold them for eating (they fill a frying pan, and can make acceptable omelettes); they were ingredients for confectioners' produce; tanners used the whites to bring up the gloss on the surface of patent leather; and collectors might pay well for unusually marked specimens. According to Smith's 1915 *Directory*, boxes were dispatched to London and elsewhere, 'a delicacy which, once tasted is evermore desired'.

> Consequently, men are to be seen dangling in a breeches-belt at the end of a line over the face of chalk cliffs which rise 400 feet sheer from the boiling surf below.

The climber effectively abseiled down a 'belt rope', using his feet to kick clear of the cliff face. There was a risk that sharp flints could razor through the line. Nevertheless, five gangs were working the cliffs according to the 1915 *Directory*. There were local professionals like Sam Leng of Flamborough, and George Longhorn, 'climbers by long inheritance', who made good livings from egg-gathering during the six-week season, bidding against others with the cut on offer to the farmer of the abutting clifftop field (**18.10**).

18.9: A climber is lowered, the third member of the gang presumably out of view, the back stop, or perhaps working the winch. The gatherer wears what looks like a Boer War period pith helmet, protection against showers of loose chalk or flint, knocked out of place by startled birds. Note the handline, for signalling to the cliff top. *[FA]*

The local tradition was that climbing began no earlier than 5th May (when the eggs were freshly laid) and continued until late June. It grew into a visitor attraction, especially on the Speeton/Bempton cliffs. This perhaps explains why it became such a well-organised, marketised industry, with climbs rented out by farmers. A reliable spike was the key to the whole operation. From this, a proper winch was used to lower the collector down to the nesting ledges. Another spike was driven into the cliff at right angles: at its end was a swivel and pulley which kept the rope clear and safe from chafing.

A number of young Filey men worked on a semi-professional basis away from rented climbs. Michael Fearon remembers Alf Gray and George Burton as experienced 'eggers' in the early '50s, with a knack of 'blowing the innards' out of especially marked eggs.[20] Collectors and dealers came to informal bazaars at the cliff top to buy the eggs.

One man, Tom *Eamen* JENKINSON, was 'absolutely fearless', a slightly bent arm being no impediment to his acrobatics. Later a coxswain of the Filey lifeboat, Tom was the son of Edmond *Eamen* JENKINSON (R87). He acquired his skills in Church Ravine: even as an eight year-old, Foster reckons, there was not a tree there that he could not climb (and some of them are huge). He sold rook eggs at 2d each to class mates. Tom could scramble down the cliffs where nobody else dared, happily shimmying up or down a single rope hanging from an iron spike on the cliff top.

The gear was provided by Walter Harper, a Filey tradesman who also found local customers for the eggs. North of The Brigg, there is a stretch of several hundred yards, Carr Naze Stacks, where the sea never leaves the cliff bottom. This was where the herring gulls nested. Here, Tom would be lowered, in a harness, by his 'crew'. Wearing plimsols and an old Great War steel helmet, he could reach some ledge perhaps 60 or 70 feet above the rocks, and then 'loose off', ie leave the harness, to move along this precarious shelf, 100 yards either way.

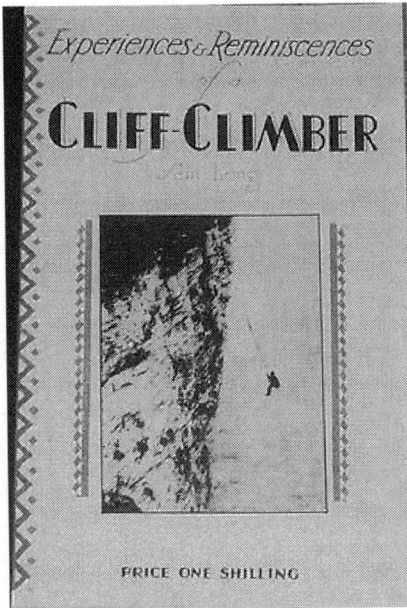

18.10: The 1931 memoir of Sam Leng of Flamborough, 'the last of the Bempton *egg climmers'*, who died in 1935.

---

[20] Fearon (2008) p2.

High above, unable to see their climber, the crew would wait anxiously for maybe a quarter of an hour whilst the collection was made. Had he missed his footing and fallen off? Then, three pulls on the signal rope - the signal to start hauling Tom back up.

One year, Harper rented a frontage on Speeton Cliffs, just north of where the trawler *Skegness* was wrecked in 1935. Foster recalls the drop, perhaps 500 feet, as terrifying: 'it made my stomach turn just to look over.' But here were thousands of eggs mostly guillemot, as well as kittiwake, puffin and razor bill. Tom thought nothing of working the cliff face in the usual way. Much of the chalk here was loose, and a swing of the rope could bring down a rock fall.

18.11: A gathering gang on the cliffs at Bempton/Speeton. *[FA]*

One day, about half a ton fell and, miraculously, only grazed Tom's leg. 'He wasn't a bit bothered,' Foster told us, 'although he did come up swearing his head off.' It is remarkable that more life-threatening accidents were uncommon. I know of no fatalities, the most serious injuries being the jagged head wound and fractured skull suffered by *Joss* Major in June 1910, when he was struck on the head and knocked unconscious by a rock fall.

Though the trade was criminalised in 1954, the *climmers* had always been mindful of their conservation responsibilities. They used to leave enough eggs to ensure the continuation of the species, and did not gather on certain parts of their territory on a rotation, a fallow year which left the colonies to recover.

They took eggs from the herring gulls, predators of the smaller, rarer birds, to keep their numbers under control. The climbers could also anticipate and warn about imminent rock falls.

A Miscellany

Finally, four unlikely jobs that men from fisher backgrounds ended up in.

Edmond JENKINSON (P52) master of the yawl *Welcome Home*, Primitive Methodist lay preacher and Sunday school teacher, spent his last years working for Filey Urban District Council as a street sweeper.

Matthew JENKINSON (P67) gave occasional help to St Oswald's gravedigger, Jimmy Douglas. 'A queer old stick,' said Terence COLLINS of Matthew,

> always wore moleskins, not cords, tied under the knees. He'd be digging a grave, you wouldn't know anyone was there, and all of a sudden his ears'd pop up and he always had a funny square bowler on - it frightened the life out of you when you saw him.

Matthew also worked on Smith's Church Farm.

Isaac ROSS and John Willie JENKINSON were consecutively chapel-keepers at Union Street, and Robert JENKINSON (Q62) was at the Quay Methodist Chapel at Bridlington.

Fearless egg climber Tom JENKINSON had an uncle, Jack *Lorty* (R84), who at 16 suffered a gruesome injury working at Nicholl's brickworks on Scarborough Road. On Saturday 30th June 1900, his arm caught in a machine's cog wheel, and was badly crushed from shoulder to elbow. Dr Foley sent him immediately to Scarborough Hospital where an amputation was carried out.[21] With the Welfare State in its infancy before 1945, those with disabilities had to eke out a living as best they could, and Filey offered as many ways on as human ingenuity could construct.

Despite his awful setback, *Lorty* made a winter living on a fish-round. He even did some garden work. His niece, Edith Horner, told us that he laid out the gardens down the slope at the bottom of Queen Street. It is good to report that his disability did not prevent him from marrying and having two sons. *Lorty* made a living posting advertising bills, but in the summer season he traced 20 foot square pictures barefooted into the sand on Filey beach, by the sea wall, using contrasting shades for effect. Each piece of beach art was framed with pebbles.

In September, during Doncaster Race Week, he always drew St George's Church and a race horse. Visitors threw coins down to him. In later life, he painted pictures, embroidered 'Sailors' Woolworks' of yawls on a tapestry frame, and at least once the proceeds of an exhibition of his work were spent on an outing for hospital patients. He lived with his disability for 68 years, dying in 1968 at the age of 83.

Like *Bonzo* the seal and the Filey yawls, Jack looked for betterment in a harbour town, and he moved to Bridlington, where he and his family were living when the *National Register* was compiled (September 1939).

---

[21] *Filey Post*, 7th July 1900.

It was on the beach at *Quay* that a young visitor saw *Lorty's* sand pictures one summer, and many years later wrote this grand dialect rhyme:

1 Ther was a blooat at Bolli't'n[22]
  Maade pickters oot o' sand
  Or ootlahned 'em wi' pebbles
  'N did it ahll bi 'and.

2 'E'd rooape a bit o' sand off
  'N scraape it sthraight 'n flat,
  Then i' bare-feeat 'e'd smoothe some
  'N staartti' dhraw o' that.

3 Ther was floowers, castles, choches,
  Ahll iv 'is pickters neat.
  Fooalks leaned ower' raailins
  'N dhropp'd pennies on 'is sheet.

4 As a bairn, ah yance seed pickters
  As waaves cem in yah daay.
  An jus' set on 'n bluther'd
  As sea wesh'd 'emawaay.

5 Yah thing ah've nut fergett'n,
  This chap, e'd bud one arm
  Ti dhraw 'n paaint 'is pickters
  Seea full o' graace 'n chaarm.

6 It's a lesson wa duc 'eed, fooalks.
  Wi' bud yah 'and ti employ,
  'E yewswd 'is preshus talent
  Tigiv us ahll sum joy.

The Primitive Methodists might say that *Lorty* simply followed his God-given calling.

18.12: Frank Cappleman JENKINSON, universally known as *Bonzo Buggins*, on account of the seal *Bonzo* that was probably his main source of income. In fact, Frank personified the huge range of income streams available to an enterprising Old Towner who did not want to go fishing. A fascinating 2019 Facebook exchange on the *Photos of Filey, old and new* site revealed a very varied portfolio in addition to *sandpoking* and seal exhibiting – taking youngsters out fishing in his rowing boat; tending a *trot*; keeping a fish and crab stall on the Coble Landing; and keeping chickens on land by his house on *Jenk Alley*! In the census, however, he wisely entered his occupation as 'Inshore Fisherman' – there was not enough space for so varied a portfolio of jobs. *[Barry Teague]*

---

[22] *Burlington* was an older version of the name Bridlington.

19 MOMENTS IN TIME: WRECKS AND RESCUES –
CASE STUDIES FROM THE 1930S

Given the hazardous nature of this stretch of coast, the town formed a volunteer rescue service as early as 1804 – reputedly, it had by 1860 saved more lives than any other RNLI station in England. The dramatic history of Filey's lifeboats is well researched[1], and even a simple chronology would be an unjustifiable repetition. This chapter therefore attempts something different.

It struck us in the 1980s how recently sail and oar power had been at the core of the town's rescue service. Until 1940, when Filey finally acquired a motor-powered lifeboat, those fishermen manning the town's first lifeboat in 1804 would have found rescue operations familiar. When we spoke to locals 40 years ago, such operations were well within living memory: by 2021, the era of oar and sail rescue has slid into the realm of the written historical record. The following five case studies from 1930s wrecks and rescues therefore seem to have a special significance, and can form the basis of a description of operational practice at the eve of the modern lifeboat service.

Case Study 1, August 1930: the Dangers of Overnight Mooring

It is in the nature of lifeboat rescue that it takes place in bad weather, and in the days of sail and oar   such extreme conditions could cause as much difficulty for the rescuers as it had for the boats they were hoping to save. One such occasion was in mid-August 1930, when Filey's 38 cobles lay at anchor in perfect summer weather. This inshore fleet was entirely unaware that it was about to suffer 'the greatest disaster it had ever known'.[2]

The fishermen had judged it safe to remain overnight south of Carr Naze, in the lee of The Brigg, a normal labour-saving practice when 'the glass is high and settled weather seems certain'. Nowadays, radio reports would have corrected this misplaced optimism - there had been extreme weather in the previous few days – a cloud burst, for example, had hit the North Yorkshire Moors where the Esk gathered its water:

> The river came down in a flood, swept away bridges, uprooted trees, foamed through Whitby harbour and tearing others from their moorings swept them out to sea.

None of this was in the minds of the Filey coblemen, when they decided to avoid all the work of beaching and launching:

---

[1] Jeff Morris, *The Story of the Filey Lifeboats* (Jeff Morris, 1991); for an update see the website *79.170.44.102/fileybay.com/lifeboat/lifeboat3*.

[2] This account is taken from Smith (1932).

On that night in August 1930 there was no sign of a change in the weather, yet early next morning it was blowing a heavy gale from ESE. Against that wind there is no protection; the bay lies open to its full fury. Fishermen out on the cliffs early in the morning saw seas breaking over the boats as they strained at their moorings – something had to be done.

The lifeboat was launched, and was somehow rowed out to the fleet's anchorage. Men jumped from her to cut the cables, and steered them through the tremendous sea to beach the boats on the sand. On a second run, the lifeboat was caught in the wind and sea, driven ashore, where she stuck in the sand and could not be refloated. Eleven cobles sank, and three were driven out to sea. One was picked up days later 12 miles from Scarborough. One was dashed to pieces on rocks, and one was simply never seen again.

Case Study 2, January 1932: *James Lay* – Fear of *Foy*-Crews

In his youth, Foster Holmes JENKINSON (R37) had a level of enthusiasm for the Filey lifeboat that most boys then devoted to steam locomotives and their numbers. His graphic recollections of the next four rescues meshed with the details contained in the duplicates of the *Returns of the Filey Life Boat*, to which we had access in the early 1980s. The originals were sent to RNLI headquarters. In combination, these two sources provide a framework for a colourful account of lifeboat operations in the decade prior to the arrival of Filey's first motor lifeboat, *Cuttle*.

The basis of salvage law lies in the recognition that to encourage the provision of help at sea, the risks involved deserve recompense. A local court or arbitrator makes an award, taking into account the danger of the operation and the value of the property salved. Anyone regularly at sea could find themselves offering salvage assistance. On such a busy shipping route as the east coast, fishermen were frequently first to encounter and offer help to vessels in distress.

The financial gains could be considerable - Nellist (1913) recorded how 27 Filey fishermen took the abandoned trawler *Hugelia* to Scarborough in 1895, and were awarded £412. A coble might have taken three months to earn its crew that sort of money. A 'rocker', ie a boat stranded on rocks, could mean a lump sum from insurers, or salvage money. 'Please God, send a rocker' was a nightly postscript to a child's prayers on this coast![3]

Unsurprisingly, fishermen were not slow to offer such help – salvage money was known as a *foy*. Indeed, it was in their interests to give help even where it was not wanted. Banks were reluctant to lend fishermen capital, and a *foy* was therefore the best chance a man had to own his own boat. As a minimum, a '*foy*-crew' needed to get a line on board a vessel to justify a claim.

---

[3] Frank (2002) p196.

It is understandable that captains delayed appeals for rescue as long as possible, aware that their owners would be displeased at the costs of any salvage claim. Men were willing to take risks in pursuit of salvage. But we can be sure that there was such a thing as helping a mate - according to the *Filey Post* of 22nd April 1899, *Jack Sled* JENKINSON (P49) leapt from his own boat to save John Watkinson's unmanned yawl from drifting to calamity on The Brigg, injuring himself in the process. I suspect *Sled* expected no more than a pint of bitter in return.

January 1932 was to be an eventful month at Filey, three vessels being stranded at different times on or near The Brigg. In the early hours of the 12th, thick fog caused the captain of *James Lay* to miscalculate his position by 30 miles. There followed a mixture of high drama and farce. The London trawler was bound for the Humber with an Icelandic catch, sailing southwards along the Yorkshire coast. The boat's log-line measuring propeller had been lost, the traditional means by which speed and therefore distance travelled could be estimated.[4] The skipper mistook Filey Brigg for Spurn Point, swung to the west to enter the Humber Estuary, and ran aground onto Reighton Sands.

Local tradition has it that a Filey coble hailed *James Lay* to see if she required help. The captain declined the offer, reasoning that the rising tide would refloat him. According to local rumour, the coble crew did not say he was at Filey, calculating that as long as he thought he was in the Humber, it would be only a matter of time before he grounded again and would need a *foy*-boat. Conspiracy theory abounds!

A few hours later, still befogged, the trawler did refloat, the captain assumed he had reached the mouth of the Humber, and was about to round Spurn Point. Moments later, at about 8.00am, he collided with the rocks of Filey Brigg, on an ebbing tide, and stuck fast in the tangle of rocks near its tip. A gale sprang up, and *James Lay* sent up distress signals. The lifeboat, *Hollon the Third*, reached the stranded boat 20 minutes later, but the captain now refused help, convinced he could again refloat at high tide.

Foster's teacher, Robert Spencer, doubled up as a free-lance reporter, sending wreck/rescue stories to national newspapers, using his fisher lad pupils as cub reporters. In pursuit of some first-hand copy, Spencer persuaded headmaster, Walter Flather, that it would be educational for the top class to go to The Brigg for the morning to see the grounded trawler.

---

[4] A ship's speed could be calculated if a line were trailed out alongside. Traditionally it was weighted with a log to stop it drifting, and knotted every seven fathoms (42 feet), as a means of calculating speed. In the 19th Century, a 'fish' rotator was devised to calculate mileage. This is the origin of *knot* and *log* in recording nautical navigation.

19.1: The London trawler *James Lay*, stranded on the south side of The Brigg, with assorted 'Filey pirates' standing alongside. The captain had mistaken the salient for Spurn Point, swung west, and ended up on its rocks. *[FM]*

This motley group of scholars was duly taken up onto the wet, muddy promontory. 'I'm going to get *plothered up*,' declared Jacky COWLING, jumping into a big pile of mud. Foster related how

> . . . all the 'rogues' of the class deliberately jumped into as much mud as possible, so that they would be unfit to return to school after dinner. As a result, half the class was missing in the afternoon, and Mr Spencer received a verbal drubbing from the headmaster.

David Smith (1932) was also a witness to the trawler's difficulties, but his and Foster's accounts do not coincide at this point, and so the order of events is uncertain. The trawler was stuck for three weeks, and at some point, five cobles got out to it, naturally eager to help. Twenty teenagers were allowed on board, the captain deciding they could assist the crew of eight to refloat – and 'to guard the swag from the pirates', as Foster put it. Strong winds from the north and north-east now reached gale force: 'great seas were breaking over the boat, and the men were frequently up to their waists in water.' Filey councillor *Titch* JENKINSON (R85) was coming ashore in his motor coble that evening, having laid some long-lines for the night. He noticed *James Lay* afloat following a change of wind, and adrift in the bay.

Once ashore, *Titch* alerted lifeboat secretary Charles Burgess, a message was sent to the tractor driver, and *Hollon the Third* launched its second rescue of *James Lay* in two days, this time to rescue the rescuers as well. It seems that floodtide and gale now combined to create the full violence of the Tide-way, and the sea rounded The Brigg end 'like a mill-race'. The boat was on the rocks when

> The lifeboat approached to within forty yards of the wreck and could make no further progress. A spectator on the cliffs timed her. For twenty minutes the crew rowed with all their strength and only managed to maintain their position. At length a buoy with a rope attached, flung overboard from the trawler, floated near enough to be caught.

The men on *James Lay* were hauling the lifeboat towards them, but when ten feet separated them, the trawler finally keeled over in the wind and current.

> Twenty-six of the twenty-eight men on board jumped for the lifeboat and landed on top of the crew. No one was hurt. At this moment the powerful motor-lifeboat from Scarborough arrived . . . .

This boat was able to get close, the engineer, mate and one Filey volunteer got on board, and managed to sail the trawler to the beach, despite it being badly holed and sinking.

When everyone was safely back, Foster rang in Mr Spencer's account of these proceedings to Driffield. A report was in the press the next day, and *James Lay* finally set off for Hull. 'Does Councillor JENKINSON get anything for bringing message?' Burgess asked the RNLI in his report next day. We never found out.

James Lay survived to be requisitioned for war service as a minesweeper in September 1939. It survived this experience too, being sold for breaking up in 1960.[5]

Case Study 3, February 1932: *Johannesburg* - Rescuing 'Pirates'

'Getting a line' to a boat in difficulties has always been at the heart of a lifeboat rescue. From 1898, the Filey crew held quarterly exercises and rocket practices in which a leadline-heaving competition was staged. The *Filey Post* always reported this spectator-spectacle in glowing terms. Matthew JENKINSON (*Brazzy?*) won first prize in May 1900 with a throw of 28½ yards. The inspecting officer was 'well pleased with the standard and smartness of the men at exercise', the *Post* crowed.

About 6.30am on 8th February 1932, just three weeks after the *James Lay* rescue, the Hull trawler *Johannesburg* ran ashore in very rough seas on the highly exposed north side of Filey Brigg. A coastguard was always on watch, and the service was therefore usually first to spot an incident. The lifeboat had been alerted within five minutes.

---

[5] *Harwich and Dovercourt* website, warships/trawlers.

19.2: The Hull trawler *Johannesburg* on Filey sands, possibly after she had been towed off the north side of The Brigg and beached for repairs. The postcard may also portray events three years later, when in thick fog, and again skippered by William Normandale, the boat ran aground on the sands. She had by then been renamed *Nordale*. *[FM]*

About 21 Filey fishermen got aboard, to render assistance to the crew of nine. The whole town watched the ensuing events from the cliff top. The lifeboat was launched, but skipper William Normandale refused help. He was also the owner and was therefore the one who stood to lose money.

In the afternoon the sea got very rough, and the trawler began to shift. The skipper changed his mind, and *Hollon the Third* went out again. We can only guess at the feelings of the volunteers who had been called away from their work twice.

The motor-lifeboat at Scarborough was always called out to assist in especially difficult weather where a wreck was on rocks. But when it arrived, it found that the Filey boat had got the whole company off 'with great danger and difficulty', presumably having thrown a line on board. This amounted to eight crew, together with 'about 20 pirates', in the secretary's words, these fishermen having been stranded on board as the sea was too heavy for their cobles to approach. Burgess was impressed, writing in his report:

> I watched through my telescope and it was very well done and the danger was very great, every minute . . . . I thought the boat would role [sic] over.

The RNLI sent a letter of appreciation to the crew, to acknowledge a particularly well-executed rescue in dangerous circumstances.[6] It is worth remembering that the reports rarely do such justice to the risks or physical hardship to which lifeboat crews exposed themselves. How could *any* boat get within feet of such a deadly headland by sail and oar power in such a 'strong gale and very heavy sea'?[7]

Normandale sought to move on with a change of name to *Nordale*, but the image makeover changed neither the trawler's nor the skipper's luck: in 1935, it was again on Filey sands, having run aground in thick fog. The boat's jinx finally brought its destruction in January 1942, when it hit the Carskey Rocks at the Mull of Kintyre, Argyllshire. The crew were evacuated by breeches buoy, but five were lost through exposure, fatigue, or being swept away by the sea.[8]

Case Study 4, September 1935: the Loss of *Skegness* - the Filey Volunteer Life Saving Rocket Brigade in Action

Sometimes, despite all efforts, the lifeboat could not save the crews of distressed boats. Such an occasion was the loss of the Hull trawler *Skegness* on the night of 24th/25th September 1935, the last of the shipwrecks to date at Speeton Cliffs. Foster suggested local rumour was that skipper Normandale of the *Johannesburg* unwittingly contributed to the disaster.

Skegness ran aground with engine trouble on a fine Tuesday evening, her nose in the rocks below Speeton Cliffs, some four miles south-east of Filey, Hull-bound from the Faeroes. By this date, wireless equipment was becoming standard on such boats, and by an odd coincidence, the captain happened to have contact with *Johannesburg/Nordale* skipper Billy Normandale at Scarborough. From the description given of the lights visible, Normandale wrongly concluded that the trawler had struck the land *north* of Filey Brigg, where he himself had been grounded three and a half years before.

He recommended the crew to abandon, but *Skegness's* captain, Richard Wright, reckoned he would be able to refloat on the next tide, around 3am. His plan was to lay an anchor in deeper water, and then winch his boat off the rocks as the tide rose, the well-known technique of 'kedging'. This may have delayed the start of rescue operations. Within an hour, a gale force easterly was driving the sea to the shore.

It was common for seamen to listen in on the *Trawler Band* for news of boats and appeals for help. Rockets were fired as assembly signals, to alert the lifeboat crew that they were needed. At night, when many of these rescues took place, a 'Knocker up' was paid to go round rousing anybody who failed to respond to the maroons.

---

[6] Morris (1991) p9.
[7] *Shipwrecks in Filey Bay* website.
[8] *wrecksite.eu/wreck* website.

Conditions that night were bad. Foster remembers coming out of the Filey cinema around 9.30pm as the rockets went up. He got to the beach as the lifeboat was being launched. A north-east gale was blowing so hard that it was barely possible to stand, even there. Ten men were bound to struggle when rowing a 35-foot lifeboat in heavy sea. But getting into the sea in the first place was especially difficult in a strong onshore wind. A major advance was the RNLI's provision in 1931 of Filey's first specially adapted tractor, to push the lifeboat well into the water.

But in these conditions, even the tractor struggled, propelling the boat into the sea only to have it blown back by the wind. The launch, around 11.10pm, had taken about three-quarters of an hour. The Flamborough lifeboat was also launched, but the swell was too heavy to let either get near. (Though their boat was motorised, the Flamborough men could not risk landing back at their station and had to make for Bridlington Harbour.) Scarborough's motor-lifeboat had initially been directed north of The Brigg, five miles from the boat's actual location, and only set off for Speeton at 4.15am.

It is heartening to discover just how the fishing community responded en masse to such situations. Normandale, for example, raised steam and set off in *Nordale* from Scarborough with other boats to assist, despite the force of the gale; and Filey fishermen set off on foot along the shoreline, but could not get to *Skegness* on account of the rising tide.

Where a boat was 'a rocker' at the foot of a cliff, the coastguard could call on the 20-strong Volunteer Rocket Brigade. Filey's station was 'under Liberal Club, Mitford Street', according to the 1905 *Scarborough Gazette Directory*, 'keys at Chief Coastguard's'. The procedure was for the Brigade, with horse-drawn launcher ('Horses: Church Farm'), to be directed by the coastguard along the cliff top and to drop a line and cradle down to the wreck.

This 'breeches buoy' technique had been developed at Great Yarmouth as early as 1808, a mortar firing a line to the stranded ship. A canvas sling, the breeches, attached to a buoy, was used to haul the men ashore through the air. In time, the mortar was superseded by a rocket with a range of about 100 yards.[9]

Foster's brother was with the Filey rocket crew that night. The coastguards finally located the *Skegness* on this occasion, and the Brigade set out from the rocket station by lorry, taking their gear to the cliff top at Speeton. This tiny village also had a Rocket Brigade company, and a maroon went up around midnight for them to turn out.

It takes a wrench of imagination to peer back just 85 years, from a time when helicopters are instrumental in such rescues, to an era when someone had to round up four grazing horses, in wind, driving rain and darkness, to harness up and haul a cart-full of rocket equipment.

---

[9] Fearon (2016) pp33-4.

19.3: The sinister, sheer 420-foot wall of rock at Speeton where on the night of 24ᵗʰ/25ᵗʰ September 1935 'a bitter wind . . . blasted up the vertical face of the chalk cliffs and tore across the cliff edge.' *Skegness* had been rammed into these rocks by the wildness of the wind and sea. *[Photo: fileybay.com/wrecks/skegness]*

Even inland, the weather was wild, but the company arrived at the cliff top to conditions that stretched language to describe. An especially graphic account relates how

> the sea grew up into white marching walls of death . . . The swells increased as the tide advanced and the fury of the sea started to ram the boat further up the rocks . . . the boat was caught in a vicious backwash from the seas as they hit the base of the cliffs and rebounded back upon themselves. The vessel was then upright on her keel but being swept from end to end by heavy seas borne of a bitter wind that blasted up the vertical face of the chalk cliffs and tore across the cliff edge.[10]

If it were barely possible to stand on Filey beach that night, how bad must things have been 420 feet up at the very edge of the North Sea? In blinding rain, the Filey and Speeton rocket crews could only get to the edge of the cliff on hands and knees. Somehow the rocket equipment was assembled, the plan being to fire a line, by which to pass down a heavier line with running block, to rig up the breeches buoy sling. But the line was simply blown back over their heads into the fields behind. A further six attempts were no more successful. Against all regulations, rockets

---

[10] Anthony Green, *The Wreck of the Skegness* (*fileybay.com/wrecks/skegness*, 2000).

were strapped together to double propulsion, but not even this desperate expedient could defeat the easterly. By their searchlight, the rocket companies could see far below that much of the boat was submerged. With the beam focused on the wheelhouse, the helpless rescuers could see the doomed men huddled inside. George Burton recalled that the lights on the vessel went out at about 1.30am. As the tide rose, the boat was forced over onto her side and in the sight of the rocket brigades she was finally swamped. All eleven men were submerged with her.

19.4: Right - Perhaps Filey's most famous wreck, apart from *Unico* and *Research* – the trawler *Skegness* after the storm. Two Filey men and a policeman somehow got to the wreck the next morning to begin a hazardous search for bodies.
[Photo: E Green]

19.5: National coverage was intense, a newspaper arranging for aerial photographs to be taken. They were later used for postcards. *[fileybay.com/wrecks/skegness]*

The following morning, George Burton, fresh out of the army, and professional footballer Matt *Sailor* JENKINSON (R117) were deemed fit enough to accompany the policeman as they struggled onto the unstable wreck to start the grim search. One man, found with a line tied around him, had tried hopelessly to swim ashore. A second search began from *Dicky Hoy's* coble in contrastingly calm summer weather a few days later. The last two bodies wrapped in nets were recovered from inside the wreck. One body was found in the trawler's fish room, the tide later washing more onto the rocks. But most were lost without trace.[11]

The impact on the fishing community at Hull could be likened to that on Filey of the *Research* loss ten years earlier. Public interest was intense, the news made national headlines, and one newspaper hired an aircraft to over fly the scene to take photographs (**19.5**). Postcards were produced, a poem *Skegness Calling* was written, and sale proceeds contributed to a relief fund for the relatives.

Lifeboat secretary Frank Wright's report has a postscript which describes the selfless heroism of the rescuers. But note the official shoestring reliance on the ingenuity of community volunteering, and back-of-an-envelope improvisation that had to muddle through if anything was to be done:

> The tractor driver was away and the assistant in bringing the boat ashore had trouble with the tackle of the tractor eventually the boat was hauled up to the boathouse by horses. The allowances should be made to Ben C JENKINSON for telephone calls and to taking rockets to Speeton Coastguard after supply was exhausted and returning to send message for Scarborough motor-boat to be sent the second time.[12]

'After the investigations,' notes Anthony Green, 'the *Skegness* was left to the ravages of the elements and man.' The wreck, still in situ 69 years later in September 2004, was surveyed by divers. Details including photographs can be found at *fileybay.com/fbi/skegness2*.

Case Study 5, February 1938: *Buckingham* – the Limitations of Oar-powered Lifeboats

The shortcomings of traditional manual operation were demonstrated yet again in one of Filey's last oar and sail rescues. On 25th February 1938, Grimsby trawler *Buckingham* ran aground two miles north-west of Filey, on rocks below the cliffs at Newbiggin Wyke. Again, Foster recalls leaving the cinema at around 9.30pm, just as the rockets were being fired to summon the lifeboat crew. He and much of Filey saw *Thomas Masterman Hardy* launched into the darkness.

---

[11] Godfrey (1974) pp38-9; Godfrey & Lassey (1982) p99; and *Filey Lifeboat Station* (*Wikipedia* entry).

[12] Presumably, *Benny Hoy*, a fish merchant, was one of the few men with access to a telephone.

The tractor driver was not immediately to hand; so all 13 crew waded into the sea, trying, without success, to hand-launch their vessel, a reminder of how demanding this had been in the old, pre-tractor days.

Eventually, the assistant driver arrived and provided the necessary force. Foster and his pals then made off across land and reached the Wyke to find that the coastguards had already rigged up searchlights to illuminate *Buckingham's* deck. Her stern was well into the water.

Several Filey cobles, loaded with *foy*-crews, had reached the scene long before the oar-powered lifeboat could. They had probably had engines for 15 years or more. The two motorised lifeboats from Whitby and Scarborough had been unable to locate the trawler. *Buckingham's* skipper, mindful perhaps of the *Skegness* disaster three years before, wisely allowed one of the cobles, *Dorothy Rose*, to tow him off the rocks. It was during these proceedings that *Thomas Masterman Hardy* laboured into view. The crew had rowed hard, for perhaps an hour and a half, to cover the four miles round The Brigg and up the coast, with little wind to assist them. A great cheer went up from the cliff top as she appeared.

The arrival of *Cuttle* in May 1940, together with a stronger tractor, revolutionised launching and propulsion – its 35 horse power petrol engine could manage 7½ knots.

19.6: The reality of oar-powered lifeboat operation – hard, physical labour. Filey Lifeboat *Hollon II* (1884–1907) c1900. **L to R:** – Edwin Martin (of The Ravine), William *Ino* CRAWFORD (both standing); *John Willie* JENKINSON, George Wheeler, Robert *Chorus* CAMMISH, ---- Scotter (?); George *Dingle* SCALES, coxswain, standing. Several men are wearing cork lifebelts. *[George SCALES Collection]*

Even more changes have occurred since: first bleepers, then mobiles, were used to summon crews. The signalman, the second cox, once so vital for flashing morse signals to other boats, or to the landing crew, has been made virtually redundant by the lifeboat's radio; whilst radar and GPS can now pinpoint positions to a few yards. British helicopter hoist lift rescues began in 1953, in the North Sea.

'. . . because they feel it's their duty'

A Bradford journalist spoke to Crompton *Crump* Wyvill in 1893, and summed up sentiments that were probably common to every Filey fisherman: 'experiences have helped to draw his sympathy out to his fellow-men'. The five case studies in this chapter show the risks that lifeboatmen faced on each call-out.

Yet still the fishermen volunteered, despite the vulnerability of a rowed craft in the heavy seas which occasioned launches. The first boats notoriously could not even right themselves after a capsize. Launching into a rough swell was as dangerous before the introduction of a tractor as for any coble.

Morris (1991, page 4) describes the near-disaster that could have overwhelmed one lifeboat before it even got to sea. *Hollon*, the first 'self-righter', was called out during the Great March Gale of 1883, but was immediately grounded, a huge wave swinging her broadside.

A large number of men waded into the roaring churn, and somehow got the boat facing 'head-to-sea', saving vessel and crew. 'Self-righters' in theory were safe once at sea, but in the worst conditions even they could be swamped. Thirty lifeboat crew drowned in four Scarborough and Whitby rescues between 1836 and 1871 alone. Lifeboats in rough seas were an act of faith: one Filey JENKINSON in the late 1950s reckoned that he felt safer in a coble than in a lifeboat, and he was a former coxswain.[13]

Payment could make volunteering attractive. Graham Taylor explained how if too many responded to an alert, 'you toss up for a belt'. In bad times, the payment could be a crucial to a household's income. One Whitby lifeboat cox, between the Wars, was visited by men made desperate by a run of bad weather: 'William,' they'd plead, 'can you give us a ticket? You know, we have nowt.' A ticket earned just three shillings. If several came to a call-out, he would throw the tokens in the air, and those who could get one in the scramble got a place.

When lives were not at risk, the Runswick crew saw salvage as 'the only real pay a lifeboatman could earn'. Fishermen getting on board stuffed clocks and compasses up jumpers.[14] But these were exceptional circumstances. And certainly

---

[13] William R Mitchell, *Life on the Yorkshire Coast* (Dalesman, 1982) p13; *coxswain* - from the French *coque*, small boat, and Old English *swain*, servant, ie man in charge of a ship's boat.

[14] Frank (2002) pp193-5.

at Filey, the lifeboat crews had scruples. For most, money was not the motive: Graham Taylor, who served from 1963 to 1998, rising to cox in 1988, summed up the prevailing attitude:

> Lifeboatmen could claim salvage, but we never did. It was a dirty word for the RNLI.

Historically, men were taken on for a rescue by order of arrival. But since the late 19th Century, trainee crew members have needed to attain a level of competence before being regarded as active. Enrolled crew were paid a retainer. Not everybody approved. David Smith (1932) reckoned four call-outs in five involved fishermen caught in sudden storms. 'It would be a gracious act to give their services free when turning out to stand by their friends,' he judged.

Crump WYVILL, coxswain of the Filey lifeboat from 1883 to 1894, told the *Bradford Daily Telegraph* in 1893 how he had been at sea since 14, and many times conditions had been so bad that he had never expected to see his friends again. This was why he had been volunteering for so long. There will also have been an element of Christian duty for some men: 80% of fishermen in Filey were Primitive Methodists.

Eighty years later, in July 1973, another coxswain, Thomas Chapman *Eamen* JENKINSON, in youth the fearless egger, explained to *Yorkshire Life* why he believed his crew volunteered. In keeping with the Old Town's culture of family, both his father and grandfather had been lifeboatmen. His brother, Frank Chapman, was then the second cox:

> We never had any shortage of men wanting to join the crew. They don't do it for personal gain. Most of the crew get a retainer, but it certainly doesn't take account of the great risk which is often involved to human life. They do it because they feel it's their duty.

19.7: 'Safely Anchored' – the gravestone of a JENKINSON coxswain of Filey's Lifeboat: *Eamen's* fine St Oswald's gravestone, with lifeboat, and Brigg to the rear may commemorate his highly commended part in the rescue in heavy seas of the crew of the coaster *Rito*, off the north side of The Brigg, 20th December 1983, after 14 attempts.[15]

---

[15] Morris (1991) p20.

It was also a tradition in some families to serve in senior positions. *Eamen* JENKINSON was succeeded in 1981 by his brother, Frank Chapman. Senior lifeboatmen were a source of family pride, gravestones often recording service.

Another well-known JENKINSON cox, *Old Brazzy*, was succeeded by his nephew, *Dicky Hoy*. Richard Cammish JENKINSON remains a well-remembered figure in Filey's lifeboat history. Cox from 1915-36, he skippered scores of rescues, including at least three of the five described in this chapter, disregarding personal danger on countless occasions. One of the most decorated lifeboatmen in the country, he was so well-known amongst the sea-going population that his death was an important piece of international news. Terence COLLINS had known the man since childhood, and was on board a ship in the Indian Ocean when in 1946 he heard *Dicky Hoy's* death announced on *All India Radio*. 'I nearly fell out of my bunk,' he told us.

A small aside from Jim Haxby hints at the sense of inner responsibility to a personal moral code, and to community, that motivated these men. *Dicky Hoy* was his grandfather, and Jim heard how he had reacted when was told he would be recommended for a medal for his part in a rescue:

19.8: One of the earliest August Lifeboat Saturday, Filey's annual carnivals. These have since the 1890s had the serious purpose in the old British charitable tradition of bringing in contributions towards running costs. The event also represents yet another social glue that historically has cohered the fishing community. The horses, presumably, were Appleby shires from *Manor Farm*. [FA]

Don't bother . . . I couldn't have done that on me own, and he refused a medal. That's the sort of men they were. He said, I'm going back to bait my line, that's about how much he bothered about medals or 'owt else.

There was family tradition, a communal expectation within a closely socially integrated few streets. The sense of belonging was crystallised in the annual 'Lifeboat Saturday', when a festival atmosphere helped to bring donations to the service. The boat was drawn round the town by horses, volunteers dressing in their best ganseys. (More recently, dramatic rescue demonstrations have been staged.) Maroons were fired, and the crowds threw coins into the boat as it passed. It would be a happy occasion. But, as *Old Brazzy's* wife said to one visitor:

Aye, it's all very nice now, but when the maroon goes at two o'clock on a January morning, with a gale from the east, there's a different feeling. I've stood down there by the lamp, watching for t'boat coming back, and worrying if the crew were all safely in it.[16]

The fishermen also belonged to a much larger, but less tangible community, most of whose members they could not know. It is hard for anyone who has no experience of the sea – me included - to appreciate the immense sense of collective maritime solidarity it seems to generate amongst fishermen and mariners. This went beyond a hope that lifeboats along the coast would reciprocate if they themselves got into distress. In 1860, Dr William Smithson Cortis, a physician who practised on Queen Street, summed up his admiration for the humanity of his fellow residents in a famous letter to *The Times*:

. . . during my own residence here, of nearly twenty years, I know that in every shipwreck our fishermen have cheerfully rushed to the rescue - men having often to be called out of the boat from too many volunteering, but never to be urged into it - and, after saving the lives of the crews, have taken them to their homes and supplied them with warm clothing and other necessities.[17]

The 19th and early 20th Century Englishman was notoriously and jingoistically xenophobic, even more so than in these Brexit years. But all such antipathy was suspended in the face of the common enemy of sea and storm. Collections were made for foreign sailors shipwrecked at Filey, and the greatest respect imaginable was shown to the nine Italian crewmen of the barque *Unico*, buried at St Oswald's in 1871, even though the names of five were unknown. An obelisk, G395, with a carving of a ship wrecked on rocks, was later erected, presumably financed by local subscription (see **27.2**).

---

[16] Ted Gower, (*Dalesman*, 1977) p6. The lamp that she refers to was a well-known landmark at the Cliff Top end of Queen Street, referred to above on p15.

[17] Quoted in the *Scarborough Mercury*, 9th June 1860.

Fishermen rescue Fishermen

The *Filey Post* regularly reported how it was the local fishermen themselves who mostly benefited from the town's lifeboat service, rather than the passing coasters and trawlers. On 16th December 1899 a storm caught 33 cobles north of The Brigg, Richard Cammish JENKINSON's *Hermione* being swamped. It was of course his uncle, *Old Brazzy*, who was called out to skipper *Dicky Hoy's* rescue. Three months later, as we have seen, the unfortunate Richard Cammish was again rescued, no doubt with some ribbing, when *Hermione* was surprised and terminally wrecked by the 1,950 ton *Water Witch*.

Dicky Hoy seems to have had a penchant for risk, despite his reputation for cautious method in logging his catches. He had succeeded his uncle as lifeboat cox in 1915, so it was, to say the least, unfortunate that he got into trouble in his coble *Pilot Me* just after Christmas 1930 and in predictably unsafe conditions. Perhaps it had been a lean time. The weather was already bad on the 27th December, a strong gale blew up and the sea got very heavy. It was left to second cox, Billy ROBINSON, to seek the secretary's permission to summon the crew. In all, 13 crew, 18 beach crew and the head launcher, two shaftmen, four horsemen and their horses, were involved in *Dicky Hoy's* hour-long rescue. 'This man should not have gone fishing this morning,' secretary Charles Burgess wrote laconically in his return that day.

There was a simple split in the attitudes of Filey fishermen to wrecks and rescues. For some, respect for life was pre-eminent, and worth taking great risks to preserve. Many men were content with 'wet money' and the retainer. But for those for whom poverty was the greater driver, equal risks were to be taken in pursuit of financial reward, especially if a salvage claim would be at the expense of some corporate boat owner, or insurance company.

An intriguing snippet which appeared as little more than a footnote in an account of the 1907 funeral of the wife of a respected fisherman captures this fundamental contrast. A fisher funeral was a solemn occasion, but the burial of the wife of Richard *Old Baggy* JENKINSON was unceremoniously interrupted when the alarm was given that a French lugger had gone ashore. The *Filey Post* of 26th October reported how the churchyard was abandoned as the town's fishermen, most of whom were attending the funeral, rushed down to the beach to give help. The lugger, however, had managed to get out of trouble herself, and so the funeral could continue as normal.

20 THE TOUGH TRADE: HARDSHIPS OF FISHING

'Before the War, I can remember them sayin', the old people, they didn't earn nothin' for mebbe six weeks. And when they went to t'butchers, all they could afford was a sheep's head. They used to boil it and mek a broth of it and dumplin's. So if you go down there and see a line o' surf on the beach tell anyone it's a Sheep's 'ead wind.' Jim Haxby, 2005

It was a trade that brought no certainty of income, or indeed of survival. Tragedies were only the most public of adversities to bring families to the brink of ruin. And it was a living that could exact a high psychological price.

This is the only chapter in this book without photographs. Poverty, hungry children and despair are not photogenic. Many current inhabitants of Filey may not realise how much chronic insecurity and want were in the town of their grandparents and great grandparents. There was no obesity problem in these east coast fishing stations, as incomes declined after about 1880. It may be likened to the coal districts which spiralled into worklessness after the pit closures of the 1980s and '90s.

Uncertain Earnings

A boat's income was at the mercy of fish, weather and market. A fisherman's typical income of 30s a week in 1913-14 was about the average for an unskilled worker. Graham Taylor reckoned a pound a day was his usual wage in the early 1960s. Fish can't be harvested and stored in a barn against better prices. Risk is inherent in the trade, even hardworking fishermen being exposed to poverty if catches are bad. It was an occupation upon which nature imposed the ultimate zero-hours contract. Jim Haxby reckoned a coble took four days to earn its expenses, and the fifth was the profit. But how many full weeks were possible in winter?

In the days of sail, if there were no wind, a boat might never even get to the fishing grounds. 'We left Filey Bay on Monday morning,' one offshoreman told Richard Harland. 'On Wednesday we could still see land.' They were home at the end of the week having shot not one line. Or there might be a strong easterly, so strong that the boats couldn't get out – the 'Sheep's head wind' that might plunge much of the Old Town into real difficulty. In the harsh winter of 1962-3, when snow was on the ground from Boxing Day until Easter and storms kept cobles ashore, Graham Taylor earned one pound in three months.

In the *Parish Magazine* of April 1910, the twilight days of the yawls' lining, Canon Cooper dolefully quoted a county newspaper. The item related how one Filey yawl had gone out 60 miles, shot 35 lines, caught just 35 fish, and earned two pounds:

> There were six men on board, so deducting six shillings for the boat (3s shillings in the £) . . . 34 shillings to divide between them, giving each man about five shillings, but leaving him still in debt for his bait. Another shot 30 lines and got two cod and a ling. Another shot sixty lines for 18 haddocks, and so goes on the dreary tale and

so it will go on, shading ever into darker hues until the men learn that the day of line fishing is past.

Nor were good catches any guarantee of solvency. The years 1883-6 exemplify how utterly unpredictable herring was as the 'harvest', the source of the Yorkshire year's principal earnings. Bad weather kept the yawls at Scarborough for days throughout the 1883 season, and catches were poor even when the weather eased. In grim contrast, catches the following three years were so heavy that prices hit rock bottom. In 1884, the landing price collapsed to 3d per hundred fish, when *eight* times that would normally be reckoned a poor price. Crews lost money, despite large catches. Canon Cooper, writing in 1885, graphically caught the desperation of the yawl sharemen:

> A penny a hundred is at times paid for herrings. At Whitby a few years since the bellman was sent round the town telling the people they could have the fish for nothing, for merely carting it away.[1]

Fortunes rarely turn as dramatically as this. Less than 20 years before, herring were the cash crop that kept men going through the hard winter and paid for new boats. Such was the effect of the *Zulu* invasion of Yorkshire waters. No wonder most of Filey abandoned the herring fishery in the 1880s. And ironically, when George Wheeler landed a 'wall of fish' off Whitby in September 1908, when prices were good, the herring that completely filled 18 of the 20 nets drifting from his mule *Euphrates* were so heavy that all sank without trace. The nets were worth £50, and the fish around £25, a local newspaper estimated.

Damage to Fishing Gear

The ultimate disaster was damage to a boat. Though much publicity surrounded the generous subscriptions that helped Filey offshoremen after the May 1860 hurricane, the hard fact was that the losses sustained were often life-changing. The best-known cases are those of Ben Simpson and Edmund Crawford, for their complete changes of career were described in their evidence to the 1863 Sea Fisheries Commission. Simpson's lugger, *Robert Newton*, was only ten years old when it was wrecked, and may have barely started to repay its capital cost.[2] They were lucky: they had skills and Crawford probably had capital from his wife to start a herring-curing house, according to Walcott's account of 1862.

Anyone would feel a pang or two of compassion for Irene's great great grandfather, Castle JENKINSON (O34) and his sharemen. They experienced a huge reverse when nearly £300 worth of herring nets disappeared in heavy winter seas right at the end of the 1867 season.[3]

---

[1] Robinson (1984) pp342-3; Frank (2002) pp144-5; Cooper (1885) p36. In contrast, Shaw reckoned, boats could earn 6s 9d a hundred in 1866 (see above, pp111-2).

[2] See above, pp246-8.

[3] *Filey Post,* 2nd Nov 1867.

Lines: 'Haddock [they] will clean off almost directly, leaving nothing on the hooks but the heads.' 1863

Drift nets: 'The greatest enemy of the fisherman will not only clear the net of its entire take, but makes great rents in it.' 1862

'Nowt's over bad for them owd dogs!' - coble fisherman, describing how if one were caught, a cork was tied to its tail and it was left to float till it died

20.1: The Common spiny dogfish – a vicious shark, up to five feet long. Packs of thousands were the fisherman's nightmare, eating alive anything hooked or netted, and tearing drifting nets in the process.

And then exactly 13 years later, the same yawl, *Admiral Hope* was terminally wrecked off Bridlington in the 1880 October Gale. Clearly Castle had neither the skills nor the capital to emulate Crawford and Simpson, for as we have seen he was possibly reduced to cheating his neighbours as a grocer. The shame in such a tightly bonded community must have been a burden too many, and it may be no coincidence that he was dead within a year of his conviction, at the early age of 58.[4]

An especially loathed irritant to offshore and inshore men alike was the scavenging dogfish (**20.1**). But this marine hyena was a minor threat compared to weather, for a fisherman's gear was far more exposed than that of virtually any other workman. Iron anchors securing lines could get fast amongst rocks, and heavily laden lines might snap, especially if snagged on *boobies*, ie seabed detritus like wrecks, lost anchors and beam-trawls. A yawl might lose ten miles of continuous great-line, with all its snoods, hooks and cod.

'Dived to get his gear back a few times from his coble *Advance* in the 1960s,' recalls Arthur Godfrey of Bill *Bullocky* COLLING.[5] Divers, of course, were simply not around to retrieve lines and pots in Filey's past.

Crab pots were shot in summer, and in shallow water, but this offered no protection from strong northerlies which could shift, smash, bundle up or sweep away whole fleets in the groundswell. The gale of May 1895 accounted for some 2,500 crab pots, 30 Filey cobles each losing around 80, a cost of £10-£12 per boat. One crab fisherman recalled in 1992 how in such weather, he might have to go out at 2am to move pots into deeper water. Very close in, the Brigg End Gulley was 'full of lobsters at the right time of year, but you could lose 200 pots in bad weather.'[6]

---

[4] See above, p249.

[5] *Photos of Filey, old and new* Facebook site, 6th March 2021.

[6] SMHC, Fishing, Filey, Malcolm JOHNSON, p4; Graham Taylor.

These risks posed by Nature may have been only marginally more tolerable than the damage wrought by other fishermen, as described in Chapter 12.

In the heyday of Filey's fishing, insurance was in its infancy, probably not readily or affordably available for fishing craft, and not likely to concern the inherently risk-taking/chancer mindset of the typical fisherman. For example, the yawls damaged in Filey Bay on Whit Monday 1860 were, according to Shaw, mostly uninsured. If men with hundreds of pounds of capital sunk in a lugger or yawl did not trouble the insurance agent, there was no chance that a coble fisherman would. Insurance agents appear in Filey directories from 1858, but seem to have been interested only in 'Fire and Life' business.

Help from the Community: Subscription

'Women outnumbered men in Filey, a fact that betrayed the brutishness of coastal life. Villagers measured their ages by the number of storms since their kinfolk were lost and made room in their cottages for widows and children left homeless by unpredictable gales.'
Deborah Valenze

The 19th Century saw the birth of the uniquely British charity movement. Parish congregations had been responding to tragedies – even foreign ones - with 'briefs' (a whip-round in church) for centuries. But secular public subscription evolved in the 19th Century - the best known Filey example is the £3,000 raised to assist the yawl owners and their crews after the 1860 Whit Monday 'hurricane'. Damage to boats and gear was put at £10,000, and half the town was said to be ruined, though only one life was lost. Remarkably, David Crawford was able to tell the 1863 Sea Fisheries inquiry that local charity and investment had made good these losses.[7]

Loss of property seems to have prompted more giving than loss of life, for without gear livelihoods vanished, and this meant long-term poverty. The gale of October 1869 threw about 860 Scarborough and Filey people area out of work. Fortunately, the locality rallied round and made donations, money coming from much further afield than the districts immediately affected. The local press emphasised how the gales had been the worst 'within the memory of the oldest fisherman.' Within seven weeks, over £1,900 had been subscribed, and was being managed by a 'Committee of Management of Funds of Distressed Fishermen of Filey.'

Thirty or so years later, the local press reported far smaller responses to the losses of *Unity* and *Trio* - in 1895, though contributions came from all over the county, the *Trio* Fund reached only £205, despite the deaths of all six crew, the bereavements of two widows and the loss of seven children's fathers. Ironically, the *Unity* Fund (1892) had only attracted around £100, despite a count of four widows with 13 children.[8]

---

[7] Shaw, *Guide to Filey* (1878) p58.
[8] More may have been given later, but most donations came soon after a disaster.

The loss of the coble *Mary*, just before Christmas 1896 – a season when even the poorest felt generous – occasioned donations of £320 for the three families. A dependent parent, as well as the widows, were catered for - Mark JENKINSON (P32) aged 61 was presumably reliant on the earnings of his son George, and was awarded five shillings a week for four years.[9]

Bad weather and the fishing tragedies that came in its wake cut donations, as visitors, often generous givers, avoided such doom-laden destinations. One beneficiary of Filey's communal generosity was *Postman Tommy*, whose mother would not allow him to go to sea after his father Tommy Avery JOHNSON was lost with *Trio*. Tommy delivered all round Filey, even on Christmas Day when he would eat in the region of five Christmas dinners. Clearly, local opinion could be very sympathetic to those viewed as especially deserving. Captain Sydney Smith told us how in September 1908, Arthur Douglas Senior, who had lost two sons in 1902, landed so large a catch in his herring coble *Jane and Priscilla* that it had to be towed by a steam trawler back to Scarborough. The weight of fish eventually sank the boat off Ravenscar. Filey raised money by public subscription, Douglas appropriately naming the Filey-built replacement *Thankful Arthur*.

But not everybody felt generous in such circumstances. 'It is feared,' wrote Cooper,

> that if people are relieved of finding their own Christmas dinner, or of providing meals for their children, or are helped to tide over a hard winter or a period of exceptional distress, they will get such a taste for the bread of dependence that they will always expect to be helped, and, indeed, get to look upon such help as a right.

In other words, the poor would be drawn into what became known in the 1980s as 'the dependency culture'. Cooper was having none of it. 'The open-handed man has been the ideal of the Bible,' he declared.[10]

Even towns further afield shared his view. After a particularly damaging storm in 1868, the people of Sheffield, perhaps with fond holiday memories of the town, established a 'Net Fund', references to its help for individual fishermen being dotted about the *Parish Magazine* and *Filey Post*. Though rolled up in the Fishermen's Charity, it was still paying out for loss of nets as recently as 1966.

Help from the Informal Community

How did families survive? In the 19th Century, the desperate could apply to the Poor Law Union relieving officer for 'out relief', ie a modest regular payment of what we might now call benefit. As a last resort, they had to enter the union workhouse.

---

[9]   *Parish Magazine*, Jan 1897.

[10] Cooper (1908) pp54-5, 60. It is interesting that the words of these Victorian opponents of charitable giving are being echoed as I proof read, in October 2020, in connection with free school meals in holidays for deprived children.

The stigma and shame associated with 'the house', however, were enough to make this the worst of all options, let alone the prison-like conditions to be faced, and the separation of children from parents, and husbands from wives. The parishes of the area lay in the Scarborough and Bridlington unions, but of their 243 and 56 workhouse inmates on census night 1881, just three were Filey-born, and none were fishermen or had Filey fisher surnames.[11]

'The Union' was just not an acceptable solution amongst the fisher population: Shaw describes how in 1856 he had met an orphaned boy at Flamborough, and learned how both parents and two elder brothers had died in the space of a single year. He'd been taken in by a widowed aunt

> who had her own large family but was determined that her sister's boy should not go to the Workhouse if she could help it (1865, Chapter VII).

The normal Filey response was to 'double up' with relatives or in-laws. But though this saved on rent, it did not feed a family. In the absence of anything like a sympathetic welfare state before the 1906-13 Liberal reforms, the relief could only come from local institutions, neighbours and family.[12] Surveys around 1900 in London and York, conducted by Booth and Rowntree respectively, found about 30% of the urban population living 'below the Poverty Line'. Filey may have been even worse in a poor fishing season. Without the customary altruism of the day, which makes even our support of food banks seem paltry, hundreds of families in the Old Town would have been seasonally pushed beyond the edge of starvation.

It is no wonder then that long before the fall-off in stocks, Cole was able to describe a 'ritualised begging' that took place annually just before Christmas. This door-to-door traipse, with collecting boxes known as Vessel Cups, anticipated the inevitable leanness of the Winter Fishing months.[13]

The churches were focal, and remarkably well supported by donations. The St Oswald's *Parish Magazine* refers often to the Widows and Orphans Fund, set up in 1892. In December 1905, in the especially hard fishing weeks, 'necessitous children' had been fed in Filey for two years. The retired doctor, Wheelhouse, was credited with 'planking down' the money to support it. This proto-breakfast club provided hot milk, cocoa and buns six mornings a week. In January 1908, around 80 children a day were judged by their teachers to be 'in real need' until the spring.

The misery went on, the scheme being necessary every year until at least 1912. Another town charity was soup kitchens, most of the money being spent on meat -

---

[11] The uncertainties of fishing clearly induced the local poor law to allow 'outdoor relief', ie weekly payments, and not insist on entry into the house. Three fishermen's widows were in receipt of 'Parochial Relief' in the 1851 Filey census returns.

[12] This new proto-welfare state catered badly for share fishermen. Under the National Insurance Act (1911) contributors who paid the stamp were entitled to unemployment benefit, but share fishermen were specifically excluded from the scheme.

[13] Cole (1828) pp135-6. There is more detail about the custom below on p309.

'the kind hearts of several people were touched by the thought of those who would be thrown out of work owing to the weather'. Sunny summer holiday shots of fashionable New Filey in the pre-1914 Edwardian sunset give only half the picture.

Members of the Clothing Club, a type of cooperative which bought in bulk, had saved nearly £194 in 1897: the 358 families each had a card recording what they had paid in and spent – 'few better aids are to be found to obtaining [a shirt] than the Clothing Club', the *Parish Magazine* enthused in January 1898.

We can well imagine that the independently-minded Filey housewives would only belong to such a charitable organisation in desperation. That membership figure of 358 families may well be an accurate guide to the numbers living 'below the Poverty Line' in the town. It is hard to be specific, but given the unpredictability of the fishing trade, it is certain that a substantial number of Old Town families would have relied on these communal initiatives.

The population of Filey in 1901 was 3,003, with an average family size of 4.5 in England and Wales. The implication is that half the families in the parish were in that Clothing Club. Remember that the national level in poverty according to Booth and Rowntree was about 30%. It was impossible for middle-class people to ignore want when the desperate lived just a few hundred yards away, and not, as today, several miles away in some entirely separate inner-city ghetto.

Some households were taken into want by a husband's alcoholism. There was often little sympathy. Cooper, more charitable than most, summed it up neatly: 'the poor women in my parish say of their drunken husbands that everyone can manage them except those that have got them.' Mothers took the brunt of poverty, however, caused: Cooper reckoned in 1908 that one Filey mother had not had shoes on in 14 years. One wonders how many Filey fisher wives around 1900 were doing 'a hell of a lot of sacrificing', as was to be far better chronicled in the 1930s Depression years throughout much of Northern England's industrial regions:

> 'Oh, I've had mine,' they'd say, but they hadn't had a bite. A good mother went without many a meal. Kids come first. And husband. She was last, though she worked harder than anyone. But you didn't find out till it was too late.[14]

But what if it were a young, child-bearing mother, who could not starve herself safely? Sunday School teacher Edward Scales JENKINSON (R38) died in 1927 at the age of 24 leaving a young family. Local tradition suggests that his decline was partly a result of him doing without during a period of poor fishing, so that his children should not go short.

It is as well that in the absence of proper state provision, there was an especially robust tradition of charitable giving. After several colliers were wrecked during the Great Gale of 10th February 1871,

---

[14] Cooper (1908) pp10-11, 43; the words of John MacNamara, a Lancashire millhand, in Juliet Gardiner, *The Thirties: An Intimate History of Britain* (Harper Press, 2010).

two Filey farmers very kindly placed teams free of charge at the disposal of any of the fishermen and poorer folk who cared to fill the bags and load the wagons.[15]

The St Oswald's *Parish Magazine* is full of local giving. In 1901, a Scarborough lady, Miss Kekwich, gave £50 (equivalent to thousands of 2021 pounds) to boost Clothing Club funds, whilst a jumble sale was held to add 1s 6d to each card, 2s 0d for widows. In March 1895, Mr Southwell financed a soup kitchen for over 40 families towards the end of an especially bad spell of fishing, a regular winter occurrence. Coal was distributed to 94 families 'on account of the exceeding severity of the weather'. A visitor donated £10 10s, as a 'small gratuity to the Pleasure Boatmen' to buy two to three stone of flour for 60 or 70 'hardworking and deserving men'. There was even a Navy Fund, presumably to support ex-sailors or those who had been in the Naval Reserve. By 1901, it had provided 5s 0d a week to Mark JENKINSON (P32) for some 4½ years, but the allocation of £59 10s was now exhausted.

Wane recorded on 9th September 1908,

> how good the Vicar was to the poor in the long dreary winter. There is a good deal of poverty in Filey but they have a well organised system of free breakfasts for children.

Canon Cooper's Leading Example

The young visitor was spot on. Few Anglican ministers can have faced so fiery a clerical baptism as Arthur Neville Cooper, inducted into the living at St Oswald's just 40 weeks before the Great Gale of October 1880, in which two Filey yawls were lost with all crew. In all, at least 18 Filey men drowned in two days, as well as eight 'names unknown' – joskins - the worst loss in any single storm in Filey's history. Nine women were widowed, and 21 children lost their fathers. I sense that the precarious realities of fisher life were seared into Cooper's conscience by the experience. Certainly he took the lead in promoting a fund to relieve the bereaved families[16], but beyond that he took an interest in the Old Town community more empathically than any other 19th Century Filey clergyman seems to have done.

Alas not every fishing station was as blessed in its clergymen. An especially outspoken opponent of such charity was the Rev CH Clissold, of St Thomas, on Scarborough's East Sandgate, which served Sandside's fishing community. 'I came here as your vicar,' this Dickensian throwback declared in 1904,

> not as a relieving officer. It has, I am afraid been the custom of some to expect, or rather demand as a right, money, coal, or groceries. I want to speak plainly so that these may not mistake me. My work amongst you is to look after your religious life, to hold services, to visit the sick.[17]

---

[15] *Filey Post*, 28th Feb 1871.

[16] Fearon (2016) p10.

[17] Friend (2010) p98.

Moving quickly on from Scarborough's Mr Bumble, Cooper's rather more literal interpretation of the Sermon on the Mount probably induced much imitation amongst his parishioners. The May 1905 *Parish Magazine* reported how a 'nobleman' sitting behind a fisherman wearing a 30 year-old coat at a St Oswald's service spontaneously gave him a new one. Estate owners near Yorkshire fishing settlements permitted unofficial 'stick days' when fisher families could collect wood from their land for fuel or pots.[18]

George CAMMISH, brother of *Jacky T* and *Bobby T*, an expert in wood, could 'do anything with cobles' that needed a repair. 'He'd do it for nothing, they had nothing', reckoned Bob Wheeler. It was often the case that those who were little better off themselves rallied round in the time of trouble. If a family were known to be in need, neighbours put aside a fish for their dinner. 'There's a fry for . . .' would be the saying.

David Smith who had first-hand knowledge of the Old Town community felt that this instinct for mutual care was 'one of the finest traits of their character. No one ever goes hungry if someone else has a dinner.' Speaking of any fatherless family, Jim Haxby insisted:

> They would give 'em a dinner, or they would give 'em clothes. They allus stuck by 'em and as soon as the eldest could work, they went into the job and they worked. But they all stuck together, they were very, very close.

Shetland fishing communities similarly kept the elderly supplied from the daily catch. On the Yorkshire coast, coal was often given to the elderly as an informal, neighbourly winter fuel allowance.[19]

Self Help

Flamborough (1809) and Filey (1811) were helped by the local moneyed to set up friendly societies, to subsidise village fishermen in the event of infirmity or loss of life, boat, or gear. Perhaps the losses caused by wartime French privateers were the impetus. Initially, these clubs had few members - Flamborough's began with just nine.[20] This mutual movement mushroomed, national societies appearing and expanding by recruiting innkeepers to accommodate monthly meetings for a new branch. Filey had at least five at different times in the 19th Century. They sported bizarre names, and could split and secede, often because younger members feared that their aged clubmates were a drain on the subscriptions.[21]

---

[18] *Scarborough Weekly Post*, 13th Jan 1913.

[19] Frank (2002) pp195, 198; *Filey Post*, 28th Feb 1871; Thompson et al (1983) pp337-8.

[20] Cole (1828) noted how Filey's first friendly society (1811) was only for those with 'business in great waters' – inshoremen were clearly not seen as able, or needing, to provide for such mishaps.

[21] Robinson (1984) pp139, 502; David Neave, *East Riding Friendly Societies* (East Yorkshire Local History Society, 1988). The *Foresters* saw Robin Hood as a mythical inspiration; the

The conviviality of these meetings, ostensibly to collect dues, typically 2d a week between the Wars, was yet another social glue that cohered the fishing fraternity. Aware of this communal draw, societies had strict rules to contain excesses - the *Hunmanby Amicable Society* forbade cursing, swearing, obscene discourse, abusive language, gaming, wagers or coming drunk into the club room. Standard sickness benefits, the main expense, were typically generous in the 19th Century East Riding, at ten shillings a week for the first six months, though Filey's *Odd Fellows* could manage only five. But injuries not illness usually caused fisher poverty – Terence COLLINS related how *Dick Stringer* CAMMISH was gutting when the boat 'took a lift'. He nearly sliced his hand off, and lost use of it for life. Long-term provision was probably beyond the means of such mutuals. There is one invalid in the Filey 1851 census returns, with an occupation 'Maintained by the Oddfellows' Society' entered. But it was clearly an unwanted piece of detail, being subsequently crossed out when the enumeration books passed up the chain. How many others were receiving such long-term assistance is impossible to say. To teach the virtue of thrift at an early age, the parish church had in 1897 established a Girls Friendly Society.

Writing in 1828, Cole had been unimpressed with the Old Town's 1811 experiment with mutuality:

> By the aid of an active originator, some charitable summer visitors, and one or two kind neighbours, a considerable fund was collected. But because, fortunately, some time elapsed without the occurrence of any signal disaster, the fishermen gradually discontinued their payments . . . .

The remnants of the fund were available for fishermen's widows and orphans,

> who . . . but for the improvidence of their lost relatives, would have been entitled to much larger allowances.

We can only marvel at the gross insensitivity with which 19th Century commentators, including newspapers, judged their fellow citizens. It was hardly the most appropriate time for the public expression of such pert opinions.

Mutual societies, with benefit entitlement earned by member subscription, were far less likely to be overwhelmed by localised sinkings or elderly membership if the risk were geographically spread. The nationally-based *Shipwrecked Fishermen and Mariners Society*, formed in 1839, clearly attracted some of the more prudent Filey men. When a storm swept Francis Haxby and the two SAYERS brothers irretrievably off a corfe in April 1859, a county newspaper noted with approval that Haxby's widow would at least be entitled to some relief from the Society, 'he having been a member of that noble institution'.[22]

Odd Fellows probably represented lesser trades, not organised into guilds; whilst the *Shepherds'* Mitford Lodge (1861) saw itself in New Testament terms. The *Oddfellows* Ravine Lodge met at the *Ship Inn* in 1835, and a second lodge, Hollon, began in 1864. The '60s was the high watermark of fishing in Filey, and membership was affordable.

[22] *Yorkshire Gazette*, 9th April 1859. The paper seems to have had a low opinion of

The habit of taking on life insurance may have increased amongst offshore crews as the century wore on, for 36 years later a newspaper judged that Filey's fishermen were 'thrifty and farsighted':

> It is satisfaction to learn that all but one of the crew of the *Trio* are insured in the local Odd-Fellows and Shepherds' Clubs and that one of them took out a policy for a considerable sum in another society shortly before he sailed.[23]

But most fishermen simply could not afford the level of contributions needed to command a regular income for their widows. The crew of *Unity* may have been no different from most inshoremen, the coble going down in May 1892 leaving four widows and 13 children 'totally unprovided for'.[24] (It was circumstances like these that first prompted the staging at Scarborough of a Boxing Day charity football match in 1893, following the loss without trace in November 1892 of the trawling ketch *Evelyn and Maud* with five of the town's fishermen. It has been an annual fixture ever since.[25])

Most Old Town widows had to eke out a week-to-week existence, barely above subsistence. It is grim to note how many widows under the age of 40 appear in Filey's census returns, usually with young children. But it was not only women who were left alone to bring up young children. One JENKINSON was left with at least four aged under twelve when his wife died in 1889, aged just 37. The especially squalid conditions in which the family was existing resulted in a prosecution for child neglect, for their father was not poor. Today, the children would have gone into care.

But it was women overwhelmingly who faced single parenthood. And since this was the lot of so many, we leave widowhood until Chapters 25 and 26, where we look in detail at the *especially* 'Tough Trade' of the Old Town fisher woman's life.

But first, we need to look at the emotional impact of the tough trade. For the grind of poverty involves a constant level of anxiety which strains every relationship within a family. Even minor wastages of food, accidental loss or breakage, and damage to clothing or shoes, all so easily overlooked in the financially comfortable household, occasion anger, over reaction, fault finding and bitter argument when every farthing is precious. Remember Graham Taylor's account of that bitter, public argument on the Coble Landing between husband and wife about going off in bad weather?[26] The poisonous impact of too many Sheep's head winds, or too few fish, was only *one* aspect of the emotional price of fishing, much of it paid by the women of the community.

---

fishermen, having criticised their failure to wear lifebelts – see above, p121.

[23] *Scarborough Gazette*, 23rd May 1895.

[24] *Leeds Mercury*, 2nd May 1892.

[25] Friend (2010) p166.

[26] See above, pp199-200.

21 FISHING AND THE PSYCHE

The concept of mental health barely existed before the 20th Century. Our ancestors had little language for the psychological disorders now recognised as widespread in modern western society. We have no obvious data by which to quantify the psychological and emotional price paid by communities like Filey for dependence on fishing, as opposed to villages reliant on non-maritime employment.

Bereavement: Coming to Terms with Loss

Psychologically, Filey Old Town was one of the best places to be widowed: death at sea was such a given that the fisher culture had come to embrace it fully. There would be no awkward crossings of the road to avoid the bereaved. Before 1914, there had been more regular grieving here than in virtually any other British community. The importance of a respectful attendance at a tragic funeral was well understood. Golf caddie George Matthew JENKINSON (Q80) was accorded this reverence, since his father was a respected fisherman. Drowned by a rising tide whilst bait-gathering, at the foot of the notorious Gristhorpe Cliff in 1907, he was buried on a particularly wet, midwinter afternoon, with a mass turn-out.

> Owing to the pathetic nature of the fatality and to the fact that the deceased was particularly well-known in the town, the funeral was attended by several hundreds of mourners, despite a drenching rain storm.[1]

During the 20th Century, death became sanitised and taken out of its community setting, so that the rituals which once eased the transition of a loved one out of immediate memory into the Beyond have largely been lost. These must have been especially elaborate in fishing villages if the 'mortuary rituals' which accompanied Staithes fisher burials at the parish church of Hinderwell were at all representative. I have been unable to find any equivalent record of traditional Filey practice, but I doubt that the Staithes fisher funeral customs arose uniquely.

For fisher widows, some comfort was furnished by the near universal Christian belief in after life, virtually everyone in the Old Town enjoying a religious literacy largely lost in modern British culture. This was solidified by the firm Primitive Methodist conviction that men were divinely 'called' to their trade, that a fisherman obeyed God's will in his work, and that his death at sea must therefore be part of some greater, unknowable purpose. Premature death was, in the words of one of its ministers, 'a Providence which we cannot, at present unravel; we shall know the reason hereafter.'[2]

---

[1] *Filey Post*, 14th Dec 1907. See below, p355, for details. His father Thomas William (*Crow*, P75) was to be killed in very different, but equally unpredictable circumstances, seven years later – see above, pp133-4.

[2] Kendall (1877) p23.

Many St Oswald's gravestones carry hopeful scriptural verses which must have permeated everyday language. Significantly, the number of richly symbolic quasi-religious maritime carvings at Filey exceeds that of any other British burial yard I know of. The commissioning of these memorials, often shortly after the death, probably reflected sincere conviction held at this most intense phase of family grief.

The phraseology, particularly relating to young men and boys lost at sea, regularly expresses a clear belief that their deaths were not the end. *'He's gone to Heaven I hope and trust/To be forever blest'*, declares the gravestone of 25 year-old Frank BAXTER, drowned on 27th November 1879, off the coble *Mary Jane*, near Atwick. *'We shall meet again'* declares the memorial to John WILLIS, 31, caught in the rigging of the herring coble *Wild Rose*, as it sank in a squall on 29th January 1903. The Scotter family stone, commemorating Mark, machine-gunned by a German submarine on 17th August 1917, has the same aspiration. The death of a parent in old age, years after the loss of a young son, was an opportunity to declare that at last the two would meet again. Especially heartfelt was the postscript at the foot of Elizabeth Ellison JENKINSON's 1964 memorial. She had died at the age of 83, 39 years after the *Research* had taken down her two teenage sons without trace:

Also Ted and George lost at sea 25th Nov 1925 'Reunited'

Unfortunately, the very frequency of death at sea may have forced fisher communities into a stiff-upper-lip response. 'The sea gat him', Shaw noted as the standard, phlegmatic reply if a fisherman were asked about a missing friend. Fisher women may have been equally undemonstrative. On the Moray coast, there was 'little weeping or wailing, at least not in public,' a typical comment to a newly-widowed woman being 'your man's away, what an awful job.'[3] Communal sanity relied on suppression of despair, and there are small hints of this social expectation on Filey gravestones.

The widow of *Research* skipper *Jack Sled*, Fanny Elizabeth, probably had more reason than any other Filey woman to succumb to grief. Yet her epitaph, 'she suffered much but murmured not', pointedly proclaims this fisher culture of resignation and restraint. Newspaper interest in the loss of *Research*, described in Chapter 13, had been intense, and even 14 years later, Fanny Elizabeth's funeral, on 30th March 1939, was widely reported. You have to wonder how this woman coped, with the heart of her family ripped out. Unusually, the *Post* allowed itself to rise above mere reportage, keying into a local collective grief that must have been akin to the Princess Diana mass-grief phenomenon of September 1997. For here was a 'there-but-for-fortune' moment, the risk of mass family wipeout being silently implicit in Filey's hermetic focus on family.

The report, a cutting of which was still, in the 1980s, kept by daughter-in-law, Rhoda Margaret, speaks powerfully of a devastated life faced, with Filey fortitude:

---

[3] Dyson (1977) p188.

THE SEA TOOK HER FAMILY: A GALLANT WOMAN OF FILEY

> There will be few of the fisherfolk of Filey absent from the funeral of Mrs F E JENKINSON, from whom the sea took husband, three sons, a grandson and the husbands of two of her daughters . . . .

You need to read that slowly, to take it in.

> Mrs JENKINSON never despaired. She turned to comforting her two daughters, each mourning a husband. . . . Although the shock of her loss was terrible she refused to give in. She was a grand lass.

If the worst did happen, these women might gain some consolation from the mass demonstration of community respect and sympathy at the burial. But this was denied to most fisher widows, for bodies were usually irretrievably lost after a drowning. In the case of offshore tragedies, especially if out on the Dogger, boat and crew usually vanished without trace. The absence of a body is known to impede the natural process of grief. Research following the Twin Towers attacks (2001) and the disappearance of Malaysian Airlines flight MH370 (2014) confirms that 'ambiguous deaths', as the psychiatric community now terms it, block the so-called 'closure' needed for successful grieving.

The often soothing importance of sight of the body, the funeral process, and the existence of a grave to visit on key dates was well understood in fishing communities. Those 11 weeks for which Eliza RICHARDSON famously sought husband Richard's body after his drowning on 27th December 1797 were immortalised by Charles Dickens in 1851. Whether Eliza truly dreamt of its location by The Brigg is less material than the story's survival within the community, for it crystallised the centrality of the body and a Christian burial to the grieving process. The Book of Revelation might insist that 'the sea gave up its dead' in readiness for judgment on the final day, but Eliza needed her husband buried *'in Mother Clay/Until the Resurrection Day'*.[4]

The fishermen understood this. There was something very important about retrieving one of their own. In June 1948, when *Lady Shirley* was swamped off Primrose Valley, Richard Ferguson *Tosh* CAMMISH was the only one of four whose body wasn't immediately found. Jim Haxby, just 12, and a witness, recalled:

> I can remember all the fishermen, Dick [his brother] and quite a few of 'em, went every low water, Scarborough one day, lookin' forrem, 'e were never found.

---

[4] Shaw, *Rambles* (1867) pp14-15. The stone survives at St Oswald's as B/16. Unfortunately, the Church's longstanding insistence that there would be *physical* resurrection meant that salvation would be denied if a body were lost or damaged. This was why executed criminals supplied the medical schools for anatomical dissection until the 19th Century: it added to the punishment by robbing the victim of a hereafter; and no Christian knowingly donated their body to medical science. Most Great War British deaths in action, however, involved near-total bodily destruction, forcing a change in church teaching. Cremation had been legalised in 1885, but only eased into social acceptability after 1918.

Memorial stones had huge importance in such circumstances, and were often erected even if the family had been plunged into penury by the loss of the main wage earner. We know that Matthew JENKINSON (O17) drowned in Boston Deeps (July 1849) solely from his gravestone. He was just 32, and the circumstances created by his death were unimaginably difficult. His pregnant widow, with two young daughters and a dependent mother, had to rely on her brother-in-law for a roof, and was never again able to keep her own house.[5] Almost certainly, the community clubbed together to pay for the stone.

Modern estimates suggest that 10-15% of bereaved people struggle to accept their loss. Such 'Complex Grief' is most likely in cases of sudden, unexpected or violent death; when a young person dies; and amongst women. Characteristics include persistent preoccupation with, and longing for the deceased; and intense emotional pain, often sparked by reminders of the death. Queen Victoria modelled this in her grieving for Prince Albert, refusing to allow his room to be rearranged for the remaining 39 years of her life.

Perhaps there was more than a hint of this in Terence COLLINS' story about Edwin and George JENKINSON, the two *Buggins* boys lost with *Research* in 1925. Liz, their mother, he told us, kept the front door unlocked on Spring Row thereafter: 'it was never shut again until the day it got knocked down. "Them lads'll come in," she said.' In fact this apparently odd behaviour was in keeping with a longstanding fisher tradition. One Filey woman could recall as recently as 2005 how in childhood her grandmother had a near-neighbour who had lost a husband and two sons:

> . . . it was often talked about . . . this lady used to burn a candle in her upstairs window. The theory was that when the souls of the lost men turned up they'd know where the house was. As children we used to ask what the candle was for . . . But that's what they used to do . . . when you haven't got a body, I suppose you never completely lose hope.[6]

No trigger could be worse than the death at sea of further family members. One June morning in 1858, John ROSS, who lived at The Cliff, was certain that this was about to happen to his mother when he spotted through the cottage window a boat coming in with a flag flying 'half-mast high'. He had the quick-wittedness to remove his missing younger brother's stockings and gansey from their mother's sight, 'for though I was only a boy when my father drowned, I very well remembered how the sight of his clothes used to affect my dear mother.'[7]

Some families seem to have carried a primal curse, as one after another of their menfolk died at sea. It seems beyond comprehension how any woman withstood the accumulation of such repeated losses.

---

[5] See below, p374.

[6] Friend (2010) p181.

[7] See ch17 for Shaw's account of William ROSS's heroic survival. The house, next door to the Coastguards' Watch House, had an especially good sea view.

21.1: One of the few well-documented insights into a woman's despair in the twilight between fear and confirmation of loss at sea is in John ROSS's account of brother William's absence overnight at sea in June 1858. His mother relived her husband's loss seven years before (see Chapter 17). The 1851 Census caught Ann and her eight fatherless children 19 days later. Gravestones became central to grief where no body was ever found, despite the poverty that such a loss must have caused. See also below, page 301.

Sarah SAYERS, a serial victim of the Rev Shaw's 'Fisher whose Name is Death', lost her husband William in the Great March Gale of 1883; her father, Tanton Chadwick, of Flamborough, had drowned in the autumn gale of 1851; and two of her brothers in January 1877.[8] Similarly, *Redux* (20th October 2017) highlights the WILLIAMSONs, another star-crossed family. John drowned in the Baltic in 1808, another Filey man engaged in that staple east coast trade; brother William was lost off Scarborough in 1818. And William's eldest boy, John, drowned on that dire June night of 1858, which William ROSS alone survived.

21.2: The news that this dove brought from the Baltic weeks after John's drowning in 1808 was not of hope, as in the biblical account of The Flood.

Isabella CAMMISH (1860-1938) was a stark victim of the Filey predilection for 'family' boats. *Bell Taffy's* roll-call of loss began in 1865, with 13 year-old brother, William, lost off *Zillah and Rachel*. We can only guess at the depletion of emotional attention available for the toddler as her mother fell into grief. Isabella lost husband Edmond Ross *Eamen* (Q64), and two more brothers, John and Richard Thomas when the herring coble *Unity* vanished in 1892.

Unsurprisingly, widows often took steps to ensure that neither they nor their families risked such suffering again. When *Bell Taffy* did remarry, her new husband, John Pockley CAPPLEMAN (*Jack Wraxer*) was *not* a fisherman but a stoker in the gasworks. Richard Cammish (*Snosh*), the youngest child by her first husband, followed in his stepfather's occupational footsteps, no doubt at Isabella's insistence. *Bell Taffy's* second son *Jack Lorty* (R84) worked in the local brickworks, but the family hex caught up there with him too – see above, page 264.

---

[8] *Redux*, 29th Oct 2019; see William and Sarah's gravestone, **1.5**.

Similarly, Mary JOHNSON lost her a husband and two elder sons with *Trio* in 1895, and was determined that her third son, Thomas, just 12 at the time, would not be going to sea but would join the Post Office. It was a prudent decision. *Postman Tommy* survived his three lost male relatives by a full 80 years, dying in his 92nd year.

Naturally, the memory of a drowning stayed with families for a lifetime. The stone recalling George Thomas JOHNSON's loss with *Mary* (1896) was finally erected 55 years later, with the death of his widow, Ann. It was their daughter Lily, just months old at the time of her father's drowning, who must have commissioned the stone.[9]

Broken Families

Redux has astutely queried the correlation between the drownings of fishermen and subsequent behavioural difficulties amongst younger male members of the family. Perhaps this was a factor in the mid-Victorian spate of juvenile delinquency in the town, reported in the *Filey Post*.[10] The police were 'aware', as is the phrase, and by June 1870 the 'many complaints' had steeled them to action. Maybe local politicians had weighed in, desperate to prevent the year's season being tainted, and hoteliers antagonised. Five 'fisher lads', perhaps contemporary New Filey shorthand for 'youfs', were up before the magistrates for 'obstructing a footpath on the Crescent'. They had been observed by PC Daniel Harvey 'standing on the footpath and larking', and then by plain-clothes

> walking four or five abreast . . . taking up nearly the whole of the pathway, which is 9 or 10 feet wide. They repeatedly jostled each other when persons were coming, so as to force them off this pathway.

Late Victorian Britain suffered a rash of gangland thuggery sufficiently alarming to convince the adult population that the country was going to hell in a handcart. 'Life in parts of Manchester is as unsafe and uncertain as it is amongst a race of savages', declared a judge in 1887, sentencing a 19 year-old gangland *scuttler* killer to 20 years. The city was plagued with youth gangs and knife-crime.[11]

The Filey mobsters were convicted and offered seven days in the cells, or fines of 6s 6d. Three other fisher lads were given the same choice for similar offences.

Redux has researched the eight June 1870 villains, viz Thomas Robinson, George Arvery, Matthew Cammish, Alfred Lowley, Abraham Sanderson, William Scotter, William Waller, and Benjamin Watson, all aged 17/19. Waller was eight when his father may have drowned; Sanderson had lost his father three days after the day of his baptism; and if Cammish were the Matthew Jenkinson Cammish born in 1854, he would have lost four uncles by the time of his conviction.

---

[9] See above p237.

[10] *Redux*, 8th Aug 2019.

[11] *bandonthewall.org/history* website, *19th-century-history/chapter-1*.

21.3: Big city youth delinquency was far more serious than the pettily anti-social larks visited on a few tender-spirited New Filey visitors in 1870. These Victorian Filey teens, propping up the doors of the Lifeboat house, don't quite look in the same league. *[FA]*

Whilst it may not be fashionable or realistic to suggest that only men can discipline boys, studies do suggest a strong correlation between fatherless boys and social maladjustment. This is in part a result of the poverty that is a common companion of single-parent families. In 1916, in the depths of the Great War, the trustees of Filey's *Ebenezer* Chapel were minuting their despair at youthful misbehaviour, amounting to 'disorder during public worship', a time when most fathers were away.[12] This is a contentious issue: but it is likely true that mothers who had lost husbands faced a harder experience in doing the parenting work for two.

Another unexplored issue is the way in which the fatherless often sought spouses who had themselves lost fathers. Human beings seem to seek intimate relationships with those with similar emotional backgrounds, and I suspect that the early loss of a father ranks as one especially formative element in our development. A clear example is the marriage of William ROSS to Mary Elizabeth WILLIAMSON.[13] But perhaps the most graphic instance concerns Lily JOHNSON, only months old when her father drowned in the coble *Mary* swamping. She was to marry *Snosh* JENKINSON, whose father was lost with the coble *Unity* before he was even born.

Anxiety: Living with Fear

Fisher wives may have processed bereavement with a stoically stiff upper-lip, but the anticipation of it was far less restrained. Shaw describes the response of Filey wives to a gale in 1865.[14] An instinctive urge took them as a body to the beach or Cliff Top, where a companionship of fear kept them together psychologically. Few sights could have been more unnerving than a 20-foot boat plunging into deep

---

[12] In the USA, 85% of youths in prison come from fatherless homes - 20 times the national average (*operation-redemption.org/statistics*); for Chapel Minutes, see below, pp337-41.

[13] See above p233. The couple can be seen after a quarter century of marriage in **3.9**.

[14] Shaw, *Adventures* (undated, chV).

troughs, only to reappear on the crest of a dwarfingly mountainous wave half a minute later. On one occasion that year, as black specks appeared in the distance on the 'foaming waters' but without any chance of landing, two women arrived from Flamborough, having walked the 12 or so miles along the coast 'through rain and storm, buffetted by the strong wind blowing straight into their faces', searching for the boats. Anything was better than doing nothing.

Wives of men at sea in storms were plunged into unrelenting dread. Kendall's description of his visit to homes of men out on the Dogger in the storm of October 1869 offers rare access to a very distressed internal world. He noted how

> . . . quiet, but inexpressible sorrow met you in every direction. It was evident that whoever might during those three or four stormy nights seek for repose in bed, there was no bed for the fisherman's wife.

In a cottage up on The Cliff, he met poor Ann ROSS, a fisher widow (**21.1**), with *five* sons out in the storm. She was

> . . . saying but little in words but the eyes and countenance discoursed touchingly to us of the sorrow and solicitude which were being carried on the mind.

21.4: Crump WYVILL's regular near-death experiences created a desire to help others in danger at sea. He was coxswain of Filey Lifeboat from 1882-94. See page 302. *[FA]*

Kendall was hugely impressed by these encounters: they 'indented the memory', he observed, in a memorable phrase. In the height of their fear, the womenfolk found connection with each other at a very deep level, a communal emotionality uniting them in their apprehension:

> . . . two or three women would resort together to spend the night and seek to keep hope alive in each other's heart. *They* wept; but not alone. Many who had no loved ones at sea wept with them, seeking to lighten the burden which pressed so heavily on their hearts.[15]

Even a 17 year-old boy could pick up such a level of anxiety. Wane (1908) noted in his diary on 31st August 1908 the effect of an onset of unseasonally wild weather:

> After tea it rained heavily and the wind rose. A great gale raged. WILLIAMSON was out between Whitby and Scarborough. His wife, Anna, said, 'I do feel anxious for him. I wish it was morning.' This was not a 'half-penny paper panic' but deep and grounded fear. We had never heard the wind so loud.

---

[15] Kendall (1877) pp22-3. Modern neurological findings recognise that such 'mirroring' of emotional reaction is central to the relief of distress.

In the later 19th Century in particular, when the mortality rate amongst Filey fishermen averaged three a year, the men themselves, whenever out in such a sea, must have lived in that constant yet unspoken state of uncertainty normally experienced only by soldiers on active service.[16]

Crump Wyvill, the coxswain of the Filey lifeboat, interviewed by the *Bradford Daily Telegraph* in 1893, had been at sea since he was 14. 'Many times when out in the terrible storms which sometimes visit the East coast,' wrote the newspaper, 'he never expected to meet his friends again. And these experiences have helped to draw his sympathy out to his fellow-men. For many times did he assist to man the lifeboat before he became coxswain.' All would have known of, and possibly even seen, friends drowning. Indeed the boat they were on daily might be swamped at any time of the year, a fellow crewman lost, and it could be their turn at any time. 'He lives with but a plank between him and eternity,' wrote one minister who worked amongst the Old Town fishermen for three years.[17]

'I've known a man to be swept overboard and brought up afterwards, dead, in a trawl belonging to another smack,' recalled 'Old Ben'. Shaw summed up what must have been a regular experience in the Old Town. Of William JENKINSON (P34) lost off a corfe in 1867 whilst taking in lines, he wrote:

> I saw him but a day or two before his death looking the picture of health and happiness, and little thought then, that I should see his face no more.[18]

Premature death was a near-neighbour in a community tightly condensed into just a few cramped streets, its inhabitants exposed to mortality from their earliest years. The Great Gale of October 1880 cost Filey at least 18 men in two days, leaving nine widows and 21 children without fathers. The Great March Gale of 1883 left five Filey cottages (five wives, 19 children) without a man. The drowning of four men off *Unity* in 1892 left four widows and 13 fatherless children, on four different streets scattered throughout the Old Town. That is 19 women and 53 children in nine years, from a total of a few hundred people.

This remorseless sequence of all-crew culls affected *every* fisher family, killing relatives, friends, neighbours, playmates and school pals. Young widows struggling to come to terms with emotional and financial loss were a given on every Filey street, yard or row.

---

[16] One soldier in five had died in the Crimean War (1854-6) the largest war involving British troops then within living memory. Filey fishermen experienced an only slightly lower mortality rate, though over a longer period - 45 drowned in the 15 years before 1895. Nationally, one in 83 fishermen drowned each year, the second most dangerous occupation, railway shunters, killing one in 179 (*Scarborough Gazette*, 30th May 1895).

[17] Robinson Cheeseman, 'Primitive Methodism among the Filey Fishermen' (*Primitive Methodist Magazine*, Vol 66, 1885).

[18] 'Old Ben' is quoted In Wood (1911); Shaw, *Our Filey Fishermen* (1867) pp78-9.

21.5: The loss of a local celebrity - photographed in Filey Red Stars strip (1891) aged 18, *Matty Wiggy*, Matthew Crawford CAPPLEMAN, drowned off *Trio* in 1895. Edmund Ross *Eamen* JENKINSON, 'prominent as a goalkeeper', had drowned off the herring coble *Unity* in 1892, with another team mate. The disappearance of three members of the Town Team in just three years could only be a regular reminder of communal loss each Saturday the team played. *[FA]*

And in such a close community, it was impossible to shield children from death in the way that later generations tried to. Kendall's account of his visit to Ann ROSS's cottage during the 1869 storm strongly suggests that her grandson, Isaac, was present throughout the visit. The emotional intensity of the occasion can hardly have eluded a nine year-old child. In 1983, at the age of 94, George CAPPLEMAN, vividly recalled that Monday in December 1896, when he had watched from the cliffs, like everyone else, as the coble *Mary* was lost in The Brigg Tide-way, none of its crew of three ever being seen again.

Trauma: Living with Memory

Drowned men retrieved from the sea do not make a pretty sight. The skin peels away after absorbing water for about a week; the head swells; and sea lice, crabs and fish nibble at the flesh. Eels dangle out of the sockets and orifices into which they have burrowed. In the 19th Century, most fishermen had seen at least one such decomposing body, as blue-grey corpses became tangled with fishing gear, especially trawl nets. Here was the ultimate *Memento Mori*. Perhaps they steeled themselves against these horrors, but less readily digestible were the terrifying storms in which men powerlessly witnessed the violent deaths of their crewmates.

Dyson (1977, p163) describes what happened on board one sailing trawler during the gale of 29th October 1880, in which the Filey yawls *Eliza* and *Sarah* went down:

> three men went up on deck to survey the damage, shouted that they had to chop away the trawl in case the boat was swung round and swamped. By the time someone found the hatchet, no one was left on deck all three had been swept overboard.

'I trembled like a leaf,' said the skipper later, 'and for half an hour I couldn't do anything, even if it had been to save my own life.'

Most fishermen suffered symptoms of shock in their time at sea, but some had far deeper psychological reactions. Post-Traumatic Stress Disorder (PTSD) is associated with military action, being known as shell-shock in the Great War. It was only accepted as a psychiatric disorder in 1980 as the unresolved mental distress of US Vietnam veterans became widely recognised. A precondition for diagnosis is experiencing or witnessing 'actual or threatened death or serious injury . . . intense fear, helplessness or horror'. Symptoms include flashbacks, nightmares, sleeping difficulties, a loss of any sense of, or interest in, the future, and outbursts of violent, uncontrolled anger, leading to 'self-medication', often alcohol abuse.[19]

Traumatisation may result from single distressing experiences or recurrently being overwhelmed. Between 5 and 30% of those exposed to trauma develop PTSD. Most recover. But PTSD can slow-boil, symptoms emerging long after the experiences. During 2014-16, the rate of probable PTSD among British ex-regular soldiers was 7.4%, compared to 4.8% among those then currently serving.[20]

It is inconceivable that men who survived that terrifying day on the Dogger during the huge Great Gale of March 1883 described in Chapter 10 did *not* develop PTSD. Take Old Ben's descriptions of these truly hair-raising episodes, memories of which must have lasted a lifetime:

> . . . a man was swept away from the deck of his smack and carried by an enormous sea straight on to the deck of another smack not far off, where he was saved by the crew, who clutched him before he could be hurled back.

Incredibly, one boat was 'turned almost completely over by one sea and then turned back by another'. And remember that trauma doesn't only result from direct threat to one's own life. Witnessing can be no less searing. Men do not drown quietly: during that 1883 Great Gale, one account tells of men hanging onto the rigging 'where their piteous appeals for help that never came were heart-rending.' Only those who experienced the 'reflex gasp' – an instinctive urge to breathe when drowning – died quickly – hence the folktales of drowning in silence. This is common, but not universal: an 'active' drowning involves a conscious victim, usually a non-swimmer or poor swimmer, no longer able to keep his head above water, who progresses from a stage of distress to actual drowning. This can take less than a minute but up to several minutes. Victims caught in a strong current (like the Filey Tide-way) could take even longer.[21]

Kendall recorded how the captain of a steam packet that sliced into Richard Haxby's *Ebenezer* out on the Dogger in the storm of October 1869, reputedly declared that 'he should not very soon forget the loud and sorrowful wail' from the yawl's Filey crew'.

---

[19] American Psychiatric Association, *Diagnostic and Statistical Manual V* (2013).

[20] *Health and Wellbeing of UK Armed Forces Personnel: A Cohort Study* (ongoing, kcl.ac.uk/kcmhr/research).

[21] *What Really Happens When Someone Drowns?* (aquaticsintl.com).

During the Great Gale that drowned around 75 men off Bridlington on 10th February 1871, 'the piercing cries of the drowning crews were frequently heard amidst the howling of the storm . . .'.[22]

But how much harder must it have been to be within a hair's breadth of saving a mate, only to witness him drowning as you watched, helplessly exhausted, just feet away? This was precisely what William Johnson COLLING experienced in 1947, aged 22, in the wintry North Atlantic. *SS Langleecrag*, a merchant ship, was wrecked on Newfoundland rocks. *Bullocky* was at the wheel, in iceberg waters. Nearly 60 years later, in 2005 in Filey, he recalled seeing his crewmate drown.

I did me best to save my mate, who lived down street 'ere . . . the air was that thin, I couldn't get enough stamina. I threw a rope at 'im . . . I threw a lifebelt just missin' 'is 'ands . . . he was unconscious with water, cold . . . I threw an 'eavin' line at 'im and it wrapped round 'is 'and. Well I thought I 'ad 'im then . . . and I towed 'im down side of boat where I thought I could get 'im.

Sea was breakin' right across deck, I was onny one on deck, rollin' . . . I gorrim right up t' side, I gorrim within very near in reach, like that (*demonstrates*), just, I just couldn't reach 'is 'and by about that (*puts fingertips of each hand almost together*) leanin' ovver. And I was so exhausted that I . . . there was nowhere I could tie it, to go and fetch somebody to 'elp me . . . I laid there exhausted and . . . at the finish I 'ad to lower 'im back inter t'sea.

21.6: William Johnson *Bullocky* COLLING lived for 68 years with the memory of seeing his mate drown, and being unable to save him. *[Richard Whitehead]*

Notice how detailed *Bullocky's* recollections are, even though he had forgotten other aspects of the wreck. We can be sure that these few critical minutes were rivetted into his memory for life.[23]

One obvious symptom of PTSD is avoidance, since even the most non-specific reminders trigger memories - the car backfire notoriously immerses traumatised veterans into combat recall. Many survivors of the 1883 Great March Gale were so shaken that they never went to sea again. 'Old Ben' got back to Hull having survived it:

I remember one young fellow who, as soon as he got into port, said, 'Look here, skipper, let's have my money. I've had enough o' the Dogger to last me a lifetime.' He was paid off, and from that time he never went out again to the Bank.[24]

---

[22] 'Old Ben' is quoted in Wood (1911); for 1869, see Kendall (1877) pp20-1; for the gale of 1871, John Mayhall, *The Annals of Yorkshire, From the Earliest Period to the Present Time* (Simpkin, Marshall & Co, 1878, Vol III).

[23] Quoted in *Redux*, 15th Nov 2017. For more detail about this wreck see below, pp407-8.

[24] Godfrey (1974) p19; Wood (1911).

It is impossible to establish how many Filey men historically suffered from PTSD after distressing sea experiences. 'It spooked some men,' reckoned one 20th Century coble fisherman. 'We all think we're tough, but three men in a boat on the North Sea - we had bilge pumps and had to use buckets too.'

Nothing has been written to my knowledge about any Filey man's Near-Death Experience, a not infrequent companion of trauma. But three accounts hint at them. Shaw (1867) described how 19 year-old William ROSS encountered something exceptional on that June night of 1858 when he very nearly died. As he was learning how to pray with surviving crewmate William JENKINSON, something mystical touched him:

> at last I believed that Jesus who died for sinners like me, and could save all sorts of sinners, could save me on a boat's bottom, out at sea on a dark night. After this, I felt all my fear go away, and had a feeling that I should not die.

The night before Francis Haxby drowned off the yawl *Ebenezer* in 1859, it is possible that he had a premonition. For his younger brother Jenkinson later reported to Rev Shaw that Francis had 'prayed with unusual fervency and power.'

21.7: Three generations of JENKINSONs - Robert (*Robin*) and his father, *Jack Sled*, with Ella and Mary Anne, cousins aged 4, *Sled's* granddaughters, at the Coble Landing. Likely to be have been taken during the summer of 1925. Both men were lost with the *Research* a few months later. *[FA]*

Ten years later, during the gale of October 1869, George JENKINSON (O16) had one of those mysterious experiences that are either divinely inspired or delusional, depending upon one's view of the mystical. For in that moment, as 'a divine power sweetly flowed into my heart', he became convinced that God was reminding him that faith meant deliverance.

What happened next must have been quite an inspiring spectacle for his storm-blasted crew. We must visualise the skipper almost certainly Old Testamently bearded:

> I again went upon deck, and again spread my hands in prayer, asking with much fervour, where is the God of Elijah? when an internal voice seemed to respond, I am in the wind and in the waves. . . . while pleading I seemed to be baptised with the Holy Ghost and with fire.

It seemed a miracle at the time that all 35 of Filey's yawls survived this ferment.[25] Many fishermen seemed quietly to have come to believe that there *was* something in the wind and the waves. 'He was quite religious but he wasn't a churchgoer,' said one Scarborough woman of her fishermen father, 'he always said anybody who had been at sea in a gale would know that there was somebody above us.'[26]

Perhaps there are clues about the psychological impact of such events in the simplest of surviving anecdotes and character sketches. Men coped differently, some throwing themselves into life with great vigour, as though trauma and loss generated energy and thirst for life. *Jack Sled* JENKINSON, lost in the *Research* disaster of 1925, was certainly no stranger to emotional hardship in his 63 years. His mother had died during his first year. He had leapt from his own boat to save John Watkinson's drifting yawl from the rocks of The Brigg, injuring himself in the process. And 12 years later (1911), he again risked his life trying to rescue the crew of the overturned corfe of the herring coble *Swanland Hall*.[27]

Sled had a great capacity to enjoy life. Every bit as distinctive as his older, larger than life half-brother, Matt *Brazzy*, *Sled* was a tough, fearless fisherman, full of life, a man who loved singing and quite a bit of drink. Despite 'ranter chapel', many fishermen drank a good deal.

Not every man exposed to danger suffers traumatic reaction. Certain features of Old Town life acted as protective, psychological cushions – like the pervasive sense of belonging, social cohesion, and often, through religion, a clear sense of meaning and purpose in life. Much in the vastness of the sea, its contrasting array of weather conditions and its many creatures, connected fishermen with the wonder of the natural world, and the strong tradition and lineage of their family involvement in a skilled craft gave them a self-esteem utterly denied to any North Sea trawlerman.

Modern research suggests that most PTSD recoverers report eventual benefit in their relationships, a sense of self, joy and meaning in life ('post-traumatic growth'). Few men exemplify this as well as *Jack Sled:* as newspaper reports of his bravery testify, and accounts from now-gone relatives and acquaintances reveal, he emerges as one of the most fascinating and compelling of the town's fishermen. He was one of the last Filey men to sail to East Anglia after the herring shoals, for he stuck to tradition. And he crewed the drifters he rented with Filey family and friends, when others depersonalised crew by giving a berth to anyone.

It is tempting to eulogise about the long-lost world of family communal identity to which *Sled* belonged. But we should remember that a fishing life was based on hardship and barely imaginable insecurity. Graham Taylor caught it perfectly when he summed up fishing as 'a tough trade'.

---

[25] Shaw, *Our Filey Fishermen* (1867, ch6); Shaw *Adventures* (undated) chV; Kendall (1877) pp27-8.

[26] Friend (2010) p164.

[27] *Filey Post*, 22nd April 1899; for *Swanland Hall*, see above, pp176-7.

22 COMING TO TERMS WITH THE BEYOND:
1: FILEY FOLKLORE AND ITS SURVIVAL

Bargaining with the Beyond

Historically, human beings have gone to great lengths to win over those forces beyond their comprehension or control. Early man painted animals on cave walls to improve hunting, whilst medieval peasants worshipped the Christian god to be spared famine, plague and damnation. Similarly, fishing communities are at the mercy of unpredictable variables such as catch size and weather. The greater this unpredictability, the more credulous these populations were in seeking magical antidotes to maritime misfortune. Even in the early 19th Century, fishermen on the Isle of Lewis sacrificed an ox or sheep to offer thanks for a good season. Later in the century, in Nairn fisher cottages, a live cockerel might be buried beneath the hearth to ensure a sick child's recovery.[1] This bargaining with the beyond is an essential feature of what sociologists call common religion, the 'silent heresy' of the folk religion, lying invisibly somewhere between paganism and Christianity.

The Christian god did not seem to figure a great deal in Filey's old folk religion. But after 1823, according to tradition, a truly momentous change came over the town - the 'Great Turnaround', Canon Cooper later called it. A general state of godlessness was replaced by a level of devoutness uncommon in most working-class communities.

The Old Town's post-1823 faith in God and Providence, together with widespread abstinence, and an adherence to a craft tradition, fired the interest of visitors, especially nonconformist ministers. Here was a New Jerusalem taking shape before their eyes. 'I have often mixed in what many would call intellectual parties,' observed Rev George Shaw in his 1867 account of a most convivial evening on a Filey yawl, 'but, have seldom heard more Christian or commonsense conversation than in the cabins of our rough and hardy fishermen.' After leaving his ministry in the town in 1867, Shaw was sufficiently intrigued by the little community to holiday there annually.

These clergymen have left a series of fascinating accounts of Filey, of a quality and insight beyond any memorial to most communities. They had an antiquarian fascination with its fisher folklore, but this alas was primarily motivated by a wish to lampoon, not to explain the survival, possibly from pre-Christian times, of its long-held beliefs and practices. These clerics, of course, held that the only guide to God's will was scripture: they believed in getting back to this original source through study and prayer – hence the movement's use of the word 'primitive'. Anything else might distract souls from the path to salvation.

---

[1] Peter Anson, *Fishing Boats and Fisherfolk on the East Coast of Scotland* (Scottish Fisheries Museum, Anstruther, 1930); Barron (2009) pp65-6.

In the scientific age of the 19th Century, the credulity of those who hung on to the old ways made entertaining copy for their books. Even Canon Cooper, who had a good deal of respect for the timeless culture of his parishioners, compared the reminiscences of a 90 year-old parishioner about her 1820s childhood to 'listening to the account of the heathen savages of some distant land'.[2]

Fisher Folklore: the Natural Order

Like all folklore, Filey's fisher belief system was a hotchpotch. Much of it was a blend of medieval Christianity with far older lore – like decking the house with willow on Palm Sunday.[3] Similarly, 'the lower order of females', Cole's shorthand for fisherwomen, went carol singing door to door just before Christmas, carrying small boxes known as 'Vessel cups'. Inside was a wax doll image of Christ, surrounded by evergreens, apples and oranges, much of which has Celtic associations. A donation of a few coppers brought luck for the new year.[4] Present and future were intertwined:

> Everything in the scheme of things had its correct place, its appropriate connections, and its proper uses. Anything out of place could only be interpreted to be a pessimistic portent for the future.[5]

So a pearl found in a mussel shell was enough of a rarity to threaten misfortune. Another natural arrangement which could only be ignored at peril was the primal gender division of labour. A man's place was outside, finding food; a woman's was in the home. In a fishing community, of course, women had as large a role in the external world of work as in the internal domestic world. Indeed, many female tasks were intensely physical and could only be performed outdoors. Perhaps the crucial male specialism was exposure to risk, a division of labour rooted in the distant human past, when the survival needs of tribal groups were key considerations. The men took the risks because males were more dispensable biologically, their procreational role being brief to the point of hours or minutes, whilst the woman's role occupied her for years.

These gender specialisations were automatically accepted by fisher men and women, their origins lost in deep history. To progressive middle-class outsiders, however, arrangements that involved women in arduous physical labour were downright oppressive. But as Frank observes, these practices dated back 'to

---

[2] Cooper (1908) pp22-3.

[3] Any Flamborough man, for example, was not to go to sea that day if he met a woman on the way to his coble, unless she were called *Anne* or *Mary*. (St Anne was supposedly the mother of the Virgin Mary.) Friend (2010) pp209-10.

[4] Cole (1828) pp135-6.

[5] David Hey's *The Oxford Companion to Local and Family History* (Oxford University Press, 1998) pp186-8. This contains Charles Phythian-Adams' excellent summary of the rationale that underpins English folklore, from which this comment is taken.

something more complex and deep-seated than the unfair and unequal conventions of Victorian and Edwardian society alone.'[6] A more mundane consideration may have required women to keep away from boats, namely the risk of a male crew being distracted in the safety-critical world of the sea.

Some pre-scientific folk healthcare cures defied explanation, rooted way beyond memory. One that was sworn by was wearing gold earrings. Annie Hoggarth (née JENKINSON, R89) as a child asked her grandfather why the fishermen did this: 'It gives them good eyesight', came the enigmatic reply. (A more prosaic explanation is that a gold ring anchored in a left ear was payment for a decent funeral if the owner were unidentifiably washed up on a strange shore.[7]) On Sunday 30th August 1908, JS Wane found *Old Baggy* JENKINSON (P35) wearing plugs of tobacco in his ears to cure toothache. Maybe it does!

Another widely-mocked conviction was that certain animals spelled disaster if associated with a marine enterprise. The fisherman's fear of seeing them on the way to a fishing trip may have been because they were *land* creatures, out of place in relation to the sea. Cats and hares (rabbits in Filey) were also feared, having associations in medieval thinking with the Devil, whilst pigs provoked real anxiety, perhaps because they were non-swimmers. Shaw gleefully quoted an 1820s Filey story of a girl sufficiently ill-advised to tell her grandfather as he prepared for a day's fishing that she had just seen one in the yard:

> Throwing the half-baited line upon the floor he exclaimed, 'out wi thea, thou nasty hussey, thou's hindered mea ganing to sea today.'[8]

These taboo words could not even be uttered, verbal acrobatics being required to avoid them – a pig was euphemistically referred to as 'the gentleman of the sty'. Similarly, salt may have been unlucky because it was a valuable commodity easily spilled, or perhaps because it belonged in the sea. There is a classic story of an Eyemouth boat needing salt, and hailing a Yarmouth drifter to ask for some:

> We need something tah we dinna want tae speak aboot,' called the skipper. 'Is it salt ye want?' The salt was handed over, but the Englishman remarked that all the rest of the Scottish crew had disappeared below rather than hear the terrible word spoken in their presence.[9]

---

[6] Frank (2002) pp169-171.

[7] Peter F Anson, *Fisher Folk-lore* (Faith Press, 1965) p33.

[8] Shaw, *Our Filey Fishermen* (1867) pp10-11; judging from Cooper (1908, pp22-4) this was Jane Chapman (née CAPPLEMAN, 1814-1907) who married Mortimer Chapman. Such beliefs survived into the 20th Century: 'In Grimsby fishing operations were once brought to a temporary halt when some boys drew the outline of a pig in the misted window of a pub crowded with fishermen, none of whom would put to sea for twenty-four hours on account of it' (Dyson, 1977, p193).

[9] Anson, *Fishing Boats and Fisherfolk,* cited above.

This notion that words are far more than labels, but have inherent power and influence, is common to many folklores. It underpinned how Christian name patterns in Filey bound generations seamlessly together over the centuries.

Natural forces were seen as personalities that could be offended – 'we only whistle while the wind is asleep and then breeze comes,' said one seaman. Casual whistling could 'whistle up' a wind that was sent to teach this lesson.[10]

Dreams as well as words could be connected with disaster. The old folklore held that disasters at sea could be foretold in the dreams of close female relatives, as well as the location of lost bodies. Filey's most famous example is that of Eliza RICHARDSON who finally found husband Richard's body after a dream directed her to The Brigg, 11 weeks after his drowning in December 1799.[11]

Such stories were common the length of the coast. William Tindall's mother, at Slingsby, 30 miles inland, dreamt of her son one morning in November 1861 'all dripping wet and covered with seaweed'. Later, news came that William had drowned during an attempt by Scarborough's lifeboat to rescue a schooner. Some women with second sight, like Filey's *Staithes Nell* COWLING, specialised in such premonitions. James Wyrill, master of the yawl *Emulous*, was lost off Scarborough in February 1844. Sixteen weeks later, *Staithes Nell* told his wife of a dream she'd just had, in which a coble was trawling in the bay. The trawl had disturbed Wyrill's body, which had lain 'sand warped', and it rose to the surface. That afternoon the body did indeed surface.[12] Many Filey women may have had similar premonitions, but kept them to themselves since clergymen disapproved.

The public face of Primitive Methodism altered in the first generation of its presence in Filey. Many organisations begin life with enthusiasm and energy which emanate from a few zealous pioneers. But whether it is a company or a religious organisation, age and expansion create a gulf between the leadership and those at ground level. The elite becomes more professional, and some of the early drive wanes. There is no better example than the contrast between Filey's pioneer Ranter preachers of the 1820s and its professional ministers of the 1860s.

'Intractable Sinners'

Primitive Methodism was less than 20 years old at the time of Filey's Great Turnaround. It had originated in open air 'Camp Meetings' around the Potteries, notably at Mow Cop, too populist and unruly for the mainstream Methodists, who expelled these zealots. But there was much else which alarmed the increasingly respectable Wesleyans. For part of the original Ranter appeal was its embrace of folk culture, notably visions, dreams, omens, magic, faith healing and even

---

[10] The Folklore Society, *Folklore of Yorkshire* (XLV, 1899) p49.

[11] For the RICHARDSON story, see above, p296.

[12] *The Allen and Truman Scarborough Fishing Families* (SMHC website). *Staithes Nell* may have been Ellen Unthank, wife of John COWLING of Filey.

witchcraft and exorcism.[13] No wonder its main constituencies of support were the miners and fishermen, whose perilous lives made them some of the most superstitious sections of the population.

Filey was a Wild West sort of place at the turn of the 19th Century. Maybe it had been coarsened by years of being a conflict zone in the war with France. It was certainly not interested in mainstream religion - when John Wesley himself attempted to preach Methodist conversion in 1806, he was famously bombarded with skate, drying to hardness all over the Old Town. Nor had Filey men created any better image at sea, and amongst the notoriously rough and ready maritime population the bar can hardly have been very high. Around 1800, the town's fishermen enjoyed, in Richard Harland's words, a reputation

> as intractable sinners prone to drink and gambling, scoffing at preachers and showing little promise of the piety of later generations.

All attempts to invade Filey spiritually from the Primitive Methodist bridgehead at Bridlington were repulsed, its preachers being regularly mobbed, abused and pelted. The fishermen's nuclear deterrent of pigs was deployed on one occasion when several were herded into a Wesleyan service. No wonder Filey was described as 'a forlorn hope', when John Oxtoby determined a final offensive. He was convinced that 'the Lord was ganin' to dea a great work in Filey.' And so it proved – in Cooper's words he 'turned the place upside down.'

Of course, this gloom and doomery about Filey was a Bridlington view, and we must remember that none of these Yorkshire coastal neighbours had a good word to say about another. But not every neighbour was quite so disparaging about Filey. Scarborough historian Thomas Hinderwell, for example, recorded in 1798 that the town's inhabitants were

> remarkable for their sobriety and industry, their cordiality as neighbours, and their intermarriages with each other.[14]

How *can* we explain the polar disparity of such views about one place?

Unfortunately, the fullest accounts we have of Filey's early 19th Century Great Turnaround were written later in the century by professional Primitive Methodist ministers, and they had an agenda. George Shaw, antiquarian and Bridlington circuit minister, published *Our Filey Fishermen (with Sketches of their Manners and Customs, Social Habits and Religious Condition)* in 1867. (The title suggests that he had recognised a social, economic and religious interconnectedness about the little community.) Henry Woodcock, a Bridlington-born minister, also describes the religious events of the 1820s, though 22 years after Shaw. Another insider source was Harvey Leigh (1856) who seems to have known John Oxtoby

---

[13] Friend (2010) p198.

[14] Thomas Hinderwell, *The History and Antiquities of Scarborough* (Thomas Wilson and Son, 1798) p259.

or at least people who had known him. His account is especially useful because it illustrates that messianic, zany wildness that characterised the pioneer Ranters.

Shaw and Woodcock in particular wanted to emphasise the heathen state of the town in order to beef up the achievement of their movement. Both did posterity a great service by recording so much about Old Town folklore, but neither were interested in the timeless 'common religion', or how it might reflect the same concerns with the Beyond that they had. They managed to create a foundation myth about Primitive Methodist and Filey which has held sway ever since.[15]

'Filey is Taken'

In the early 1800s, these two nonconformist zealots insisted, the place had truly been a fleshpot, Yorkshire's Sodom and Gomorrah . . . 'long noted for wickedness of every description', as Woodcock colourfully put it. Such enormities as drunkenness, Sabbath-breaking, swearing, cockfighting, card playing and 'similar evils', were the town's way of life. Enter the town's saviour.

For a messiah, *Praying Johnny* hardly cut much of a figure – 'his personal appearance, though by no means despicable, yet had nothing in it particularly attractive,' even his sympathetic biographer Harvey Leigh had to admit. But he was a star performer in religious histrionics, known to lie down on his face 'groaning and moaning aloud', and even writhing, when in the throes of prayer. In short, he was not the sort of guest that you wanted at a family function.

Needless to say, according to Leigh, Oxtoby prepared himself spiritually for the Filey campaign:

> John reached Muston Hill, where he could see Filey in the distance. He fell to his knees to pray about the work . . . he received the assurance that his prayers had been answered, and he stood and said:
>
> 'It is done, Lord! It is done! Filey is taken! Filey is taken!'

Woodcock describes how Oxtoby

> entered the village and sung [*sic*] along the streets to the beach, where he preached to a rough and rude audience. Presently, backs straightened, cheeks flushed, hearts softened, tears began to flow and numbers were convinced of the wickedness of their lives.

'The Lord gave me 80 souls while I was praying in a ditch this morning,' *Praying Johnny* declared later. A personal amalgam of piety, preaching and powers of healing brought unparalleled success. 'Six hours each day he usually spent on his knees, pleading with God, in behalf of himself, the Church and sinners.'

---

[15] This account of Filey's moral darkness, and the subsequent 'Great Turnaround', relies on Harvey Leigh, *'Praying Johnny' or the Life and Labours of John Oxtoby* (Conference Offices, 1856); Shaw, *Our Filey Fishermen* (1867) and Woodcock (1889).

1 War raised food prices, the peace of 1815 lowered them. The price of fish did not recover until the 1830s. Dissatisfaction with *this* world focuses minds on The Beyond

2 The Yorkshire Coast was suffering economically in the 1820s - the wartime French blockade on British trade hurt Scarborough's economy, and cannot have done Filey any good

6 The Church of England had a poor presence in Filey, its eccentric, contrary curate having little interest in his religious responsibilities

Why was there a religious revival in 1820s Filey?

3 Primitive Methodism emphasised the value of prayer – God *could* be lobbied, for safe winds and big catches

5 The early Ranters believed in omens, visions, dreams, faith healing, magic, witches and exorcism, and this fitted in comfortably with an existing culture steeped in susperstition and magical belief

4 A Great Yorkshire Religious Revival (1792-6) passed Filey by: it was not the sort of place that accepted outside trends. Only a highly charismatic, personalised approach had any chance of succeeding

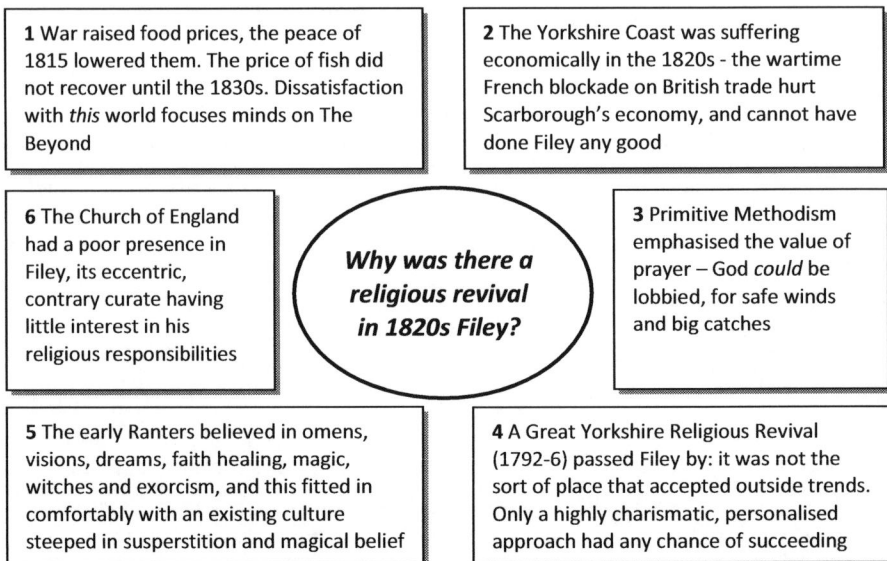

22.1: 'Filey is taken!' How miraculous *was* the Primitive Methodist takeover of Filey? The town's conversion was a mix of religious and secular, but writers emphasised the former.

Shaw describes how Oxtoby's prayers for a child unable to walk or stand led to what appeared a complete recovery within 24 hours.

In Filey, the man graduated into a prophet, with his own hotline to Heaven, and a crudely bastardised biblical delivery. 'Thou wilt to get better and be able to walk as ever thou did, for the Lord has told me so,' he told a fisherwoman with legs 'stiff and hard, as though they had not a joint in them.' And according to the account, 'she could soon run up and down the cliff with as heavy a load upon her head as any fisherman's wife in the place.' Such miracle working must have convinced the Old Town that it had been divinely selected to stage the Second Coming. How could there *not* be a great Christian revival after 1823?

Another early Primitive Methodist historian said of Filey's transformation:

> . . . it was noted for vice and wickedness of every description. The fisher-folk of that time were even more superstitious than the miners. They worked as hard on the Sabbath as on any day of the week. Now, the fishermen of Filey are, as a class, orderly, Sabbath-keeping, God-fearing.[16]

Woodcock's summary was pithier: 'Many of the fisher-folk became as exemplary for virtue as they had been for vice', and the Filey Primitive Methodist Society

---

[16] Rev HB Kendall, *History of the Primitive Methodist Connexion* (Joseph Toulson, 1888); Frank (2002) pp206-9.

was by 1889 'numerically larger in proportion to its population than in any other town in England, except Cleethorpes.' (Modern cynics might consider this unfashionable Lincolnshire coastal town an unlikely yardstick for religiosity.)

Nor were nonconformists like Shaw, Woodcock and Kendall the only clergymen to be impressed by the Old Town's remarkable transition to godliness. Of the Filey fishermen, Anglican clergyman Mackenzie Walcott (1862) reckoned:

> In the matter of temperate habits they stand at an immeasurable superiority above those of their own class at Flamborough and Scarborough; tea is their strongest drink, and sweet-cakes are their favourite food.

To be fair, the Primitive Methodists didn't face much spiritual competition in Filey. Staying at *Cliff House* in 1852, Charlotte Brontë wrote of the 'well-meaning but utterly inactive clergyman . . . .'. But at the time of the Great Turnaround, 30 years earlier, the Church of England's presence was unimaginably worse even than this. Summarising the situation with his usual tartness of humour, Canon Cooper acidly described how the care of Filey souls

> seemed to be thrown in as a makeweight, very much as you see the butcher fling a morsel of fat or bone to turn the scale. Sometimes it was flung in with Muston, sometimes with Folkton, sometimes with Reighton, the stipend for doing the work of the two places was £25.[17]

Put simply, the lord of the manor was hanging on to the Church's tithe income from the parish – ie payment of one tenth of the produce of the soil and sea. In 1823, when *Praying Johnny* first came to Filey, St Oswald's was in the hands of an oddball perpetual curate, Rev Evan Williams. This was a budget post very much at the bottom end of the Anglican food chain, with low pay, and even lower status. The Church got what it paid for. Living alone in *Church House*, Williams would allow no woman through the door, and reputedly received his milk delivery in a pitcher lowered on a rope from an upstairs window. He often suspended services without a sermon, and made himself especially unpopular by launching a law suit over the parishioners' right to appoint both the parish's churchwardens.[18]

By March 1832, a new man had taken over, and was having to clean up the mess. Some parent was clearly annoyed that one of his children had been missed out of the baptismal register. The exasperation of the new curate sings out in the comment he wrote in the register - that the 'deranged state of mind' of his predecessor was responsible for the omission. That unfortunate advertisement for the Church of England had been responsible for Filey's spiritual needs since 1809. Anglican vacuum was every bit as responsible for handing the parish over so convincingly to nonconformity as *Praying Johnny's* evangelism. 'The aloofness of the physical situation of the church fitly symbolised the remoteness of its influence on the moral life of the village,' noted one commentator.

---

[17] Cooper (1886) p14.
[18] *roys-roy.blogspot.com* website, *2013/11/unusual-church-stories-3*.

Ridiculing Filey Customs and Folklore

As well as the swearing, cockfighting, card playing and drinking, Shaw and Woodcock had a field day on the town's customs and superstitions. Shaw especially seems to have been very much of the fewer-units-than-thou school. Weddings, and funerals especially, he thundered, were the occasions when large numbers attended, and got 'something to drink'. And once the formalities of weddings were over, 'order gradually broke down'. On their way home from church, the wedding party were usually beset by invitations to drink at door after door as they passed, jugs of strong liquor were bravely drained, and the whole company joined in the revelry which followed. Local youths charged down Queen Street, in an unseemly race for a ribbon, silk handkerchief or the bride's garter.[19] 'Romish', Shaw spat out, when decrying 'Carling Sunday' (the fifth in Lent) for specially prepared peas were eaten 'in the public houses of the town'. It may have been a survival of an old funeral custom of eating steeped beans, as a communal confession of sins. *Carling* could be from the German *Karr*, atonement.

Wagons and carts were driven to the cliff-top on the third Saturday night after the departure of the herring fleet, in the belief that this would drive herrings into the nets. But Shaw had no curiosity in the origins of what sounds like the fishing equivalent of a Christian harvest thanksgiving: he was concerned solely with the work that would be required on the Sabbath, to have them all back and ready for work by Monday morning.

He would have been apoplectic at one communal pastime, had it not escaped his rage by dying out perhaps in the later 18th Century. Each village in turn hosted what sounds like a gymkhana, involving dancing, sports and horse racing - Filey's took place on the beach. George Beswick witnessed Lebberston's in 1744, and in what was probably a deliberate double entendre, he noted that 'the young men and the young women adjourned to the ale houses to conclude their sports indoors. Ale was one penny a flaggon.'[20]

Many special occasions in the Filey calendar were celebrated solely by the fishing population. These are equally tut-tuttingly described by Shaw. The Easter seizing of shawls and hats by the young men and women, for example, seems to have had no especial relevance to fishing, save as a speed-dating opportunity. Its timing may have been to allow such trysting to evolve over the summer before the fleet set off to the Yarmouth herring fishery. Prior to departure, in late September, on 'Boat Sunday',

> they sent a 'piece of sea-loaf onshore from each boat to such of their friends as they wished *weel teea* [well to].' This led to a 'bit of a supper at which those who are going away and those who remain meet to enjoy a good cheer, heightened with mutual good will.'?

[19] Friend (2010) p174.
[20] Lady Diana Beswick, *History of Gristhorpe* (SMHC website).

22.2: Three clergymen who wrote about Filey - **L to R**: the Primitive Methodists George Shaw and Henry Woodcock dismissed the fisher community's traditional beliefs as irrational superstition, but neither spent long in Filey; in contrast, Anglican Arthur Cooper was vicar at St Oswald's for 55 years, and developed a healthy respect for what he saw as a timelessly old heritage of belief and dialect that was rapidly vanishing. *[FA]*

Note Shaw's dismissive question mark, no doubt to register disapproval of the alcohol that would be consumed. 'Scarcely anything could be done without drink being circulated freely', he lamented of the old ways. The social benefits that might result from this farewell gathering seem to have eluded him. Yet it takes little imagination to recognise the communal stress release that must have been needed prior to so risky a voyage, physically and financially, into deteriorating autumn maritime conditions. We need only delve a little into most of the so-called irrational superstitions and practices to recognise the clear rationale from the 'common religion' that underpinned them.

Just as important was the repetition of behaviours, which is the definition of ritual, by which all human groups, from married couples to nations, bind themselves together. Boat Sunday also had strong Christian parallels with the Last Supper, but this linkage between two related belief systems too was lost on Shaw.

Fortunately for the longer-term survival of Primitive Methodism in Filey, there were preachers who recognised these bridges between the common religion and Christianity. The salaried full-timers like Shaw may well have been the official spearhead of the movement. They were trained crowd movers. 'The whole congregation was moved to tears, or transports of spiritual delight,' declared one obituarist of a well-remembered Shaw sermon. But they moved on every two or three years, and were not as well-known or well-established as the lay preachers, who were members of the community. 'Don't take any notice of ministers,' one older Primitive Methodist said to David Clark at Staithes in 1975, 'don't let them get the whip hand over you, because they're only ships that pass in the night.'[21]

---

[21] Clark (1982) p78.

In contrast, the lay preachers, often from the JENKINSON and Haxby families at Filey, were the lifeblood of the movement. They were some of the first families to embrace the Primitive Methodist cause. William JENKINSON (N8) was a key convert. Tradition has it that Oxtoby stayed at his house 'at the top of Spring Row' whilst engaged in his earliest evangelical work. William's young sons John, William and George were also converted, and became lay preachers. Shaw's hagiographic account of the elder William's death in 1865 has some lovely detail about the responsibilities of a skipper as knocker-up, and the hours yawl masters had to keep:

> He trained up his family in the nurture and admonition of the Lord, and had the happiness of seeing, before his, death, his sons office-bearers, and about one hundred of his relatives members of our Filey Society.

> His son, George, who is a local-preacher and class-leader, was going up the street one morning, about two o'clock, to call up his men for sea, when, as he drew near the window of the parlour where his father slept, he was surprised to hear a voice, - and pausing - found it to be his father's, who was engaged in prayer.

> With much feeling he listened to the voice he knew so well, and heard his reverend parent pray for his aged wife and his family, supplicating earnestly for their spiritual prosperity, and then for their temporal welfare.

According to Shaw, the saintly William JENKINSON was famously instrumental in bringing an end to Sunday fishing. 'No Sunday in ten fathoms of water' lamented a writer in *Sailors' Magazine* (December 1823), despairing of a widespread practice that was possibly insisted on by the boat owners.[22] Only men with their own boats were in a position to refuse.

JENKINSON joined Thomas COWLING and John Shippey to buy a yawl so they could observe the Sabbath.[23] JENKINSON's sons, John, William and George, followed suit, bought a boat and named it *Three Brothers*. 'They will sean come to nowt' was the word on the street, but 'earnest prayer was offered for their success . . . in the firm persuasion that "God would vindicate the right".' And apparently He did, for the three JENKINSONs hugely outfished their competitors in that week of the 'Yarmouth fishing', despite not sailing on the Saturday night. 'From that time,' declared Shaw, 'Sunday fishing was doomed'.[24]

---

[22] *Filey Ebenezer: The Romance of the Filey Fisherman's Ranter Chapel, Souvenir, 1871-1971*, p3; quotation in Shaw (1867). Four years later, George's personal faith was to get him through that wild night on his yawl *Good Intent* during the Oct 1869 gale.

[23] The JENKINSON pedigree (Appendix E, chart **E5**) indicates that this JENKINSON, COWLING and Shippey were related by marriage, in the usual Filey way.

[24] Note the simple nature of this explanation, so similar to the folklore brand of thinking, which disregards any sophisticated consideration. This refusal to fish on Sundays was probably as much to do with challenging the boatowners' oppressive working conditions as religious observance. Shaw, incidentally, confuses the elder William with his younger brother John: the *Three Brothers* are clearly John, William and George.

It became a Filey truism, part of the foundation myth, that 'if there were twea herrings in the sea, *Ranter Jack* would be seaar to git yam [one] on em.' And 'if a ranter went to sea in a wesh-tub he would come home wiv mair than anybody else'. Fishing on the Sabbath remained taboo for some older coble fishermen into the 1960s - Saturday's catch was 'iced down' to be sold on Monday morning. Smith (1932) reckoned that Lord's Day observance had been very precise:

> I have heard it said that in 'the old days' men would assemble by their boats on Sunday night at five minutes before midnight, wait until the Parish Church clock struck Monday morning, then away to the fishing grounds.

Good money was made by coblemen leaving at that time, for fish supplies were in short supply over the weekend, and fresh fish fetched good prices early on a Monday, before the bigger boats got back with their larger catches. Perhaps economic self interest underpinned this pre-lark Monday start as much as religious devotion. Another change, noted Shaw, 'significant of the altered habits of the people,' was the increased gravitas of Filey's yawl names: *Ebenezer, Unity, Concord, Eye of Providence, Tranquility, Hope, Integrity, Good Intent, Faith, Amity,* and *William Clowes.*[25] Such respectful, thought-provoking names were far less common elsewhere. There, you might expect to find 'a quite different class of name, as *Bitter Beer, Catch-em-alive, What's that to you . . .'*.

Clergymen were keen to suppress the old beliefs whenever they could, but these had a limpet-like resilience. Colours were notoriously significant in the traditional fisher mind. Red had a reputation for warding off evil, which is why Yorkshire fishwives wore red petticoats. At Staithes, white was avoided. And universally, green was and is taboo. Maybe it was associated with creation and birth, and therefore naturally with death, or perhaps it is the colour of land foliage.

Green's reputation has not diminished amongst fishermen. As late as 1990, Hull City Council were receiving complaints when painting doors, park benches or lamp posts green. Haberdashers on Hessle Road found it wasn't worthwhile stocking green wool. Famously, in 1931, Rev Thomas Tardrew had his pews at the nearby St John's painted green, perhaps to counter what he felt were pagan beliefs. Whenever he held a function in his copious garden, 'the air would be thick with bricks, stones, eggs, dead cats and huge pieces of codfish', though the reverend's new broom had been provoking this response from the youth of this traditional parish for years![26]

Some of Filey's beliefs were at the darker end of the 'common religion'. There is very little evidence of the Old Town's acceptance of witchcraft and its associated practices. But the Yorkshire Coast was notorious for it in the 19th Century.

---

[25] William Clowes was a Burslem potter, dancer and preacher, expelled by the Methodists and one of the founders of the 'Primitive Methodist Connexion' in 1810.

[26] Alan Gill, *Hull's Fishing Heritage: Aspects of Life in the Hessle Road Fishing Community* (Wharncliffe Publishing, 2003) chs6 and 7.

There were at least three practitioners in Flamborough, and one in Scarborough. Flamborough's dark arts celebrity was Milcah Lawrence, whose merry party tricks included that old favourite of sitting in the church or churchyard on St Mark's Eve (24th April) in order to witness a spectral procession of those locals who were to die in the coming year. Presumably she then frightened the wits out of her more credulous neighbours by directing knowing looks at them.[27]

George Shaw of course had no time for 'ghosts, hobgoblings *[sic]*, witches and wizards' and did his best to rid the Old Town of such beliefs. His short account is the only reference I have found to witchcraft in Filey, and it is very revealing:

> I remember going some time ago to visit a sick girl, and on asking the mother the cause of her complaint, I was gravely assured that she was 'wronged, poor thing'. Not comprehending her at the moment, I enquired what that was, and a neighbour replied with a frightened look, 'Bewitched, sir'. While I was trying to show them the folly of entertaining such notions, the poor child exclaimed 'you're right, sir, I am sure nobody has wronged me unless my mother has, for she won't pray for me, though I have asked her again and again.'

Shaw's was exasperated, the neighbour frightened, the mother probably reluctant to cross the Old Religion with Christian prayer, and the girl seems to have believed witchcraft was nonsense. This perhaps was a microcosm of East Riding attitudes in the 1860s. Twenty years later, Woodcock ridiculed fear of 'ghosts and hobgoblins' that had supposedly terrified travellers on the lonely road between Wetwang and Fimber, and insisted that such nonsense had been eradicated by Primitive Methodism.[28] I wonder how many Filey people believed him.

Local Ribbing

Primitive Methodism offered a stark world view of good and bad, as binary as that of the old folklore. Perhaps this made the transition to godliness easier. But there was a local backlash against this religious absolutism, perhaps amongst the drunks, Sabbath-breakers, cockfighters and card players. Thus, the complete turnaround on alcohol generated a few wry tales, many possibly apocryphal, but their survival suggests some didn't take Filey's Great Turnaround too seriously.

Those just 'brought in' (converted) were butts for humour. George Burton told us how newly-saved *Ginger* Bill Scotter hadn't quite got the hang of abstention, taking a bottle of rum onto a boat to wash down his breakfast. 'Shamon thee sen', the outraged ranter skipper growled as he spotted the bottle. 'Here, maister, have a drink with me,' *Ginger* suggested politely, but this riled the skipper further. The captain took the bottle and promptly supped the lot in one go.[29]

---

[27] Friend (2010) p208.

[28] Shaw, *Our Filey Fishermen* (1867) pp7-8; Woodcock (1887) ch17.

[29] This William Scotter may well have been the Filey *scuttler* fined 6s 6d for anti-social behaviour on The Crescent in 1870 – see above, p299.

George also reckoned that sometime after the Turnaround, a ship laden with brandy was wrecked at Filey. Barrels were hastily retrieved by the 'converts', and the brandy drunk at once out of sou'westers, so that nothing incriminating came back to the town. Barrows and flat carts had to be used to bring the men home.

At Staithes, where Primitive Methodism was also vehemently taken up in the 1820s, Lord's Day observance was taken to even greater extremes. As at Filey, bait-gathering, skeining and baiting were unacceptable, but in Staithes even basic household chores fell into the same category. In the mid-1970s, one man recalled wryly how

> me mother wouldn't even wash up of a Sunday, she used to put dirty pots away in a cupboard rather than wash em. Same as kids, there was no playing about – you were in your Sunday best and that were it.[30]

Continuity

However much Shaw might have disliked and denied it, there was a good deal of intermingled grey, common ground between the old folk religion and the less sophisticated aspects of Christianity. And if the roll-call of highly localised superstitions on Scotland's east coast is any guide, this was generally true early on of all the more extreme species of nonconformity. This may be why the folklore rootstock took the evangelical graft so well. Did fishermen give their boats those spiritually uplifting names for the magical protection they offered, just like the ring-shaped 'luck stones' Clark noticed fastened as talismans to some Staithes cobles?[31] Present-day descendants of fishing families will be well aware that Filey superstition long outlived Rev Shaw. They all have personal memories of elderly relatives alive well into the 20th Century who subscribed viscerally to aspects of this body of pre-Christian belief. In the 1920s, according to Jim Haxby, a single unwise word earned Bob *Tewy* HUNTER a beating. He had been out playing in Church Ravine. Once back home he told his father that he and his brother had seen a rabbit:

> Well Bob didn't know any better, he was onny a young lad. He says he hit me so hard, he says, I saw sun, moon and morning star all at once.

Jim's brother, Dick, tells a similar story from even more recent years. Speaking of their own father, Jim, born as late as 1899, Richard describes a conversation around the time of World War II. As a child, he was helping his father push a barrow of baited lines down Church Ravine to the Coble Landing:

> there was a bank and . . . bit of a waterfall and I says to me father, lookee there, dad, a rabbit. Why, he looked at me and he went mad, saying a thing like that, rabbit and he were touching fishing lines. And he wanted to tek that barrer back 'ome. He said, we needn't go to sea . . . we won't get no fish.

---

[30] Clark (1982) p56.

[31] Anson, *Fishing Boats and Fisherfolk,* cited above; Clark (1982) p150.

George William *Tewy* HUNTER and Jim Haxby, the two fathers named, would, in normal circumstances, be aware that these ancient beliefs were widely ridiculed. It would be in a moment of anger like these that they might betray adherence to such non-rational convictions.

Fishermen often affected disregard for the less plausible beliefs of their parents and grandparents, but when push came to shove they held them too. One 1970s story from Staithes, Filey's cultural doppelganger, suggests that these fisher superstitions were not merely instinctive spur-of-the-moment-reactions. Two fishermen were eager to take delivery of a new coble, but nevertheless postponed its arrival beyond a Friday even though it was available for collection. Friday, for no clear reason, was an unlucky day to start anything. Was it Christian awe of Friday as 'the Devil's day'? (Somehow the medieval church calculated Friday as the day when Adam and Eve were expelled from Eden); and was it not the day of Christ's crucifixion?

Especially ambiguous was the ominous reputation of Friday 13th, a conjunction which aroused even more apprehension than amongst the population at large. Was this Christian disgust at Judas the traitor, the 13th person to arrive at the Last Supper? Did the belief survive from pagan Norse mythology, in which the 13th god Loki was an evil trickster? Or were these fishermen responding to a far older pre-Christian belief, the roots of which went back far beyond folk memory? Perhaps the number had associations with the feminine menstrual cycle, stemming from Neolithic worship of the moon goddess, and her 13 lunar months. In short, were women *just* unlucky?

Whatever their ancestry, such beliefs survived in part because they were self-perpetuating. The 99 occasions when a Friday start proved harmless did not register; but if the 100th were attended with difficulty, this pooled into the collective consciousness. One retired Norfolk fisherman recounted *this* Century how he would not start anything on a Friday:

> . . . perhaps it's something in the Bible. When I was herring-catching on the drifters, it was Friday 13th, we were setting away from Yarmouth, everyone was uptight about it but the owner wanted us to go. These tubes in the engine blew, so we turned round and go back in - we put it down to Friday 13th![32]

However much Shaw may have stressed the Great Turnaround in Filey life styles, I have a hunch that there simply had to be an easy coexistence. I like Terence COLLINS' vignette about painter/spawer James *Fatty* CAMMISH, of Mariner's Terrace, who was rather partial to a bet on the horses (preoccupations with risk and luck had been in Filey genes since its first boat went out onto the North Sea):

> He was always singing hymns. He was always betting, and he'd come out of the betting shop singing: 'When I Survey the Wond'rous Cross'.

---

[32] Weatherhead (2011) p16.

Prayer, Miracle and Magic

Perhaps Filey fishing people stepped effortlessly into the new 'sacred culture' as merely a Christianised version of what they had always believed. Primitive Methodists, for example, held that God would intervene in human lives in response to earnest prayer. The 'miracle' of how the *Three Brothers* outfished the competition was earnestly prayed for; and Shaw pointedly quoted William ROSS, who on that June night in 1858, witnessed the drownings of his two crewmates when their coble capsized five miles out. This fortunate young man somehow defied all odds and survived to describe his chastening brush with mortality:

> . . . though the wind got still higher and blew very strong, and the waves washed over me, I never lost hope. I believed the prayers that had been offered for me by my parents and brothers, would not be in vain.[33]

If God *did* respond to lobbying from the devout, then no wonder there was as much bargaining with the beyond under the new regime as there had been under the old. Writing of 1820s Filey, Canon Cooper described a popular 'cash for catches' deal. He had been told of a 'crone'

> in a house overlooking the bay, who in bad times made her money by selling the desired wind, always a northerly one, to the credulous fishermen who believed her. In bad times, when there was scarcely money to buy bread, the fishermen would find sixpence to buy a favourable wind.

Cooper's nonagenarian informant, likely to be Jane Chapman, also recalled a custom with pagan Scandinavian roots of 'paying for the fish':

> When the nets were being let down, one of the men would cut a slit in one of the corks attached to them, and insert a coin in it. If a silver coin, then so much the better chance of luck.[34]

After the Great Turnaround, certain women maintained the crone's tradition, exploiting fishermen's continuing credulity by implying that their Christian devoutness gave them privileged access to God's Ear. What safer bet than to pay sixpence in return for the promise of a good wind? John JENKINSON (O12) of *Three Brothers* fame married Ann COOLING in 1833, after which time she was always referred to as *Nan Jenk*. Woodcock notes that this early Oxtoby convert's skill in soliciting contributions to the Society's box earned her the title 'Queen of Filey Missionary Collectors'.[35] It is no coincidence that this enterprising woman was the selfsame lady of entrepreneurship we met in Chapter 18. According to an 1860 directory she managed her husband's diverse portfolio of business interests – viz 'fisherman, grocer, draper, and lodging house'. Yet even *Nan Jenk's* trading in good luck was somehow to be far outstripped by Mrs Jane Kirkpatrick Gordon,

---

[33] *Our Filey Fishermen* (1867) p57.

[34] Cooper (1908) pp26-8.

[35] COOLING was an early variation of the COLLIN/COLLING/COWLING stable of surname.

a Filey mariner's wife, who had spent time in large docks. Considering Oxtoby her spiritual father, she went

> from wharf to wharf, from office to office, from warehouse to warehouse, begging for missions; the results for 1868 being £105.

The Filey Society eventually established a regular system by which it effectively received a tithe from the fishermen's catch. Terence COLLINS told us that Primitive Methodist coble fishermen shot a tenth line with every nine of theirs. Whatever it caught was sold for the benefit of the Chapel.

Some practices survived the Turnaround even though they had no Christian associations whatsoever. One famous instance, still around a century or more on, was 'First Footing'. A man of dark complexion had to enter a house immediately after midnight on New Year's Eve. In Filey, he had to carry a piece of coal, to wish warmth for the household in the coming year.[36] This custom, widespread in the North of England within living memory, has no Christian basis: the medieval Church's year began on 25th March, Lady Day, deemed to be when Christ was immaculately conceived. First Footing's prevalence in regions as far apart as Scandinavia and south-eastern Europe suggests origins with the Indo-European people who spread across Europe at least four to six thousand years ago. With a lineage like that, no wonder some beliefs would simply not go away.

Some of the darkest appeals to the old gods that controlled fishing are only known elsewhere – Friend notes (page 207) that at Staithes, as late as the 1870s, folk memory recalled wives of men having bad catches killing a pigeon, removing its heart, pricking it with pins, and roasting it - a ritual which attracted the witch who had hexed the coble. The next woman to show up was presumably the witch, and could be placated with presents. Did anything like this ever happen at Filey? Of course not – that sort of thing could only happen at Staithes . . . or could it?

The continuity between the old folk beliefs and the new 'sacred culture' offered by Primitive Methodism guaranteed its initial acceptance. But there was far more to the lure of this vibrant, energetic brand of Christianity. In the next chapter, we look at the unique appeal offered to Filey fisher people by Ranter Chapel.

---

[36] Clark (1982) pp92-3. At Filey, something similar also had to occur on Christmas morning – no one could go out until the 'the threshold had been consecrated by the entrance of a male' (Shaw, *Our Filey Fishermen*, 1867, p9).

23 COMING TO TERMS WITH THE BEYOND: 2: PRIMITIVE METHODISM TAKES ROOT

Calling

Within a few years of the Great Turnaround, Primitive Methodism was rooted deeply in the psyche of the Filey fishing community. Central to its beliefs was the idea of a Calling. This concerned not only social behaviour, but also a man's dedication to the livelihood, no matter how humble, to which God had called him – hence the use of the word *vocation* for occupation. Medieval Catholicism had emphasised that God could be fully served only by withdrawal from the world, whereas the Protestant reformers found in scripture clear evidence that a man could obey God's will in the proper discharge of his everyday work:

> . . . no task will be so sordid and base, provided you obey your calling in it, that it will not shine and be reckoned very precious in God's sight.[1]

We see now the significance of those wonderful St Oswald's gravestones with their sculpted images of working life – sails, oars, anchors, cobles. John Sumpton Fox, the likely carver of many, may have had Primitive Methodist leanings, despite once serving as parish clerk. For the 'brought in', such occupational equipment was central to a man's service to God. And surely God would bless with fruitful outcomes those who followed their calling diligently. No wonder the Ranter caught more in six days, in popular tradition, than those who godlessly shot all seven.

God was indeed meshed into the everyday, and the everyday was an ongoing opportunity to commune with him. There is a lovely memory of Robert Pearson *Tewy* HUNTER, recalled as a 'true Christian man', who would say a prayer in the skeining shed as he began his work. Similarly, an anonymous contributor to the Scarborough Maritime Heritage Centre's collection of written memories recalled his CAMMISH grandparents' house on Sandside, in Scarborough's fishing quarter, around the time of the Great War. Of an evening, the whole family would be in the kitchen, baiting long-lines by candle light:

> They sang at their work, the women and men alike. Songs of praise, all of them an acknowledgement of their love and trust of the lord above in whatever should befall.

The notion of accepting one's calling required a resignation to God's purposes, which of course were beyond human understanding. But this should not involve fear, for the Ranter also believed in divine good intent. God would ultimately provide – hence the repeated theme of *Providence* (divine provision) on their gravestones. He would come up with the goods, and if he didn't, well, he had a special reason not to.

---

[1] John Calvin, *Institutes of the Christian Religion* (1536).

23.1: The 1849 gravestone of John Stockdale is an early example of how the most mundane items of daily toil could be celebrated as a devout compliance with God's calling. Hence the respectfully detailed portrayal of anchor, rudder, and rope, down even to the correct knot.

This neat fit with divine will gave the Old Town community the resilience to cope with the hazardous nature of their lives. Captain Sydney Smith told us how a man might complain of a poor catch with the words 'not much of a shot': the Ranter would console him with the words: 'That's what the Lord says you should have, so be glad of it!' As Calvin also observed in *Institutes*:

> Each man will bear and swallow the vexations, weariness and anxieties in his way of life, when he has been persuaded that the burden was laid upon him by God.

All fishermen must somehow come to terms with the high risks of their profession. Most became philosophically resigned. 'We're used to being drowned' was a catchphrase used by many fishermen.[2] Shaw noted that the Filey men specialised in euphemism for the risks of their trade (see below, pages 415-6). But the Primitive Methodist fisherman took consolation in the acknowledgment that even tragedy could be part of God's unknowable purpose. It was a religion that suited admirably so dangerous a vocation.

Ministers and Preachers

'I leads them to the tree of life', said John Oxtoby, explaining in homely if ungrammatical vernacular how he rooted all his preaching in everyday experience. Christ himself took his first apostles from a fishing community, and so there was much in their working lives which offered potent metaphors for the Christian message. Primitive Methodist success in Filey was largely due to its emphasis on simple, spontaneous, and passionate public oratory, centred on fishing themes. 'Ranter' became the movement's by-name, and the word was still used in Filey in the 1980s, even though the Filey congregation had by then lost its separate identity. The traditional lay preaching was maintained by many Filey fishermen, and the intimate knowledge of the fisherman's life they shared with their audiences gave their message a relevance, authenticity and immediacy which the sermons of more staid clergymen must have lacked.

---

[2] Dyson (1977) p167.

23.2: Despite a lifetime of meanderings around Primitive Methodist circuits as a minister, Castle ROSS (1840-1928) never lost his Filey roots. Brought up in a fishing family, his father had been lost without trace when Castle was just 11. All five of his brothers were fishermen. Castle himself worked initially as a tailor, but trained for the ministry in his twenties, and spent over 40 years in different parts of England. Widowed in 1914, he finally returned to Filey, dying in *Cliff Top Cottage*, his childhood home, in 1928, aged 87. *[FA]*

They preached 'rudely but earnestly', Arthur Munby declared, having watched a fisherman-preacher at a Scarborough service in 1865.[3] Filey people would say 'tarribly in earnest', according to Canon Cooper. These fine communicators commanded attention and respect. We cannot now experience such a sermon, or imagine being part of a congregation that so fully embraced the imagery and commonality of the fishing life, nor have the far simpler, less sophisticated life experiences of those vanished communities. And once back at sea, every fisherman had plenty of time for reflection on these spiritual essences. Of *Ranter Jack* CAMMISH, who became a preacher, it was recalled that

> Whilst pursuing his occupation as a fisherman, a deep sense of conviction of sin overtook him out on the great deep, and, like many another, after a severe inward struggle, even there on the billows he found peace with God through Christ Jesus.[4]

Even the fulltime ministers could fill any room with energy and presence, despite being strangers – they spent just two or three years with each circuit. Take Filey-born Castle ROSS who moved to 19 different circuits, ranging from Yorkshire to Somerset. To his credit, he seems never to have lost the common touch:

> His sermons and speeches were never dull. His temperament was quick, sensitive, emotional and sympathetic. Pathos, and humour, and passion, alternated; and face, voice and gesture combined in effective utterance.[5]

Yet despite the experience and polish of these professional ministers, it is my sense that they were not the backbone of the movement.

---

[3] Frank (2002) p213. The name came from Primitive Methodism's similarities to a shadowy 17th Century sect, dismissed as 'Ranters' because of their robust and often noisy preaching, which were mostly 'rants' against hierarchy and civil obedience. But Ranters had also attacked private property, which they believed to be a sin. There were of course, shades of this way of living in the communality of Filey's social and working practices.

[4] *Christian Messenger*, 1910/280, quoted in *My Primitive Methodists* website.

[5] Entry for Castle ROSS, in *My Primitive Methodists* website.

23.3: Thirty five years of preaching gave Matt Haxby (1834-1902) an especially robust delivery. He also had a passion for hymns, and was the leading singer at *Ebenezer* for most of his life. Son Matthew and grandson James also went out singing with the Mission Band. As Chapel attendance declined, the focus of the town's public singing shifted from the Sunday services. Fittingly, when the Filey Fisherman's Choir was formed in 1960, Matt's great grandson, *Jim* Jenkinson Haxby was a founder member, he and brother *Dick* Jenkinson continuing a tradition from the movement's earliest days.

'He loved the old tunes; the tunes with body and soul in them,' Matt's obituary recorded. *[FA]*

There was huge gulf between the trained, salaried circuit ministers, and the lay 'paras', the part-timers. Canon Cooper, a fellow full-timer, wrote to George Shaw's wife at his death that her husband had been 'delightful and cultivated'. That would never have been said of the passionately raw, down-to-earth fisher preachers like Matt Haxby (**23.3**), far more representative of Ranter preaching.[6]

Younger brother of Jenkinson Haxby, we met him in Chapter 7, in what were perhaps the most traumatic two days of his life. He was with Jenkinson on the *Felicity* during that terrifying storm of 1869 which all 34 Filey yawls somehow survived. Matt had been a local preacher since 1856, and seems to have had no ambition to become a salaried minister. Though he was 'no butterfly preacher', he was moved to tears when at the height of the storm, and when all hope seemed lost, his eldest son, 11 year-old Matthew Crawford Haxby, sang a hymn. And like every Filey fisherman, he was well aware of the pain of bereavement that the sea exacted. His second son, Frank Jenkinson Haxby, was lost off the yawl *Amity*, aged 23, in the Great March Gale of 1883. These personal reverses seemed to hone a particularly heartfelt dedication to his religious engagement:

> No journey was too long – no day too wet – no night too dark – and no congregation too small for Matthew Haxby to fulfil all his appointments. When his boat was late in getting ashore, he has walked on the Sunday morning, from Scarborough to Filey, a distance of eight miles; and then from Filey to Staxton and back, sixteen more miles, to preach 'the glorious Gospel of the blessed God.'

Dedication in one sphere of life is often matched in the rest, which probably explains how this conscientious man acquired so many boats. All naturally carried spiritually-appropriate names – his yawls were *Felicity*, *Ebenezer* and *William Clowes*, whilst his herring coble rejoiced in the name *Piety*.

---

[6] Shaw's obituary is online, in *Primitive Methodist Magazine* 1904/489. This account of Matt Haxby, and its quotations, comes from his obituary (*Primitive Methodist Magazine*, 1904/71, *My Primitive Methodists* website), and from Captain Sydney Smith.

His crew, of course, were chapel-going Filey men. He was a man who could conjure up, and breathe immediacy into the lives of Christ's first disciples, fishermen of Galilee, potent precursors for the Ranter mission to embrace and save souls. Its lay preaching has been called 'experiential', and the following account shows why.

In a 1980s Newlands Park front room, Captain Smith took us effortlessly back to some dark chapel interior at the other end of the century, with his brilliant dialect rendition of Matthew's favourite sermon, on Christ's Calling of Peter and Andrew. 'He was like an Old Testament prophet,' said Sid, 'a great white beard he had'. ('The stalwartness of his physique in some measure represented the majesty of his soul,' it was said.) And he addressed his fisher congregation in terms they understood, and in broad Yorkshire, which was what he knew:

> And Jesus said, y'ar day 'I'll gannay have a walk on t'sand' . . . then he gets doon there he sees old coble pulled up on t' beach . . . and then he gets there . . . there's ould Zebedee sat in there an' t'lads with him . . . an' there they are mendin' nets. Bad state they was in - all rove t'pieces - must have been a noutherly wind that night. He had a yarn to 'em there . . . and thee had a yarn back, an' he says to 'un, 'what der they call thoo?' He says 'they call me Simon.'

> 'Well,' he says, 'I'm gonna call thee Peter in future . . . thoo an' thee brother 'ere Andrew . . . an' him an' all . . . better come with me . . . I can fine summat better than this for you lot t'dae . . . I can show you better fishing than these herrings . . . I'll mak thee fishers o' men - thoo come wi' me!' And straightaway they left ol' Zebedee in t'coble an' away they went . . . an' that was a funny thing t'dae, 'cos when you sign up for fishin' you're supposed to finish that fishin'. . . you're not supposed te leave 'alf way through it . . . what was he gannae to do for another crew when he wanted them the next mornin'? O ah it was a rum do altogether . . . but anyway that's where they went . . . and that's how he cum t'call them disciples.[7]

Sid could repeat another of Matt Haxby's spellbinding renditions, which would begin: 'And the Israelites descended into gross darkness.' Then leaning over the pulpit, his voice rising for effect, he would say to any who looked uncomprehending:

> You know what gross darkness is, don't yer? Well, if yer don't I'll tell yer . . . it's a 'undred an' fouty four darknesses, that's what it is!

You cannot picture Rev Shaw preaching like that! Primitive Methodist preachers were famous for improvising an appropriate prayer to fit any occasion, in the fashion favoured by Wesley himself. Captain Smith remembered an instance his father had told him about during a service at the Scarborough Seamen's Mission, perhaps around 1900. Filey men were often invited along to preach, and there was

---

[7] What a tribute to the penetrative spell of Ranter preaching that 80 years later octogenarian Sid could recite this fiery piece word perfect! And Matt had died five years before Captain Smith was born, so he must have remembered it second-hand, probably from his father Thomas.

a supper afterwards, 'a good slap-up do'. On this particular evening, after a poor winter of catches, nobody had much, so it was not much of a spread. A Filey fisherman was asked to say grace. With commendable tact, he intoned this couplet:

> We thank the Lord fer what we've getten.
>
> If ther had a' been maer it would've been etten.

Primitive Methodism was 'born in the open air', and such services were a regular feature of the movement. JS Wane listened to one on Sunday 30th August 1908, on the cliff top, and recorded in his diary:

> All the fishermen strolled slowly to it. The preaching is rough, but it is one of the old Filey institutions.

'Camp Meetings' were popular in the East Riding. Those held in the 1840s and '50s were at nearby villages like Kilham, Langtoft and Weaverthorpe, a few hours walk away, alternatives to 'wakes' celebrations - known to descend into bad behaviour![8]

'Rough preaching' by the likes of Matt Haxby was the real motive power of the movement. Filey was one of 20 or more villages in the Bridlington and Scarborough branch of the Hull Circuit in the early days, and each had at least one service on Sundays, some two or three, as well as on other days.

The quarterly Circuit Plan, which carouseled lay preachers around each, had the complexity of a Victorian railway timetable. The logistics mostly involved cycles and foot-power of course, though a kind-hearted Society member might well have a horse and cart free on a Sunday.

23.4: *John Willie Jenk* (Q41) at 18 - owner of the alcoholic dray horse that obligingly delivered the Ranter circuit preachers round the rural chapels. In old age he was 'A nice old gentleman, a genuine Christian . . . nowt boastful about him, a wonderful speaker.' *John Willie* was successively an offshore fisherman, fish-salesman and chapel-keeper. And naturally, he was a lifeboatman. *[George SCALES Collection]*

One benefactor was *John Willie Jenk* who took up a fish-round after retiring from fishing. Each Sunday, he lent himself, his horse, and his humble flat-cart to the Chapel, to ferry the preachers to the tiny village chapels.

---

[8] Truss (2016) pp114-5.

Terence COLLINS related a great story about the horse, formerly a dray horse for Bentley's Yorkshire Brewery. *John Willie* dropped off fellow preachers at a succession of places - Muston, Flotmanby, Hunmanby, Flixton and Staxton. Incongruously, however, he had to load about eight cans of beer alongside the teetotal preachers since the horse would come to a halt outside a pub and not budge until it had had a guzzle. 'Here's Chapel Beer Horse comin' ' was a common refrain on this Sunday circuit. Fittingly, this sad equine advertisement for Primitive Methodist abstinence finally died outside the *Ship Inn* at Muston.[9]

For those who had to spend the Sabbath in some distant fish-dock, Filey boats had their own 'local preacher' – *Ranter Jack* CAMMISH was John Crawford's 'Sunday Man', on his yawl *Indiana*, whilst John ROSS was on *Charity*. Prayer meetings were held on some yawls every evening. It's likely these included prayers for a good catch, as was the practice on some Scottish boats.[10] If a boat were forced to be out on the Sabbath, it was a point of honour that these nautical chaplains wore a distinctive top hat, as a mark of respect to the Lord. The presence of a Sunday Man on board was yet another adhesive that drew Filey men into the Chapel fold.

Democrats at Prayer

Primitive Methodism was socially progressive in a way that must have unnerved the British ruling elites of the early 19th Century, the French Revolution being a recent memory. Democratically and locally controlled, the movement offered an alternative to the more middle-class Wesleyan Methodists and the establishment-controlled Church of England, which were the opposite of democratic. In marked contrast, there were no Ranter hierarchies – all were Brothers and Sisters; equal before God, an inclusivity which would please any 21st Century fan of the Diversity Agenda. The mainline Wesleyan Methodists had rejected female preachers in 1803, for had not the Bible insisted that women should 'remain quiet' and 'learn in silence'? But Primitive Methodism gave even teenage girls a chance to preach.

The wordy, turgid, vallium-like hymns which dulled 19th Century Anglican services emphasised deference, resignation and unworthiness. But the Ranter hymnal was awash with subversion and empowerment. Take this simple but potent, almost communistic verse from Primitive Methodist composer Richard Jukes:

> Your gold will waste and wear away,
>
> Your honours perish in a day;
>
> My portion never can decay;
>
> Christ for me. Christ for me.

---

[9] The bicycle kept these circuits in existence. *John Willie Jenk,* clearly unlucky with horses, ran into one at Reighton whilst cycling home from a Bridlington meeting one night in 1913. 'He was thrown over the handlebars of his machine,' the *Filey Post* reported, 'and fell heavily on his head, being rendered unconscious.' Fortunately, he recovered.

[10] Kendall (1877) pp19-20; Shaw (undated) chV; Friend (2010) p201.

No wonder, according to Cooper's estimate, three-quarters of agricultural labourers in the area, and seven-eighths of its fishermen, were Primitive Methodists. There was little point in Anglican parsons 'telling a Dissenter he was committing a sin by going to chapel.'[11] They didn't believe him.

Nationally, Primitive Methodism may have become institutionalised after about 1850, losing its spiritual momentum and revivalism. There was less emphasis on outdoor preaching, and more on chapel building and financial considerations.[12] But as we will see, this secularisation simply did not happen in Filey.

The Filey Church Mission Band

As well as being the backbone of the circuit preaching, local preachers were not afraid to broadcast their presence in the town. 'We have noticed as many as 600 people in the streets singing the praises of God with all their might,' eulogised Rev Isaiah Potts, Filey's minister from 1901-5. 'We visited the public-houses, and sang Gospel hymns for the tipplers, which moved many of them very deeply.' They were taking a big risk, for these visits could easily have ended badly late in the evening.[13]

Nor were they afraid of venturing further afield, offering 'services of song' to towns and villages felt in need of evangelising. From about 1880, brothers Jenkinson and Matt Haxby led 'revival services', and became known as the 'Filey Fishermen.' Three or four ardent 'missionaries' could make up such Church Mission Bands. They travelled modestly, some setting out to heathen darkness on bicycles. The Filey band borrowed a horse and cart from some sympathetic tradesman. For hadn't Jesus entered Jerusalem unpretentiously on a donkey the week before his death?

As part of Jenkinson Haxby's 1908 funeral obituary, the *Scarborough Mercury* noted of the 'Filey Fishermen' that

> . . . their breezy utterances were looked forward to in many places as a relief from the ordinary pulpit supply.

'Pulpit supply'! That is truly a phrase which makes you cringe with Sunday afternoon ecclesiastical boredom! But Ranter preaching made an impact; it was different. The 'Filey Fishermen' visited local fishing ports, and those stations further south that they knew from the Norfolk fishing. 'On one occasion, at West Street, Hull,' declared this account, '£5 of the £9 collection was in copper coins.'

> They come straight from the sea to the rostrum. And occasionally they have scarcely time to get off their fishing clothes. Once, when advertised for Hull, they landed at Scarborough just in time to catch the last train down the coast. At Filey the resourceful wives waited on the station platform with Sunday clothes under their aprons.

---

[11] *Wikipedia* entry for Richard Jukes; Cooper (1908) pp207, 224-5.

[12] Truss (2016) p116.

[13] *Christian Messenger*, 1903/6, quoted in *My Primitive Methodists* website.

Why do people flock to their services? The fishermen are not preachers. One or two are on the [circuit] plan . . . but most do no public speaking whatever. We get simple addresses and testimonies . . . . They themselves are definitely, radically, gloriously saved, and they can tell others both the experience and how to get it.

The charm is largely in the setting of the truth. These men live, move, and have their being in the sea-world, and they bring their world with them – the sea, the rocks, the storms, the fishing vessel, Filey village, and the Filey dialect as well.

Sometimes they have doubted if they could make the harbour, but they never feared making the heavenly port. After an expression of this nature a speaker will lapse into Hebrew and cry 'Hallelujah!' They are full of fishing reminiscences, and tell thrilling stories of peril . . . .

Let any reader try to imagine the effect when this bronzed-faced, blue-guernseyed choir sings, 'Rocks and storms', 'Does your anchor hold?' or 'Throw out the life-line.' The singing of these men makes it easy to believe in Christ. Jenkinson Haxby will stand up and quietly talk of heaven and salvation and of being ready to die. 'Now,' he will say, 'let us sing a verse. Sing it softly; not too fast; sing it with power.'

'When I go down the stream of Time,

When death shall shake this frame . . .

Prepare me, prepare me, Lord,

When death shall shake this frame.'

And the congregation is ushered into the realm of the unseen and the eternal.

'They can fill our largest chapels,' one minister wrote.[14] These graphic descriptions of the Filey Band's charismatic missionary activity come closest to bridging the vast spiritual gap of the very long century that separates us from our great grandparents' generation.

Healand SAYERS was another well-known, eccentric Ranter preacher in Filey, known as something of an oddball. He might be baiting when he received news that someone had been 'brought in' to the faith, converted after a lifetime of dissipation. He would run out into the yard on receipt of the good news and shout: 'Look not on the wine when it is red!' or 'wine is a mocker and strong drink is raging!' Despite these biblical strictures, he was himself partial to 'a glass of rum'.[15]

Self-Improvement

Finally, we should consider another facet of the appeal of Primitive Methodism to poor, working class people. There is no doubt that it raised the aspirations of any

---

[14] *Primitive Methodist Magazine,* 1905/153; 1883, p662, quoted in *My Primitive Methodists* website.

[15] Healand was in old age regularly thrown out of Liz JOHNSON's house for arguing and spitting (p367). He was younger brother to the William and Edmond SAYERS, just 12 when they drowned on the Dogger in 1859; and of the disturbed Jane (pp28-9).

number of Filey people. Whether it was developing confidence in public speaking, chapel administration, or basic literacy, involvement at the Union Street Chapel brought on those who wished it.

Shaw tells a fine story[16] which begins with a simple conversation near Flamborough Head in 1856, where a nine year-old boy was fishing from a rock. But it is template, and was intended as such, for the betterment a Calling could bring:

> 'How are beaaks gannin' t'day, sir?' he asked.
>
> 'Books going today? Why, what do you mean?'
>
> 'Why sir, begging your pardon, but I thought that if they were gannin' cheap, I wud try to buy yan or twea ov 'em.'
>
> 'And what sort would you like?'
>
> 'Well I wad like 'em to be about the Bible, and they wad be neaan the warse if they hed a picture or twea in 'em.'
>
> 'And what made you think I could let you have such books?'
>
> 'Why, ye see, sir, I saw you gannin' about Flambro' yesterday, with some in yaer hands, and you went first into yan hoose, and then intiv another, so I thowt you were selling 'em laakly.'

Shaw had been delivering monthly magazines, and he explained that the price did not vary like the price of fish, as the boy had thought. He learned David was an orphan – his father and two older brothers had been lost in a storm a few years ago, his mother had died a year later, and he'd been taken in by a widowed aunt. She had her own large family but had taken him in to ensure her sister's boy did not go into Bridlington Union Workhouse.

David told Shaw that he went only to Sunday School, he could only just read and spell using the books there, but if he had his own he would learn faster. He had saved 4d from running errands towards this goal. Shaw made him a present of a picture book of scripture. David was soon doing well with his books, and within six months could read fluently. When old enough, he became a fisherman, and helped out his widowed aunt with his earnings.

The story has a delightful ending! Twenty-one years later, Shaw was in Norfolk opening a new chapel. At the end of the service, he felt 'a large, firm hand on his shoulder':

> 'And how are beaaks gannin' t'day, sir?'

Turning round, he found David, now 30, with a handsome wife, prospering in the fishing and net trade. He had heard of Shaw's planned visit and had driven over to see and hear him.[17]

---

[16] Shaw (1865) chVIII, *Short Stories – The Fisher Boy*.

[17] It would be gratifying to be able to identify 'David' but alas, an 1861 Flamborough Census search reveals no possible candidate.

24 THE UNION STREET CHAPEL

The 'Fisherman's Chapel'

The chronology of nonconformist rise and decline in *any* locality can make for turgid reading, but the spirited presence and communal energy of the Filey Primitive Methodist Society, even now, half a century after its individual existence slipped into history has lessons for us, despite the dustiness of the detail. In an atomised age, in which private wealth sits uneasily alongside pot-holed public poverty, the collective enterprise, responsibility and identity encapsulated in Filey's 'Chapel' is from another age, beyond our general experience.

24.1: 'The Fisherman's Chapel' at completion, 1871 – 'red brick with stone dressing in an ornate Italian style' - anyone who has commissioned even a modest kitchen extension will appreciate the detailed planning, and the sums that might be involved, in a four-storey building capable of holding 1,000 people. Imagine the cost of the materials - 200,000 bricks, the decorative capitals, ironwork and intricate brickwork, not to mention all the internal plastering, woodwork and decoration . . . and the cost of employing for a year the fine craftsmen photographed here. Visible below steps-level is the large, basement Sunday School. Behind the Chapel were two houses for the ministers, and one for the chapel-keeper. *[FA]*

The history of chapel building in Filey has been well covered elsewhere.[1] The Society soon outgrew 'the capabilities of the barn'. But how *did* a fishing community of perhaps 200 families raise the huge amounts of capital over the half century from the 1820s to the 1870s for large public building projects that would cost millions today? The doubling in size of the original *Bethesda* chapel (1859-60) on Mitford Street cost £500 pounds, at a time when a fisherman's weekly income was around one pound, with no savings surplus. The cost ten years later of what was later known as *Ebenezer*, on Union Street, must have run into thousands. True, these decades were the golden years of traditional fishing, but only corporate business money can now afford capital schemes of this magnitude.

Roman Catholicism always emphasised the centrality of the priest and the rituals and ceremonies he performed. All protestant sects, in contrast, believed in the importance of the sermon, and its value in guiding worshippers through the scriptures. But *nobody*, even amongst the protestants, took preaching as seriously as the Primitive Methodists, hence the huge central pulpit at *Ebenezer*, a full eight steps above the congregation. Decor was kept to a minimum, so as not to distract spiritual focus. The diminishing number of people who still remember the rousing sermons at the Union Street Chapel will agree with Sokell's 1899 description of the magical impact that this arrangement had:

> . . . a splendid rostrum forms a somewhat central ornament to the whole, and the sound of an ordinary orator's voice travels high and low to the uttermost corner of the Sanctuary [ie the body of the chapel].

Here indeed were heard 'the burning truths of the Gospel'! The acoustics also produced 'superb singing', Michael Fearon reckoned, even in the 1960s, as attendances were no longer filling even the Sanctuary. Filey Chapel was synonymous with singing. William CAPPLEMAN's description of his father, William, could probably have been applied to most of the congregation:

> . . . he had a wonderful voice and he could sing nearly all the hymns there were. He knew all the tunes and he knew all the words and I think one of his big disappointments was that I couldn't sing. He said to me once, he says, I was a good singer before they invented tunes.

We can only guess at the power and charge in the atmosphere when special occasions crammed up to 1,000 into the body of the chapel. And the electricity must have been intensified by the fact that the worshippers were bound together by far more than membership of a religious sect. For virtually everybody present was from the same few streets and yards. Even outsiders found the people 'homely and warm-hearted'.

It truly was the 'Fisherman's Chapel'. In Filey, Methodism was almost precisely split on social and political lines. Before the 1960s, when a joint youth group was established, the Wesleyan Methodist Chapel on Murray Street was a separate

---

[1] Fearon (2008) p103; (2016) pp41-2.

universe, drawing its worshippers from New Filey, from amongst the middle and skilled/semi-skilled working-class. 'Tories', one local recently opined!

In our sceptical, secular century, we can no more understand this all-pervading sense of congregational community than we can imagine the atmosphere in that tightly-packed chapel. These services were hardly events you could invisibly drift in and out of. For especially important were 'Exhorters', prototypes of our century's 'meeters and greeters'. They made the newly arrived welcome, but their roles went much further, for this was an interventionist faith. They were befrienders and spiritual advisers. Exhorters risked exposing their own doubts and vulnerabilities, sharing their own shortcomings and weaknesses – they spiritually walked alongside, as companions rather than superiors. This was truly religion 'not at but by the poor themselves'. There was no spiritual privacy:

> every convert has come bodily forward to the communion-rail, and in the presence of the large congregation have consecrated their lives to Jesus Christ.[2]

Certainly at Union Street, as Terence COLLINS related, everyone was expected regularly to come to this rail to say in turn what the Lord had done for them that week and finish with an impromptu prayer as they knelt.[3] There may even have been a 'penitent seat' to be used in services: there was elsewhere.

It was difficult to slip unobtrusively out of active observance after such communal exposure. The social adhesion glued into Old Filey by such a public commitment was intensified by the deep penetration of Primitive Methodism into everyday life. The Chapel was used every evening of the week, and we were impressed in the 1980s by those elderly informants who remembered with fond smiles how its activities were the focus of so many families' social lives. And this involvement began early, for beneath *Ebenezer* lay a large Sunday school of six classrooms, in which the Old Town's youngsters began a lifetime of close association with the spiritual soul of their community.

Keeping it all going

The organisation ran as a worshippers' cooperative. Its trustees, probably yawlmasters and local tradesmen, met regularly to manage the Chapel's affairs. Within all their administrative minutiae, the first two minute books which record their debates and decisions up to 1937 vividly immerse the reader into an older, far different version of Filey.[4]

---

[2] *Christian Messenger*, 1903/6, quoted in *My Primitive Methodists* website.

[3] Being Filey, this may not always have been taken seriously. Terence reckoned *Billy Calam* CAMMISH took out a red spotted white handkerchief, at least once, shook it, placed it on the floor before he knelt (he didn't wish to spoil his suit) and followed with his 'prayer': 'You have a crown for Peter and a crown for John . . . and you know my size, 6⅞!' Imagine doing that at St Oswald's!

[4] *Ebenezer's* surviving records are now in the Fisher-Crimlisk Archive, at Filey Archives.

Much of the business was to do with the chapel fabric: the preacher's (ie minister's) house was to have the luxury of gas laid on 'in the three lowest rooms and the study', to be fitted by Mr ROSS (26th September 1868)[5]; the house was to be papered, but the paper was 'not to exceed in price 6d per role' *[sic]*. There were familiar problems with the weather: it was resolved 'that something be done to prevent the water from blowing in at front doors of the Chapel' (20th September 1872). 'Our apparatus does not warm the Chapel sufficiently', they minuted on 9th January 1875, adding that 'piping burst in several places with the frost.' The room in which they had to meet was probably freezing too.

The passing of Society members, such as Richard Thomas CAMMISH, was very formally observed, and minuted:

> A letter of condolence to be sent to the widow and family of the late Bro RT CAMMISH . . . a loyal follower of the Lord Jesus Christ. It was passed in the usual way, all the Brethren standing. Bro Fenby to send a wreath from the trustees (3rd June 1922).

The minutes secretary had a frustrated poet in him: he crafted drippingly mellifluous images for a tribute to retiring organist, Miss M Towse, that 'the well tone of the loving Jesus may let her soul to the sweetest music.' On a more mundane note, it was agreed next 'that we advertise for an organist in the *Scarbro' Mercury* and the *Filey Post* . . . £10 a year' (10th September 1894).

Godliness was encouraged wherever possible: a bible and hymn book were to be presented to the first couple to be married in the Chapel (28th January 1874). Moral dereliction was to be prevented: on 29th August 1868, it was solemnly recorded 'that no gambling be allowed at the bazaar'. (Coffee and tea, incidentally, were to be provided at 1½d a cup).

Initially, wealthy members primed the financial pump. Jenkinson Haxby paid the deposit for the purchase of the land, whilst men like Vickerman Mainprize of Flamborough lent money. But fund-raising activities were ongoingly essential, for 'estate' upkeep must have been a constant expense. There was a perennial concern with the collection of pew rents, which were not always forthcoming: sums still outstanding for 1875 were to be collected 'as far as practical' (20th January 1876); and nine years later it was decided 'that the financial state of the Chapel be mentioned from the pulpit, people to be urged to pay their seat rents' (9th January 1885).

First-hand memory of the annual fund-raising 'fish pie suppers' will now be easing into history, for it seems they died out before the Second World War. Four or five were held each year, in the Chapel basement. 'Something you looked forward to in

---

[5] John ROSS established an ironmongering and gas-fitting business in Filey on King Street in the 1850s – he was from Castleton Danby, in the Esk Valley. There is no known connection with the ROSS fishing family.

Winter,' recalled Foster Holmes JENKINSON, who could remember even in the 1980s the tantalising smell of the fish pie! Requests were made to the local fishermen for the necessary fish. This seems to have fallen on deaf ears in 1902, perhaps a bad year, for a 'coals to Newcastle' decision was made to buy them in Scarborough. The suppers sold at around 9d to a shilling, the proceeds used to buy ingredients and materials for a 'sale of work' bazaar weeks before Christmas.

In preparation, all manner of food and clothing was made by the women of the Society, and set out on stalls around the walls of the cellar. There was 'a hat trimming contest first night, stocking darning on second night' and a 'fish pond as usual' (6th November 1899). Filey really knew how to have a good time. Isn't it all so delightfully English, the simple quintessence of small community life? Oh, and plays in the evening.

One innocent little caper was 'Postman and Letterbox', notes written by boys confidentially delivered to girls of choice, for 1d. Then there were 'faith teas', people sending 'tea, sugar, milk, bread, butter, beef, ham, cheesecakes, tarts, and, indeed, everything that was necessary . . .'. In 1902, after feeding about 700, there was enough left of the 'loaves and fishes', so to speak, to send '80 parcels of wholesome food . . . to God's poor.'[6] The Good Friday fish supper in particular seems to have been one of the culinary high spots of the year, judging from the *Filey Post's* account of April 1906:

24.2: Back-room girls, Chapel Bazaar, c1920 – some of the women who made the tea, sandwiches and fish-pie; ran the bring-and-buy stalls; and knitted things to sell. **L to R**: *Bella* JENKINSON née Wheeler, wife of *John Willie*, Mrs Clarke, and Priscilla JENKINSON née Scotter. *[George Scales Collection]*

> . . . huge cods cooked whole, and stuffed, steaks crumbed; fish inside fish to mingle flavours . . . fish swimming in sauces, stranded . . . in batter, caught fast in crust; buttered, lemoned, flavoured with ham . . . the king among them all is the Seven-Decker. A great erection of pie-crust, enclosing alternate layers of varied fish and bacon. There is nothing to beat fish cooked in this way.[7]

All that was missing was a lemon drizzle.

---

[6] *Christian Messenger*, 1903/6, quoted in *My Primitive Methodists* website.
[7] Quoted in Fearon (2016) p42.

The Great War brought its own problems - the bombardment of Scarborough in December 1914 perhaps moved the trustees to insure their property 'against war risks'; spring blinds were to be fitted on certain windows and the rest pasted over with paper (1915). By 1917, however, it was concluded that the 'brown paper be removed from the lower portion of the Chapel Windows'. In fact, the trustees were by then more worried about the rampages of the British forces. The soldiers, who were lodged in their schoolroom, were to be requested not to smoke there before 7pm on Sundays.

All these policy decisions were passed on to the volunteer back-room staff, whose activities were to be coordinated by the Chapel Steward, and under him the Chapel-keeper. This seems to have been truly a dogsbody role. The ever-obliging *John Willie Jenk* (Q41), whom we met in the last chapter, was associated with the Primitive Methodist Chapel for many years as a lay preacher, trustee and in his later days as Chapel-keeper. He took over from Old Isaac ROSS. 'Why he was chapel-keeper I don't know,' Terence COLLINS said. 'It wasn't for the money. He made a lot of money from fishing. It must have been for the love of the Chapel.' Perhaps it was a Calling.

The duties in *John Willie's* 'job description', dated 1st April 1930, seem overwhelming - for £1 0s 0d a week, he was the Chapel's cleaner (inside and out, *and* he had to provide all 'cleaning material'), pavement sweeper, gaslight operator, toilet-cleaner, setter-out of chairs, boiler of water, and master of the 'heating apparatus'. This rudimentary central heating was 'in frosty weather to be lighted on Saturdays for Sunday services' - temperatures to be kept within a miserly 55-65° Fahrenheit. Given the all-hours nature of this job (the Chapel was of course in use daily) the provision of a house behind the building was some consolation, although there must have been times when *John Willie* wished he lived in Scarborough, or better still, Hull.[8] His wife *Bella* (née Wheeler) will have taken much of the burden. The couple lasted seven years - *John Willie* retired in 1937, aged 64, by which time the seven-day week drudgery was probably too much for them.

Laiking round t'Chapel

People who believe that the behaviour of children has seriously declined could be surprised by some of the minutes in the Chapel Trustees' books. There were, enigmatically, 'the boys who misbehave themselves at the top of the gallery' (1875) and 'the Boys in the body of the Chapel' (1889). It looks like the horseplay had spilled out onto the street, for it was later resolved, barely legally, 'that we ask the Policeman to keep the children in order during the Sabbath in front of the Chapel and the Chapel Steward to offer a small gratuity as an inducement' (1892).

Names of wrongdoers were to be taken 'with a view to further action' (1892); young people were failing to stand in the gallery 'during the singing' (1902); and

---

[8] *Trustees' Minute Books, Ebenezer* Chapel, Filey.

with so many fathers away at war, rock bottom seems to have been reached in 1916, when the trustees bemoaned 'disorder during public worship' and the need for 'more reverence'.

Perhaps these 'youfs' were all chapelled-out! It is hard for anyone of 2021 to take in how completely God muscled in on a child's Sunday a century ago. William CAPPLEMAN was at Sunday School from 9.30 till 10.30am, in Chapel until midday, home for dinner till 1.30pm, back to Sunday School for an hour. Then:

> Half past two till four o'clock we could please ourselves . . . walkin' to Flotmanby out there pickin' snowdrops and later on we'd go pickin' primroses, Primrose Valley . . . then at six o'clock we 'ad to go to Chapel again.

Despite the disruptions caused by high-spirited young chapelgoers and indisciplined soldiery, it is the memories of countless communal functions organised by the Chapel that figured most strongly in the minds of elderly people we spoke to in the 1980s. Activities were timed to coincide with 'sinful events', ie traditional popular festivities like wakes customarily awash with drink.

Apart from fish-pie suppers and the bazaars, Chapel Anniversary Weekend was the high spot of the year. The Sunday 'scholars', in brand-new clothes of course, assembled outside the Chapel at 9.00am, set off with a banner down Hope Street and Mitford Street, and returned up Queen Street. At the top of virtually every yard, the procession stopped to sing an anniversary hymn, to the accompaniment of the little organ that came with them on its barrow. The whole circuit, including perhaps ten stops, took about an hour.

24.3: *Bob 'ush* CAPPLEMAN (1860-1931) was one of a number of men remembered for the tight ship they ran in the Chapel. A preacher and Sunday School teacher, he got his nickname from his habit of quietening the children with the simple command 'ush'! Another respected ever-present was Chapel-keeper Old Isaac ROSS, a strict disciplinarian who in the 1910s and '20s kept the Chapel front clear of street corner children. 'He was a bugger if you went laiking round t'Chapel,' George Burton told us.

This grand photograph of *Bob 'ush* shows to perfection how Union Street was truly the 'Fisherman's Chapel', for every level of personnel was actively from this background. Note the coil of long-line [**Right**]. He was also a grocer. *[FA]*

The Building Service followed, a series of 'display pieces of poetry' performed at the Chapel: the primary scholars in the morning, senior in the evening. Terence COLLINS remembered special hymns being written each year by a Filey minister, Tom Jones[9] - he probably penned hundreds altogether, in the movement's DIY hymnal tradition. Sadly, the custom died out along with much else around the time of the Second World War. Sunday School Teacher Edward Scales JENKINSON (Q35) used to teach the children their 'pieces'.

St Oswald's: 'Church First and Last'

Why are there so many Primitive Methodist gravestones at St Oswald's? Why did the Ranters have no yard of their own? In much of England and Wales, there had been perennial tension between the Church of England and the nonconformist dissenting sects. Anglican ministers were known to refuse to bury non-Anglicans in the parish churchyard. The Liberal Government's Burial Act of 1880 finally allowed *any* parishioner to be buried in an Anglican graveyard, with a service conducted by their own minister. Yet despite the staunchness of the Ranter tradition in Filey, even the strictest Primitive Methodists were buried at St Oswald's, before and after 1880. There was never any question of a Ranter burial ground, and not simply because it would have involved expense.

The Primitive Methodists accepted John Wesley's foundational belief that his movement was no more than a preaching add-on to the Church of England, to which he wished to remain 'sweetly united together in Love'. Hence the well-known Filey saying 'Church First and Last'. For so traditionally a minded community, this was after all *their* parish church, the 'Fish Church'[10], and it was the Church of *England*. Generations of their ancestors had been christened, married and were at peace there, or at least their gravestones were.

Similarly, though baptisms could easily be performed in a Primitive Methodist chapel, they don't seem to have been in the early years - there was no sudden depletion in the St Oswald's register in the 1820s/30s, after the Great Turnaround. It has been argued that working people had a sense of a special potency in the Anglican christening service.[11] For some reason, things changed in 1863, when a Filey Primitive Methodist register of baptisms began. Immediately, there was a collapse in fisher-family baptisms at St Oswald's. By the 1870s, they averaged 24.2 a year at Union Street, but just 3.5 at St Oswald's. Then in 1880 all changed, and in a new 'Great Turnaround', the imbalance reversed (**24.4**). Early that year, Arthur Neville Cooper began his 55 years of incumbency at St Oswald's.

---

[9] Jones was an evangelist preacher who had moved onwards and upwards – from Filey to the Midlands. He reputedly married *Bob 'ush* CAPPLEMAN's daughter, Sarah.

[10] So called because of its weather vane – Cooper reckoned only Bradford-on-Avon shared the distinction. It was an early Christian symbol as well as the source of much of the parish's livelihood (*Filey Parish Magazine*, Sept 1911).

[11] Friend (2010) p136; Valenze (1985) p267.

24.4: Fishing-family baptisms, 1858-1913, at Ranter Chapel and St Oswald's: the 'Great Turnaround' of 1880. The dotted line shows numbers of Primitive Methodist baptisms (based on Friend, 2010, pp307-9).

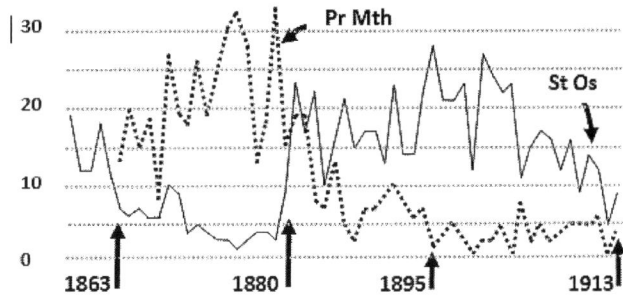

This had nothing whatsoever to do with Society membership – in the 10 years from 1875 to 1884 this never fell below 300, a consistency equalled neither before nor since. It must exclusively have been Cooper's arrival. His energetic response to the Great Gale in the October may have convinced the Old Town's fishing folk that the Anglican Church actually cared for them. Cooper encouraged rebaptism at St Oswald's of babies already christened at Union Street, parish register entries after 1880, often stating 'Received into the church . . . previously baptised'.

Similarly, joint burial services, involving both chapel and church, became the norm, the Chapel Superintendent reading the lesson. The Burial Act, which had become law in September 1880, seems to have passed Filey by completely. Even Jenkinson Haxby, affectionately known as the Primitive Methodist 'Bishop of Filey', was dispatched in this ecumenical way, the parish church, in the words of the *Parish Magazine*, being 'filled to the very end.'

This was far more than simply 'nominal Anglicanism.' We need only read the homely prose of Cooper's many books to recognise a genuine affection for his adopted town (he was originally from Windsor) and its fisher people. It was the humanity of his sermons and pastoral work which set him apart from his predecessors. He and his curate alternated Sunday mornings between St Oswald's and St John's on West Street, and fishermen often waited outside his house on Church Street to see which way he was going. A local story has it that the window sills were worn down by the frequency with which they were sat on! Even if untrue, its survival clearly chimed with a basis in local belief if not in fact. John S Wane recorded in his diary on Sunday 6th September 1908 that Cooper had drawn so many to St Oswald's for his 10.30am service that the sidesman had difficulty finding seats for him and his parents. By 1884, there were four services on Sundays, Cooper claiming a regular attendance of 500, rising to 1,200 in summer.[12]

Not everybody in the nonconformist camp approved of this ecumenicalism. One frustrated Primitive Methodist moaned in 1921 that the Filey Society was not marching with the times,

---

[12] Fisher, *History* (1970) *Churches*, p5. Anglican attendance had not always been so good
 – see Appendix C for the respective figures in the 1851 Religious Census (30th March).

for in 11 years there have been only 14 marriages at Union Street, the only place registered for marriages in the circuit. . . . the people have a deep-rooted idea that all marrying, burying and baptising should be done by the church parson!'[13]

Filey people did not seem to care. Asked about the number of dissenters in the parish, the vicar reported with resignation in 1865,

I am almost incapable of affording a direct answer, as very many of the Methodists . . . divide their attendance between Church and Chapel.[14]

To use an appropriate metaphor, Cooper sang from the very same hymn sheet. There was 'general indifference to doctrine preached, and the ritual that is practised', he wrote in 1908. He cited an earnest vicar elsewhere in the county who called his flock together asking if they wanted psalms sung, or candles lighted, or the congregation to rise as the choir came in. 'You can do as you please, sir,' declared the churchwarden summing up the feeling of the meeting, 'provided you loose us by twelve o'clock!'[15] Cooper may have been speaking from his experience of the Anglican Church, where committed enthusiasm was actually frowned upon. But he really had grasped the whole point of Ranterism – that psalms, candles and choirs were immaterial when a man was truly connecting with the Christian god.

Fisher Funerals in Filey

'A fantastic affair. I never saw them anywhere else.' Foster Holmes JENKINSON (1983)

I have been unable to find an account of traditional Filey fisher funeral customs as comprehensive as that recorded in 1975 for Staithes practice around 1900.[16] There are scraps of clues, but much can be assumed from the close cultural and social similarities of the two communities. In 18th Century Filey,

. . . all the houses . . . threw their doors wide open during the wake and anybody might enter who chose. Cakes and tea were supplied to all comers.[17]

This was to allow the living in, but windows too were opened, allowing exits for the soul of the deceased, unimpeded by malevolent spirits. Shaw recorded in 1867 that fishing families customarily held a prayer meeting on the eve of the funeral in the house of the departed, a clear christianisation of the wake. It was common along the east coast to stop clocks, and cover mirrors and pictures, for fear that the soul would be captured in the glass reflection.

---

[13] *Christian Messenger*, 1921/58, quoted in *My Primitive Methodists* website. Since 1898, a nonconformist chapel could be registered for marriages, though a registrar had to attend to register each ceremony.

[14] Friend (2010) p95.

[15] Cooper (1908) pp227-8.

[16] Clark (1982, ch7), from whom my Staithes references in this chapter are taken, suggests that the practices he described were still extant in the early 20th Century.

[17] The Folklore Society, *Folklore of Yorkshire* (LXIX, 1911) p155.

Another north Yorkshire custom was for a 'bidder' to go from house to house advising those 'bidden to t'funeral' of the timing. This was Staithes practice into the 20th Century. Also at Staithes, Sunday funerals were favoured, to counter the folk belief that 'if a body lays over a Sunday, there'll be two more to follow'.[18] (A cursory sampling of early 19th Century Filey's burial register shows that all seven days were used fairly equally, with a slight preference for Fridays.)

When choosing coffin bearers, one Staithes informant suggested you 'always go as near as you could' in kinship, and their gender was normally that of the deceased. The coffins of females were commonly carried by women pallbearers. This also seems to have been Filey practice.[19]

In the 1980s we heard funeral accounts from Lizzie HUNTER who had lived between the Wars at 89, Queen Street, next door to undertaker Tom Chapman, at no 87. The coffin rested on trestles or chairs outside the deceased's house on the day of the burial, and the mourners gathered to form the procession. This went first to the Chapel, and then with rich symbolism over Church Ravine from the world of the living to that of the dead. There was a class division as to how the coffin reached St Oswald's, a hearse being the preserve of the wealthy. According to Terence COLLINS, 'the coffins were carried on scarves through the handles.' Those of drowned fishermen and sailors were traditionally carried shoulder high.[20]

Women bearers at Staithes had an elaborate dress code of white hats and shawls, and black skirts, with white bows or rosettes for male bearers. In 1828, Cole observed that the mourners following Filey coffins carried timeless, pre-Christian evergreen symbols such as ivy, laurel and rosemary to indicate the immortality of the soul.

One medieval practice which survived in remote fishing communities on the Yorkshire coast from pre-Reformation times involved 'maidens' garlands'. These were hoops wrapped in white paper from which hung lengths of white garland, to accompany the coffin of a woman who had died young, usually in tragic circumstances. The custom's antiquity is unknown but the Catholic church adapted it to their cult of Mary, the 'Virgin Unspotted', testimony to a chaste girl's 'triumphant victory over the lusts of the flesh'.

24.5: Two ancient maiden's garlands at St Steven's, Fylingdales.

Cole encountered Filey informants in the 1820s who could remember the practice being observed, with:

---

[18] Rev John C Atkinson, *Forty Years in a Moorland Parish* (Macmillan & Co, 1892) p226.

[19] 'Memoir of Jenkinson Haxby', in *Primitive Methodist Magazine,* 1909/238-9, quoted in *My Primitive Methodists* website. See also below, p373.

[20] This was also Flamborough practice as late as 1912.

a hand, cut in white paper . . . inserted in the middle of the hoop or hoops upon which is fairly written the name of the deceased maiden, with her age.

The garlands were subsequently displayed inside the church (**24.5**).[21]

Foster Holmes JENKINSON, living on Ebenezer Terrace, just next to Church Street, often witnessed these walking funerals, coffins carried by fishermen, always in their best ganseys, followed by all the mourners singing appropriate fishermen's hymns, sometimes by the full Chapel choir:

They stopped opposite any relative's house, put the coffin on trestles and sang a hymn. A good sight.

Michael Fearon quotes an outsider's 1908 impressions, watching in awe from the north side of Church Bridge as a funeral procession came down Church Street:

Looking in the direction from which the music came . . . I saw a solid mass of people coming at a foot pace down the slope towards the other end of the bridge from where I stood. In front was a group of thirty or forty fishermen, four abreast, all in their spotless dark blue knitted jerseys, all slowly stepping on, and all joining in Dr Watts' well-known hymn, 'There is a land of pure delight'. . . . Behind them the coffin with one or two wreaths of flowers upon it, was carried by six stalwart brother toilers of the deep, and it was followed by the widow and the more distant relatives of the deceased, while closing the procession came the wives and sisters of the fishermen, and other sympathising friends . . . .[22]

These 'walking' fisher funerals, which ended early in the Second World War, were such dramatic, moving events that they often led to conversions.

A church window was always left open during the service, presumably to allow the soul to depart.[23] The funerals of two especially respected Chapel 'celebrities', each active members of the Filey Primitive Methodist Society for over 50 years, illustrate how they were 'nicely packed up', in the local phrase, their funerals being staged on a scale nowadays reserved for royalty. That of Jenkinson Haxby, in 1908, was reckoned to be possibly the largest so far to have been seen in Filey. 'Business was suspended. Blinds drawn down in respect. Friends came from far and near.'[24]

Edmond JENKINSON (P52), Chapel Superintendent (the highest official within the district society), died 18 months later. On the day of his funeral, Monday 9th May 1910, Terence COLLINS reckoned that not a boat went to sea from Filey, Scarborough, Flamborough or Bridlington.

---

[21] Cole (1828) pp138, 149; *maidensgarlands.com* website.

[22] Michael Fearon, *Filey, From Fishing Village to Edwardian Resort* (Blackthorn Press, 2008) pp125-6.

[23] Valenze (1985) p266.

[24] *Memoir of Jenkinson HAXBY.*

Postscript

Edmond had been Sunday School Superintendent, and evidently kept a tight rein on the children. He remained a clear memory for life with those in his care. Why else would Mary Elizabeth ROBINSON recall, 75 years on, that 'he died the very time when King Edward died'?[25] She had a lasting image of her and her friends cutting through 'Salvation Army passage' to Queen Street. 'He'd always used to send us back, and it was a short cut', she told us.

In his sixties, after he had given up his yawl, *Welcome Home*, this self-assured, dignified man became a street sweeper in Filey. Convinced that any job done properly obeyed God's calling, he would see no debasement in this change of status. He seems to have been one of those few men in the town whose respect defied the attribution of any nickname.

Much of this regard may have come from the fact that he could speak to his faith truly through wounded experience – two wives

24.6: This sternly-posed photograph of lay preacher and Chapel Superintendent Edmond JENKINSON is still remembered as hanging over the pulpit at *Ebenezer*. As we saw in Chapter 7, he skippered a North Sea yawl for several decades, but never let its harsh conditions jeopardise his faith. *[FA]*

had died, the first when he was just 24; he had no memory of a father lost at sea when he was just two; and his elder brother and married son had also drowned. The civilising influence of his serene presence did not only extend to children. Terence COLLINS told us his progress along a street would silence swearing amongst an assembled group of even the coarsest men.

The communal respect in which Jenkinson Haxby and Edmond Ross JENKINSON were held illustrates the unbridgeable gulf between the lay preachers and the professional ministers. We notice that the likes of Rev George Shaw were customarily addressed as *sir*, an ascribed status natural in a deferential society. Lay preachers, however, do not seem to have been considered part of the imposed class system. They were after all part of the fishing community, part of its egalitarian share culture, with a rootedness resulting from their status as neighbours and crewmates. Their influence probably kept Ranter Chapel in touch with its original entanglement with the ancient folk culture. This had made such it a close fit with fishing and mining communities.

---

[25] Edward VII died on the 6th May 1910, Edmond on the 7th, his widow Mary on the 17th.

'Chapel People': Bringing them Alive

Time and again we encountered little anecdotes and vignettes about active Primitive Methodists who had made a deep impression amongst the Old Town community, not least by the example they set. Take Sunday School teacher Edward Scales JENKINSON (R38), the man who according to local tradition sacrificed food during a period of poor fishing so that his children should not go short. His father, who had the same name, was always referred to as *Neddy Rasp* (Q35). *Neddy* the elder was still well remembered in Filey in the 1980s, a rather gloomy preacher and teacher at the Chapel. As well as being a member of the 'Band of Hope' temperance movement, he was still remembered for the fine models of cobles and full masted sailing ships he made in his spare time. They were such sought after by visitors. Foster recalled his yawls were 'lovely sailers'.

Another spiritual beacon in the town was John William JENKINSON (Q4l), the only surviving son of the saturnine *Old Marky* and Mary JENKINSON. (Mark's younger son George, *John Willie's* only brother, had drowned off the coble *Mary* in 1896.) The dutiful *John Willie* was associated with the Union Street Chapel for most of his life. 'He had a great depth of knowledge of human nature,' said Terence. And he had seen it at its worst, directly witnessing the one known German war crime against Filey fishermen - the machine-gunning of his skipper Mark Scotter on the yawl *Susie* in 1917.

These impressions of the old Chapel Folk percolate down the generations. From its earlier days came the memory of John JENKINSON (O12), one of the first converts, who held family prayers three times a day.[26] More recently, Mary Smith has a lovely pen portrait of her Uncle Jack and Aunt Susie JOHNSON. Jack was never without his gansey:

> Aunt Susie knitted them and my Dad inherited his old one. He wore it with pride for years. Alchohol never entered their house and the only book in the house was the family bible. I had it rebound and have it still. It was always open on the sideboard and read every day. They were Chapel people.

In his eighties, Captain Sydney Smith could remember how, in 1923, aged 15, he acted as cook for Mary's Uncle Jack. Whilst midsummering, bad weather lost the boat its herring nets. 'He didn't turn a hair', Captain Smith recalled. 'I took him a cup of tea up to the wheelhouse . . . and he was stood at the wheel there and he was singing 'I know that my Redeemer liveth'!'

William CAPPLEMAN (born 1917) said of his father, also William:

> . . . 'e didn't preach, 'e wasn't a Sunday School teacher but he was very religious. I only ever knew 'im go in a pub once and that was the day I got married.

And despite the institutional decline of Filey's Primitive Methodism, and the eventual closure of the Chapel, people who had been brought up under its influence

---

[26] *Primitive Methodist Magazine* (1883) p662 (*My Primitive Methodists* website).

carried on in the old ways. 'Graham, do you eat at home with your cap on?' Graham Taylor remembered, from a Primitive Methodist skipper – they were out midsummering in the 1960s. The skipper insisted on the hat being removed, despite the fact that the crew were snatching a food break during two or three days of very intense, exhausting work.

Travelling preacher Matthew Denton knew the Filey Society well:

> Let those who talk much about religion not reaching the humbler classes visit the Primitive Methodist Chapel at Filey, especially on a Sunday evening. The multitude of blue blouses will interest them, and the fisher-lads arrayed in rows if under the pulpit . . . hundreds of souls crowd the church.[27]

Primitive Methodism attracted people who had a keen conscience about the evils of *this* world. It would be intriguing to know how typical was poet Edward Anderson of Old Town opinion. A Wesleyan convert to the faith, and later in life a resident in Filey, he had spent half his life at sea and seen at first hand the savage transatlantic slave trade, from which British ports like Bristol and Liverpool profited before abolition in 1807. In a poem, written about that time, he wrote of 'poor negroes as my fellow men', asking the obvious question:

> Can Christians join in such a trade as this!
> 'Tis not the way to gain eternal bliss.[28]

Human nature being what it is, however, no earthly organisation or its members can hope for perfection. An engaging little project for the prurient would be to salivate over the annual Filey circuit returns (also known as the station reports), at North Yorkshire Archives, Northallerton. For as well as recording membership numbers, naming local preachers and Sunday school teachers, and giving the number of 'fallen', they include details of disciplinary action taken against members for drunkenness, sexual misconduct and financial irregularities.[29] There may of course be no such instances at Filey!

Perhaps the last word on the spiritual calibre of the town's fishing community should be left to a religious outsider, a Wesleyan Methodist clergyman, who knew many British fishing communities. Rev HB Kendall reckoned he knew 'none equal to the Filey fishermen; and . . . their superiority was entirely owing to the successful labours of the Primitive Methodist Connexion.'[30]

---

[27] *Primitive Methodist Magazine* (1883) cited above.

[28] *My Primitive Methodists* website.

[29] Truss (2016) p20.

[30] Rev HB Kendall, *History of the Primitive Methodist Connexion* (Joseph Toulson, 1888).

25 FILEY WOMEN: 1: KEEPING THE BOAT AFLOAT

'What men did was definite, well defined and limited. What women did was all the rest.'
Mary Prior

The Centrality of Women

Significantly, references to Filey women in the town's books and guides were until the 20th Century scattered around the fishing chapters, which was men's work. Women were incidental: in 1867, Shaw quoted the common fisher adage, 'a woman 'at won't work for a man is nea worth yan'. Whilst he was clearly attributing this view to the fishing community, most middle-class Victorian men were equally dismissive of female worth. Another Filey truism rated women who wouldn't gather or hook bait 'as much use as a ship without a rudder'. Yet many men did appreciate how hard the women worked, and how *they* really held family fortunes together. James Cole, in his nineties, admitted in the 1970s that 'to tell you the truth, a woman in Staithes did more work than a man that went off to sea'. And Frank Meadow Sutcliffe, who as a photographer in Whitby had in the years around 1900 captured images of the drudgery of the fisherwoman's life, concluded that 'the woman's work by daylight is even harder than the fishermen's toil and danger at sea by night'. Shaw summed it up:

> The men have only to catch the fish, their labour, as a rule, being over as soon as the boat touches to the sand.

At Filey on a bad weather day, one visitor noticed the men *laakin* about the streets in crowds, playing at *pickaback*, while the women were indoors mending nets.[1] Indeed it is noticeable that there are many photographs of groups of unoccupied Filey fishermen standing around, but very few of unoccupied women. As late as 1904, a visitor to Staithes saw men mostly watching their womenfolk at work,

> mere spectators in the arduous working of hauling the cobles one by one on to the steep bank of shingle.

As at Filey, it was 'an accepted state of things at Staithes that the work of putting out to sea and the actual catching of the fish is sufficient for the menfolk'. At least Filey fishermen paid for horses to get the cobles up to the landing: Staithes wives carried the catch up into the town on their heads, in baskets, with

> the best part of a hundredweight, they toiled up the rough zigzag to the village. The result was that they had good figures and an upright bearing, but were rather too drudged and weather-beaten for what townspeople would call good looks.[2]

---

[1] Frank (2002) pp160, 169.

[2] Gordon Home, *Yorkshire Coast and Moorland Scenes* (A & C Black, 1904); Thomas Mozley, *Reminiscences Chiefly of Towns and Villages and Schools* (Longmans, Green, 1885) p450.

25.1: Church Well in Church Ravine, and the likely origin of the name Spring Row - the steps in front of the women are still there, below the graveyard. At least one of them is five or six months pregnant, yet will be carrying that keg once filled down to a boat. Eva CAMMISH (born 1884) wouldn't drink this water - the *drizzles* of dead folk would be in it! *[JC]*

As well as her work ethic, the fisherwoman's financial nous was critical in keeping the typical fishing family out of poverty. 'We leave all that to the women,' said one Brixham fisherman, of the crew's wage calculation.[3] A man's earnings could so easily drop below the cost of his bait; and there was the risk of loss of gear, which was rarely insured. And if the worst did happen, and given the mortality rate amongst Filey fishermen it often did, it fell to a woman to keep the family together in the most straitened of financial and emotional circumstances.

The Offshore Wives' Tasks

Few modern Filey housewives born later than the 1950s can credit the hard labour that their 19th Century equivalents endured. No Yorkshire fishing community lived so far from, or so much above, its boat landing. And remember that Church Ravine had no made-up road for cart traffic until 1871, when the streams that run down it were culverted.[4] So until the 1870s, when the yawls were still based in Filey, wives and daughters helped the fishermen carry baited lines, *me-at* and water down to the boats on shoulder yokes, and the gear home on return.

> . . . their strength is almost equal [to the men's]; they carry the water-kegs upon their heads, and huge bales of nets up the steep cliff-paths with an ease akin to grace (Walcott, 1862).

Mercifully, the Moray Firth practice of women wading to the boat carrying a dry husband does not seem to have spread to Filey. Kegs were filled from the only convenient and usable wells, in Church Ravine, below the churchyard (**25.1**).

---

[3] Dyson (1977) p226.
[4] Fearon (2016) p44; Fisher, *History* (1970) *Introduction*, p1.

When the yawls moved to harbour towns, womenfolk initially accompanied their men on the train each Monday morning, and then helped carry the week's provisions down to the harbour on their heads or over their shoulders. In the 1980s, Elizabeth HUNTER (née RICHARDSON) told us how her mother and three other women skeined for her father, Edmond Cammish, George Jenkinson Mainprize and the other crew of herring coble *Faith* when it was lining. The women accompanied them on the train to Scarborough, the bait travelling in buckets in the guardsvan. At least they had the tram the mile down to the harbour.

By the early 1900s, however, our Scarborough informants of the early 1980s, in their seventies and eighties, remembered only the men arriving. Similarly, in 1908, diarist John S Wane saw no women joining the first Monday morning train out of Filey with the fishermen. By then, the yawls were probably catching their own bait as they sailed for the fishing grounds - or they had degraded to crabbing.

The Inshore Wives' Day

Women who kept a coble fisherman afloat in the Winter Fishing faced near-continuous exertion, on a daily basis, six days in seven. And it started early, often before 5.00am. Fisher people were expert at getting up early. Mary Bradley told us how two 'solicitor lads', staying at the *Crescent Hotel*, were to go out spawing with her father, *Titch* JENKINSON. 'Be at the Coble Landing by five,' they were told. 'How do we get up?' they asked. *Titch* told them to put an alarm clock in a bucket, and they successfully woke up the whole hotel the following morning.

Bait-Collecting - Filey offshoremen generally got their mussels from Boston Deeps, but those from the beds at the mouth of the Tees were especially prized, 'big and plump . . . you only needed one'. They were deposited by Carr Naze[5], the southern, landward portion of The Brigg, to maintain mussel beds or 'gardens'.

One good spot for limpets and mussels was *Aggie Point* on Filey Brigg, more formally *Agony Point*, which probably took its name from the serious risk of being cut off by the incoming tide. At some time, numbers were chiselled into the rock every 80 yards, to ration access.

Local supplies of limpets (*flithers*) grew in importance for inshore fishing as supplies of mussels depleted. They were a free substitute, if you did not factor into the calculation the extra female work required. Territorial rights were hotly disputed. Frank cites the *scratting* that broke out at Runswick Bay between local women and interlopers from Staithes. This was only settled when local magistrates allocated certain days of the week to the Staithes women. Lampreys came from Nottingham, and snails were even collected by children.

---

[5] From the Norse *Scar*, 'protruding rock'; and *naze* – 'nose, ness, headland'.

Lug worms could easily be dug up at night on the beach, as they neared the surface. '*Gravin*' for worms entails much hard labour,' explained Smith in 1932, 'the creatures' powers of rapid retreat being considerable. The weapon used in their pursuit is a three-pronged fork on the end of a six-foot pole.' Razor fish (known locally as *war fish*) needed stalking. Being sensitive to the vibrations caused by the approach of a bait-collector, they could shoot down into the sand, though a frost would slow them down. A strong breeze would wash them out. Candles marking the night's progress of the bait-collectors created a magical flickering of lights, twinkling over a distance of two or three miles, a delicate image sharply at odds with the tiring drudgery involved, at the end of an already long day.

25.2: Number *9* chiselled into the rock on Carr Naze, delineating a mussel-gathering, or perhaps salmon-fishing boundary. *[JC]* Stephen Eblet has been unable to find number 13!

> The lights of the many lanterns, carried by those who are seeking this bait at night, often mark the curve of the Bay from the Brigg to Primrose Valley or even further – with a very fine and picturesque effect.[6]

But Filey's Brigg and beach could supply only a fraction of what was needed, and local women, as at Staithes, had to range further afield. The distances walked by flither women increased as local stocks declined. If they could not get bait in Filey Bay in the winter months, they ranged to Gristhorpe and Cayton Bay, along the cliffs to Flamborough, or over rocks and beaches to Scarborough. Gristhorpe Cliff was four miles there, four back. If they were going 'picking' on a Monday then it was out of bed at 5am to do the washing before setting off to collect a 'tide' of bait. They carried as many as eight baskets (*mawns*) strung to back and shoulders, with food for the day. Knitting came too so as not to waste meal breaks. As the tide receded, flithers and periwinkles were left clamped to the rocks. For a few hours it was safe to walk beneath the cliffs. Tides varied, so if few molluscs were found, on they went to Cayton Bay and beyond.

The dangers the women risked may not be appreciated today. These cliff bases are lethal places for the unwary. Five children drowned at Reighton Gap in August 1902, 'suddenly surrounded by the tide in the presence of their mothers'. The following August, a six year-old boy was crushed at Filey 'by the falling of the cliff beneath which he was sitting' even though he was with a mother and nurse.[7]

---

[6] Pettitt (1868). He provides this account of flithering northwards of Filey.
[7] Nellist (1913).

The bait-gatherers spent hard winter days in far more dangerous places. The seashore walk northwards from The Brigg is rough-going, a death trap for the unwary if the tide is misjudged and you are 'flowed in'. Even today, with mobile phones and modern walking gear, it is not a place to be trifled with. Nor was it work for the ageing, although some were still *flithering* into their sixties.

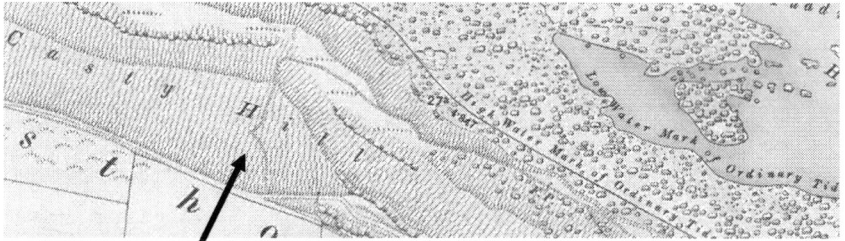

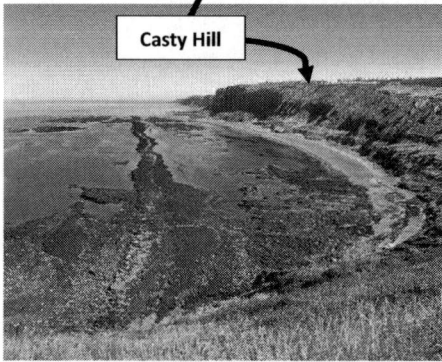

Casty Hill

25.3: Even in sunshine, these remote rocks and *binks* (sea ledges) by Gristhorpe Cliff have a sinister, haunted isolation. High and low water marks on the 1891 25 inch map indicate that the whole platform was covered at high tide, a deadly trap for boat and bait-gatherer alike. When there was snow and ice on Casty Hill, women had 'ti sholl doon because it was si slipe', getting backsides wet, and their work clothes sodden.

As the wife aged, it was increasingly the strong daughters on those long winter trudges. They were often in bitter easterlies or north-easterlies, continuously and laboriously stooping to knife limpets off rocks. Each woman ended up with full *mawns* slung on the back or perched on the head, on a wooden or cloth ring, the *bun*. And this was not in specialist outdoor winter gear to resist snow and rain, but in everyday clothing - shawls, with frocks pinned up clear of the lapping sea water. They often wore just flimsy shoes, but even with lace-up boots or wooden-soled clogs it was easy to become vulnerably drenched, through slipping on the seaweed and falling into rock pools.

It was possible to head north more easily along the cliff top, dropping down to favoured sites. This route allowed the women to keep an eye seaward on the off chance that they spotted a coble in trouble. There were many descents, but landslides and erosion have probably destroyed most of those used in the 19th Century. One surviving drop that we have already encountered in Chapter 18 descends a precariously steep stretch of Gristhorpe Cliff, and was known as the 'Baitgatherer's Descent', or 'The Chimney'. It was also used by beachcombers.

The women dropped 40 feet, steadying themselves with a rope attached to 'a very small and unsafe-looking stake . . . [they] gain what additional help they can by planting their feet against the perpendicular cliff-side'. Such spots were always visited by two or more women together, since numbers offered help and collective judgment (**25.3**). And this risk-assessment procedure worked, for the 'loyal sisterhood' looked out for each other. The only misadventure anyone could remember dated back, in oral tradition at Flamborough, to the early 18th Century. *Old Nan* Cross could relate how one woman had gone down before anyone else had arrived at the climb head:

> There was yan woman, she wad gan doon t'ropes bi hersen foor tahm, and when t'others coomd, they fund 'er deead on t'rocks below but that's lang sin.

The reason for this aberration remains a 300 year-old mystery, 'for none would dream of going down the ropes before all were assembled at the appointed time'.[8] The hazards of being in these dangerous locations alone, even if only bait-gathering, were shown in December 1907, when George Matthew JENKINSON (Q80) drowned at the foot of Gristhorpe Cliff. The *Filey Post* of the 14th described how he had been 'flowed in' (ie cut off by a rising tide). His death had been so avoidable: like many of the Old Town, even those who regularly went to sea, George could not swim. He probably had only limited practice in marking the tide's progress by the disappearance of certain rocks, as the sea rose. This was the advantage of having an older, experienced woman in the party.

By the 1860s, women were getting the train to Scarborough to *flither pick* along the shore to Cloughton or Robin Hood's Bay. The North Eastern Railway issued 3rd class 'Fishwoman' tickets, 3d each way, after pressure from some sympathetic ladies. In 1868, Pettitt noted how a carriage was attached especially, with a truck for the bait, perhaps to spare the noses of fellow passengers as much to prioritise the *flitherers*. Women were walking from Filey, setting off as early as half past midnight. Tradition says a wealthy lady met them on the road, and arranged to subsidise their rail fare. The women could spread the cost of the ticket over two or more days' worth of bait by staying overnight at Mrs Cockerill's, 3d a night, three to a bed. *Sal Jin* (Sarah Jane CAPPLEMAN) told Arthur Munby 'we taks a bit o'bacon, sweet cake, a bit o'pie or owt o'that and summat ti drink.'[9]

Mary Elizabeth ROBINSON remembered her mother staying overnight in Cloughton if she misjudged the tide and missed the last train. An elderly couple provided B&B, though the going rate by the early 1900s was 6d. The special 'bait-gatherer's' return ticket cost 4½d at the beginning of the 20th Century.[10]

---

8 Ann Fearon, *The Flither Girls of Filey* (SMHC).
9 Census returns suggests their digs were provided by Fanny Cockerill, a widowed laundress on Cloughton's High Street. Several widows, living in old, stone, thatched cottages, 'walls a foot thick', also offered this B&B.
10 Frank (2002) pp162-4; Terence COLLINS; Kendall (1877) pp8-9.

Some of the last women to have made the journey to Cloughton regularly were still living in Providence Place in the 1980s. One was George Burton's aunt, Liz JOHNSON. But some Filey women still went occasionally to The Brigg, Gristhorpe and Robin Hood's Bay in the 1970s.

The Diaries of Arthur Joseph Munby

In modern times, the interest that this good-natured Victorian eccentric took in working women would be dismissed as perverted, but contrary to widespread current belief, 19th Century Britain was far less publicly sexualised than our 21st Century version. Munby regularly approached women in their work clothes, asking would they be photographed for a fee of one shilling. He seems virtually never to have been taken as sexually motivated, and was disgusted when at one sleazy photographer's he was asked if he might like to have photographs of a girl 'with her clothes up'.

From 1864-75, he came annually to the Filey and Flamborough coasts, striking up some very close friendships with the bait-gatherers, and speaking to them in detail about their work. He filled many pages of detailed diaries with what he learned from Filey fisherwomen.[11]

In October 1864, Munby noted down a conversation with Filey photographer Walter Fisher near the station:

> He often takes photos, he says, of Filey fish girls, for artists, and sends them to London. . . . the girls will come readily, if you give them a copy of the portrait. They are big strong lasses, with hands and arms 'very large', says Mr Fisher.

25.4: Fisher outdoor portrait, 1873 - flimsy shoes and non-waterproof everyday clothing. The cloth ring, known in dialect as the *roller*, *bun* or *raith*, seated loads on the head. *[FA]*

---

[11] Infuriatingly all this local detail has been omitted from the edited version of his diaries, Derek Hudson's *Munby: Man of Two Worlds* (John Murray, 1972). Munby even mastered the local dialect. The original diary volumes are at Trinity College, Cambridge, and are not readily accessible.

25.5: 'Barbarian fisher girls' as Munby reckoned outsiders thought of them: an 1867 Walter Fisher shot of exhausted Flamborough bait-gatherers, Molly Nettleton, left, and Sally Mainprize, right, amidst rocks and seaweed. The shot catches the hard physicality of cliff-climbing and constant stooping along a stony sea shore far more accurately than anything posed in a studio. Skirts were gathered up at the back between the knees, 'kilted' up and pinned, with strings tied around each knee to create breeches. Work finished, the women restored their skirts, 'legs and thin worn boots soaked with wading in the pools,' as Arthur Munby put it. They then carried home up to eight full baskets, each weighing a stone or more. *[FA]*

Munby now began his collection of such commercially-taken photographs from the north-east coast, asking the photographer to endorse each with the name of the woman, if possible, for the sake of authenticity.

In researching this edition, I have been amazed at how busy as thoroughfares the huge sea cliff faces were. Beach-watchers, seekers after sea-gift and egg climmers all roped their precarious ways down hundreds of feet of vertical and often unstable rock face as though they were merely slightly awkward extensions of paths down to the seashore. But the risks that flither girls took are especially remarkable.

25.6: Munby's on-the-spot pencil sketch of his four *flither picker* friends on the sheer cliff face at Breil Head, Flamborough. Molly (top); and Ann sitting on the 'windy corner ledge', c60 feet up – 'the figures are too large in proportion', he noted. The girls often climbed one-handed, *mawns* in the other. Note the absence of a lifeline. *[Trinity College, Cambridge]*

The fearlessness of these women so amazed Munby that he wrote detailed accounts of the climbs they undertook – like scaling 150-foot cliffs near Flamborough, the girls actually using only one hand on the rope, steadying their baskets with the other.

One girl, Molly Nettleton, born in Flamborough in 1846, had been working the cliffs since she was 11 years-old. She and Munby developed a special bond across the social chasm between them, and when in 1867 some 'lads' stole her rope to be used in a net, he paid 8s 3d for a 'stout well-tarred rope', a stone in weight. Picture any 21 year-old of today as you read this diary entry:

> Molly joyously took up the tarry coil and carried it home on her arm, I going with her. She thanked me as if 24 fathoms of ship's rope were the prettiest present a woman could have.

The following year, he stayed in Filey at the start of the Winter Fishing, walking to Breil Head, Flamborough, to catch the local flither girls for the first time this visit:

> And then, looking down, I saw the new rope, my gift and Molly's treasure, hanging from the stake . . . down the whole height of the cliff, to the broad platform of table rock at the bottom.

Four local girls had climbed down at daybreak to gather bait. It must have been barely light. Molly's rope was knotted to a single stake, 150 feet or so above the shore. She clambered up to appear first, six hours later:

> Hand over hand, sticking her toes into the crevices of the chalk wall, she went up as easily as one might walk upstairs. And having thus climbed some 50 feet, she turned round, and with her back to the cliff, worked her way along a level ledge that just supported her heels, to an overhanging point. There, stooping forward as coolly as possible, she hauled up her own full basket and her fellow's . . . . When the baskets came up, she just loosened them, and hoisted them up, with one hand, upon a broader ledge above her head . . . a windy corner-ledge . . . on which Sally Mainprize used to sit and shout and whistle to the ships at sea.

Once Molly Nettleton and Ann Mainprize were at the top of the rope, they sat to await the others. But a strong south-westerly brought rain, and they had no jackets:

> So Molly stood up [and] shouted to the far off folk, 'Noo then, coom on we're gahin'! And at last the rope at our feet began to tremble again. Instantly Molly and Nan started up, and saying 'Wa min gan an' help 'em', these fearless lasses seized the rope, and . . . began to run, Molly first, head-foremost down the dizzy slope of rock, until they both disappeared over the edge of the cliff wall below.[12]

Munby was also on very good terms with a number of Filey *flither-lasses*.[13] By 1864, they were travelling by train 'in troops' to Scarborough. But having filled 'their creels or sacks', they walked back loaded all the way to Filey. Presumably they caught the train to catch the tide, but could not afford the 3d back.

Munby's intimate knowledge of these women's arduous lives intensified his great concern for the welfare of working women generally. He was acutely sensitive of the oppressive social class gradations that weighed down on them, noting how conspicuous the women were outside Old Filey: 'Folks stopped to look at 'em, boys shouted "flitherlasses"... . The well-dressed mobs on the platform looked astounded at the strange dress and stalwart forms of the barbarian fisher girls.'[14]

Typically of his generosity of spirit, Munby intervened in the small ways that were available to him. One opportunity presented itself in the depths of winter, December 1869, when he met a group of flitherers on the platform at Scarborough, with an hour to wait for a Filey train. They began to take off some of their wet clothes to the astonishment of the ladies and gentlemen waiting nearby.

They must have been even more astonished when Munby spoke to the girls in dialect: 'Wat are ye boon ti dea while then?' They told him they would walk up and down to keep themselves warm. 'Wad ye like a cup of tea?' They had no idea how to get one.

He led them to the refreshment room, cleared some men from the fire, and sat the girls in front of it, explaining they were cold, wet and thirsty. The girls were served tea whilst their wet boots steamed. They were, he wrote, 'fine seafaring women - to me far nobler and more interesting than anyone there.'

---

[12] Ann Mainprize was probably daughter of Sarah (née JENKINSON, O45) and the George Mainprize who drowned off The Brigg in 1874 (see above, pp236-7). Sarah was probably the 28 year-old spinster living with widowed mother Mary in the 1871 Flamborough Census.

[13] Some of Munby's Filey girls can be identified within fisher families in the 1861 Census: Sarah Jane CAMMISH, 17, bait-gatherer, daughter of William and Jane, Suggit's Yard; Jenny/Jane CAPPLEMAN, 17, bait-gatherer, daughter of Thomas and Elizabeth, King Street; Anne Born (née CAPPLEMAN), 21, daughter of William and Sarah, Beach Cottage; and Jane SAYERS, 18, daughter of William and Susannah, Ocean Place.

[14] Quoted in Ann Fearon, *The Flither Girls of Filey* (SMHC).

Back Home

When these exhausted bait-gatherers finally got home in darkness, some *skeining* was necessary.[15] Several thousand flithers had to be ready for the morning, 'fresh off the knife' for the long-lines, once the men came in from the morning's fishing. These were soaked, then spooned out of the shell, far less demanding than skeining mussels (**25.7**).

25.7: Joan CAPPLEMAN, wife of *Granddad Cap,* skeining mussels in a Filey kitchen, half a century ago, but using the technique of her 18th Century ancestors. Skilled, tedious knife work – 'squeeze the mussel, put yer knife in and go round . . . they 'ad to come out whole, you weren't allowed to rag them', all in a three or four-second action.

Skeining could be painful, for barnacles clinging to the shells cut into the flesh, and the salty liquid inside would then inflame the open wound. 'Never learn how to skein mussels,' Ruth Canning's mother told her, 'you never get rid of the smell.'

By the later 20th Century, women could find outside jobs, and simply would no longer work for the family in the old way. Buying in mussels (sack in foreground) pushed up costs and this has contributed to the demise of long-lining from the Yorkshire coast. *[FFF]*

In the 1920s, the pay was 9d for skeining a sack of mussels, two being usual for one man's lines. Stephen Eblet recalls coming from school to dinner at his gran, Fanny Elizabeth (née Temple)'s house, eating it next to her as she skeined. 'As a Sheffield lad, I found it a bit of a challenge with the smell,' he says.

Lugworm though more accessible (from the beach) was a last resort - it 'tendered the fingers and made them sore.' It was common for a woman from another household to be put to skein if a family had insufficient women or girls of their own. Foster Holmes JENKINSON recalled his sister, Mary, being knocked up to start skeining at 3.30am.

Baiting - two women skeined for one fisherman, but a third person, maybe a retired fisherman, helped bait anything from the 2,000 to 3,000 hooks or more, ready for the day's fishing.

---

[15] Most of the quotations in the following accounts are taken from *Exploring Filey's Past: Oral Interviews, 2005-6* (Transcripts at Filey Museum).

25.8: ?Susan SCALES, baiting a long-line, c1948 - the *caved* line (old bait and seaweed removed) is coiled on the right; skeined mussels are taken from the bowl (regularly refilled) and pulled onto a hook; the line is then coiled onto a *skep* (left) so that all baited hooks lie at one side – hence the apparent pile of mussels. *[FA]*

Ideally, this was done in a separate baiting shed, which left the living quarters free of mess and smell. (Baiting sheds were specially built by the Council behind its houses.) But many kitchens had to be used, atmospherically described by the anonymous CAMMISH writer already quoted on page 325. Imagine it, one 1920s evening in a house on Scarborough's Sandside:

> The winter line-fishing bought about a dramatic change in the domestic aspect. One half of the kitchen table augmented by planks and trestles was given over to baiting of long-lines ready to be taken to sea the following morning, whilst in the scullery or the 'back spot', as it was known, the ladies of the house were busy steaming the mussels, that were used for bait, by candle light. They sang at their work, the women and men alike, lusty voices carried the very breath of the sea itself beyond the confines of the house. Songs of praise, all of them an acknowledgement of their love and trust of the lord above in whatever should befall. [16]

---

[16] *smhc.hqtdevelopment.co.uk* (SMHC website).

Some women tipped the shellfish into a tin bath, pouring on cold water to firm them up ready for baiting, though too much of a soaking might me counterproductive – see above pages 202-3). There were two parts to the mussel, tongue and gristle, and they had to be cut out in one, so that both could be hooked on – 'through the black, turn it and through the white so they didn't come off,' as Jim Haxby put it. Hooking cold, wet molluscs did the hands no good. In fine weather, it was a common sight well into the 20th Century to see women skeining and baiting in the yards off Queen Street. The smaller the mussels, the more they had to use, and the longer it took. 'When they used to bring mussels from Boston by road,' Jim recalled, 'they used to feel the bags. Were they big uns?' One big mussel was as good as six or seven. The work might be finished by 8.00 am if they had started early, and women might be out shopping by 8.30am. Life got easier when fridges appeared in the 1950s and '60s, for skeined bait would not go sour so quickly.

Servicing the Coble also fell within the women's job description. They carried buckets of water, suspended from shoulder yokes, from the spring in Church Ravine to the landing. Women and donkeys helped the men carry baited lines down to the cobles. (Readers may consider the juxtapositioning of those words highly indicative of the status of women in 19th Century fishing communities.)

Line-spinning; Netmaking and Repairing - earlier in the 20th Century, lines were spun by women in the evenings, and new nets were braided – perhaps there were the same tell-tale brass rails for this process on some outside walls in the Old Town, as in Hessle Road, Hull. Gear had to be maintained regularly, lines usually being tanned at Christmas and after the Winter Fishing. Nets were repaired and tanned. The spare set of oilskins had to be oiled, varnished and hung up to dry. Much of this work was done by women.

Gladys Thompson told a story of a visit to a Fife cottage probably before World War II. It could easily have been on Filey's Queen Street. She chatted to the cottager, sharing gansey patterns. Would she like to meet 'Granny in the attic', the woman asked, for Granny had been a great knitter in her day:

> Granny was standing by a window at the far end, repairing a net. Yards and yards of net - she'd a netting shuttle in her right hand, and a small pair of scissors in her left. She worked at a tremendous pace - her hands flashing in and out, snipping and netting and talking at the same time . . . . She kept all the family nets repaired and at busy times worked in the attic the entire day.[17]

It really was demanding work. Men might have to get involved on bad weather days, and on retirement from the sea. How it must have tested old eyes used to the long-sighted work of the fisherman. William Johnson *Billy Bullocky* COLLING (1925-2015) didn't specify the age he was recalling, but his account conveys the weariness of it all, and will resonate with a new generation of computer users:

---

[17] Gladys Thompson, *Patterns for Guernseys Jerseys and Arans [sic]. Fishermen's Sweaters from the British Isles* (Dover, 1971, first published 1955) p95.

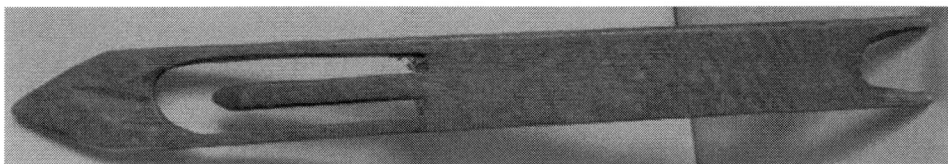

25.9: A netmender, or netting shuttle - used for repairs. Made of wood or horn. *[JC]*

I used t' braid the net in. I used ter start at four in the mornin' when it was bad weather and I used ter be gooin' till eleven or twelve at night. . . . I used t'get up again at four, lay me fire, 'ave a cup o' tea and start again. At night I could 'ardly see out o' me eyes, burr I kept gooin'.

Hawking the Catch

Before the railway age, most of the catch was disposed of at markets on Filey Beach (**25.10**) as at Scarborough and Staithes. Any surplus was hawked around the district by women or retired fishermen, sold on to local fish-dealers, or sent inland by packhorse.

25.10: Perhaps the earliest image we have of a working Filey beach scene, c1860, taken by Belle Vue Street photographer Walter Fisher (1832-1911) - sales direct from a freshly beached coble, before the Landing was any more than sand. The preponderance of men suggests they are dealing rather than buying for tonight's tea. *[FA]*

Arthur Munby was told in the 1860s that Filey women went selling as far as Pickering. One 1950 account of childhood in a harbour town in north-east Scotland around 1900 could probably have been written about such formidable Filey female hawkers:

> ... we had a regular supply of fish brought to the door by fish-wives who had their regular customers and could deal effectually with anyone trying to poach. I remember the prices well because it was fun to be at the door when *Meggie*, or *Cauld Annie*, came with a basket. It was always assumed that the fish would be bought. Indeed it would have been impolitic to refuse.

Any haggling over price would be met with 'Eh woman! The wather! Think o'the storm!'[18] Or perhaps some variant of 'it's men's lives you're buying!'

Let's pause for breath. The modern woman would rate this workload beyond human capability. For each year, her Old Town predecessor collected, carried, skeined and baited possibly dozens of tons of worms and molluscs. Yet this was only half of it, for the fisherman's wife somehow had to be a mother, *and* manage housework too.

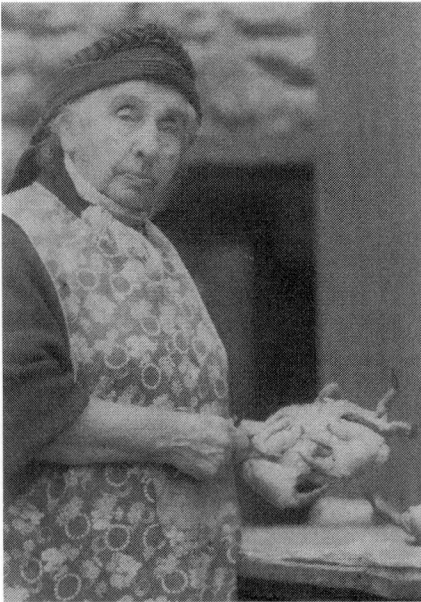

25.11: The archetypal Filey fisherwoman, who kept boat *and* home afloat. Moll Ann Wyvill (née Wright) of 11, Queen Street, wife of *Jimmy Bass*, known as *The Crab Lady*, is dressing her namesake – cutting off legs, and scooping meat out of the shell. *[FA]*

She wears traditional headgear, a Filey edition of the 'Staithes Bonnet', with cloth ring, known in dialect as the *roller, bun* or *raith*, to seat loads on the head – skeps, kegs, catch. The corded peak (the *poke*) kept some sun out of the eyes, whilst the rear frill kept rain and spray off the neck.

These bonnets were universally worn in Filey Old Town well into the 20th Century.

---

18 Quoted in Dyson (1977) pp194-5.

'Once the flither girls had finished their backbreaking work of gathering flithers, then baiting their husbands' fishing lines, they were of course wives and mothers who looked after the house, fed the family, knitted guernseys, socks and stockings for their children and husbands. When the man came home from fishing, he was met by a bright fire burning in the grate, a chair set by the hearth and a bowl of warm water. His wife sat him down, removed his seaboots and socks, washed and dried his feet and set a meal in front of him – the breadwinner!' Ann Fearon, The Flither Girls of Filey (SMHC)

Motherhood and Homemaking

Daunting amounts of childcare were generated by the large families that inevitably resulted from early marriage in the pre-contraception era.[1] In a herculean 24 years of childbearing, for example, Thomas JENKINSON (N11) and Mary Castle begat nine children who lived to marry, and five who died within 24 months. Pregnant for virtually half that span, and nursing one or more young children for the remainder, the sheer physicality of the unenviable existence of women like Mary was more akin to breed-livestock than human beings. In comparison, the mere ten childbirths generated by younger brother George JENKINSON (N12) and Mary SCALES seem a model of reproductive restraint.

Women marrying widowers could inherit children to look after, before they even started conceiving their own. In a two-bedroomed cottage, there was often so little bedspace that it became a question of 'get one to sleep in bed, lift out onto the floor and on to the next.'

There could be a lackadaisical disregard for the vulnerability of pregnant women within these hardworking fisher communities (25.1), shockingly illustrated by the childhood recollection of Martha Boddington, born at Staithes in 1901.

26.1: 5, Mariners Terrace - Betsy (née JENKINSON, P13) and husband William COLLING had 12 children, according to the 1911 Census. Three had died. 'All immaculately clean and tidy.' Betsy herself was the youngest of ten. *[JC]*

---

[1] The vulcanisation of rubber after 1844 led to the manufacture of rubber condoms in Britain from the 1870s, though easily mistaken for inner tubes. Impressionistic parish register and census evidence suggests they were in use in Filey by the late 19th Century.

She and her mother walked the six miles to Whitby to collect sea-coal off the shoreline. It was March, yet her mother, nearly five months gone, was up to her waist in cold sea water. She suddenly felt ill, dropped onto the sand, and the baby was born. She put the dead baby into her pinned-up skirt, and they walked back:

> She had forty or fifty steps to climb . . . and just dropped the basket of coal in the yard. . . . The doctor said she was a lucky person that she was alive . . . it was the intense cold and the weight on her head that had caused her to have the miscarriage.[2]

The basket of coal was clearly being carried on a *bun*. If this could have happened in the 20th Century, whatever can it have been like in the 19th, let alone the 18th?

Without help from the wider family, women with large families simply could not manage the near full-time job as a fisherwoman. Census returns regularly show the older generation in the same terrace or yard, if not next door. Older and unmarried relatives helped with baiting, and provided the childcare that freed mothers to skein and bait. In such domestic circumstances, with only the fire or a side oven for cooking, meals had to be bulky, wholesome and simple to prepare. Apart from fish, the Yorkshire coast specialty *Pan Aggie* was easy - left-over beef, lamb or pork, layered with sliced potato and onion, prepared in the morning and left to simmer all day over the fire, with rashers on top.

It was hard to make these tiny cottages comfortable. There was little light, and amidst the homely smells of cooking, you simply could not escape from fishing. The blend of stench from flithers, worms and mussels, wet gear and clothing drying by the fire in the small kitchen/living area were Old Town givens. But women were proud of their house, and as with Betsy COLLING (**26.1**) she kept things as she wanted them, whatever the difficulties. Fisher houses were known for warmth and cleanliness, a fire being the focus of the home. It meant warmth, but also the means to cook, and to heat water to clean wash and launder. Arthur Munby visited a house in Quay Street, Scarborough which was a 'neat houseplace, sanded floor, bright fire, tea set, china ornaments.' At Staithes, it was said, 'So long as you had a good fire you were all right.'[3] This traditional and abiding sense that indoors was the woman's jurisdiction enhanced her authority there. Ultimately, she set the tone, and the standards, and in many fisher homes laid down the law. This was certainly the case with George Burton's grandmother, Liz CAPPLEMAN.

Matt JENKINSON (P46) known universally in his later days as *Old Brazzy*, was a rough diamond, often very bad tempered, who would struggle with any 'tone'. Yet his Flamborough wife, Ann Knaggs was remembered by Elizabeth HUNTER as 'spotless . . . a lady.'

---

[2] Frank (2002) p172.
[3] Frank (2002) pp52, 54.

George Burton recalled how *Brazzy* and Healand SAYERS came round to his grandparents' house every night, during the time that his grandfather George CAPPLEMAN was ill. These two classic curmudgeons would always argue. The three old men would be sitting round the open fire, on which his grandmother lavished much time. The *rakens* in particular, suspended within the fireplace, were sacrosanct:

> They were my granny's pride, and she used to black lead them every day. And *Brazzy* used to come and sit on a night and spit baccy juice all over them. Smoke used to come right out - it used to sizzle. She used to play hell - '*Old Brazzy's* black sickenin'', she would say.[4]

The cantankerous Healand and *Brazzy* were always waiting to catch one another out:

> *Brazzy* might say: 'It was August Bank Holiday . . . .' So, as a matter of course, Healand would say:
>
> 'I know it warn't then!'
> 'Well I know it was then!'
> 'Well thoo's a liar then!'
> 'Thoo's a liar then!'

26.2: Chalk and cheese! Matt and Ann JENKINSON. Two more contrasting personalities would be hard to find. *Brazzy* was a rough diamond, spitting into the fire, and quite ready to relieve himself off a coble full of spawers, 'never bothered about nobody', whereas his wife was 'spotless . . . a lady.' *[FA]*

And so it would go on, with the two arguing, George's granddad sitting 'saying nowt', and the *rakens* periodically sizzling, until Grandma had had enough:

> She would turn them out, just like a pub: 'you've gone far enough the pair of you, it's time you were going.' And out into the street they would go.

Women without dependent children could effectively run crèches for their fertile neighbours. George Burton reckoned that *Sal Tiny* (Sarah Ann, daughter of George Simmons *Tiny* CAMMISH) 'brought the whole of Filey up' – like a number of women, she made toffee for children, out of vinegar and treacle. She was married to *Jack Black* JENKINSON (P93), and effectively kept open house - a 'heart of gold', 'an angel'. Medical adviser to much of the fishing community, she could

---

[4] *Rakens* is usually rendered elsewhere as *rakentines* - vertical iron band with hooks from which the kettle and cooking pots would hang.

cure an infectious wound from a hook, helped as a midwife when aged only 11, and did so for the rest of her life; local tradition has it that doctors consulted her if they had a difficult case, though this story may reflect hostility to the well-heeled medical profession. At a time when doctors' charges were beyond working-class families, this village 'wise woman' treated all manner of complaints from bad fingers to poisoned hands and bad sores (by the rubbing in of salt, on the assumption that this was always used to cure meat). There was much quaintness in folklore medicine, timelessly rooted way beyond modern memory, and passed down in the female line.

Jobs

If a fisherman had more womenfolk than he needed for fishing support, there were plenty who didn't. There were 20 'bait-gatherers' in the 1861 Census, all single-women, and aged 15 to 28, except one widow. These 20 were working for a wage outside the family, to be singled out like this. *Tommy Laffy* JENKINSON's mother, Alice Ann née COLLING, earned about five shillings a tide in the early 1900s. There was also paid work as skeiners and baiters: in the early 20th Century, as the decline took husbands out of Filey, women were free to work for others. From the mid-1800s, the herring-houses offered seasonal work. Females were expected to do heavy or arduous work, nowadays acknowledged to be the preserve of men, simply because men were at sea and unavailable.

And they started young: Frank (page 172) cites an 1883 example of a school log book at Staithes which noted as fact rather than child abuse how attendance had been poor, girls of nine and younger being kept at home to carry coals from a collier, anchored in the bay. Children of course worked young, leaving school on their tenth birthday. This rose to 11 in 1893, and 12 in 1899.

One woman who single-handedly encapsulated the varied female job portfolio, was a Filey woman, Lizzie Ann, admiringly portrayed by Gladys Thompson:

> . . . a remarkable woman, and though she only had one hand (the other arm ended up at the knuckles) she was one of the hardest workers in Filey. A great Chapel supporter, she also helped at the Vicarage and on other days went out cleaning and whitewashing. During the summer her house was overflowing with visitors and the same people came to her year after year. She was also a great knitter, and through her I came to know many of the Filey patterns and to learn the names of the different stitches. I often slipped up to her cottage in the evenings and listened to her lovely East Yorkshire dialect.[5]

Two sources in Filey identify *Lizzie Ann* as Elizabeth Cammish RICHARDSON (1913-2000) who married Bob *Tewy* HUNTER.

---

[5] Gladys Thompson, *Patterns for Guernseys, Jerseys and Arans. Fishermen's Sweaters from the British Isles* (Dover, 1971, first published 1955) p22.

Knitting Ganseys

Lizzie Ann was an acknowledged expert in one of Filey's great crafts, the knitting of ganseys, *the* characteristic garment of the Yorkshire fisherman. They were thickly and tightly knitted with oiled wool, seamlessly in one piece ('in the round') for warmth, wind-proofing and water-resistance, and worn under a smock and/or oilskins. The close fit prevented loose clothing dangerously catching tackle or hooks when at sea. Sleeves were kept above the hand so as not to impede working.

Some women used a *shear* when knitting, a small case, inches long, filled tightly with feather quills. Tucked under an arm to lodge one needle, it freed a hand to work the wool faster. Knitters also wore wooden sheaths, often elaborately carved, and tucked in the waistband. Sheringham too had a strong home-knitting fisher tradition: early in the 20th Century women were paid between four and nine shillings by a Yarmouth firm which sold ganseys on to fishermen. It was skilled, time-consuming work for such a return, each one involving 50 hours knitting with up to five *pins* (needles). The large number of Filey knitting photographs suggests that some Old Town women similarly made a living out of knitting, as well as ganseying all their menfolk, including boys. One retired Norfolk fisherman remembered his grandmother demanding silence as she concentrated to 'set up the pattern' for the first two rows.[6]

Gladys Thompson collected fisher knitting patterns from all over the country. But she found Filey particularly beguiling:

> When I first remember Filey, every doorway in the old town held a knitter, in a black or coloured sun bonnet, with her needles flicking in and out so quickly, that it was impossible to follow their movement.

> One day I found myself in Queen Street . . . and I called at a whitewashed stone cottage with walls at least a foot thick. An old lady opened the door, and when she heard I wanted guernsey patterns she asked me into the kitchen. A tortoiseshell cat sat by the fire, and an old man lay asleep on a horsehair sofa. She asked me to sit down and went to fetch some guernseys from up the yard. She showed me one or two, and then pointing to the sofa said, 'Tak a leeak at yon gansey he's wearing; yer can tun him over and see t'pattern!' Thank goodness our talking woke him, and I had a look without having to 'tun him over'.[7]

There is a widespread belief that each town or village on the Yorkshire Coast had its own specific gansey pattern so that drowned fishermen could be identified with a particular place.[8] The sea's propulsion of bodies was utterly unpredictable, in direction, speed and distance. A corpse sinks to the sea bottom, but surfaces after a few weeks, bloated by the gas generated in the process of decomposition.

---

[6] Weatherhead (2011) pp16-17.

[7] Thompson (1971) pp23-4. As the account refers to them as the parents of George Overy, they will be Thomas CAMMISH and Sarah Overy.

[8] The same conviction was repeated to me in the Devonshire port of Appledore in 2019.

26.3: Filey had at least 14 patterns, with traditional combinations of ladders, cables, netting, and herring bone motifs. This group illustrates some of the variety. Back row, **L to R**: John William *Jackdaw* JOHNSON, Jimmy Douglas, Dick CAMMISH; *Topper* CAMMISH in suit; front, Matt Haxby, William *Gussy* COWLING, Bill Freeman - c1920. *[SE]*

Currents then take it anywhere. A Bridlington man, William Welburn, drowning off a coble in 1878 six miles south of *Quay* was found nearly 20 miles south, on the sands at Mappleton after two days.[9] Men were usually soon completely unrecognisable after being fed on, and knocked around against rocks. Any aid to identification would make sense, and in a preliterate age, something as distinctive as a pattern may have been memorable.

But the notion that patterns could link drowned men to a specific place has only limited truth. There is, for example, some evidence that herring girls picked up ideas from the different ganseys they saw as they worked. Thompson found that local patterns were adapted and embellished, so that fishing stations had many variations, a wife incorporating detail from her home village – a Filey man's gansey might have sleeves in a Flamborough or Staithes style (**26.3**). It is even difficult to match them to particular surnames, since the unwritten instructions for each inevitably came down female lines. A wife could personalise any gansey, often by displaying a man's count of children. This was usually shown by the number of welts (ribs) or ridges, on the sleeves or waist, created by alternately knitting and

[9] *Driffield Times*, 16th Nov 1878. A bottle containing a distress message thrown from a sinking ship near the Canaries in January 1865 was found on Filey beach six months later *(Filey local and social history group Facebook site, posted by Suzanne Pollard, 1st January 2018)*.

purling rows. Another Filey motif was the zig-zag, anecdotally the 'marriage lines' which symbolised the ups and downs of wedlock. Of her husband's great grandfather Robert CAMMISH, Joanne CAMMISH explains how he had a highly allegorical 'everyday gansey . . . rope steps down to the coble landing, moss stitch shingle and sand beach.' The diamonds were nets. Folk belief perhaps held that an inherited pattern was a charm against disaster.

Perhaps ganseys distinguished men if a specific coble were lost. A personalised gansey may have identified Jack Bell, drowned at Scarborough in 1890, so badly deteriorated when found a mile away nine days later, that his gansey *was* the only clue. Captain Smith's story, relating to this uncle, is the only clear instance I have encountered. I have found no example of such identification cited in the St Oswald parish registers. If ganseys were so distinctive, why in September 1833, for example, were the three men found drowned in the space of three days not named in the St Oswald's burial register, either then or later? (It seems logical to assume they were off the same coble, and likely therefore to have been from the same nearby place.) As literacy grew, it became customary at Staithes and Filey to embroider initials on items of a fisherman's working clothing, usually just above the decorative lower border (the welt) to facilitate this grim personalisation.[10] The following account of the aftermath of the Great Gale of February 1871, taken presumably from newspaper reports, illustrates the macabre process. About 30 boats had been wrecked off Bridlington:

> . . . in twos and threes they washed ashore, bloated, battered and bruised. They were laid out in the back of *The Albion* public house on Hilderthorpe Road, and, in the days that followed, relatives of the victims would come and identify their loved ones. The clothes . . . were hung on rails, still wet, tattered and merely rags.

They could be identified only by buttons, initials, and distinctive clothing items.[11]

Conclusive evidence comes from Historic England's *National Record of the Historic Environment*. This online database of 400,000 entries from primary sources contains references to 2,655 fishing vessels lost between 1750 and 1950. A recent study of this mass of data yielded no instance of a fisherman identified by clothing or gansey, but many examples of passenger vessel drownings where bodies were identified by items of clothing or jewellery.[12] James Wyrill, master of the yawl *Emulous*, could only be identified by his buttons, when his body was recovered 16 weeks after boat and crew were lost off Scarborough in 1844.[13]

---

[10] Clark (1982) p145; Joanne CAMMISH.

[11] Richard Jones, *The Great Gale of 1871* (Memoir Books, 2013) pp50-1.

[12] Historic England Blog, Wreck of the Week, *No 65 A Complete Absence of Fishermen's Ganseys*. The myth, not widely believed by fishermen, seems to have originated in the fertile imagination of a German fantasist, Heinz Edgar Kiewe, an Oxford yarn shop owner whose flaky *The Sacred History of Knitting* (1967) invented any number of knitting fables, no doubt for commercial publicity. He is well-mocked on the internet!

[13] *The Allen and Truman Scarborough Fishing Families* (SMHC website).

Drowned East Anglian fishermen were likely to be distinguished by the colour of jumper, type of trousers, or colour of neckerchief (worn to counter abrasion by oilskins) and that this tradition continued into the early 20th Century.[14]

The Filey Sisterhood

. . . the Filey women are rarely seen gossipping about; if they are, it is always with work in their hands. Canon Cooper (1886) p35

One compensation for the intensity of women's work was the communal cohesion amongst them. In fine weather, many of the tasks allowed them out onto their steps (if their cottage had one) where this neighbourliness was cemented. Anglican clergyman Mackenzie Walcott (1862) caught this intangible feminine clubbability in his perceptive and revealing account of everyday life in the Old Town. Having watched four Filey girls in a herring-house, nimbly spiking 10,000 herrings in two hours, 20 to each hazel 'spit', ready for smoking, he noted how they eased the monotony 'by a vivacious and almost unbroken conversation, often interrupted by peals of hearty laughter.'

26.4: The sisterhood, Cliff Top, c1890 – virtually any female task was a social opportunity, like this proto 'Knit and Natter' session. **L to R:** bearded, Matthew *Walsher* JENKINSON (O40); Mary Jane COWLING; a non-fisherwoman with toy dog, immaculate dress and shoes, in stark contrast with the other three; Maud COWLING (*shear* in hand) and Ann ROBINSON née JENKINSON (P12), perhaps with a grandchild. *[FA]*

---

[14] Ian Robb, *Memories of the East Anglian Fishing Industry* (Countryside Books, 2010) pp84-6.

Knitting was especially communal, the old sloping sea wall being a favoured spot. George Burton's grandmother could sit *callin* (gossiping) on her step for hours, knitting as she talked, never once looking down at the garment. But this sense of communal sisterhood extended far beyond knitting and tittle-tattle. A real female solidarity and identity existed in a way that is difficult to define, but is beautifully illustrated by the funeral of Agnes Wheelhouse, on 1st May 1911, widow of the highly respected doctor who had in retirement been an active force on the Lifeboat Committee. The coffin was carried to the churchyard exclusively by women pallbearers, no doubt as a mark of respect and gratitude.[15]

Visitors

A seven-page typescript of nearly 500 visitors staying at Filey in August 1876 can be found in the Scarborough Maritime Heritage Centre. It was probably drawn up as a result of the 1875 Public Health Act which required councils to keep registers of common lodging-houses and the number of lodgers authorised to stay in each. On the list were the eminently respectable hotels of the New Town, hardly the target of the statute! Just three addresses on Queen Street, and five on Alma Terrace, figure from Old Filey. Yet it is pretty obvious that this was the tip of a ubiquitous iceberg, for possibly a majority of fisher wives with – or without - spare room was unofficially taking in visitors in the late 19th Century.

Though economically essential, this seasonal visitor economy serially piled on these women cooking and cleaning for a complete extra family some weeks after the Winter Fishing, when they could have had a breather from drudgery. As with the case of *Lizzie Annie*, whose house Gladys Thompson described as 'overflowing with visitors' each summer, it was the same people who came each year, and probably in their town's fixed wakes week, so the whole system could be completely informal, requiring only a confirmatory letter. JS Wane's 1908 diary entries make it clear that Ann WILLIAMSON (née JENKINSON, Q37) treated the visiting family virtually as personal friends.

Taking in visitors was far from a breather, for the women relied on their reputations for this regular custom, cleanliness and the provision of good food being crucial. Sokell stated in his 1856 guide that

> the landladies at Filey are of a very high order of ability and cleverness as housekeepers and scrupulously conscientious.

And all this might well have to be undertaken without a proper night's sleep, for the Old Town families often condensed themselves into a single room, or possibly even into an outhouse, to make their beds available. As late as the 1960s on Hoxton Road in Scarborough, Irene Allen, co-writer of this book's first edition, was as a child hauled out of bed occasionally at advanced hours, and dispatched to the attic, to make her bed available for surprise visitors. She was lucky - her brother ended

---

[15] Nellist (1913); Clark (1982) p129.

up in the cellar. Her mother, *Connie*, born in 1917 on Queen Street, and brought up there, went to any lengths to please her long-term regulars, always known by first names. Even in the 1980s, she slept in the kitchen to make room; and if a breakfast egg-yolk broke during frying, a fresh egg *had* to used.

Sokell recommended that the visitor should avoid 'inconsiderateness' if he wanted a pleasurable stay. 'Bear in mind,' he said, in terms that he would not get away with today, 'that stroking down the right way of the fur makes it smooth and the opposite rough.'

Surviving Widowhood in Filey

'I was seven years old when the Fleetwood trawler Evelyn Rose *went down on New Year's Day 1954. My father was Chief Engineer on board and my mother never recovered.'* Sam Barton, quoted by Ron Freethy.

Sam Barton was referring to the emotional legacy of such a loss, but the fallout of becoming a seaman's widow extended far beyond the psychological.

'Doubling up'

When 32 year-old Matthew JENKINSON (O17) drowned in Boston Deeps in July 1849, the plight of his widow was truly unenviable. Left with two young daughters, and pregnant with a third, Margaret had also been giving a home to her 66 year-old mother for at least eight years. By the time of the 1851 Census, with no wage-earner, she, her three daughters, *and* her mother, were somehow squeezed into Robert Shaw's tiny terraced cottage in Victoria Passage. Robert, a fisherman, was married to Margaret's younger sister, and the couple also had two young daughters – so nine had to be crammed in. It beggars belief how a man and eight females coped in what must have been a modest dwelling, a growing family sharing with out-of-season fishing gear and three generations of in-laws.

Would any man you know open their homes to so many of their wife's relatives today? What strains were put on their marriage? And the in-laws were still there, minus the aged mother, ten years on. Twenty years later still (1871), Margaret, 64, was living with one of her daughters' family. Such 'doubling up' with relatives was how the working-class dealt with economic hardship. But Margaret (née Shippey) lived in such overcrowded circumstances for at least 40 years.

These extended families did not always rub along so well, and in such crowded streets and yards it was hard to keep this a secret. One woman who gave her married son a home simply could not abide her daughter-in-law's company:

'Mum, what's Mrs CAPPLEMAN doing sitting out there?'

'Never you mind.'

Terence COLLINS recalled this childhood memory in the 1980s. Mrs CAPPLEMAN was only allowed in just before her husband got in from work.

Class Contrasts

We need to leave Filey briefly to compare the lot of the fisher widow with that of her middle-class equivalent. One branch of an Old Town family, the senior line of the JENKINSONs, master mariners, did well for themselves. One daughter, Marion (P4), was able to marry in more elevated social circles than her second cousins down Queen Street. Her first husband, a mineral water manufacturer, died in Leeds after just nine years of marriage, leaving her an estate worth 'under £200' according to the probate valuation. Marion was 31, with one daughter, but clearly marketable, for she secured the post of live-in housekeeper to a 28 year-old bachelor in a respectable Bradford suburb. It must have been unusual for a housekeeper to be able to bring a young daughter to her position, perhaps an indication of her nubility.

At some stage, her employer's requirements of his housekeeper warranted marriage. The more cynical readers may be assuming that their 1885 wedding simply legitimised a cohabitation. But there was probably no *need* to marry – their one child was born in 1887. Unfortunately, this marriage did not end happily either. John Reddie was a medical electrician – ie delivering focused electric shocks primarily to treat muscle pain and atrophy. At some stage, he was admitted to the nearby Menston Asylum, where he died in 1900. His estate was valued at a modest £79 11s 1d.

There were around 1900 far fewer openings in respectable employment for middle-class women than for Filey fisherwomen. But Marion followed on from her husband's electrical specialism, taking up the bizarre line as an 'agent for magnetic bells', according to the 1901 Census. Presumably, these were doorbells. There were capable genes in this family, son John Alexander becoming a bacteriologist at Bradford's municipal sewage works. By 1911, she had a lodger. So, like her Filey widow cousins, she got by, and kept the marital home together.

26.5: Arthur Douglas – probably photographed at his marriage, in May 1902, aged 20. Three days into married life, he and his brother Richard had drowned off Ravenscar. *[FA]*

Social Capital

This was a world away from Margaret Shippey's experience. Those fisher widows whose husbands had been unable to make contributions to a friendly society's insurance policy faced an insecure future. One does not need to be too cynical about the male psyche to appreciate that a self-sufficient widow was a better prospect in the remarriage market than a woman like Margaret, whose impecunious existence was summed up by that 1871 Census entry, a widowed tag-on at the end of a married daughter's family.

The emerging 20th Century welfare state made things no better. Widows of share fishermen were excluded from the contributory state pension scheme set up in 1925, a situation only remedied 25 years later by the postwar Attlee government.

The more children a widow had, the less likely presumably she was to receive a fresh proposal of marriage. Sarah SAYERS was left with four youngsters after husband William drowned in the Great March Gale of 1883. Women who could, or would, not remarry often faced a long widowhood. In Sarah's case, it ran to over 38 years. Ann JOHNSON's lasted from her husband's drowning on *Mary* in 1896 to her death in 1951. Like many fisher widows, she survived by charring.

Some women lost husbands so shortly after marriage as to become 'widowed brides', cruelly back at the same church, but in black rather than white. These stories made good copy for the *Filey Post*, but the reality was that remarriage was far more likely for them than in the case of a middle-aged widow. William JENKINSON (P34) drowned off a corfe in March 1867 (page 121). He had married Jane CAPPLEMAN on Christmas Day 1866, less than ten weeks before his death. Without children, she could at least make a fresh marital start. But the most dramatic example of instant widowhood was that of Mary COLLEY, just 18 when she married Arthur Douglas in May 1902, three days before he drowned. A daughter, Maud, was born shortly afterwards, but lived for only six months.[16] Mary remarried to bricklayer's labourer Benjamin Simpson COLLING in 1911, perhaps determined to avoid a repeat of the emotional trauma.

Income

Some women benefited from the providence of a husband's contributing a few pence a month to one of the friendly societies. Unfortunately, such dues were unlikely to pay for much more than the funeral and funeral tea. Of Staithes, Clark was told in 1975-6 by a man in his seventies that in the past 'the poorer class o' person often had to spend his last penny paying for everything'.[17] A callous observer might say that the 'lucky' ones were those whose husbands were never found, and who were therefore spared the funeral expenses and the cost of the smoked ham, 'funeral bread' (fruit cake) and Madeira cake . . . or drowned in a big disaster, preferably during the visitor season, or near Christmas.

The dramatic loss of the coble *Mary*, in full view of the fishing community and just 11 days before Christmas 1896, generated a relief fund able initially to pay the three bereaved families annuities of over a pound a week, though this fell away as children became wage earners. In January 1897, the *Parish Magazine* listed what the fund could now afford to pay. There was no respecting the privacy of these bereft people – everybody knew what they were living off, and each of them would have to live with the judgment of their less sympathetic neighbours, should they indulge themselves even slightly:

---

[16] *Yorkshire Evening News*, 28th May 1902; *Redux*, 27th May 2018.
[17] Clark (1982) pp131-2.

Total sum collected £320 0s 0d. Mrs Skelton whose youngest boy is 8 years-old will have 8 shillings a week for 6 years. Mrs JOHNSON whose youngest girl is only 1 year-old will have 4 shillings a week for 12 years. At the end of these periods, the children may then be able to work for themselves. These payments will exhaust £240 or £120 each. Mark JENKINSON, father of the drowned lad, will have 5 shillings a week for 4 years and Mrs JOHNSON senior, mother of one of the drowned men will have 2s 6d a week for 5 years.

In contrast, the *Trio* fund a year earlier only offered five pounds per annum for the six families, since five of the six were insured with clubs – offshoremen commanded higher earnings. If there were children of working age, a woman could just about keep a home together. She would need to char, or work for another fisher family. Ann Watkinson WILLIS (née Day) had lost her husband John in 1903 when he had become tangled in the rigging of the herring coble *Wild Rose*. She too went charring to support her five young children. Son George worked as a golf caddie, but also made a seasonal income on Filey beach.

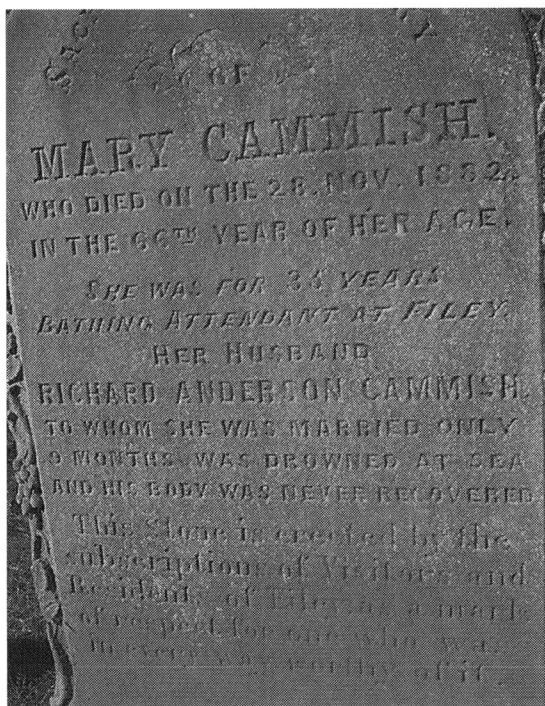

26.6: Surviving widowhood - one of the most remarkable gravestones at St Oswald's is that of Mary CAMMISH, bathing attendant/well-woman for 35 years. She really did have a life marred by misfortune. Married in 1843, but for just nine months, Fate arranged an especially ironic end for her - being knocked down by a runaway 'bathing machine' on Crescent Hill, and dying of her injuries. It cannot have been a painless death, given the likely state of pre-NHS end-of-life care in 1882. *[JC]*

JS Wane described George WILLIS in 1908, none too sympathetically, as

> the boy sand artist who we have known since 1904. I threw a penny down to him. He had drawn on the sand the notice of a woman suffrage meeting to be held at 3pm near the bathing vans in addition to the usual tale about his father being drowned.[18]

There was paid work helping fishermen with insufficient women. And 'well-women' like Mary CAMMISH (**26.6**) could earn coppers carrying kegs of water down from Church Well to the cobles and visiting boats. In summer they became bathing attendants, bringing down water for bathers to wash themselves down; and there were 'Ladies Conveniences Attendants.'

For some women, the worst of circumstances could be ridden by a combination of luck and steady work. Mary JOHNSON (née CAPPLEMAN), somehow had enough capital to open a 'goodie shop' (ie sweets) at 35, Mitford Street, despite the most unimaginable family reverse. When *Trio* disappeared in 1895, she lost not only her husband, Thomas Avery, but also their teenage sons Frank Cappleman and William. Despite the loss of three incomes, Mary's takings were evidently enough to bring up three small children. The earnings of two older daughters, in service, could hardly have contributed much. Her son, Thomas, was 12 when his father disappeared, and his earnings as *Postman Tommy* would subsequently have been indispensable (page 287).

Homemaking: Ruling the Roost

Chapters 25 and 26 confirm that working women were one of the most exploited groups in 19th Century Britain. But other than the women who worked in coalpits, still legal until 1842, fisherwomen must have had *the* hardest of lives. Unpaid ancillaries when unmarried, their wedding day passed them seamlessly into the same round of mind-numbing drudgery, much of it now pregnant, with perhaps a season or two away at the herring fishery beforehand. But were they passive victims of their harsh economic lot? One 1970 account of English herring girls who started the season in Scotland indicates that they were anything but:

> They came from places such as Scarborough and Hull in search of adventure. Although they worked hard, many managed to find husbands. The girls were lodged in organised digs ruled over by morally austere landladies. . . . their language according to my grandma would even shock the men but they had a fantastic sense of humour.[19]

We can only guess if any Filey women were the subject of such observations. But Old Town women certainly resembled these viragos in that they were definitely not

---

[18] Born in 1897, George would have been just seven if he began his beach artistry in 1904, his youth no doubt evoking much sympathy.

[19] Ron Freethy, *Memories of the Yorkshire Fishing Industry* (Countryside Books, 2012) pp13-14.

some feminist archetype of a subjugated walkover. Just listen to this 1958 recollection of the Filey fisherwoman:

> Her manners were of the rough and ready description, her dialect a lingo not to be understood of the inland people, but having a cadence of its own. It was a primitive dialect, full of keen idioms, and strong descriptive words, with a dash of salt-water phrases and remarkable capacities of objurgation [harsh criticism]. He would be a bold man . . . who could stand for five minutes of fire of a Filey flither girl's tongue, even if not enforced by a sprinkling of empty shells from the collective forces of the sisterhood.[20]

Fisherwomen were made of stern stuff, but muscularly charitable. Deborah Valenze has suggested they were the ones who formed the links with the wealthier classes of the town or village, collecting for good causes, and distributing the proceeds throughout the fishing community, especially after sea disasters.[21] No doubt they targeted the wives of the local elites, hence the close relationship that had clearly evolved between Filey fisherwomen and Dr Wheelhouse's widow, already noted. The arrival of Primitive Methodism gave them an extra goad to conscience. We noticed in Chapter 22 how *Nan Jenk* and Mrs Jane Kirkpatrick Gordon used this prod to excellent effect. Canon Cooper reckoned that this robust altruism was seen during the two great storms of 1880 and 1883, which had marked the first years of his ministry:

> . . . the women were even more anxious about the saving of life than the men were, and in one case where the Lifeboatmen hesitated to face the dangerous sea, the taunts of the women, who called them 'cowards' drove them out against their will.

Cooper had been told that when in 1902 Arthur Douglas had been knocked off the family coble *Margaret* by a swinging boom, a mile off Ravenscar, his brother Richard had told his father as he jumped in after him that 'he dared not face his mother without him.' This sense of obligation may have been enhanced by him being three years older, and skipper. Facing the women back home, Cooper thought, seemed to have been an abiding fear for Filey fishermen:

> I remember one mother listening to the account of the drowning of the other brother told by another. The mother asked with infinite scorn 'How come you to survive?'

It was clearly a common feature of seafaring family dynamics. One mother and son had fallen out after he and his father had been shipwrecked off the Welsh coast. He alone had survived, the rupture only being mended when the drowned father had 'come again' to assure his widow that their son was blameless.[22]

---

[20] 'The Flither Girls', *Scarborough Mercury*, 2nd July 1958.

[21] Deborah M Valenze, *Prophetic Sons and Daughters: Female Preaching and Popular Religion in Industrial England* (Princeton University Press, 1985) ch11.

[22] SMHC; Cooper (1893) p30.

Bell Taffy

So, when we encounter, time and again, strong, determined women in Filey Old Town we should not be surprised – it was in their DNA. And few match the description better than *Bell Taffy* CAMMISH, whom we met in Chapter 21, a victim of the deadly practice of kin-crewed boats. She lost a husband and two elder brothers when *Unity* went down in May 1892. The crew of the herring coble, alas, may have been no different from most inshoremen, for the four widows and 13 orphans were 'totally unprovided for'.[23]

Poor Isabella was, like so many Filey widows, left to bring up a young family. In this case, there were six children, the eldest just ten years-old. The sixth, Richard Cammish *Snosh* JENKINSON (R88) was probably born posthumously, since the press refer to five fatherless children. Here was a woman who must have had dollops of something, for with no regular annuity, and six young children, she managed to remarry three years later, to a man eight years her junior - and to have two children by him.

Making toffee, incidentally, seems to have been a common Filey matriarchal accomplishment, for like *Sal Tiny*, *Bell Taffy* was known for it, hence her by-name. That aside, Isabella had had to assume a male role perhaps as the surviving parent of six, for her refusal to accept a stereotypical identity was legendary. In later life, she cut a daunting figure in Queen Street, in black cap, black apron, black bombasine dress, and a little black shawl if it were a Sunday. She wore glasses and smoked a pipe. 'Everybody used to get out of the way,' we were told, and it took a brave person to call her *oul four een* as Esther HOGGARTH had the nerve to do. Daughter of *Ranter Jack* CAMMISH, *Bell Taffy* no doubt inherited very robust genes. 'The hardest woman I knew,' one near-neighbour told us.

Other Filey women didn't fit a Victorian shrinking-female template. When Sarah Jane JOHNSON (née HUNTER) died in June 1939, the *Filey Post* reported how she had been 'an ardent supporter of local football'. Two wreaths placed on the grave came from 'The Football Club' and 'The Supporters' Club'.

George Burton knew the *Buggins* family well, being a neighbour on Providence Place. With grandchildren living with the old couple[24], it must have been a full house. *Old Jossie's* wife, *Pris*, however, was a firebrand who 'could straighten them up: her word was law up that yard with the kids, the bairns and the old man an' all'. With an extended family to control, in a confined space, robust management would have been essential.

Such forceful female qualities may not solely have been a question of individual psychology. In the north-east of Scotland, the economic importance of women to the fishing household has earned these fisher families the title 'matriarchy'.

---

[23] *Leeds Mercury*, 2nd May 1892.

[24] George *Old Jossie* (P91) and Priscilla JENKINSON, née Scotter.

26.7: Men and women relaxing on equal terms, 1894. It is rare to see women doing nothing, as well as their husbands, but notice that two women are hard at work with washing at the other end of the Cliff Top, and all three of the other women have their sleeves rolled up! Perhaps they are taking a break from washing too. *[Peter Croft]*

To quote Thompson et al (1983, p177):

> Their responsibility for both preparation for the fishery and sale of the catch gave women a clear practical basis for power. 'Them that sell the goods guide the purse – them that guide the purse rule the house.'

A very similar analysis was offered in 1885 by a Filey circuit minister who rejoiced in the especially memorable name Robinson Cheeseman:

> All the household management is left to them; indeed they seem to have a genius for financiering; the husbands being well aware of this, are content to leave this vital branch of household economy to their wives, well knowing that it will be duly cared for.[25]

The fact is that in a different age these women could have managed without husbands. Yet I know of no case in Filey to equal that of Milcah Lawrence, the mysterious Flamborough sorceress we met in Chapter 22, ghoulishly spending St Mark's Eve in the churchyard hoping to divine which of her neighbours would soon be freshly underground there. Unsurprisingly, *Milkey* never married, and actually

---

[25] Robinson Cheeseman, 'Primitive Methodism among the Filey Fishermen' (*Primitive Methodist Magazine*, 1885) Vol 66 (*My Primitive Methodists* website).

proved that feminine self-sufficiency was entirely possible by working in the mid-19th Century as what we would now have to call 'a fisherperson'. Details are sparse, for she was clearly pushing the envelope beyond anything that the local census enumerator could comprehend. Her occupation was therefore left as blank! But what a fascinating case study she could prove to be.[26]

There were of course many different balances of power in these Old Town marriages. It is often said that men marry their mothers, but Jim *Buggins* JENKINSON (Q91) was the exception to the rule. If his mother, Priscilla, was the *Jenk Alley* firebrand, his wife Violet May was the complete opposite. Despite the *Buggins* family's venture into the glamorous world of seaside seal showmanship, Jim's income was always uncertain. In summer, he went salmon fishing and 'pleasuring' (he was well-known to the visitors). Violet May was a devoted wife who thought the world of Jim, even though she had to keep in full-time work to keep the family afloat. 'He's a wonderful fellow to me,' she would tell George Burton; 'by - I was lucky to get him. Do you know, he allus pays for beef.'

And that, George told us, was his sum total to keeping the house. 'Them's the sort of wives you want,' George concluded. We finish this look at the lot of Filey Old Town wives with one delightful tale, the subject of which is best left unidentified, beyond his membership of the Fishermen's Choir. Jim Haxby explained in 2006 how the wife of this ideal husband was setting off out - *Black and White Minstrels:*

'E said, look, yer know I go to choir practice, don't yer? 'E says, tell yer what, get yer coat on and I'll tek your sister . . . . Drop yer there, I'll go to t'practice, go to *t'Star* fer a drink or two, pick you up and we'll come back. So, he did this. When he came out the gale were in north and it were swillin' down wi' rain. Alec Gibson 'ad a car then, says c'mon I'll give yer a lift up. So he jumps in, this is 'ow absent minded 'e was, 'e jumped in, dropped 'im off at 'is 'ouse, 'ad a cup o' tea and went to bed. Checkin' 'is football pools and their daughter came in. Everybody in? He looks round. Where's yer mother? She says she went out wi' you. Good God, 'e says, I've forgotten 'er. Surely she'll stop where she is tonight, she won't come up 'ere while mornin'.

'Owever, after a bit 'e was gonna turn the light out, front door din't bang, the whole 'ouse wrapped itself round wi' such a crash whitewash kem off ceilin' onto bed. 'E 'eard runnin' upstairs. The last step, she tripped ovver it and as she was laid on floor, oilskins, sou' wester and sea boots an 'all on 'er, he looked over 'is glasses and said, don't mek me any tea, love, will yer? I won't tell yer what she said.

The fact that the 'hero' of this yarn was clearly the original narrator, and probably with some glee, may say more about male perceptions of 'good marriages' than any other source!

---

[26] Friend (2010) p208.

27 FILEY CHARACTER AND CULTURE:
1: LYING APART FROM THE REST OF THE WORLD

'. . . forming the apex of a triangle lying apart from the rest of the world.'
Canon Cooper (1886) describing Filey's remote location at the tip of its promontory.

This chapter, and the next two, hope to catch the feel of Old Filey, pulling together a number of threads to get as close as we can to its very special essence.

1 '. . . most favourably situated for preserving its primitive character'

This was Canon Cooper's verdict six years after taking up his benefice. Things didn't change quickly. As recently as 1958, the *Filey Advertiser's Directory* suggested that nobody came to Filey unless they have 'cause for doing so', since the main road from Scarborough to Bridlington by-passed the town completely. Penetration from the outside world was slow: though the York-Scarborough road was gradually improved by a turnpike trust after 1752, it seems to have taken 30 or more years for the whole 52 miles to acquire a decent road surface.[1] As more people took the waters after 1826, when Scarborough's spa company was formed, those seeking the peace and quiet, 'free from all vulgarity', came the further nine miles for a day or more at Filey.

And Filey *was* remote. Most communication seems to have been by boat along the coast (**27.1**). Inland travel was slow – in the 1840s, just before the railway arrived, the stage coach took 11 hours to drift from Leeds to Scarborough via Filey. Twenty years later, Bridlington minister George Shaw reckoned Filey was just as remote from human awareness, despite the new railway - a letter from a neighbouring county addressed to 'Filey near York' took six months to arrive, having been to *New York*, USA! And even in the north of England, an enquiry at a railway station booking office 'not fifty miles from Leeds' was met with the response: 'Who knows anything about an outlandish place like Filey?'[2]

Old Filey wasn't the sort of place to go out of its way to attract visitors. Preacher John Oxtoby told one potential helper in 1824 that he had better not come

> unless he could put up with a 'cawd taty' tea (cold potato) for supper, and a 'caff' (chaff) bed to sleep on afterwards.[3]

Local people rarely strayed far from home:

> Ah dee'ant gan banboskin about leyke sum on 'em, ah stick to 't'heeaf . . . .[4]

---

[1] Cooper (1886) p30; (1908) p10; KA Macmahon, *Roads and Turnpike Trusts in Eastern Yorkshire* (East Yorkshire Local History Society, 1964) pp28-9.
[2] Shaw, *Rambles* (1867) pp9, 114.
[3] Matthew Denton, *Primitive Methodist Magazine* (1883) p662.
[4] Cooper (1900, p19) reckoned this was a phrase in use as recently as 1880.

27.1: Geographical remoteness – virtually everything reached Filey from the sea. Coal is being discharged from this square-rigged collier by means of a hoist. Oxen seem to be ready to haul the chaldron up to the village. Though the drawing could easily date from the 1700s, the initial traces of the New Town dates it to the 1850s. *(FA)*

As late as 1908, Cooper could write of a woman in a village just a mile and a half from Filey Bay who had never seen the sea. How much more self-contained must the district have been a century before? People had little call to go very far beyond their immediate environment: even the top end of Queen Street was 'foreign territory' in childhood, an elderly native told us in the 1980s.

Filey knew little of the outside world, beyond what was bellowed out by the Bellman/Town Crier, or passed on in the sermons of the more widely-travelled preachers.[5] Offshoremen saw a few harbours, maybe 100 miles away, and even coble men probably journeyed out to sea further than they ever did inland. What cause did they have to visit the cities their catches went to? One Filey man who perhaps did more *banboskin* than most was Matthew *Brazzy* JENKINSON (P46).

---

[5] The last Town Crier, Robert Stork, still going strong at 80 in 1902, used to announce 'concerts, meetings and shows, as well as acting as a lost and found agency and arranging, in stentorian voice, assignations between anonymous young ladies and gentlemen. One wonders how many hopefuls turned up after hearing "A gentleman wishes to meet a certain lady in Church Ravine at 7 o'clock . . .".' *(Victorian Filey,* undated typescript, 1970s, Filey Archives).

A classic *Brazzy* story has him going down by train to visit an ill relative in London. Arriving in seaboots at King's Cross, and without a clue where he was, he approached the first policeman he saw with the question: 'can thoo direct me to our Mary Lizzie's?' *Brazzy's* grasp of geography of course was notoriously weak. Jim Haxby had a grand story which must have come down the family.[6] A group of fishermen was on the Cliff Top, one afternoon in 1899, waiting for the old *Scarborough Post* to be delivered by the man on horseback. It cost a penny:

> And *Brazzy* used to wait 'till somebody bought one, 'e never bought one. 'E says, owt in it, Bill? Bill was lookin' through it and all of a sudden Bill says, we're all gunna be killed, we're all gunna be killed. 'E says, calm down, what's matter. 'E says, Boers 'ave started war in South Africa. 'E says, don't you worry, Bill, we'll win am sure o' that. We will win, all them foreign countries like Grimsby an' 'artlepool will come an' 'elp us.

2 'I do not presume to understand one-tenth of what is said' (Pettitt, 1868)

Arthur Pettitt was watching the *flither* gatherers returning to Filey Station:

> Numbers of friends welcome their return . . . [a] merry, many coloured, chattering, throng that crowds around the railway truck and then breaks up in little parcels, of warm the hearts and helping hands.

Every 19th Century visitor was as uncomprehending. Canon Cooper was intrigued by the dialect of his fisher parishioners. 'When I first came to Filey, twenty years ago,' he wrote in 1900,

> the fishermen seeing my vacant stare when they addressed me in their own tongue, would hasten to add, 'bud as thou'd say.'

And then they would translate. Significantly, he noted that other 'natives' of the parish simply did not know these dialect words. There is no better way of remaining remote than speaking a different language. Cooper's now little-read *Guide* is full of the Scandinavian usages that both fascinated and bewildered him, and contains some delightful thousand year-old echoes of the speech of the original Danish settlers – like the poignant tale of the Filey fisherman, taken terminally ill at Bridlington Quay, who asked simply to be buried 'in Filey garth'.[7] As late as the 1980s, the town's fishing families were still using Scandinavian dialect terms like *laik* for 'play/lark about', as well as more obscure

---

[6] Mary Elizabeth JENKINSON (R58), Jim's mother, was *Brazzy's* great niece.

[7] Cooper (1900) pp19-21. *Garth* was Old Norse for 'yard, enclosure', in this case the churchyard. Cooper relates how King Christian VIII of Denmark, aware of the number of Danish words extant in Yorkshire but extinct in their country of origin, commissioned in 1846 a professor to collect such living relics of his kingdom's lost linguistic past – eg the Yorkshire 'Ridings' derivation from Old Norse *thriding*, 'three-thing'. See Cooper's *East Yorkshire Dialect* chapter in *Across the Broad Acres* (1908).

phrases and words - like *all-uh-wand* as an expression of surprise, *wear-be-or-zit* - to whom does it belong, *skellit* - a pan, and *ewn* - an oven. There has always been a tradition at Filey of Viking origins, which Storm also found amongst older families of Robin Hood's Bay. Cooper had recognised as soon as he arrived in the parish that this was a linguistic heritage that was disappearing. He seems to have started to record it right away:

> How I opened my eyes when a woman told me her son was nothing but a *shack back*, and not until this year did I know its derivation to be from *shack* the Danish word to rove. *Slape* is from *slebber*, which means slippery. A *runty* ie short man, is from *ryndel*, meaning a little heap (Cooper, 1886, pages 32-3; see caption, **25.3**).

Within 20 years of his arrival, he was noticing that many of the dialect words commonly used in 1880 had become rare. The spread of newspapers and elementary education took their toll. By the 1930s, if the Primitive Methodist ladies were composing a dialect piece, someone had to 'go and ask *Old Bella*'. Isabella JENKINSON née Wheeler (1872-1957) was the local expert.

But dialect didn't vanish overnight. As late as 1914, there is a story about Filey fishermen from the Naval Reserve on York station, waiting for a train south. It was during that feverish period when rumours were rife about Russian reinforcements for the Western Front.[8] The Filey men, speaking in their broad and unintelligible dialect, were supposedly taken for Russian soldiers. As late as the 1980s, Filey fishermen were still occasionally nicknamed 'Filey Russians'.

3 'Uniformly Civil to Strangers'

Despite this long history of isolation, Sokell's 1899 *Guide*, a kind of *Hitchhiker's Guide* to this vanished way of life, deemed Filey people 'possessed of kindliness with much civility and trueheartedness'. Outsiders would be treated with courtesy; for if you 'put yourself in a communicative turn of mind',

> depend upon it, if you are from John O' Groats or Land's End, you will begin to feel by the second morning of your appearance . . . you are no stranger, and begin to imagine that they had known you, and you them, all your life.

Those who failed to abide by this basic rule, however, could be dealt with more rudimentarily. *Jack Black* JENKINSON (P93) was a street sweeper known for terseness of speech. One day, early in the 20th Century, he was hailed by two Leeds chaps in a motor car. 'Hey, granddad, come here,' one called impudently, 'can you tell us the road to Scarborough?' 'Aye,' replied Jack, 'if you go to the bottom of this road, you'll see a signpost.' Sensing the opportunity for further mickey-taking, one asked him, 'but what if I can't read?' 'Then it'll just suit a grand bugger like you,' came the reply, 'there's nowt on it.'

---

[8] Foreign soldiers had supposedly landed in Scotland, indisputably Russian because they had 'snow on the boots'!

Those in motor cars with pretensions to grandeur generally elicited hardheaded treatment. One party of visitors got in some difficulties in April 1907 when driving onto the beach at Primrose Valley. Having stopped to take photographs they found the car was sinking in the sand, and the tide was coming in:

> Fortunately, help was at hand in the shape of horses drawing of fish carts, and an urgent request for assistance was made. The cartmen clearly saw an opportunity not to be missed and made a bargain by which the party was required to purchase the total load of fish before rescue would be attempted.[9]

Generally, however, Filey was infinitely more civil to visitors than Staithes, where the leisure and tourism hospitality ethos had clearly yet to be fully embraced. According to one 1904 observer, it was

> less than fifty years ago that the fisherfolk were hostile to a stranger on a very small provocation, and only the entirely inoffensive could expect to sojourn in the village without being a target for stones.[10]

In contrast, visitors to Filey were impressed by the homely disposition of the people in this backwater. George Walker visited probably just before 1814 to sketch local dress, and commented that they were 'a hardy, industrious race':

> From the little intercourse they have with the world, there is a singular simplicity in their manners and deportment, and their behaviour, though unpolished, is uniformly civil to strangers.[11]

Half a century later, Anglican clergyman Mackenzie Walcott (1862) came to a similar conclusion:

> Every place has its characteristic, and that of Filey is its hardy race of fishermen, stout, broad-chested, wide-shouldered; blunt and honest in speech, but kindly-hearted and open to every advance of truthful interest on the part of strangers.

This altruism towards strangers reflected a strong sense of community in the Old Town which was itself mirrored at sea. The offshore fleet sailed together, docked together in 'foreign' overnight harbours, and - when fishing - stayed close enough to help boats in trouble. The inshore cobles were sometimes more solitary, skippers desperate to keep secret the location of good grounds.

But the hazards of launching and beaching demanded communal experience, and team effort. Primitive Methodism probably encouraged what already was second nature in Filey. Kendall's account of the Great Gale of October 1869 gives a particularly poignant example of such a sense of camaraderie that went far deeper. Richard Haxby, skipper of the *Unity*, insisted that he and his son should stay on the wave-swept deck to man the tiller, whilst the crew took refuge in the cabin:

---

[9] Fearon (2008) p61.

[10] Gordon Home, *Yorkshire Coast and Moorland Scenes* (A & C Black, 1904).

[11] George Walker, *The Costume of Yorkshire* (Robinson, Son, & Holdsworth, 1814).

> Now some of you have a wife and young children dependent upon you, I have a wife that I well prize, but no young children . . . besides, you are not ready for another world. I and Francis are insured for eternal life, therefore lash us to the tiller and you go below where there will be less danger.[12]

In a trade that has always had by far the highest rate of fatalities of any occupation, this willingness to risk one's own life for family members and crewmates was coded in the fisherman's genes. There are other examples, but so many must have taken place unreported, in disasters that no one survived.[13]

27.2: The treatment of the sole survivor and 12 drowned crewmen of the Italian barque *Unico* is almost certainly characteristic of the Filey fishing community. *[Redux]*

This spirit of humanity extended to strangers imperilled by the sea. On Friday night, 4th September 1908, John S Wane recorded in his diary how he had heard 'about a hundred men [who] must have clattered past before I fell asleep.' Next day he learned that a young woman had been cut off by the tide. 'Every man in the fishing quarter turned out in boats and a woman was found in a dying condition.' There was of course no prospect of salvage payments to muddy the charitable waters.

In the case of seamen wrecked in their bay, the response of the town's fishermen was especially selfless. Dr William Cortis, who had known the fishermen of Filey for 20 years, famously wrote to *The Times* after the Whit Monday hurricane of 1860, to emphasise how deserving of help they were. They risked their lives in lifeboat rescues, and frequently looked after survivors in their own homes. Cortis must have visited the fishermen's cottages when treating the shipwrecked men: 'a more industrious, sober, well-disposed set of men cannot be found if you search the Kingdom through,' he judged.'[14]

After the Italian Barque, *Unico*, was wrecked on The Brigg (16th January 1871) the sole survivor, Litano Maccouchi, was found sitting on a rock, 'fearfully

---

[12] Kendall (1877) p30. This tale is an instance of the snowball accretion of myth. By 1899, Kendall *himself* was writing that the 'Haxby Brothers' 'tied themselves to the mast of their fishing boat' and sending the crew below deck. It sounded dramatically classical, as when Ulysses wanted to hear the enticing, deadly song of the Sirens.

[13] Men who died trying to save relatives included Richard Douglas (1902) and Richard Ferguson *Sorta* CAMMISH (1948) – see ch17.

[14] Quoted in the *Scarborough Mercury*, 9th June 1860.

bruised and bewildered, and shivering. Two fishermen carried him over rocks and to the *Ship Inn*, where every care and comfort was bestowed upon him.' Funerals of foreign sailors were always well attended and treated with great respect by fishermen, wreaths and flowers being commonplace. The gravestone for 12 Italians lost off *Unico* was paid for by local subscription.[15] There were other instances of Filey hospitality proffered to survivors of marine disaster. Take the account of a man given accommodation in Norway by a former mariner:

> He had once been master of a vessel, and alone of all on board had been saved from a watery grave by Filey fishermen. By the wreck he had lost everything, yet he got a fresh start in life owing to a collection of £20 having been made for him in Filey Church.[16]

How then can we square these testimonials with the darker reputation that Cooper drew attention to, the superstition that it was unlucky to save a drowning man, that strangers had an evil eye? 'The old people,' he wrote, 'could tell tales of men nearly dragged ashore, and then, by the advice of the elders, abandoned to their fate lest ill fortune should result from saving them.' Cooper also quoted the dubious authority of George Crabbe, whose dour poetry obsessively dwelt on the topic of the wrecking by coastal populations of boats for plunder. Living in his native Aldborough, Suffolk, Crabbe wrote in 1778 of locals waiting on the shore, and 'as the waves run high, On the tost vessel bend their eager eye'.[17]

Unsurprisingly, Cooper shared the opinion of the nonconformist ministers Shaw and Woodcock, whom we encountered in Chapter 22, that it was the Great Turnaround of 1823 that had civilised Filey. But like them, Cooper failed to appreciate that folk culture changes only very slowly, and if such predatory 'wrecking' behaviour had existed before 1823, there would have been traces of it surviving years afterwards. I'm far more inclined to believe that it was in the interests of any coastal settlement to have a reputation for benign charity, on the grounds that what goes round comes around. A kind of maritime trade unionism bound seafarers together, solidarity and mutuality being the only way that anyone had a chance at sea. In the later 19th Century heyday of the North Sea sailing trawlers, fishing boats were described as 'the lifeboats of the offshore':

> the lives of hundreds of sailors and passengers, British and foreign, were saved by fishermen who considered it all in a day's work. One smack set out from Yarmouth three times and each time was back within a few days with a crew of a wrecked ship; the skipper was heard to mutter that he been warned by his owner to stop catching Dutchmen and bring home a few fish.[18]

---

[15] *Driffield Times*, 21st Jan 1871 (*Redux*, 16th Jan 2018; *Scarborough Mercury*, 6th Nov 1880).

[16] Cooper (1908) pp28-9.

[17] Rev George Crabbe, *The Poetical Works of the Rev George Crabbe*, Vol I (John Murray, 1834) p47.

[18] Dyson (1977) p166.

And as we saw in Chapter 7, nobody could accuse North Sea trawlermen of any great Christian turnaround! We should also note that there were genuine bonds with other fishing stations. Terence COLLINS told us how *Old Titch* JENKINSON (R85) as a young man, was drifting off Staithes one foggy night. Finding a local boat at sea, the Filey men called to it to ask if there were any fish.

> 'None' came the reply; then, as an afterthought, 'who are you?'
>
> 'Filey', they answered.
>
> 'Get your nets down, there's plenty here.'

And this was *Stears*, with its well-known distaste for strangers. But let us remember that most contentions have an alternative perspective. It is after all rather difficult to square a Filey reputation for welcoming strangers with the dismissive treatment meted out early on to many of the Norfolk *joskins*.[19]

4 The Natural World

People who are embedded in community and well-disposed to their fellow men often have a sense of connectedness with their natural surroundings. It would be anachronistic to liken the Old Town community to 21st Century eco-warriors, for when starvation threatened, Filey men would go trawling despite their timeless hostility to its destructiveness. Yet there was a rootedness in the natural world that seems appealingly enlightened; and a healthy respect for the moods of the sea, the fishing seasons, the weather cycle, and even the random swings between bounty and shortage. Nature's rotations and rhythms were understood and complied with.

The sun was *the* reference point – along with the meets of the landscape and seascape, it gave direction. It told the time of day, and year. 'I was born on the day the Sun got the other side of the Head,' one Filey woman had been told by her mother. She was referring to a specific day in September, for after the longest day, the sun retreats southwards in the sky, rising over The Brigg in June, but over Flamborough Head by September. At Nairn, any boat leaving the shore and needing to turn would do so with the sun in a clockwise direction, or risk alienating this natural order.[20] Jim Haxby characteristically summed up this compliance with the natural world:

> In a coble you had six fishings, six different ways of earning a living through the year. We were farmers. As a farmer farms his land, various things coming on through the year, we farmed the sea and if it had been kept that way there'd have been fish water deep today. But the trawlers came . . . .

Terence COLLINS quoted a traditional Filey saying, 'sons to come after, and sons after that'.

---

[19] See above, pp68-9.

[20] Cooper (1900) pp26-7; Barron (2009) p64.

28 FILEY CHARACTER AND CULTURE: 2: ENGAGING WITH THE WORLD

1 Hardheadedness and *Laikin'*

Having lived in Lancashire all my life, I must be careful how I phrase this section. Call it stubbornness, persistence, determination and add a dash of competitiveness – and we have what I might diplomatically call Yorkshireness.

28.1: Three generations of a characterful JENKINSON family group, early 1920s. **L to R**: *Old Brazzy* (Matthew, P46); *Benny Hoy* (Benjamin Cross, R59); and *Dicky Hoy* (Richard Cammish, Q45). *[FA]* The upwards trajectory of the three generations can be judged from the three Filey addresses at which each died:

Matthew	1929	3, Richardson's Yard
Richard Cammish	1946	50, Mitford Street
Benjamin Cross	1965	37, Station Avenue

What is not in doubt is the hardheaded work ethic into which every Old Town child was immersed from toddlerhood. Around 1930, William CAPPLEMAN, aged about 13, was helping Billy Cullan, a coble fisherman who lived next door on Ravine View at the bottom of Queen Street:

> . . . they used to tek twelve lines, four for each and a lot of the lads used to carry the lines down to the coble landing, carry two lines down and carry two lines up and you had a pair of yokes which fitted over your shoulder. And you left school at twelve o'clock, ran like hell home, bolted your dinner down, took your pair of yokes

and down on the coble landing with a pair of lines and then hope that the coble you 'ad was ashore, then you got your pair o' lines and carried them up; you had to be back at school by quarter past one.

And schoolgirls worked just as hard, as Ann Hartas testifies:

I used to skein a quarter bag of mussels before I went to school for me granddad [Charlie ROBINSON] and helped to pull and straighten lines on Clark ashphalt [end of Mariner's Terrace and Hope Street] for him too. My gran used to send me down to Coble Landing on a Friday after school to fetch fry up for tea bloody cod was bigger than me sometimes used to put my hands through its gills and walk back up to Mariners Terrace with it on me back with a bit of sacking on me back (*Photos of Filey, old and new,* Facebook, 2019).

The *Sled* JENKINSONs (**28.1**) had both work ethic and hardheadedness in abundance. Matt *Brazzy* had no children, but was uncle or great uncle to a whole fleet of enterprising descendants of his brother *Dick Sled* (Richard Cammish, P44). We have already encountered *Brazzy's* nephew, *Dicky Hoy*, Filey's 'top coble' on account of 'that booook'. *Dicky Hoy's* second son, Ben Cross, seems to have decided that fish-selling was the wiser career choice in the lean 1920s.

We have no way of knowing if the core Primitive Methodist belief in each man's Calling lay behind the dedication of successful Filey men. Though religious conviction may have originated habits of diligent application, these may simply have become central to a family's culture long after any derivation from godliness had been forgotten. If success is to be measured by bank balance, then there was certainly some link between the town's wealthiest family and Primitive Methodist faith. John ROSS for example was 'a devoted local preacher and class-leader' and father of Thomas, founder of the multi-million Ross Frozen Food Group.

But along with this work ethic, there was a rich, irreverent strain of mischief, *laikin'*, which was never far from the surface. Remember *Billy Calam* and his 'Crown of Peter' line? One of my favourite Filey tales, full of sociological revelation, concerns an episode, sometime around 1900, and is told by Cooper (1910, pages 51-3). A small band, hired for the season, performed daily on the bandstand in the seafront gardens. The musicians were in the habit of taking a half hour interval, 'round the corner', which was a euphemism for the nearby pub. Several young fishermen were hanging about 'by the railings of the gardens',

in the hopes of booking some visitor for a sail on the morrow, or on the off-chance of somebody standing them a drink. They were not as a rule allowed in the gardens, but during the half-hour's interval, the officials as well as the band were in the habit of going round the corner. They wandered in, and one of them began to 'strum on the harmonium'.

Others took the example, and in a few minutes the violins, violas, 'cello, and double bass were in the hands of fishermen, mimicking the actions of the musicians as best they could, while another seized the cornet, and, by dint of swelling out his cheeks near to bursting, managed to produce a few ear-splitting sounds . . . and, on the harmonium player taking off his hat, after the fashion of the leader of the band when a piece was specially applauded, a gentleman threw a penny into it.

Behind some windbreak shrubs, unable to see what was going on, sat a lady with 'no ear for music . . . a deficiency she by no means acknowledged'.

> When the sounds so wild and discordant began she recognised something from the ordinary music of the band . . . . 'What a note that trumpet has, to be sure! Those fishermen are handy men,' she said to herself. 'Last Sunday I saw they relieved the minister of the Primitive Methodist Chapel of his duties, and conducted the service themselves - they could have relieved the organist too . . .'.

And in appreciation, she dropped into the hat the largest coin she had in her purse – half a crown (2s 6d). It represented maybe a day's wage to these young men. 'The average reader,' concludes Cooper,

> with an average ear for music, will think the foregoing impossible, or at least exaggerated, but it is strictly true, and goes far to account for the number of incompetent performers, with worn-out and cracked instruments, or who sing with tuneless voices, and yet year after year, make a visit to the seaside . . . and have a fair sum over to carry back home. No doubt something must be put down to the pence being given by those who wish to be rid of the nuisance . . . .

As with so many sources, it is the incidentals, the asides, that reveal what was taken as normal at that time. This short item, for example, tells us on the surface about the playful antics of 'off-duty' fishermen, and Cooper's low opinion of the seafront live music, of which he had, by 1910, been exposed to 30 excruciating seasons. But look at what else we learn – that fishermen hung around the rim of Crescent Gardens in the hope of selling a sail round the bay or cadging a drink; and that their alien presence in New Filey was tolerated as long as they did not lower its tone by entering the gardens themselves.

Also, 'officials' were likely to enforce this 'rule' (when they weren't in the pub) although by what legal authority is difficult to judge. Furthermore, the fishermen accepted this custom, and Cooper too, despite his good relations with the Old Town, seems to have treated it as an enforceable norm. Here is evidence that socially, Filey was indeed a tale of two cities, as we discovered earlier. Incidentally, we learn from this account, that the Union Street Chapel thought nothing of its services being 'taken over' by fishermen. Imagine that degree of congregational involvement at St Oswald's in 1900!

2 Liberal Politics

That strain of independence in religion, and irreverence towards the social elites, expressed itself politically too. Boys brought up under the influence of hardy, independent relatives, with very little exposure to any different cultural values, grew unsurprisingly into hardy, independent adults. They naturally objected robustly to any government regulation of their affairs. In short, they were by nature old-style Liberals, impatient of anything they saw as a meddlesome restriction of their personal liberty. For some, these instincts converted into a keen interest in contemporary politics. All the Filey fishermen were Liberal in sympathy – except one. *Old Naz* could be very awkward and stubborn, his grandson, Robert Hall, told us:

> . . . he was certainly not afraid of being different. Mother (*Sally Naz*) told me that he was at one time the only Tory fisherman, all the others being Liberals.

John *Ranter Jack* CAMMISH (**28.2**) was probably typical of many Old Town fishermen, combining robust Christianity with informed support of the Liberal cause. *Ranter Jack's* read of choice, *The Daily News*, had been founded in 1846 as a Liberal rival to Conservative newspapers like *The Times*. Its first editor, Charles Dickens, started a long tradition of pressing for reform – civil and religious liberty, wider popular education, and votes for working people. A cover price of 1d made the paper accessible, whilst communal reading (note the several photographs of men at the Fisherman's Look out) may have reached a much larger number of Filey men, but probably to fewer women.[1]

Before 1885, few Filey fishermen, and none of their wives, had the parliamentary vote. The town lay in the two-member constituency of East Riding, solidly if unrepresentatively Tory. In 1885, however, boundary changes split the constituency, and Filey came under the newly created single-member Buckrose.

One of the sitting East Riding Tory members, Christopher Sykes, son of a baronet, must have recognised that the Liberal Government's plan to extend the franchise deeper into the working-class spelt trouble for him and his party. This may explain his generosity towards his prospective voters (**28.3**). For Sykes had hardly been a vigorous MP. Between 1868 and 1892, he made only six Commons speeches, his only significant trace of activity being to champion the bill which passed as the Sea Birds Preservation Act of 1869. As a result, he earned the unenviable nickname 'The Gull's friend'.

28.2: *Ranter Jack* CAMMISH – 'He is a constant reader of the *London Daily News*, and watches with keen interest the political situation,' the *Christian Messenger* noted (1910/280).

---

[1] Lucy Brown, *Victorian News and Newspapers* (Clarendon Press, 1985) p31.

28.3: As the franchise widened, even fishermen became worth courting. Luke White, Liberal MP for Buckrose after 1900, gave the Filey fishermen new oilskins, probably in defiance of electoral law. But it is likely that this bedraggled scene dates from 1882, when a Tory predecessor, Christopher Sykes, set the precedent - John ROBINSON, c70, is clearly identifiable on the second row from the front, seventh from the left, fourth from the right, with distinctively white mutton-chop sideburns. Compare with **4.3**, c1881.

Perhaps the photographer wanted authenticity, hence the rain, and lack of smiles – or perhaps they were suspicious of his camera! *[FA]*

The Third Reform Act of 1884 had extended the franchise to about 60% of the adult male population. The new Buckrose constituency swung left, yet somehow The Gull's friend won – maybe the oilskins helped. But history was against him, and thereafter Buckrose returned a Liberal MP in all seven elections from 1892 to 1922. Surprisingly, the Labour Party never got a look in, despite being formed in 1900 to gain representation for the working man.[2]

This is hardly surprising, for Filey fishermen were Old Liberals, with little or no interest in the ideological changes that transformed the party after Gladstone. What use was traditional liberty, asked the New Liberals, if a man - and woman - could not vote, read, enjoy good health, or earn a decent wage in safe working conditions? But Filey men didn't want a bigger state to deliver this - we met their Old Liberal

---

[2] Henry Pelling, *Social Geography of British Elections 1885–1910* (Springer, 1967); *Wikipedia* entry, Christopher Sykes.

opposition to the 1883 Fishing Boats Act, and its requirements of proper reporting of accidents, and skippers having certificates of competence (Chapter 12).[3]

A tiny hint of the limited interest with which Filey greeted New Liberal progressive reforming politics is caught in JS Wane's September 1908 diary entry about a women's suffrage meeting on the beach. The mix of interest, apathy and downright hostility was probably typical of the whole country:

> The resolution was put and carried. I voted for it. Father abstained. We had left mother asleep on the sofa in our little Queen St parlour. Then came the questions. One fat youth asked, 'Can a Christian support women's suffrage,' and quoted St Paul. Other questions were, 'Do you want women MPs?'

Between the Wars, the Labour Party took away the Liberal Party's natural working-class voter base, and its support leaked away. But Filey always retained a vein of Liberalism, long after the party's national collapse. Ryedale, in which constituency the town then lay, famously but briefly returned a Liberal Democrat MP from 1986-7. Irene's mother, Elizabeth Jenkinson Allen, born in Filey in 1917, remained a Liberal supporter all her life.

Well into the 20th Century, there was a rugged individualism in the Filey fisherman that contrasted markedly with the subjugated condition of other workers in the same parish. In 1983, Terence COLLINS provided an illuminating story about the employment conditions beyond fishing, related to him by Irene's grandfather, William Thomas Hoggarth, who worked as a labourer for Queen Street builder James Sawdon.

> Now Hoggarth.
>
> Yes Maister.
>
> You're going to work at North Burton Grange. Do yer know where that is?
>
> Yesssss, *Click 'em.*
>
> *Click 'em*? What do yer mean, *Click 'em*, Hoggarth?
>
> Well I'll tell you. Billy Picken lives there, and he's maister over there . . . an' he'll come after dinner . . . twenty past twelve . . . you only have 20 minutes fer dinner . . . takes his watch out . . . and when it got te 19 minutes past he says, righto lads, click 'em. Get hold of your horses and out again.

And to that day, reckoned Terence, North Burton Grange was known as *Click 'em.* Just imagine *Old Naz, Dicky Hoy* or *Old Brazzy* putting up with that treatment off a farmer.

---

[3] It may well be, of course, that the most vocal opposition to the bill came from the skipper/owners, whilst their crew had nothing to lose. If this were so, then it would suggest a growing crystallisation of class differences amongst traditional fishermen.

3 Striking lucky

The Filey fisherman's lack of interest in a national welfare safety net may have been because the uncertainties of their trade prevented future planning. Many made no attempt to insure their lives with one of the town's several friendly societies - modest and seasonally unpredictable earnings often precluded that anyway. But it may also have stemmed from the devil-may-care recklessness characteristic of men who lead dangerous lives.

Share fishermen were convinced that one day, especially in the herring season, their number would come up in a good way. Herring fishing held a special excitement, for a boat might come to shore with a huge catch, when everyone else had found thin swims, and prices were soaring. Peter Frank catches precisely the surges of addictive adrenaline that such an utterly unpredictable trade generated:

> It is always in the back of their minds that they will strike lucky, 'get among the fish', and take the top of the market. Such occasions stand out, become talking points, and are savoured over and over again many years afterwards.

These monster bonus payouts became embedded in folklore. In the early 1970s, as an old man, Whitby fisherman James Cole could clearly remember drifting, back at the other end of the century. Deep in reverie with *Billy Butter*, the two of them recalled the 1907 season, when the three-man cobles each of them was on came into Whitby on a particular Friday morning with well over 100,000 herring:

28.4: Matthew *Matty Airy* Crimlisk, elegantly attired, as befits a man who has done well from two years risking German mines. Grandson of the founder of the Crimlisk line in Filey, any Irish luck ran out for him on *Emulator* in 1919, when he and his two sons were blown up without trace. *[Crimlisk One Name Study website]*

We landed 110 cran; and when we reckoned o' t'Saturday night we had £50 . . . . And we got £13 apiece, which was talked about. It was a *lot* of money . . . me and *Billy Butter* - he was a Filey man really - sat on t'pier just afore he died, he says, 'Dis tha remember that Friday morning, Jim?'

I says, 'Aye, I mind t'morning.' It was in the paper about a coble getting all that money in one week.[4]

4 Risk-taking

Steam and Minefields - ironically, in view of their natural conservatism, it can only have been this herring adrenaline that induced Filey men to take a leap into the future by buying and introducing second-hand steam drifters into the Scarborough district. 'Banks did not lend to fishermen,' recalled Terence COLLINS in 1983. 'There was no money for drifters, they relied on a "lord" or a *foy*.'

Unsurprisingly, it was again three descendants of *Dick Sled* who saw an eye to the main chance. *Sled's* son, *Billy Trummy*, William JENKINSON (Q46) and his young nephew, Richard Cammish (R53), partnered Matthew *Matty Airy* Crimlisk and bought *Emulator* in 1913, for herring and line-fishing. *Billy Butter* senior, whose son in old age was to reminisce with James Cole 'on t'pier' at Whitby, was next, but shrewdly rented the steam drifter *Lord Kitchener* before buying.[5]

The *Butters* were on the up, disposing of the yawl in which they had a half-share with 'a lord' in the shape of the Scarborough Sellars family, in order to buy *Lord Kitchener* outright. And by some chance spin of the roulette wheel, these Filey risktakers were in the right place to strike it lucky, at the right time and with the right boats. But for *Emulator* it did not end well.

Never was there a greater chance to 'get among the fish', and 'take the top of the market' than with a steam drifter during the First World War. The Admiralty saw minesweeping as a priority from the outset: trawlers in particular were therefore commandeered, along with their crews, and put onto mine clearance and anti-submarine work, on account of their size and power.

With much of the fishing fleet otherwise engaged, catches fell away, and dockside prices rose fast. There was no control of fish prices until 1918, and they soared, twice as fast as general food prices, which themselves shot up by around 25% per year. In Filey, flour was simply not available at times. Fish and chip shops closed. Even dogfish were now marketable:

---

[4] Frank (2002) p145.

[5] Scales, *A-Z Boat Index. Lord Kitchener* was the second steam drifter to be registered at Scarborough, but the first to work there. (The *Butters*, both called William Jenkinson Watkinson, also had the same by-name.)

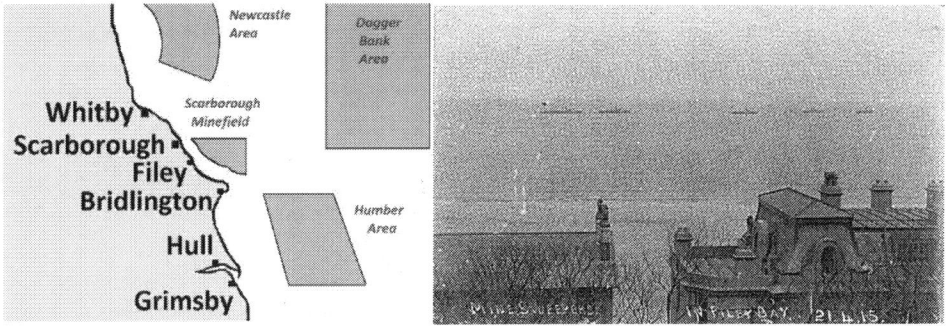

28.5: Left: Map based on the British Admiralty chart showing the minefields laid by the German Navy off the north-east coast during the Great War.

28.6: Right: Minesweepers in Filey Bay, April 1915, *Ackworth House* right foreground - 'one minesweeper lost for every mine swept.' *[Photo: FM]*

> According to *Fishing News*, Scottish boats working herring from Yarmouth during the 1915 season 'only had to go to sea and put their noses in the fishing grounds to come back with at least a catch worth £100'.[6]

Skippers and crews did well if they were lucky enough to be too old or too young to be called up immediately. *Matty Airy*, 42 in 1914, and *Trummy* 39, were in the Royal Naval Reserve, but it took two years for them and their boat to be needed. Boats over ten years old, and under 110 feet in length, had not been wanted in 1914, leaving many drifter owners free to take the risk of their lives. Largely undisturbed, the fish population in the minefields, and fish size, grew rapidly - and profitably, for chancers. *Matty Airy* and *Trummy* risked these precarious waters until 1916 - when the Admiralty requisitioned their boat for sweeping.

This new work really was out of the fishing frying pan and into the sweeping fire. The mines they dealt with were moored to the seabed with a length of wire or even sisal rope. The boats swept for the mines using wires to sever the moorings. Once these had floated to the surface, they could be detonated by gunfire. Unfortunately, as the tide went out, many mines might be within a boat's draught, the subsequent detonation often killing the whole crew of as many as ten.

The Admiralty banned fishing boats from the minefields in 1914, but relented in 1915, perhaps because of food shortages. Bans, however, had not been universally observed. David Smith summed it up in 1932:

> A fisherman said to me 'haddocks know nothing about regulations'. So they went where haddocks were to be found, and damned the consequences.

---

[6] This account of Great War minesweeping is taken from John Worrall, *Fishermen in WWI - Sweeping all before* (*Fishing News* website, Oct 2015); *ww1hull* website, *Hull's Minesweeping war*; and *Scarborough Evening News*, 1st Jan 2000.

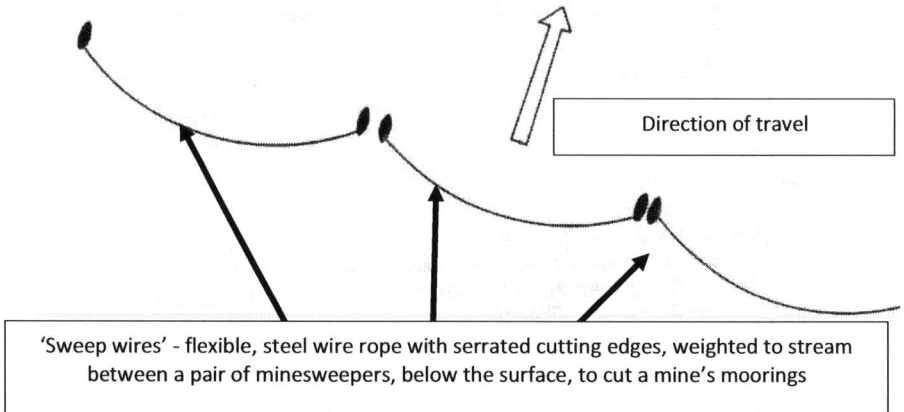

'Sweep wires' - flexible, steel wire rope with serrated cutting edges, weighted to stream between a pair of minesweepers, below the surface, to cut a mine's moorings

28.7: German mines were moored below the surface, designed to be exploded by a passing vessel. This early method of minesweeping, 1914-16, shown above, involved 'tandem pairs' of trawlers, 800 feet apart, three pairs abreast, thereby clearing a lane 2,400 feet wide. Drifters, less powerful, worked closer together.

Whether fishing or minesweeping, fishermen took a huge risk, and this increased dramatically as U-Boats laid more mines, and German technology grew beyond the ability of sweepers to detect and remove them. In all, 670 fishing vessels were lost from the Humberside region alone, 214 being minesweepers. A single U-Boat, UC-47, of the new UC-1 class, sank 56 British and allied ships in just 13 months – one a week.[7] Captain Sydney Smith quoted an old Scarborough saying, 'one minesweeper lost for every mine swept.'

Yet somehow, luck held for *Matty Airy* and *Trummy*. But ironically, having been at sea throughout the War, and minesweeping for two of the years, *Emulator's* luck eventually ran out, and on its first peace-time fishing trip from her home port.

Scarborough Harbour had been closed again by the Admiralty in 1917, to prevent the loss of fishing boats, so the drifter had fished out of Grimsby after release from minesweeping duties. By April 1919, *Emulator* was back in Scarborough. On the afternoon of Tuesday 15th she set off for the fishing grounds to go line-fishing in the old way, with drifters *Fear Not* and *Tryphena*. Accounts then differ. We spoke in the early 1980s to Tommy Flynn, deckhand on *Fear Not*, quarter of a mile to the starboard. About 26 miles off Flamborough Head, *Emulator*, came round and cut in between *Fear Not* and *Tryphena*.

---

[7] *Independent*, 7th Aug 2020.

At this point, there was an immense explosion. Tommy Flynn saw it all:

> . . . it shook the boat we were on . . . we thought it was really us. She just blew to pieces . . . we never saw anything - just maybe an odd basket or something - but no wreckage . . . everything went.

The *Hull Daily Mail* (17th April 1919) seems to have got its account from *Tryphena*, which was back first:

> shortly before ten o'clock on Tuesday night they heard a terrific explosion in the direction where they last saw the *Emulator* fishing. They missed the *Emulator's* lights, and later, whilst cruising round, discovered traces of oil on the water, but there was no sign of any crew. A search was made at daylight by the *Fear Not*, but nothing could be seen, and after getting in their own lines the two drifters returned to port.

Either way, 66 tons of boat had completely vanished, along with all her crew. Like most drifters, *Emulator* was made almost entirely of wood, and could offer no resistance to 20-odd pounds of explosive. This truly was a family tragedy in the old Filey way. Three of the crew were sons of the two owners, being too young to be conscribed, and had probably been with them since 1914. Skipper *Matty Airy* died with sons Wilfred (19) and Tom Robert (16).

28.8: A Fisher studio portrait of Richard Baxter COWLING (*Dick Fipney*) deckhand on *Emulator,* and his wife Alice née Bayes. She was left with their seven children. *[FA]*

Mate *Billy Trummy* died with 15 year-old son Thomas Castle JENKINSON (*Toye*, R67) and nephew Richard Cammish (R53) son of his elder brother *Dicky Hoy*. Richard Cammish junior had only recently returned from the Mediterranean where at just 21 he had skippered a minesweeper. The seventh man, just back from service with the Royal Navy, was Richard Baxter COWLING (*Dick Fipney*) a cousin of both *Trummy* and *Matty Airy*.[8]

The other Filey risk-taker, *Billy Butter* Watkinson, was known as a capable and lucky skipper. As his drifter was not immediately needed, he had a few months to risk fishing in and around the North Sea minefields before active service. And of course, he had a state-of-the-art steam drifter.

---

[8] *Redux,* 22nd April 2018.

28.9: The Dardanelles, spring 1915 – the Allied fleet tried to force this strait, intending to land forces in order to take Constantinople. The Turks had lain ten lines of mines under German supervision across 'The Narrows', two miles wide in parts. Yorkshire trawlers and drifters, acting as mine-sweepers, were part of the naval force. The mines were the reason for the fleet's failure. [*Wikipedia* entry]

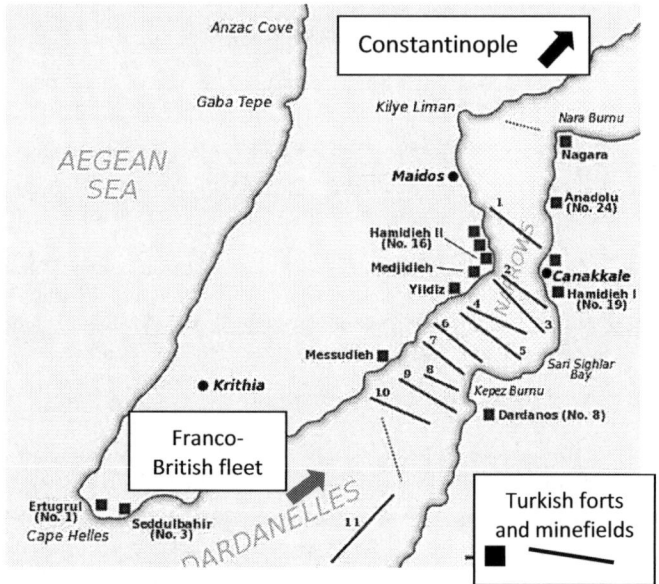

As a naval reservist, he, drifter and crew were inevitably requisitioned eventually. They were dispatched for minesweeping duties in the abortive Dardanelles campaign (1915). Ironically, *Butter* survived the mines both in the North Sea, *and* the Dardanelles Strait (guns too), but within two days of landing in Portsmouth he was ill, and he died a few days later, at the Haslar Military Hospital, Gosport. His funeral, at St Oswald's, was that of a war hero, and may have been one of the largest ever attended in Filey. Figure **28.10** shows how these early steam drifter entrepreneurs profited, financially at least, from their abandonment of sail, and their gamble with the German mines, though three of them lost the ultimate stake.

Filey's Last Yawl - another man who took the ultimate risk of wartime fishing was Mark Scotter, co-owner with son Reuben of *Susie*, possibly one of the last yawls to be built on the east coast, and by 1917 the last to be fishing. These were even deadlier times, as stakes were being raised: the especially effective 'Super-Weapon', the Type UC-1 mine-laying U-Boat, was now in service, and the German submarine fleet had recently resumed unrestricted attacks on merchant shipping. Much ill will was in the air.

In April 1917, nine year-old Sydney Smith witnessed the infamous surfacing of a U-Boat close to the Foreshore at Scarborough. It opened fire, a shell cleaving a woman's leg off as she leant on the seafront railings. 'There was a lot of bitterness,' he said. 'If they'd been caught, they would have been lynched.'[9]

---

[9] Sound recording 14621, Imperial War Museum (produced 1994). Available online.

Testator	Died	Value of effects	Equivalent in 2017
William Jenkinson Watkinson *Billy Butter*	1915	£2,915 11s 10d	£171,997.17
Matthew Crimlisk *Matty Airy*	1919	£1,798 19s 6d	£52,274.08
William JENKINSON *Trummy*	1919	£1,529 4s 0d	£44,435.03

28.10: The profits of steam - probate valuations for the estates of the Filey men who first risked abandoning sail. In contrast, the estate of deckhand Richard Baxter COWLING came to a mere £41 3s 4d (2017 value £1,196.21).[10]

The Germans had also begun sinking fishing boats, coming close to the British coast to do so. The crew were normally removed first, the boat either being shelled or scuttled, for the UC-1 class had no torpedoes. As the U-Boats treated even the smallest three-man cobles as prey, the lone yawl's crew must have known that their 38-ton, 61-foot boat, visible for miles if in sail, was a compelling target. The Admiralty had sent Yorkshire trawlers away from this danger area, to fish off northeast Scotland, after especially heavy losses in 1916.

In such circumstances, rocketing fish prices really had drawn the Scotters and their crew into a deadly situation. *Susie* was now one of the biggest fishing boats at sea on this coast. On 17th August 1917, she was line-fishing ten miles out of Scarborough, with three of her crew tending lines in the corfe, completely vulnerable. At this point, UC-16 surfaced nearby. The captain must have assumed the yawl was an armed 'Naval Trawler', engaged in minesweeping, an entirely legitimate target. There were several operating out of Scarborough at the time. Indeed officially, *Susie* was described as a trawler, of the Mercantile Marine Unit. UC-16 opened fire with her deck-mounted Maxim machine gun, hitting Mark Scotter fatally in the head. Scuttling charges were placed below deck, and the crew dispatched in the corfe with the skipper's body. They were picked up by *Billy Butter's* old drifter *Lord Kitchener*, still risk-taking though in new hands.

The Navy had commissioned a number of armed drifters ready to take on U-Boats, and this will explain why UC-16 opened fire so peremptorily. David Smith (1932) heard a bizarre story of one coble skipper who risked lining in a prohibited area in the hope of good wartime prices, but lost far more than he profited. As he was hauling in his lines, a drifter appeared nearby, and a U-Boat surfaced. The unsuspecting coble ended up hauling-in slap bang in the middle of a naval battle. The coble skipper was later fined £32 10s for fishing in a prohibited area, and for obstructing the drifter in the execution of her duty by being in the line of fire.

---

[10] For an explanation of probate valuations, and how modern equivalent values can be calculated, see Appendix D.

28.11: The yawl *Susie* in Scarborough Harbour - a photograph of 'lasts'. The last working yawl at Scarborough; probably the last great herring season, 1913; the last known image of a Filey offshore sailing crew on board a yawl; and the last known photograph of its doomed skipper, Mark Scotter. **L to R**: Mat Wright*; Bill *Coddy* CAMMISH; Mark Scotter*; George *Brittany/Britner* CAMMISH (standing); *John Willie* JENKINSON*; Reuben Scotter*.

Those marked with an asterisk * were to be on board on 17th August 1917 when *Susie* was scuttled by a German U-Boat, its skipper Mark Scotter being killed by a deck-mounted machine gun. This photograph has been published before, in mirror image, but the position of the Old Pier, with slipway at the north end of the Old Harbour, confirms that *Susie* was moored port-side, facing north, as shown. *[Photo: Rev JSW Stanwell; FA]*

In 1918, four motorised fishing vessels were sunk by U-Boats – *Botha*, *Brotherly Love*, *Honora* and *Coronation*. All were crewed by Filey men.[11]

Sunday Schools, Sandwiches and Cinemas

Let's round off this grim section on a lighter note. Great War German U-Boat captains were often at pains to counter the 'murderous Hun' image invariably presented by the British popular press. George William *Tewy* HUNTER was yet another Filey man who liked to live dangerously, provocatively naming his 1916 motor herring coble *Edith Cavell*. The Germans were sensitive about that name, for it commemorated the Norfolk-born nurse who had become a symbol for the Allied cause, widely used on recruitment posters in Britain. In what might best be

---

[11] *Scarborough Mercury*, 24th May 1917; David Scotter, *Spawned in Norfolk caught in Filey* (posted in three parts, *Looking at Filey* website, 2011).

described as a PR own-goal, the German Army had executed her in Brussels in October 1915, for her indiscriminate humanitarianism, an act which had provoked disgust in the USA, on whose neutrality Germany was relying.

Tewy must have been made of solid stuff – some fishermen changed partisan names to keep out of trouble. But *Tewy* sailed this floating affront to teutonic sensitivities the length of the Yorkshire coast, right under the nose of the Imperial German Navy's submarine fleet. (A modern analogy might be the waving of a Manchester City scarf at Old Trafford, when United were losing.) It was only a matter of time before he ran into trouble: the miracle was he got away with it for as long as a year. The end came on 5th May 1916, when *Tewy* was fishing off Flamborough Head, characteristically contrary to Admiralty advice in a high-risk area, known to be patrolled by U-Boats. It seems *Tewy* was a bit like that.

The captain of the U-Boat that finally sank *Edith Cavell* was remarkably magnanimous, being at pains to get the crew back to Filey for the following Sunday once he had learned that the skipper's son, George (*Young Tewy*) attended the Union Street Chapel on the Sabbath. Half the population famously turned out to meet the crew at Filey railway station when they get home.[12]

Interactions between German submariners and their Yorkshire combatants often have a comic flavour to them. In May 1916 one U-Boat captain captured *Osprey*, a Bridlington fishing boat, handed the crew coffee and cigarettes, and dispatched them in their corfe. 'Spurn Point is sixteen miles, west by north,' he told them:

> So it is a fine morning, you will land safely I hope. Here are some sandwiches I have had made up for you, and now good day, and remember, not all Germans are killers.[13]

Several U-Boats were reported as surfacing alongside Yorkshire fishing boats to ask for fish for their crews, although whether this was simply wry humorous Filey fantasy we will never know. One U-Boat skipper took wartime fraternisation to a bizarre extreme, allegedly rowing ashore at Scarborough under cover of darkness to watch a film at the cinema. After the War he produced tickets to prove he had done it. Another U-Boat captain claimed to have surfaced in the South Bay on a number of occasions to listen to bands playing in the Spa.[14]

Unlike *Matty Airy*, *Trummy*, *Billy Butter*, *Mark Scotter*, and the provocative *Tewy*, some Filey men did not dice with death and German U-Boats with an eye to the main chance. Some had had enough dicing in their early years to last a lifetime. William ROSS knew the sea's power - his father had drowned in 1851, when he was 12, and his brother, also Isaac in 1872. Add to this his own brush with death, aged 19, on that June night of 1858, when he survived the capsize of a coble, five

---

[12] Arthur Godfrey, 'Scarborough fishermen and the U-boats' (*Scarborough Evening News*, 29th Aug 1985); Godfrey (1974) pp44-9.

[13] Mike Wilson, *History of Bridlington* (bridlington.net website, 2008-18).

[14] Godfrey, 'Scarborough fishermen and the U-boats'.

miles offshore. The father of his future wife, Mary Ellen WILLIAMSON, had drowned in his sight that night, and two of her uncles had already died at sea. How could this family history *not* make him careful? In 1872, he inherited a half-share in the yawl *Tranquility* from his childless brother Isaac, and continued great-lining from it until at least 1911. William ROSS never risked steam, and certainly not the North Sea minefield.

His nephew, Thomas ROSS was similarly careful, but a risk-taker in other ways. He famously moved to Grimsby, as a fish merchant, and founded the food dynasty, which, by the 1960s, had turned the Ross Frozen Food Group into the largest trawler owner in Europe, with eight fleets. Yet Thomas never forgot his roots – he named his home at Cleethorpes *Filey House*. His grandson, David, has reportedly amassed personal wealth of £873 million.[15]

But Uncle William took no risks. Aged 76, his decision to have *Tranquility* broken up (1915) was possibly a shrewd acknowledgement that great-lining by sail was done – and anyway, scrap prices had risen on account of wartime demand for wood and metal. His estate was valued at a modest £331, a fraction of *Trummy's*, and *Billy Butter's*, but the photograph of him in middle age (**3.9**) catches him in his prime – a man with solid Christian faith, rooted in a supportive community, at ease in marriage, master of his own boat, and in a comfortable house. This was probably as much as he and most of his neighbours ever wanted. Which branch of the family – Grimsby or Chapel Street - got the most out of this life is a moot question.

5 Beyond the Horizon

Distant Drownings: St Abbs Head, 11th January 1891

I'm unaware of any attempt to determine how many Filey men joined the Merchant Navy or peace-time Royal Navy. The risks weren't much different. Robert Jenkinson WATKINSON, son of William and Mary (née JENKINSON, P79), appears on the list of drowned fishermen on the 1900 St Oswald's window (**10.9**). In fact, that he was one of 12, from a crew of 14, that had drowned off St Abbs Head when the cargo ship *SS Bear* sank after a collision. It was unglamorously carrying pig iron from Middlesbrough to Grangemouth.[16]

---

[15] *Redux*, 23rd Nov 2019; At his death in 1937, Thomas's estate was valued at £14,302 1s.

[16] Rarely can a woman have experienced quite so much adversity as Robert Jenkinson's widow, Annie Elizabeth née RICKABY. The couple had lost their three infant children in the space of just 10½ months (October 1889 to August 1890). Eighteen weeks after that last burial, their father drowned. Perhaps it was a mercy that Annie Elizabeth was one month pregnant, and that this baby somehow survived. Unsurprisingly she named him Robert Jenkinson WATKINSON, after his father.

The widowed Annie Elizabeth was taken in by her father, she and her little boy earning their keep in his bootmaking shop, 31, Queen Street. Her father's name, Jonah, may explain a lot.

Distant Drownings: Sacred Island, 15th November 1947

Another case that has come to light, this time through the *National Probate Calendar of Wills and Administrations*, and the researches of *Redux*, concerns William Cammish COLLING, who drowned in a shipwreck off Newfoundland in mid-November 1947.

28.12: Record card detailing the death of a Filey man far from home – William Cammish COLLING, the fourth generation of an Old Town fishing family, drowned in icy Newfoundland waters in November 1947. He had possibly been in the Merchant Navy since the 1930s. His second cousin, crewmate William Johnson COLLING, had attempted to rescue him. *[UK, Merchant Seamen Deaths, 1939-53, National Maritime Museum]*

Also on board was his second cousin, William Johnson COLLING (*Bill Bullocky*). They may have joined the Hull cargo boat together. *SS Langleecrag* was sailing to Quebec to collect a load of grain. But in the November dawn of the 15th, she 'bounced over rocks' at Great Sacred Island, Strait of Belle Isle, off the northernmost tip of the Canadian island of Newfoundland, and broke in two. His cousin was plunged into the sea and drowned, despite *Bullocky's* despairing efforts.

It seems that she became incapacitated by illness, for the 1911 Census found her in Scarborough Workhouse on Dean Road. She died there in November 1912, at the age of 46, just a few months after her father. Her only son, Robert Jenkinson WATKINSON, was killed in a night air attack on the Western Front in 1917. Fortunately, death had spared his mother their yet another heartbreak. *[Redux, 18th Aug 2017]*

William's body was recovered, and buried in a small graveyard at Flower's Cove, about 50 miles south-west of the site of the wreck.[17] Both men were away from Filey in September 1939, according to the *National Register*, so it is possible that they had been at sea for at least eight years – they could well have begun as Merchant Navy apprentices at the age of 14.

Survival on 'Monkey Island'

In later life, *Jacky* Wheeler lived on Spring Road, with daughter *Bella* and her husband *John Willie Jenk*. *Jacky* had started and finished a long working life as a fisherman, but had also been to sea as a mariner, probably in the 1870s/80s as the fishing decline set in. Bob *Lano* Wheeler told us the story in 1984:

> My granfeyther sailed three times 'roun the world in *windjammers*[18], bringin' grain from Australia. On the last one – an' this is a true story – they were shipwrecked off the West African coast. Well they got to shore, an' there were trees. An' lots o' inquisitive monkeys. Well we all had lots of chewin' baccy. 'Giv 'em a lump,' ses one chap. Well it sent 'em berserk. Shot up trees and pelted 'em wi' coconuts. And that's how they lived for six weeks.

Well, it probably wasn't an island, but the Filey men involved in this story might have appreciated the reference! I'll leave readers to judge its likely veracity. But it's a classic Filey story of crafty survival in a world that can throw just about anything at you.

---

[17] *wrecksite.eu/wreck* website; *Redux*, 15th Nov 2017. *Bullocky's* memories of the failed rescue attempt can be found above, p305.

[18] A commercial sailing ship with multiple masts - this was an informal late 19th Century term, used as a term of derision by steamship crews, rather like diesel locomotive drivers referred to steam engines as *kettles*!

1 Family

As organisational employment mushroomed in the 19th Century, fishing remained one of the few trades in which a man learned the skills from his father. Evidence taken by the 1863 Sea Fisheries Commission revealed that men were at sea by nine, ten or 11. They were 'fishing off the wall with a little land-line', according to Richard Haxby; and finding their sea legs well before that, if Colin *Dilt* JENKINSON is at all typical. Born in 1935, he was out on his father's motor boat just before the outbreak of war in September 1939, at the age of four.[1]

This was quite deliberate of course, for as Allison choicely put it in his 1856 *Guide*, it meant that they lost all dread of the sea:

> Hardy nurslings of Neptune are the men of Filey, rocked on the ocean from their boyhood . . . .

They were, as George Walker put it in 1814, 'inured from infancy to a hazardous employment and to boisterous elements.'

They were also inured to physical punishment. Terence COLLINS could remember parental cries of 'I'll smack oor arse!' echoing down Queen Street more than once. It was a harsh age, in which corporal punishment was common. And life at sea could be far tougher than homelife. Boys condemned to the living hell of North Sea trawling could be thrashed, tortured and even murdered by sadistic skippers, but 'family boats' might be no picnic:

> The old fisherman went to sea when he was eight years old. His father was not sparing in the rope's end, in the efficacy of which he was a firm believer, Robert and his brother Jim often carrying marks for days together.[2]

This description refers to a trawling environment, but we should beware of conjuring out of wishfulness a contrastingly idyllic picture of family coherence and male bonding at sea amongst the Filey family crews.

---

[1] William JENKINSON (N8) baptised at St Oswald's on 24th Sept 1786, reckoned in 1863 he had been a fisherman 'upwards of 70 years'; his younger brother John (N10) baptised 7th Aug 1791, claimed 'about 63 years'; William CAMMISH went to sea 'when I was 11 years old'. John CAPPLEMAN claimed in 1803 that he had been 'going to the Yarmouth fishing since 1758'. He died at 91 in March 1841, according to the Filey burial register, so can only have been eight or nine on this first voyage - see ch11. *Dilt* JENKINSON was a working fisherman with his Filey-born father Charlie *Dilt* (R2) by 1948, at the age of 13 (*Scarborough Evening News*, 24th Dec 2019).

[2] *The Allen and Truman Scarborough Fishing Families* (SMHC website). Robert Allen was born in 1824.

29.1: 'Hardy nurslings of Neptune', c1900 - **L to R:** 1 ?; 2 --- Mason; 3 ?; 4 Jack Wright; 5 Jack ROSS. Before 1870, there was little legal requirement for children to be at school, employment keeping them economically useful, and out of trouble. Of his 1920s childhood, William CAPPLEMAN describes fishing with hook and line, and being 'all among fishin' boats, going to Jack Chapman's shop where he built boats, and mekkin' wooden boats to sell, and Billy Guinn's shop when he first started with motor engines.' [FA]

Yet boys who have been brutalised or bullied by their fathers and uncles do not normally seek their company as adults, and virtually every Filey fisherman worked with these relatives in later life. We should also remember that these crews came home to women who were not passive or blind, for in crowded cottages bruises wouldn't be missed. Michael Fearon suggested to me that individual fishermen were respected in the town if they treated boys well at sea. Chapel membership may have been central to this. Also, I know of no accounts of grave physical abuse in such a Filey boyhood apprenticeship, and the photographic evidence, whilst limited (eg **4.3**, **7.5**) does not show cowering, frightened children.

Looking back from his seventies, in 2006, Jim Haxby gave an insightful account of what may have been a common father-son relationship:

> My father was the best friend I ever had. But, by he treated me, in fact I've said to my wife in this very room, I'm sick as 'ell of this. She says, get finished, get another

boat. But I knew my father wanted me as good as 'im. Don't think I ever was but I had 'im up 'ere, my father, that's how good he was, but, erm, this was their way. The fishermen set here they'd wrap up, they wouldn't stand for what we took. But we knew it was for our own good and when you look back, you know, oh, what men they were, what men they were.

Jim senior had a gentler side. Like his grandfather, the gifted preacher Matt Haxby, and his father Matthew Crawford, elder Jim too went out singing with the Filey Church Mission Band, as did his son Jim.

Not every father-son working relationship worked out as well as Jim Haxby's. I was told how one such pair fell out whilst midsummering, a notoriously hard-worked time. The son had been brought on board to make up numbers and was a reluctant recruit. The intensity of the work brought matters to a head, and in the end the father had to hold the door of the wheelhouse shut with his foot whilst his son brandished a knife outside.

Often, it is easier to discipline someone else's children than your own, and some men deliberately refused to take out their sons, to avoid having constantly to shout at them. Increasingly, the family crew in Filey became rarer as men told their sons to 'learn a trade first'. Yet crew cohesion survived, increasingly based on respect rather than on family seniority: 'You were loyal to each other,' Graham Taylor suggested, reflecting on the 11 years he spent on Matt Haxby's coble. Even if a man were taken on for winter or summer, 'you wouldn't finish in the middle of a fishing'.

The contrast with the family relations that came in the wake of the corporate trawling industry could not be more marked. Such visible evidence of its destructive effects that carried over into family life on land was simply absent in traditional fishing communities. At Fleetwood, for example, as traditional inshore fishing declined, and trawling increased, nothing could have been clearer than how separate and disparate the two communities had become. The five 'inshore' streets to the north of the town were occupied by families; trawlermen in contrast were often single men, more in the pub when ashore than in their lodging houses. An identical contrast existed at Aberdeen, where there were no community institutions amongst the trawlermen, whilst the incidence of domestic violence amongst those who were married far exceeded anything amongst the inshore families. Writing in 1886, six years into his ministry, Canon Cooper reflected on the moral fibre of the Old Town, writing that

> A fisherman never strikes his wife, or leaves her. The Divorce Act has never been taken advantage of in Filey. Blessed be the Great God![3]

Of course, even the most discordant couple might be careful not to brawl before the parish priest. So we can only hope that the following account of a mid-20th Century 'domestic' was not typical of the fishing community:

---

[3] Thompson et al (1983) pp90-8, 130-1; Cooper (1886) p37.

> . . . 'e'd been married and 'e gerra row with 'is wife and smashed all the 'ouse up.
> It were in Scarborough paper about it, she took 'im to court ovver it. And then, he
> said, like a fool, 'e said, after the divorce I married 'er again, then I divorced 'er
> again. That was the sort of bloke 'e was.[4]

Not every Filey family got on perfectly, of course! One coble fisherman told me
how he once asked for a job:

> 'I believe there's a berth going.'
>
> 'Can you ride a bike?'
>
> 'Tom, what do I want a bike for, to go to sea in a boat?'
>
> 'To ride up and get our lad out of bed.'

Rather more serious was the bust-up between two half-brothers, probably in the
1930s – they and the reminiscer had better remain nameless. They had to spend
hours filleting together in a shed:

> They didn't get on well . . . had an argument one day and one stabbed the other
> with a gutting knife . . . a hell of a goin' on about it . . . it never got to court, they
> made it out to be an accident . . . one brother had irritated the other so much . . .
> It was a hospital job for a day or two . . . . They hushed it up.

Any work in confined and dangerous conditions, in unsocial hours, could tax
working relationships. But given that coble fishermen were forced into the
company of just one or two others, with all the additional strains of any family
disharmony, you had the seeds of potentially explosive situations. It is, perhaps,
again diplomatic to conceal the identities involved in this next account of family
strife at sea, related by the Haxby brothers, and to be found in Filey Museum's *Oral
Interviews, 2005-6.*

The story concerns two brothers, with tough reputations, 'allus at sea, bad weather
and any weather,' reckoned Jim; 'two of the hardest in Filey', his brother Dick said,
and having been at sea with them, he knew. Family discord at sea could get
dangerous, for there was no walking away from it. Here is Dick's account:

> If there was two boats at sea, we were one of them. I'd just got married, 1953. I'd
> been in keel boats at Scarborough for over ten years. I'd finished with them and
> come back 'ere. Well the difference in the humour and everything. You could 'ave
> a bit of a joke with seven men and if you couldn't do a job there was always one to
> 'elp yer, but when you got into a Filey coble, them days, it was hard, winter time.
> But I was with two fellers, you were expected to be as good as them, I was onny
> twenty-four. They were big drinkers . . . and one Christmas they were drinking all
> Christmas week. And the New Year's Day they said they would go to sea to mek
> sure they didn't get any more drink. . . . as we were going down bay, you could
> realise the tension, they didn't want to go, they knew they were missing the
> drinking, but they were going.

---

[4] It is probably diplomatic to name neither the subject of the tale, nor its originator.

In this difficult atmosphere, the brothers disagreed about where there'd be fish, after a week's break.

> It was an old-fashioned saying 'a fish don't ring any bells'. You 'ave to tek pot chance, pot luck. Well, before we got to Bell Buoy, they started arguing so much. They were telling each other how much they had in bank, we can go back now if you wan. They started swearing at one another, playing 'ell up, and I'm stood in middle.
>
> All of a sudden, the chap for'ard fetched the prod out . . . pokes his brother in the belly with it. Nearly knocks 'im ovver. He teks the tiller off rudder and takes a swipe at 'is brother. If it 'ad 'it me I'd 'ave been goin' yet. They knocked off using utensils and they locked together in the midships of the boat, scrappin'. They fetched blood. They 'ad 'ooks in their 'ands.

Dick had been warned by his predecessor, 'fetch the boat ashore and go 'ome', if they ever started fighting.

> So I did summat I'd never done in my life before, I steered the coble back to shore, turned it round, pushed it ashore as best way I could, and they were still fightin' in bottom of boat. I got out of t'boat, got me bag and was goin' 'ome. The old men that 'elped you on with wheels . . . they said, ' 'ave you broken down lad?' I says no we 'aven't broken down, there's two in coble breaking down. They're breaking one another up.

Dick went home, determined to finish with the brothers, but within half-an-hour there was a knock at the door:

> . . . [he] said, come on, we're goin' to sea. All forgotten. I said no. I've finished. He said no it's all right come on. Well, I wanted some wages, so I bent and went back. And I stopped eight years. Two nicer fellas as you could 'ave . . . . But they both liked their drink.

These explosions of violence were exceptional. Somehow, every crew had to rub along, or no one caught any fish. Cooperation was key. Smith (1932) noted how men could agree to take it in turns to sleep in a salmon coble – once the net was shot, and the boat anchored at its end, there was nothing more to do. And in salmon season, men could be tired and irritable, having probably been out spawing and crabbing already, getting no sleep.

Older men managed best - Tommy *Laffy* JENKINSON (Q108) went out for years with one other man, probably his brother *Watto*, in the 1930 salmon coble *Joan and Robin*. Even men who prized their own way, like the brothers Thomas Robert and Richard Cammish JENKINSON (Q44, Q45) became consummate salmoners, despite regularly falling out whilst fishing. For decades, this alpha-male pair, *Old Naz* and *Dicky Hoy*, improbably lived as neighbours, at 57 and 59, Mitford Street, fishing together in *Daybreak* for a similar length of time.[5]

---

[5] Robert Hall, grandson of *Old Naz*.

One suspects that it was the archly-resourceful *Dicky Hoy* who had learned how to handle his contrary elder brother.

Robert Hall's cousin, Thomas Jenkinson Watkinson, remembered *Old Naz* and *Dicky Hoy* as 'a thrifty hardworking pair, who owed no one and were proud of their heritage. They were strong silent men not given to many words who kept aloof from their fellows and minded their own business.' They were Robert's grandfather and great uncle. He remembered as a child going out salmon fishing with them. His last memory of this venerable pair was of him

> . . . sitting quietly in the boat whilst the two elderly - more or less retired - gentlemen got on with their work. I was fascinated by the rhythm of their rowing.

Silence at sea was not uncommon. George Burton knew fishermen who went to sea together all their lives and never spoke to one another, other than 'give us that' or similarly necessary communications. They might even pass in the street a thousand times and never speak. This partly stemmed from a long-held belief that it was wise to say nothing when sailing out to sea, 'lest it should prove ominous':

> Whatever may from accident be necessary to express, is done by significant signs.[6]

Shaw had observed in 1866, as the corfe he was in 'looked on' a fleet of nets, that as the men rowed 'not a word was spoken.'[7] Perhaps this made sense, since empty conversation could be a distraction in a safety-critical environment. 'In a calm, under sail,' wrote David Smith (1932), 'a man learned infinite patience, that power to sit still and wait which the hurry of modern life tends to kill.'

Nowadays it might be called mindfulness, but being able to clear the mind and think about nothing was a skill mastered by most seamen, even those on relatively short voyages. It may well have been a way of being that was difficult to leave behind once back on shore.

2 'Got a Lartle'

Fishermen generally learned when to be quiet, not mentioning grounds kept secret in the family for generations, or the meets and marks that got them there. They said little about their catches - they did not even trust to the discretion of their vicar. 'Got a lartle,' was about as much as Rev Cooper could get out of them if he asked whether they'd 'got a good haul'.[8] Fellow fishermen were told little; outsiders nothing; officialdom even less.

An undated newscutting at SMHC, perhaps from the late 1920s, caught the Filey 'got a lartle' script very accurately. Inshoremen, the reporter explained, were annoyed at reports of their bumper catches:

---

[6] The Folklore Society, *Folklore of Yorkshire* (XLV, 1899) p48.

[7] See above, p110.

[8] Cooper (1900) p19.

> Filey fishermen are neither flattered nor too well pleased at the broadcasting of such figures as have been recently published and suggesting catches worth £10 per boat on some days, for they give to the world in general, and perhaps to the Inland Revenue people in particular, a false idea of prosperity.
>
> It must be remembered, firstly, that the last winter season was not a good one, and, secondly that during last autumn most of the fishermen, although they 'went off' in gales and fog, at great risk to life and tackle, did not earn more than 5s a week and frequently lost valuable gear, that had to be replaced.

It seems that the journalist had been well and truly hooked into being an apologist for these struggling fishermen! Old Towners had this veil of secrecy, especially with regard to fishing profitability, down to a fine art. The following exchange, between Professor Huxley of the 1863 Sea Fisheries Commission and 79 year-old William CAMMISH, who had lived in the Old Town most of that time, is a peach:

> Have you any notion how well the fishing population as a general rule stand here; are they doing well or are they in difficulties? - That I cannot tell.
>
> Have you no general notion, have you no idea at all? - It is not my business to interfere with regard to other people's circumstances.

Understatement was wired into the Yorkshire fishermen's way of being. If forced to reveal something, they were masters of creative euphemism. 'He's about ready for the North Ridin'' meant at death's door. 'Went downstairs' meant sunk. If asked what had happened to one of their missing fellows, the phlegmatic Filey reply, Rev Shaw noted, would be 'the sea gat him'. Storms were 'breezes'. Scarborough trawlerman 'Old Ben' summed up the Great March Gale of 1883, probably the worst of the century, as if it had been poor holiday beach weather:

> during the whole of the breeze it was touch and go with us - all the time it was 'just as near as mak's nae matter.'

This was a storm that killed probably 250 Yorkshire fishermen, and filled four Hull dock basins with crippled fishing boats that had somehow limped back from the Dogger. As with the extremes of active service in wartime, it is probably impossible to communicate the impact on a man's deepest core of a really violent offshore storm. This may well be why soldiers and mariners very often do not even try to talk of such searing experiences. But writing of 1883's Great March Gale, Ben reckoned some men might open up:

> Sometimes, if you know them well, they will take their memories back to the gale and tell of grim things that happened on the edge of the Dogger when many a son of the North Sea was gathered to his fathers.[9]

In general, Filey men avoided emotional declaration. Cooper (1900, p29) cites delightful examples of how any such outbursts of feeling could get a man to compromise himself, noting a gravestone extant 120 years ago, which bore:

---

[9] 'Old Ben', quoted in Wood (1911).

a deleted inscription in which a bereaved husband announced his intention to live in solitude. As time went on he thought better of it and took another mate, and so the inscription was rather out of place.

3 'There or Thereabouts'

Graham Taylor described Matt Haxby's rough and ready weekly accounting system (page 211). David Smith probably caught the 'cig packet' culture better than most offcomers in his 1932 account of the Filey inshoreman, 'Cobblemen'. 'Fishermen have methods of doing business with each other which do not commend themselves to chartered accountants,' he noted dryly.

Cash changed hands far less than in most economies, for money is only necessary in transactions with people you have no reason to trust, or are unlikely to see again. Neither was normally the case in a small fishing community. Smith seems to have relied for much of his information on John Matthew *Jossie* JENKINSON (Q89) eldest of the three *Buggins* brothers. After the Great War, this distinctive trio somehow scratched out an accounts-free living from sandpoking, trotting, and seal-exhibiting, at the very margins of the black economy. 'The system of barter is very prevalent,' Smith continued, recalling how a friend was delivered 'a barrow-load of codfish' in settlement of a £5 loan:

> Buckets of mussels are exchanged for lengths of line or anything else that is wanted, making the keeping of accounts almost impossible and entirely unnecessary, except for the satisfaction of tax collectors.

An economy based on fluctuating catches does not lend itself to taxation, and the traditional Filey fisherman saw it as an intrusion - one 'ancient mariner' with a spread of income, including lettings to visitors, told Smith he would be declaring

> My pension . . . that is all the money belonging to Government that I have got. I don't see that my private money is anything to do with them.

In many barter transactions, the phrases 'that'll do' or 'there or thereabouts' commonly settled an account, having the added advantage of leaving no paper trail. The unruffled philosophy 'there or thereabouts' was almost a way of life, extending far beyond this shadowy *gig* economy. Dick *Crackem* JENKINSON (John Richard, Q84), for example, drove the Hunmanby-Scarborough bus, and if a regular were not at their normal stop, he thought nothing of going and knocking on their door. His bus would get to its destination on time – 'there or thereabouts' presumably.

'They do as they have a mind,' Smith reckoned:

> The Board of Fisheries makes regulations for them which are obeyed 'there or thereabouts.' They are one of the few remaining bands of free men in a regulation-sick age. [10]

---

[10] Smith, 'Cobblemen' (1932) pp200-1; we met the *Buggins* JENKINSON family in ch18.

It may be hard to believe, but in the previous century, Filey fishermen had been even *less* amenable to civil obedience. Despite certain regulations on net size and close seasons for particular species of fish, Benjamin Simpson insisted to the 1863 Sea Fisheries inquiry that he had no firsthand experience of any inspection. And that was how the Filey fisherman liked it, even if the rules sought to protect him.

In that inquiry, Professor Huxley had questioned Edmund Crawford about the fact that Filey herring boats carried just one lantern:

> Did you ever hear of any law obliging you to have two?
>
> Yes, I have.
>
> Did you ever trouble your heads about it?
>
> I do not think we ever have.

Crawford was generally selective in the laws he obeyed: he was questioned about shooting herring nets from decked and undecked boats. Huxley reminded him how the law required these craft to be kept well apart, so that the larger yawls did not foul the operations of cobles. Crawford had never heard of this legislation. Patiently, the professor read out the relevant clauses verbatim: 'It is a very bad law,' Crawford told Huxley:

> If we rouse a shoal of herring in the water, then of course we will have our nets among them if we can . . . it is of no use going to land without herring.
>
> Would you rather take your chance of being fouled, in order that you may get what fish you can? - Yes.

How Huxley must have struggled, a well-intentioned, beneficent bureaucrat, convinced he was explaining a perfectly sensible regulation to a beneficiary of its wisdom. But instead he was confronted with a man who had absolutely *no* intention of being legislated at, even for his own good. Here was the very epitome of Old Liberalism. Truly, the newly evolving interventionist style of government represented a different culture.

The Commissioners had little time for men such as these whom they considered beyond the appeal of reason: 'fishermen, as a class, are exceedingly unobservant of anything about fish which is not absolutely forced upon them,' its report observed. Historians could not disagree. 'The fisherman was the last to accept any refinement of a technique that had served perfectly well. It could be said that the fisherman's virtue of persistence scored his brain, or that continuous hardship dulled his vision.'[11]

---

[11] Dyson (1977) p20. The *Report* and *Minutes of Evidence* that emerged from the commissioners' investigations is, in itself, evidence of the two non-contiguous worlds that government officials and traditional fishermen inhabited. For in all those thousands of pages, there is not one hint of the rich dialect in which the evidence was given. It was a miracle that anyone understood anyone else in those question and answer sessions.

29.2: A magnificently sharp photograph that oozes social history. Townsmen and fishermen, at the Filey Homing Pigeon Club's race from Cottingham, September 1920 - for the newly-landed 165 birds, many veterans of flights from the south coast, this was just a local flutter. Science has yet to account for the pigeon's near-miraculous homing instinct.

The real winners, however, were William Simpson, the 'great trainer' who seems to have been retained by most of the successful owners; and John Fawcett Potter, landlord of the *Star Hotel*, on Mitford Street, who will be counting up the day's takings on Sunday morning. White waistcoated, he is the tallest in the group, and probably needs to be – they look a tough lot, most home from the Great War for less than two years, and they will be spending much of the Saturday in his public bar. The barmaids, in white, will not be relishing the day, or earning, so much.

The fishermen seem mostly to be on the left – perhaps they drank in a separate bar? One or more of the smartly dressed men on the right could have been be keeping what would then be illegal books of bets, so that the men too could have a flutter. *[FA]*

4 Leisure

Given the competitiveness between boats at sea, it is no surprise that the same spirit permeated fishermen's recreational pastimes. The interest shown in pigeon racing, for example, was intense.

According to Nellist (1913) in May 1898, 57 Filey birds were released in Doncaster, the winner covering the distance home at a breathtaking 960 yards per minute, nearly 33 miles an hour. In 1900, the winning pigeon got back from Brighton in 12 hours. The suspense must have been massive: it is inconceivable that some illicit wagering did not take place. Only when off-course betting was legalised in 1960 could gambling emerge from the shadows.

Rather more sinisterly, there were 'repeated complaints of gangs of men infesting the cliff tops for gambling purposes', and in January 1908 the local press reported eight men heathenishly 'caught gambling at cards on the sands on Christmas Day', after PC Stathers had secreted himself behind a windbreak, perhaps on a tip-off.

This urge to bet could be applied to contests that involved extreme cruelty to animals. The following dark report probably represents the tiniest tip of a huge iceberg: for the regular activities of a horrible group of Filey men only came into the light after two participants were sufficiently appalled to squeal. And given the Old Town's *cosa nostra* philosophy, such 'grassing up' must have happened rarely. Perhaps it is as well for the many descendants of these reprobates that most are not named, so that the skeletons in ancestral cupboards are left unrattled. Anyone sensitive to animal suffering should consider skipping to the next page.

In 1864, sixty year-old Charles Coyle, of Gofton's Yard, off Church Street, appeared before Bridlington magistrates – his 'filthy' quarters were renowned for 'dog-fighting, cock-fighting, and the worrying of cats'. A rag and bone carter, Coyle was described unflatteringly in one newspaper as 'a dirty old son of Erin'. He seems to have been an inveterate mistreater of animals.

As a result of the distressing evidence that the JPs had to hear, he was sentenced to three months hard labour at Bridlington House of Correction – he had set several dogs on a cat, a source of especially distasteful entertainment for 'several young scamps residing at Filey'. An accomplice, William Featherstone, probably a Scarborough fisherman, 22, got away with a 45s fine. The details of the case are sickening. Two youths who attended had been so troubled by what they saw at Coyle's that they alerted the local Royal Humane Society. A member brought the prosecution. The young men, William WILLIS, c21, and William Wiseman, 22, both fishermen, confirmed that the regulars caught cats, and brought these to Coyle's:

> . . . it was not an uncommon thing for him to tie the cats to his bedpoles until a favourable opportunity arrived for torturing them to death, selling the skins, and giving the carcases to his dogs for food . . . .

Featherstone was a petty dealer in these skins. Perhaps they ended up as *bowls* and floats on some long-line. WILLIS described how on the night in question, 20 or 30 youths watched as a cat, delivered to Coyle's by one Tom JENKINSON, in a sack,

> was brought forward to the centre of the room and held by a string. Coyle held one dog and Featherstone another. The cat was partly worried by Coyle's dog, and finished by Featherstone's. Before the cat was dead it got away, while it was in great agony, and was again brought forward and two dogs got hold of it and were each pulling in opposite directions. The cat screamed loudly, &c., and died.[12]

---

[12] *The Bridlington Free Press,* 19th March 1864; *Yorkshire Gazette*, same date, both quoted in *Redux*, 15th Sept 2020. WILLIS died in 1865; Wiseman drowned in the Great Gale of Oct 1880, probably off the yawl *Sarah*.

Cruelty was never far from the early 19th Century surface, of course. We should remember that bear, bull and badger-baiting, cock and dog-fighting had only been outlawed in 1835, and were notoriously popular gambling 'sports'. Until 1868, it was still possible for people of any age to watch a public hanging in Britain. And before we judge too harshly, we should also note that it was perfectly legal in the UK for a pack of hounds to rip a live fox in half as recently as 2003.

5 Bonds across Time

In a lighter tone . . . we are omitting the Filey fisherman's main source of private recreation, pure reverie, a capacity to melt the present day, and drift into the past. In old age, men and women must have found solace in their declining years from a wealth of shared memory, virtuously compounded by the commonality of occupational experience, a resource denied to an increasingly large majority of us, as we live away from our birthplaces.

What joy for women of any age to sit on a doorstep, *callin'* and knitting, or for men looking out to sea from the bench at the end of Queen Street, using a lifetime's experience to identify the incoming cobles of a morning, when they were but specks on the horizon. 'That's *Tommy Laffy'*, some old timer would observe, when a non-fisherman would be unaware that a boat was even in view. And by an evening fireside, old men like *Brazzy* JENKINSON and Healand SAYERS might turn reminiscence into a field sport of combat. Graham Taylor remembers coming home some days to find his uncle, Matt CAMMISH, round to see his granddad. The two would have settled down 'to have a *yarn*: pipe smoke, smell of drink, plenty of it!'

29.3: Many of these men will have come up here as soon as they'd finished a morning's fishing, joining the retired men who had been competing to identify them when their cobles were the size of seagull chicks on the seascape. *[FA]*

These forays into the past often continued a long tradition of sharing 'Filey Death Tales', folk memory that, according to Cole, went back at least as far as 'The November Gale' of 1696. But perhaps there was even beyond that, a deeper, collective unconscious, reaching through scores of generations, back to the Dark Ages and beyond, as long as men and women had had language to yarn about storms on this coast.[13]

As with any community so rooted in the past tense, Filey's ancient parish churchyard seems always to have held an especially revered place in its heart. According to Terence COLLINS, speaking of his interwar childhood,

> that was Filey's walk then. On top of *Monkey Island*[14], Queen Street, down Church Hill, to the churchyard and have a look at the graves and say hello to everybody.

Many urban burial places are now visited only by the irreverent and loutish, toting beer cans, drugs and aerosols. In contrast, whenever I have been to St Oswald's yard, soberly-deporting families bring blooms, trowels, secateurs and respectful reverie. The graveyard is often bedecked with flowers, and this is no new phenomenon. Cooper noted in the *Parish Magazine* of March 1911 how delightful it was to see so many fresh flowers brought to the graves of dear ones. Unfortunately, there was a downside, for there were none of those ornamental flower pots now affixed as a standard accessory to modern graves: 'It is much to be desired', he wrote,

> that no tins bearing labels or advertisements be placed on the graves in the Churchyard. A few pennyworth of dark, olive green paint will soon make tins sightly and the flowers will look ever so much better in consequence.

Oh, and one other thing:

> Will they also kindly remove any dead wreaths or flowers?

The families in the graves and their visitors ran like the fisherman's long-lines through the stationary generations. As Michael Fearon has pointed out (2008, page 20) the population of 505 in 1801 was probably about the same as it had been in 1600. We know from earlier chapters it was the same core stock. Such constancy created an intertwining of families, and it was a source of pride amongst Filey's elderly to untangle them. In 1908, young diarist John S Wane recorded a conversation with the Lifeboat-house caretaker, about family history going back to the mid-19th Century:

> 'Ye stayed at JENKINSON's' he said, and explained at great length how he was related to the JENKINSON family.

---

[13] See above, pp47-8.

[14] *Monkey Island* – slang for the lookout at the top of a ship's mast; Filey's is the hill behind the Lifeboat house, from which there were uninterrupted views across the Bay.

Mary Elizabeth ROBINSON's skills in this regard were probably even better. In the 1980s, she could slot scores of people whom she had known up to 80 years before into their respective positions on our family group sheets. Cooper had an eye for this Filey sense of generations across time. In the July 1911 *Magazine*, he described the ox roast for the over-sixties, and the bonfire by which the parish had celebrated the coronation of George V on the 22nd June of that year. The first slice of the cooked beast was dispatched to Miss Isabel Rudston, aged 91, by the hand of Isabel WILLIS, aged three.

> If the child lives as long as the lady has done, we shall have linked together the year 1820 (the year Miss Rudston was born) and the year 1999.

The elder Isabel, Cooper noted, could remember the coronation of Queen Victoria in 1838, and the Filey ox roast that had accompanied it.

Filey's antiquarian-minded minister was not alone in prizing local heritage. In 1839, he recorded, a destructive modernisation programme had been inflicted on St Oswald's interior. 'Every ancient feature was obliterated', Cooper lamented. Any medieval decorations on the walls were lost under many coats of whitewash. It seems that there was an image of 'an ecclesiastic' in the south wall of the nave, believed to represent a boy bishop who died in office. It was

> only preserved from demolition by the promise of a pint of ale to the destroying workman. If you look at the shoulder of the figure you will see the mark where the pick had already fallen.

It was the parish clerk, John Fox, the father of the monumental mason John Sumpton Fox, who had intervened with the beer bribe.[15]

6 'Fair teems it down'

'In the matter of temperate habits they stand at an immeasurable superiority above those of their own class at Flamborough and Scarborough; tea is their strongest drink, and sweet-cakes are their favourite food.' Walcott, 1862

The town had of course had a reputation for hard drinking as its principal leisure activity, as Cooper admitted:

> 'The eating and drinking, specially the drinking which followed every baptism, and in which, if report is correct, the Filey parsons were not backward to join. All are gone. The old order has passed away . . . .'[16]

Mrs Zillah Suggit, who died in January 1898 at the age of 84, could remember the stocks on Church Street, at its junction with the main street, opposite the site of

---

[15] Cooper (1886) p20.
[16] Cooper (1886) p16.

what is now the *Station Hotel*.[17] Presumably, before the 'old order' did pass away, they were in regular use for the attempted rehabilitation of inebriates.

Alas, all this talk of an 'old order' vanishing in a sudden alcoholic turnaround was wishful clerical thinking. The Primitive Methodist ministry may have been 90% teetotal in 1881, but amongst the fishermen, as Foster Holmes JENKINSON put it, 'there were a lot that weren't'. Most were willing to embrace temperance (ie modest intake) but no more. But some were not even willing to go that far, if the fishing were good! At Christmas they always used to get 'well and truly oiled, whatever the fishing'. A good number of their fellow townspeople would 'stand on one side and look down on them.' The state of the local water supply alone probably required a fair proportion of East Riding Primitive Methodists to drink alcohol.[18]

We have seen from newspaper comments how fishermen were urged to join friendly societies. These mutuals met in public houses, where drinking was inevitable. The societies had a pre-Reformation flavour, redolent of guilds and confraternities, recycling medieval concepts of the 'Feast Day', often on the parish church's patronal saint's day. Filey's was an exception, probably because St Oswald's August 3rd was in the middle of the busy Yorkshire herring season.

In 1983, Foster fondly drifted into 1920s childhood memories for us, recalling Filey's Saturday 'Club Feast' each June, when the town closed down for the day. There was a grand, pomp-filled procession, of the town's friendly society members to a special church service. Members wore sashes, the Odd Fellows for example carrying blue staffs with gold tops; whilst the Shepherds had green sashes, their staffs topped with a brass crook. This was followed by banquets at each club's headquarter public house. Travelling showmen turned up with rides and peep shows, and later there were children's games on the football ground. In the evening there was drinking and dancing - revelry which, in Richard Harland's words, 'became exceedingly rampant before the day was over', reflecting the friendly societies' links with what has been called 'an older, rougher village culture'.[19]

It was the wife and family who suffered the consequences of a man of whom it could be said, disapprovingly, 'he fair teems it down'. But as Cooper shrewdly pointed out, 'everyone can manage them except those that have got them.'[20] Physically tiring jobs like fishing have always been associated with alcohol, and the adrenalin raised by the exhilaration and risk of a spell at sea could be quickly countered by beer. *The Foord's* in particular was a regular fishermen's haunt: it was even known for some men in the 19th Century to go to the back window and help themselves on their way down to the Coble Landing. Unfortunately, it is when

---

[17] *Parish Magazine*, Feb 1898.
[18] Truss (2016) pp239, 294.
[19] Truss (2016) pp239-41; Filey information, Foster Holmes JENKINSON (R37), and
 Fearon (2008) p35.
[20] Cooper (1908) p40.

alcohol got an upper hand and turned men to violence that records were created. It is worth remembering that the newspaper accounts of court cases comprise a tiny fraction of the town's alcohol profile.

Fearon (2008, page 42) cites reports of how large-scale, drunken fights sporadically broke out in Filey. In September 1910, a hostile crowd of 100 surrounded the courageous police superintendent who broke up a brawl outside the *Three Tuns* on Queen Street. One man who got more than his share of exposure in the local press was local bad boy George Whiteley *Baltic* Boynton, an ex-mariner who may well have learned how to look after himself in bar fights the length of the Baltic's extensive coastline. Marriage in 1864 did not settle him down, nor did the imminent appearance of his third child, judging from an 1868 court case. Filey was of course all 'Sunday Boats', invariably back on Saturdays, and Boynton seems usually to have been in an Old Town pub shortly after getting onto dry land. One George Gage was selling nuts from a basket, and *Baltic* had helped himself to a handful:

> About that some words followed, when defendant struck complainant on the face and took a piece out of his nose. The next day the defendant again attacked complainant, tried to throw him over some rails down the cliff, and cut his cheek very much.

It sounds like Boynton was lucky, getting away with a one pound fine, and 24 shillings costs, or a month in jail. Brawling seems to have been accepted as part of 19th Century working-class life in these fishing stations.[21] We met *Baltic* in Chapter 8, 'wilfully interfering with the comfort of the passengers' (ie fighting) at Bridlington Station in October 1877, when he also got the usual one pound fine.

In the early 1930s, alcohol got one Filey man, from a fish-dealing family, into more serious trouble. The story's source and subject had better remain unknown:

> In drink he was the devil incarnate, and he kicked a policeman to death in Cayton. Well, he died within a year. It cost his father an awful lot of money in barristers' expenses, and he got him off with manslaughter and a heavy fine.

In contrast, someone whom alcohol seems to have eased into sentimentality rather than violence was *Jack Sled* JENKINSON (P49). We have already encountered him as a man who had more than his share of misfortune. In the 1980s, many Filey people could still remember him, even though he had drowned with four of his family six decades earlier. He was a tough fisherman, full of life, who loved singing and a bit of a drink.

He seems to have had a great capacity to enjoy life. His wedding, on Sunday 9th April 1882, part of local lore even 100 years on, was said to have featured a barrel of ale. There was much singing, and the company got so drunk that eventually one

---

[21] *Hull Packet*, 10th April 1868, quoted by *Redux*, 4th Nov 2019; how just two policemen and the odd unpaid parish constable coped with brawls beggars the imagination. Filey only got a third officer in 1905.

of the mothers came and pulled the plug out, the contents spilling out down the yard. His boats were anything but Primitive Methodist bastions of abstention - Tommy Flynn remembered two of the crew falling overboard into the harbour at Lowestoft - 'they'd maybe had a drink too many,' he said. It was that kind of boat.

Jack had a sensitive side as well, and prized family very highly. Perhaps this had been a result of the death of his mother when he was just a year old, or the loss at sea of various members of his family. He was comfortable with children, and they warmed to him - remember how fondly Sydney Smith reminisced about his formative, childhood years helping out *Sled's* Filey crew in Scarborough Harbour in the early years of the 20th Century?

Lizzie HUNTER, as a small child, remembered him and a few of his friends coming round to visit her father, Edmond Cammish RICHARDSON, one Christmas. Her mother proudly showed them the Christmas tree. 'Mrs,' he said, pointing to Elizabeth and her two young brothers, 'these are your best Christmas tree'. Christmas was always a special time on fishing streets, for it could always be the last one that a family had together.

There seems to have been a splash of godliness in the Old Town drinking culture, for there was probably plenty of hymn singing in Filey bars, lubricated by beer. Clark reckoned that this, and story-telling, formed the basis of a customary evening in the old pubs of Staithes village. Indeed, with the addition of popular religious songs on a juke box, the practice was still around in 1975-6, when he was living there.[22] It seems unlikely that Filey was much different.

Hymn singing was *Jack Sled's* great forte. George Burton, something of a chorister himself, remembered a 'funny-pitched voice, with a bit of a wobble.' *Sled* helped to form a 'comrade's choir', a group of drinking men which came round singing at Christmas to collect for fishermen's widows. Jack's favourite hymn was *I will sing of My Redeemer*. He lived at 5, Clifford's Terrace, and his wife, Fanny Elizabeth, always knew when he was on his way home from the pub, for his strains of *My Redeemer* would be heard growing in volume as he approached along Queen Street. Bob Dale told us how carol singers at Christmas always stopped at the corner of the terrace and sang this favourite of his.

Perhaps it is fitting that this account of Old Town Filey, fishing, and family should conclude with this reference to *Sled* and his wife. Their biographies, as well as any, catch this past way of life. We wouldn't want to live it now, for it was hard and often dramatically cut short, but the sense of belongingness that their remarkable community took for granted is something few of us can even imagine today.

---

[22] Clark (1982) pp19, 151.

SIX LITTLE ORPHANS OF THE STORM

29.4: 'Your best Christmas tree'. The children of Robert *Robin* JENKINSON (Q52) grandchildren of *Jack Sled,* after the *Research* disaster of November 1925. It's a pity that a better version of this contemporary newscutting hasn't survived, though there is a fitting poignancy to its deteriorated condition. **L to R:** James Henry Newby, Lilian Ethel, twins Jane Baxter and Alice, Mary Anne, and baby Robert. The children still had a mother, so they were not actually orphaned – but why let the truth spoil a good headline? *[FA]*

30 POSTSCRIPT: A MOMENT IN TIME: FILEY, AUTUMN 2020

'The days of cobles are gone.' Graham Taylor

Irene and I were wrong in 1982 when we walked around Queen Street and the churchyard, and assumed that the Filey fishing community would last timelessly. Nearly forty years on, there are no cobles working regularly off the Coble Landing, although a few smaller boats go out. 'Many of those cottages are in darkness,' Michael Fearon told me, as the holiday season eased into winter. Visitors are no longer content to stay at hotels or with local families; now they want to stay in an authentic fisher cottage. Many are now the homes of retirees from west and south Yorkshire, Lancashire, the Midlands and Tyneside.

30.1: c1900 - the herring bone outline of Filey Old Town was gutted in 1936, after 119 buildings (in 17 yards and places) had been condemned the previous year. The *Filey Post* reported a storm of protest from those who grieved the loss of 'the homes of their parents and grandparents'. Included in the clearance were these cramped early 19th Century fishermen's cottages, which faced late 19th Century shops of quality (**Left**) at the western end of Queen Street. The girls are standing at the turn to Spring Road. *[FA]*

1948	13	2000	5	**30.2**: Filey's coble numbers since World War II.
1959	9	2006	4	The all-time peak was around 1867, when
1970	12	2011	3	Shaw counted 64. Since 2013, 'The Filey Few',
1970s	18	2013	1	have fished the bay from Scarborough.

In 1969, when he moved onto Queen Street, near *The Grapes*, Graham Taylor reckoned there were six working fishermen in just that row. Now, a handful live in the whole of Filey, though their boats are elsewhere. There are just six former fishermen on the whole of Queen Street. But many descendants of the old fisher families are still in the Old Town, and some older women might say, if prompted, 'Oh yes, I used to skein.'

In the 19th Century, most of the fishing community lived and died within a few minutes' walk of where they had been born – unless they were lost at sea. Irene's grandmother, Esther Mainprize, was born, married and buried from Queen Street addresses no more than 150 yards apart. But as fishing declined and families moved, this lifetime range stretched to scores, and even hundreds of miles. Plenty went to Scarborough and Bridlington, or perhaps further south to Hull. But we have also seen migrations to Derbyshire, York, West Hartlepool, Middlesbrough, Milford Haven and London (see family tree charts, Appendix E).

Plenty of women in Filey may be glad that fishing has declined and all but disappeared. For the trade has got no safer, however much technology might have changed it. From 1991-5, the fatal accident rate for fishermen was *76.6 times* higher than for all workers in Great Britain.[1]

And yet against this sea-tide of change, some have stayed in fishing. Colin *Dilt* JENKINSON was born in Eastborough, in the Scarborough fisher quarter, in 1935, son of Filey's *Charlie Dilt* (R2). He recalls how, in the school holidays of 1948, he went out with his father as fourth hand on Irene's uncle Castle Mainprize's *Rosemary*, lining and potting from Scarborough:

> He put me on a quarter share, and my best week was £15, which was a lot back then, when some Scarborough fishermen were going labouring for the council at a fiver a week because the fishing was poor.

His uncle, *Billy Wemp* JENKINSON, had drowned at Primrose Valley a few weeks before. At his retirement in 2019, after 70 years of full-time fishing, *Dilt* commented on the changes:

> The lads who were in cobles at Filey have now got bigger boats and work out of Scarborough . . . most of them are potting, because shellfish look okay. But there aren't any finfish. Some who've tried trawling the last couple of years have got

---

[1] SE Roberts, 'Occupational mortality in British commercial fishing, 1976–95', *BMJ Journals, bmj.com/content/61/1/16* (Jan 2004).

nothing. There's no cod. I think the last really good year for whitefish around here was about 1999.[2]

Dilt's dad advised him against the sea, but he took up fishing nonetheless. Many did not – a glance at the *National Calendar of Probate Grants* lists executors of many 20th Century Filey fishermen (usually their sons) with other occupations.

'Lining died,' said Graham Taylor, who finished fishing in 1974. 'It got to the stage where the cod was getting less, mussels more expensive, and work was 15 hours a day.' Traditional line fishers maintain that the trawlers have played a big part in the collapse of their trade, just as they did to that series of 19th Century government inquiries.

They were right. More and more data emerge to confirm their case. As this edition is being finalised, the debate about the impact of 'super-trawlers' on North Sea stocks has resurfaced.[3] Trawlers continue to deplete the very stock that inshoremen relied on, even in so called Marine Protected Areas. 'For every hour spent fishing today, in boats bristling with the latest fish-finding electronics, fishers land a mere 6% of what they did 120 years ago. Put another way, fishers today have to work *17* times harder to get the same catch as people did in the 19th Century.'[4]

Bill COLLING pinned the blame on foreign trawlers fitted out only for herring:

> . . . they were catchin' everything else, skates, plaice and cod. They were gerrin' tons of it in their nets and chuckin' it overboard in the bay. And when we were trawlin' on a night we'd tow 'em up, great big plaice. And that's what they'd chucked overboard . . . we went alongside one, one night and they give us thirty stone of big cod, biggest cod you've seen . . . they didn't want them.

30.3: March 1986 - Bob and Lizzie HUNTER, chatting to Irene outside their house on Queen Street, which had a working bait shed - an archetypal Old Filey fishing couple. 'A bit rough and ready,' said Lizzie, not expecting company. 'In your natural element,' said Bob!

---

[2] *Scarborough News* website, *thescarboroughnews.co.uk*, 24th Dec 2019.

[3] *The Guardian*, 9th May 2019.

[4] *The Guardian*, 10th Feb 2014. Compare with the figures given on p153. It seems that in one hour, the modern fisherman lands less than 1% of what his early 19th Century ancestor did.

But it was local trawlers too. Jim Haxby crystallised a century or more of grievance and economic loss to the town:

> . . . that year there was a tremendous lot of 'addocks in Filey Bay, just come at right time, September, 'cos we were startin' in October. They marked these 'addocks, did these two trawlers, comin' from Scarborough, and they shot their nets and they absolutely filled 'em. By the end of the week the Brid men were there, the Scarborough and the Whitby men and they just about got the lot. 'Addocks were very slow swimmers. I talked to [one trawlerman] and I ses to 'im, you've tekken a livin' from a town, becos' when the fishermen did well, they spent well in the town, electric shops whatever.
>
> Jimmy Brown, the 'airdresser, used to say, when fishermen are doin' well they get their 'air cut every fortnight, when they aren't it's a month. This is 'ow the fishin' in the winter did so much good for this town.

Bill and Jim's early memories were recorded in 2006, in the *Filey's Past* project, transcripts of which are at the Museum. By this time the number of cobles at the Landing were falling to a tipping point. A cooperative, the Filey Fisherman's Society, had been formed to provide the tractor and cut out the middle man, but even these lesser costs were spread over a diminishing number of boats - Filey had become uneconomic, hence the draw to harbour towns.

There is still sand-fishing, the traditional means of catching salmon, though this is now mostly sea trout. But this is under threat, for the Environment Agency has just proposed (2020) restricting the season again, to just four months, which will curtail even the sea trout fishery.[5] Crabbing, Graham reckons, has changed out of all recognition – 'the days of using the natural swell to shoot 250 pots from a rolling coble are gone' – fast, stable catamarans now deploy 3,000 pots, hauling in with hydraulic winches. An encyclopaedic knowledge of 'meets' is redundant, for GPS now takes the fisherman to the precise locations of individual pots in these huge fleets.[6] Jim Haxby charted the decline in 2006:

> When I first started, late fifties, we used to work two 'undred and fifty pots a day. . . sometimes getting 'undred stone o' crabs, mebbe twenty lobsters. When I finished, four or five years since, we were working nearly seven 'undred pots and weren't catching as much.

David Pockley managed, until 2016, to make a year-round living from netting salmon and trout, and fishing for lobster in the winter, when so few were caught that prices doubled.[7] The disappearance of Filey's fishing industry has been mirrored in several ways. Names like *Herring Hill*, the cobbled slope to the beach at the end of Ravine Road, and bait sheds and smoke-houses, ease into history, known now only to those with an interest in the past.

---

[5] *The Skipper* website, *the skipper.ie*, 7th April 2020.

[6] Graham Taylor; Fearon (2016) p70.

[7] *Filey: Last of the Coble Fishermen* (*Around and About Yorkshire*, Youtube, Oct 2020).

30.4: Some of the last brothers to be out lining together, Jim and Dick Haxby (**L to R**) with Peter Warcup (back to the camera) – a brilliant no-frills late 20th Century study of working coble-fishermen. The brothers' boat *Pilot Me* tosses gently on the ever-changeable North Sea, in the last decades of Filey traditional fishing. You can almost feel the spray, hear the screeching of the gulls, smell the stench of gutted fish, and taste the brine. *[Photo: Bob Dale; FA]*

Many bait sheds were converted into 'summer houses' where families could live in the season, releasing their house for lettings.

Symbolically, ganseys, once seen often on Queen Street as daily wear, are now far rarer. When Joanne CAMMISH recognised *Trab* CAMMISH's Sunday best gansey in a charity shop after his death, she knew it marked the end of an age, and that she had to buy it, to ensure it didn't pass into the hands of someone who would not appreciate its significance – note that she could recognise the pattern.

Decline is always marked by a succession of 'lasts'. *Windsor Lad II*, was the last coble built in Filey, in 1949. The last regularly working coble left Filey in 2013. On Union Street, the Fisherman's Chapel held its last service in 1975. Once, 900 regularly attended, but as faith and fishing declined, so did support. By the end, just a handful of fishing families continued the tradition. After ignominious use as a builder's store, Ranter Chapel has gone the way of so many large buildings in Britain and become apartments.

Now, for £344 (2020) visitors can rent one for a week and enjoy the Xbox 360, DVD player and genuine drift wood chair to seat up to seven people. No doubt, the building's modern 'heating apparatus' manages better than the 55-65° Fahrenheit stipulated by the trustees in 1875. Pipes 'bursting in several places with the frost' are long gone, we hope. But perhaps in the silences of night time, those who now live or stay in this former focus of communal worship may just be able to tune in to disembodied hymn singing from generations ago, when on 'crush occasions' up to 1,000 filled the sanctuary pews.

30.5: One late user of Filey dialect was George Cappleman Burton, of *Jenk Alley*, who died in 2002 – 'one of the town's last remaining characters', said his friend Jim Haxby. Egger, angler, artist, member of the Fisherman's Choir, brilliant yarner (in the *Brazzy* tradition), World War II veteran, fireman, rider of a motor cycle with fishbox as 'sidecar', and for many years Filey's ratcatcher, George's affability, immense network of acquaintances, and gleeful memory for a good story must have greatly added to his fund of anecdotes, many of which we have used! *[Photo: Mary Smith]*

Terence COLLINS' wife Nancy remembered *Bella* JENKINSON née Wheeler, who died in 1957, as one of the last authorities on Filey dialect. She was effectively the 'go-to' translator of the old speech, as it faded from common usage in the 1920s and '30s. With Filey dialect, it is hard to pinpoint any lasts other than that.

And it has been a long-term decline. Writing as long ago as 1908, Canon Cooper described how a neighbouring clergyman spoke at a St Oswald's parish tea a few years before. He had given a specimen of dialect to amuse the audience. 'Why, that's how grandfeeather used to talk,' someone commented.[8]

Before the 1920s, people born in the Old Town would have heard virtually no one speak other than those born within a day's walk. Visitors would be too fleeting to make any linguistic impression.

Fishermen were exposed slightly to other accents, as were those who joined the armed services. But it is radio and television which has boiled down accent and dialect. What is surprising is how long some of the traces have lasted - Clark noted of 1975-6 Staithes, for example, how the use of *thee* and *thou* had been common in living memory.[9]

---

[8] Cooper (1908) ch on 'East Yorkshire Dialect'.
[9] Clark (1982) p31.

By 2050, hundreds of dialect words in daily use by a thousand years of fishermen will have died out with them.

30.6: Ghostly traces of the Old Town. This half-demolished wall in Reynolds Yard with its series of bricked-up doors and windows offers stark though transient evidence of just how tiny these cottages were. *[SE]*

30.7: Once you have spoken to a few Old Towners about the fishing past, you can wander round Filey churchyard and feel as though you are bumping into old friends. But how much more profound that experience must be for people who have lived here all their lives. **Left:** Matt *Lampler* Haxby and crew of *Janet and Carol*, forever now in the potting season.

And finally, what of the churchyard, where we began this project in 1982? Another 'last' occurred there in 2014, the final burial in 1,000 or more years, as the yard closed. Except that one man was determined there would be one more. We have spoken of the determination and sense of purpose that characterised so many Filey fishermen. But few can have taken methodical determination into and *beyond* the grave in quite the same way as Jim Haxby. Fresh off the press early in 2019 came Filey's *Illegal Burial Case*, as Jim's spirit defied statute and canon law to secure for himself what *will* now be the last ever burial at St Oswald's.

The national media couldn't resist it. Filey men have often had to settle for a last resting place in the North Sea, so unsurprisingly they have universally declared an ambition to be buried in 'Filey garth', as a kind of assertion against that fate. In recent decades, many of the last former fishermen in the town have been joining maybe ten or more generations of ancestors in the former North Riding, and this long association gives an added charge to an already fervent wish.

Jim's direct male line has been in Filey since the 18th Century, and he had insisted to his family that he was determined to join the scores of Haxbys in St Oswald's 'even if he had to be buried upright or left in his box in the graveyard'. He particularly wished to lie next to Richard, his elder brother, who had died in 2005.

Unfortunately, when Jim died in 2018, the yard had been closed for four years, and Rev Nigel Chapman advised the undertaker to this effect. But by some Filey providence, the vicar was on a course at the time of the funeral, and was 'shocked' on his return that a fresh burial had been 'slotted in between two graves'. No less a body than the Consistory Court of the Diocese of York declared the burial illegal, and told Vic Bowes, the Scarborough Road undertaker, who as a good friend had helped out the family, to stump up all the legal costs. Good sense prevailed, however, and Jim remains (however illegally!) exactly where he always intended his remains to be.[10]

But isn't it all classic Filey! A 950 year-old church court had heard evidence from Vic that he'd 'sorted everything out over a cup of tea with the vicar', whereas Rev Chapman said, yes, Mr Bowes had indeed visited him, but he'd made the position quite clear . . . and they certainly did *not* have a cup of tea. Doesn't it all have a ring of *Lampler's* Friday teatime 'back of a cig packet' reckoning up?! Jim went Ovver t'North Ridin' with as big a splash as he and Dick might ever have encountered in *Pilot Me*.

30.7: Autumn 2020 - Jim Haxby in the spot he had wanted since 2005, when brother Dick died. In 2018, he got his wish, despite only fitting in with burial law and ecclesiastical procedures 'There or Thereabouts'!

---

[10] *Daily Telegraph*, 30th Dec 2019; *Scarborough Evening News*, 9th Jan 2020; *Church Times*, 31st Jan 2020.

Appendix A: Muster List of the Filey Fencibles, 28th Aug - 18th Sept, submitted 20th Sept 1803

N°	Names	Quality	Aug 28	Spt 4	Spt 11	Spt 18	Total days	Paid	Signed
	John Cammish Sen	Officr	1	1	1	-	3	7-6	Y
	Marmaduke Cammish	Prvte	1	1	1	-	3	3	X
	Wm Cammish Sen	Prvte	-	-	-	-	-	-	-
	Robt Cappleman Jun	Prvte	1	1	-	-	2	2	Y
5	Robt Edmond Senr	Prvte	-	-	-	-	-	-	-
	Richd Crowfoot[1]	Prvte	1	1	1	1	4	4	Y
	Robt Jenkinson	Prvte	1	1	1	1	4	4	X
	Geo: Dixon	Prvte	-	-	-	-	-	-	-
	Frans Edmond	Prvte	1	1	1	-	3	3	Y
10	Edwd Bays	Prvte	-	-	-	-	-	-	-
	John Johnson	Prvte	1	1	1	-	3	3	X
	Thos Johnson	Prvte	1	1	1	-	3	3	X
	Robt Chew	Prvte	1	1	1	-	3	3	X
	Wm Wyvel	Prvte	1	1	1	1	4	4	Y
15	Wm Chambers	Prvte	1	1	1	-	3	3	Y
	John Miller	Prvte	1	1	1	1	4	4	Y
	John Brown[2]	Prvte	1	1	1	1	4	4	Y
	Richd Cammish	Prvte	1	1	-	1	3	3	Y
	Jams Chambers	Prvte	1	1	1	-	3	3	X
20	Thos Segworth	Prvte	1	1	1	1	4	4	X
	Timothy Hopper	Prvte	1	1	1	-	3	3	X
	Marmaduke Couling	Prvte	1	1	1	-	3	3	X
	Robt Crowfoot	Prvte	1	1	1	-	3	3	X
	Robt Edmond Junr	Prvte	1	-	1	-	2	2	X
25	Wm Dixon	Prvte	1	1	1	-	3	3	Y
	Wm Sayers	Prvte	1	1	1	-	3	3	Y
	John Willis Sen	Prvte	1	1	1	-	3	3	Y
	Wm Williamson	Prvte	1	1	1	-	3	3	Y
	Wm Anderson Sen	Prvte	1	-	1	-	2	2	Y
30	John Cappleman	Prvte	1	1	1	1	4	4	Y
	Wm Edmond	Prvte	-	-	-	-	-	-	-
	Frans Williamson	Prvte	1	1	1	-	-	3	X
	Richd Anderson	Prvte	1	1	1	-	3	3	X
	Mark Baxter	Prvte	1	-	-	-	1	1	Y
35	Richd Crumpton	Prvte	1	1	1	1	4	4	Y
	David Smith Junr	Prvte	-	1	1	1	3	3	Y

---

[1] Early version of *Crawford*.

[2] His signature was *Broun*. Several children of John Brown, Day Labourer, were baptised at St Oswald's from 1815 onwards.

Nº	Names	Quality	Aug 28	Spt 4	Spt 11	Spt 18	Total days	Paid	Signed
					Day of Exercises				
	John COULING	Prvte	1	1	1	1	4	4	Y
	Richd RICHARDSON	Prvte	1	1	1	-	3	3	Y
	Jam^s ROSE	Prvte	-	-	-	-	-	-	-
40	Edwd WILLIAMS	Prvte	-	-	-	-	-	-	-
	John FELL	Prvte	1	1	1	-	3	3	X
	Jam^s CHEW	Prvte	1	1	-	-	2	2	X
	John BAYS	Prvte	1	1	-	-	2	2	Y
	Wm COULING	Prvte	1	1	-	-	2	2	X
45	Joseph CAMMISH	Prvte	1	1	1	-	3	3	X
	John SIMPSON	Prvte	1	1	-	-	2	2	Y
	Fran^s CHEW	Prvte	1	-	1	-	2	2	X
	Wm DUNN[3]	Prvte	1	-	1	-	2	2	Y
	Alexander YOUNGER[4]	Prvte	1	1	1	1	4	4	Y
50	Thos HOGGOT	Prvte	1	1	1	1	4	4	X
	John HALL	Prvte	1	1	1	1	4	4	X
	Matthew TELFORD[5]	Prvte	1	1	1	1	4	4	X
	Peter CAPPLEMAN	Prvte	1	1	1	-	3	3	Y
	Wm HALL	Prvte	1	1	1	-	3	3	X
55	Charles S DUNNEL	Prvte	1	1	1	1	4	4	X
	Wm CAMMISH Junr	Prvte	1	1	-	-	2	2	X
	Thos HUNTER Senr	Prvte	1	1	1	-	3	3	Y
	Richd MILLER	Prvte	1	1	1	1	4	4	X
	Ralph PARKIN	Prvte	1	-	1	1	3	3	Y
60	Wm SYMON[D]S[6]	Prvte	1	1	1	-	3	3	X
	Wm LORRIMAN	Prvte	1	1	1	1	4	4	X
	Jam^s BULMER	Prvte	1	1	1	1	4	4	Y
	Wm HORNBY	Prvte	-	1	1	-	2	2	Y
65	Chris RICHARDSON [64]	Prvte	1	1	-	-	2	2	Y
	Wilson CAMMISH	Prvte	-	-	-	-	-	-	-
	Saml CAMMISH	Prvte	1	1	-	-	2	2	X
	Saml ROSS	Prvte	1	1	1	-	3	3	Y
	Isaac ROSS	Prvte	1	1	-	-	2	2	Y
70	David SMITH Senr [69]	Prvte	-	-	-	-	-	-	-
	Richd MOSEY	Prvte	1	1	-	-	2	2	X
	Geo^r RICHARDSON	Prvte	1	1	1	-	3	3	X
	John RICHARDSON	Prvte	1	1	-	-	2	2	Y
	Thos RICHARDSON	Prvte	1	1	-	-	2	2	Y
	Wm HUTHORN	Prvte	1	1	1	-	3	3	Y
75	Joseph WADKINSON	Prvte	1	1	1	1	4	4	X

The incorrect position of no 70 is in the original list.

[3] ?The Fishmonger who married 1820, or the Farmer, aged 65, in the 1841 Census, Filey.
[4] Likely to be the Yeoman who married in 1811.
[5] Matthew Telford, Agricultural Labourer, aged 68, 1841 Census, Filey.
[6] The compiling officer, Nathaniel Cook, wrote different spellings in the two columns.

N°	Names	Quality	Aug 28	Spt 4	Spt 11	Spt 18	Total days	Paid	Signed
						Day of Exercises			
	John GAGE	Prvte	1	1	1	1	4	4	X
	Wᵐ WILSON	Prvte	1	1	1	1	4	4	Y
	Jamˢ SMITH	Prvte	1	-	-	-	1	1	Y
	Robᵗ CAPPLEMAN	Prvte	1	1	1	1	4	4	Y
80	Wᵐ BULMER	Prvte	1	1	1	-	3	3	Y
	Richᵈ SCALES	Prvte	1	1	1	-	3	3	X
	Wᵐ CAPPLEMAN	Prvte	-	-	-	-	-	-	-
	Thoˢ CAPPLEMAN	Prvte	1	1	1	-	3	3	Y
	Wᵐ COOK	Prvte	-	-	1	1	2	2	X
85	Wᵐ CAMMISH Youngr	Prvte	1	1	1	-	3	3	X
	Edwᵈ COULING	Prvte	1	1	1	-	3	3	X
	Robᵗ LANE	Prvte	1	1	1	-	3	3	X
	Robᵗ WILLIAMSON	Prvte	1	1	-	-	2	2	X
	Joseph SHEPY [sic]	Prvte	1	1	1	-	3	3	Y
90	Rickman SKELTON	Prvte	1	1	1	-	3	3	Y
	John WILLIS Junʳ	Prvte	1	1	1	-	3	3	Y
	Jamˢ ROBINSON	Prvte	1	1	1	-	3	3	Y
	Wᵐ ANDERSON	Prvte	1	1	1	-	3	3	Y
	John LORRIMAN	Prvte	1	1	1	-	3	3	X
95	Chrisʳ CLARK	Prvte	1	1	1	-	3	3	Y
	John CAMMISH Jun	Prvte	1	1	1	-	3	3	Y
	William DOUSLING	Prvte	1	1	1	-	3	3	X
	Thoˢ HUNTER Junʳ	Prvte	1	1	1	-	3	3	X
	Thoˢ ANDERSON	Prvte	1	1	1	-	3	3	X
100	John RACE	Prvte	1	-	-	1	2	2	Y
	Geor CAPPLEMAN	Prvte	1	1	1	-	3	3	X
	Joseph COULING	Prvte	1	1	1	-	3	3	X
	Benj SMITH	Prvte	1	1	1	1	4	4	X
	Thoˢ MILLER	Prvte	1	1	-	1	3	3	X
105	Wᵐ FENBY	Prvte	1	-	-	-	1	1	X
	Samˡ MURGANTROYD [sic]	Prvte	-	-	-	-	-	-	-
	Crumpton SKELTON	Prvte	1	-	1	1	3	3	Y
	Lancelot SIMPSON	Prvte	1	1	-	1	3	3	Y
	Matthew DAY	Officʳ	1	1	1	1	4	10	Y
110	Thoˢ FRANK	Prvte	1	1	1	1	4	4	X
	Chris EDMOND	Prvte	1	1	-	-	2	2	Y
	Thoˢ CHAPMAN	Prvte	1	1	-	-	2	2	X
	Nathaniel COOK	Officʳ	1	1	1	1	4	10	Y
	Robᵗ ROW[7]	Prvte	-	-	-	-	-	-	-
115	Edwᵈ CROSIER[8]	Officʳ	1	1	1	1	4	10	Y

---

[7] Robert Rowe, buried St Oswald's, 5ᵗʰ Feb 1815, aged 59.

[8] Edward Crosier, Farmer, aged 78, 1841 Census, Filey. Signed 'Croser'.

What can we learn from the Muster List?

The breakdown in May 1803 of the efforts to forge a permanent peace with revolutionary France finally prompted the Admiralty to implement a 1798 scheme to recruit a naval volunteer militia, known as the Sea Fencibles. A total of 36 units was raised, men recruited for home service, for the duration of the War. Each was based in a port, and given responsibility for the stretch of coastline nearest to it. Fear of invasion hung over the years preceding Nelson's 1805 victory at Trafalgar, much like in the summer days of 1940. Unsurprisingly, the muster lists surviving for the first years of the Filey Fencibles' existence contain the most names, for this decisive battle extinguished the French naval threat.

There were 115 men listed at Filey in August 1803, from whom four non-commissioned officers had been elected by the privates, no doubt one for each of the town's three companies, and one as an adjutant. It may be that these elected men had military experience, for three did not have local fisher surnames. The last return, March 1810, had just 28 names, implying that the unit had been collapsed into a single company. Several questions arise:

1 Were all the men fishermen?

The muster of 1803 records 115 men, though 11 of them seem to have expressed an interest but did not enlist or take part in any exercise days.

How many of the 115 men were fishermen? This was certainly the scheme's target group. Yet the total 1801 population of the whole township was just 505. We know from the parish register that there were many non-fisher occupations in the town, so it seems probable that at least some of these volunteers were not active fishermen.

There are three ways to clarify the issue:

a) **Surnames** – 29 of the 115 surnames figure as fisher names in no other source. We would therefore need other proof that these men were truly fishermen, for we know that casual entry into the trade was unusual.

b) **The 1841 Census and Parish Registers** – five of this 29 can be fairly conclusively identified from the baptismal and marriage registers as having non-fisher occupations, as are shown in footnotes. Predictably, four of the five were present at the 18th September exercise, since as non-fishermen they would not be going to Norfolk. The fifth, William Dunn, seems to have been away with the herring fleet: his occupation of fishmonger may have concealed some fishing involvement or interest.

c) **The Norfolk Fishing** - the last Sunday of the 1803 return, 18th September, was the worst attended of the four: 68 men were absent, yet in most cases they had attended all three previous exercises. The inescapable conclusion is that the Filey fleet had sailed for the Yarmouth herring fishery. Twelve of the non-fisher surnames were borne by men also missing from this fourth exercise day, making it possible that they *were* nevertheless fishermen. For some reason, these surnames did not become established fisher names. A figure of 68 fishermen going to the Yarmouth Fishery, incidentally, is consistent with the 12 luggers cited as being at Filey in the 1820s.[9] We can assume that some men who *did* attend the fourth day were inshoremen.

It seems reasonable to conclude that about 100 of these 115 men (87%) were fishermen. Only the inclusion of youngsters and elderly men can explain so high a proportion of the total population of the town.

2 What is the significance of the order in which the names were recorded?

The volunteers were not alphabetically listed, almost certainly being in order of enlistment. This will have taken place in Filey, probably on a specified Sunday, and at a public house, the usual location of public business at the time.

The men seem to be in clusters, representing the senior, core crewmates of each Filey lugger, ie the men who either owned shares in the boat or contributed gear:

a) The decision to enlist would be made by the **skippers and gearmen**, and naturally they would sign up together, to ensure collective compliance. Men on a particular boat would almost certainly attend on the same Sundays, since they could not go fishing if one or more joined the Fencibles. Their boats would be used in training. There were usually two, three or four gearmen per boat, judging by this pattern of attendance.

b) Luggers were **family concerns**, hence the clusters of twos and threes with the same surname. In so patriarchal a community, the order of enlistment within each cluster almost certainly reflected seniority, even if this were not specified by the suffixes *senior* and *junior*. Family reconstitution focused on the surviving muster lists may confirm this. Men recorded consecutively who shared a surname attended the same Sunday exercises, evidence that they most probably belonged to one boat. Relationships by marriage are hidden but implied, a rich vein of future family research for those wanting to squeeze even more out of this fascinating source. One likely example is apparent from entry numbers 6 and 7, Richard Crowfoot (Crawford) and Robert JENKINSON (N5) clearly being connected by the 1801 marriage between Robert JENKINSON and Mary Crowfoot.

Only those names in this muster that can be securely identified in other sources are included in the indexes.

---

[9] These 'five-man boats' would carry additional waged crew, especially in the herring season. For numbers, see above, p89.

APPENDIX B: THE FILEY FISHER SURNAMES: BRIEF HISTORIES

Filey Old Town's 15 core names were introduced in Chapter 4. I have defined them as those that figured in the fishing community broadly from 1800 to the Great War, a period of about four generations. The 1803 Muster List of naval volunteers, the Filey Fencibles (Appendix A) and the 1911 Census are convenient bookends for this 'long 19th Century'.

Explanatory Notes for Figure B.1

Core surnames – the first number after each name denotes its rank in the descending order of commonness in Great Britain (England, Scotland and Wales) in the 1881 Census – ie the number 1 would signify the most common name. The number in bold represents the total number of people in Great Britain with the name in that year's returns. It is remarkable how some of the Old Town names have been nationally very common, notably the patronymics ending in -*son*. *JOHNSON*, for example, was borne by over 100,000 people all over the country in 1881. In contrast, *CAMMISH* and *CAPPLEMAN* each mustered fewer than 150. And these two handfuls were each focused entirely in the Filey area.

Column 1 Muster of the 115 Filey Fencibles, dated 20th Sept 1803. Extant from 1798 to 1810, the volunteer force comprised 'all fishermen and other persons', the latter presumably a reference to anyone with some maritime experience. Given that probably no merchant shipping used Filey as its home port, it seems certain that most of these men were fishermen. This is confirmed by parish register and sometimes 1841 Census entries.

The remaining four columns give the number of fishermen of each core surname returned for Filey in a spread of four censuses.

These national enumerations, apart from 1841's, were held in the spring, to catch seasonally mobile workers at home. Yorkshire fishermen who engaged in the herring trade traditionally did not venture away in the direction of East Anglia until late September, and so were mostly enumerated at home. By 1881, diminishing catches were drawing boats further away from traditional offshore waters, with the result that some long-lining luggers and yawls were away from home in an east coast dock on census night. The Filey men have been traced by the online digital index, and are included in the Columns 4 and 5 figures.

The totals – the bottom row totals up the core surnames in each source, and shows them as a percentage of the number of fishermen in Filey recorded in that source. The core names consistently made up around three-fifths of the active fisher workforce. The increased percentage in 1911 may imply that the core remained loyal to the trade even though a decline was setting in.

CORE SURNAME	Ordinal Position (ie how common) in GB, 1881	Total no of people with each name in GB, 1881 (in bold)	Col 1 1803 Fencibles	Col 2 1841 Census	Col 3 1871 Census	Col 4 1881 Census	Col 5 1911 Census
BAXTER	214TH	**17,813**	1	3	4	6	6
CAMMISH	16,117^TH	**142**	10	16	20	20	21
CAPPLEMAN	19,237^TH	**106**	7	5	11	16	17
COLLEY/	*1,209^TH*	***3,788***	-	-	*2*	-	*3*
COLLING/	*4,863^RD*	***761***	-	*1*	*2*	*16*	*11*
COOLING/COULING	*9,002^ND*	***339***	*5*	-	-	-	-
COWLING	*1,700^TH*	***2,619***	-	*8*	*6*	-	*6*
Total of all the above COLLING variants		**7,507**	*5*	*9*	*10*	*16*	*20*
HUNTER	104TH	**30,724**	2	1	7	5	3
JENKINSON	854TH	**5,237**	1	15	29	34	34
JOHNSON	15TH	**100,242**	2	5	10	9	10
LANE	179TH	**20,557**	1	1	1	2	2
RICHARDSON	54TH	**50,876**	5	6	6	4	2
ROBINSON	16TH	**95,282**	1	1	3	9	13
ROSS (ROSE/ROW early versions) 98TH/**32,695** (Ross only)			4	2	4	3	4
SAYERS	1,383^RD	**3,296**	1	3	7	7	10
SCALES	2,451^ST	**1,769**	1	3	5	4	8
WILLIAMSON	121ST	**26,794**	3	1	1	2	1
WILLIS/WILLAS	248TH	**15,885**	2	2	4	6	4
NO WITH CORE NAMES IN EACH YEAR/			46/	73/	122/	143/	155/
TOTAL WITH FISHER NAMES IN EACH YEAR			78	120	217	244	212
PROPORTION WITH CORE SURNAMES			59%	61%	56%	59%	73%

B.1: Continuity in the 19th Century, 1803 to 1911 – the core 15 fisher surnames, as shown by the number of fishermen with each name in five sources. The figures are taken from Archer's *British 19th Century Surname Atlas – full reference, p446n*.

Surprises – we can understand that the names which came to Filey from Norfolk in the 1850s and '60s, mentioned in Chapter 6, were too late to be classed as core, even though some became well-established. Integration is reflected in their use as middle names by core families. But there are several other families missing from the 15 that Filey people would automatically associate with fishing.

Perhaps the two most puzzling absences from the core are ***Chapman*** and ***Haxby***. ***Chapman*** (meaning 'merchant/monger') was, by the late 19ᵗʰ Century, indisputably a member of the core, but there were no fishermen with the name in Filey until the 1820s/30s. The earliest bearer, origins unknown, was Thomas, a joiner. He married Mary JENKINSON (N7) in 1801, daughter of the famous Robert and Margaret 'Clapham Junction' of the JENKINSON dynasty. Enlisting as a Fencible in 1803, Thomas Chapman probably accompanied the herring fleet to Norfolk, for he missed the last two attendances of the four in the 1803 muster. Perhaps he was Filey's on-board handyman in wood, making running repairs during the two-month absence. The Yorkshiremen may have been stung before by East Anglian joiners. Son John kept up the trade, whilst a later Chapman, John William, still a joiner, had a boat-builder's 'shop' at Undercliff into the 20ᵗʰ Century. Later, a Tom was an undertaker. William and Mortimer, sons of the original Thomas, became fishermen, no doubt because of their father's associations. This may be the start of *Mortimer* as a Christian name in the town.[1]

There were five ***Haxby*** fishermen in the 1841 Census, and seven in 1871. The first family in the town seems to have been that of William Haxby who married Mary WILAS (presumably WILLIS) at Filey in 1787. The name derives from the inland village of Haxby four miles north-east of York, and had reached Bempton and Hunmanby by the 1740s. There are no Haxbys in the surviving musters of 1803, 1809 and 1810, and this seems to suggest that they retained landed occupations initially, after they had arrived in the town.

The first proven fishing Haxby was Richard, owner of the yawl *Unity*, born at Speeton in 1789: after 1814, with Elizabeth née JENKINSON (N9), he fathered the stock from which the Filey Old Town Haxbys descend. An additional line came from Scrayingham, represented by *Old Tom*, the butcher who threatened violence to Bob Wheeler for trespassing in pursuit of apples (Chapter 5). Any connection with the fisher line will be centuries back.

---

[1] The only baptism that remotely fits Thomas Chapman's age at death of 66 (1841) was in 1777 at Brantingham, near Brough, 40 miles away by road. In such cases of a 'Lone Migrant', arriving unaccompanied in a parish, we can only look for a package of clues that may identify him in his parish of origin. In this case we have three clues that we could look for in Brantingham, or elsewhere – a fairly exact year of birth; a likely family occupation; and some association with a surname Mortimer/Morton. Such genealogical methods are explained in Andrew Todd, *Family History Nuts and Bolts: Problem-Solving through Family Reconstitution Techniques* (Andrew Todd, 2015).

Crawford appeared in Filey in the early 19th Century, though there were occasional **Crawforths** and **Crowfoots** in the 18th. The name's original home must be the Lanarkshire village near Abington, some bearers clearly migrating to the east coast – by 1881 there was a large concentration around the mouth of the Tyne, the likely source of the Filey family. The name there solidified into *Crawford* in the 1800s, and gave rise to a line of fish-merchants. Strangely, it drifts off the radar in the 30 years between 1881 and 1911, by which time the town's active fishermen of that name seem to have gone to Bridlington.

Another constant in the late 19th and 20th Century Old Town was *Crimlisk*: its only presence in Great Britain is along the Yorkshire coast, in Scarborough, Filey, Flamborough and Hull, all bearers descending from Thomas Crimlisk. Born in Ardara, County Donegal, in 1803, and joining the Coastguard Service, he was moved to Rottingdean in Sussex, then Flamborough in 1839 and Filey by 1842. Of five sons by Catherine McDevitt, one died at sea, and three married, to *Haxby*, *JENKINSON* and *JOHNSON* fisher girls. Chance male births and survivals created seven fishing families in the town by 1881.[2] It is a Gaelic nickname, 'drooping eye'.

B.2: Thomas Crimlis(k) 1803-86, coastguard, and founder of a prolific Filey fisher family. Born in County Donegal, like all members of the service he was moved around, to pre-empt local connections which might compromise his ability to combat smuggling. *[Crimlisk One Name Study website]*

Douglas was a late arrival at Filey, fish merchant Gordon Douglas settling in the 1860s. The Christian name confirms a Scottish origin.[3] The first *Douglas* fisherman was in the 1881 Census. A topographical name, meaning 'black stream', there are many Scottish locations from which Filey's line could derive. A large 1881 cluster in Sunderland suggests that the fishing stations in this area were likely stepping stones to the town, a feature of much Scottish movement down the east coast.

Douglas is only one of several Scots names - *Alexander*, *Donkin/Duncan*, *Ferguson*, *McPherson*, *ROSS*, and *Younger* - that could have come from the Highlands of Scotland. There was much movement southwards, as a result of the clearances of tenants by indebted landlords, mostly in the period 1750 to 1860.

---

[2] *Crimlisk One Name Study* website, *pchurch.org.uk/crimlisk*. Thomas died in Leeds.

[3] Jimmy (1860-1944) the Filey gravedigger, was from Easington; the Arthur in Hull in 1871 probably belonged to a separate branch.

CATEGORY	RATIONALE	FILEY EXAMPLES
Personal	Use of a father's Christian name, or a patronymic, ie ending in *-s* or *-son*	COLLIN; PEARSON (son of Peter); ROBINSON
Nickname	Involuntarily imposed name, often uncomplimentary	CAMMISH (possibly); CRIMLISK
Topographical	Given to those on the village fringe, living near an obvious landscape feature	BAYES/BOYES; FELL; HALL; LANE; SCALES
Locative	Derived from the name of the village, town, county or country of origin	HAXBY; BOYNTON; SKELTON; ROSS; ENGLAND
Occupational	The job, craft or position of a man, or his master	BAXTER; HUNTER; SHIPPY WHEELER; WRIGHT

B.3: How men with the same Christian name in a village were distinguished in the Middle Ages. Any medieval *by-name* inherited by a son had become a *surname* (French 'over name' meaning superior to the Christian name).

Many migrated to the coast, where fishing could have been an inviting alternative to the many landowner attempts to harvest seaweed for the chemical industry. NB *Arthur Douglas* was a regular combination nationally for bearers of the surname, implying an early common origin.

The Flamborough *Mainprizes*, present at Filey during the census period, 1841-1911, and connected by marriage with several core families, are now primarily a Scarborough family. A rare East Riding name, meaning 'one who acts as security for bail', there were less than 200 in Great Britain in 1881.

Overy was a far later arrival, its first migrant, Charles, who married a *CAMMISH*, giving a bewildering sequence of birthplaces from 1871 to 1911. These ranged from London to Newark, to Canterbury, and again London, before finally settling on Canterbury, a reminder that such data is only as reliable as the memory, or truthfulness, of its recorder. *Overy* may derive from a lost Norfolk place name.

Watkinson is another surprising absence from the core 15. Common in Lancashire, Yorkshire and the East Midlands, it is a patronymic, from the old Christian name *Watkin*, which itself means 'Little Wat', a familiar form of Walter. Fishermen with that name have figured in all the Filey censuses from 1841 to 1911. Yet parish register entries record the first Joseph Watkinson as a day labourer, probably born in Spofforth. He enlisted in 1803 as a Fencible, and attended all four exercises, which strongly suggests he was not involved in the Norfolk fishing.

William **Wheeler** first appeared in Filey in the 1840s, as Chief Boatman of the Coastguard, born Hull, son of George. Family tradition connects George with the

Battle of Trafalgar, 1805 (but see above, page 56, footnote 9) and takes the family origins to London. William's son John founded the Queen Street fisher line, marrying Elizabeth CAPPLEMAN. *Wheeler* is occupational, 'wheelwright', and its 1881 distribution suggests it has originated separately in many areas.

The rarest surname to appear as a fisher name at Filey was *Wyvill(e)*, sometimes appearing as *Wyvel* or *Warvel*. The marriage of a John in 1757 marks the earliest entry in St Oswald's parish registers. There were just 97 in the whole of Great Britain in 1881, yet the name retained a modest presence in the Old Town fishing ranks throughout much of the core period. This East Riding name is believed to have originated from one of the several *Vauville* place names in Normandy, borne by a knight in the service of William the Conqueror. There was just one in the 1803 muster, William, almost certainly born in Folkton. He was a shoemaker according to the parish register, a 'saylor' briefly in 1815, and then a miller's labourer in 1820. As with Joseph Watkinson, he attended all four exercises. Single surname presences in the 1803 list usually prove not to be fishermen, given the close family/multi-generational nature of the trade.

Some names began the 19th Century as fisher names but had disappeared by 1911. One was *Crompton*, first in Filey in the 1720s. This line is clearly connected with the two *Crumpton* baptisms at neighbouring Cayton in the following decade. The variation in spelling was probably due to the auditory capabilities of the two clergymen involved in registration. The sources of locative names like this, deriving from a specific place name, are normally the easiest to fix on. But in this case, there is no town or village which is an obvious candidate. The ancestors of these fishermen are self-evidently not from the inland Lancashire township of that name, near Rochdale, 100 miles away, and 30 miles from any sea fish. The jury remains out.

There were no less than five fishermen surnamed *Edmond* in the 1803 muster, exceeded only by *CAMMISH* and *CAPPLEMAN*. But the surname soon faded into near extinction, though surviving today as a fisher Christian name. In 1881, the largest cluster as a surname in the country was around Filey, but where it came from is unclear. It derives from the personal name Edmund. Similarly, *Bayes/Boyes* was core until the 1870s, a Yorkshire name, focused on Malton. Deriving from the French *bois*, it is topographical, 'dweller by a wood'. *Fenby*, overwhelmingly concentrated on the Yorkshire coast, deriving from the Lincolnshire village name, and the topographical *Hall* each retained a persistent, if slight, presence until 1881, figuring as middle names in various families. *Shipp(e)y*, a Staithes/Whitby name, 'shepherd', was also core until the 1870s.

Another surprising omission from the core 15 is *Skelton*, a locative surname that derived from the village name four miles north of York. In Filey since at least the 1590s, with six fishermen in 1881, its disappearance from the trade by 1911 is difficult to explain. The decades of fishing decline began in the 1870s, and this coupled with drownings may explain such changes.

General Observations on Researching the Core Fifteen

Filey lay in the Manor of Hunmanby, and some of the earliest names, like *CAPPLEMAN* and *JOHNSON*, appear amongst 18th Century lists of its farming tenants. It is unclear if these names were also borne by fishermen at that time, since occupations were absent from most pre-1813 Filey parish register entries. Bearers may only have come into fishing later, as farming families sprouted junior lines without access to land, making fishing the only livelihood. Without more evidence, there remains a question mark over this hypothesis.

Unfortunately, four factors make it difficult to determine the precise town or village from which many of the Filey fisher surnames originated[4]:

1 Distance – Chapter 6 discussed how fishermen were unusual in the distances they might travel to resettle their families. With inland population, a rule of thumb is that movement, even in the railway age, was overwhelmingly over short distances, typically eight or ten miles. One remarkable result is that surname distribution well into the 20th Century was virtually the same as in the 14th.

Surname specialist, Colin Rogers, in a memorable simile, likens the 600-700 year spread of surnames from their medieval homelands to a teaspoonful of Marmite spending an unstirred half hour in a tumbler of hot water - enough will have seeped out to give the water only the hint of a pale brown tint. But the originating lump remains largely undisturbed. An inexpensive database of all 400,000+ surnames in the 1881 Census therefore offers instant identification of the likely geographic origins of most surnames extant in Britain in late Victorian times.[5] This is therefore useful in offering clues about fisher origins.

The big problem is that the greater the move, the more unfamiliar would be the migrant's surname and his accent. No wonder out-of-district names caused havoc with their spelling in local records. We saw on page 102, how the Staithes name *Trattles* became *Truckles* 200 miles away in East Anglia. Foreign names were equally vulnerable: the Scottish pronunciation of the vowel *u* in *Duncan*, for example, is probably close enough to the English *o* for the name to have been rendered *Donkin* when migrants came to Yorkshire.

2 Surname assimilation is another confusing linguistic process, and can conceal a name's origins. An Old Town example is how the unfamiliar *COLLING*, likely to be from Berwickshire, was probably associated with the Yorkshire place name Cowling, in the Aire Valley, hence this version in Filey. The Norkfolk *Bullamore*

---

[4] These problems are covered in more detail in my *Surnames, Christian Names and Practical Family History Research: Shadows of Ancestors* (in preparation).

[5] Steve Archer's interactive CD, *The British 19th Century Surname Atlas* (version 1.2, 2011, upgraded 2017; £15 post free from *www.archersoftware.co.uk*) shows totals by county or poor law union for every surname and forename found in the 1881 Census of England, Scotland, and Wales. It displays these distributions and densities on national base maps.

sometimes gets assimilated by the Yorkshire *Bulmer*. In a pre-literate period, immigrants might find it impossible to prevent their identity being swallowed up by a similar-sounding local name.

3 Records get scarce before the 19th Century. Most of the core Filey fisher surnames had arrived in the town before anyone was recording where they had come from. There are no exact places of birth in census returns until 1851, and it doesn't help that one of Canon Cooper's servants threw at least one 18th Century parish register on the fire, assuming it was far too old to have any further use.[6]

4 Common surnames, like the patronymics, which are especially common in the north of England, rarely have any precise geographic homeland. Thus some Filey names of this type – *JENKINSON, JOHNSON, RICHARDSON, ROBINSON* and *WILLIAMSON* – sprang up independently in too many districts to carry any clues as to origins. Occupational names like *BAXTER* ('baker') and *HUNTER* aren't a lot better.

Filey's Fifteen Core Fisher Surnames

Let's now look at when each of the core 15 arrived, their likely origins, and meanings.

1 *BAXTER* only just qualifies. Mark, the man who brought the name to the town, can only have been in his early twenties when he was mustered as a Fencible in 1803.[7] This version of the name for 'baker' was concentrated almost entirely in Kent and Surrey in 1881, so the baptism, at Tynemouth in 1780, which fits his age at death, is an isolated outlier. North Shields, in Tynemouth ancient parish, was one of the largest fishing stations on the east coast, famous for herring. There is no other Mark BAXTER in *FamilySearch* which can rival this Northumbrian candidate, so the case seems compelling. This biblical Christian name never became common in Filey, appearing only once more in the 19th Century.[8]

Mark BAXTER's name was listed in the 1803 muster after Richard Anderson, with whom his daughter Ann was later connected by marriage. Mark's 1803 marriage to Ann WILLIAMSON was propitious, for he inherited a cottage, a third

---

[6] A parallel but incomplete series of Bishop's Transcripts is at York's Borthwick Institute.

[7] He was 23 when he married Ann WILLIAMSON at Filey in April 1803; she was a daughter of Francis WILLIAMSON, next but two before him in the muster list.

[8] Mark Baxter JENKINSON (P32, *Old Marky Jenk*) his grandson. Note that this is an early example at Filey of 'entity naming', as described in Chapter 5. Mark BAXTER did give a birthplace as Filey in the 1851 and '61 Censuses, but it was common practice for a man to adopt wherever he was living as a birthplace, in case he fell into poverty. There was a real risk that the poor law authorities would remove paupers to their place of origin to escape the cost of maintaining them.

share in the lugger *Endeavour*, and 'fishing materials' (ie gear) from his mother-in-law.[9] This set the BAXTERs up as offshore fishermen at an early date.

2 *CAMMISH* remained the commonest name in the Old Town for centuries, only overtaken by *JENKINSON* in the 1860s. There are intriguing local assertions that the surname derives from the Vikings, but such associations are beyond proof, other than by genetic genealogy.

In fact, the earliest *CAMMISH* parish register entry in Britain, listed in the Mormons' *FamilySearch*, is the baptism of an Emot, daughter of John, at Filey on 15th October 1612. A dispute of 1625-6, about payment of church tithes, concerned one John GAMAGE of Filey, probably the same man. He was alleged that year to have caught 73,000 fish, including 40,000 herring.[10] A William CAMMISH was 'drowned and buried' in March 1718, offering further evidence of the surname's occupational constancy at Filey.

It may be a nickname surname, deriving from the Old French *camus*, 'short, flat nose, pug-nose'. But since the first recorded instance in any medieval record is Adam le Camhus, in the 1256 Assize Rolls of Northumberland, my sense is it could be locative, referring to a man living at 'The Cam House'.[11] Unfortunately, there is no proof that this 13th Century entry has any connection with the Filey name.

The Old Norman French *camise, kemise*, 'shirt', arising from the occupation of shirtmaking, seems to be the source of the name *Kemmish* in the English South, especially Kent, and this also may have evolved into *CAMMISH*. A third possibility is that some medieval migrant took his surname from the Normandy place name, Campeaux. Both these alternatives seem improbable, given their southern associations.[12]

Intriguingly, the name figured only in the Scarborough registration district in 1881, which included Filey. This strongly suggests that *CAMMISH* came in a single migration from outside the country. If the migrant came from somewhere in Britain, why is there no clear trace of it elsewhere in any set of records? The name's origin remains a mystery.[13]

---

[9] Will of Ann WILLIAMSON (née CAMMISH), proved 1811, Exchequer Court, York.

[10] Fisher, *History* (1970) *Fishing and Shipping*. Clearly a mistranscription of CAMAGE.

[11] *Cam* is Celtic, 'crooked', and could refer to any location by a river bend.

[12] Hanks, Patrick, & Hodges, Flavia, *A Dictionary of Surnames* (Oxford University Press, 1988).

[13] The Scandinavian theory breaks down for several reasons. First, Vikings had patronymic surnames, like the Welsh – *CAMMISH* is not of this type; second, a combined google search of *CAMMISH*/Denmark, Norway and Sweden produced nothing; and third, Orkney and Shetland have historically no *CAMMISH* presence, despite being part of Norway/Denmark until 1468, and strong connections after that.

3 The early 17th Century also saw the first ***CAPPLEMAN*** entries in Filey's parish registers. Of German or Dutch origin, there is intriguingly, according to *FamilySearch*, a 17th Century smattering at Alkmaar, in North Holland. It is tempting, though speculative, to suggest that brief sojourns by Dutch herring-boats at Filey were the occasions of the two early summer *CAPPLEMAN* marriages at St Oswald, in 1606 and 1635, to women with local surnames. Herring girls must have been just as necessary in the 17th Century as in the 20th.

A contemporary account speaks of 1,000 craft leaving the Dutch river mouths each June 'for to catch herrings in the North-seas'.[14] The Dutch War of Independence against Spain recommenced in 1621, these river mouths being war zones throughout the 1620s. If this were the origin of the name in Filey, it could be that the *CAPPLEMAN* tenants of Hunmanby Manor mentioned above were refugee farmer/fishermen, devoting time to each according to the season. Again, the name was confined to the Scarborough registration district in 1881, strongly suggesting a single migration from outside the country. The name may be occupational (someone employed in a chapel) or topographical, ie given to families that lived near what must have been a distinctive feature in the German/Dutch landscape, either natural, or as in this case, a man-made one.

4 ***COLLING*** and its several variants all very probably derive from the east Scotland name, *Collen*. Unusually for a patronymic, it seems to have a concentrated origin in Berwickshire, although the name also has an English heartland in Cambridgeshire, likely to have been entirely of separate origin. The name means 'son of Col', or derives from *Nicholas* (ie 'Little Colin').

There was a William COLLIN in Filey in the early 1700s, and the Christian name *Francis* descends during that century. Local tradition specifies the major Berwickshire fishing station of Eyemouth as the origin of the migrants to Filey – before the great disaster of 1881, in which 129 of the town's fishermen drowned, there were 100 Eyemouth boats engaged in the herring fishery. The size of the harbour was constrained by the narrowness of the River Eye's valley as it reaches the sea, whilst the problem of the entrance to the harbour silting up with sand was longstanding.

As with Filey in later years, overcrowding could have been a spur to an early 18th Century emigration. Local men engaging in the annual herring fishery knew the Yorkshire coast well. The 1881 distribution confirms a Berwickshire concentration, though there was a major cluster of a local version *COLLING/COWLING* at Sunderland, entirely consistent with a staged move down the east coast from Scotland.

If fisher migration were to take place from Scandinavia, these islands would be the obvious destination. See *North Isles Family History* website, *bayanne.info/Shetland/surnames*.

[14] Tobias Gentleman's 1614 account is quoted by Frank (2002) pp132-3.

At Filey, after some uncertainty (see **B.1**) the favoured version crystallised as *COLLING* in the 1870s, perhaps with the growth of literacy, though this may reflect the preference of the enumerators rather than the families themselves. Note how *COWLING* was digested by *COLLING* in 1881, but had reasserted itself by 1911, strongly implying varying enumerator versions.

5 *HUNTER* is a north country occupational name, especially common in Scotland and Lancashire; the east coast concentration will have moved from the inland forest and chase districts of Northumberland and Durham, wide expanses of fell and moorland reserved by crown and nobility for hunting. The two *Thomases*, senior and junior, in the 1803 muster, father and son no doubt, are the founders of the Filey *HUNTER* line. Since both were dead by the time of the 1851 Census, we have no clues as to the family's origins.

6 *JENKINSON* is another patronymic, in this case meaning 'son of Jenkin', itself a diminutive of *John* – ie 'Little John'. It was especially common in Lancashire and Yorkshire, but like most surnames deriving from common personal names will have arisen independently in many places.

The first of the Filey JENKINSONs, William (L1) appeared in the St Oswald registers in 1749, having married Mary CAPPLEMAN in Hornsea, on 3rd May 1748. *CAPPLEMAN* was a uniquely Filey name at this time, so why this event took place 30 or so miles south along the Holderness coast is unknown. It seems unlikely the bride was in service, or that Hornsea attracted 'herring girls', and certainly not in May! William's origins may have been in Norfolk, but nothing connects him with Runton, near Cromer, with which local tradition links the JENKINSONs. The descent of the whole *JENKINSON* fishing clan can be traced from William and Mary's son, Robert (M4), baptised at Filey in 1756. The pattern of intermarriage amongst the core Filey families now connects the name down the generations like vertebrae. Most of the Filey, Bridlington and Scarborough fishing communities are descended from this 1748 marriage.

The senior, uniquely non-fishing line, descending illegitimately from William and Mary's daughter, Elizabeth (M2), is a study in social elevation. Father and son William and Edmond (N2 and O4) were master mariners, ie captains of merchant vessels. They were licensed to take charge of a ship of any size and type, sailing anywhere in the world, the highest position in the British Merchant Navy. We saw how seamen at sea were dealt with in census enumeration in Chapter 7. A momentous shaft of historical revelation caught Edmond in charge of the 615-ton barque[15] *Eleanor Olive* on census night in 1861 – she had about 15 times the displacement of the yawls that his second cousins in Filey were used to. Based at Gloucester, the crew of 15 were about 300 miles west of the Irish coast at the

---

[15] A generic term for a square-rigged, three-masted ship. The *barque* was the 'workhorse of the golden age of sail in the mid-19th Century.' They were able nearly to match the performances of ships which had much larger crews (*Wikipedia* entry).

moment of enumeration, midnight 7th April, bound for America perhaps with cotton goods. If they made their destination in time, they could soon have been returning with one of the last cargoes of raw cotton from the South – the Union naval blockade of the Confederate ports was to begin on the 19th of that month.

7 The origins of ***JOHNSON***, one of the earliest fishing families still in Filey in its final fishing years, are a mystery. The name has been in Filey continuously for 450 years, figuring in the 1570s in some of the earliest parish register entries, in the reign of Elizabeth I. It was the 11th commonest surname in Britain according to the 1881 Census, simply because *John* was the commonest medieval name; and many villages inevitably distinguished sons by means of a patroymic by-name, ie adding the suffix *-son* to their father's Christian name.

Ancestors of these Tudor JOHNSONs had probably been in Filey parish 'time immemorial', ie 'time whereof the memory of man runneth not to the contrary'. As late as the 1720s, one George JOHNSON was a farming tenant in the Manor of Hunmanby, appearing in its court records for overstocking the commons - there is therefore doubt as to how long this surname was associated with fishing.

8 *LANE* is nationally common, and typically of topographical names has no obvious originating geographic cluster. Many families lived on a highway away from the village centre, distinguishable by this name. William's marriage in 1769 marks the start of the Filey line, his son Robert appearing in the 1803 muster.

9 *RICHARDSON* is another claimant to be the oldest fishing family in Filey, with entries in the parish register, like *JOHNSON*, as early as the 1570s. As with the other patronymics, we have no idea where it originated, for in 1881 it was the 54th most common surname in Britain. It was concentrated in the old Danelaw, the 15 northern/eastern counties of England settled by the Danes in the 9th Century.

10 *ROBINSON* is a third claimant to the earliest presence. It was the 16th most common British surname in 1881, rampantly common north of the Mersey/Humber as far as the Scottish border. And like the other two primal Filey names, *JOHNSON* and *RICHARDSON,* it is likely to have been in the town at least as far back as the growth of surnames in the 14th Century. It means simply 'son of Robin', itself a diminutive or pet name of *Robert*.

11 *ROSS* appeared at Filey with the baptisms of children of an Allan ROSS, after March 1695/6. There were at least two families in the next generation, but there is no documentary evidence that they were fishermen. There seems to be an unbroken descent to the Isaac (1764/5-1844) from whom the *ROSS* fishing clan sprang. The original Allan was probably baptised in 1671/2 at North Burton (now known as Burton Fleming, and six miles south of Filey). Whilst the *Bruce* family, Earls of Carrick, held manors in Yorkshire in the 14th Century, any connection with the *ROSS* name three centuries later seems improbable. Scottish migration into England was more likely after the union of crowns in 1603.

The 1851 Census shows many ROSS families in Yorkshire, virtually all born there. This locative name's homeland is predictably in the far north of Scotland, indicating origins in Ross-shire, but there was also a cluster inland west of Aberdeen. A presence around Sunderland is compatible with a drift down the coast in connection with herring fishing.

12 The first **SAYERS** family in Filey was headed by William who had married Hannah Edmond at Whitby in 1806. A string of subsequent baptisms registered at St Oswald's marks the foundation of the line. William was recorded as a 78 year-old Skipsea-born fisherman in the 1861 Filey Census, consistent with the birthplace he had given in 1851. He was recorded in the 1803 muster.

The name derives from a Christian name *Saher* or *Seir*, a shortened version of the Germanic *Sigiheri* (meaning 'victory army') which came to England after the Norman Conquest. The Filey version is the common variation with the final *s* which suggests 'son of Sayer'. Despite an 1881 concentration in Sussex, the County Durham cluster will be the source of the name's moves to Yorkshire. *Sayer* without a final *s*, has a different origin, *sayhare*, ie 'sawyer'.[16] That variation was common in Norfolk and Kent.

13 The **SCALES** family is reputed to have come from Lowestoft in Suffolk: there was certainly a cluster inland from Yarmouth. But the distribution in Yorkshire in 1881 suggests a homeland in the Pickering area, movement later radiating out along the coast from Whitby to Hornsea. The surname derives from the Scandinavian word *skali*, 'a hut or temporary shelter'. As a topographical surname, it refers therefore to someone who lived at an outlying hut, away from any settlement. *SCALES* and its many variants (notably *Scholes* in Lancashire) is also common throughout the 15 counties of Danelaw. *SCALES* was in Filey by the 1690s, and could have come from anywhere on the east coast. One identifier is the Christian name *Christopher*, which occurs in the family from the earliest days in Filey and well into the 18th Century.

14 **WILLIAMSON** is another exclusively north-country patronymic, including Scotland, 'son of William'. The earliest known recorded presence in Filey is of the 1694 marriage to a *JOHNSON* bride. If as is likely the traditional pattern of intermarriage dates back that far, this entry is possible evidence that both were already fisher names.

15 **WILLIS** is a nationally common name, though with a particular cluster around Newcastle in 1881, and with effectively the same meaning as *WILLIAMSON* – a patronymic, 'son of Will'. There were two John WILLISs, senior and junior, in the 1803 muster (nos 27 and 92), later baptismal entries confirming a fisher association.

---

[16] Hanks & Hodges (1988) cited above.

APPENDIX C: FILEY CENSUS STATISTICS, 1801-1911

1 Population - the ancient parish of Filey, served by St Oswald's church, comprised the townships of Filey, Gristhorpe and Lebberston. The 1851 Census revealed that in Filey township there were only seven men to every eight women. Shaw believed this was due to the drowning of fishermen. The difference increased – from 1861 to 1911, there were consistently just four males to every five females.[1] The following statistics relate only to Filey township.

Census	Males	% of total	Females	% of total	Total
1801	249	49.3	256	50.7	505
1811	270	46.6	309	53.4	579
1821	366	47.3	407	52.7	773
1831	376	46.9	426	53.1	802
1841	563	45.7	668	54.3	1,231
1851	703	46.5	808	53.5	1,511
1861	827	44.0	1,054	56.0	1,881
1871	1,004	44.3	1,263	55.7	2,267
1881	1,036	44.3	1,301	55.7	2,337
1891	1,100	44.3	1,381	55.7	2,481
1901	1,368	45.6	1,635	55.4	3,003
1911	1,437	44.5	1,792	55.5	3,229

2 Religious Census, Sunday 30th March 1851: Attendance at Church /Chapel

	Services			Sunday School	
	am	pm	evening	am	pm
St Oswald's	-	80	-	-	45
Wesleyan Methodists	84	-	-	-	-
Primitive Methodists	120	-	300	107	107

---

[1] Filey was exceptional - in 1851, Englishmen, at 49%, were only marginally outnumbered by their womenfolk. The ratio at the neighbouring agricultural parish of Hunmanby was a more normal 50.2% males to 49.8% females. The 1851 imbalance at Staithes was even more stark than Filey's (four men for every five women). This could have resulted from yawls being at sea over census weekend, or men working away, factors unlikely to apply to Filey in 1851. As the Old Town's two enumeration districts included some non-fishing streets, the fisher gender imbalance could have been even more pronounced.

APPENDIX D: WHAT WERE THEY WORTH?
PROBATE VALUATIONS, 1858-1950

These tables cover virtually all the people mentioned in this book whose estates went through probate between 1858 and 1950. They are therefore a small but representative sample of those involved in the Filey fishing trade (and some non-fishing sons). Women connected with these families are also included.

The *Calendar of Probate Grants, England & Wales, 1858-present* is freely accessible online. It usually gives the date of death, value of effects, and names of executors/administrators. See *gov.uk/search-will-probate* website. The *National Archives currency-converter* website will show the modern value of any sum between 1270 and 2017, for years ending in *0* (*0* and *5* after 1900).

But average wage levels are far higher in real terms today than in the period 1858-1950. The converter site, for example, shows that trawler owner *Clicker* CAMMISH's 1940 estate of £15,209 16s 2d (worth £598,451.20 in 2017) would have taken 10,711 days to earn in 1940. A man working those hours in 2017 would have earned £1,231,765, twice the 2017 value based solely on purchasing power.

The format 'gr1883' indicates a grant of probate made one or more years after the death.

	Died	Final address	Probate value £ s d	2017 value £.p
BOAT BUILDERS				
SKELTON Robert	1860	Scarborough	Under 1,500	88,693.00
FISHERMEN				
COWLING Elizabeth, *Spnstr, Exec* John JENKINSON, *Shpkpr*	1859	Filey	Under 20	1,182.58
HAXBY Francis, gr1879	1859	Filey	Under 100	5,912.92
CAMMISH Thomas	1864	Filey	Under 100	5,912.92
CAMMISH William	1870	Filey	Under 100	6,260.90
CAMMISH William, *?Old Traf*	1872	Filey	Under 300	18,782.70
CAPPLEMAN William	1877	Beach Cottage	Under 100	6,618.47
JENKINSON Mary, *Wid of Thos, N11*	1878	Filey	Under 450	29,783.12
HAXBY James, gr1880	1879	Queen St	Under 100	6,618.47
HAXBY Francis, gr1881	1880	Filey	Under 100	6,618.47
COWLING Thomas, gr1882	1881	Sand-lane	107 0 0	7,081. 76
JENKINSON Castle, *O34*	1882	Filey	80 0 0	5,294.78
JENKINSON Mary, *Wid of Edmond, O21,* gr1883	1882	Filey	12 0 0	794.22
JENKINSON Mary, *Wid of Castle, O34*	1883	Filey	59 8 8	3,936.89
CRAWFORD William	1891	Hilderthorpe *(Execs of Filey)*	144 0 2	11,815.78

	Died	Final address	Probate value £ s d	2017 value £.p
HAXBY Richard	1894	Filey	83 16 0	6,875.73
CAPPLEMAN Matthew Crawford *Matty Wiggy*	1895	Filey	Under 100	7,817.22
CAMMISH Joseph	1899	Filey	140 0 0	10,944.11
CAMMISH Edmond	1901	89, Queen St	368 15 0	28,826.00
HAXBY Matthew, gr1903	1902	16, Mitford St	263 0 0	20,559.29
HAXBY Jane nee, *Wid of above*	1905	16, Mitford St	438 12 10	34,463.86
JENKINSON William, *Bill Penny, P27*	1908	20, Queen St	363 15 0	28,435.14
JENKINSON Matthew, *Walsher, O40*	1911	Filey	1,252 10 0	97,910.68
WATKINSON William Jenkinson, *Billy Butter,* gr1916	1915	*Seadale,* Mitford St	2,915 11 10	171,997.17
JENKINSON Richard Cammish, *Dick Sled, P44*	1918	Filey	290 0 0	8,426.73
JENKINSON Richard, *Old Baggy, P35*	1918	95, Queen St	525 5 6	15,263.28
CRIMLISK Matthew, *Matty Airy,* gr1920	1919	4, Queen St	1,798 19 6	52,274.08
COWLING Richard Baxter, *Dick Fipney*	1919	70, Queen St	41 3 4	1,196.21
JENKINSON William, *Billy Trummy, Q46*	1919	Filey	1,529 4 0	44,435.03
JENKINSON Matthew, *Brazzy, P46*	1929	3, Richardson's Yd	115 15 3	5,300.23
HAXBY John Richard	1929	1, Chapel Trrce	630 12 10	28,874.18
HAXBY Matthew Crawford	1936	16, Mitford St	330 0 0	16,718.66
COLLING Frank	1937	Colling's Yd, Queen St	891 4 11	45,152.83
COWLING Jenkinson	1937	14, Hope St	352 17 0	17,876.30
COLLING Benjamin Simpson	1938	3, Reynolds St	626 9 11	24,650.36
ROSS Isaac	1938	41, Newlands	171 9 7	6,747.09
CAMMISH Thomas Simpson	1939	54, Queen St	918 13 11	36,147.37
CAMMISH William	1939	47, Mitford St	246 15 3	9,709.22
HAXBY Mary Jane	1940	16, Mitford St	1,636 11 8	64,393.66
CAMMISH John Richard, *Son of Fshrmn,* war svce, gr1942	1941	3, Raincliffe Ave	98 5 9	3,867.26
COLLING Elizabeth Sarah, gr1944, to John William COLLING	1943	32, Hope St	576 2 0	20,481.22
CAPPLEMAN John Pockley, gr1946	1945	21, Reynolds St	735 16 9	26,160.13
JENKINSON Richard Cammish, *Dicky Hoy, Q45*	1946	50, Mitford St	1,993 1 11	70,857.55
COLLING William Cammish, *Mrchnt smn,* gr1948	1947	Sacred Island, Newfoundland (but of 1, Sand Hill La, Filey)	169 7 7	6,021.68
CAMMISH Jenkinson Haxby, gr1948	1947	4, Raincliffe Ave	1,246 13 4	44,320.87
COLLING Thomas, gr1949	1948	85, Queen St	321 4 5	10,024.85
CAMMISH Francis	1948	54, Queen St	637 16 7	19,905.76

	Died	Final address	Probate value £ s d	2017 value £.p
CAMMISH Mary Emily Simpson	1948	30, Hope St	1,765 0 0	55,083.18
CAMMISH William Watkinson	1948	12, Mariners Trrce	719 4 9	22,446.40
JENKINSON William Robinson, *Billy Wemp, R3*	1948	19, Victoria Ave	259 4 7	8,090.18
COLLING Thomas Jenkinson, gr1949	1948	1, Sand Hill La	315 17 9	9,858.41
CAMMISH Richard Ferguson, gr1949	1948	49, Mitford St	495 15 11	15,473.09
CAMMISH Frances, *Wid of William,* d1939	1950	47, Mitford St	1,202 10 0	37,528.34
CAPPLEMAN Francis Edward	1950	4, Providence Plce	427 7 2	13,337.26

FISHING TACKLE DEALER
CAMMISH Robert	1927	18, West Parade	1,469 8 6	60,332.97

FISH MERCHANTS
CRAWFORD David Dunn	1890	Filey	5,753 6 9	172,057.31
CRAWFORD Dunn	1904	Filey	9,889 11 9	777,019.95
HAXBY Jenkinson	1908	6, Chapel St	1,500 18 0	117,328.65
HAXBY Sophia, *Wid of Jenkinson*	1921	Filey	1,082 16 0	31,463.68
CRAWFORD William, *Ino*	1930	35, Queen St	1,472 9 2	67,417.09
CRAWFORD Newman	1937	Newby (Herring House, West Parade, 1914)	6,971 0 3	353,169.62
ROSS Thomas	1937	*Filey House*, Cleethorpes	14,302 10 0	724,601.84
CAMMISH Richard Ferguson, *Clicker, Filey Utd Steam Trwling Co*	1940	3, Raincliffe Ave	15,209 16 2	598,451.20

GROCERS
CAMMISH William, *Grcr & coal mcht, Son of Fshrmn*	1900	King St	3,651 18 10	285,480.31
CAPPLEMAN Robert, *former Fshrmn*	1931	Filey	485 2 5	22,211.45

MASTER MARINER
CAMMISH William	1868	Filey, died at sea	Under 300	18,782.70

MISCELLANEOUS
FOX John Sumpton, *Monumental mason*	1901	2, Church St	704 18 2	55,104.24
ROSS Rev Castle, *PM minister*	1928	*Cliff Top Cottage*	1,023 15 8	46,874.33
POTTER John Fawcett, *Rtd Publican*	1943	East Ayton	3,956 1 3	140,643.96
CAMMISH Robert, *Bobbin, Btmaker*	1946	15, Reynolds St	511 9 7	18,183.85

APPENDIX E: THE FILEY SPINE: SEVEN GENERATIONS OF THE JENKINSON FAMILY

The fold-out pedigree chart, *The Jenkinson Family of Filey*, at the end of the 1985 edition of this book, has been impossible to replicate: so much more information has become digitally available in the intervening 35 years. Its expanded content has therefore been spread over eight pages, focused upon the descent from each of the five sons of Robert and Margaret JENKINSON. The family can be seen as a spine, for every Old Town surname connects with it. Young men from the CAMMISH, CAPPLEMAN, CHAPMAN, COLLEY, COLLING, COWLING, CRAWFORD, CRIMLISK, HAXBY, JOHNSON, ROBINSON and WILLIAMSON families had married JENKINSON brides by the 1850s, and the other fishing families were not far behind. The earlier such a marriage took place, the more likely that JENKINSON genes can be found in *anybody* now bearing the groom's surname. The CHAPMAN and HAXBY marriages in Generation *N*, for example, are ancestral to everybody from fishing stock in the Filey area with those names.

The Mathematics of Ancestral Descent

The genesis of this immense Filey family is described at the other end of this book in Chapter 1, notably the chance fertility of Robert and Margaret JENKINSON and their five surviving sons – see page 5. By about 1914, there were 141 known great great great grandchildren, born JENKINSON, all shown on these charts. They had spread the length of the Yorkshire Coast, but the majority were in and around Scarborough, Filey, or Bridlington.

It would have required a book of encyclopaedic length to show the *full* descent to 2021 from Robert and Margaret. On average, half a couple's grandchildren are born with a different surname, daughters traditionally changing their names at marriage. Therefore, that figure of 141 only represented about one sixteenth of Robert and Margaret's great great great grandchildren. Of course, being Filey, the majority of these people would have been descended from the couple several times over. A conservative estimate might therefore bring the 1914 figure down to 1,000. By now, they must have getting on for 5,000 living descendants – any one reading this book could be in the same boat in a few centuries. Or they might be like Henry VIII – no known living descendants, despite plenty of wives.

Things to look out for on the Charts

Anyone with Filey connections will soon connect up with generation *R*; but for more detailed use of the data, a magnifying glass or sheet is essential. Many of the characteristics of the fishing families described in Chapters 4, 5 and 6 will be apparent:

1 Intermarriage between families – notice how two siblings often marry spouses who are themselves siblings, or cousins.

2 The descent of nicknames – known by-names are in italics after the surname.

3 'Family boats' – where fishing disasters are specified, two or more close relatives can often be seen dying together.

4 Entity-naming - explained on page 53. Abraham Cole, second child of Robert Jenkinson (O31) is a classic example of how this practice always perpetuates the name of a significant ancestor. Robert's wife, Elizabeth COLE, was born in Staithes, daughter of Abram COLE.

5 The decline of fishing – the charts show starkly the preponderance of fishing as an occupation in the earlier generations, and the growing intrusion of a wider variety of occupations later on. The yawls gradually disappear from the charts as offshore fishing sank into penury. This decline is also reflected in:

- **The breakdown of the traditional custom of 'marrying in'** – marriage horizons extend beyond the traditional fisher surnames in the later generations
- **The increasing movement of families** away from Filey

Taking your line further

The presence of an arrow after any couple on the charts **E2** to **E6** is an invitation to do some research of your own. Especially useful are *Ancestry.co.uk* for the census returns and the 1939 *National Register*, but I would be very careful about using *Ancestry's Public Member Trees* section.

The immense database index to parish registers available on *FamilySearch* is indispensable, as are the *Pedigree Resource File* entries (known as *Filey Genealogy and Connections*) in the *Genealogies* section. *Freebmd.org.uk* is a freely available online index to the civil registration system of births, marriages and deaths which began on 1ˢᵗ July 1837. Some births are missing before 1875, non-registration only then becoming subject to fines. Taken from the local registers, the marriages in particular seem to be rather more reliably indexed than the national General Register Office quarterly returns. The index currently comes as far as 1992. The free online *Calendar of Probate Grants, England & Wales, 1858-present* (*gov.uk/search-will-probate* website) allows easy discovery of exact dates of death, names of executors, and valuations of estate, if a deceased's person's estate were subject to probate.

The best source for bringing to life any kind of family history research is the written and oral evidence of people who knew, or knew someone who knew, the person you are researching. In the 1980s, a large number of our leads came from these sources. They should certainly not be ignored now, just because so much is available online. We can never *truly* know the past, but sometimes we can have an eerie sense of getting pretty close to what a community *was* like, and it is always the personal that allows us on those rare occasions to get 'between the sheets of history'.

L   **1 William JENKINSON** m Hornsea 3rd May 1748 **Mary CAPPLEMAN**
died 1762

M¹

1	2	3	4
John 1749-	Elizabeth 1752- ✝	Rachel 1780-	Robert 1756-1808 Lugger *Prospect* m Great Yarmouth 1st Nov 1778 Margaret TRUCKLES (?TRATTLES) ?1754-1823 ?bn Staithes, dau of Thomas; died Filey

N

1	2	3	4	5	6	7	8	9	10	11	12	13
John 1773-	Captain William 1776-1844 Master of Luggers *Friends and Ark* Elder Brother of Trinity House; d Kronstadt, Russia	m Filey 7th April 1804 Mary EDMOND c1778-1867	Hannah 1789-1847 m John SIMPSON 1795-1820 Butcher	**Robert** c1780- 1844 Fshrmn m Mary CROWFOOT/ CRAWFORD	**Mary** 1784-1864 m Thomas CHAPMAN 1775-1841 Joiner		**Elizabeth** 1788-1868 m Richard HAXBY 1789-1869 Fshrmn, Yawl *Unity* All the Filey, Scbro & Brdingtn HAXBY fishing families descend from this couple		**Thomas** 1793-1863 Fshrmn, Luggers *Flora* and *York* m Mary CASTLE 1795-1878	**John** 1791-1872 Fshrmn, Lugger *Vigilant* m Mary EDMOND 1791-1856	**Matthew** 1797-8

Rachel 1780-

O

1	2	3	4	5	6
Mary bn1807	William 1812-30	Rachel 1816-	Captain Edmond 1815-73 Master mariner m Mary Ann HUTCHINSON c1814-95	John 1819-	

Elizabeth 1810-68 m William STORY c1810-86 Draper, Grocer & Postmaster, Queen St

Matthew 1781-

E2

William 1786-1865 Fshrmn m Isabella ANDERSON 1788-1870

E3

George 1795-1860 Fshrmn, First Yawl *Integrity* m Mary SCALES 1798-1881

E4

E5

E6

Capt Edmond and Mary Ann were living with her brother, Christopher, in Muston, in the 1871 Census

P

1	2	3	4
John bn Muston 1840	Elizabeth bn Muston 1842	(?John) William bn Muston 1844 Shipbroker Agent m Mary HOLMES bnc1843 in Stoke Newington 1891 Census	Marion 1848-1932 m1 William WHITTLE Mineral Water Manufacturer bn Whitehaven Cumberland 1848, d Leeds 1879

m2 John REDDIE, Medical electrician, bn Perth c1850, d Menston Yorks 1900

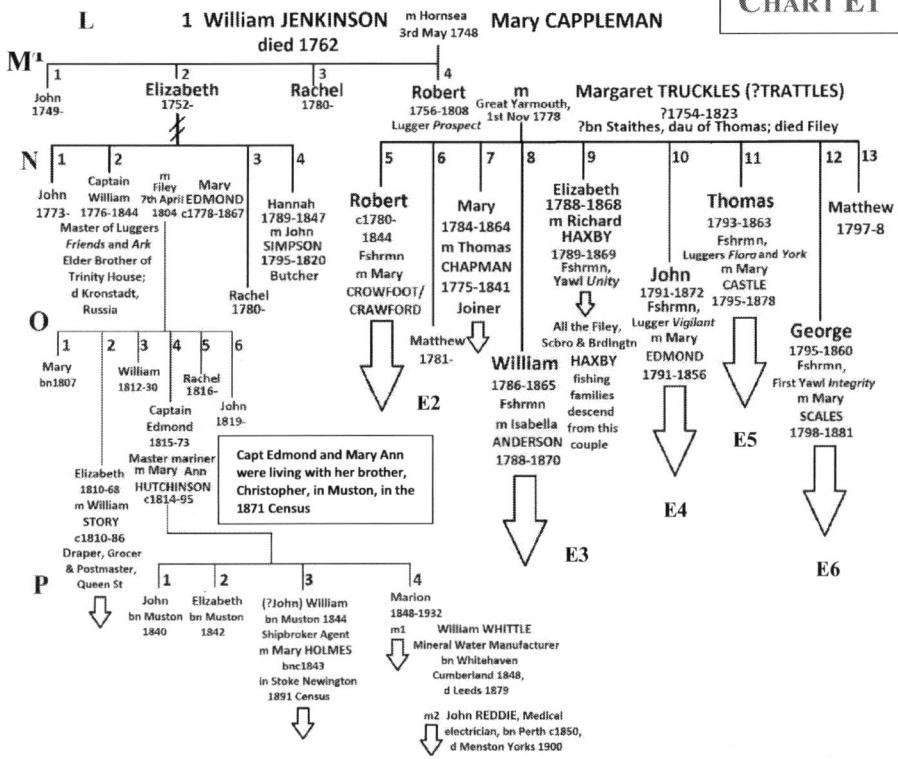

Lack of space prevents any attempt to index the names on the six charts in this Appendix.

KEY TO CHARTS E.1 TO E.6

⇩ Marriage known to have produced children
○ No known children to this marriage
⋈ No known marriage
✝ Parents unmarried at the time of this birth
1821* Child died in the calendar year of its birth
bn - born; m - married; d in i - died in infancy; k in a - killed in action
● Drowned/died at sea
✝ Officer and/or lay preacher at 'Ranter Chapel'

Some hints to help you find your way around the charts:

All surnames are in BLOCK CAPITALS, to prevent confusion with surnames used as middle names.

Unless otherwise specified, everyone on these charts was born a JENKINSON and lived in Filey.

N 5 Robert JENKINSON

c1780-1844 Fisherman

O

7

Matthew
1802-51
Fshrmn
Yawl *Integrity*
m
Ann DONKIN

P

5	6	7	8	9	10	11	12	13
	Elizabeth 1827-31			Matthew 1832-76 Fshrmn	Charles 1834-1900 Fshrmn m Jane SIMPSON née COWLING c1830-1913 ⭕		Ann 1839-1917 m James ROBINSON Fshrmn ⇩	Betsy 1845-1912 m William COLLING Fshrmn ⇩

Robert 1826-49

Mary 1830* William 1830*
twins

m 1
Mary Jane PROCTOR c1831-63

m 2
Mary Selina EASTON c1839-

William *Nanny Billy* 1837-96 Fshrmn m Ann CAPPLEMAN c1839-1905

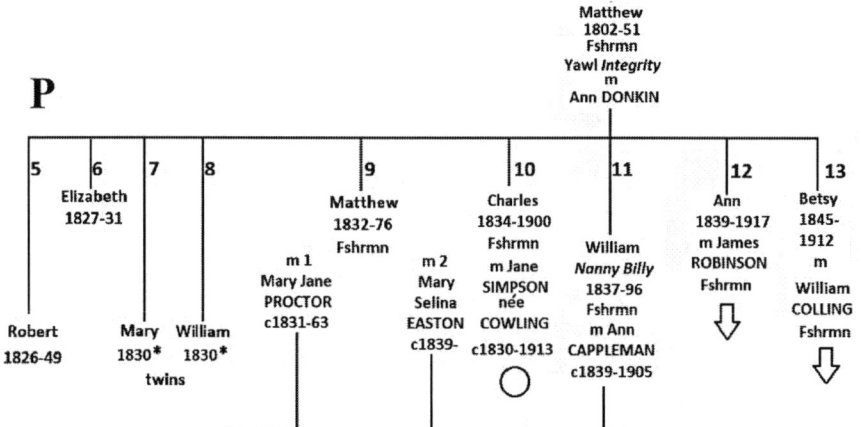

Q

1	2	3	4	5	6	7	8	9	10
	Betsy Ann 1858-		Matthew John 1863*			Robert 1873-1938 Agricultural labourer Carnaby, 1891, Shepherd, Willerby (Staxton) 1911 unmarried			Robert 1869-1923 Line fshrmn

Betsy 1855-

Robert 1862*

Matthew *Wemp* 1868-1922 Fshrmn m Grace ROBINSON 1869-1946

William 1871-1947 Line fshrmn m Elizabeth Ann WHEELER 1870-1945

Charles 1877- Rly porter, goods clerk m Emily WALSHAM, at least six chdn born Sculcoates

Sarah Ann 1859-1935 m Charles ⚫ HUNTER bn 1857
Washed off yawl *Decision*, Great March Gale 1883 ⇩

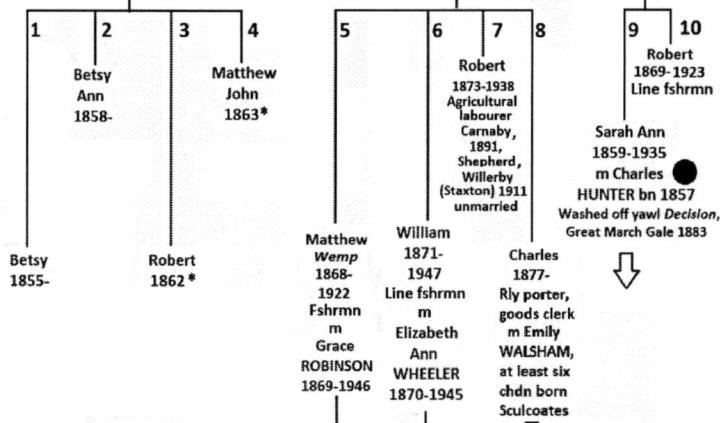

R

1	2	3	4	5	6	7	8	9	10	11	12	13	14	15	16	17	18	19
	Charles *Dilt* 1891- Fshrmn m1 Alice Jane COLLING c1892-1931 m2 Kitty	Marjorie Lindsay 1896- m JEFFERSON ⚫			Matthew 1900-1				Mary 1904-	Grace 1910-		Matthew 1891-1973 Fshrmn m Emma Elizabeth HUNTER 1898-1977 ⇩	Ruth 1893- m John W JOHNSON 1890- Farm horseman ⇩		William 1900*		Olive 1905- m Thomas Dobson SAWDON 1902- Gardener ⇩	

Grace 1890*

William Robinson *Billy Wemp* 1893-1948 drowned Primrose Bay, coble *Lady Shirley* m Jennie 1897-

Jane 1898- m Billy WHITE

Annie 1902-41

John Matthew 1906- Fshrmn m Ann M WOOD Living Scrbro 1939 ⇩

Daisy 1914-

John Wheeler 1892-1918 Fshrmn d Naval Hsp Granton, Edinburgh

Mary Elizabeth 1896-1985 m1 John Rowland OXTOBY ⚫ 1896-1917 k i a Mediterranean m2 James M ROBINSON ⇩

Isabella 1904- d young

William 1908-9

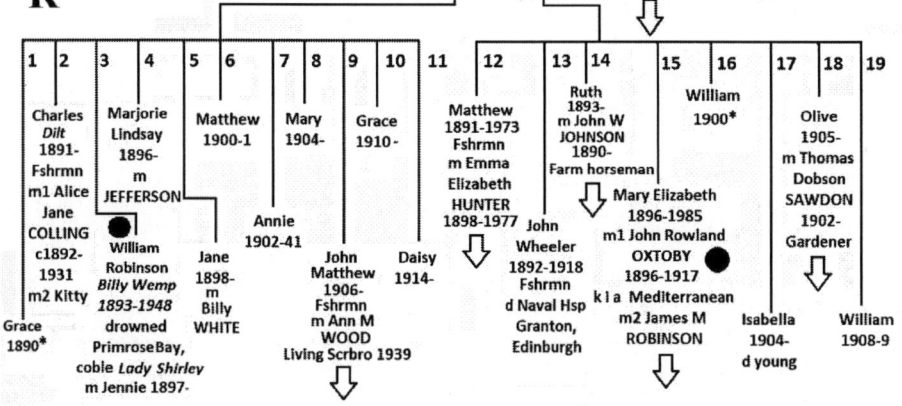

Mary CROWFOOT [CRAWFORD]

m Filey 26th Feb 1801

c1769-1849

8
Richard 1804-74 Fshrmn
m 1 Elizabeth QUINN
m2 Jane PARKER

9
Robert 1807-

10
Ann 1809-89 m Frank DAY c1800-80 Carrier/House agent/ Post messenger

Elizabeth 1 m SIMPSON c1814-40

11
George 1812-90 Fshrmn
m 2 Elizabeth HALL

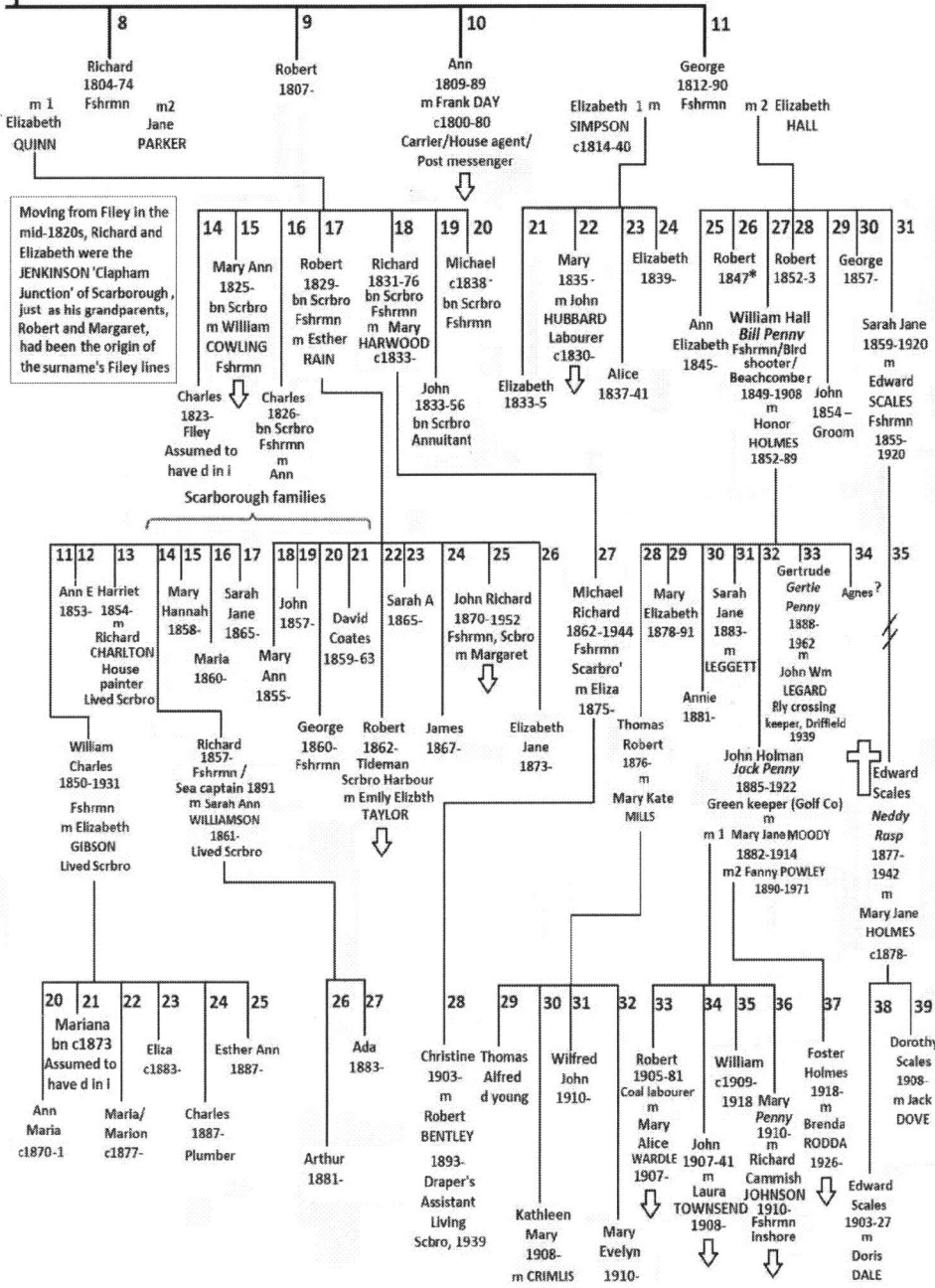

Moving from Filey in the mid-1820s, Richard and Elizabeth were the JENKINSON 'Clapham Junction' of Scarborough, just as his grandparents, Robert and Margaret, had been the origin of the surname's Filey lines

14 **15**
Mary Ann 1825- bn Scrbro m William COWLING Fshrmn

16 **17**
Robert 1829- bn Scrbro Fshrmn m Esther RAIN

18
Richard 1831-76 bn Scrbro Fshrmn m Mary HARWOOD c1833-

19 **20**
Michael c1838- bn Scrbro Fshrmn

21 **22**
Mary 1835 - m John HUBBARD Labourer c1830-

23 **24**
Elizabeth 1839-

25 **26**
Robert 1847*
Ann Elizabeth 1845-

27 **28**
Robert 1852-3
William Hall *Bill Penny* Fshrmn/Bird shooter/ Beachcomber 1849-1908 m Honor HOLMES 1852-89

29 **30**
George 1857-
John 1854 – Groom

31
Sarah Jane 1859-1920 m Edward SCALES 1855-1920

Charles 1823- Filey Assumed to have d in i

Charles 1826- bn Scrbro Fshrmn m Ann

Elizabeth 1833-5

Alice 1837-41

John 1833-56 bn Scrbro Annuitant

Scarborough families

11 **12** **13**
Ann E 1853-
Harriet 1854- m Richard CHARLTON House painter Lived Scrbro

14 **15** **16** **17**
Mary Hannah 1858-
Sarah Jane 1865-
Maria 1860-

18 **19** **20** **21**
John 1857-
David Coates 1859-63
Mary Ann 1855-

22 **23**
Sarah A 1865-

24 **25** **26**
John Richard 1870-1952 Fshrmn, Scbro m Margaret

27
Michael Richard 1862-1944 Fshrmn Scarbro' m Eliza 1875-

28 **29**
Mary Elizabeth 1878-91
Annie 1881-

30 **31** **32** **33**
Sarah Jane 1883- m LEGGETT
Gertrude *Gertie Penny* 1888-1962 m John Wm LEGARD Rly crossing keeper, Driffield 1939

34 **35**
Agnes ?

William Charles 1850-1931 Fshrmn m Elizabeth GIBSON Lived Scrbro

Richard 1857- Fshrmn / Sea captain 1891 m Sarah Ann WILLIAMSON 1861- Lived Scrbro

George 1860- Fshrmn

Robert 1862- Tideman Scrbro Harbour m Emily Elizbth TAYLOR

James 1867-

Elizabeth Jane 1873-

Thomas Robert 1876- m Mary Kate MILLS

John Holman *Jack Penny* 1885-1922 Green keeper (Golf Co) m m 1 Mary Jane MOODY 1882-1914 m2 Fanny POWLEY 1890-1971

Edward Scales *Neddy Rasp* 1877-1942 m Mary Jane HOLMES c1878-

20 **21**
Mariana bn c1873 Assumed to have d in i
Ann Maria c1870-1

22 **23**
Eliza c1883-
Maria/ Marion c1877-

24 **25**
Esther Ann 1887-
Charles 1887- Plumber

26 **27**
Ada 1883-
Arthur 1881-

28
Christine 1903- m Robert BENTLEY 1893- Draper's Assistant Living Scbro, 1939

29 **30** **31**
Thomas Alfred d young
Wilfred John 1910-
Kathleen Mary 1908- m CRIMLIS

32 **33**
Robert 1905-81 Coal labourer m Mary Alice WARDLE 1907-
Mary Evelyn 1910-

34 **35** **36** **37**
William c1909-1918
Mary Penny 1910- m Richard JOHNSON 1910- Fshrmn inshore
John 1907-41 m Laura TOWNSEND 1908-
Foster Holmes 1918- m Brenda RODDA 1926-

38 **39**
Dorothy Scales 1908- m Jack DOVE
Edward Scales 1903-27 m Doris DALE

N 8 William JENKINSON
1786-1865 Fisherman

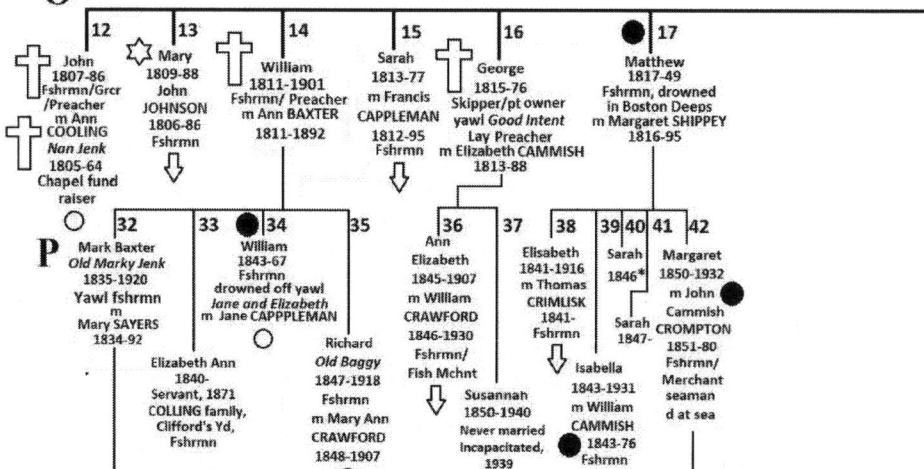

O

12 John 1807-86 Fshrmn/Grcr /Preacher m Ann COOLING *Nan Jenk* 1805-64 Chapel fund raiser

13 Mary 1809-88 John JOHNSON 1806-86 Fshrmn

14 William 1811-1901 Fshrmn/ Preacher m Ann BAXTER 1811-1892

15 Sarah 1813-77 m Francis CAPPLEMAN 1812-95 Fshrmn

16 George 1815-76 Skipper/pt owner yawl *Good Intent* Lay Preacher m Elizabeth CAMMISH 1813-88

17 Matthew 1817-49 Fshrmn, drowned in Boston Deeps m Margaret SHIPPEY 1816-95

P

32 Mark Baxter *Old Marky Jenk* 1835-1920 Yawl fshrmn m Mary SAYERS 1834-92

33 34 William 1843-67 Fshrmn drowned off yawl *Jane and Elizabeth* m Jane CAPPPLEMAN

35
Elizabeth Ann 1840- Servant, 1871 COLLING family, Clifford's Yd, Fshrmn

Richard *Old Baggy* 1847-1918 Fshrmn m Mary Ann CRAWFORD 1848-1907

36 37 Ann Elizabeth 1845-1907 m William CRAWFORD 1846-1930 Fshrmn/ Fish Mchnt

38 Elisabeth 1841-1916 m Thomas CRIMLISK 1841- Fshrmn

Susannah 1850-1940 Never married incapacitated, 1939

Isabella 1843-1931 m William CAMMISH 1843-76 Fshrmn

39 40 41 Sarah 1846*

Sarah 1847-

42 Margaret 1850-1932 m John Cammish CROMPTON 1851-80 Fshrmn/ Merchant seaman d at sea

Q

36 Mary Edmond SAYERS 1863- aka Mary Elisabeth JENKINSON Living with fthr, unmrrd, aged 47, 1911 Census

Ann 1865-1934 m Thomas WILLIAMSON 1862-1918 Fshrmn

37 38 39 Margaret Baxter 1866-1945 m Robert EDMOND Fshrmn 1864-95 drowned in yawl *Trio* unknown location

Elizabeth 1868-1945 m John WHEELER c1868 -1932 Fshrmn

40 Sarah 1872-1942 m Thomas Cammish OVERY Fshrmn 1868-1946

John William *John Willie Jenk* 1873-1944 Fshrmn, Chapel keeper, Preacher m Isabella WHEELER 1872-1957

41 42 George 1876-96 Fshrmn drowned in the Coble *Mary,* off Filey Brigg

43 Matthew Crompton 1868-1946 Bricklayer's Labourer m Emily/Emma JAMES c1869-1936

44 Thomas Robert *Old Naz* 1869 -1951 Fshrmn m Elizabeth TOWSE c1869 -1934

R

40 Elizabeth Ann 1898-1975 m Harold ROBINSON

41 42 George 1900-26

Mary 1900*

43 John Richard School- master *Dicky Jenk* 1903- m Gladys Leila COOPLAND 1908- Lived Scrbro

44 45 Sarah Elizabeth 1893- General svnt

John Crompton 1890-1909

46 47 Frances Crompton 1898-

Matthew Crompton 1895-1917 Newsboy 1911 d of wounds, Filey Royal Engineers

48 49 twins Nesfield Crompton 1900*

George Crompton 1900*

50 George James Crompton 1902-61 m 1 Bertha KING

51 Tom Fenby Crompton 1905-68 Fshrmn Inshore m 1 Lilian Mabel CLAYTON 1906-63 m2 Ann WICKEN 1910-80

52 53 Richard Cammish 1893-1919 blown up in *Emulator* by a German mine

Mary Elizabeth *Mary Naz* 1896-1915

54 55 Sarah *Sally Naz* 1900-67 Teacher m Milton HALL 1899-1940 Insurance agent bn Newing- ton, Hull RAF WWI

Thomas 1891-1966 m William WATKINSON 1891-1973 Deep sea skipper

Mary Elizabeth Naz 1891-1966 m William JENKINSON k in a, Fortuyn, France

56 57 Fanny Elizabeth 1900*

Richard Cammish 1898-1919

☆ Confirmation that this Mary was O13 and not O1:

1 The 1838 St Oswald marriage entry gives her father as William JENKINSON *fisherman,* not *mariner*

2 One of the witnesses was Matthew JENKINSON, clearly O17, her younger brother

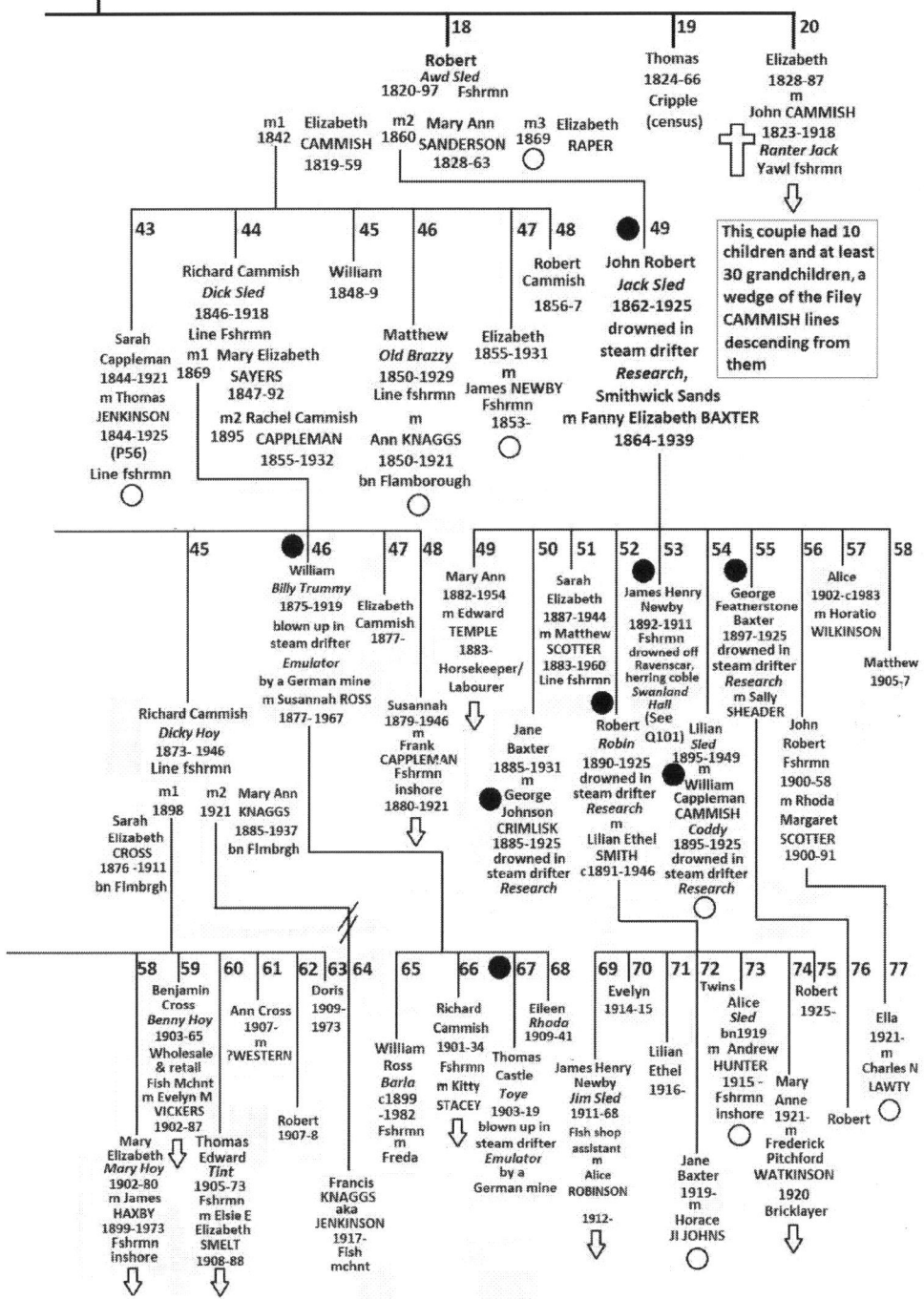

m
Filey
24th May
1806

Isabella ANDERSON
1788-1870

18
Robert
Awd Sled Fshrmn
1820-97

19
Thomas
1824-66
Cripple
(census)

20
Elizabeth
1828-87
m
John CAMMISH
1823-1918
Ranter Jack
Yawl fshrmn

m1 1842 **Elizabeth CAMMISH** 1819-59
m2 1860 **Mary Ann SANDERSON** 1828-63
m3 1869 **Elizabeth RAPER** ○

This couple had 10 children and at least 30 grandchildren, a wedge of the Filey CAMMISH lines descending from them

43
Sarah Cappleman 1844-1921 m Thomas JENKINSON 1844-1925 (P56) Line fshrmn ○

44
Richard Cammish *Dick Sled* 1846-1918 Line Fshrmn m1 1869 Mary Elizabeth SAYERS 1847-92 m2 1895 Rachel Cammish CAPPLEMAN 1855-1932

45
William 1848-9

46
Matthew *Old Brazzy* 1850-1929 Line fshrmn m Ann KNAGGS 1850-1921 bn Flamborough ○

47 48
Elizabeth 1855-1931 m James NEWBY Fshrmn 1853- ○

49 ●
Robert Cammish 1856-7

John Robert *Jack Sled* 1862-1925 drowned in steam drifter *Research*, Smithwick Sands m Fanny Elizabeth BAXTER 1864-1939

45
Richard Cammish *Dicky Hoy* 1873-1946 Line fshrmn m1 1898 Sarah Elizabeth CROSS 1876-1911 bn Flmbrgh m2 1921 Mary Ann KNAGGS 1885-1937 bn Flmbrgh

46 ●
William *Billy Trummy* 1875-1919 blown up in steam drifter *Emulator* by a German mine m Susannah ROSS 1877-1967

47 48
Susannah 1879-1946 m Frank CAPPLEMAN Fshrmn inshore 1880-1921

49
Mary Ann 1882-1954 m Edward TEMPLE 1883- Horsekeeper/Labourer

50 51
Sarah Elizabeth 1887-1944 m Matthew SCOTTER 1883-1960 Line fshrmn

Jane Baxter 1885-1931 m ● George Johnson CRIMLISK 1885-1925 drowned in steam drifter *Research*

52 53 ●
James Henry Newby 1892-1911 Fshrmn drowned off Ravenscar, herring coble *Swanland Hall* (See Q101)

Robert *Robin* 1890-1925 drowned in steam drifter *Research* m Lilian Ethel SMITH c1891-1946

54 55 ●
George Featherstone Baxter 1897-1925 drowned in steam drifter *Research* m Sally SHEADER

Lilian *Sled* 1895-1949 m William Cappleman CAMMISH *Coddy* 1895-1925 drowned in steam drifter *Research*

56 57 58
Alice 1902-c1983 m Horatio WILKINSON

Matthew 1905-7

John Robert Fshrmn 1900-58 m Rhoda Margaret SCOTTER 1900-91

---

58 59
Benjamin Cross *Benny Hoy* 1903-65 Wholesale & retail Fish Mchnt m Evelyn M VICKERS 1902-87

Mary Elizabeth *Mary Hoy* 1902-80 m James HAXBY 1899-1973 Fshrmn inshore ⇩

Ann Cross 1907- m ?WESTERN

Thomas Edward *Tint* 1905-73 Fshrmn m Elsie E SMELT 1908-88 ⇩

60 61
Doris 1909-1973

Robert 1907-8

62 63 64
Francis KNAGGS aka JENKINSON 1917- Fish mchnt

65
William Ross *Barla* c1899-1982 Fshrmn m Freda

66 ●
Richard Cammish 1901-34 Fshrmn m Kitty STACEY ⇩

67 68
Thomas Castle *Toye* 1903-19 blown up in steam drifter *Emulator* by a German mine

Eileen *Rhoda* 1909-41

69 70
James Henry Newby 1911-68 Fish shop assistant m Alice ROBINSON 1912- ⇩

71 72 73
Evelyn 1914-15

Lilian Ethel 1916-

Twins Alice *Sled* bn1919 m Andrew HUNTER 1915- Fshrmn inshore

Jane Baxter 1919- m Horace JI JOHNS ○

74 75 76 77
Robert 1925-

Mary Anne 1921- m Frederick Pitchford WATKINSON 1920 Bricklayer ⇩

Robert

Ella 1921- m Charles N LAWTY ○

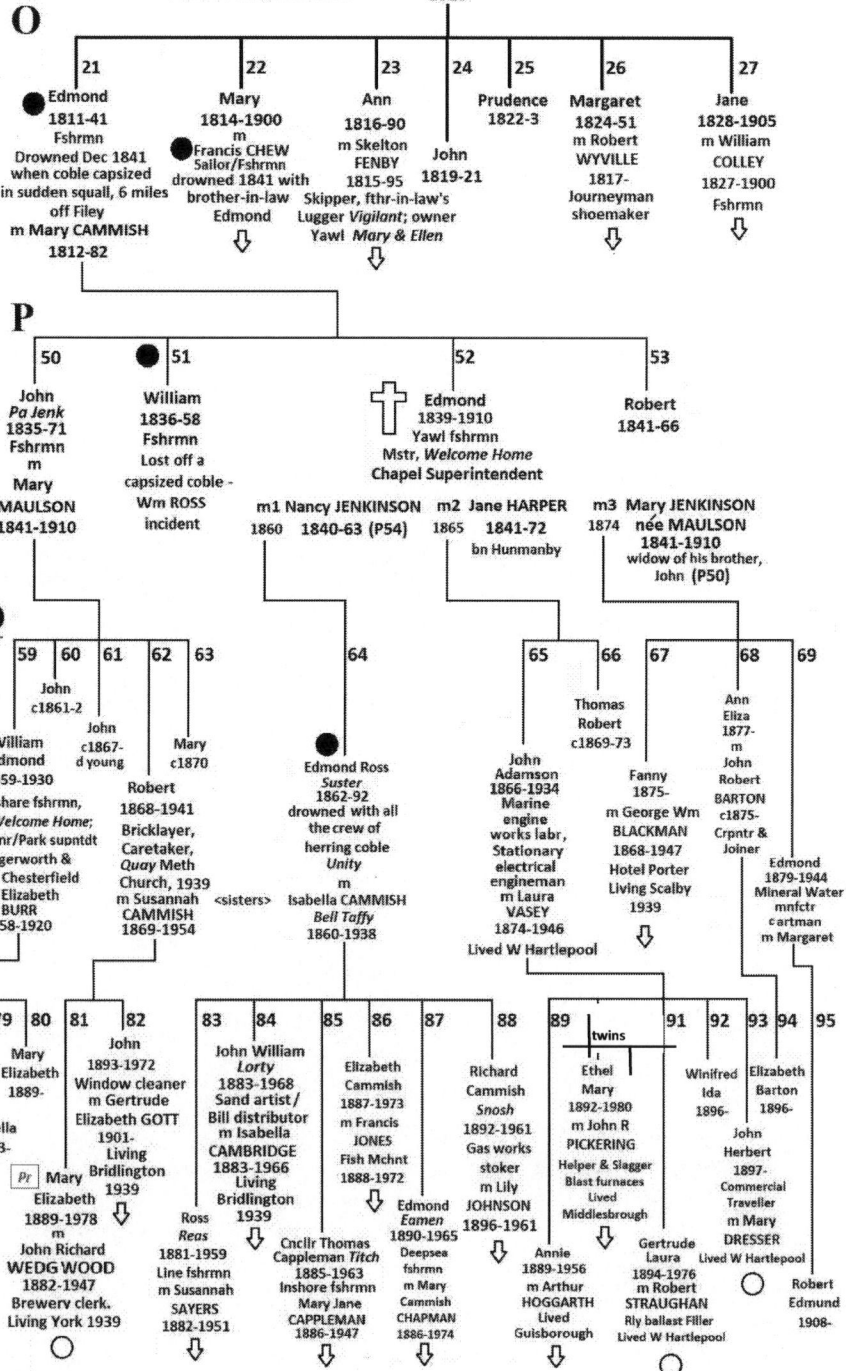

John JENKINSON m **Mary EDMOND**

1791-1872 Fisherman
owned Lugger *Valiant*

Filey
18th Dec
1810

1791-1856

O

21
● Edmond
1811-41
Fshrmn
Drowned Dec 1841
when coble capsized
in sudden squall, 6 miles
off Filey
m Mary CAMMISH
1812-82

22
Mary
1814-1900
m
● Francis CHEW
Sailor/Fshrmn
drowned 1841 with
brother-in-law
Edmond ⇩

23
Ann
1816-90
m Skelton
FENBY
1815-95
Skipper, fthr-in-law's
Lugger *Vigilant*; owner
Yawl *Mary & Ellen* ⇩

24
John
1819-21

25
Prudence
1822-3

26
Margaret
1824-51
m Robert
WYVILLE
1817-
Journeyman
shoemaker ⇩

27
Jane
1828-1905
m William
COLLEY
1827-1900
Fshrmn ⇩

P

50
John
Pa Jenk
1835-71
Fshrmn
m
Mary
MAULSON
1841-1910

51 ●
William
1836-58
Fshrmn
Lost off a
capsized coble -
Wm ROSS
incident

52 ✝
Edmond
1839-1910
Yawl fshrmn
Mstr, *Welcome Home*
Chapel Superintendent

53
Robert
1841-66

m1 Nancy JENKINSON
1860 1840-63 (P54)

m2 Jane HARPER
1865 1841-72
bn Hunmanby

m3 Mary JENKINSON
1874 née MAULSON
1841-1910
widow of his brother,
John (P50)

Q

59 | **60** | **61**
John
c1861-2

William
Edmond
1859-1930
Yawl share fshrmn,
1881 *Welcome Home*;
1891 Grdnr/Park supntdt
Wingerworth &
1901 Chesterfield
m Elizabeth
BURR
1858-1920

John
c1867-
d young

62 | **63**
Mary
c1870

Robert
1868-1941
Bricklayer,
Caretaker,
Quay Meth
Church, 1939
m Susannah
CAMMISH
1869-1954

64
● Edmond Ross
Suster
1862-92
drowned with all
the crew of
herring coble
Unity
m
<sisters> Isabella CAMMISH
Bell Taffy
1860-1938

65
John
Adamson
1866-1934
Marine
engine
works labr,
Stationary
electrical
engineman
m Laura
VASEY
1874-1946
Lived W Hartlepool

66
Thomas
Robert
c1869-73

67
Fanny
1875-
m George Wm
BLACKMAN
1868-1947
Hotel Porter
Living Scalby
1939 ⇩

68 | **69**
Ann
Eliza
1877-
m
John
Robert
BARTON
c1875-
Crpntr &
Joiner

Edmond
1879-1944
Mineral Water
mnfctr
cartman
m Margaret

R

78 | **79** | **80**

John
1881-

Isabella
1883-

Mary
Elizabeth
1889-

Pr Mary
Elizabeth
1889-1978
m
John Richard
WEDGWOOD
1882-1947
Brewery clerk.
Living York 1939 ○

81 | **82**
John
1893-1972
Window cleaner
m Gertrude
Elizabeth GOTT
1901-
Living
Bridlington
1939 ⇩

Ross
Reas
1881-1959
Line fshrmn
m Susannah
SAYERS
1882-1951 ⇩

83 | **84**
John William
Lorty
1883-1968
Sand artist/
Bill distributor
m Isabella
CAMBRIDGE
1883-1966
Living
Bridlington
1939 ⇩

Cncllr Thomas
Cappleman *Titch*
1885-1963
Inshore fshrmn
Mary Jane
CAPPLEMAN
1886-1947 ⇩

85 | **86** | **87**
Elizabeth
Cammish
1887-1973
m Francis
JONES
Fish Mchnt
1888-1972 ⇩

Edmond
Eamen
1890-1965
Deepsea
fshrmn
m Mary
Cammish
CHAPMAN
1886-1974 ⇩

88
Richard
Cammish
Snosh
1892-1961
Gas works
stoker
m Lily
JOHNSON
1896-1961 ⇩

89 twins **91**
Ethel
Mary
1892-1980
m John R
PICKERING
Helper & Slagger
Blast furnaces
Lived
Middlesbrough ⇩

Annie
1889-1956
m Arthur
HOGGARTH
Lived
Guisborough ⇩

92 | **93** | **94**
Winifred
Ida
1896-

Gertrude
Laura
1894-1976
m Robert
STRAUGHAN
Rly ballast Filler
Lived W Hartlepool ○

Elizabeth
Barton
1896-

John
Herbert
1897-
Commercial
Traveller
m Mary
DRESSER
Lived W Hartlepool ○

95

Robert
Edmund
1908-

⬩ Thomas JENKINSON m ⬩ Mary CASTLE

1793-1863 Fisherman, part owned Filey **1795-1878**
Lugger *Flora* and Yawl *Admiral Mitford* 23rd April bn Thwing
1814

O

28 Jane 1815-18

29 ⬩ Thomas 1817-90 Yawl fshrmn m Rachel JOHNSON 1815-1900
Margaret 1816-90 m William COWLING 1815-90 Fshrmn

⬩ Robert 1819-1904 Yawl fshrmn m Elizabeth COLE 1824-1900 bn Staithes

In the later 1800s these eight relatives had shares in at least four yawls, viz *Admiral Mitford*, *Eliza, Elizabeth & Emma*, and *Refuge*. This may represent a deliberate spreading of personal and financial risk, as well as inheritance.

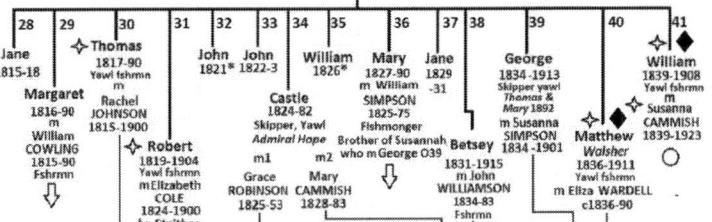

30

31

32 33 34 35 John 1821* John 1822-3 William 1826* Castle 1824-82 Skipper, Yawl *Admiral Hope* m1 Grace ROBINSON 1825-53

36 Mary 1827-90 m William SIMPSON 1825-75 m2 Mary CAMMISH 1828-83

37 38 Jane 1829 -31 Brother of Susannah who m George O39 Betsey 1831-1915 m John WILLIAMSON 1834-83 Fshrmn

39 George 1834-1913 Skipper yawl *Thomas & Mary* 1892 m Susanna SIMPSON 1834-1901

40 ⬩ Matthew 1836-1911 Yawl fshrmn m Eliza WARDELL c1836-90 ◯

41 ◆ William 1839-1908 Yawl fshrmn m Susanna CAMMISH 1839-1923

⬩ Walsher

P

54 55 ● Ross 1841-80 skipper of yawl *Eliza*; lost off *Eliza* Great Gale, Oct 1880 m Eliza CRAWFORD 1841-1920

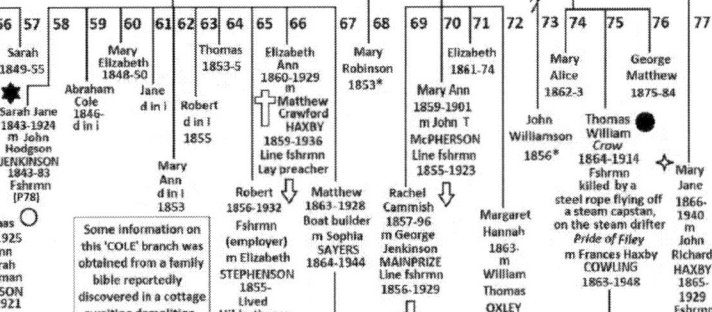

Nancy 1840-63 m Edmund JENKINSON (for their son see under P52) ⬇

56 57 58 Sarah 1849-55
★ Sarah Jane 1843-1924 m John Hodgson JENKINSON 1843-83 Fshrmn (P78) ◯
Thomas 1844-1925 Fshrmn m Sarah Cappleman JENKINSON 1844-1921 (P43) ⬇

59 60 Mary Elizabeth 1848-50
Abraham Cole 1846- d in i
Jane d in i

61 62 63 64 Thomas 1853-5
Robert d in i 1855
Mary Ann d in i 1853

Some information on this 'COLE' branch was obtained from a family bible reportedly discovered in a cottage awaiting demolition

65 66 Elizabeth Ann 1860-1929 m ✝ Matthew Crawford HAXBY 1859-1936 Line fshrmn Lay preacher
Robert 1856-1932 Fshrmn (employer) m Elizabeth STEPHENSON 1855- Lived Hilderthorpe ⬇

67 68 Mary Robinson 1853*
Matthew 1863-1928 Boat builder m Sophia SAYERS 1864-1944 ⬇

69 70 71 Elizabeth 1861-74
Mary Ann 1859-1901 m John T McPHERSON Line fshrmn 1855-1923
Rachel Cammish 1857-96 m George Jenkinson MAINPRIZE Line fshrmn 1856-1929 ⬇

72 73 74 John Williamson 1856*
Margaret Hannah 1863- m William Thomas OXLEY

75 Mary Alice 1862-3
● Thomas William Crow 1864-1914 Fshrmn killed by a steel rope flying off a steam capstan, on the steam drifter *Pride of Filey* m Frances Haxby COWLING 1863-1948

76 77 George Matthew 1875-84
⬩ Mary Jane 1866-1940 m John Richard HAXBY 1865-1929 Fshrmn

Q

70 Sarah Elizabeth 1882-

71

72 73 Mary Jane 1889-
Robert 1886- Chalk quarryman Brdlngtn
John Hodgson 1884-1956 Lighterman, Hull m Laura DEAN 1881-

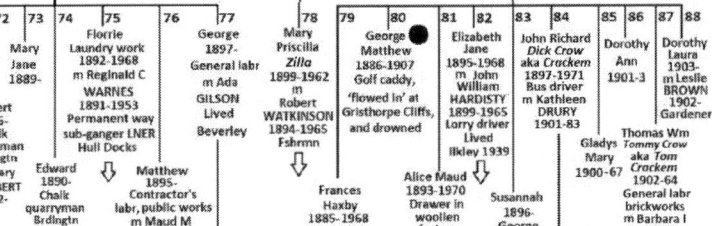

74 75 76 Florrie 1892-1968 Laundry work m Reginald C WARNES 1891-1953 Permanent way sub-ganger LNER Hull Docks
Edward 1890- Chalk quarryman Brdlngtn
Matthew 1895- Contractor's labr, public works m Maud M SULLIVAN Lived Beverley

77 George 1897- General labr m Ada GILSON Lived Beverley

78 Mary Priscilla *Zilla* 1899-1962 m Robert WATKINSON 1894-1965 Fshrmn
Frances Haxby 1885-1968 m George SMITH 1889-1964 Motor driver ⬇

79 80 ● George Matthew 1886-1907 Golf caddy, 'flowed in' at Gristhorpe Cliffs, and drowned

81 82 Elizabeth Jane 1895-1968 m John William HARDISTY 1899-1965 Lorry driver Lived Ilkley 1939
Alice Maud 1893-1970 Drawer in woollen factory Lived Ilkley 1939 unmarried with John W & Elizbth J HARDISTY

83 84 John Richard *Dick Crow* aka *Crackem* 1897-1971 Bus driver m Kathleen DRURY 1901-83
Susannah 1896- George William SAYERS 1898- Gas works labourer ◯

85 86 Dorothy Ann 1901-3
Gladys Mary 1900-67

87 88 Dorothy Laura 1903- m Leslie BROWN 1902- Gardener
Thomas Wm *Tommy Crow* aka *Tom Crackem* 1902-64 General labr brickworks m Barbara I SMITH

R

96 John Hodgson bn Brd1906 Lighterman Hull

97 98 Matthew 1913-77 bn Hull Lighterman Hull m Agnes Mary LISTER 1914-84

Laura bn Hull 1909

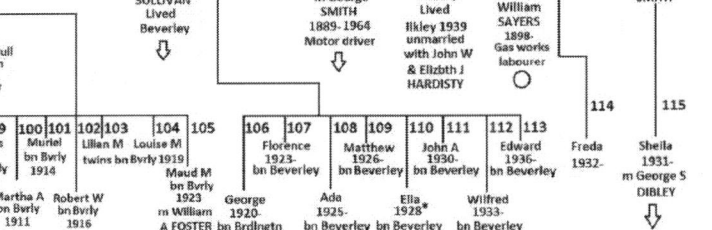

99 100 101 Gladys Bell bn Bvrly 1907
Muriel bn Bvrly 1914
Martha A bn Bvrly 1911

102 103 Lilian M twins bn Bvrly 1919
Robert W bn Bvrly 1916

104 105 Louise M
Maud M bn Bvrly 1923 m William A FOSTER

106 107 Florence 1923- bn Beverley
George 1920- bn Brdlngtn

108 109 Matthew 1926- bn Beverley
Ada 1925- bn Beverley

110 111 John A 1930- bn Beverley
Ella 1928* bn Beverley

112 113 Edward 1936- bn Beverley
Wilfred 1933- bn Beverley

114 Freda 1932-

115 Sheila 1931- m George S DIBLEY ⬇

★ **Proof that Sarah Jane married John Hodgson JENKINSON (P78) - Sarah Jane, widow, sister-in-law of Matthew HAXBY and Elizabeth Ann (P66) in 1891 Census, Filey**

◆ **Owners of the yawl *Elizabeth & Susannah*. Wrecked at the back of the Outer Pier, Scrbro, Feb 1884**

George JENKINSON m Mary SCALES

Filey
14th April
1795-1860 Fisherman 1816 1798-1881
Bought first yawl *Integrity*, 1833

42	43	44	45	46	47	48	49		50	51

42 Robert
1817*
twins

43 George
1817*

44 Robert
1819-82
Fshrmn
part owner
/skipper of
yawl *George
Peabody*
m Rachel
HODGSON
1818-94

45 Sarah
1821-91 ☆
m George
MAINPRIZE
1818-74
yawl /coble fshrmn
bn Flmbro drwnd off
The Brigg with nephew
(P80) when their coble
was caught in the Tide-way

46 George
1824-96 ☆
Master
Tailor
Unmrrd

47 John
1826-1900
yawl fshrmn
m Mary
HODGSON
1824-84 ○

48 William ●
1829-61
master of yawl
Hope, swept
overboard
and drwnd
m Frances SCALES
c1831-1908
Remarried to
Thos SEXTON
Fshrmn

49 Matthew ●
1832-63 m
Fshrmn
Drwnd Filey
Bay when 'a
huge breaker
overturned the
coble'

Jane
COATES ✗ ?
c1832-
Remarried
1870
to John
PRESTON
Fshrmn

50 Thomas ☆
1835-95
Fshrmn
m
Rachael
FELL
1835-99

51 Mary
1837-83 ☆

These men held
shares in the yawl
Elizabeth & Emma,
built Scrbro 1867,
wrecked Rbn Hds
Bay, Oct 1880, Thos
the skipper

78	79 ●	80	81	82	83	84	85	86	87	88	89	90	91	92	93	94	95	96	97	98	99	100	101

78 John
Hodgson
1843-83
Skipper, yawl
Monarch
transferred to
Brdlngton 1877
m Sarah
Jane
JENKINSON
1843-1924
(P58) ○

Mary
1845-1926
m William
WATKINSON
Labr/Carter
1839-1934
⇩

79 George
1847-74
Fshrmn
drwnd off
The Brigg
with Uncle
George
MAINPRIZE

Sarah Ann
1849*

80 Edmond
1851*

Robert
1852-62

84 Catherine
aka Kate
1857-1926
m Robert
LANE
1856-1932
Line fshrmn
⇩ Edmund
1859-60

Rachel
1855-81

87 Mary
Elizabeth
1860-1915
m David
WILLIS
Fshrmn
⇩ Edmund
Line fshrmn
1848-1917

Mary
Elizabeth
1858*

89 Mary
1858-
m
William
Cammish
BAXTER
Fshrmn
1856-78

George
*Old
Jossie Buggins*
1860-1933
Line fshrmn
m
Priscilla SCOTTER
1859-1948

William
1856-78

92 Matthew
1862-?1928
Fshrmn
m Kate PICKERING
1863-1949
bn Brdlngtn; they
moved there early
1880s

John Robert
Jack Block
1864-1936
Bricklayer
& labourer
m Sarah Ann
CAMMISH
Sal Tiny
1867-1954

93 Jane
1867-
✗

94 Martin
GULLEN

95 John
1862-1935
Fshrmn
m Eliza
JOHNSON
c1865-1941

George
William
1860-1936
Painter
m
Mary Jane
ELLIOTT
1863-1945

97 Mary E
1866-1958
Ldgng hse kpr
/Confectioner
Never mrrd

Richard
?Andrew
c1870-1

Thomas
Laffy
1864-1944
Line fshrmn
m
Alice Ann
COLLING
c1865-1949

99 William Mtthw
1868-1945
Lbr fshrmn /
Lbr river side
Gainsborough
m Sarah
TURNER
⇩

Sarah Jane
1877-1936
m John Wm
PASHBY
c1867-1924
Brcklyr's labr

89	90	91	92	93	94	95	96	97	98	99	100	101	102	103	104	105	106	107	108	109

All children bn Brdlngtn

89 Francis
Cappleman
Bonzo Buggins
1883-1957
Line fshrmn/
beachcomber
m
Bertha
Laura/Louisa
COLLEY
1883-1961

John
Matthew
Jossie Buggins
1880-1957
Line fshrmn
m Elizabeth
Ellison CHAPMAN
1881-1964
bn Scrbro ○

91 George Wm
1892-
Golf caddy
Left children
with his Filey
family, 1930s?
Died Sacramento,
California
m
Juliet Annett SEYMOUR
bn Newcastle 1891

James
Scotter
Jim Buggins
1889-1965
Line fshrmn/
beachcomber
m Violet May
WHITE
c1895-1981

123 Jane G
1915-
m John Wm
JENKINSON
bn 1912,
son of
Edmond (R87)

124 John M
1917-

93 Elizabeth
Annie
1885-1967
m Alfred
WRIGHT
Joiner
1885-1956

94 Margaret
1891-

Matthew
1887-1969
Fshrmn
m Florence
Annie
SPECK
1889-1954
Living
Brdlngtn

95 Florence
1899-

Robert
1897-1974
Inshore
fshrmn
m
Lilian Hardy
BURRELL
1898-1979
Living Brdlngtn
after c1920

98 Sarah Jane
1887-1957
m Robert
Jenkinson
HAXBY
?*Cock Robin*
1886-1956

George
Matthew
1890-
Coal
trimmer
m Elsie
INMAN
1894-
In Hull
1939

99 Susannah
1892-1951
m Edmond
Tot
Cammish
CHAPMAN
Line fshrmn net &
line weekly
articles, 1939

101 Jane
1887-1974
m George
William
FORDEN
1887-1947
Rly Inspector
engineering

102 *Pr*
Thomas
Francis
1890-
bn Leeds,
Teacher,
Cayton
Bay

Mary
Ellen
1895-
m James
Henry
Newby
JENKINSON
(Q53)

104 Olive May
1899-1949
m Maurice
WOOD
Jrnyman
painter
1895-1955

Wilfred
bn c1894
Draper
Pte, Yorks
Rgt, k i a
1st July 1916

106 Annie
1891-1971
m
Frank
FELL
1890-1956
Builder &
contractor ○

Eliza
1888-
m
David Page
FOX
1879-
bn Pickering

Thomas *Laffy*
1894-1964
Line fshrmn
m1 Annie Theresa
HUNT
c1893-1927

m2 Mary
Elizabeth
CARTWRIGHT
1888-1971 ○

109 William
Colling
Watta
1898-1973
Licensee
Star Inn
m
Eleanor
Ferguson
COLLEY
1898-1982

116 ●	117 ●	118	119	120	121	122	125	126	127	128	129	130	131	132	133	134	135	136	137	138	139	140	141

All children bn Brdlngtn

116 Edwin
Chapman
Teddy Fat
1904-25
drowned
in drifter
Research

Matthew
Sailor
Fshrmn
Footballer,
York City
1906-79
m Jane
JOHNSON
1908-81
⇩

117 George
1909-25
drowned
in drifter
Research

Francis
Cappleman
1916-19

Elizabeth
Chapman
1918-
m
? Harold
PARKER

120 Priscilla
1917-
m
Leonard
G SMALL

George
William
1919-
Fshrmn
Inshore

122 Matthew
1913-

Marjorie
1915-
m Harold
COLBECK
Motor Mchnc
Living Scrbro
1939
⇩

126 Elsie
1918-
?m
William

Betty
1920-

128 Arthur
1921-
Painter &
decorator
m Marie
Doreen
SMITH
1922-72

Leslie
1928-
?m Dorothy

130 Robert
1920-
Lorry
driver's
mate

? Annie

132 Margaret
1928-

June
1933-

135 Raymond
1918-
bn Hull

George
1916-
bn Filey
Coal trimmer
m Kitty MORRILL
1916-
Living Hull 1939

136 Doris
Irene
1920-
bn Hull

137 Richard
Cammish
Dick Black
1911-81
Boot &
shoe repairer
m Barbara J
LANCASTER
1909-

138 Jane Baxter
1911-83
m Reginald
BURDETT
1905-71
bn Malton
Electrical
Travelling
Salesman
⇩

Thomas
Gordon
Laffy
1916-74
Bricklayer
m Nancy
JENKINSON
1917-
dau of Richard
Cammish and Lily
JENKINSON
Snosh (R88)
⇩

141 Alice Lundy
1924-2017
m
Thomas
Moore
Reginald
LISTER
1922-81

Sources

Oral

ALLEN, Mrs Elizabeth Jenkinson,
née HOGGARTH (1917-99)
BRADLEY, Mrs Mary, née JENKINSON
BURDETT, Mrs Jane (d1983)
BURTON, George Cappleman (1911-2002)
CAMMISH, Joanne
CAPPLEMAN, George (bn1889)
COLLINS, Terence (bn1923) - an authority on
Filey families
CRIMLISK, John & Maisy – transcribers of
Filey parish registers, census returns, and
gravestones; collectors of press cuttings
DALE, Bob (died 1984)
DOWSON, Mrs Sue
EBLET, Stephen – collector of photographs,
which he makes freely available
ELSOM, Ian – fount of local knowledge
FEARON, Michael - introduced Irene and
myself to many elderly Filey people, and
encouraged me to revisit this research 33
years on
HALL, Rev Robert
HORNER, Mrs Edith
HOUSLEY, Mrs Constance C
HOWE, Mrs Marjorie
HUNTER, Robert Pearson *Tewy* (1917-95)
HUNTER, Mrs Elizabeth Cammish
(1913-2000)
JENKINSON, Edmund Ross
JENKINSON, Foster Holmes (bn1918)
JENKINSON, Mrs Rhoda Margaret
(1900-91)
JENKINSON, Robert Edmund
JOHNSON, Richard Cammish (bn1910) -
coble fishing in the days of sail
LONGBOTTOM, Bernard
MAINPRIZE, Mrs M

MAITLAND, Mrs E
MIDWOOD, Steve – authoritative Filey
Archives volunteer and leading light
OLIVER, Mrs Ethel
ROBINSON, Mary Elizabeth, née
JENKINSON (1896-1985) - accurate
recall of early 20th Century Filey families
RUDD, Steve
SAYERS, Peter
SCALES, George - Scarborough and Filey
fishing
SMITH, Captain Sydney T (1907-2000) –
Scarborough's Deputy Harbour Master
to 1974; expert on Yorkshire maritime
history
SWIFT, Mrs Betty
TAYLOR, Graham - coble fisherman
1959-74; experienced lifeboatman
WATKINSON, Peter
WATKINSON, Tom Jenkinson
WELBURN née HOGGARTH - 'Aunt
Mary' (1915-83); initial memories made
us realise how special these families are
WHEELER, Robert Lane (1900-92)
WILKIE, Kath – enthusiastic researcher
WOOD, Robin (died 1984)

Transcriptions of Oral Interviews *Exploring
Filey's Past: Oral Interviews, 2005-6*
(Transcripts at Filey Museum):
COLLING, William Johnson (1925-2015)
HAXBY, Jim (1935-2018)
HAXBY, Richard Jenkinson (1928-2005)

Fishing Project (Box 6, Filey Archives)
CAPPLEMAN, William (1917-2009) undated
typescript

Primary Sources

Calendar of Probate Grants, England & Wales, 1858-present (*gov.uk/search-will-probate*
website); Census Returns 1841-1911, and *National Register*, 1939 (all digitised, indexed and
available at *Ancestry.co.uk*, *Findmypast* and *UK Census online*); Monumental Inscriptions, St
Oswald's; Parish Registers and Bishops' Transcripts; Directories and Almanacks; Newspapers
– accessible at *britishnewspaperarchive.co.uk; Filey Post* cuttings (John Crimlisk) at Filey
Archives; Cappleman Account Book, 1872-93 (Scarborough Maritime Heritage Centre, Filey

History, Vol 4, item 12) rescued by John Crimlisk some years ago, it contains the working accounts of a Filey boat-builder and repairer who worked on the Coble Landing and names many boats and owners, often detailing parts replaced and charge made); *Report from the Commissioners on the Sea Fisheries of the United Kingdom, with Appendix and Minutes of Evidence, 1866; Report of the Inspectors of Fisheries for England and Wales and Commissions for Commissioners for Sea Fisheries on the Sea Fisheries of England and Wales, 1879; Report by the Inspectors for England and Wales and Commissioners on Trawl Net and Beam Trawl Fishing, with Minutes of Evidence and Appendix, 1885;* Returns of the Filey Life Boat; *Sailing Fishing Vessels registered at Scarborough* (all Filey cobles were registered after 1869; larger fishing vessels from 1786 - registers give names and dimensions of boats, naming owners and (larger boats only) skippers.

Secondary Sources

The following are cited in in several chapters, in abbreviated form (ie author, year, page). The full references are given here.

Barron, Alan, *The Fishertown of Nairn: Echoes of a Byegone Age* (Alan Barron, 2009)

Blaikie, Andrew, 'Coastal Communities in Victorian Scotland: What makes North-East Fisher Families distinctive?' (*Local Population Studies,* 69, Autumn 2002). Available online

Cole, John, *The History and Antiquities of Filey in the County of York* (John Cole, 1828)

Cooper, Canon Arthur N, *Filey and its Church* (ETW Dennis, 1886)

Cooper, Canon Arthur N, *Illustrated Guide to Filey: Descriptive and Historical* (Sokell, 1900)

Cooper, Canon Arthur N, *Across the Broad Acres. Being Sketches of Yorkshire Life and Character* (A Brown & Sons, 1908)

Cooper, Canon Arthur N, *Round the Home of a Yorkshire Parson: Stories of Yorkshire Life* (WH Smith, New and Revised Ed, 1910)

Cortis, Dr William S, *An Historical and Descriptive Guide to Filey* (Kendall, 1860)

Dyson, John, *Business in Great Waters: The Story of British Fishermen* (Angus & Robertson, 1977)

Fearon, Michael, *The History of Filey North Yorkshire from Fishing Village to Edwardian Resort* (Blackthorn Press, 2008)

Fearon, Michael, *Old Filey: A Remarkable Fishing Community* (Blackthorn Press, 2016)

Fisher, Fred, *History* (typescript, c1970, at Filey Archives)

Frank, Peter, *Yorkshire Fisherfolk: A Social History of the Yorkshire inshore fishing community* (Phillimore, 2002)

Friend, Stephen Frederick, *A Sense of Belonging: Religion and Identity in Yorkshire and Humber Fishing Communities, c1815-1914* (Hull PhD Thesis, 2010). Available online

Godfrey, Arthur, *Yorkshire Fishing Fleets* (Dalesman, 1974)

Godfrey, Arthur & Lassey, Peter J, *Shipwrecks of the Yorkshire Coast* (Dalesman, 1982)

Harland, Richard, *Filey, a Short History* (unpaginated typescript, c1970, Filey Archives)

Harland, Richard, *Fishermen of Filey* (unpaginated typescript, c1970, Filey Archives)

Harland, Richard, *Society at the Seaside* (unpaginated typescript, c1970, Filey Archives)

Kendall, Rev Charles, *God's Hand in the Storm* (1877; first published Lamb & Newton, 1870)

Kurlansky, Mark, *Cod: A Biography of the Fish that changed the World* (Vintage, 1999)

McKee, JEG (ed), *The English Coble* (Trustees of the National Maritime Museum, 1978)

Morris, Jeff, *The Story of the Filey Lifeboats* (Jeff Morris, 1991)

Parkin, Dean, *A Maritime Miscellany: Vol 1: Whitby to Great Yarmouth* (Tyndale & Panda Publishing, 1989)

Pettitt, Rev Arthur, *The Filey Hand-Book* (1868)

Pritchard, Dr Edward William, *Observations on Filey as a Watering Place: a Guide for Visitors* (1854)

Robinson, Norman William, *The English Fishing Industry 1790-1914: A Case Study of the Yorkshire Coast* (Hull PhD Thesis, 1984). Available online

Robinson, Robb, *A History of the Yorkshire Coast Fishing Industry 1780-1914* (Hull University Press, 1987)

Shaw, Rev George, *Our Filey Fishermen with Sketches of their Manners and Customs, Social Habits and Condition* (Hamilton Adams, 1867)

Shaw, Rev George, *Rambles around Filey* (Hamilton Adams, 1867)

Shaw, Rev George, *Scenes and Adventure on the Sea* (Knapp, undated)

Smith, David T, 'Cobblemen' [*sic*] (*Blackwood's Edinburgh Magazine,* Aug 1932). Partial copy at Scarborough Maritime Heritage Centre

Smith, Malcolm, 'The Demography of Coastal Communities' (*Local Population Studies,* 70, Spring 2003)

Smylie, Mike, *The Perilous Catch: A History of Commercial Fishing* (History Press, 2015)

Sokell, John T, *The Visitors Illustrated and Descriptive Guide to Filey and Neighbourhood* (1899)

Starkey, David J, Reid, Chris & Ashcroft, Neil, *England's Sea Fisheries. The Commercial Sea Fisheries of England and Wales since 1300* (Chatham, 2000)

Storm, Alan, *Family and Maritime Community: Robin Hood's Bay, c1653-c1867* (Leicester PhD Thesis, 1991). Available online

Thompson, Paul; Wailey, Tony; & Lummis, Trevor, *Living the Fishing* (Routledge & Kegan Paul, 1983)

Truss, Priscilla Mary, *Primitive Methodism in the Yorkshire Wolds c1820-1932* (Leeds PhD Thesis, 2016). Available online

Valenze, Deborah M, *Prophetic Sons and Daughters: Female Preaching and Popular Religion in Industrial England* (Princeton University Press, 1985)

Walcott, Rev Mackenzie EC, 'Filey Fishermen in 1862 - Yawls and Cobles' (*Once a Week,* 1862). Article available online at Scarborough Maritime Heritage Museum website

Walker, George, *The Costume of Yorkshire* (Robinson, Son, & Holdsworth, 1814)

Weatherhead, Fran, *North Norfolk Fishermen* (The History Press, 2011)

Wane, JS, *Diary of a Schoolboy on Holiday in Filey 1908* (K Clegg, 1998)[1]

Woodcock, Rev Henry, *Piety among the Peasantry: Being sketches of Primitive Methodism in the Wolds* (Joseph Toulson, 1889)

Online

Much material can now be found on the internet, and only a fraction is cited in footnotes. *Ancestry.co.uk's Public Trees*, and *FamilySearch* provide access in seconds to what took hours to find in the 1980s – though beware of some of the more creative genealogical inventiveness displayed in some of the family trees submitted – one of Robert JENKINSON (M3)'s descendants has him born in Linton-in-Craven, near Skipton. We are especially fortunate, however, to have the *Pedigree Resource File* entries (known as *Filey Genealogy and Connections*) in the *Genealogies* section of *FamilySearch* – submitted over a period of years, there are now tens of thousands of the town's inhabitants included. Also invaluable are Ian Elsom's numerous posts (*Redux*), *Looking at Filey: Adventures in the kin trade;* and George Scales' extensive *Scarborough A-Z Boat Index* (SMHC website, 2018) – a searchable database, with comprehensive detail on all Scarborough's 1,603 fishing vessels registered from 1877 to 1960; Scarborough Maritime Heritage Museum has posted extracts from many of its sources – see SMHC website.

---

[1] The availability of online, digitised and indexed census returns has at last permitted an identification of this mysterious teenage author. John S Waine was born in Wigan in late 1890, and as well as holidaying in Filey seems to have been enumerated in the US Federal Census of 1930 in the Allegheny, Pennsylvania.

INDEX TO PEOPLE NAMED IN THE TEXT

GENERAL INDEX

Printed in Great Britain
by Amazon